CLACHTOLL

AN IRON AGE BROCH SETTLEMENT IN ASSYNT, NORTH-WEST SCOTLAND

Edited by

GRAEME CAVERS

Written by John Barber, Graeme Cavers, Andy Heald, Nick Johnstone, Dawn McLaren, Jackaline Robertson and Lynne Roy

with contributions from

Enid Allison, Helen Chittock, Anne Crone, Leanne Demay, Charlotte Douglas, David Dungworth, Julie Dunne, Richard P. Evershed, Toby Gillard, Jen Harland, Richard Jones, Louisa Matthews, Fiona McGibbon, Penelope Walton Rogers, and Alex Wood

OXBOW | books
Oxford & Philadelphia

Published in the United Kingdom in 2022 by
OXBOW BOOKS
The Old Music Hall, 106–108 Cowley Road, Oxford, OX4 1JE

and in the United States by
OXBOW BOOKS
1950 Lawrence Road, Havertown, PA 19083

Hardcover Edition: ISBN 978-1-78925-847-9
Digital Edition: ISBN 978-1-78925-848-6

A CIP record for this book is available from the British Library

Library of Congress Control Number: 2022939409

Printed in Malta by Melita Press

Typeset in India by Lapiz Digital Services, Chennai.

For a complete list of Oxbow titles, please contact:

UNITED KINGDOM
Oxbow Books
Telephone (01865) 241249
Email: oxbow@oxbowbooks.com
www.oxbowbooks.com

UNITED STATES OF AMERICA
Oxbow Books
Telephone (610) 853-9131, Fax (610) 853-9146
Email: queries@casemateacademic.com
www.casemateacademic.com/oxbow

Oxbow Books is part of the Casemate Group

Front cover: Aerial view of Clachtoll bay, facing south, with the broch in the foreground and the Split Rock stack behind
(image: John Town)
Back cover: Excavation of the hearth complex in progress in 2017 (image: AOC)

Contents

Acknowledgements

The list of contributors to the successful completion of the Clachtoll Broch Project is a long one, and regrettably we cannot thank every volunteer, participant and supporter by name; we would like to record our sincere thanks to every one, however, for the hours, days and weeks spent in helping to make such a remarkable community heritage initiative happen. In particular, the contribution of Historic Assynt members and the North of Scotland Archaeology Society (NoSAS) was invaluable throughout, providing an enthusiastic workforce in often demanding conditions. Training and supervision of all project volunteers was delivered by AOC Archaeology's field team, Alan Duffy, Leanne Demay, Charlotte Douglas, Vanessa Jackson, Lindsey Stirling, Stuart Wilson and Alex Wood, led by Nick Johnstone, whose dedication and organisational skills were a major reason for the success of the project. As a model for cross-sector collaboration, we believe the Clachtoll broch project is an exemplar of what can be achieved by statutory, professional and voluntary groups working together, and this could not have been achieved without the support of Historic Environment Scotland's heritage team, particularly John Raven, Simon Stronach, Steven Watt and Joss Durnan; the authors and Historic Assynt are sincerely grateful for their advice throughout.

The post-excavation analysis involved a large team of specialists, each supported by colleagues from numerous organisations and we are grateful to colleagues at NMS, Gemma Cruickshanks for her comments and to Fraser Hunter for access to unpublished material. AOC's survey and graphics team, Jamie Humble, Gemma Hudson, Sam O'Leary, Orlene McIlfatrick and Marta Pilarska deserve credit for their thoughtful approach to the presentation of the results, and for their work on converting academic data into accessible formats, both in this publication and through interpretation media. Martyn Robertson and his team at UrbanCroft Films helped to provide the vehicle for dissemination of the project results, and we are also grateful to John Town for making his drone footage available to the project.

Many local people contributed to the logistical organisation of the fieldwork and associated events, and we would like to thank the Assynt Crofters' Trust, and particularly Iain Matheson and subsequently his daughter Katie, for leasing the broch to Historic Assynt. Many others contributed to the various public meetings and consultations held in Assynt to discuss the strategy for work at the broch, and we are grateful for all the opinions and support received. Several local people contributed skills and knowledge to experiments, demonstrations and workshops designed to make the broch's archaeology more accessible, and we are grateful to Marc Campbell and Fergus Stewart for their input to these. Andy Summers was a reliably knowledgeable and supportive source of advice throughout, and always on hand to help coordinate tours, school visits and other activities. Historic Assynt's 'broch liaison officers', Mandy Haggith, Richard Pease and Roz Summers along with Brenda Gibson and Sharon Bartram enthusiastically engaged the many visitors and school groups over the course of the fieldwork, as well as in the period leading up to and after the excavations themselves.

Professional advice and guidance was received at all stages of the project from Dr Dimitris Theodossopoulos (University of Edinburgh) and Stuart Burke Associates (Engineers), while the skill and practical experience of Brian Wilson, Craig Neate and Martin Callus were vital to the successful completion of the conservation works.

Louisa Matthews is grateful to The Assynt Crofters' Trust, Mr W. Smith, Dr Kirsty Owen, Mrs M. Macphail and Mr E. Mackenzie for their help with site access and fieldwork. Financial or grant-in-kind support was provided by NERC IAPETUS Doctoral Training Partnership, NERC Radiocarbon Fund and the British Ocean Sediment Core Research Facility, Southampton. Constructive comments on chapter 8 were provided by

Drs Althea Davies, Maarten van Hardenbroek, Andrew Henderson, and Helen MacKay. Radiocarbon dates were funded by the NERC Radiocarbon Fund. Richard Jones is indebted to Dr Iain Allison for the identification of the stone as serpentinite.

No project of this type obtains funding support without the hard work of a dedicated project management team, and Pat Buchanan deserves much of the credit for the design of a funding strategy that fit the ambitious scale of the project. From the inception of the Coigach and Assynt Living Landscape Partnership, the management skills and advice of Boyd Alexander and his colleagues ensured the project remained on track, while Richard Williams provided invaluable advice in the early stages of the project's design.

Most of all, however, credit is due to Historic Assynt, a local heritage organisation with an impressive track record in conservation, outreach and education projects, and led by an equally impressive committee and membership group: Scottie Sutherland, Fin and Jen Valentine, Dave McBain, Nigel Goldie, Mandy Haggith and others. The broch project would not have progressed at all without the vision and dedication of two people, Robin Noble, former Community Council Chair and Historic Assynt member who played a key role in the early stages of the work at Clachtoll and Historic Assynt's Broch Project Leader, Gordon Sleight. In particular, the Clachtoll project became a full-time job for Gordon and its successful completion is testament to his passion for Highland archaeology, sharing and celebrating Assynt's heritage and to his people management skills; it is no exaggeration to say that none of this work would have taken place without his continuous commitment.

The Clachtoll Broch Project was part of the Coigach and Assynt Living Landscape Project, and received funding from the National Lottery Heritage Fund, Historic Environment Scotland, SSE Sustainable Development Fund, the Pilgrim Trust, Highland Council via the Scottish Communities Landfill Fund, the Robert Kiln Trust, and private donors.

AOC Archaeology Project Team
December 2021

List of contributors

ENID ALLISON
Canterbury Archaeological Trust Ltd,
92a Broad Street,
Canterbury,
Kent CT1 2LU

JOHN BARBER
AOC Archaeology Group,
Edgefield Road,
Loanhead,
Midlothian EH20 9SY

GRAEME CAVERS
AOC Archaeology Group,
Edgefield Road,
Loanhead,
Midlothian EH20 9SY

HELEN CHITTOCK
AOC Archaeology Group,
Edgefield Road,
Loanhead,
Midlothian EH20 9SY

ANNE CRONE
AOC Archaeology Group,
Edgefield Road,
Loanhead,
Midlothian EH20 9SY

LEANNE DEMAY
AOC Archaeology Group,
Edgefield Road,
Loanhead,
Midlothian EH20 9SY

CHARLOTTE DOUGLAS
AOC Archaeology Group,
Edgefield Road,
Loanhead,
Midlothian EH20 9SY

DAVID DUNGWORTH
Heritage Science Solutions,
Stage 2 Business Centre,
Dundas Lane,
Portsmouth PO3 5ND

JULIE DUNNE
Organic Geochemistry Unit,
School of Chemistry,
University of Bristol,
Cantock's Close,
Bristol BS8 1TS

RICHARD P. EVERSHED
Organic Geochemistry Unit,
School of Chemistry,
University of Bristol,
Cantock's Close,
Bristol BS8 1TS

TOBY GILLARD
Organic Geochemistry Unit,
School of Chemistry,
University of Bristol,
Cantock's Close,
Bristol BS8 1TS

JEN HARLAND
Orkney College UHI,
East Road,
Kirkwall,
Orkney KW15 1LX

ANDY HEALD
AOC Archaeology Group,
Edgefield Road,
Loanhead,
Midlothian EH20 9SY

NICHOLAS JOHNSTONE
AOC Archaeology Group,
Edgefield Road,
Loanhead,
Midlothian EH20 9SY

RICHARD JONES
Department of Archaeology,
University of Glasgow,
Gregory Building,
Glasgow G12 8QQ

FIONA McGIBBON
National Museums Scotland,
Chambers Street,
Edinburgh

DAWN McLAREN
AOC Archaeology Group,
Edgefield Road,
Loanhead,
Midlothian EH20 9SY

LOUISA MATTHEWS
School of Geography, Politics and Sociology,
Newcastle University,
2nd Floor,
Henry Daysh Building,
Newcastle upon Tyne NE1 7RU

JACKALINE ROBERTSON
AOC Archaeology Group,
Edgefield Road,
Loanhead,
Midlothian EH20 9SY

LYNNE ROY
AOC Archaeology Group,
Edgefield Road,
Loanhead,
Midlothian EH20 9SY

GORDON SLEIGHT
Historic Assynt

PENELOPE WALTON ROGERS
The Anglo-Saxon Laboratory,
Bootham House,
61 Bootham,
York YO30 7BT

ALEX WOOD
AOC Archaeology Group,
Edgefield Road,
Loanhead,
Midlothian EH20 9SY

Foreword

Lots of people enjoy clambering around ruins especially if the ruins are unprotected and lie beside a well-used coastal path dominated by a mound of rubble spilling down from a rocky outcrop. A clamber over the loose rubble to the top of the mound reveals half-blocked entrances and passages which invite further exploration and the end result is that loose stonework gets dislodged and the surviving remains destabilised. Add in winter gales whipping up huge waves which crash over the ruins, animals taking shelter in the recesses or burrowing into the softer material and, as stonework shifts, the whole structure becomes less safe. Exposed walling and precariously balanced lintels can fall suddenly and without warning. Anyone caught in such a collapse could be seriously injured or even killed.

The ruins of Clachtoll Broch, which stand sentinel over Stoer Bay in Assynt on the exposed west coast of Sutherland, were in precisely that situation in the early years of this century. Local concerns were brought to the Assynt Community Council where it was suggested that Historic Assynt be asked to investigate what might be done. They had developed some experience of this kind of work having been set up in 1998 to conserve the ruins of Ardvreck Castle and Calda House and restore the former Parish Kirk in the medieval heart of Assynt at Inchnadamph. That project was drawing to an end and they had begun to turn their attention to understanding more about the wider archaeological heritage of Assynt. They had no thought of moving straight into another major project but agreed to jointly sponsor a public meeting with other concerned groups. That meeting revealed widespread worry about the safety of the broch and of its visitors, but also a hope that any eventual conservation work might provide an opportunity to discover more about the broch's origins and use, and to improve public access and understanding. The meeting concluded that Historic Assynt should seek funding for a feasibility study and so began a close relationship between Historic Assynt and Clachtoll Broch which is ongoing nearly 15 years later!

The feasibility study suggested that the broch's instability was more serious than realised and this led Historic Scotland (now Historic Environment Scotland) to commission and fund a Conservation Management Plan by AOC Archaeology. Their plan highlighted that, despite a minor intervention in the entrance by Historic Scotland in 2001, more work was urgently needed in that area and that other parts of the structure needed conservation in the longer term. Much of the conservation work they proposed would also expose underlying archaeological material which would need to be simultaneously excavated and subsequently analysed to reveal as much as possible of the broch's story. The combined conservation and excavation would allow for new access arrangements to reduce the amount of damage caused by people climbing all over the broch.

While all this was going on Historic Assynt had become a participant in the nationwide Scotland's Rural Past Project as part of its exploration of the wider archaeological heritage of the area. This served to highlight the rich diversity of Assynt's archaeological heritage but also revealed how little of that heritage had been investigated. Unless more understanding of this wider picture could be gained the proposed conservation and excavation at the broch would be lacking any comprehensive local context.

So, by 2008 the Inchnadamph Project was completed and twin foci for Historic Assynt's work for the foreseeable future were identified:

- To work towards conservation, excavation, interpretation and improved access at Clachtoll Broch.
- To explore, survey and record the wider archaeological heritage of Assynt.

Three interrelated professionally led projects were developed over the next few years and funding secured. 'Assynt's Hidden Lives' surveyed large parts of the most accessible areas of the parish and gave a much clearer overview of the extensive and varied archaeology. It was followed up by 'Life and Death in Assynt's Past' which focussed on excavation and consolidation work at three very different sites in different parts of the parish – the Neolithic Loch Borralan East Chambered Cairn, the Iron Age Clachtoll Broch and an 18th-century long house in the cleared township of Glenleraig. 'Fire and Water' completed the trio with excavations at a Bronze Age burnt mound at Stronchrubie and a medieval moated site close to the church at nearby Inchnadamph. The information from all of these projects immensely enriched understanding of Assynt's wider built heritage and the work at Clachtoll stabilised the dangerous entrance passage and provided valuable insights into the condition of the structure and some intriguing pointers to part of its complex story.

The sorts of damage found on the newly exposed stonework around the broch entrance and the patterns of collapse discernible in the rubble of the interior suggested to John Barber and his colleagues from AOC Archaeology that the broch tower may have suffered quite a sudden and dramatic collapse which might also have been associated with a fire; charcoal found on an internal ledge provided a date in the mid-1st century AD. It would have been unlikely to have survived undisturbed over the subsequent two thousand years if the broch had ever been reused and so there was a strong possibility that below the rubble in the broch interior were undisturbed signs of the lives of the last inhabitants.

The conservation work at the broch was followed up by some modelling of the surviving remains of the structure and the associated rubble inside and around it. This work was undertaken by engineering students at Edinburgh University under the direction of Dr Dimitris Theodossopoulos and indicated that the rubble in the interior was exerting a constant pressure on the surviving broch walls, pushing them outwards with the real possibility of ongoing collapses in the future if that pressure was not relieved.

All these findings and many more have been regularly fed back to the local community and their ideas and wishes have also played a part in the eventual design of the current project as reported in the pages that follow.

Involvement with Clachtoll Broch project has been exhilarating! The excitement of excavation, discovery and the results of post-excavation analysis have more than compensated for the long and often tedious hours of background administration – seeking the necessary permissions and funds, consulting the local community and more widely, dealing with the wide range of inevitable frustrations and stresses that come with major projects of this kind.

Historic Assynt is immensely grateful for the help, support and involvement of a huge number of organisations and individuals over the years as the list of acknowledgements will indicate. Many, many thanks to one and all!

At the time of writing we are in the midst of Coronavirus restrictions and the final stages of the project involving access and interpretation are in suspended animation, but we still hope to have everything completed during 2022. Beyond that Historic Assynt will continue working towards further explorations into Assynt's archaeological riches.

Gordon Sleight
Historic Assynt Project Leader
December 2021

Introduction and background, conservation context

Clachtoll: topography and geology

Clachtoll is located in Assynt, Sutherland, on the north-west coast of Mainland Scotland (Fig. 1.1). The area is well known for its dramatic scenery, which provides some of the UK's most spectacular and beautiful views across white sandy beaches of the coast and inland, over the 'inselberg' landscape created by the peaks of Suilven, Canisp and Quinag. Popular with tourists, the area is nonetheless relatively sparsely populated, even by Highland standards, and Assynt itself has only around 1000 inhabitants. The population in summer months grows considerably, however, and the settlement of Clachtoll, located on machair fringes on the western coast of the parish, is a popular destination for campers and holiday makers.

Assynt is well known for its complex geology and was the field laboratory of 19th-century geologists Benjamin Peach and John Horne, who pioneered geological mapping techniques and the modern understanding of processes of geological thrust, opening up new possibilities in the study of landscape formation and evolution. Some of the world's oldest rocks are found in Assynt, gneisses formed over 2600 million years ago, which were in turn overlain by Torridonian c. 1000 Ma, encompassing the sandstones from which Clachtoll broch is constructed. The position of the broch itself is significant in geological terms, being located on Torridonian sandstone but close to the boundary between the coastal Torridonian and the gneiss of the western Assynt coast (Fig. 1.2). This has translated into a practical division in agricultural viability in the north-west of the parish, with the inland areas over gneiss typically poorly drained and giving rise to peat-dominated knock-and-lochan landscape while the coastal areas, with more freely draining geology, have given rise to coastal machair and good agricultural land, now mainly used as common grazings. Clachtoll broch therefore occupies a topographic niche common to many Atlantic Iron Age settlements in that it is close to the coast, controlling likely harbours at Clachtoll and Stoer bays and associated with better agricultural land. The geology of the immediate locale was undoubtedly a determining factor in the siting of the settlement, with the sandstone bedrock quarrying easily into tabular blocks, unlike the hard and irregular gneiss of the areas to the north and south of Stoer.

The broch itself occupies a rocky crag on a prominent shoulder of rock to the south of Stoer Bay, only 2–3 m above the MHWS, in a particularly exposed position that is prone to the impact of westerly storms (Fig. 1.3). Reconstruction of sea level in later prehistory at Clachtoll is complicated by the complex interplay between isostatic rebound and post-glacial sea level rise, and relative sea level (RSL) models are too coarse to reconstruct this reliably, but current models indicate a probable RSL in the first millennium BC that was 1 to 2 m higher than at present (Hamilton *et al.* 2015). This is unlikely to have been high enough to have isolate the broch from the low, level ground to the east during its occupation, but would certainly have provided more immediate access to the sea, albeit that this would presumably also have entailed greater vulnerability to wave damage in winter storms.

In its rocky and coastal location the Clachtoll broch perhaps shares more in common with brochs found in the Western Isles and along the west coast than those in the Caithness and Northern Isles group, which are more often built on flat, cultivable land which saw the development of deep enhanced soils comprising a productive infield during the period of the settlement's use (*e.g.* Dockrill *et al.* 2015, 58–62). Modern maps of capability for agriculture class most of Assynt as low-quality land, given the predominance of peat and poorly drained gleys, but small coastal pockets, such as the areas around both Stoer and Clachtoll bays, to the north and south of the broch, provide significant tracts of machair that were cultivated

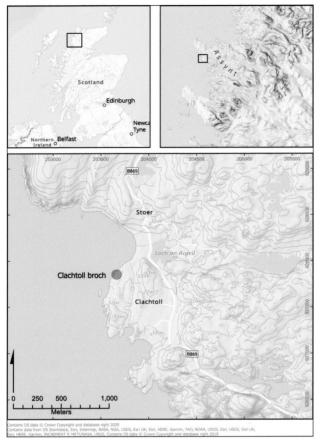

Figure 1.1 Location of Clachtoll broch

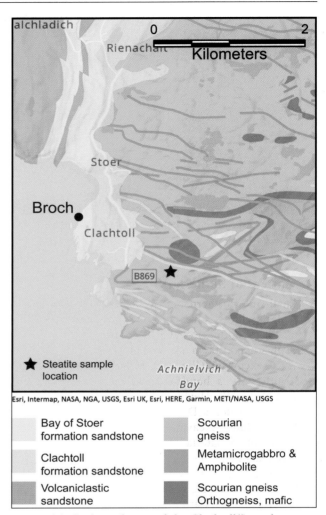

Figure 1.2 Geological map of the Clachtoll/Stoer bay area, indicating the position of the broch and the steatite sample location referred to in section 4.8

until the modern period and it is likely that these were the main crop-producing lands held by the broch occupants.

Archaeological context

In archaeological terms, Assynt – and western Sutherland more generally – remains one of the least studied areas of Scotland. There have been few concerted programmes of archaeological research undertaken in the area, and most of the region's historic environment records derive from early 20th-century inventory entries and minimal record updates in the 1950s to 70s. A significant contribution to the records of the archaeology in Assynt was made by Historic Assynt's survey work carried out under the auspices of the *Scotland's Rural Past* project, which mapped many medieval and later townships as well as coastal prehistoric settlements across the Stoer peninsula, at Clachtoll and Ardbhair. A significant update to the record in Assynt was provided by the *Assynt's Hidden Lives* project, carried out in 2009/10 as a community survey project by AOC and Historic Assynt. The survey visited around 200 sites, providing record updates and measured surveys, along with an overview of settlement patterns from prehistory to the post-medieval period, commenting on the notable

concentration of later prehistoric settlements on the coastal fringes of Assynt, in marked contrast to the prevalence of earlier prehistoric funerary monuments in the 'limestone corridor' around Loch Assynt and Borralan (Cavers and Hudson 2010). Identifiable settlements likely to date to the first millennia cluster around the Stoer peninsula, north of Clachtoll, including the 'duns' at Clashnessie and Rubh an Dunain and an islet settlement at Loch na Claise; none had been excavated prior to the commencement of the Clachtoll project. To the east, on Assynt's north coast, there are two further brochs at Loch Ardbhair and Kylesku, but despite evidence for excavation at the former site (Cavers and Hudson 2010, 111) there is no recorded information about either, other than MacKie's survey data (MacKie 2007b, NC13 1). The only other evidence for Iron Age activity in the area comes from a few stray finds: a bronze needle and pot sherds from Stoer bay (PSAS 1960, 253) and a steatite cup found *c.* 400 m south of the broch (Canmore ID: 4501).

Figure 1.3 Aerial image of the broch looking southward over Clachtoll Bay

The brochs of Sutherland

Although the northern mainland counties (Caithness, Sutherland, Ross-shire and Inverness-shire) contain about 300 definite, probable and possible brochs and although some of them are well preserved, few are well known or excavated (Fig. 1.4). Modern explorations are rare with only a handful undertaken in Caithness (*e.g.* Calder 1948; Heald and Jackson 2002) and only one in Sutherland, at Durcha in Strath Oykel (Dunwell 1999). This latter excavation was on a very small scale and provided no material evidence from which the broch and associated remains could be accurately dated. Other excavations of Sutherland brochs are exclusively on the east of the county, the majority excavated in the 19th century, *e.g.* Carrol, Carn Liath, Kintradwell (Joass 1865; Joass and Aitken 1890) and Backies (Stuart 1870). Atlantic roundhouses in Wester Ross have seen more attention, through MacKie's work at Dun an Ruigh Ruaidh (MacKie 1980) and latterly via community excavations at Applecross (Peteranna 2012) though the sample size is still small.

Our present understanding of Sutherland brochs is therefore largely based on survey. It is a reflection of our current knowledge that discussions still largely rest on the report of the Royal Commission on the Ancient and Historical Monuments of Scotland (1911) under-taken almost a hundred years ago and on the work of 19th-century scholars such as Joseph Anderson (1878). The RCAHMS Inventory of Sutherland presented descriptions of the 67 Sutherland sites recorded at that time as brochs. These lists were subsequently updated by Graham (1949, 94–6), Hamilton (1968, 175–9) and MacKie (1965b). In 1996 the National Monuments Record of Scotland recorded 84 sites in Sutherland as 'brochs' with numerous further roundhouses described as duns. Our understanding of the architectural details of the Sutherland brochs has been greatly enhanced by the work of Euan MacKie (2002; 2007b) which standardised

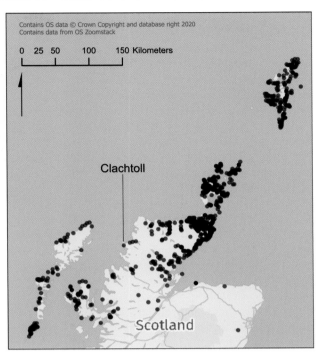

Figure 1.4 Distribution of brochs and 'possible brochs' in the north mainland, Western Isles and Northern Isles of Scotland (data from Canmore, used under Open Government License 2021)

and collated the available data, but the majority of our knowledge is still derived from surface survey.

Irrespective of number the distribution of brochs in Sutherland is weighted heavily to the northern and eastern areas of the county (Anderson 1878; Rivet 1966, foldout; Gourlay 1996, 12, 69; Cowley 1999, 70). There are comparatively few known brochs on the west coast area of the county, with only three specifically mentioned by MacKie (2007b, 614–7): Clachtoll, Loch Ardbhair and Kylestrome (An Dun, Kylesku). To the south, there is an isolated example at Loch Poll An Dunain, Achiltibuie (Cavers and Hudson 2016) and a cluster around Loch Broom, but based on current knowledge the area is remarkably sparsely populated by broch settlements, and nowhere in Wester Ross or western Sutherland do brochs appear in the numbers found in the Hebrides, Caithness or the Northern Isles.

The origin, development, use and abandonment of Sutherland brochs is therefore one of the least well-understood aspects of Iron Age societies in northern Scotland (Dunwell 1999, 283), and their affinity or otherwise to the better-known areas has been uncertain. Fairhurst (1984, 183) regarded the Sutherland brochs as representing a secondary spread from an Orkney/Caithness core area and drew a distinction between the distribution of sites along the coastal edge, often attended by extra-mural settlements, and the mostly isolated structures occupying the more rugged inland areas (see also Young 1964, 173–5,

184–9). More recent writing has emphasised that, although brochs and their variants were built and used across Atlantic Scotland it is probable that there were different zones of interaction and development within adjacent areas. Such discussions have been based largely on analysis of artefacts and, to a lesser degree, architectural traits. MacKie suggested (2000b; 2005) that the flat plain of Caithness and the eastern coastal zone of Sutherland represents a transitional or hybrid zone, indicated not by the architecture but by the impression that there is a gradual stylistic transition in material culture from 'typical' Atlantic assemblages found in the north (with abundant fine pottery and masses of bone implements) to more impoverished assemblages in the south, which are more closely aligned to non-Atlantic mainland cultures. In MacKie's view (2005, 24), the north-west mainland should be a similar transitional or hybrid zone where brochs were built and used by groups with material culture different to that found in other areas, particularly in the Hebrides. As MacKie would himself have admitted, the identification of frontier zones or cultural boundaries between Atlantic Iron Age groups is fraught with difficulty, however, and the lack of evidence from excavated sites in Sutherland makes this a particularly difficult area to define.

The depiction of the north-west mainland as a transitional zone nonetheless persists in current literature. Henderson (2007, 151) draws a clear distinction between the 'Northern Settlement Sequence' – that is northern and eastern Sutherland, Caithness, Orkney and Shetland – and the 'Western Isles and Skye Settlement Sequence', with the few west-coast mainland brochs, including Clachtoll, viewed as part of this latter group. Architectural form provides the other main basis for the assessment of affinity. MacKie (2000b, 101) argued for two distinct forms of broch, with a few transitional examples. In the *ground-galleried* form the hollow wall is constructed directly on the ground, the wall base tends to be slimmer and the central court larger; these are concentrated heavily in the Western Isles with a few outliers in the Northern Isles. In the *solid-based brochs* the galleried wall is built from a massive base which is solid masonry, except for the entrance passage and one or more isolated intramural cells. This type, dominant in the northern islands and the north-east mainland, tends to have thicker wall bases and a smaller central court or garth (*cf.* MacKie 1971, fig. 1). Clachtoll lies on the boundary between the two zones and, with no local excavations to provide context, prior to excavation might equally well have been expected to relate to either.

A key research objective of the archaeological work at the broch, therefore, was to investigate the extent to which the Clachtoll broch could be said to share characteristics of the Western Isles or north-east mainland and Northern Isles Atlantic groups. While this issue is fundamental to the investigation of the Sutherland Iron Age in general, the question has importance beyond characterisation of a hitherto little-studied area, and has the potential to clarify the relationships between neighbouring communities in the Iron Age and the mechanisms by which 'broch-building culture' (MacKie 2008) spread to the north-west mainland.

History prior to 2000

Early cartographic sources are of little assistance in assessing the modern history of Clachtoll. The first depiction of the area is on Bleau's map (1654), where the settlement of Clachtoll is depicted as *Clawhoill*. The first detailed map of the area is Roy's military survey of Scotland, which dates from 1747–1755 and shows a settlement of *Ballclachinhole* immediately south of the broch and *Stoir* (Stoer) immediately north-west of it, along with areas of cultivation to both the north and south. John Home's survey of Assynt, from 1774, is the first map which depicts the Clachtoll broch, which is shown as an 'Old Castle' (Fig. 1.5). Home's survey shows the extent of pre-Clearance settlement and agriculture in the Clachtoll/Stoir area, at least 13 occupied buildings are depicted in Clachtoll, and cornfields are shown north, east and south and settlements both north and south-east of the broch. The first edition Ordnance Survey map (1:10,560) dates from 1878 and is the first to depict the site with any accuracy (Fig. 1.6). It shows the Clachtoll broch as '*An Dun (Pictish)*' and its surroundings in detail. It also depicts 'tumuli' immediately south of the broch, and the findspots of a silver coin of the reign of Charles II and a stone cup south-east of it. '*An Dun*' is shown north-east of the Clachtoll broch, where, according to the map, a stone cist was found in 1871. These antiquities refer to the steatite cup (Canmore ID 4501) and silver coin (Canmore ID 4500) referred to in the OS Name Book; it is probable that the cup was found at or near the broch, but this cannot be reliably established. The 'tumulus' is most likely a reference to a natural shingle bar that is very prominent on the rocky foreshore to the south of the broch. This was recently dug into by a local resident, but nothing of archaeological significance was found.

Condition of the broch in 2007

In 2007 AOC undertook a 3D laser scan and topographic survey of the broch at the request of Historic Assynt, with a view to providing the basis for a condition assessment and Conservation Management Plan (Fig. 1.7). This survey identified several threats to the broch, both related to the structure and its associated archaeological deposits but also in relation to visitor safety. In several places, capping lintels over the intramural cells were loose or

Figure 1.5 The Clachtoll area as depicted on Home's map of 1774 (Reproduced by kind permission of the Trustees of the National Library of Scotland)

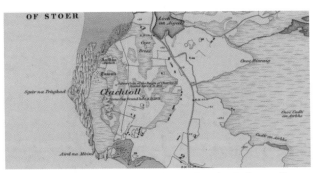

Figure 1.6 The Clachtoll area as depicted on the Ordnance Survey map of 1878 (surveyed 1875) (Reproduced by kind permission of the Trustees of the National Library of Scotland)

missing, presenting the risk of a fall of several metres into the voids below. In numerous places the upper stonework of the broch was in a very precarious state, and one of the major lintels over the stair foot cell had been broken and chocked for support, an intervention that had probably prevented the collapse of a large section of the upper walling in the south-east of the broch.

Most alarmingly, the lowest sections of the outer wall on the south side of the monument, where it rises up and over the craggy and stepping bedrock, had begun to slip outward, with several of the lowest stones missing and leaving an unsupported arch of masonry, behind which was the stair gallery and one of the highest surviving sections of walling. Monitoring of this area of the broch in subsequent years showed that stones were continuing to be lost in this area, and that a collapse was probably imminent. Through a series of experimental studies carried out by the University of Edinburgh led by Dr Dimitris Theodossopoulos (Theodossopoulos *et al.* 2012), it was determined that the breach in the seaward side of the broch and the loss of basal stones on the south meant that there were significant unresolved forces in the surviving structure, and that these were likely to bring about further structural failures. Assessment of the depth of internal rubble and associated archaeological deposits based on analysis of the 3D survey data led the project team to conclude that should a further major collapse occur, the internal deposits were likely to be irreversibly damaged, with significant loss of archaeological information.

Interim works

Some earlier intervention in the broch had been carried out by Historic Scotland, when the entrance passage was cleared of rubble and the lintels excavated from above to allow the installation of a bronze armature support around one, and a propping marble pillar under the end of another. In 2012 the entrance passage was returned to as part of the *Life and Death in Assynt's Past* project, and

consolidation of the damaged lintels in the entrance was completed by reseating displaced and damaged stones and repairing the relieving corbelling over the entrance passage (Barber 2012). As part of this work the displaced corbel capstone over Cell 4 was also reinstated and as a consequence the broch was considerably safer for visitors and at far less risk of further collapse. During this work, clearance of upper levels of the rubble close to the end of the entrance passage temporarily exposed the scarcement ledge, and a deposit of charcoal found on it was sampled and radiocarbon dated. The determination returned, calibrating in the range 153 to 55 BC (SUERC-36728, see Chapter 3) gave the first indication that intact Iron Age occupation deposits were preserved within the broch, and the prospect that there had been little activity within the structure in later centuries.

As a temporary measure to address the threat of the eroding south wall, steel props were inserted under the void created by the missing stonework, dowelled into the bedrock with stainless steel rods to prevent further slippage. It was clear, however, that the long-term solution to the undermining of the south wall involved a significantly larger project, and this was the rationale for the 2017 excavation and conservation programme.

Conservation and excavation strategy

In consultation with Historic Environment Scotland and consulting engineers, a Conservation Management Plan (CMP) and Conservation Strategy and Research Design (CSRD) (Cavers, Barber and Heald 2015) were devised. In summary, this entailed the downtaking of the south wall of the broch following stone-by-stone recording and labelling, installation of a concrete plinth secured to the bedrock beneath the unsupported walling and reinstatement of the wall above. The consequence of this strategy, however, was that the interior rubble deposits would be unsupported by the outer walls and as such would need to be removed prior to carrying out the downtaking

Figure 1.7 View of the broch, from the north, prior to the commencement of the 2017 fieldwork

exercise. The knock-on effect of this was that sensitive deposits relating to the use of the broch would be put at risk, and it was agreed that in order to secure the future of the structure, the interior deposits would need to be fully excavated under archaeological conditions.

The resulting programme of excavation and conservation work was designed for a three-month season in 2017, funded through the Coigach and Assynt Living Landscape Partnership (CALLP) project. AOC Archaeology Group was awarded the contract to lead the archaeological programme, and a project team involving stonemasons and consulting engineers was assembled to carry out the work over July to September 2017. The project was run as a public initiative, with volunteers invited to take part in the excavations and receive training in field archaeology techniques from the supervising archaeological team. A concurrent programme of outreach and education ran alongside the excavations (see below).

Excavation of the broch inevitably presented daily challenges and new conservation issues that had to be addressed. The structure was damaged and unstable in areas and ways that could not have been foreseen prior to the excavations taking place, and the project team were required to work closely with the project stonemasons and HES in order to devise appropriate responses to new problems. In all responses, the strategy was guided by the conservation principles set out in the CMP; in summary, the aim was to conserve the monument using as light a touch as possible, aiming to preserve the 'legibility' of the structure and ensuring that conservation interventions were identifiable. Throughout, a collaborative approach that balanced consideration of health and safety, structural stability, archaeological authenticity and feasibility was needed, and the ultimate success of the project was attributable in no small part to the project partners' ability to strike this balance.

Research questions

While the project was driven by conservation imperatives, the project team was acutely aware of the archaeological importance of the excavation and the academic research design was integral to the development of the field strategy. The suggestion that intact Iron Age occupation levels might survive, as suggested by the C14 date obtained during the 2012 work, raised the possibility that the structure may have collapsed shortly after use and remained undisturbed by significant activity ever since. This would be a particularly rare situation, since the majority of Atlantic roundhouses excavated contain clear evidence of Late Iron Age and Early medieval reuse, in both the Western Isles and northern sequences, where secondary buildings typically take the form of cellular houses of various formats, inserted into or on top of the broch, which by that stage may have been considerably reduced from its tower-like form (Gilmour 2005, 84; Harding 2009a, 476). The prospect of undisturbed Iron Age levels from a western broch, therefore, presented the opportunity for major advances in our understanding of how Atlantic roundhouses were used in their unmodified state.

As outlined above, the geographical position of Clachtoll furthermore presented opportunities to expand our understanding of the north Atlantic Iron Age. Clachtoll would be the first west Sutherland broch to be excavated, and one of the very few on the north-western mainland. In turn, this presented the possibility of the exploration of community connections through the study of the settlement's material culture, along with comparative studies of the economic basis of the occupant community. In its physical position within the Atlantic province, Clachtoll offered the opportunity to explore issues of cultural affinity and connectivity that could further our understanding of the broch building tradition and the transmission of ideas over space and through time (Hunter and Carruthers 2012, 5.8).

In doing so, the establishment of a reliable chronology was always going to be of key importance. It is well known that broch studies have been consistently hampered and confused by the difficulty in obtaining reliable dating sources that allow confidence to be placed in the construction date of the building. While the initial radiocarbon date from the scarcement obtained in 2012 gave reason for optimism that Iron Age occupation was undisturbed within the interior, the relatively late date range it indicated suggested that the occupation sequence within may not extend back to the earliest horizon of known broch construction, at least in an undisturbed state. It was clear, nevertheless, that the opportunity existed for the establishment of a reliable chronology for the duration of occupation, whatever that chronology might be. The close control of stratigraphic excavation and the identification of suitable dating samples was therefore central to decision-making during the fieldwork.

Figure 1.8 Excavation of the upper occupation deposits in progress, in early September 2017

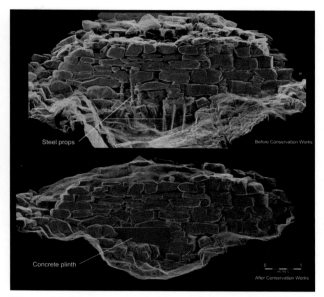

Figure 1.9 Laser scan orthoimage of the south wall before (above) and after downtaking and installation of the supporting concrete plinth

The research questions formulated prior to the commencement of fieldwork were, then, as follows Barber and Heald 2015, 9):

- What was the construction date of the broch?
- What was the duration of occupation, or other use of the primary broch structure?
- Can secondary phases of occupation, or other use of the remains be identified, and how do these relate to the form of the broch structure over the course of its use?
- Can we be confident that the broch was in continuous and consistent use over the period prior to its abandonment?
- When was the broch abandoned as a settlement, assuming it had been one, and what evidence is there for gaps in the history of its use?

This monograph sets out our attempts to address the research questions formulated in the project CSRD, and to contribute to the bigger questions that still dominate Atlantic Iron Age archaeology from a new geographical perspective.

For reasons of practicality the details of the conservation works carried out have not been included in this report, but are reported separately. The full record, including photographic and 3D data, is included in the site archive.

Methodology

The excavation was carried out entirely by hand (Fig. 1.8). In the early stages of the project this meant a daunting task for the excavation team: the interior of the broch was filled with stones that were regularly too large to lift single-handedly, and required the use of rope slings to manoeuvre carefully out of the structure. Even those stones small enough for one person to lift presented a challenge, since all had to be taken out of the broch carefully, so as to avoid damage to the surviving structure. As a consequence, progress in the rubble removal stages was slow, and well over half of the fieldwork season was spent removing the upper rubble layers. In total, 105 m³ of rubble was removed from the broch interior before the excavation of deposits could even begin.

Given the importance of documenting the three-dimensional structure of the archaeology within the broch, both for the purposes of archaeological recording and for conservation planning, the excavations were recorded on a regular basis using 3D laser scanning, with a Trimble TX5 laser scanner, and using photogrammetry. The 3D data provided by both techniques has proven invaluable to the analysis of the structure, providing high-resolution cross-sections through cells, galleries and lintel pockets, and was the basis for the stone-by-stone downtaking of the south wall (Fig. 1.9). It is difficult to imagine undertaking a similar project without the benefit of 3D recording techniques to facilitate analysis (Cavers, Barber and Ritchie 2015), and 3D scanning is now an essential tool of the broch archaeologist. Artefacts were recorded by positioning with a Trimble S6 total station, working from control points established using differential GPS, and the resulting find positions provide the data for the spatial analysis incorporated into the artefact reports.

During the excavation, all soft deposits were 100% dry sieved by the field team and the project volunteers. Where artefacts were recovered from sieving, these were bagged and labelled by context, and are included in the specialist analyses reported in Chapter 6. A minimum bulk sample of 10 litres was recovered from every context, and Context 042, the burning layer, was sampled on a 50 cm grid in order to provide the basis for the spatial analysis of the macroplant assemblage discussed in Chapter 7. Where highly stratified floor deposits were encountered, these were sampled using kubiena tins for soil micromorphology.

The outreach programme and community collaboration

Alongside the archaeological fieldwork, a programme of outreach and training was delivered. This involved on-site workshops in excavation recording techniques, finds identification and cataloguing, and environmental sampling and processing. A project website provided an ongoing blog of the excavation progress, and there were regular social media posts throughout the project. Towards the middle of the 2017 excavation season, a film crew from UrbanCroft Films captured footage for a short film documenting the volunteers' experience (Fig. 1.10); the film can now be found on the project website at *clachtollbroch.com*. Over 180 tours of the site were delivered during the fieldwork in 2017 to over 1500 visitors. Local school children were also regularly involved, with pupils from both primary schools and Ullapool High School visiting site and attending 'Iron Age Survival' workshops and working with traditional craftsmen on possible solutions to the problem of roofing broch towers.

As the excavations were completed and the project moved into the post-excavation analysis stages, the outreach initiative was maintained through regular talks by the archaeological team, both in person in Assynt and at regional and national conferences, but also via video conferencing after the Covid-19 pandemic limited

Figure 1.10 Volunteers sieving the excavated deposits while a film crew from UrbanCroft Films conducts an interview

physical gatherings in 2020. The modern model for public interaction with archaeological research suited the Clachtoll project well, and the 3D models of the artefact assemblage, created by AOC's digital documentation team for conservation and analysis purposes, also allowed the creation of a 'virtual' exhibition of the objects during the post-excavation analysis stages.

Throughout the project, the relationship between professional archaeological team and Historic Assynt and other community groups, particularly the North of Scotland Archaeology Society (NoSAS) was a model for how community participation can be the driving force behind major conservation and archaeological research initiatives, working in partnership with national heritage agencies, consulting archaeologists and the wider public to deliver long-lasting public benefit. Recognition for the success of the collaboration came in 2020, when the Current Archaeology Awards awarded Historic Assynt and AOC Archaeology Group 'Rescue Project of the Year'.

Structure of the monograph and terminology

The following report is structured as follows. Chapter 2 sets out the interpretation of the structure and provides a descriptive narrative of the internal stratigraphy, including the intramural cells, entrance passage and a description of rubble clearance works undertaken at the entrance to the outer enclosure surrounding the broch. Chapter 3 discusses the radiocarbon dates obtained from samples contained in the internal deposits, and provides the chronological framework for the interpretation of the site. Chapter 4 provides the specialist analyses and discussion of the artefact assemblage, while Chapter 5 reports the assessment of the environmental evidence: plant macrofossils, charcoal, animal and fish bone. Chapter 6 reports on the soil micromorphology analysis carried out on the internal flooring deposits, while Chapter 7 is dedicated to the spatial analysis of the macroplant remains contained within the final burning layer that marked the end of occupation at the site, context 042. Chapter 8 sets the broch in its physical and palaeoenvironmental context with an overview of the available evidence compiled by Louisa Matthews, who was in the early stages of a PhD on proxy environmental evidence for late prehistoric activity in Assynt at the time of publication. Chapter 9 reports on the investigation of three sites near Clachtoll: at the Split Rock fortification south of Clachtoll beach, at Loch na Claise islet settlement and at Clashnessie dun, on the north of the Stoer peninsula. Chapter 10 discusses the results of the project, considering the contribution of the project results to our knowledge and understanding of brochs in the north-west.

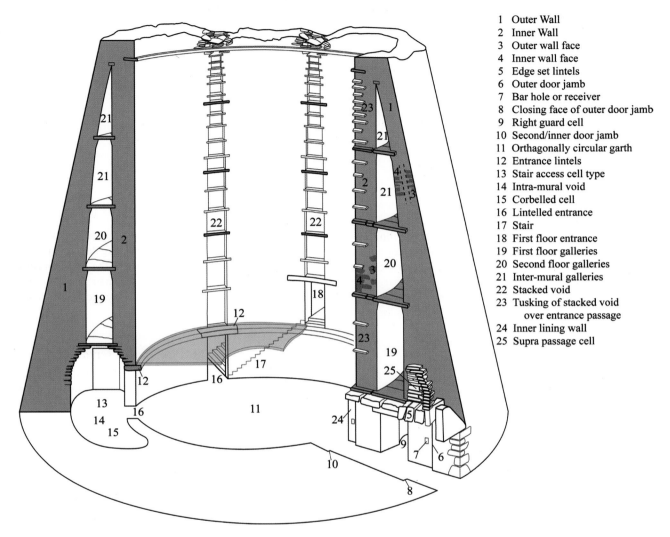

1 Outer Wall
2 Inner Wall
3 Outer wall face
4 Inner wall face
5 Edge set lintels
6 Outer door jamb
7 Bar hole or receiver
8 Closing face of outer door jamb
9 Right guard cell
10 Second/inner door jamb
11 Orthagonally circular garth
12 Entrance lintels
13 Stair access cell type
14 Intra-mural void
15 Corbelled cell
16 Lintelled entrance
17 Stair
18 First floor entrance
19 First floor galleries
20 Second floor galleries
21 Inter-mural galleries
22 Stacked void
23 Tusking of stacked void
      over entrance passage
24 Inner lining wall
25 Supra passage cell

Figure 1.11 Barber's (2017) Revised Standard Model (RSM) for broch architectural features

Throughout this monograph the authors make use of the structural terminology set out by Euan MacKie (2002), and further developed by Barber (2017), whose 'Revised Standard Model' (RSM) for broch architecture is illustrated in Figure 1.11. This scheme uses MacKie's 'clock-face' notation, whereby the entrance to the broch is considered to be at 6 o'clock, and the positions of structural features in the wall are described in relation to this position: *e.g.* at Clachtoll Cell 2 is at the 9 o'clock position. The central internal space within the broch is referred to as the 'garth' – with the recognition that this is perhaps an unsatisfactory term given the implication of an unroofed yard in later fortified buildings – in the interests of consistency with other studies. Issues of roofing and possible solutions for internal furnishing are discussed in detail in Chapter 10.

2

The structure and the archaeological excavations

Graeme Cavers, John Barber and Nick Johnstone

Structural analysis

John Barber and Graeme Cavers

The pre-excavation monument

The monument as we understood it from survey and preliminary investigations could be described as a RSM broch ('revised standard model', see Barber 2017), meaning that it featured most of the architectural traits taken as diagnostic, with some variations to fit the landscape context and with no evidence for alterations after a primary collapse. The major variation from a pure RSM form was that caused by the gross irregularities of the construction site. Taking elements from various laser scans we set out in Figures 2A.1 to 2A.4 images of the monument and the ground levels from which the masonry of the broch walls was initiated. It will be clear that the basal courses on the east side lay almost 3 m below the level of the wall base on the west. Given the existence of steep steps in the bedrock of the knoll, more than one isolated segment of walling was initiated, the whole only becoming a continuous circle at the level of the western bedrock, where both inner and outer walls are missing, lost to coastal erosion. A significant level of surveying competence on the part of the builders must have been necessary to enable construction to proceed different levels and yet form a coherent structure once the separate built elements united. The cognitive challenge required understanding of the concept of a survey plane, from which the separate elements could be demarcated by projection onto the varying ground surfaces beneath. This was all the more challenging in the outer wall, with its sloped wall-face whose diameter changed with height.

The broch entrance

The entrance passage to the broch seems in all respects to comply with the RSM ideal (Fig. 2A.5). Its left-hand side (LHS), looking into the interior, is radial to the structure but its right-hand side (RHS) is set about 10 degrees out of radial symmetry. This suggests that this side may have been remodelled.

The guard cells – RHS

The guard cells seem somewhat atypical (see Figs 2A.4 and 2A.6). The entrance to RHS guard cell (Cell 4), in plan, follows the outer wall-face of the broch's inner wall, on the broch side, but the passage's outer wall-face recurves towards the outside, and a chamber of sorts is formed by a widening of the passage into the outer wall. A very restricted passage gives access to the garth and is less than 60 cm high. It is not impossible that in the primary configuration of the broch, a simple gallery curved round to the broch entrance but this was partly destroyed and rebuilt in antiquity, prior to the formation of the occupation levels excavated in 2017. In remaking the broch wall on the west side, the guard cell would necessarily have been re-formed along the rather eccentric floor plan it now displays. In such a situation, the fact that the anticlockwise wall of the Cell and the garth entrances side wall are colinear and could have functioned as a blocking wall across a damaged gallery and inner broch wall.

The guard cells – LHS

The LHS guard cell (Cell 1) seems to consist of two discrete elements; the first is a segment of gallery, roughly concentric with the broch's inner wall, but with a strangely linear outer wall-face which fits under the inner edge of the outer wall. The second is a short access passage that cuts through part of the thickness of the broch's inner wall. Excavation revealed that a significant step downwards in the crag on which the broch was built presents a near vertical face immediately

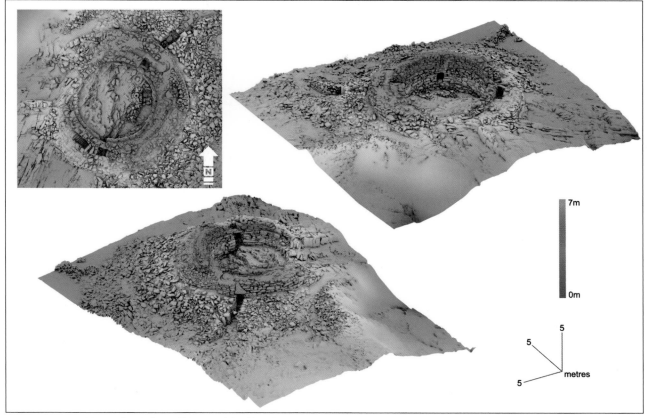

Figure 2A.1 Overall 3D model of broch, post-excavation, showing the principal structural features

inside the guard cell entrance. On balance, this evidence suggests that the cell was rebuilt in antiquity.

The wall cells

Clockwise from the broch entrance, roughly between the 8 and 9 o'clock position (the broch entrance being 6 o'clock) a cell entrance could be seen and the cell that it accessed (Cell 2) could be entered from the then wall-head, through an ope forced through the top of the cell's corbelled capping. Before excavation, the cell was seen to be at least 3 m tall, which meant that its upper levels would have projected through the gallery floor of the second level (Fig. 2A.7). This phenomenon is observed at other brochs, like Gurness, where the ground/first level gallery floor was compressed and downshifted by the failure of the broch walls (Hedges 1987; Barber 2017). The elevation of the discernible cell entrance lintel suggests that the entrance ope is high in the structure as, for example, at Dunbeath (MacKie 2007b, 429; Cavers, Barber and Johnstone 2018) where it is a secondary structure, or at Kintradwell, where it must also be a secondary structure given that it pierces the inner lining wall which, as MacKie acknowledges, is secondary (MacKie 2007b, 649). It seemed safe to argue that the height of Cell 2 suggests it was a secondary modification of the original broch layout.

The end walls of the cell are clearly linear in horizontal cross-section and approximately radial to the curvature of the broch. These walls are not curved in the horizontal plane, as corbelled cell walls normally are, and neither are they keyed into the curving inner and outer walls, save at their upper-most levels. The cell walls include in their visible faces large edge-set slabs, a style of building more compatible with the external structures around eastern and northern brochs and repaired or wholly secondary wall-faces within these brochs (see Gurness and Midhowe respectively).

It was hypothesised that Cell 2 was originally a segment of a much larger ground level gallery and was created by isolating the cell from the rest of the gallery by construction of the cross walls and by capping off above the second-level gallery floor with a crudely corbelled upper structure.

The stairwell

The entrance to the stairwell could be discerned just clockwise of the 11 o'clock position (Figs 2A.7 and 2A.8). The stairway was not visible but is reliably reported in earlier reports. The wall above the lintels of the entrance to the stair cell from the broch interior was in part clearly of modern construction, as shown by the absence or inversion of lichen growth. The broken lintel was apparently

Figure 2A.2 Plan of the broch at wall head level, with the ground level footprint shown as shaded grey. The cell numbers are indicated

supported by a stone block and clearance in the area suggested the existence of a stairfoot cell, opposite the stairway. The masonry separating the stairway assembly from Cell 2 could not have been much more than 1 m thick, along the circumference.

Above the stairway, immediately clockwise of the garth entrance, three large stone slabs crossed the just perceptible gallery segment into which the stairway was set. These were, inadequately, explained away as elements of an upper stair or upper gallery floor. At the probable head

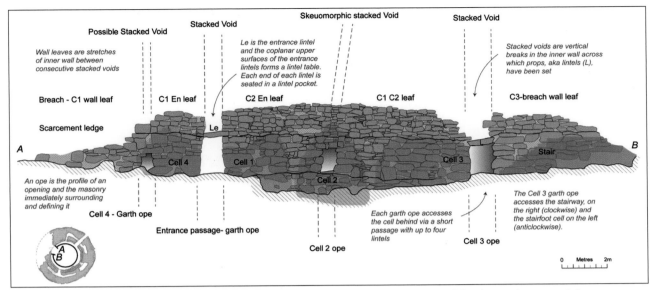

Figure 2A.3 'Unrolled' elevation of the internal broch wall, showing the position of the principal structural features

of the stairway, the outer wall-face of the inner wall was smoothly built and recurved, in a shallow curve into the inner wall. This seemed to imply the existence of a cell at the stair head, a feature not known previously in brochs. Overall, the stairway assembly runs from 9:30 to 11 o'clock.

The first level gallery

Preliminary excavations in the area of the broch entrance revealed a distinct, but badly damaged gallery at the wall-head, 0.88 m in width. Anticlockwise of the entrance passage the gallery formed a short chamber but on the clockwise side it continued over at least 4.5 m. The outer wall was much lower than the inner wall across the NE quadrant and towards the east, the outer wall was all but absent, or at least not visible above the rubble over much of the circuit. The gallery remains obscured roughly the areas between the 9 and 10 o'clock positions and the visibility of wall core material (below) between 8 and 9 o'clock indicated that there was gallery in this area.

A wall core

At the surviving wall-head, between the stairfoot and Cell 2, it seems that no gallery existed. Instead, a wall core of long (500 mm) prismatic stones, typically 100 by 100 mm in cross-section, was observed. These stones were densely stacked and while soil indurated at the extant wall-head were probably soil free beneath. It was hypothesised that this unification of the inner and outer walls may have been intended to carry a stairway from the first level to the second, but no direct evidence for this survives. This arrangement is, however, clear evidence that the first level gallery did not continue uninterrupted around the circuit of the monument, as is the norm save only where interrupted by stairways.

The breach

Between 1 and 3 o'clock the broch wall has been removed by the sea. The 1 o'clock terminal is reasonably well defined but the clockwise (3 o'clock) terminus ends in a jumble of masonry debris. It is unlikely that the wall breach formed a tidy lesion, with clear masonry lines still in their original positions at either terminal. On balance, it seemed possible that the bulk of the masonry loss lay between the 2 and 3 o'clock positions but that this pulled masonry from either side of it so that the damage extended, in the outer wall, from the 12:40 to the 3:30 o'clock positions.

It is possible that the damage north of the breach extended to the broch entrance passage, but probably rising as it curved round that quadrant. If major masonry disturbance had occurred there, only to be rebuilt, this would explain the absence of the gallery north of the breach, the non-canonical form of Cell 4, lack of radial symmetry of the passage's RHS and the projection of Cell 4's roofline above the gallery floor level; thus blocking off the gallery and forming the cell west of the broch's entrance passage. This was the hypothesis prior to the main excavation.

The planform of the monument

MacKie has claimed that true circularity is a diagnostic of broch towers (MacKie 2002, 1 and at many points thereafter) and claimed for specific monuments that their planform does not deviate from the truly circular by more than ±2 cm. In a forthcoming paper (Barber, Hudson and

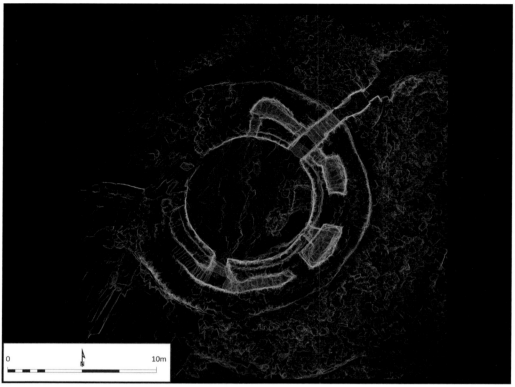

Figure 2A.4 Orthoimage of the broch post-excavation derived from terrestrial laser scanning, showing the position of the intramural galleries, stair, scarcement and internal 'souterrain'

Cavers in prep) experiments in broch metrics will be shown to challenge such hyper-precision whilst supporting the idea that brochs were laid out to a level of precision that militates against vernacular construction. Clachtoll is a particularly important test case for the exploration of this subject since, as noted above, it has been constructed across the pinnacle of a rocky ridge with foundation heights varying over about 3 m.

Even at the visible wall-head the circularity of the built monument was obvious; loose stones and obviously recent rebuilds being discounted. Where the first-floor gallery could be discerned, it was largely concentric with the inner wall. Despite the problems associated with uneven burial under fallen masonry even the outer wall seemed largely concentric also. Deviations from circularity were therefore considered to be evidence, not of poor initial survey but of poor repair and rebuild.

The entrance and chamber of the RHS gallery (Cell 4) were not concentric with the monument's planform and the garth entrance from Cell 4 was not set radially to the latter. As already suggested, this implies that this ensemble is a secondary insertion. Despite evidence for its disturbance, the gallery of the stairway is clearly concentric but the stairfoot cell deviates from concentricity. Cell 2, although concentric with the planform is wider than it and deviates a little from

it at both circumferential ends. This implies some disturbance to the cell, and may indicate that its origins were as a stacked void, converted to a wall cell following the impact of a collapse episode of the surrounding masonry.

Excavation would show that the foot of the inner wall in the arc between the 9 o'clock and 11 o'clock positions projected well beyond the line of the wall-face (Fig. 2A.1). The masonry segment concerned is 0.9 m high, projecting *c*. 0.4 m out of concentricity. This feature is considered likely to represent the walling of the primary broch tower, damaged by a collapse that required a major rebuild on a similar, but detectably different footprint. The significance of this is discussed further in Chapter 9.

The outer enclosure

The entire broch and its immediate surroundings are enclosed by a massive enclosure wall, which at various points in its circuit appears to function both as a wall and a revetment. To the NE of the broch, a wide entrance is formed by two massive boulders, each *c*. 1.0 by 1.0 by 1.0 m. The northern section of walling continues northward to the cliff edge for *c*. 8 m, but is ruinous and has collapsed. The wall is massive, composed of blocks over 1 m across. To the south, the wall is similarly massive, again using blocks over a metre across. This section of

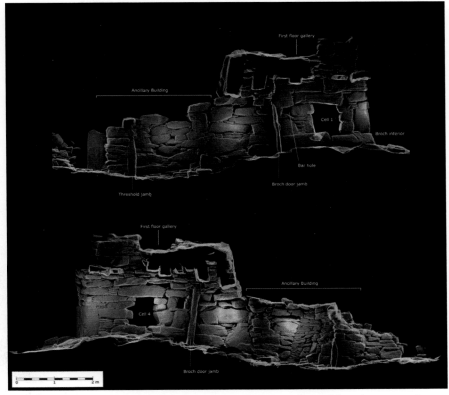

Figure 2A.5 Entrance passage elevations, orthoimages derived from laser scanning

wall continues around the broch to the south, where it is largely buried by rubble debris. In the areas to the south, the walling stands to almost 2 m in height and retains a mass of rubble debris above. In the southern areas, there is a considerable mass of stone debris between the broch and the perimeter wall, and it is possible that there are structures within this debris. No surface evidence is visible, however.

Several later walls have been constructed abutting the rubble debris from the broch site. These are generally of poor-quality build and are likely to be considerably later than the original broch constructions. It is probable that these walls are related to agricultural activity around the broch.

The excavations

Graeme Cavers, Nicholas Johnstone and John Barber

The bedrock knoll

The broch builders selected a prominent knoll of outcropping bedrock located on a spur of Torridonian sandstone, flanked by sharp crags to the seaward (west) side, and a steep slope toward the land (Figs 2A.1 and 2A.2). The basal course of the broch on the west, now sea-adjacent

side, had been quarried away, not beneath the broch wall, but inside the garth, to provide a rough even surface. No reduction of the bedrock to form a better footing for the broch was observed on this side, and it is hypothesised that glacial deposits lay over the bedrock under the broch walls and seaward of them. As Figure 2A.1 shows, the relatively steep slope of the bedrock would have proven hard to found upon without some attempt at quarrying to a level, at least locally.

The average altitude of the bedrock reduced from west to east in a series of abrupt steps, comprising a roche moutonnée feature with glacial plucking from the lateral and downstream sides of the crag, which formed the high point of a coarse crag-and-tail structure. The geometry of these clefts also reflects palaeo erosion among the beds of the steeply pitched bedrock substrate. The resulting and uneven footing required the builders to accommodate a change in elevation of over 1.7 m from west to east. A bedrock shelf bisects the interior of the broch, running N/S from the interior threshold of the entrance passage to the entrance to Gallery 3, where the stairs rise from the bedrock surface, clockwise, to the west. The broch wall steps over this ledge, accommodating it within the entrance to Gallery 3, requiring the entrance opening to step up almost 1 m to the west. Thus, the wall-foot immediately east of

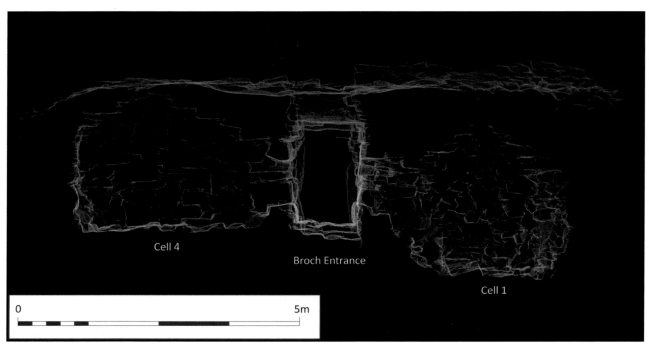

Figure 2A.6 Sections through 'guard cells' and entrance passage, orthoimages derived from laser scanning

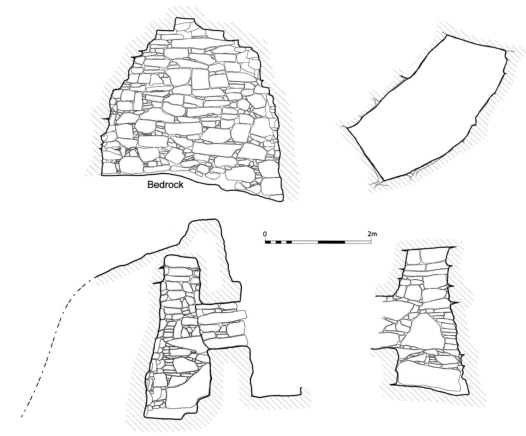

Figure 2A.7 Elevations and plans of Cell 2

Figure 2A.8 The remnants of the primary broch wall, below the dashed line indicated, surviving as a stub of coarse and disturbed masonry overlain by the later rebuild of the broch

Figure 2B.1 Rounded cobbles deposited as levelling material into clefts in the bedrock, beneath the primary floor deposits

Gallery 3's ope is some 0.52 m below the wall-foot in the entrance and under the stair.

Where not quarried, the bedrock was covered by a thin sandy till, patchy yellow/brown and white/grey in colour (075) and (116) and averaging around 0.01 to 0.05 m in thickness. It is likely that a thin skeletal soil had developed over the bedrock knoll in places prior to construction on the site. In several places, clefts and crevasses in the bedrock had been levelled up at an early stage in the construction using rounded cobbles and small stones (Fig. 2B.1). The structures and deposits found within the broch are described below from earliest to latest, and are shown in Sections AA to WW (Figs 2B.Sect-01 to 2B.Sect-25).

Hearth 1 and the earliest floors

The earliest surviving hearth, Hearth 1, constructed within the interior of the broch was [139] (Figs 2B.2 and 2B.3). This hearth had been constructed on a thin layer of flooring deposits, represented by a humic layer of green-brown silty clay (124), *c.* 0.05 to 0.3 m thick and containing charcoal flecks, patches of peat ash and lenses of inorganic sand. This layer was similar in character to later flooring deposits, described further below, and comprised humified organic materials such as rushes, reeds and grasses laid down as flooring (see Chapter 6). Lain directly onto this early floor, and very close to the diametrical centre point of the interior was a flat sandstone flag hearthstone [117] (Figs 2B.2 and 2B.3), 1.35 m in length and 0.75 m wide; the stone was heavily heat-affected, leaving it fragmentary and fragile. It was retained in place on the east side by a large, fragmentary edge-set stone [126], similarly heat-damaged. Around the east and south-east periphery of this hearth a line of edge-set stones may have formed a partial surround [127] at this time. This surround was angular in plan and was

set between 0.3 m to 0.5 m out from the hearth slabs. The platform created by this surround was continued to the west of the hearth by an upstanding bedrock shelf which would have projected above the contemporary floor surface. It is likely that Hearth 1 was replaced as it became fragmented through use and as the surrounding floor deposits accumulated to the extent that they began to envelop the hearth. The floor layers which began to accumulate ((111) and (118)) comprised banded grey/brown, highly organic silt/clays *c.* 0.2 m thick.

The composition of the floors themselves was difficult to determine during the excavation; for the most part they were represented by humified organic silts and clays, typically containing frequent charcoal flecks and fragments of burnt bone as well as patches of inorganic sand, clay and lenses of orange/yellow peat ash. However, in some places (for example (118) around the south of the hearth complex) flooring was well preserved, with woody fragments and fibrous organic material surviving. The floors were apparently refurbished repeatedly (see detailed analysis in Chapter 6), with debris from hearth rake-out evident throughout as bands of orange/yellow peat ash interleaved with organic layers. It is probable that this refurbishment took place on an ad hoc basis, as and when the floor surfaces were deemed too wet or foul to be serviceable and involved covering up the existing floor with new material. Kubiena samples were collected from the floor sequences in several locations for analysis of microstratigraphy and resolution of refurbishment episodes that were not identifiable by eye (Fig. 2B.4); the analysis of these samples is reported in Chapter 6.

The sub-layers that comprised the floor deposits were, for the most part, indistinguishable during excavation. Distinctions were made between the earliest floor (124) and the secondary floor (111/118) based on the uppermost level of the primary hearth [139]. A similar distinction was made between the secondary flooring (118/111) and the

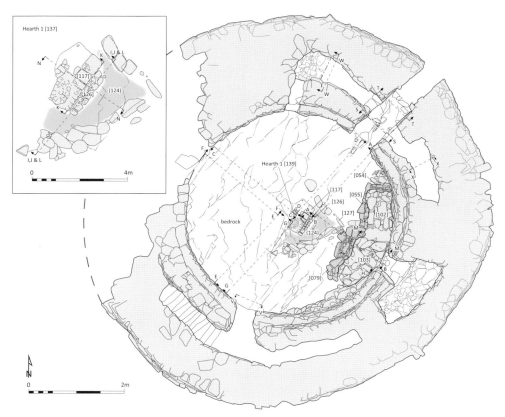

Figure 2B.2 Plan of the primary hearth and associated deposits, with the 'souterrain' structure in the low eastern area of the garth. The positions of the sections are marked

later flooring (049/062) by the construction of the secondary hearth [138]. Following the secondary hearth, the floor build-up was regarded as a continual process: (049) north side and (062) at the south side, until the demolition of the broch. This deposit was later subdivided (in the northern area) into (087), (086), (085) and (084) for purposes of sampling and finds recovery. These deposits encompassed the entire period of occupation for which evidence survived. An

additional deposit (091) was recorded around the secondary [138] and final [051] hearths where it had accumulated within the confines of the hearth surround (Sections I, J, K, L and N, Figs 2B.Sect-9 to 12, 2B.Sect-14).

In the southern half of the broch, around the entrance to the stair cell, Gallery 3, the flooring appeared to have developed differently. This may have been a consequence of a substantial vertical bedrock face at a higher level than

Figure 2B.3 The primary hearth, laid directly onto the bedrock in the centre of the garth

Figure 2B.4 Kubiena tins inserted through the highly laminar flooring deposits within the broch

Figure 2B.5 The stone drain (059), leading to the entrance passage

Figure 2B.6 The 'souterrian' structure, formed by lining walls [054], [055] and [079] in the low area of the garth

elsewhere in the interior. The presence of this feature may have prevented the continued accumulation of material in the same manner as elsewhere. Directly overlying this outcrop, and in deeper hollows in this area a similar organic flooring (067) had accumulated to a limited extent but the predominant deposit here was a mixed midden deposit (047), rich in shell and animal bone.

Floor drainage

At some point, either during the use of this hearth or during the early use of the secondary hearth, a drainage channel [059], capped with flagstones, was constructed between the north edge of the hearth complex and the thresholds to the guard cells in the entrance passage (Figs 2B.5; 2B.Sect-18). This was between 1 m and 1.6 m wide and constructed of thin, flat flagstones over bedrock ledges and edge-set stones, creating an irregular drainage channel within the existing organic floor deposits (049). The floor at this time had built up to a depth of around 0.15 m of layered organic matting, peat ash and clay. It is possible that waterlogging and puddling of this build-up led to the requirement for better drainage, especially across the frequently travelled route to and from the entrance. The drain itself was filled with a wet, mixed deposit of brown/red clay and silt (100); no finds were recovered from its contents. Although this drain did not have any clear path for outflow it did efficiently draw away the water from the surrounding floor deposits during the excavation work. Similar stone drains are a common feature of Iron Age stone buildings, and most often seem to function more as soakaway sumps (*e.g.* at Dun Mor Vaul, MacKie 1974, 12 where the bedrock blocks the flow of the drain in numerous places). The Clachtoll 'drain' seems to have been required to assist in the drying of the trampled organic surfaces, the refurbishment and maintenance of which seems to have been a constant concern for the occupants.

The lifespan of this feature does not appear to have been particularly long as it was overlain by frequently replenished floor deposits, until it was buried by around 0.25 m of stratified flooring. These upper flooring layers contained frequent inclusions of stone ((053) – north and (068) – south) and sand (077), lain directly onto existing floor horizons prior to replenishment. These stony deposits included fire-cracked stones, hearth waste and burnt beach cobbles. These had filled many of the irregularities in the underlying bedrock and were ubiquitous throughout the flooring from the north to the south-west of the broch interior.

Revetment of the lower area: the 'souterrain' [069]

Integral to the design of the broch internal layout was a deep step in the natural bedrock across the south-east side of the structure. This had been enclosed by the broch walls and was lined inside with a series of dry-stone walls. During excavation this was termed structure [069] (Fig. 2B.2). The space created by the lowest bedrock shelf

Figure 2B.7 The upper infill of the 'souterrain' structure

was lined by three distinct sections of walling: to the south by [079], in the centre by [055] and to the north by [054] (Fig. 2B.6). None of these sections of walling was particularly well constructed and were evidently prone to collapse. The wall section [079] appeared to form a 'kidney' shaped chamber which may have originally abutted the broch wall to either end. A possible wall scar [101] in the flagstone floor [102/103] appeared to continue the walling to this point. To the north of this, wall sections [055] and [054] formed an additional, rather square annex. By the time of the later occupation, the two chambers were combined to form a long continuous passage along the foot of the broch wall, creating a curving space in the lower part of the broch interior, similar in character to a souterrain.

The floor of this 'souterrain' was paved with sandstone flags [102] and [103], which overlay a dark grey/black organic clay (104), which in turn directly overlay the bedrock (Fig. 2B.Sect-13). The upper stone of a rotary quern was found lying flat on this flagstone floor (SF 208). To the south of [069] was an additional section of deep internal space between the bedrock shelf and the broch wall. Unlike [069] however, this was not lined with walling and filled with a mixture of deposits, [067], [079] and stones (Fig. 2B.Sect-8). It is possible that this deep space had been intentionally backfilled, or that surrounding structures collapsed into this area: the fill was particularly dense in finds and may have incorporated midden/waste material (Fig. 2B.Sect-2).

How structure [069] integrated with the remainder of the broch floor is not certain from the excavated evidence. However, two features lend weight to the interpretation that in the original design it may have been roofed, or floored over, providing a continuation of the broch floor and creating a subterranean passage. Firstly, the entrance to Cell 2 is located *c.* 1 m above the foot of the inner broch wall, roughly at the same level

as the top of the revetment wall [055], so that a timber or wicker floor spanning the passage [069] might have rested on the revetment wall [055] and met the broch wall at the threshold to Cell 2. The projecting ledge of rough stonework south of the entrance to Cell 2 (interpreted as the remnants of an earlier arrangement of the broch wall) may have provided additional support for this roofing. If [069] was roofed, it seems likely that the sub-floor space would have been accessed from the south, where the bedrock steps down to the flagstone floor. This floor/roof itself would most likely have been lightweight, perhaps wicker, and there was no evidence for designed integration with the broch wall.

It is not possible to be certain as to the function of structure [069], but the sub-floor space shares characteristics with 'souterrain' and well-like sub-floor voids commonly found in brochs of the north mainland and Orkney. Such features have often been described as wells, though their practical function as a source of fresh water is dubious, and this cannot have been the purpose of the Clachtoll structure. It is more probable that structure [069] was formed by necessity in accommodating the bedrock knoll, and that by continuing the floor across to the entrance to Cell 2, a convenient sub-floor space was created. This, however, is not to deny any possible special function that this feature may have acquired for the occupants.

The fill of [069] was unlike other deposits in the broch, being composed of a very dry and loose intermixed collection of rubble and soil deposits. These deposits were a mixture of charcoal (including remnants of the final conflagration (042)), yellow clay/peat ash (048), mixed clay/midden deposit (containing large quantities of animal bone and charcoal flecks) (047), and a dry sandy rubble deposit (078) containing numerous finds including spindle whorls, stone lamps, ceramics and worked bone. This occupation debris could be interpreted as infill or deliberate dumping of refuse into [069], but it was considered at the time of excavation that this might instead represent the collapse of the flooring over [069] and associated internal structures in this area.

Hearth 2

The second hearth [138] was constructed after mixed debris, including shattered stone and ash was spread over Hearth 1 to level it (112), before a new slab [095] was placed on top, slightly off-centre within the broch, to the west of the centre of Hearth 1 (Fig. 2B.8). This brought the level of the hearth up to the top of the shelf of bedrock against which the previous hearth had been built. The centre of the replacement hearth was a large flat sandstone flag [095], which survived as a fragmented, badly heat-affected slab 0.95 m long and 0.58 m wide. To the west of the slab, a linear setting of badly heat-affected

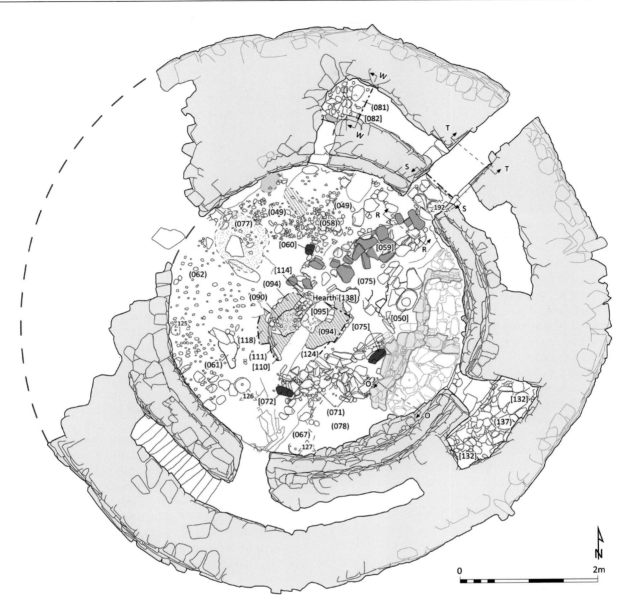

Figure 2B.8 Plan of the second phase hearth [138], stone drain [059] and associated deposits

stones [114] may have provided a surround for the hearth stone. A thin deposit of hearth debris within (094), containing charcoal and peat ash, *c.* 0.05 m thick, was spread over the slab [095], probably representing debris of the last use of Hearth 2 (see Fig. 2B.9).

Surrounding the hearth to the SW was a kerb-like setting of rounded stones [110] set into the organic flooring (118). This curved in an arc around the SW defining a roughly circular area around the hearth that may have acted as an activity surface. This kerb was likely laid down at the same time as the hearth stones [095] and [114]. A deep deposit of organic flooring deposits (091), some 0.4 m thick, interleaved with ashy

hearth rake-out accumulated around the hearth burying this kerb (Fig. 2B.Sect-12). These floors apparently continued to accumulate to the point where the central hearth was becoming unusable, at which stage this hearth was also levelled and refurbished. The flooring deposits beyond the hearth were largely organic ((049) and (062)), and contained occupation debris including a cache of hazelnut shells.

Between this hearth and the broch entrance the partially articulated remains of two small sheep/goats (SF 201) (Fig. 2B.10) were uncovered. Although no cut could be defined in the organic flooring it is considered that this animal must have been intentionally buried

Figure 2B.9 Secondary hearth [138]

Figure 2B.10 The partial carcassess of two sheep/goat (SF201)

for its articulation to have remained intact. Within the surrounding floor deposits (049/087), deep pockets of flooring had become completely waterlogged, preserving small fragments of wood (SF 202 and SF 205). To the west and south-west of the hearth, the character of the deposits was very mixed; floor surfaces (067), (062) and (049) were mixed with deposits of clean, shelly beach sand, (076) and (077), and stone (053/068), apparently to consolidate wet surfaces. To the south, the floor in this phase became almost entirely composed of midden material (047) containing large quantities of marine shell (limpet and cockle).

During the use of this hearth there was also the noticeable phenomenon of reusing broken or discarded quern stones for construction material. Within the floor build-up in the south half of the broch, querns (SF 125, 126, 127, and 150) were uncovered within various deposits laid down to level up the floor. In addition to these, two more broken querns (SF 193 and 194) were used in the construction of the next hearth level. Another quern (SF 192) was also used as consolidation material in the flooring of the entrance passage.

Figure 2B.11 The final hearth slab [066]

Hearth 3 and the stone tank

As Hearth 2 became unusable, it was levelled with a thick deposit of ash (090) and rubble (099), before a third hearth complex was built over the top (Figs 2B.11, 2B.12, 2B.12a, 2B.12b, 2B-Sect.9, 10 and 11). This was composed of a central slab (066) surrounded by closely laid smaller flagstones. As a whole the setting measured approximately 1.5 m by 1.5 m and was covered by a patchy layer of orange ash and black charcoal (074). It seems that hearth debris, and particularly peat ash, was at regular intervals raked out and spread around the hearth, perhaps in the process of cleaning and maintenance and possibly as a way of consolidating damp and dirty flooring.

Construction of this third hearth included another kerb revetment around its SW quadrant, this time with more substantial edge-set stones [064] (Fig. 2B.12). These stones were set within a deep cut [092] through the flooring (091)/(062) around the previous hearth. The stones were then packed in with a mix of redeposited clay and large rounded cobbles (093) to support the upright kerb surround. To the south end of the hearth this surround terminated with a large vertical post stone [072] set upright within cut [092]. This was held in place which a large quantity of rounded cobbles, pebbles and a broken quern stone (SF 194). The substantial post comprised a large, rounded beach cobble with a cylindrical shape and rounded ends, measuring 0.22 m by 0.22 m by 0.75 m long.

Two similar post stones were uncovered with one to the north [060] (at the corner of the stone tank [052]) and one to the east [073] (at the edge of the deep area [069]). These were of similar size and shape and appear to have demarcated three points of a square surround around the hearth complex. There was also less certain evidence for the remains of linear arrangements of supporting stones for a stone kerb connecting these posts. This, however, was difficult to define amid the substantial rubble debris and collapse in the eastern side of the broch (071). It is

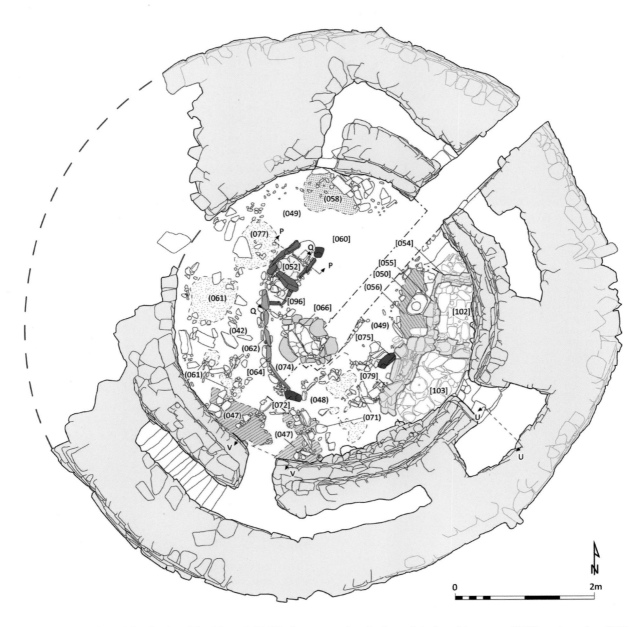

Figure 2B.12 Plan of the third and final hearth [066], the surrounding kerb, and the knocking stone [050] set into clay (056)

furthermore possible, but not demonstrable, that earlier incarnations of these surrounding walls also enclosed earlier phases of the hearth.

With the construction of this new level, the hearth complex was over 0.5 m deep (Fig. 2BSect-9), with associated floor accumulations to a similar level. The third and final hearth was of a similar design to the earlier ones, comprising flat flagstones with a kerb surround. Hearth 3 was the final hearth to be used in the broch. Around the south and south-west quadrant of the broch deposits of orange peat ash (074) had been spread across the organic flooring

(062) and midden (047). This was likely the final phase of the continual process of floor replenishment uncovered within the deeply stratified flooring to the north.

Still in use at the time of the abandonment of the broch was a stone tank or setting [052], measuring 0.7 m by 0.8 m and 0.55 m deep, located immediately NW of the hearth (Figs 2B.13, 2B.Sect-16 and 17). The stones of [052] rested directly on bedrock, and there was no evidence for clay lining or other waterproofing, so that the stone box may have been lined with hide or other organic material to allow it to hold water. The fill of [052] was

Figure 2B.12a Section through the hearth stack sequence, with the final hearth stone [066] at the top, and the primary hearth [137] visible at the base

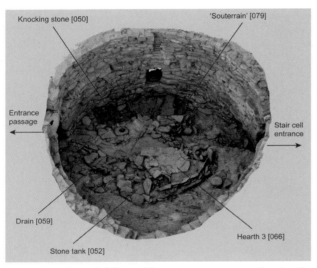

Figure 2B.12b Model derived from photogrammetry showing the position of the central hearth, the knocking stone and souterrain

a mix of large quantities of fire-cracked stone, animal bone and shell in a matrix of silty grey clay (053). The character of this fill, coupled with the proximity to the hearth suggests that the function of structure [052] was related to cooking or food preparation.

In addition to the large stone tank, a second smaller stone box [096] was uncovered between [052] and the hearth slab [066]. This was a simple feature constructed using the edges of stone tank [052] and the surround [064] as two of its edges. In addition, two edge-set stones were added making a small box no more than 0.6 m² in plan. This feature was shallow (*c.* 0.3 m deep) and poorly preserved, but appeared to have a distinct fill (097) of gritty clay flecked with red/orange ash and fire-cracked stones.

The entire SE quadrant at this time was covered by a mixed deposit of stone rubble (071) and yellow clay/ash (048) which sloped downward from west to east into the subterranean feature [069]. While little sense could be made of these remains it is possible that they had once formed the south-eastern section of the hearth surround, as well as upper portion of the walls of feature [069]. The severe disturbance of this area was unfortunate as it obscured the area of interaction between the upper broch floor and the lower subterranean chamber [069]. It is possible that the yellow ash [048] found in this area was the remains of an organic flooring which overlay revetment wall [071], but this could not be confirmed.

The knocking stone

In the NE quadrant of the broch interior, immediately above the 'souterrain' structure [069], a spread of compact brown-orange clay (056) formed a floor over roughly set flagstones [105], into which a large igneous boulder had been set. This boulder was a mortar or 'knocking stone' with a central V-shaped hole (050) *c.* 0.25 m deep which, on discovery, was full of carbonised grain (045) (Fig. 2B.14). Floor surface [105]/(056) had a distinct edge to the west, suggesting that the knocking stone may have been located within an internal compartment within the broch, though no superstructure relating to this survived. At the very least, it was surrounded by a prepared clay surface, perhaps designed to facilitate sweeping up spilled grain. Given the carbonisation of the grain within the stone, it is highly likely that the mortar was in use when the broch was destroyed, *i.e.* that it relates to the latest phase of flooring and hearth construction. Whether it was in place prior to these later phases cannot be demonstrated.

The burning, context 042

The occupation surfaces and hearth sequence described above were sealed by an event that seems likely to mark the end of significant occupation within the broch. Covering nearly all of the interior was a thick layer of charred debris (042), containing a range of materials including roundwoods, burnt heather and grasses and cereal grains (Fig. 2B.15). This deposit varied in thickness across the interior, but was virtually continuous, overlying all of the *in situ* archaeological deposits and structures, with the exception of the souterrain feature [069], where the collapse of rubble and mixed debris described above into the 'souterrain' void had apparently badly disturbed the destruction layer.

In an attempt to recover spatial patterning in context (042), the layer was sampled on a 50 cm grid (Fig. 2B.16), with a sample of approximately 0.5 litres recovered from each grid square. During excavation, specific context numbers were assigned to identifiable

Figure 2B.14 The grain-filled knocking stone (050), as discovered (top left), after excavation and sampling (bottom left) and set into the clay-covered flag floor (right)

Figure 2B.13 The ruinous stone tank [052], after removal of the surrounding flooring deposits.

patches of charcoal when sampled (contexts 007, 010, 017, 018, 019, 020, 021, 035, 037, 038, 039, 041 are all subdivisions of context (042)). Context (042) is interpreted as a single burning event that marked the end of occupation of the building.

The fire seems to have destroyed much of the internal organic furnishing of the broch, and post-excavation analysis has identified a range of organic materials that could feasibly be interpreted as internal structural material as well as possible roofing (see Chapter 5). It was notable during excavation that a large proportion of the artefacts recovered were found in the SW quadrant, in the lowest areas of the site, as though objects that had been lying on raised floors or platforms or shelving and had slid downwards as these structures collapsed. The analysis of the contents of context 042 and its spatial composition is discussed in Chapters 5 and 7.

Cell 1

Excavation of Cell 1 could not be undertaken in 2017 owing to time constraints, and this was completed in summer 2018. Before excavation, the interior was nearly three-quarters full, leaving a space only around 0.4 m high between the passage lintels and the rubble infill. The upper rubble fill (143) was around 0.25 m thick, comprising loose rubble similar in character to the debris removed from the broch interior; it is suggested that the majority of this material derived from slumping of the broch collapse debris into Cell 1 in the relatively recent past. Beneath this upper rubble a thick layer of wind-blown sand *c.* 0.4 m deep (144) had accumulated (Figs 2B.17, 2B.Sect-24). This sand deposit was largely sterile, but contained modern plastic and other debris in the upper levels.

Immediately beneath (144) was a thick, brown-black organic silt (145). This deposit was very mixed, containing fragments of unburnt bone, pottery and occasional

fragments of waterlogged wood. In several places, large patches of white animal fat were contained within (145) and near the top of the deposit was the majority of an intact, though partially burnt, sheep skeleton (155).

The lower deposit within Cell 1 was a similar greasy organic silt (159), though lighter in colour and containing lenses of charcoal. Like (145), this deposit was wet and contained numerous woody fragments, including a spatula (SF 248) and a possible bowl rough-out (SF 217). Other organic items included remarkably well-preserved woven fibres, surviving as fragments of string or cord (SF 230, SF 229). All of the pottery fragments recovered from deposits (145) and (159) were isolated and did not appear to comprise vessels broken *in situ*. Given the character of the artefacts recovered from the deposits in Cell 1, it seems likely that this space was used as a midden or dump. Radiocarbon dates from these deposits establish their contemporaneity with the main excavated occupation deposits within the broch interior (see Chapter 3).

The structure of Cell 1 itself is noteworthy. The internal space was accessed via a short, descending flight of steps leading off the broch entrance passage (Fig. 2B.18). The cell had to accommodate the sharply dropping bedrock in this area, meaning that the internal floor of the cell is *c.* 0.7 m below the level of the bedrock in the entrance passage. Thus, the corbelled roof of the cell is relatively tall for a broch guard cell, reaching a maximum height of 2.8 m. In plan, the chamber is unusually angular, while the short entrance passage opens into the cell at the latter's north-east corner, rather than in line with the long axis of the chamber: this is similarly atypical of the conventional broch arrangement. Evidence that Cell 1 had been remodelled or entirely rebuilt is also presented in the rear (south-western) wall, which is not bonded in to either the outer or inner broch walls, suggesting it may have been inserted into a longer, continuous ground gallery when Cell 1 was rebuilt and capped with the existing corbelling. This evidence for a substantial rebuild of the broch in the Iron Age is

Figure 2B.15 Burnt organics within context (042)

Figure 2B.16 Sampling the burning layer (042) on a 50 cm grid

supported in other areas of the structure and is discussed further in Chapter 9.

Cell 2

Cell 2 is the tallest intramural space in the broch, and was excavated during the main programme in 2017. The cell is rather angular in plan, with straight ends aligned radially to the broch wall (Figs 2A.7, 2B.19). Unusually, Cell 2 is accessed via an entrance doorway located *c.* 1 m above the inner wall foot; once inside there is a step down into the interior of the cell *c.* 1.5 m below, suggesting that access to and from the cell was probably via a wooden ladder or steps. The character of the stonework of Cell 2, incorporating large vertical slabs overlain by horizontal infilling courses, indicates that it was not part of the original design of the broch, or that it witnessed significant rebuilding at some stage in the history of the broch's use.

Within Cell 2, the upper floor layers were similar to the post-abandonment levels within the broch interior, comprising sandy and rubbly debris (122), overlying a layer of charcoal relating to the conflagration context (042) and (123). Beneath this were a series of floor layers and probable refurbishments, the lowest of which was a floor surface of sandstone flags [132] within a thin grey organic clay (137) (Figs 2B.20, 2B.Sect-21). Above this was a thin layer of light brown clay (136) and a deposit of charred organics (137), in turn sealed by a layer of clean beach sand (135), perhaps laid down as a refurbishment of the cell floor. Above these deposits was a further brown clay layer (125), onto which a grey-blue organic layer with an unusual 'fluffy' texture (140/141/133) and a thick deposit of burnt cereal grain and charcoal (123) had been deposited. The nature of these deposits was only identified in the post-excavation analysis stage, when ED-SEM imaging established that

they represent carbonised and vitrified cereal sheaves. It seems likely, therefore, that Cell 2 was used as a storage area for cereals, perhaps both unprocessed sheaves and processed grain.

Gallery 3: the stairs and stair-foot cell

Gallery 3 is located on the south side of the broch, immediately above the area on the south wall face that was the focus of the primary remedial works. This intramural space is the largest of those surviving in the broch wall, comprising the stair to the first floor of the tower and encompassing a ground-level stair-foot cell running to the west for a distance of over 3.5 m. The stair itself comprises 13 steps ascending clockwise to the east, leading to a short surviving landing at first floor level (Fig. 2B.21). Prior to excavation commencing, Gallery 3 was filled close to the level of the wall-head with rubble debris and wind-blown sand. On removal of this material, it became clear that the majority of the soft sediment accumulation in this area was of relatively modern date, with the upper sandy deposit producing pieces of fishing float, fragments of plastic and a penny dating to 1944. Within this accumulated sand, several large, long sandstone blocks were removed from Gallery 3, interpreted as fallen lintels that originally spanned the gallery above head height. During excavation, the surviving unstable lintels that spanned the stair gallery were removed, marked and set aside for reinstatement after the completion of consolidation works.

At the foot of the stair, removal of the same rubble and sandy deposits encountered in the broch interior uncovered a steep step in the bedrock, over which Gallery 3 had been constructed; the lowest stair tread was placed at the edge of this bedrock shelf, meaning that the floor space within Gallery 3 would have been uneven and presumably floored with timber or wicker to allow access. Within the

Figure 2B.17 Section through deposits in Cell 1

Figure 2B.18 The steps down into Cell 1, seen from inside the cell

upper sandy deposits at the foot of the stair, a large whale vertebra was recovered (SF 24).

Following inspection of the walling within the stair foot cell to the west of Gallery 3, it was considered unsafe to remove the infilling rubble and sediment without risking destabilisation of the inner broch wall and the capping lintels in this area. During removal of the rubble at the foot of the stair, these deposits were stepped back into the stair foot cell, and during the final consolidation works, revetted with drystone walling to prevent visitor access. The interior deposits in this area remain unexcavated.

Cell 4

Cell 4, the right-hand guard cell [032] off the entrance passage in the NW quadrant of the broch was fully excavated. As in the entrance passage and other intramural cells, the uppermost deposits (080) were inorganic sand and brashy rubble, likely derived from post-abandonment processes and wind-blow. Beneath (080) was a somewhat disturbed flagstone floor (108), composed of flat sandstone slabs averaging around 0.4 by 0.35 m across. These

flagstones were packed and levelled with a rubbly infill (109), which lay within a thick deposit of organic green-brown humic silty clay (081) (Fig. 2B.Sect-23). (081) was banded, with visible layers in section, suggesting that the deposit represented flooring material that had been repeatedly refurbished in a similar manner to the organic floors encountered within the broch interior (see analysis in Chapter 6). These flooring deposits directly overlay bedrock; no finds were recovered during their excavation.

Cell/Gallery 5

During the removal of rubble from the seaward-side broken wall end prior to consolidation works, the vestigial remains of a probable further gallery, labelled Gallery 5, were uncovered on the south wall end, indicating that a further intramural cell had been located on the west side of the broch. It is probable that this cell was accessed at ground level from a doorway located close to the 3 o'clock position within the broch, within the segment of walling now lost to coastal erosion, but too little of the cell remained to establish more of its character. Evidence

Figure 2B.19 Cell 2 interior, showing the vertical slabbing and horizontal coursing in the south (left) and north (right) walls, which is not integrated with the internal wall of the broch.

Figure 2B.20 Section through deposits in Cell2, with the paving slabs visible at the base of the section

for the cell was restricted to a curving alignment of facing boulders (Fig. 2B.22), placed on the bedrock at the position of the inner wall face of the outer wall. Within the space created by Cell 5 was a mixed, brashy-rubble deposit, primarily composed of relatively recent sandy soil and tumbled boulders.

Post abandonment and collapse

The fire represented by (042) and its constituent contexts must have occurred close to or at the end of occupation of the broch, as no disturbance of this layer or any other evidence of occupation after this event was apparent. Over the top of the charcoal layer was a layer of brown-pink sand (028); this likely constituted a combination of material eroded from the still-standing broch walls without a roof, material eroded from the overlying rubble and wind-blown sands undergoing natural processes of soil development.

The quantity and disposition of the rubble lying inside the building clearly derived from the collapse of upper levels of the wall of the structure that must have occurred after abandonment. In several places during the process of rubble removal, rectangular slabs were encountered in imbricated blocks, as though representing masonry that had tumbled as a near-intact unit from the wall above. Given the frequency with which broch collapse rubble is reused in the construction of post-broch buildings, care was taken during stone removal to ensure that evidence for any secondary stone structures relating to post-broch activity was assessed and fully recorded. Although, as noted, several intact blocks of stacked masonry were observed within the rubble, the majority of these were deemed more likely to be structured collapse of the broch wall than secondary constructions (Fig. 2B.24). One exception to this was a small semicircular block of possible walling, built against the broch wall in the SE quadrant, described as [008] (Fig. 2B.25). This walling was poorly built, to the extent that in some areas it was inconclusive whether it in fact represented fortuitous

Figure 2B.21a View of the stair gallery, after excavation and consolidation

Figure 2B.21b View of the stairs from the stair foot cell

Figure 2B.22 View of the vestigial remains of a ground-level gallery, beneath the ruinous south wall end of the broch

collapse and abutted the broch wall above the scarcement ledge to form a small cell *c.* 2.5 m across. As removal of the rubble layers surrounding [008] progressed, it became clear that the walling rested on unstructured collapse debris, and there were no associated soil deposits. It was concluded that, if walling [008] indeed represented a structure built within the broch rubble, it was very temporary in nature and likely to relate to relatively recent use of the site. Local knowledge of casual use of the broch in recent times as a shepherd's shelter and other expedient uses were reported to the excavators by several visitors.

The rubble deposits themselves were described in three layers – an uppermost, very disturbed layer of sandstone blocks with demonstrable evidence of movement and disturbance in recent times (004), a middle, more voided layer containing a large percentage of shattered, brash-like and sandy material (005) and a lower, less obviously disturbed layer of somewhat larger blocks (011), immediately overlying the destruction (042) and post-abandonment (028) layers. The rubble debris was laser scanned at each of these levels (Fig. 2B.23) and the

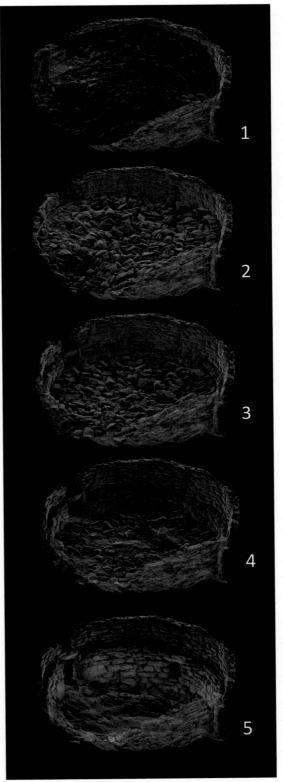

Figure 2B.23 Laser scan images showing the stages of rubble removal from pre-excavation (1) to the removal of deposits to bedrock (5). The upper level of the occupation deposits is shown in image 4

Figure 2B.24 Semi-structured rubble in the upper levels of the collapse debris

Figure 2B.25 Ruinous structure [008] built in the upper levels of the broch collapse debris

volume of rubble overlying the occupation deposits was calculated as 105.36 m³.

The entrance passage and the approach to the broch

Although cleared out prior to the project starting at the broch, the entrance passage was filled with soft sediments and rubble left exposed and vulnerable by the rubble removal from the interior of the garth (Figs 2B.Sect-19 and 2B.Sect-20). The upper levels of the passage were an inorganic orange-brown sand (082) overlying a dark humic clay layer (083), containing numerous lenses of ashy/charcoally deposits, sampled as (113). A fragment of quern stone (SF 192) and a ceramic sherd (SF 211) were recovered from this deposit. Immediately inside the door jambs of the entrance passage, a discrete patch of charcoal (106) was also sampled, though this was too degraded to be identifiable as structural in the field. Beneath these soft deposits, the flagstone covering of drain [059] ran into the entrance passage directly for a length of around 2 m, directly overlying the bedrock. The drain ran somewhat to the eastern side of the entrance passage, though this is considered to be simply a response to the landward-sloping bedrock, which drops away in this direction.

The entrance area was returned to in 2018 in order to complete the removal of rubble and soil deposits which blocked direct access to the broch interior through the entrance passage. In July 2018, the passage between the external buildings located to the NE of the broch was cleared of debris and the deposits excavated (Figs 2B.27, 2B.Sect-19 and 2B.Sect-20). Beneath a layer of loose rubble and wind-blown sand (082) a dark organic layer (146) – equivalent to (083) – was encountered. This deposit was very mixed, containing lenses of charcoal and ash, fire-cracked stones and rounded pebbles. Directly beneath, a rubble layer (153) comprising irregular stones up to

0.25 m across, probably representing collapse debris or rubble – perhaps relating to an earlier reconstruction of the broch tower – contained several large sandstone slabs (154) which had the appearance of rough, secondary paving laid down to level debris in the entrance passage (Fig. 2B.28). Beneath (154) a dark, humic soil (158) containing charcoal, shattered stone and shell fragments overlay the primary paving in the passage [152]. This paving was composed of slab-like quarried sandstone blocks, laid directly onto the uneven bedrock surface. The mixed humic deposit (158) surrounded the paving slabs, and a bulk sample was collected from beneath one slab before it was replaced.

The lintel spanning the passage approach outside the broch was broken, and removed prior to excavation of the passage and set aside for the duration of the works. On completion, the lintel was dowelled back together using 10 mm stainless steel threaded bar and resin mortar, before being replaced in its original location.

The position of the lintel marked the threshold to an ancillary building constructed against the northern outer wall of the broch. This structure is clearly secondary to the broch build, and is not bonded to the broch in any way (see Fig. 2A.5), but how much later than the broch this structure is cannot be demonstrated. During removal of the rubble in the access passage to the north of the broch entrance, the lintel mentioned above was found to cap a doorway defined by two upright door jambs forming an antechamber inside the building immediately to the north of the broch entrance. The walling abutting the NE of the broch entrance formed a solid triangular block of masonry [147], effectively extending the broch entrance passage into an accessway. The outer, eastern face of this masonry block is somewhat rounded, though little could be seen of the outer wall beneath the rubble debris to the east. In its interior, this walling stood to a maximum of 1.85 m in height, coming close to the level of the outermost triangular lintel of the broch's entrance passage.

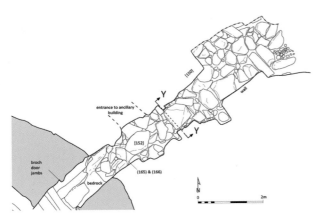

Figure 2B.26 Plan of the paved entrance passage outside the broch, between the ancilliary buildings to the north and south

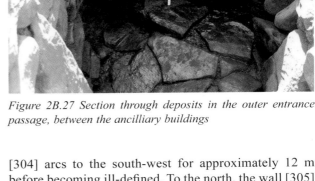

Figure 2B.27 Section through deposits in the outer entrance passage, between the ancilliary buildings

On the opposite side, to the NW of the broch entrance, the walling of the ancillary building stood to 1.71 m in height, with a pronounced corbel, away from the broch, towards the upper levels of the 11 courses of sandstone blocks [148]. Within this wall, a doorway led in to the ancillary building to the west of the broch access passage. This opening was 0.5 m wide and again had a notable corbel, suggesting that the outer walls of the structure corbelled toward their upper levels in order to reduce the roofing span. The void within the ancillary building was filled with loose rubble which was not disturbed; the project stonemason stabilised this by revetting a stone face against it. The arrangement of the visible areas of walling in the ancillary building suggests that this building survives to at least 1.8 m in height, is rubble filled and largely undisturbed since collapse.

Immediately to the north of the wall of the ancillary building, a low revetment of sandstone slabs [150] was constructed, probably in response to the slumping of the outer wall of the building. This revetment was demonstrably a secondary addition since it overlay paving [152], which otherwise respected the walling of the ancillary building. The paving slabs [152] continued to the north of the ancillary structure, lining the access passage for a distance of at least 7.5 m from the broch entrance threshold. It seems likely that this paving extends around the ancillary structures north of the broch, and possibly as far as the entrance in the encircling outer enclosure.

The outer enclosure
Leanne Demay

Surrounding the broch, and visible in places beneath piles of collapse rubble, is a substantial stone wall forming an enclosure. The entrance through this outer wall is located in the north-east, and comprises a paved threshold giving access to the passage leading to the broch entrance. To the south of the entrance the wall

[304] arcs to the south-west for approximately 12 m before becoming ill-defined. To the north, the wall [305] arcs to the north-west for approximately 9 m before becoming ill-defined. At the entrance, the walls terminate at substantial sandstone orthostats measuring 1.05 m and 0.7 m respectively, creating an imposing entrance into a walled passage 1.8 m wide.

The outer passage

The northern wall [307] in the outer passage extends west-south-west from boundary wall entrance stone [305] for 2.5 m and abuts a stone stack beside an upright post stone [309]. The northern wall has almost completely collapsed and only the lowest courses remain. The southern wall [306] survives as three courses of large sandstone blocks and boulders, stands 0.7 m high, and extends 2.9 m from boundary wall entrance stone [304] towards the west where it abuts an equivalent post stone [308].

The uppermost deposit in the outer passage was turf-covered rubble (301) comprising large sub-angular sandstone boulders of various sizes up to 0.7 m in length. Shallow topsoil (302) was present between the rubble, over a layer of eroded material comprising mixed pink and red sand with fragments of sandstone (303). Removal of these upper deposits revealed a dark reddish-brown silty sand with frequent charcoal inclusions, localised around the area of post-stone [309] and wall [307]. A further deposit of rubble (312) consisting of a mix of sub-angular and sub-rounded sandstone up to 0.5 m in length extended across the outer passage area and is likely to represent collapse from first activity post-abandonment.

Around the exterior of the outer passage entrance, removal of rubble (312) revealed paving [316] consisting of substantial flat sandstone slabs up to 0.85 m by 0.7 m by 0.15 m. The slabs were set into dark brown silty

Figure 2B.28 View of the outer entrance passage, showing the paved approach to the broch between the (unexcavated) ancilliary buildings

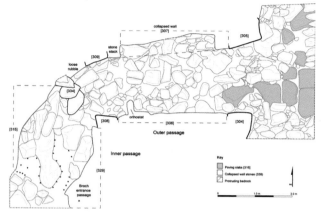

Figure 2B.29 Plan of the entrance through the outer enclosure, following removal of rubble

sand containing occasional charcoal flecks and charred material (331; 332). It was unclear whether these deposits represented bedding material or an *in situ* ground surface present prior to the passage construction. In the outer passage, removal of rubble (312) revealed a lower deposit of stones (319) comprising flat sandstone flags up to 0.48 m in length and sub-rounded sandstone blocks up to 0.5 m in length. Deposits in the outer passage were limited; many stones directly overlay bedrock or a natural accumulation of dark brown sandy silt (314). Occasional pockets of waterlogged dark brownish black silty sand (327) and (328) containing woody fragments, burnt bone and charcoal were encountered directly overlying bedrock and sealed by collapsed structural stones probably associated with early post-abandonment.

The substantial paving slabs [316] observed at the entrance exterior did not extend into the passage. While lower stones (319) appear to have been deliberately positioned to fill voids in the undulating bedrock, the function of others were unclear and may represent collapsed structural stones. During excavation in wet weather, significant water seepage was noted in the outer passage. The elevation and natural rise in the bedrock towards the inner passage and volume of seepage suggests this area may never have been paved and was probably left exposed, with stones (319) placed in the deeper cavities around protruding bedrock to level the surface, whilst retaining maximum drainage properties.

The inner passage

Two large upright post stones [308] and [309] form a threshold and a distinct transition from the outer passage to the inner passage as it arcs sharply to towards the south-west. Post stone [308] stands 1 m high and adjoins outer passage wall [306] to the east and inner passage wall [329] to the south. Post stone [309] stands 0.76 m high and adjoins a stack of flat, square-edged stones to the east.

A rubble filled void to the west continues for approximately 0.5 m before encountering three large slab-like stones in a stepped arrangement [334]. It is likely these form an entrance from the inner passage leading to the ancillary building discussed above.

Within the limits of the excavation, the remains of southern wall [329] extended 2.5 m towards the southwest from post stone [308] and northern wall [315] extended 2.8 m NE–SW from stone steps [334]. Although both walls survive to 0.5 m high and consist of three courses of large sandstone blocks and boulders, [315] is notably of inferior build, consisting of rubble topped by two large flat sandstone slab-like stones.

Upper deposits in the inner passage consisted of loose, partially turf-covered rubble overlying mid-reddish-brown loamy sand (317) containing sub-angular and sub-rounded stones (80%) with an average length of 0.12 m. Removal of the upper deposits revealed blackish brown silty sand (318) with patches of darker staining containing charcoal which extended across and was contained within the inner passage area only.

The deposits encountered in the inner passage differed greatly to those in the outer passage. Whilst those in the outer passage were limited in depth and extent, the inner passage contained a substantial deposit of levelling material packed into cavities and around protruding bedrock. Removal of (318) revealed waterlogged dark blackish-brown sandy silt (320) with inclusions of burnt bone, woody fragments, white quartz pebbles and containing angular and broken sandstone fragments (322) up to 0.2 m (80%). Lenses of mid-orange sand with burnt bone (323) and brownish-orange sand with woody fragments (324) within (320) may represent remains of organic flooring material within a maintained floor surface. A large fragment of possible whalebone (SF 286) was recovered from the lower extent of (320). Collapsed structural blocks (338) concentrated around the edges of the inner passage overlying (320) are associated with post-abandonment of this phase.

The entrance passage was cleared of rubble and deposits were excavated to the underlying bedrock. All large paving slabs at the entrance exterior were preserved *in situ*. To create a safe access for visitors, voids and cavities around protruding bedrock were backfilled and the passages were levelled utilising the larger, flat stones removed during excavation which were bedded into sand for stability.

Summary of the structural and occupation sequence

The following description sets out the sequence of construction and occupation of the broch and associated settlement, as interpreted by the excavators.

Stage 1A

Stage 1A comprises the construction of the primary monument. The weight of evidence points towards this monument being a broch, but this cannot be demonstrated conclusively. The only structural evidence for this element is the stub of damaged walling located in the 9 o'clock to 11 o'clock positions in the interior, in the southern half of the 'souterrain' structure. The Stage 1B structure was evidently damaged by a catastrophic structural failure, most evident in the eastern half of the surviving monument.

Stage 1B

Following Stage 1A, the structure was rebuilt along the template of an RSM broch and must have had tower-like proportions. Structural elements necessary for the attainment of height were incorporated into the walls, including relieving stacked voids over the cell threshold lintels, edge-set lintels over the entrance passage and a clockwise ascending stair providing access to a first-floor gallery. This structure in turn suffered significant damage, probably including a large-scale collapse that damaged both the inner and outer walls of the broch, with this disruption most detectable in the outer walling either side of the entrance passage, in the higher levels of the stair cell and in much of the inner wall face.

There is no direct dating evidence for Stage 1A or 1B. Early dates within the determinations from samples recovered from the occupation deposits, which calibrate in the 4th to 3rd century BC, could be related to this phase (see Chapter 3), but this cannot be demonstrated.

Stage 2A

At some stage following the collapse that brought about the end of the Stage 1 use of the monument, the structure was cleared out to ground level and rebuilt for a second time. At this point, the inner wall-face was largely reconstructed on a plan close to that of the original Stage 1 monument but involving a resetting of the inner wall face and the incorporation of large edge-set slabs in the inner wall face and Cell 2. It is probable that it was during Stage 2A that the ground floor gallery was sub-divided to create isolated cells from a previously continuous gallery. Vestigial elements of the original tower were retained, including skeuomorphic versions of the stacked voids above Cells 2 and 4, and perhaps through an awkward reconstruction of the stair gallery and its capping. The outer wall of the broch either side of the entrance was substantially rebuilt over the debris of the earlier tower and may have involved resetting of the triangular threshold lintel.

Stage 2A marks the beginning of the Middle Iron Age occupation of the site, including all of the occupation debris excavated within the interior and the three sequential hearth settings, and came to an end with the burning event represented by context (042). Radiocarbon dates suggest this phase took place within a span of around 50 years following 50 BC, but its duration may have been shorter.

Stage 2B

Following the reconstruction of the building in the Middle Iron Age, and perhaps not long after, additional buildings were constructed against the outer wall of the broch. These remain unexcavated, and as such no information is available on their function or duration of use, but radiocarbon dates from deposits beneath and above paving integral to these structures suggests they were in use at the same time as the MIA occupation of the broch (Chapter 3).

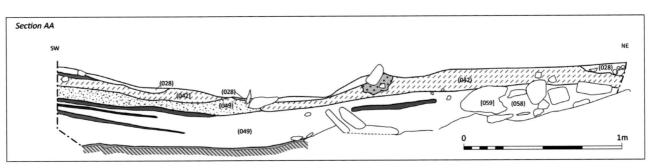

Figure 2B.Sect-1 North baulk, east-facing section through occupation deposits

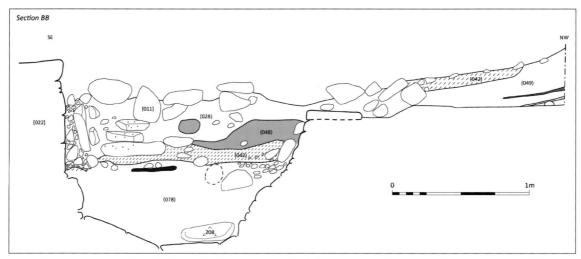

Figure 2B.Sect-2 East baulk, north-facing section through occupation deposits and upper souterrain fill

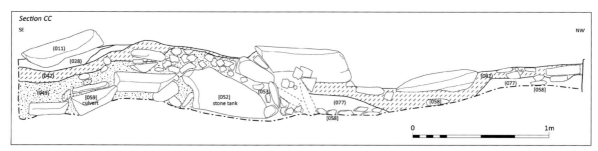

Figure 2B.Sect-3 West baulk, north facing section through occupation deposits, the stone tank and drain/culvert 059

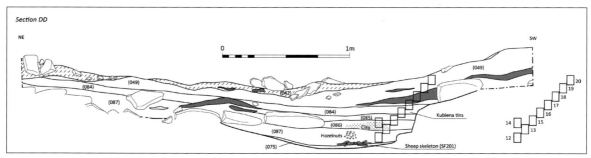

Figure 2B.Sect-4 North baulk, west facing section through occupation deposits

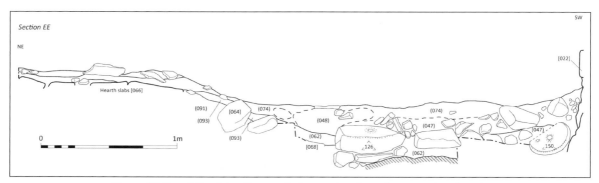

Figure 2B.Sect-5 South baulk, west facing section through occupation deposits

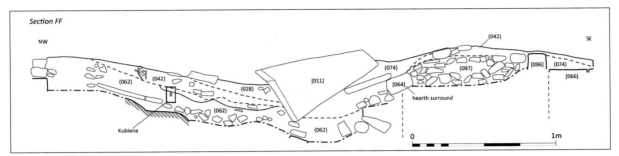

Figure 2B.Sect-6 West baulk, south facing section through occupation deposits

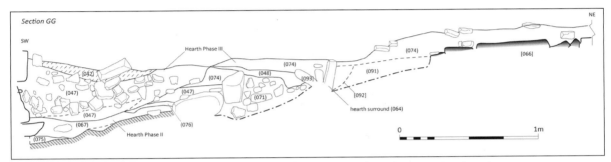

Figure 2B.Sect-7 South baulk, east facing section through occupation deposits

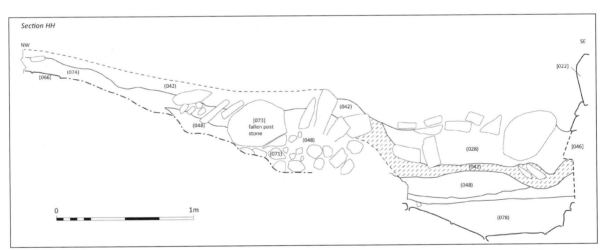

Figure 2B.Sect-8 East baulk, south facing section through occupation deposits and souterrain fill

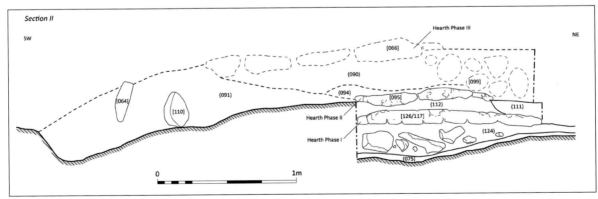

Figure 2B.Sect-9 Composite section through the hearth stack

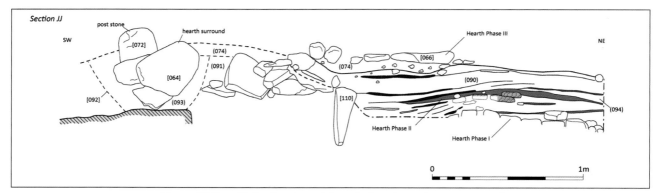

Figure 2B.Sect-10 Section through hearth deposits and stone surround

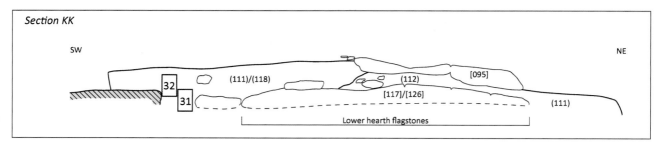

Figure 2B.Sect-11 Section through the primary hearth and associated deposits

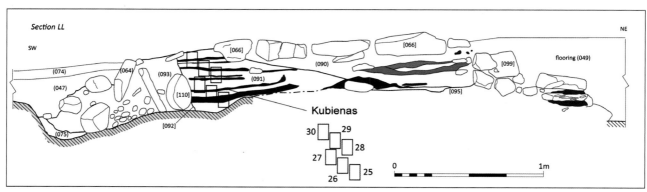

Figure 2B.Sect-12 East facing section through hearth complex deposits

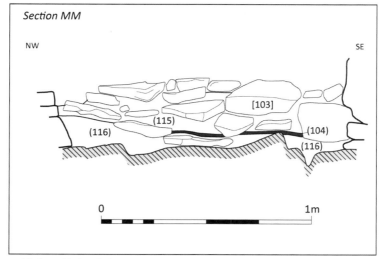

Figure 2B.Sect-13 South-facing section through flag floor [103], within the souterrain

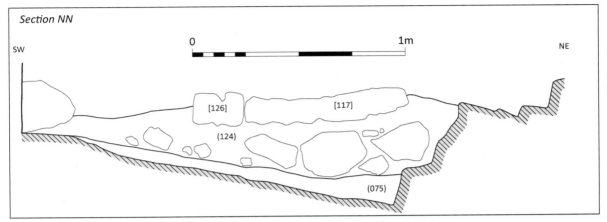

Figure 2B.Sect-14 Section through the primary hearth

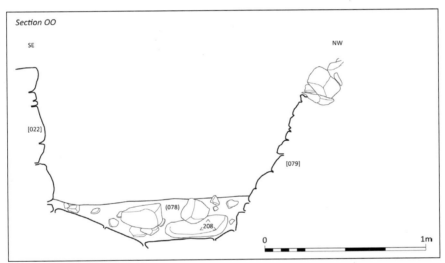

Figure 2B.Sect-15 Section through lower fill deposits within the souterrain

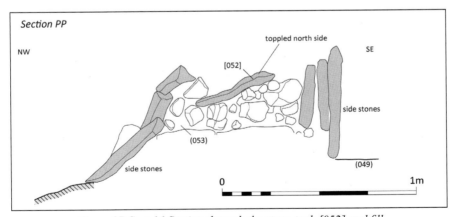

Figure 2B.Sect-16 Section through the stone tank [052] and fill

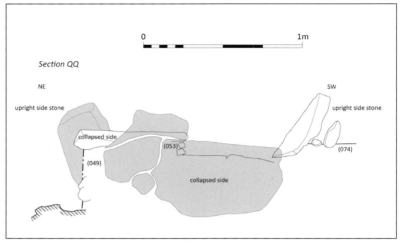

Figure 2B.Sect-17 Longitudinal section through the stone tank [052]

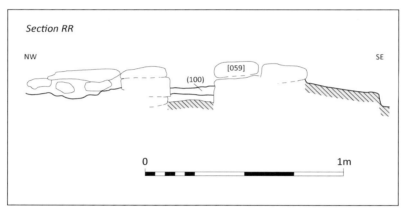

Figure 2B.Sect-18 Section through the stone drain [059]

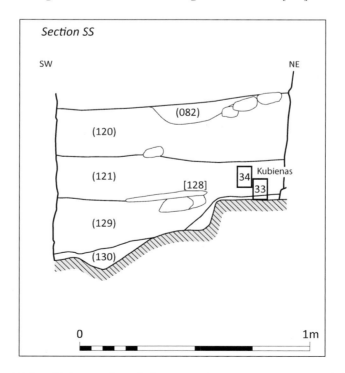

Figure 2B.Sect-19 Section through deposits in the entrance passage, south facing

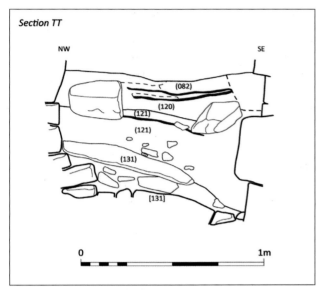

Figure 2B.Sect-20 Section through deposits in the entrance passage, north facing

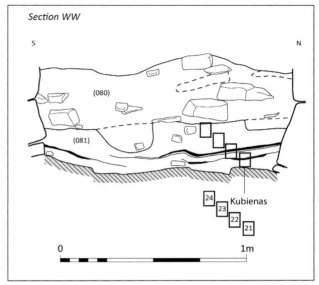

Figure 2B.Sect-23 Section through deposits in Cell 4

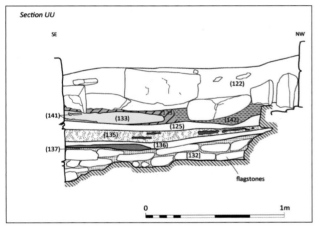

Figure 2B.Sect-21 Section through deposits and flag flooring in Cell 2

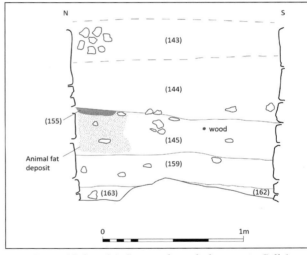

Figure 2B.Sect-24: Section through deposits in Cell 1

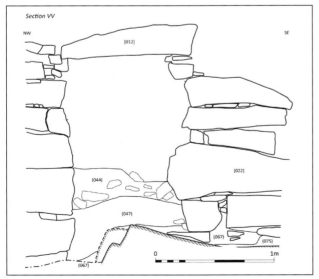

Figure 2B.Sect-22 Section through deposits filling the stair cell entrance

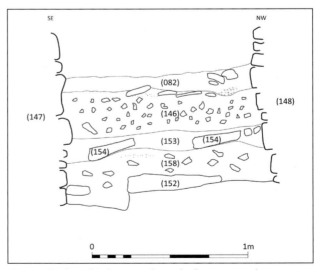

Figure 2B.Sect-25 Section through deposits in the entrance passage approach to the broch

3

Radiocarbon dating

John Barber and Graeme Cavers

Dating strategy

Twenty radiocarbon determinations[1] were obtained for samples from deposits within the broch and from surrounding structures. All of the radiocarbon dates were provided by the SUERC facility in East Kilbride, and calibration was undertaken using OxCal 4.4 using the IntCal20 calibration curve (Reimer *et al.* 2020). The initial batch of dates were selected to construct a chronological framework for the sediments within the broch, while a second set were selected to test the interpretation of that outline chronology. A third tranche of dates were selected to establish the relationship of external structures to the broch.

The conflagration context (042), together with the date from the scarcement (taken in 2012), on archaeological grounds,[2] is taken to represent the final event in the occupation of the broch and there is no archaeological evidence for settlement or other significant human activity within the interior after this event.

The outliers

The data set of 20 determinations spread over a range of 718 ^{14}C-years[3] is illustrated in Table 3.1 and Figure 3.1; this group of determinations is graphed in Figure 3.2. The distribution of age determinations is almost rectangular with three outliers, two earlier than the main dataset and one later. The temptation to dismiss these as statistical outliers must be tempered by the knowledge that, at ±2σ (the 95% confidence interval) only one date should be expected to fall outside the main body of the data, on the random hypothesis. The two earlier dates represent single years in the intervals 535 cal BC to 392 cal BC and 416 cal BC to 262 cal BC,[4] with a 24 year overlap range of 416 to 392 cal BC (a mere 46 ^{14}C-years separates these two older age determinations).

The 46 ^{14}C-year interval between them is not significant with respect to the precision of the radiocarbon method; both have counting errors of ±26 ^{14}C-years and each lies within 2σ of the others cited age. If it be hypothesised that they represent an event in the primary use of the monument, or its locus, then the age of that event would best be represented by the weighted mean, ±1/σ², of these two determinations, viz; 2348±18 BP (Long and Rippeteau 1974, 2) It is concluded that these two early dates are residual elements on the monument as excavated but may reflect a real event in the biography of the primary Clachtoll broch monument (see Chapter 10). The closeness of the determinations, and the differences in their stratigraphic find spots, add some weight to the idea that, although residual, these bones were not random survivors of intermittent-discard origins.

These two dates are inconsistent in the contexts and deposits in which they were found. Therefore, an additional Quality Assurance statement was sought and received from SUERC, who could not find any technical reason for the dates falling so far from the core group. An additional bone date was commissioned for bone from context (087), to explore whether bone dates from the site produced systematically anomalous results. The additional date proved close to the group norm and so this possibility was rejected. Both bone samples were too small and abraded to be identifiable to species level and the possibility was considered that they evidenced a marine reservoir effect, with naturally relict ^{14}C from marine environments. However, the possibility that these bones were either those of marine mammals or from terrestrial mammals fed on marine matter, like seaweed or fish meal, was ruled out by the fact that their delta C[13] values fall in the range typical of terrestrial mammals. Neither was their sampling nor

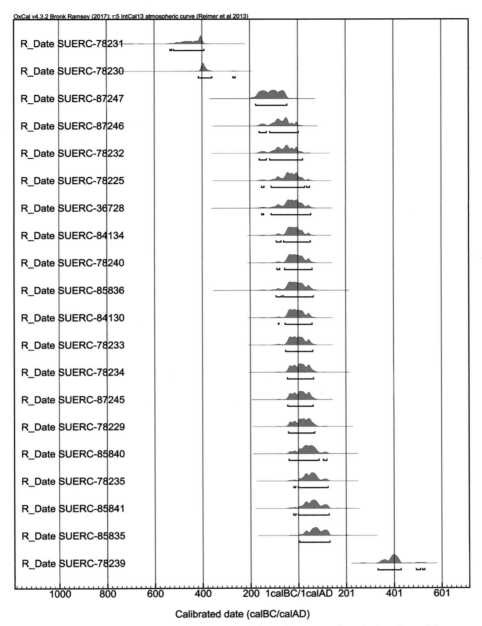

OxCal v4.3.2 Bronk Ramsey (2017); r:5 IntCal13 atmospheric curve (Reimer et al 2013)

R_Date SUERC-78231
R_Date SUERC-78230
R_Date SUERC-87247
R_Date SUERC-87246
R_Date SUERC-78232
R_Date SUERC-78225
R_Date SUERC-36728
R_Date SUERC-84134
R_Date SUERC-78240
R_Date SUERC-85836
R_Date SUERC-84130
R_Date SUERC-78233
R_Date SUERC-78234
R_Date SUERC-87245
R_Date SUERC-78229
R_Date SUERC-85840
R_Date SUERC-78235
R_Date SUERC-85841
R_Date SUERC-85835
R_Date SUERC-78239

1000   800   600   400   200 1calBC/1calAD 201   401   601

Calibrated date (calBC/calAD)

Figure 3.1 Calibration distributions of radiocarbon determinations from deposits within the broch, and from structures outside the broch tabulated in Table 3.1

processing different in any way from those of the rest of the dated samples. There is therefore no reason to reject these dates as aberrant.

One of the dated samples (SUERC-87247) came from a floor level relatively high in the stratigraphy whilst the other (2053 BC, SUERC-87246) was close to the bottom. Their stratigraphically distinct contexts suggests that this material does not derive from *in situ* early occupation levels but rather from the inclusion and burning of debris

found nearby, perhaps from small refuse spreads relating to an earlier period of activity.

Consequently, the early dates from the burnt bones are considered accurate and it is concluded that the material was residual, from an earlier phase of activity at the site.

The younger of the two early dates is separated from the oldest determination from the main body of the data by some 237 ^{14}C-years and on statistical grounds, could not legitimately be averaged with them. On this

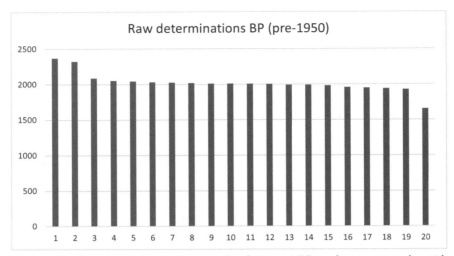

Figure 3.2 The distribution of radiocarbon determinations, rendered as years BP is almost rectangular with two earlier and one later outliers

evidence, and in the absence of dating technology reasons or sedimentary or structural evidence to the contrary, it is assumed that this interval indicates a *circa* two-century hiatus in the monument's biography.

The youngest radiocarbon determination is 275 ^{14}C-years younger than the core group of determinations (Table 3.1). The dated sample was burnt bone, and in this instance, it is suggested that it probably infiltrated down through open voids in the masonry rubble of the monument's final collapse. As noted above, the radiocarbon laboratory has confirmed that it can find no procedural reason to suspect bias in the determination of the burnt bone dates and their ΔC^{13} levels do not indicate marine origins or marine reservoir effect. It is concluded therefore that this bone is displaced from some transient deposit formed within the broch garth and filtered thence into the lower levels of the broch's masonry infill, probably in the 4th or 5th century AD.

As noted in Chapter 2, two stadia were observed in the masonry infill, in which sandy soil deposits amongst the stones indicated temporary and discontinuous ground surfaces. Activity on either of these could have generated the recovered bone, as waste material from a cooking site for example. The *ad hoc* reuse of abandoned brochs is well attested and Curle has noted, regarding the abandoned Dun Troddan Broch, that 'there had at all times been shelter here for the fugitive and the vagrant' (Curle 1921, 88). Some evidence for activity in the form of transient shelters or huts built within the rubble of the broch's collapse was noted in the early stages of the excavation (*supra*), but this can only have happened long after the main structural collapse and, given the continuity of the covering charcoal layer from the conflagration event, evidently did not disturb the main occupation deposits in the interior. It

is probable that this late date derives from debris relating to some unknown phase of post-abandonment activity.

The core group of dates
Radiocarbon dates and stratigraphy

The distribution of the dated elements through the stratigraphy of the occupation deposits demonstrates firstly that the entire excavated sequence from bedrock to the conflagration belongs within the Middle Iron Age activity horizon, within the ^{14}C-year range from 176 BC to AD 65, and secondly that reworking of floor components, inclusions and hearth debris has resulted in residual and contaminant material being incorporated into otherwise undisturbed deposits. As a consequence, the early outliers discussed above come from contexts with relative stratigraphic positions *above* the earliest Middle Iron Age layers, *i.e.* from debris relating to Hearths 2 (context 094) and 3 (context 074). This seems likely to be a result of the floor formation processes, which evidently involved occasional rake-out and replacement, in consolidation of the organic materials around the accumulating hearth sites (see Roy, Chapter 6). During this process, it would not be difficult to envisage some mixing and cross-contamination of burnt bone or charcoal fragments between superimposed floor layers. In effect, the core group of dates represent a single block of activity, spanning several decades and the stratigraphic phases identified during the excavation of the deposits cannot be equated to the chronological distribution of C14 determinations. However, the dates are so close to each other and their calibrated ranges overlap to such a great extent (see Figs 3.1 and 3.4) that the apparent conflict between their numerical sequence

Table 3.1 Radiocarbon determinations from samples within the broch structure and surrounding structures

Area	Type	Species	Context	Lab Code	BP Determination	Calibrated Date (2 σ)
Charcoal layer over interior, sealing occupation	Charcoal	Corylus	42	SUERC-78233	2004±26	53 BC–AD 62
Charcoal layer over interior, sealing occupation	Charred cereal grain	Hordeum (hulled barley)	42	SUERC-78234	1992±26	46 BC–AD 65
Scarcement charcoal from 2012 works	Charcoal	Corylus	Scarcement	SUERC-36728	2025±30	153 BC–AD 55
Hearth debris relating to use of Hearth 3	Burnt bone	Burnt bone, L/M fragment	74	SUERC-78231	2371±26	535–392 BC
Hearth debris relating to use of Hearth 3	Charcoal	Sorbus	74	SUERC-78232	2045±26	161 BC–AD 21
Bone date test from flooring	Bone	Cattle	049	SUERC-87245	1991±25	45 BC–AD 63
Articulated skeleton in flooring	Bone – rib	Sheep/goat	087	SUERC-87247	2088±24	176–45 BC
Hearth debris relating to use of Hearth 2	Burnt bone	Burnt bone, carpal L/M	94	SUERC-78230	2325±26	416–262 BC
Dark silty organic deposit beneath flagstones in 'souterrain' [069]	Carbonised hazelnut shell	Corylus	104	SUERC-78225	2032±26	152 BC–AD 50
Early floor layers on S half of interior	Burnt bone	Burnt bone, L/M fragment	67	SUERC-78239	1655±26	AD 332–528
Early floor layers on S half of interior	Charcoal	Betula	67	SUERC-78240	2010±26	88 BC–AD 60
Charcoal from mixed debris layer	Charcoal	Betula	078 East	SUERC-87246	2053±21	161 BC–AD 3
Organic flooring deposit beneath Hearth 1 (primary)	Carbonised hazelnut shell	Corylus	124	SUERC-78229	1982±26	42 BC–AD 69
Charred materials including cereals within Cell 2	Charred cereal grain	Hordeum (6 row barley)	123	SUERC-78235	1949±26	20 BC–AD 125
Entrance to enclosure	Cereal caryopses	Hordeum (Hulled barley)	333	SUERC-85840	1960±30	40 BC–AD 121
Entrance to enclosure	Charcoal	Corylus	337	SUERC-85841	1941±30	21 BC–AD 129
Cell 1 upper midden deposit	Charcoal	Salix	145	SUERC-84130	2008±25	83 BC–AD 59
Cell 1 lower midden deposit	Charred nutshell	Corylus	159	SUERC-84134	2019±24	91 BC–AD 53
Ancillary passage N of broch	Cereal caryopses	Hordeum (Hulled barley)	158	SUERC-85835	1928±30	AD 5–132
Ancillary passage N of broch	Cereal caryopses	Hordeum (Hulled barley)	165	SUERC-85836	2010±30	92 BC–AD 65

Table 3.2 Excluding the 2088 and 2053 determinations, it is legitimate on statistical grounds alone to average each sequential pair of determinations from Clachtoll

Determination	± Error	Averageable
2088	24	
2053	21	NO
2045	26	YES
2032	26	YES
2025	30	YES
2019	24	YES
2010	26	YES
2010	30	YES
2008	25	YES
2004	26	YES
1992	26	YES
1991	25	YES
1982	26	YES
1960	30	YES
1949	26	YES
1941	30	YES
1928	30	YES

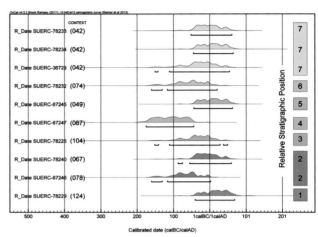

Figure 3.3 The 'core' group of C14 dates for deposits within the garth, in relative stratigraphic order from lowest (1) to highest (7). The outliers are excluded

and their stratigraphic sequence can be explained by the counting statistics and calibration process alone.

Seven stratigraphic units across the occupation sequence were dated, ranging from the lowest/earliest deposits associated with the primary hearth to three determinations relating to the final conflagration (two from the conflagration layer (042) and the third from 'The Scarcement' date). These chrono-stratigraphic start and end points to the core activity in the garth constrain the modelling discussed below.

Excluding the earliest and latest 'outliers', the core group of dates is represented by 17 determinations over the 160 ^{14}C-year determination range 2088 to 1928 (Fig. 3.1). If the separation of the data along the x-axis of Figure 3.2 correlated with actual depth in a single sedimentary column, *which they do not*, it would be interpreted as indicative as a steady accumulation of sediments (represented by their radiocarbon determinations) in the earliest six sedimentary units followed by a greater but uneven rate of deposition in the middle seven units (more deposits in shorter timespan) and a return to the earlier profile in the final three (Fig. 3.3). Given that the scale of the x-axis is a variable and not fixed units of a set time interval, then the clustering of dates along the 'time/depth' curve may nonetheless indicate intermittent activity with one or more hiatuses between episodes of use of the monument.

Ignoring their stratigraphic relationships, it is possible to interrogate the dataset with a view to revealing its intrinsic clustering, founding on the work of Long and Rippeteau 1974).

An iterative process is employed to test in the first instance whether each date can legitimately be averaged with its neighbours. Those sequential dates that cannot be so averaged must have between them an interval which is significant with respect to the precision of the radiocarbon method.

Such intervals, if discovered, may be attributable to:

i. The taphonomic process; not all periods of use represented in surviving deposits

   a. Episodes of cessation of deposition but settlement activities continue elsewhere on the site

   b. Episodes of cessation of settlement on the site

   c. Clearance of deposits in site cleaning or refurbishment

      i. Tidying the margins of the spread onto its top, at intervals, to keep passage clear would displace and mix materials of different ages at different levels

ii. Short periods of temporary site abandonment with natural erosion of the ash heap and mixing of materials of different ages, mainly later material displaced to earlier sediments

iii. Sampling bias in the selection of our samples. This was not a random sample of the available dating material but was selected to address specific questions (see above).

However, the radiocarbon determinations alone cannot distinguish between these alternatives; for that we must

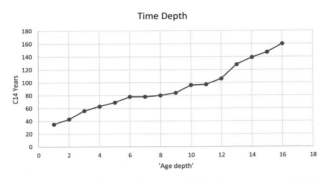

Figure 3.4 Simplified age-depth model for the core group of C14 determinations

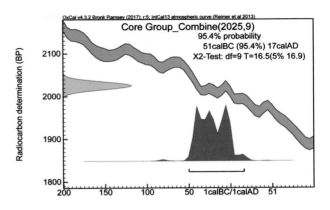

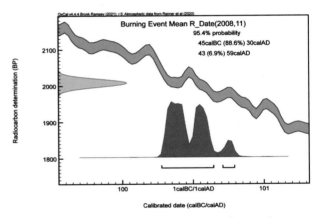

Figure 3.5 OxCal combined determinations for the core date group (above) and for the final burning event (context 042, below). The combined dates suggest that the occupation spanned the second half of the first century BC, with an 89.4% probability that the final conflagration occurred before AD 30

rely on further observational evidence from the excavation and post excavation processes. For example, Roy's micromorphological study (Chapter 6) of the deposits records observed evidence for interruption in the sedimentation of some taphonomic units which she has attributed to cleaning out of sediments from time to time (*infra*). Accepting that this is correct, the suggestion at point i.c.i above might credibly explain the presence of dated material above their original deposition locus, as we have in fact discovered (Fig. 3.1). In fact, and to pre-empt the result before presenting the analysis, there is no statistical evidence for the existence of any significant hiatus period (*i.e.* significant with respect to the precision of the radiocarbon dating method) within the deposits.

The initial hypothesis tested was that each date, considered in numerical order, could be legitimately averaged to its adjacent neighbours, as were the two earliest examples, noted above. The results of this test are presented in Table 3.2. The statistical legitimacy of pairwise averaging of 16 of the 17 radiocarbon determinations does not support the hypothesis that the 16-group is subdivided by significant hiatuses, save that separating the earliest, the 17th determination, from the rest. It does not reject the hypothesis that these dates indicate a continuous process, and this is not surprising, given that the 16 determinations in the 160 ^{14}C-year span are, on average, separated from each other by 8.33±5.42 ^{14}C-years.

Further subgrouping

Testing the hypothesis that statistically significant subgroups exist within the 16 determinations is not possible on statistics alone. For example, let us select the group of determinations between 2025 and 2004, because they span a mere 21 ^{14}C-years, and test the probability that they may be averaged as a group, *i.e.* test the probability that they represent separate assays of the date of a single event. Tested for legitimacy of group averaging, the statistics suggest that they could in fact be averaged,

yielding 2008±11 as an estimate of the event, or very short process, represented by the group of dates. However, if a single earlier or later determination is added into the calculations, this grouping breaks down and it is no longer legitimate to combine these series determinations. By moving the sampling frame (the start and end determinations) up or down the list of determinations many apparent subgroups can be identified, but none can be justified by the mere fact of their existence nor can statistics alone distinguish between the 'reality' of one subgroup over another.

The date of occupation: conclusion

The 'core' group of 17 determinations cannot be pairwise averaged in full, because the earliest date is separated from the second date by too large an interval. This might indicate an hiatus between an activity that created original deposition on site and the remainder of the on-site activities represented by the other dates. However, given

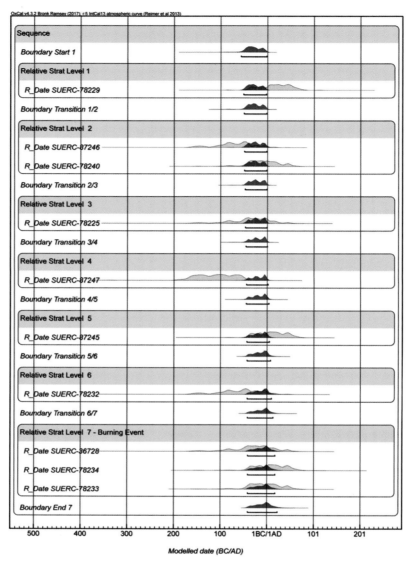

OxCal v4.3.2 Bronk Ramsey (2017); r:5 IntCal13 atmospheric curve (Reimer et al 2013)

Figure 3.6 Modelled chronology of the phases within the core group of dates, where Phase 1 is the primary hearth and Phase 7 is the final conflagration. The model supports the interpretation that the entire excavated occupation sequence occurred within less than half a century after 50 BC

the close contiguity of the group of 16 determinations, it may well be that the interval between the first and second dates in the sequence simply represents a lack of sampled deposits from the earliest part of the sequence and given the direct evidence for intermittent removal of material in antiquity (Roy, Chapter 6) this would not be an unreasonable assumption. Similarly, mechanical processes seem likely to have resulted in contamination by intermixing of occupation deposits within and across the phases deduced from the post-excavation soil analyses.

The remaining 16 determinations are all pairwise averageable and do not negate the hypothesis that they represent a continuous process rather than intermittent

or episodic events or processes the intervals between which are significant with respect to the radiocarbon method. Despite the apparent 160 ^{14}C-years span of the determinations, it is improbable that the depositional sequence was long exposed to erosion by wind and rain before the conflagration and collapse of the broch superstructure sealed it *in situ*. Indeed, exposure of only a decade or two would probably have washed down or blown out the peat ash and charred organics. There can be little doubt that the broch walls collapsed onto the burnt remains of the interior soon after, or during, the fire and it is conceivable that the collapse of some part of the wall initiated the fire.

One of the samples from the conflagration layer, retrieved from the scarcement, returned a determination of 2025±30BP and is the seventh oldest date from the monument: the fifth oldest in the core group of dates. The other two dates from the charcoal layer representing the terminal burning event are respectively the 10th and 11th dates, counting from the oldest of the core group dates. The three dates cover a span of 33 ^{14}C-years. Given their common causation we might expect identical dates and in fact, the spread of their dates is not significant with respect to the precision of the dating method. Their weighted mean ± √Σ(1/σ²) 2008±16, best reflects their estimated age, and this calibrates to the interval 45 BC to AD 61 at 95.4% probability.

Since the events or processes conducted in the settlement or use of the site all predated the conflagration, it is possible and reasonable to conclude that all the site dates should predate our estimate of the age of this event. That being the case, the 97 ^{14}C-year spread of the youngest 13 radiocarbon determinations is necessarily reduced to zero or near zero. Stated thus, this seems improbable but, as noted above, the group of determinations 2019 to 1992 uncal BC, could be represented by a single or short duration event dating to 2008±11 uncal BC.

The excavated stratification (Chapter 2) establishes that the events or processes conducted in the settlement use of the site, all predated its conflagration. Thus, it is possible and reasonable to conclude that all the site determinations listed in Table 3.2 should predate our best estimate of the age of this event. The weighted mean and estimated variance of the three determinations from the conflagration event were established above as 2008±11. The determination of the sample from the upper midden deposit within Cell 1 is, coincidentally, 2008 (albeit, ±25) and may serve as a useful marker in Table 3.2 for where the conflagration's best estimate determination would lie. This date is the eighth from lowest in Table 3.2 and lies immediately above two of the conflagration determinations (2004 and 1992).

Two factors need consideration here, firstly, the most recent determinations, 2010 to 2008, indicate dates earlier than the conflagration event's best estimate determination, which, in terms of the stratification's evidence for the sequence of events, is what is expected. Determinations between 1928 and 1991/2 indicate dates later than the conflagration which is logically impossible and must be an artefact of the imprecision of the radiocarbon method. The real-world existence of the conflagration sets a terminal date, albeit that the actual date is unknown, for the deposition process in the broch and rejects the calibrated values of these dates, taken at face value.

In Table 3.2 and in this discussion, we have focussed on the actual dating data, the determinations returned by the laboratory, rather than derived properties arising from the calibration process or a combination of our prior assumptions and Bayesian statistical analyses. The fixed, if unknown, but effectively instantaneous event of the conflagration in or about 2008±11 anchors a sequence of determinations in ^{14}C space and offers no support for an assumption that the settlement debris in this monument accumulated over a lengthy time interval, and that is just about all that the radiocarbon programme offers on issues of site duration.

The end date

The calibrated ranges of the conflagration dates have been calculated as 2008±16 uncal BC and of the 2019/1992 group's weighted mean and SD, 2008±11 uncal BC, which are near identical and can be cited, respectively, as:

  i) Between 151 cal BC and 143 cal BC (0.9%) or between 112 cal BC and 55 cal AD (94.5%)
  ii) Between 45 cal BC and 26 cal AD (95.4%)

The determinations relating to the seven dated stratigraphic units through the depositional sequence were modelled as contiguous phases using OxCal v4.3.2 to produce the refined chronology set out in Figure 3.6. These modelled dates do not reject the hypothesis that all of the deposits excavated within the garth of the broch belong to the latter half of the 1st century BC, or the possibility that the burning event that ended occupation occurred early in the 1st century AD.

It will be clear from Figure 3.6 that a dating model constrained by the stratigraphic phasing produces no conflicts between the patterns of the radiocarbon and stratigraphic evidence. This indicates that all the core dates could lie in the last 50 years of the 1st century BC but cannot indicate the duration of the events involved. The fragility of the sediments, which are virtually all peat ash with carbonised inclusions, has been referred to above in explaining the absence of hiatus periods embedded in the chronological sequence. It also supports the idea that the total duration of sediment accumulation is brief. The identity of the weighted means of the final event on the monument, its burning and collapse, and the central subgroup of determinations, does not refute the hypothesis that the duration of events in the broch was very brief. We do not suggest that the central group of dates is a statistically significant subgroup (above) we merely observe an aspect of the distribution of the core dates.

Dates from the external structures

During the excavation of the broch entrance passage and the paving associated with the ancillary building, samples were retrieved from deposits beneath paving that runs under the building abutting the outer broch wall (contexts 158 and 165, Table 3.1). These produced determinations in close agreement with the core group from the broch interior, 1928±30 BP (SUERC-85835) and 2010±30 BP (SUERC-85836), calibrating between AD 5 to 132 and 92 BC to AD 65 respectively, suggesting that the structures built outside the broch tower belong with this Middle Iron Age occupation horizon.

Further samples from deposits surrounding the paving associated with the outer enclosure of the site provide similar agreement, with determinations from deposits beneath the paving returned at 1960±30 BP (SUERC-85840) and 1941±30 BP (SUERC-85841), calibrating in the range 40 BC to AD 121 and 21 BC to AD 129 respectively. While these results do not conclusively date the construction of the outer enclosure wall, they demonstrate that this entrance, at least, was in use during the Middle Iron Age occupation of the broch at the time of the main excavated occupation. As discussed above, the enclosure entrance was probably refurbished several times during the use of the site, however, an earlier origin for the outer enclosure wall is not ruled out.

Notes

1　Two further samples were undatable for lack of carbon.
2　Archaeological grounds and archaeological evidence in this instance refer to the fact that the conflagration deposits were observed to overlie all the sediments inside the broch (Context 42 dates) and to lie undisturbed on the scarcement (the 'scarcement' date in Table 3.1).
3　^{14}C-years are conceptual years, corresponding to the units of the determination values returned by the radiocarbon process and adjusted to the global base of 1950.
4　To avoid the circumlocution *single year/s in the interval/s* the following convention, *e.g.* 535 x 392 cal BC or 416 x 262 cal BC, has been adopted, allowing that the 'x' conveys the sense of 'one year in the enumerated interval'.

4

The artefacts

Andy Heald and Dawn McLaren

4.1 The pottery

Andy Heald and Dawn McLaren

Summary

The assemblage from Clachtoll comprises 300 sherds, probably representing no more than 15 to 20 vessels. Despite the small number of finds the assemblage is of significance for several reasons. First, it represents one of the few securely dated Middle Iron Age pottery assemblages from mainland Scotland and, indeed, from Atlantic Scotland. Second, the catastrophic collapse of the roundhouse means that the vessels should be viewed as a 'closed group', a snapshot into the collective household repertoire of one family or extended group. Third, the thorough digital recording of all the finds allows rare insight into the context of discovery of the pottery and household activities within the roundhouse and, from that, understanding of wider social interactions. Fourth, the assemblage allows one to place Clachtoll, and by inference, west coast mainland Sutherland, into wider cultural and geographical landscapes; until now it has been unclear whether the inhabitants of Clachtoll were more aligned with their west coast neighbours or their more distant neighbours to the north-east and Northern Isles. Fifth, the application of scientific techniques (digital reconstruction and residue analysis) allows better understanding of the form, function and use of the vessels, allowing greater insight into cooking and consumption within the household. Finally, by considering aspects such as decoration and symbolism we can begin to suggest wider narratives from pottery that move beyond typology and chronology and relate the assemblage to wider issues of the natural environment, cultural contacts and the wider social context of use and meaning.

Methodology

The pottery was analysed on two levels. First, the assemblage was catalogued by fabric type, vessel form, number of sherds, weight, sherd dimensions, surface treatment, decoration, surface adherences and manufacturing technique. Details of abrasion, sooting and residues were also noted. This allowed the pottery to be divided into fabric groups and a description (where possible) was written of vessel forms/types, methods of construction, surface finish and decoration. Second, the assemblage was considered within the contextual findings of the excavations. The full catalogue can be found in the site archive.

Technology

All vessels were hand-thrown. Most surface finish was by smoothing (90%); the remaining pottery had coarse surfaces with grass impressions (5%; Type G, *e.g.*, Vessels 9 and 10) or vertical scrapes with occasional organic impressions (5%; Type J). Four 'grades' of clay were used, categorised as 1 (coarse sandy clay), 2 (fine sandy), 3 (fine sandy clay) and 4 (sandy clay). Although some sherds had no obvious sign of temper most had a variety of temper added including organics (grass and straw), mica, sand and grits. Most of the pottery had different colours including a range of beiges, oranges and browns. It is important to note that some sherds that were found to join had completely different colouring suggesting that the colouring of pottery fabrics was differentially altered post deposition, presumably during the fire that ended the occupation.

Decoration

Decoration included applied, impressed and incised. Where the position of decoration could be determined, it was restricted to the upper part of the vessel, from the shoulder upwards to the rim.

Applied decoration

The most usual from of applied decoration was a cordon around the shoulder of the vessel; no applied neckbands below the rim were noted. The applied cordon came in various forms: wavy cordon (Type F and G); incised lines (Type C); pinched up and impressed decoration (Type A).

The other form of applied decoration was ring-shaped impressed boss (Type H).

Incised decoration

Aside from the incisions on the cordon other incised decoration was used on the pottery, usually on the top area above the shoulder and below the rim. Most of the incised decoration was fine incision creating various geometric shapes (*e.g.*, Types A, B, C); one vessel has more pronounced grooved decoration (Type C). One vessel (V7, Type E) is decorated with a configuration of short crescentic fingernail impression; another (Type J) has vertical scrapes creating deliberate texturing for decorative purposes; another (V8, Type F) has vertical scratch marks across the profile made during smoothing of the surfaces when the clay was still damp, prior to firing.

Impressed decoration

Various tools and implements were used for impressing decoration including pointed tools (*e.g.*, V1 (rim), Type A) and a ring-headed pin (V2, Type B).

Many sherds have finger imprints below the rim (*e.g.*, V7, Type E; V8, Type F, etc.) or on the interior surface of the base (*e.g.*, V17). However, these indents are probably more a reflection of how one made the everted rim, as opposed to a distinctive and deliberate decorative trait.

Morphology

Most of the sherds are small, undiagnostic and/or body sherds: only 23 rims and 10 bases were recovered. That said several sherds allow the partial reconstruction of various vessel forms. In keeping with most Atlantic Iron Age assemblages, the vessels fall into two general types: smaller vases and larger urns/jars.

No complete vessels were recovered. In an attempt to reconstruct the vessels all relevant sherds were digitised, and the dimensions recorded, and then used to extrapolate a probable digital reconstruction of the body shape. As well as suggesting form the models were also used to elucidate capacity of said vessels (Table 4.1.1).

Rim sherds can only be constructed in a number of ways, and they generally fall into one of three categories; everted rim, straight rim or inverted rim (and all the variants in between). The predominant rim form at Clachtoll was the everted rim. This type is the best way of constructing a rim that is needed for pouring, and, hence, such rim types are recovered from numerous sites and periods on many northern Atlantic sites in various guises. A few examples of flared (Type B) or out-turned rims (Type J) were also recovered. The rims range in size from *c.* 110 mm to about 220 mm suggesting a range of vessel sizes.

Wall thickness is between 3 mm and 18 mm. Overall most vessels (79%) have wall thicknesses between 6–10 mm, with a smaller number (17%) of thinner walled vessels (less than 5 mm thick) and 4% of thick-walled vessels (11 to 18 mm).

Ten pottery types were recovered from Clachtoll, represented by around 17 vessels.

Type A

Everted rim vessel with applied cordon and impressed and incised decoration. Although not enough survives to be sure it is likely that the vessel was an everted vase, with a rim diameter of *c.* 130 mm and height around 180 mm (Figure 4.1.1).

One sherd (SF 174) forms the main part of the distinctive vessel; two other sherds (SF 174 and 191) are likely to be either part of the same vessel or an associated type.

Residue analysis showed that the vessel was associated with dairy and plant products.

VESSEL 1

SF 174. Everted rim, flattened at tip and decorated and a body sherd. Applied cordon around shoulder impressed with elongated ovoid pairs to mimic shape of ear of barley; row of small, impressed dots on rim (D 1 mm); below rim twin rows of closely spaced oval incised dots (D 6 mm); between twin dots and cordon are a widely spaced pair of nested inverted V-shaped incised lines; between the two incised motifs, towards the right-hand decoration is a slightly curving incised line superimposed by a column of dots which go outside the line towards the cordon. Smoothed; shallow vertical scrapes between rim and horizontal decorated cordon. Dark and slight sheen in this neck area. Buff brown exterior; dark grey-brown core and interior (stained). Fine sandy clay. Occasional grits; occasional organics (grass/straw) seen as burnt-out voids and carbonised inclusions. Abundant sooting. Abundant residue. Minimal abrasion. Rim Dia: 133 mm; Rim T: 4.5 mm; Body T: 6.5 mm. Probable girth: 180 mm. Probable height: 180 mm. Context 078 (Figure 4.1.11).

SF 174. Plain body sherd, joins rim sherd described above. T: 6.5 mm. Residue on interior (Bristol

Figure 4.1.1 Possible reconstruction of Vessel 1, Type A. Front view (left), profile (right)

University Residue Analysis sample CLT 18). Context 078.

SF 191. Plain body sherd. T: 7 mm. Context 078.

In general form the Clachtoll vessel is similar to pottery often referred to as *Balevullin Ware,* a type of vase first characterised by MacKie (1963, figs 2 and 3) in his analysis of pottery from that site. Although there are no radiocarbon dates (the work was carried out in 1912 by A.H. Bishop) Balevullin is generally assumed to date to the Late Bronze Age or Early Iron Age (see MacKie 1963; 2007b, 995; but see Topping 1987, 80). The overall pottery assemblage is dominated by quantities of coarse, gritty sherds, presumed to be from large barrel- and bucket-shaped vessels, some of which are sparsely decorated with incised lines and fingertip marks, and a relatively small number of small, beaker-like pots a few of which are finely ornamented with applied cordons and incised and punctuated designs. Three main categories of sherds were distinguished, termed Classes A, B and C (see MacKie 1963 for a summary); only sub-class Ai concerns us here.

Sub-type Ai are small thin-walled urns with an S-shaped profile, a slightly everted lip and a body tapering to a relatively narrow footed base (MacKie 1963, fig. 2, nos. 1 and 2; fig. 3, nos. 26–38). The three most intact vases (nos. 1, 26 and 27) all have a diameter of around 10.5 cm and a height between 12 to 13.5 cm. The general type is characterised as being decorated with an applied cordon, sometimes slashed or punctuated, around the waist; above this, incised lines or punctuated marks in simple geometric patterns. The everted foot of the base is sometimes slightly finger indented. However, it is important to note that variations in design occur within this sub-group. For example, one of the vases (no. 1) does not have an applied cordon around the waist, but instead has an impressed decoration; the fine example (no. 27) has no incised decoration above the applied cordon.

These Ballevulin vases are often discussed in relation to similar vases found at Dun Mor Vaul and called *Vaul Ware vases,* a sub-type of *Vaul Ware.* The vases from Dun Mor Vaul are small vessels, with a delicate S-shaped profile, a footed base and a slightly out-turned rim (see MacKie 1974, fig. 11, nos. 20–22, 27, 40, fig. 12, nos. 66–69, 76, fig. 14, nos. 206–207, fig. 17, no. 339, fig. 19, nos. 456–463, 468 and 470 for examples; and MacKie 2007b, 995).

Five vases from Dun Ardtreck (MacKie 2000a, 323–5, illus. 21–22, vases 1 to 5) appear to be part of this general vase series. Four (Vases 1, 3 to 5) are classed by MacKie (*ibid.*, 323) as *Vaul Ware vases.* The other vase (2), with its distinctive cordon and linear decoration above, was classed as a Balevullin vase. These vases have been dated by MacKie (*ibid.*) to the first centuries AD, showing that use of the type continued into the Middle Iron Age. The Dun Ardtreck vases range in height between 14 cm and 18 cm showing that said vases can be different in size. Further, the design around the waist of vase 5 appears to be an incised skeuomorph or imitation of applied cordons (*ibid.*, 325, 379, illus. 22).

Vaul Ware vases and Balevullin vases also occur at Dun Bharabhat (Harding and Dixon 2000, 43, fig. 21, nos. 15, 17 and 18; 86, fig. 43, *e.g.*, nos. 2, 4 and 5; see MacKie 2007b, 1080–2 for further discussion); one of the vases (no. 18) has the applied chevron decoration that is very similar to the Clachtoll example. The other vases from Bharabhat also have the distinctive nested V and/or chevron decoration (*ibid.*, 85–86, fig. 43, 93–4, 93, fig. 48, no. 11) also found at Clachtoll.

Pottery Type 1b from Dun Vulan was believed to be comparable to Balevullin Ware and argued to date to between the 1st and 3rd centuries AD (Parker-Pearson 1999, 210). As with Bharabhat the type was also associated with 'thick plait-like cordons' which were recovered from the earliest layers in the wall chamber (*ibid.*, 70, 72, fig. 4.13, nos. 1, 3, 9 and 10); this cordon is very similar to the 'cereal' cordon from Clachtoll (see below).

Although not classified as such in the report, one of the surviving vessels from Baleshare (MacSween 2003, 126–7, 129, fig. 75, b and d, vessel 81/98) seems remarkably similar, at least in form, to one of the Balevullin vessels (MacKie 1963, 167, fig. 3, no. 27). If this identification is correct then it is one of the few dated examples, dating to the 1st century BC/AD (J. Barber pers. comm.). Like the examples from Dun Ardtreck they are larger than the typical Balevullin vases with a diameter of 14 cm and a height of 20 cm.

Although many are undated and/or unstratified, other pottery from Hebridean excavations may also be part of this wider group as they have superficial similarities, for example: Kilpheder (Lethbridge 1952, fig. 7, nos. 4, 6 and 8; MacKie 2007b, 1130, 1234, illus. 9.83, esp. nos. 6

and 8); Tigh Talamhanta (Young 1953, 93, fig. 7; MacKie 2007b, 1113, 1228, fig. 9.77) and Á Cheardach Bheag (Fairhurst 1971; MacKie 2007b, 1137, 1239, fig. 9.89). It is possible that one unstratified vessel from Eilean Olabhat (Armit, Campbell and Dunwell 2008, 67, 77, illus. 29, no. 144) is of Campbell's (1991) Sollas Form B – smaller, lighter vessels of a general bucket-shaped form. Frustrated by the classification, MacKie (2007b, 1165) argues that some Sollas Form B types are similar to Vaul Ware vases and should be viewed within this general vase group. An intact shouldered vessel from Cnip (MacSween 2006, 111, illus. 3.5a) may also be part of this group.

That the Clachtoll pot is best viewed within this general 'vase' group is also supported by having similar decoration on other known vases within the broader group. For example, the distinctive applied 'cereal' cordon is also found on another vase from Dun Bharabhat (Harding and Dixon 2000, 43, fig. 21, no. 18). Other examples of thick plait-like cordons, although not identical in size to the Clachtoll examples, are known from Hornish Point (Barber 2003, 130, fig. 76, c) and Dun Vulan (Parker Pearson and Sharples 1999, 72, fig. 4.13, nos. 1, 3, 9 and 10, 214–217, fig. 9.2 Type 15).

Similarly, although nested chevrons are a known general decoration type of the Middle Iron Age (Topping 1987, 69, illus. 2, no. 9) and, as with so many potters' designs these can come in a variety of forms and elaboration, the Clachtoll examples are very similar to the decoration on a vase from Dun Ardtreck (MacKie 2000a, 324, illus. 21, no. 12). Finally, one of the vases from Balevullin (MacKie 1963, 167, fig. 3, no. 26, 179) also has impressed dots around the rim (although only a single row, unlike the double row found at Clachtoll). Thus, although there is not an identical example to the Clachtoll pot the individual traits (size, form, applied cordon, barley decoration, impressed dots, nested v-shaped decoration) suggests that the Clachtoll pot is part of the general 'Vaul/Balevullin Vase' ware found on Tiree, Skye, Lewis and the Uists.

In terms of form and size the closest parallels for the Clachtoll vessel are pottery from Baleshare (MacSween 2003, 129, fig. 75d), Dun Bharabhat (Harding and Dixon 2000, 86, fig. 43) and Balevullin (MacKie 1963, 167, fig. 3, nos. 26 and 27); all have more pronounced 'S-shape' profiles than other examples within the general group. Further, all of these examples have an applied cordon (although of different types) and two of the pots have incised decoration above the cordon and below the rim. All of their rim diameters are around 14 cm and the pots around 20 cm in height, which is very similar to the Clachtoll example.

Type B

Thin-walled vessel with flared rim; finger impression under rim, presumably related to manufacture of the rim. Decorated with a combination of a ring and incised V

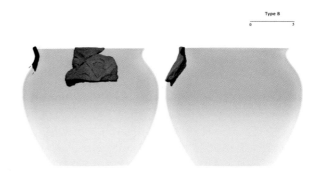

Figure 4.1.2 Possible reconstruction of Vessel 2, Type B. Front view (left), profile (right)

decoration around rim and body, the circular impression made with a ring-headed pin. Not enough survives of the pot to reconstruct the vessel but it is likely to have had a rim diameter of around 120 mm and a probable height of 130 mm (Fig. 4.1.2).

Vessel 2

SF 35. Body sherd with incised wide zigzag line, within the angles of which (both below and above) are impressions made by the head of a projecting ring-headed pin (D 14 mm). Smoothed surfaces prior to decoration. Re-joined with rim from SF 41. Buff. Sandy clay. Occasional grits, frequent burnt-out organics (grass/straw). No sooting. No residue. Minimal abrasion. Body T: 6 mm. Context 042. Refitted with SF 41 (Fig. 4.1.11).

SF 41. Flared rim. Wide partial finger impression directly under rim, impressed with head of projecting ring-headed pin (D *c.* 13 mm), occasional short organic impressions on interior. Smoothed exterior surface prior to decoration. Buff-red; evenly fired. Sandy clay. Occasional grits, frequent burnt-out organics (grass/straw). Re-joined with SF 35 (body sherd). No sooting. No residue. Minimal abrasion. Rim Dia: 120 mm; Rim T: 5 mm; Body T: 6 mm. Context 042. Refitted with SF 35 (Fig. 4.1.11).

SF 41. Body sherds (2); 1 sherd plain; 1 damaged but partial impression from projecting ring-headed pin survives (D 15.5 mm). Smoothed, some short organic impressions on interior. Buff-red; evenly fired. Sandy clay. Occasional grits, frequent burnt-out organics (grass/straw). No sooting. No residue (Bristol University Residue analysis sample CLT 25). Minimal abrasion. Body T: 6 mm. Context 042.

Many Inner and Outer Hebridean sites have pottery that appear to have impressions created by circular rings or the heads of pins (see also Topping 1987, 69, illus. 2, no. 26). Examples are known from Allasdale (Young 1953, 93, fig. 7, nos. 61, 62, 65, 67), Sithean a' Phiobaire (Lethbridge 1952, 188, fig. 8, no. 3), Garry Iochdrach (MacKie 2007b, 1271, illus. 9.122, no. 35), the Udal (MacKie 2007b, 1259, illus. 9.110, no. 13), Sollas (Campbell 1991, 151, illus. 15, no. 360), Cnoc a' Comhdhalach (Young 1953, pl. IX, no. 1), Eye Peninsula (*ibid.*), Dun Cuier (Young 1956, 310, fig. 12, no. 109), Á Cheardach Mhor (Young and Richardson 1960, 144, fig. 5, 17), Balelone (Barber 2003, 127, fig. 74, a and b), Dun Bharabhat (Harding and Dixon 2000, 41, fig. 20, no. 7), Dun Ardtreck (MacKie 2000a, 325, illus. 22, no, 31) and Dun Mor Vaul (MacKie 1974, fig. 11, no. 16, fig. 12, no. 87).

Conversely, the evidence from other Atlantic areas is sparse. In Shetland, a rare Middle Iron Age example was recovered at Clickhimin (Hamilton 1968, 95, fig. 44, no. 9; and see also 121). Examples from Orkney are equally rare with the few known examples from the Howe (Ross 1994, 244–6, illus. 144, no. 7542, illus. 145, no. 5672, illus. 146, no. 4052), Lingro (MacKie 2002, 333–4, illus. 5.113, no. 1, NMS X.GE56. illus. 5.114, nos. 5 and 6, NMS X.GE 104, GE 44) and Ayre (Graeme 1914; Young 1953, pl. IX, no. 3). Finally, the authors' do not know of a single piece of Middle Iron Age pottery from Caithness or north-east Sutherland with definitive evidence of ring-impressed decoration.

Although impressed ring decoration can be found on its own – Garry Iochdrach (MacKie 2007, 1271, no. 35), Dun Bharabhat (Harding and Dixon 2000, 41, fig. 20, no. 7) and Dun Mor Vaul (MacKie 1974, fig. 12, no. 87) – or beside applied decoration (*e.g.*, Á Cheardach Mhor (Young and Richardson 1960, 144, fig. 5, 17)), in the overwhelming number of cases (as at Clachtoll) it is found alongside other incised motifs of varying complexity: Allasdale (Young 1953, 93, fig. 7, nos. 61, 62, 65, 67), Kilpheder (Lethbridge 1952, 188, fig. 8, no. 3), Dun Cuier (Young 1956, 310, fig. 12, no. 109), Cnoc a' Comhdhalach (Young 1953, pl. IX, no. 1), Sollas (Campbell 1991, 151, illus. 15, no. 360), Balelone (Barber 2003, 127, fig. 74, a and b), Dun Ardtreck (MacKie 2000a, 325, illus. 22, no. 31), Howe (Ross 1994, 244–6, illus. 144, no. 7542, illus. 145, no. 5672, illus. 146, no. 4052), Lingro (MacKie 2002, 333–4, illus. 5.113, no. 1, NMS X.GE56. illus. 5.114, nos. 5 and 6, NMS X.GE 104, GE 44) and Ayre (Young 1953, pl. IX, no. 3).

Arguably the closest parallels for the Clachtoll piece (with circular decoration beside a simple linear triangular design) is the pottery from Balelone (Barber 2003, 127, fig. 74, a) and, further afield, the Howe (Ross 1994, 245, illus. 145, no. 5672). Various forms of Middle Iron Age pots have ring decoration just below the rim. For example, the holemouth jars from Dun Bharabhat (Harding and Dixon 2000, 41, fig. 20, no. 7) and Dun Mor Vaul

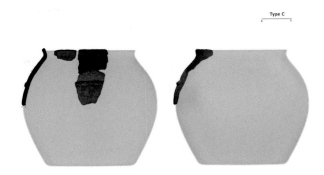

Figure 4.1.3 Possible reconstruction of Vessel 3, Type C. Front view (left), profile (right)

(MacKie 1974, fig. 12, no. 87) and the beaded rim from Eye Peninsula, Lewis (Young 1953, pl. IX, no. 4). The out turned and decorated rims from Cnoc A' Comhdhalach (Young 1953, pl. IX, no. 1) and Dun Ardtreck (MacKie 2000a, 325, illus. 22, no. 31) are also good comparisons for the Clachtoll sherd.

Type C

Thin-walled globular vessel with everted rim. Decorated with a row of shallow incised dots (made with tip of finger?) immediately below rim, haphazard horizontal incised line; series of diagonal incised lines above an applied or pinched up narrow cordon, the cordon interrupted by regularly spaced incised lines giving corrugated or notched appearance. Likely that the vessel had a diameter of *c.* 160 mm and a height of around 200 mm (Fig. 4.1.3).

This type appears to be represented by two vessels, although they might actually be from the same vessel.

VESSEL 3

SF 81.   Body sherd. Joins SF 204. Coil junction between rim and body not masked. Series of diagonal incised lines above an applied or pinched up narrow cordon (W 5.5 mm), interrupted by regularly spaced incised lines giving corrugated appearance. Below this the sherd looks burnished but abraded. Smoothed surfaces, no organic impressions on interior, some present in exterior? Lightly burnished below cordon. Sandy clay. Small grits (look natural) and occasional (*c.* 5%) organic inclusions (grass?). Minimal sooting. No residue. Severe abrasion. Body T: 6 mm. Context 042 (Fig. 4.1.11).

SF 155. Everted rim with row of finger impressions below rim. Smoothed; some organic (grass) impressions on rim and interior. Beige; evenly fired. Sandy clay. Small grits (look natural) and occasional (*c.* 5%) organic inclusions (grass?). No sooting.

No residue. Minimal abrasion. Rim T: 5 mm; Body T: 6.5 mm. Unstratified (Fig. 4.1.11).

SF 204. Everted rim. Joins SF 81. Row of shallow incised dots (made with tip of finger?) immediately below rim, haphazard horizontal incised line; series of diagonal incised lines. Smoothed surfaces, no organic impressions on interior, some present in exterior? Lightly burnished. Mid-brown evenly fired. Sandy clay. Small grits (look natural) and occasional (*c.* 5%) organic inclusions (grass?). Minimal sooting. Minimal residue. Minimal abrasion. Rim Dia: 154 mm; Rim T: 5.3 mm; Body T: 6.5 mm. Context 078 (Fig. 4.1.11).

VESSEL 4

SF 16. Body sherd. Pinched up cordon superimposed with short, incised lines. Smoothed surfaces, no organic impressions on interior, some present on exterior? Lightly burnished below cordon. Red-beige exterior; beige. Quite evenly fired. Sandy clay. Small grits (look natural) and occasional (*c.* 5%) organic inclusions (grass?). Minimal sooting. No residue. Minimal abrasion. Likely to be the same type as SF 81/204 and may even be from the same vessel. Body T: 6.5–8 mm. Context 028 (Fig. 4.1.11).

Linear decoration on everted rim pottery is well known from a variety of Hebridean sites (Topping 1987, 69, illus. 2, nos. 8 to 18) and, as at Clachtoll, is usually restricted to the upper third of the vessel and can often be found above a cordon (see Campbell 1991, 154). Examples include Cnip (MacSween 2006, 95–100, 106–115, illus. 3.2 to 3.7 for examples), Sollas (Campbell 1991, 153, illus. 17, *e.g.*, nos. 184 and 232), Bharabhat (Harding and Dixon 2000, 43, fig. 21; MacKie 2007b, 1175, illus. 9.4 for examples); Beirgh (Harding 2000, 23; Harding and Gilmour 2000; MacKie 2007b, 1187, illus. 9.21) and Allasdale (Young 1953, 93, fig. 7).

This linear decoration is different from 'other' linear decoration consisting of shallow grooves forming arches of asymmetric waves (see Topping 1987, 69, illus. 2, no. 25); this is the type of decoration scholars such as MacKie (1974, 81) used to define as 'Clettraval Ware'. Young (1966, 52) thought that channelled decoration replaced linear-incised decoration at the time of the introduction of everted-rim pottery but work at, for example, Sollas (Campbell 1991, 154) has shown that this is not the case and it is currently not clear if this difference in technique has a specific chronological implication aside from being part of the wider Middle Iron Age tradition. Examples are known from Sollas (Campbell 1991, 153, illus. no. 17, 176; 156, illus. 18, no. 32) and Dun Vulan (Parker-Pearson 1999, 210).

Linear decoration on Middle Iron Age Orcadian pottery is, in fact, quite rare; indeed, when discussing the pottery from Lingro MacKie (2002, 243) notes that, 'it is not always realised how rare this incised ware is amongst the Orkney brochs, being more or less confined to Lingro and Ayre, and also to the Howe'. Linear decoration is known from Howe (Ross 1994, 243–50, illus. 145–149), Lingro (MacKie 2002, 330, 333) and Ayre (Graeme 1914). A few pieces from Midhowe 'showed an attempt at decoration, and this consisted of simple incised lines' (Callander and Grant 1934, 512). A pot from Burrian (MacGregor 1974, 98–9, fig. 22, no. 284; MacKie 2002, illus. 5.135, no. 21) has an incised zigzag pattern, beneath an applied cordon. Incised decoration is also known from a few sherds from Gurness (Hedges 1987, 83, 173, 265, fig. 2.97, no. 1276, fig. 2.107, nos. 1873, 1886 and 1889; MacKie 2002, 307, 310, 379–81, illus. 5.73, no. 23; and perhaps 24 and 25; illus. 5.76, no. 10). Two sherds from St Boniface (MacSween 1998a, 127–8, illus. 152 and 154) have incised lines/grooves for decoration.

A similar situation is also apparent in Shetland. A handful of decorated pottery was assigned to the late wheelhouse period of Jarlshof (Hamilton 1956, 77–8, fig. 40, nos. 1 to 7). All of the pottery sherds are variations of marks made by incising lines, many in an informal way (*e.g.*, *ibid.*, nos. 1 and 7). One sherd (no. 4) has a 'Celtic' volute pattern and another (no. 2) may have been made with a brush. Incised decoration was used during the Iron Age fort phases at Clickhimin where curved decoration was created using a thumbnail (Hamilton 1968, 95, fig. 44, no. 8); during the broch phases at the same site some of the everted rims were decorated by slashed lines (*ibid.*, 121, 123, fig. 54, nos. 9 to 13). Various incised decorations (triangles, curves) were also used during the Clickhimin wheelhouse phase (*ibid.*, 144, 147–8, figs 66 and 67); a decorated form with chevron meander and key and herringbone band being the most impressive. Incised decorated pottery was recovered from Middle and Later Iron Age levels at Kebister; one sherd has tracing of scoring which may have been deliberate decoration (Dalland and MacSween 1999, 184, illus. 162, no. 2), the others are sherds decorated with a series of incised motifs (*ibid.*, 185–6, illus. 163); Dalland and MacSween (*ibid.*) note that the decorated pottery from Kebister is similar to the aforementioned pottery from Jarlshof and Clickhimin in phases immediately following the use of the broch (AD 200–500). Various forms of incised pottery were also recovered from Scalloway; designs included incised herringbone decoration, lines and dots, and chevron and lozenge-type decoration; one pot combines incised and relief decoration (see MacSween 1998a, 122 for summary). Incised decoration was found at Scatness (Brown 2015, 321, 325–8, pls 7.2.13 and 7.2.19, fig. 7.2.9, no.

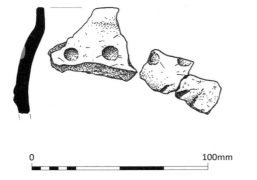

0   100mm

Figure 4.1.4 Illustration of rim sherd of Vessel 5, Type D

28722). Incised decoration on rim sherds was noted at Bayanne (MacSween 2014, 124, fig. 3.37, no. 348) as well as incisions on body sherds (*ibid.*, fig. 3.37 no. 344, fig. 3.38, no. 898).

Type D

Thin-walled vessel with impressed and applied cordon decoration (Fig. 4.1.4). Not enough survives to reconstruct the diameter or possible shape although it has a probable rim diameter of around 130 mm. The type appears to be represented by two vessels.

VESSEL 5

SF 235. Body sherd. Smoothed (but damaged; detached cordon?). Dark brown. Fine sandy clay. Occasional small grits, frequent burnt-out organics. Minimal sooting. Minimal residue (Bristol University Residue Analysis Sample CLT 23). Minimal abrasion. Body T: 7 mm. Context 145.

SF 239. Everted rim. Two widely spaced, shallow, circular dots (D 7 mm) made by boring flat tipped implement into surface. Possibly globular jar. Smoothed; short fine? Grass impressions on both surfaces. Mid-to dark brown exterior; mid-brown interior; dark grey core. Fine sandy clay. Occasional small grits, frequent burnt-out organics. Minimal sooting. No residue. Minimal abrasion. Rim Dia: 130 mm; Rim T: 5 mm; Body T: 5 mm. Context 145. (Fig. 4.1.11)

RT.   Body sherd. Smoothed; short fine? Grass impressions on both surfaces. Dark brown. Fine sandy clay. Occasional small grits, frequent burnt-out organics. Minimal sooting. Minimal residue. Minimal abrasion. Body T: 5 mm. Context 145.

RT.   Body sherds (3). Vestiges of applied/pinched up cordon, interrupted with diagonal incised lines. Smoothed; short fine? Grass impressions on both surfaces. Mid- to dark brown. Fine sandy clay. Minimal sooting. Minimal residue. Minimal abrasion. Body T: 5 mm. Context 145.

RT.   Body sherds (2). Two partial circular bored dots (D 6 mm) below which are the vestiges of applied/ pinched up cordon, interrupted with diagonal incised lines. Smoothed; short fine? Grass impressions on both surfaces. Mid-to dark brown. Fine sandy. Occasional small grits, frequent burnt-out organics. Minimal sooting. Minimal residue. Minimal abrasion. Body T: 5 mm. Context 145.

VESSEL 6 (NOT ILLUSTRATED)

SF 92.   Body sherd. T: 8 mm. Context 049.

SF 165. Body sherd. T: 8 mm. Context 049.

RT.   Body sherds; two; decorated. Larger sherd has the vestiges of an applied or pinched up cordon interrupted in diagonal incised lines; second sherd is a detached fragment of cordon. Vessel I. T: 5 mm. Context 049. NW Quadrant.

RT.   Body sherd. T: 5 mm. Context 049.

Numerous Hebridean sites have evidence of notched cordon: Galson (Edwards 1924, 197, fig. 8, no. 15), Garry Iochdrach (Beveridge and Callander 1932; MacKie 2007b, 1271, illus. 9.122, no. 31), Foshigarry (Beveridge and Callander 1931; MacKie 2007b, 1262, illus. 9.113, X.NMS GNA 388), Clettraval (MacKie 2007b, 1258, illus. 9.109, no. 1241), Á Cheardach Mhor (Young and Richardson 1960, 144, fig. 5, no. 4), Kilpheder (Lethbridge 1952, 186, fig. 7, nos. 6 and 8); Allasdale (Young 1953, 91, fig. 6, nos. 56, 59 and 60; 93, fig. 7, no. 68), Dun Cuier (Young 1956, 309, fig. 11, nos. 97 and 98), Á Cheardach Bheag (Fairhurst 1971, 97, fig. 8, nos. 4–5), Bharabhat (Harding and Dixon 2000, 36, fig. 17, nos. 11–14; 90, fig. 46, no. 5), Balelone (MacSween 2003, 127, fig. 74 a); Baleshare (*ibid.*, 129, fig. 75 c), Hornish Point (*ibid.*, 130, fig. 76 b), Cnip (MacSween 2006, 93–95, 123, illus. 3.11 e) and Dun Vulan (Parker Pearson 1999, 115, fig. 5.18, no. 7; 152, fig. 6.16, no. 5). Notched cordon is also known from Dun Mor Vaul (MacKie 1974, fig. 18, no. 392), Dun Ardtreck (MacKie 2000a, 327, illus. 23, no. 54), Dun Beag (Callander 1921; MacSween 2002, 148, fig. 45, no. 13) and Dun Nan Nighean (McIlfatrick 2013, 709, illus. 34, NMS X. HD 372).

The use of punched decoration is also common in the Hebrides, for example at Á Cheardach Bheag (Fairhurst 1971), Tigh Talamhanta (Young 1966, pl. 2a, no. 6) and Balelone (Barber 2003, 127, fig. 74 a).

Although notched cordon was an applied decorative motif on the rim of vessels, definitive evidence of applied notched cordon on the body of the of vessels in mainland Sutherland, Caithness, Shetland and Orkney is rare. There is one example of such pottery in the National Museums Scotland classed as 'Caithness unprovenanced' (*e.g.*, McIlfatrick 2013, 686, illus. 11, GA 894) but we cannot be sure it was from a Middle Iron Age site in

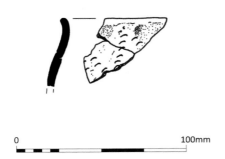

0   100mm

Figure 4.1.5 Illustration of rim sherd of Vessel 7, Type E

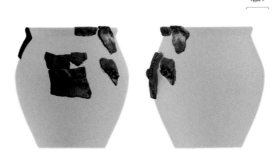

Figure 4.1.6 Possible reconstruction of Vessel 8, Type F. Front view (left), profile (right)

the county. To the author's knowledge there is not a single example from Middle Iron Age Shetland. Some sherds from Howe (Ross 1994, 246, 250, illus. 146, nos. 4055 and 4846) may be some of the rare examples from Orkney sites.

Type E

Thin-walled flared rim vessel decorated with a haphazard series of short fine incised lines; row of shallow finger impressions immediately below rim (Fig. 4.1.5). Rim diameter likely to be around 120 mm.

Vessel 7

SF 210. Flared rim. Joins body sherd SF 220. Haphazard series of short fine incised radial lines on flattened flared rim; row of shallow finger impressions (W 6 mm) immediately below rim; tip of inverted V-shaped configuration of short fine crescentic impressions made with fingernail tip (W 3 mm). Buff. Sandy clay. Occasional burnt-out organics. Minimal sooting. Minimal residue. Minimal abrasion. Rim Dia: 120 mm; Rim T: 5 mm; Body T: 5 mm. Context 078.

SF 220. Body sherd. Joins rim from SF 210. V-shaped configuration of short crescentic fingernail impressions (W 5 mm). Buff-red; evenly fired. Sandy clay. Occasional burnt-out organics. No sooting. No residue (Bristol University Residue Analysis Sample CLT 24). Minimal abrasion. Context 078. (Fig. 4.1.11)

Type F

Thick-walled jar with finger impressions below the everted rim and applied wavy cordon around the shoulder. The diameter of the vessel is likely to have been around 180 mm at the rim with a maximum external diameter around the shoulder of around 200 mm; not enough survives to reconstruct the height although, reconstructed, the vessel may have been around 27 cm in height (Fig. 4.1.6).

Residue analysis shows that the pottery was associated with dairy products and marine oils.

Vessel 8

SF 107. Rim and body sherd. Everted rim. Finger impressions below rim. Vertical scratch-marks across profile. Applied thick zigzag cordon (?around shoulder). Smoothed exterior; series shallow vertical scrape-marks below rim and applied cordon. Orange-mid-brown exterior; pale brown interior. Coarse sandy clay. Mica flecks give sparkly appearance; occasional grits (D 4 mm or less) <10%; rare organics <5%; short organic impressions on both faces. Joins sherds from SF 181 and SF 188; coil junction very clear. Abundant sooting. Minimal abrasion. Abundant residue. Rim T 8 mm. Body dia: 260 mm. Body T: 8.5 mm. Context 067 (Fig. 4.1.11).

SF 181. Rim and body sherd. Everted rim. Vertical scratch-marks across profile, applied thick zigzag cordon (?around shoulder); wide (W 18 mm) finger impressions below rim. Smoothed exterior; series shallow vertical scrape-marks below rim and applied cordon. Orange-mid-brown exterior; pale brown interior. Coarse sandy clay. Mica flecks give sparkly appearance; occasional grits (D 4 mm or less) <10%; rare organics <5%; short organic impressions on both faces. Joins sherds from SF 107 and SF 188; coil junction very clear. Abundant sooting. Minimal abrasion. Abundant residue. Rim Dia: 220 mm; Rim T: 8 mm. Body T: 9.5 mm. Context 067.

SF 188. Body sherds (2). Vertical scratch-marks across profile, applied thick zigzag cordon (?around shoulder); wide (W 18 mm) finger impressions below rim. Smoothed exterior; series shallow vertical scrape-marks below rim and applied cordon. Orange-mid-brown exterior (blackened by sooting); pale brown interior. Coarse sandy clay. Mica flecks give sparkly appearance;

occasional grits (D 4 mm or less) <10%; rare organics <5%; short organic impressions on both faces. Joins sherds from SF 107 and SF 181; coil junction very clear. Abundant sooting. Minimal abrasion. Abundant residue. Bristol University sample CLT 28: Dairy/Marine. Context 067.

SF 162. Body sherd. Vertical scratch-marks across profile. Smoothed exterior; series shallow vertical scrape-marks below rim and applied cordon. Orange-mid-brown exterior (blackened by sooting); pale brown interior. Coarse sandy clay. Mica flecks give sparkly appearance; occasional grits (D 4 mm or less) <10%; rare organics <5%; short organic impressions on both faces. Joins sherds from SF 107 and SF 181; coil junction very clear. Abundant sooting. Minimal abrasion. Abundant residue. Body T: 7.5 mm to 10.5 mm. Context 067.

SF 162. Body sherd. Vertical scratch-marks across profile. Smoothed exterior; series shallow vertical scrape-marks below rim and applied cordon. Orange-mid-brown exterior (blackened by sooting); pale brown interior. Coarse sandy clay. Mica flecks give sparkly appearance; occasional grits (D 4 mm or less) <10%; rare organics <5%; short organic impressions on both faces. Joins sherds from SF 107 and SF 181; coil junction very clear. Abundant sooting. Minimal abrasion. Abundant residue. Bristol University sample CLT 27: Dairy/Marine. Body T: 8 mm to 12 mm. Context 067.

Type G

These are other body sherds with wavy cordon; however, none have surviving rims and all are thinner than Type F, suggesting that they are a related, but different form of vessel, if only in thickness.

Vessel 9

SF 18. Body sherds (7). Globular? Applied horizontal wavy cordon (protrudes *c.* 10 mm from exterior face). Smoothed when wet, distinct swipe marks on rounded upper body. Skim of wet clay applied on interior surface. Beige/buff surfaces; pale grey core. Sandy clay. Organic inclusions; very occasional sub-rounded grits (*c.* D 4–14 mm). No sooting. Minimal residue. Minimal abrasion. Body T: 7.5 mm. Context 028. (Fig. 4.1.12)

Vessel 10

SF 26. Base sherd. Bristol University Residue Sample CLT 21. Context 042. T: 11 mm.

SF 29. Body sherds (15). Globular? one wavy cordon decorated sherd, very pronounced, up to 10 mm

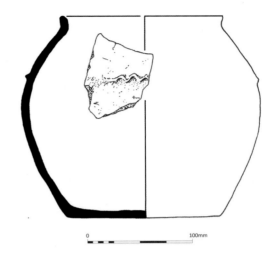

Figure 4.1.7 Possible reconstruction of Vessel 9, Type G. The shape of the vessel is speculative

protrudence. Smoothed, rough in patches, some sherds show wipe marks. Skim of wet clay applied on interior surface. Beige/buff surfaces; pale grey core. Sandy clay. Organic inclusions; very occasional sub-rounded grits (*c.* D 4–14 mm). No sooting. Minimal residue. Minimal abrasion. Body T: 5–9 mm. Context 042 (Fig. 4.1.12).

SF 29. Body sherd. Tiny portion of applied or pinched up cordon. Skim of wet clay applied on interior surface. Beige/buff surfaces; pale grey core. Sandy clay. Organic inclusions; very occasional sub-rounded grits. Bristol University Residue Sample CLT 22. Context 042.

SF 29. Body sherd. T: 10 mm. Context 042.

SF 30. Base sherd. Context 042.

SF 53. Body sherd. Context 042.

SF 56. Body sherd. Context 042. SW Quad.

SF 89. Body sherds (8). Context 042.

SF 113. Body sherd. Context 042.

The use of various forms of applied cordon on Hebridean Iron Age pottery has been well documented (*e.g.*, Topping 1987, 69, illus. 2). The cordon is usually around the widest part of the body although it can also be applied as a neckband, as is more common in Orkney and Shetland. As we have seen, applied decoration can exhibit a wide variety of forms, depending on the application of the applied strip. Typical examples include: wavy/zigzag cordon (as at Clachtoll); fingertip impressed cordon, thumbnail impressed cordon and notched cordon.

Examples of actual wavy cordoned pottery, either from complete examples, but more usually from body sherds, are known from a huge range of Hebridean sites, such as Galson (Edwards, 1924, 197, fig. 8, nos. 14, 16 and 17), Garry

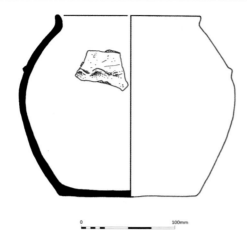

Figure 4.1.8 Possible reconstruction of Vessel 10, Type G. The shape of the vessel is speculative

Iochdrach (Beveridge and Callander 1932; MacKie 2007b, 1271, illus. 9.122, no. 23), Foshigarry (MacKie 2007b, 1262, illus. 9.113, X.NMS GNA 323 and 343), Clettraval (MacKie 2007b, 1258, illus. 9.109, no. 1202), Kilpheder (Lethbridge 1952, 186, fig. 7, nos. 1 and 3), Allasdale (Young 1953, 85, fig. 5, no. 15; 91, fig. 6), Dun Cuier (Young 1956, 308, fig. 10), Á Cheardach Mhor (Young and Richardson 1960, 145, fig. 6, nos. 28, 30, 31), Á Cheardach Bheag (Fairhurst 1971, 97, fig. 8, nos. 7–11), Dun Vulan (La Trobe-Bateman 1999, 152–7, figs 6.16–21), Dun Bharabhat (Harding and Dixon 2000, 36–37, fig. 17, nos. 1–10, fig. 18, no. 1, fig. 43, no. 1), Baleshare (MacSween 2003, 129, fig. 75 d), Hornish Point (*ibid.*, 130, fig. 76 d), An Dunan (MacSween and Johnson 2013, 179, illus. 19, SF 280) and Cnip (MacSween 2006, 93–5, 108, illus. 3.3a, b and d, 112, illus. 3.6(a) f, 117, illus. 3.8 g, 123, illus. 3.11 a and d).

When discussing the assemblage from Cnip, MacSween (*ibid.*, 93) noted that the most usual form of applied decoration from the site was the zigzag cordon and that it was usually found in combination with everted rims (but not always). Although often the zigzag is the only decoration on a vessel (*e.g.*, Sollas (Campbell 1991, microfiche table 7); Cnip (MacSween 2006, 112, illus. 3.6(a) f, 117, illus. 3.8g)) it often serves as the lower border for incised decoration in the area between the neck and the shoulder.

Wavy-cordoned pottery is also known from a number of sites on Skye and Tiree including Dun Ardtreck (MacKie 2000a, 327, illus. 23, nos. 48, 51–54, 57), Dun Mor Vaul (MacKie 1974, fig. 12, nos. 107–109, fig. 13, nos. 118, 125, 135, 171, 177), Dun Cul Bhuirg (Topping 1985a, 203, illus. 2, no. 123, 205, illus. 3, nos. 163–164), Dun Beag (Callander 1921, 129–30; MacSween 2002, 147, illus. 44, nos. 6 and 8), Dun Fiadhairt (MacKie 2007b, 887, illus. 8.34), Dun an Iardhard (MacLeod 1915, 67–70, figs 13 and 14), Dun Flodigarry (Martlew 1985) and Tungadale (Miket 2002, 99, fig. 31, nos. 6,7 and 22).

The potters of Shetland and Orkney used applied cordons, but these were usually around the neck; vessels with actual cordon on the body are rare, with the applied cordons from Jarlshof (Hamilton 1956, 66, fig. 35, nos. 21–22) and Scalloway (MacSween 1998b, 134–6, fig. 81, nos. 7 and 9) rare examples. Examples from Orkney are equally sparse. Discussing the Howe pottery (Ross 1994, 250, illus. 146, no. 4055 and 4846) stated 'body sherds with applied cordons at Howe were few and only two examples…are worthy of mention'. Even amongst the elaborate decorated pottery at Ayre there were few examples of applied cordon on the body (Graeme 1914, fig. 12; MacKie 2002, 384, illus. 5.110, nos. 9 and 11); there are none among the decorated examples at Lingro. When discussing the pottery from Gurness Hedges (1987) noted that 'decoration is so rare as to be virtually absent'; a rare sherd has applied cordon on the body (MacKie 2002, 307, 379, illus. 5.73, no. 22). The lack of applied decoration in the Northern Isles cannot be due to a lack of modern excavations. For example, in recent years Shetland has seen a swathe of modern excavations such as Kebister (Owen and Lowe 1999), Scalloway (Sharples 1998), Bayanne (Moore and Wilson 2014) and Scatness (Dockrill *et al.* 2015).

Examples of applied cordon of any form (not just wavy) from Caithness and other Sutherland sites are equally rare, with only a handful of examples known from Wag of Forse (Curle 1948, 279, 285, fig. 3, no. 2), Keiss West (MacKie 2007b, 597), Wester broch (Anderson 1901, NMS X.GK 96), Yarrows (Anderson 1890, X.NMS GK 96; McIlfatrick 2013, 681, illus. 6), Skirza (Anderson 1901, NMS X.GA 911; MacKie 2007b, 480, 612, illus. 7.174; McIlfatrick 2013, 679, illus. 4) and Applecross (McIlfatrick 2013, 696, illus. 21, SF 70). Edwards (1924, 198) notes two fragments from Everley broch having applied wavy cordon being in NMS although these were not previously recorded by Anderson (1901). Again, this paucity of cordoned pottery cannot be explained by recourse to the lack of modern excavations; numerous Middle Iron Age roundhouses across Caithness have recently been excavated, for example, Crosskirk (Fairhurst 1984), Thrumster, Nybster, Whitegate, Keiss and Everley – not a single piece of pottery from these recent excavations has applied cordon decoration of any kind.

Regarding actual wavy cordoned examples (either on the body or below the rim) the author knows of only one provenance example: from Skirza, Caithness (*op. cit.*) the pottery classed by MacKie (2007b, 480) as 'a native sherd with a cordon decoration, similar to that found commonly in the Hebrides'. There are other examples of wavy cordoned pottery in the National Museums Scotland classed as 'Caithness unprovenanced' (*e.g.*, McIlfatrick 2013, 684–5, illus. 9 to 10, GA 881; GA 883; GA 885) but we cannot even be sure they were from Iron Age sites in the county.

Type H

Figure 4.1.9 Possible reconstructions of Vessel 11, Type H. Both possible interpretations are shown: squat globular vase (left) and taller vase (right)

Type H

Everted rim with finger impressions below the rim, the body decorated with applied dimple bosses. Not enough of the vessel survives and with the available assemblage the sherds may either represent a smaller vase (height *c.* 200 mm) or a larger vessel (height *c.* 255 mm) (Fig. 4.1.9).

Likely that vessels 11 to 14 are all of the same type; possible that some may actually be part of the same vessel.

VESSEL 11

SF 220 (bag 1). Rim and body. Out-turned rim, distinct internal bevel. Globular body. Eight rim sherds and 14 body sherds. Series of applied ring-shaped bosses *c.* 54 mm below rim (9 survive); row of finger impressions immediately below the rim, evenly spaced, D 8.5 mm from which radiate shallow finger fluting. Smoothed; short fine ?grass impressions on both surfaces; closely spaced vertical and diagonal scratched lines on surface (confined to lower body below bosses). Red-orange-buff exterior; pale grey core; orange buff interior. Coarse sandy clay. Occasional grits (D 5.5 mm), frequent burnt-out organics. The sherds towards the base of the vessel still have organics present but these seem less abundant than those from the upper body and the fabric as a whole is more compact/denser. Minimal sooting. Minimal abrasion. No residue. Rim Dia: 160 mm; Rim T: 7 mm; Body T: 9 mm. Context 078 (Fig. 4.1.12).

SF 220 (bag 2). Base and body sherds. Flat base, only very slight hints towards a foot; body sherds the lower body sherd joins the base. Smoothed; short fine? grass impressions on both surfaces; closely spaced vertical and? diagonal scratched lines on surface. Orange-buff surfaces, pale grey core. Coarse sandy clay. Occasional grits (D 5.5 mm), frequent burnt-out organics. The sherds towards

the base of the vessel still have organics present but these seem less abundant than those from the upper body and the fabric as a whole is more compact/denser. Minimal sooting. Minimal abrasion. No residue. Body T: 10 mm; Base Dia: 120 mm; Base T: 8 mm. Context 078.

SF 220 (bag 3). Body sherd. Smoothed on both surfaces. Orange-buff surfaces, pale grey core. Coarse sandy clay. Occasional grits (D 5.5 mm), frequent burnt-out organics. The sherds towards the base of the vessel still have organics present but these seem less abundant than those from the upper body and the fabric as a whole is more compact/denser. Minimal sooting. Fractured. No residue (Bristol University Residue Analysis Sample CLT 16). Body T: 10 mm. Context 078.

SF 220 (bag 4). Rim sherd. Orange-buff surfaces, pale grey core. Coarse Sandy clay. Minimal sooting. Fractured. No residue (Bristol University Residue Analysis Sample CLT 17). T: 8 mm.

VESSEL 12

SF 41. Body sherd. T: 11 mm. Context 042.

SF 48b. Body sherd. T: 7 mm. Context 042.

SF 51. Body sherds (3) with a hollowed boss. Smoothed; short fine grass impressions on both surfaces. Buff ochre exterior, paler interior, no core. Fine sandy clay. Frequent grass impressions and pores from vegetable temper. No sooting. Minimal residue. No abrasion. Body T: 3–6 mm. Context 042.

SF 57. Body sherd. Applied ring-shaped boss 20 × 20 mm, *c.* 3 mm. Smoothed exterior, some organic impressions; organic impressions on interior. Pale beige-buff with patches of dark sooting; buff interior; black core. Sandy clay. Abundant organic inclusions (burnt out). Minimal sooting. Minimal residue. Minimal abrasion. Body T: 7 mm. Context 042 (Fig. 4.1.12).

RT Base sherd. T: 16 mm. Context 042. Next to hearth; SW Quad.

VESSEL 13

SF 176. Everted rim and 5 body sherds, four of which join. Two applied bosses (D 18.5, W 3, internal D 13.5); possibly part of a row. Smoothed; diagonal and vertical series of shallow scrape marks below bosses (shoulder). Orange-buff surfaces, pale grey core. Coarse sandy clay. Occasional grits (D 5.5 mm), frequent organic impressions. Minimal sooting. No residue. Minimal abrasion. Rim T: 5.5 mm; Body T: 8.5 mm. Context 071 (Fig. 4.1.12).

VESSEL 14

SF 188. Rim and two body sherds. Everted rim with shallow internal bevel. Two widely spaced finger pad impressions (D 6 mm) apparently forming a row. Smoothed both surfaces; short organic impressions frequent. Pale beige-buff; pale brown interior; dark grey core. Sandy clay. Abundant organic (grass and straw), mostly burnt out but some carbonised remains survive. White substance filling some organic impressions on one sherd. Sooting on rim. Moderate abrasion. Patches of residue. Rim T: 5.5 mm; Body T: 7 mm. Context 067 (Fig. 4.1.12).

SF 188. Body sherd. Patches of residue (Bristol University Residue Analysis Sample CTL 14). Rim T: 5.5 mm; Body T: 7 mm. Context 067.

SF 181. Rim. Everted. Finger pad impression (L 9.4 mm; W 6.8 mm), shallow, 27 mm below top of rim; diagonal incised line below rim (W 1 mm) crossing extent of surviving face. Smoothed both surfaces; short organic impressions frequent. Pale beige-buff; pale brown interior; dark grey core. Abundant organic (grass and straw), mostly burnt out but some carbonised remains survive. White substance filling some organic impressions on one sherd. Minimal sooting. Minimal abrasion. Joins rim sherd from SF 188. Rim T: 5.3 mm; Body T: 7.5 mm. Context 067.

SF 181. Body sherds (2). Applied ring-shaped boss 20 x 20 mm, *c*. 3 mm T, on one sherd only; other sherd has very faint shallow finger pad impression (sherd from just below rim. Smoothed both surfaces; short organic impressions frequent. Sandy clay. Abundant organic (grass and straw), mostly burnt out but some carbonised remains survive. White substance filling some organic impressions on one sherd. Minimal sooting. Minimal abrasion. Encrusted carbonised residue and staining. Body T: 7.5 mm. Context 067.

VESSEL 15

SF 02. Three body sherds, two joining. Applied or pinched up ring-shaped boss (ext. D 17.3 mm; H 3 mm) on largest sherd. Body to one side of the boss (orientation unclear if above or below boss) has series of slightly haphazard shallow radial lines made by impressing and dragging the tip or edge of a bone implement or comb into the clay when the surfaces were still slightly damp. Short organic impressions frequent on both surfaces. Orange-red-buff colour, completely oxidised, medium-hard fired. Fine sandy clay with frequent fine organic inclusions (burnt out). Clear finger impressions from production on interior. Moderate abrasion. Body T: 6 mm. Context 008 (2011 excavation) (Fig. 4.1.12).

BODY SHERDS (NOT ILLUSTRATED)

It is likely that body sherds from context 078 (SF 160; SF 210), context 047 (SF 111), context 145 (RT) and context 049 (SF 132) are Type H vessels.

Type I

These are other body sherds with applied or pinched up ring-shaped bosses (ext. D 13 x 12.5 mm; W 2 mm; Internal D 9.5 mm); however, none have surviving rims and all are thinner than Type H suggesting that they are a related, but different form of vessel, if only in thickness; the vessel is likely to be a vase.

VESSEL 16

SF 238. Two body sherds. May be of a similar type to the applied bosses found in Context 145 and 155.

RT. Body sherds (3). One sherd with an applied or pinched up ring-shaped bosses (ext. D 13 x 12.5 mm; W 2 mm; Internal D 9.5 mm). Smoothed; short fine grass impressions on both surfaces. Mid-brown to dark brown. Fine sandy clay. Occasional small grits, frequent burnt-out organics. Minimal sooting. Staining and encrusted residue. Minimal abrasion. Body T: 6–8 mm. Context 145.

RT. Body sherds (7). Two widely spaced applied or pinched up ring-shaped bosses (ext. D 13 x 12.5 mm; W 2 mm; Internal D 9.5 mm). Smoothed; short fine grass impressions on both surfaces. Mid-brown to dark brown. Fine sandy clay. Occasional small grits, frequent burnt-out organics. Minimal sooting. Encrusted residue. Minimal abrasion. Body T: 7 mm. Context 155 (Fig. 4.1.12).

Applied bosses have long been known to be part of the wider Iron Age decorative motifs (see Topping 1987, 69, illus. 2, 22); most are indented by a thumb and often referred to as 'dimpled bosses'. Again, various Hebridean sites have pottery with applied bosses: Foshigarry (MacKie 2007b, 1263, illus. 9.114, X.NMS GNA 366); Garry Iochdrach (MacKie 2007b, 1271, illus. 9.122, nos. 29, 39 and 42); Allasdale (Young 1953, 95, fig. 8, nos. 75 and 76); Á Cheardach Mhor (Young and Richardson 1960, 144, fig. 5, nos. 17 and 18, pl. XI. nos. 5 and 8); Eilean Olabhat (Armit, Campbell and Dunwell 2008, 68, 71, illus. 25, no. 24); Dun Vulan (Parker Pearson and

Sharples 1999, 81, fig. 4.19, no. 13, 112, fig. 5.15, no. 3, fig. 5.21, fig. 6.18); An Dunan (MacSween and Johnson 2013, 179–82, illus. 19, SF 216); and Cnip (MacSween 2006, 95–6, tab. 3.15, 130 illus. 3.16c).

Examples are also known from Skye, for example Dun Beag (MacSween 2002, 147–8, illus. 45, no. 12), Dun Iardhard (MacLeod 1915, 67–70, fig. 13) and Tungadale (Miket 2002, 99, fig. 31, no. 16). Unfortunately, these are all body sherds so it is not possible to ascertain the overall body form. More intact vessels with bosses are known from Hornish Point (MacSween 2003, 130, fig. 76 a); Baleshare (*ibid.*, 129, fig. 75 b) and Dun Bharabhat (Harding and Dixon 2000, 40–1, fig. 20, no. 4). On many of these Hebridean sites the total number of vessels with said decoration is one, far fewer than other types of applied decoration, such as cordon.

Like other forms of applied decoration (*e.g.*, cordoned) the evidence of boss decoration from Caithness and Sutherland is rare. One example is known from Cross-kirk (Fairhurst 1984, 108–9, illus. 62, no. 749), although it is noted by the excavator as being pre-broch so may actually date to the pre-Middle Iron Age period. Other examples are from 'New R' (assumed to be Keiss Road) in Caithness (McIlfatrick 2013, 677, illus. 2; X.GA 897) and a solitary find from recent excavations at Everley broch (McIlfatrick 2013, 687, illus. 12, SF 836). Other applied boss pottery is in the NMS classed as Caithness unprovenanced (*e.g.*, McIlfatrick 2013, 683, 685, illus. 8, 10, X.GA 862 and X.GA 892).

Applied bosses seem to be equally rare in Shetland and Orkney with none of the pottery from Jarlshof, Keb-ister, Scalloway, Bayanne or Scatness having such applied decoration; a solitary example was found at Clickhimin (Hamilton 1968, 95, fig. 44, no. 7). The few examples of applied bosses from Orkney are from the Howe (Ross 1994, 247–9, illus. 147, nos. 2635 and 7114, illus. 153, no. 4388) and Lingro (MacKie 2002, 333, illus. 5.113, NMS X.GE56). None of the other major Orcadian assemblages such as Gurness, Midhowe, Burrian and Ayre have said decoration.

Type J

Out-turned rim 'decorated' with vertical scrapes. No joining sherds were recognised making it impossible to determine minimal number of vessels. Further, not enough survives to be sure of its proportions but the curvature of the body sherds is suggestive of a broadly globular shape.

SF 9.   Out-turned rim from probably globular jar. Vertical scrapes below rim; series of three shallow finger impressions immediately below out-turned rim on exterior. Interior surface has shallow vertical scrapes and occasional organic impressions.

Red-brown surfaces, dark grey core = incompletely oxidised. Fine sandy clay. Frequent organic inclusions (possible straw); organics well preserved. Minimal sooting. Stained interior residue. Minimal abrasion. Rim T: 5 mm; Body T: 6 mm. Context 028.

SF 34.   Body sherds (15). Vertical scrapes follow vessel curvature; occasional organic impressions. T: 7 mm. Context 042.

SF 54.   Body sherds (3). Vertical scrapes follow vessel curvature; occasional organic impressions. T: 7 mm. Context 042.

SF 48.   Body sherd. Closely spaced vertical scrapes on exterior. Buff exterior; dark brown core. Fine sandy clay. Frequent organics (? Grass) *c.* 30%; mica flecks – sparkle. Minimal sooting. Minimal residue. Minimal abrasion. Body T: 8 mm. Context 042.

SF 139.   Body sherd. Vertical scrapes on exterior, closely spaced. Deliberate texturing for decorative purposes. Exterior blackened with a light sheen? Burnished. Two-tone beige-grey/black exterior; black core and interior surface. Sandy clay. Extensive sooting. Encrusted carbonised residue and staining. Bristol University Residue Analysis Sample CLT 20: Dairy/Plant. Minimal abrasion. Body T: 6 mm. Context 062.

SF 224.   Body sherds (4). Vertical scrapes follow vessel curvature; occasional organic impressions. T: 7 mm. Context 078.

No *num.*   Body sherd. Vertical scrapes on exterior, closely spaced. Deliberate texturing for decorative purposes. Pale brown surfaces, occasional glimpse of a grey core. Fine sandy clay. Frequent organic inclusions. No sooting. No residue. Minimal abrasion. Body T: 7 mm. Spoil heap 2017.

No *num.*   Globular jar? See finish. Vertical scrapes on exterior, closely spaced. Deliberate texturing for decorative purposes. Interior surface has shallow vertical scrapes and occasional organic impressions. Buff-mid brown exterior; dark grey/brown core; pale beige/grey interior. Fine sandy clay. Occasional organic inclusions (preserved as impressions) and surface impressions -?grass/ straw. Minimal sooting. Minimal residue. Minimal abrasion. Body T: 6 mm. Spoil heap.

Body and base sherds: unassigned to type

VESSEL 17

Forty-seven sherds from context 042 including a dimpled base sherd (see below) representing the basal and lower portion of a vessel of unknown type. The fabric of this vessel is distinct from the vessels above. Although in appearance the surfaces and colouration bear similarities to Type G, vessels 9 and 10. It is possible that the sherds from SF 26 could be the lower portion of one or both of these vessels but are sufficiently different in colour and fabric is distinct to merit recording as a separate vessel.

SF 26.   45 body sherds and 2 base sherds from a narrow-based flat-bottomed vessel, upper portion of vessel lost and all sherds appear to be from lower body. From context 042 including a dimpled base sherd (see below) representing the basal and lower portion of a vessel of unknown type. The surfaces have been roughly smoothed probably whilst wet leaving swipe marks and scrapes surviving. The fabric is a fine sandy clay, pale buff in colour throughout with very minimal patches of mid-grey core, no obvious temper or inclusions are present. Staining on interior Similar to V 9 and V 10. Minimal abrasion. Looks heavily heat affected. Body T: 8 mm. Context 042.

A further 52 sherds were not assigned to type or to vessel. These include four sherds (SF 29, SF 45, SF 55, SF 64) all from context 042 and three sherds (SF 178) from context 078 which show similarities in form and fabric and may represent a globular jar (Vessel 18?) or jars with a similar surface finish to Type F but are sufficiently different in profile and thickness to suggest that they are probably from a separate vessel or vessels,

The remaining body rim and body sherds (45 sherds) are different are sufficiently different from the Types and Vessels described above that they cannot be closely ascribed, however, as noted earlier, the effects of the fire on many of the sherds has altered their colour and texture. Many of these comprise very small and sometimes abraded sherds recovered during soil sample processing or extracted from collections of animal bones. These sherds encompass: 1 body (SF 81), context 042, T: 6 mm; 2 body (SF 90), context 042, T: 6 mm; 1 body (SF 119), context 048, T: 4 mm; 2 body (SF 122), context 048, T: 8 mm; 1 body (SF 156), context 048, T: 8 mm; 2 body (SF 167), context 049), T: 6.5 mm; 3 body (SF 170), context 078, T: 6mm; 1 body (SF 203), context 078, T: 6 mm; 1 rim, heat affected (SF 211), context 082, T: 6 mm; and small sherds from soil sample retents from contexts 042, 047, 067, 078, 091, 094, 121, 145 and 146.

Bases

Ten base sherds were recovered, two of which had dimpled fingerprints.

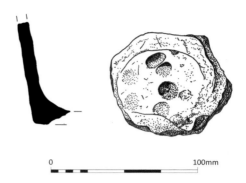

Figure 4.1.10 Dimpled base sherd probably from Vessel 17, not assigned to Type

SF 26.   Base is dimpled with fingerprints internally. Roughly smoothed on surfaces, probably white wet. Buff throughout, occasional glimpse of grey in core. Sandy clay. No obvious temper. No sooting. No residue. Heavy abrasion. Vessel 17. Body T: 8–11 mm. Context 042 (Figs 4.1.10 and 4.1.12).

SF 162.   Base sherd. Flat; finger impressed above foot. Found in context with sherds from vessel F but is this from a separate vessel based on fabric and thickness. Coarse surfaces, some grass impressions, finger impressions at foot of base. Orange-mid-brown exterior; interior obscured by residue. Coarse sandy clay. Abundant sooting. Abundant residue. Minimal abrasion. Vessel 18. Body T: 9 mm; Base Dia: 200 m (9–11 radius, not precise); Base T: 9 mm. Context 067.

Dimpled bases have been recovered from various sites across Atlantic Scotland including Á Cheardach Mhor (Young and Richardson 1960, 145, fig. 6 nos. 35–36), Garry Iochdrach (Beveridge and Callander 1932; MacKie 2007b, 1271, no. 25), Cnip (MacSween 2006, 98), Dun Bharabhat (Harding and Dixon 2000, 46, fig. 23), Dun Mor Vaul (MacKie 1974, fig. 11, 31), Howe, Orkney (Ross 1994, 250–1, illus. 150, nos. 5672a and 5672b), Keiss Road (McIlfatrick 2013, 165) and Everley (McIlfatrick 2013, 192).

Like finger-impressions around rims it is doubtful whether these can be classed as decoration, to stand alongside the geometric and lattice designs recovered from Clickhimin (Hamilton 1968, 144, 149, fig. 68, nos. 2, 5 and 6), Scalloway (MacSween 1998b, 134, fig. 80, no. 1) and Howe (Ross 1994, 250. Illus. 150, no. 2635) or the finger-impressed spirals or concentric rings from Clickhimin (Hamilton 1968, 95, fig. 44, nos. 10–11; 144,

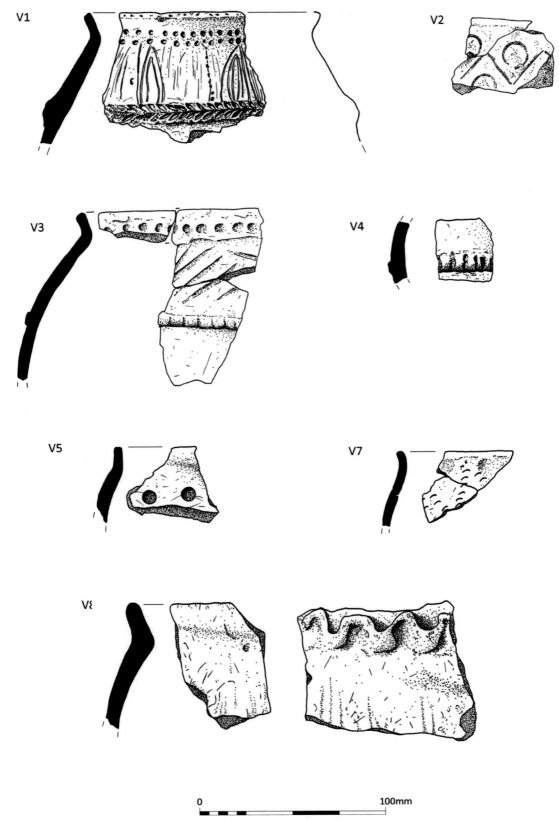

Figure 4.1.11 Feature sherds identified amongst the pottery assemblage (V1-17, V6 not illustrated)

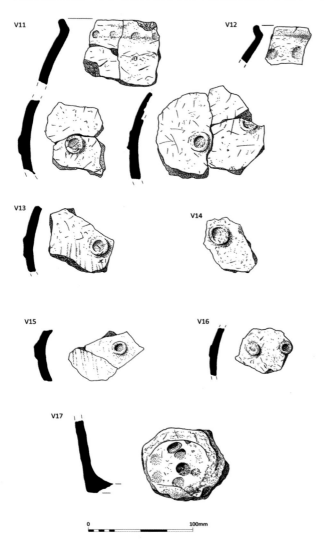

Figure 4.1.12 Feature sherds identified amongst the pottery assemblage (V1-17, V6 not illustrated)

149, fig. 68, nos. 1, 3 and 4), Bayanne (MacSween 2014, 133, fig. 3.37, no. 377; 135, fig. 3.39, no. 337) or the Howe (Ross 1994, 250–1, illus. 150, no. 4487).

Discussion

Despite the small number of finds the assemblage is of particular significance for a number of reasons. First, it represents the first securely dated Middle Iron Age pottery assemblage from mainland Scotland. Thus, it allows the formation of a dating and established typology for Middle Iron Age north-west mainland Scotland, a model to be tested through future excavations. Second, the 3D recording of all finds allows detailed reconstruction of the context of discovery of the pottery which, in turn, allows rare insight into household activities within the

roundhouse and, from that, understandings of wider social interactions. Third, the assemblage allows one to place Clachtoll, and by inference, west coast mainland Sutherland into wider cultural and geographical land-scapes; until now there has been no clarity whether the inhabitants with Clachtoll were more aligned with their west coast neighbours or their more distant neighbours to the north-east and Northern Isles. Fourth, the application of scientific techniques (digital reconstruction and residue analysis) allows better understanding of the form, function and use of the vessels, allowing greater insight into cooking and consumption within the Clachtoll household. Finally, by moving beyond typology and chronology and considering aspects such as symbolism we can begin to glean wider narratives from the pottery that move beyond the functional and relate the assemblage to wider issues of the natural environment, cultural contacts and the wider context of use. In the following sections we consider each of these five key research areas in turn.

Dating and establishing a typology

Since the beginning of the discipline, archaeologists have attempted to create relative and absolute chronologies for pottery sequences but more often than not, and particularly for mainland Sutherland and Caithness, these are from sites and assemblages without secure stratigraphic sequences and/or scientific, chronological control. Well-dated Middle Iron Age sites with pottery from northern mainland Scotland are incredibly rare with only the recent excavations at Nybster, Thrumster and Everley returning pottery and associated Middle Iron Age radiocarbon dates (Heald, Cavers and Barber in prep). Thus, Clachtoll is incredibly important as the extreme taphonomic processes that led to the pottery deposition, survival and recovery make it one of the few dated and sealed assemblages in northern mainland Scotland, and indeed northern Britain.

As described above there are ten general types from Clachtoll, probably represented by no more than 15 to 20 vessels. Although they were found in different contexts (from the roundhouse interior and the guard cells) there can be little doubt that all the different types were effectively contemporary and probably used by one family. Thus, we have an incredible snapshot of the different types of pottery used at Clachtoll between the 1st centuries BC and AD. The vessels talk of different sizes and forms being used, decorated with a variety of applied, incised and impressed decoration.

The dominant pottery rim form is the everted rim. Vessels with everted rims are a characteristic of the Middle Iron Age sequence across all of Atlantic Scotland and, as at Clachtoll, it is equally clear that everted rims appear on a range of vessels and the term covers a range of types. For example, in his discussion of the

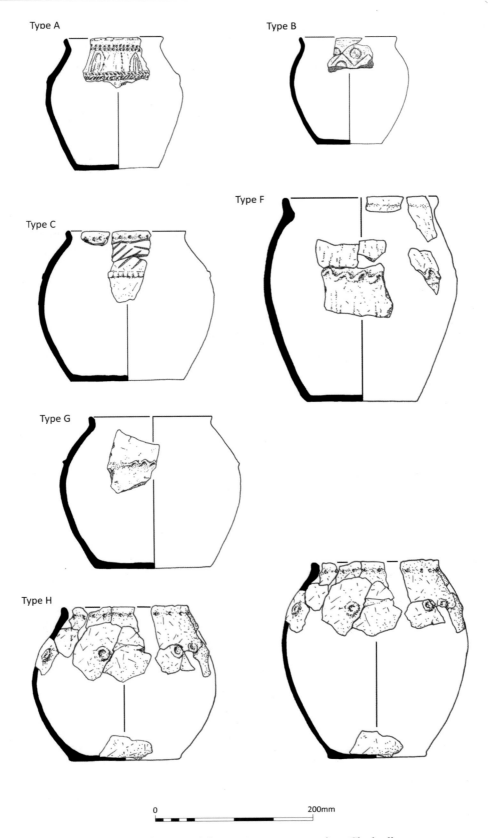

Figure 4.1.13 Schematic of diagnostic pottery types from Clachtoll

Dun Mor Vaul pottery MacKie (1974; 1997) defined a series of everted types – 'Everted Rim ware', 'Cordoned Everted Rim Ware' and 'Clettraval Ware' – the types distinguished by the addition of single decorative traits such as cordons and channelled arch decoration. Similarly, Campbell (1991, 154) noted four variations of decoration on everted pottery – plain[1] cordoned, incised and channelled – from the same 1st/2nd-century AD deposits at Sollas, all contemporaneous variations of a single class of vessel rather than different wares. Further, some everted pottery has a distinctive facetted or fluted rim; that is where the neck of the vessel has a smooth curve on the exterior, but on the interior has an angled 'facet' at the point of inflection.[2] Finally, as noted above, some everted rim pottery often had applied decoration around the neck.[3]

Regarding the date of everted rim pottery Campbell (1991; 2002) suggested an appearance and/or floruit around the 1st or 2nd century AD. MacSween (2006) argues for an earlier date; everted rims were present at Cnip in some quantity during Phase 1, a phase that almost certainly ends during the 1st century BC. MacSween (2003, 131–3), also suggested that everted rims appear between *c.* 550 and 220 cal BC at Balelone and Hornish Point and 'supports MacKie's theory of an early date for everted rims rather than their introduction in the first/second century AD' (MacSween 2003, 133). Others (*e.g.*, Parker Pearson 1999, 210) have suggested everted rims may have been used beyond the 2nd century AD.

Irrespective, as Campbell (1991) points out there seems little doubt that everted rim pottery achieves a prominence at the time of the occupation of brochs and the building of wheelhouses; as Campbell highlights (*ibid.*, 157) it is noticeable that everted rims are found in the lowest levels of all the wheelhouses excavated in modern times such as Sollas, Clettraval, Á Cheardach Mhor, Á Cheardach Bheag, Tigh Talamhanta, Kilpheder and Cnip. Everted rims are undoubtedly a preponderant type and reached their zenith during the Middle Iron Age, probably across the entire Atlantic province; for example, at the Howe, everted rims accounted for more than 65% of the rims from Middle Iron Age levels (Ross 1994, 242).

It is important to note that many of the typical Middle Atlantic Iron Age types – faceted everted rims; necked band cordon everted rims; straight-sided jars/vessels/buckets and ovoid-shaped vessels (where the top bends inwards to almost become enclosed and look like an egg with its top sliced off) – were not, for whatever reason, recovered from Clachtoll.

Cultural and geographical interactions

Given the lack of mainland regional comparisons and geographical location of Clachtoll a critical question when studying the pottery was ascertaining what connections and similarities it had with pottery assemblages from other areas. It has long been suggested that the Atlantic Zone can be divided into three broad zones: the Western Isles and Skye Settlement Sequence; the Argyll and the Inner Isles; and the Northern Settlement Sequence (see Harding 2004, 123–7; Henderson 2007, 151, 154–7, fig. 5.1). Reference to Henderson's map (2007, fig. 5.1) shows that Clachtoll is normally placed within the Western Isles and Skye Settlement sequence.

However, these 'zones' are largely constructed on analysis of structures, as opposed to material culture – arguably only Euan MacKie has tried to systematically study both structures and artefacts to construct wider narratives of these areas (*e.g.*, MacKie 1965b; 2000b; 2002; 2007b). Irrespective, the perceived geographical difference in structural types is also believed to be replicated in pottery, summarised by Lane (1990, 108):

> pottery seems to be the one main thing which differentiates the Hebrides from the Northern Isles, mainland Scotland and Ireland. Later prehistoric pottery is known from Orkney and Shetland but the evidence of sites such as Jarlshof (Hamilton 1956), Clickhimin (Hamilton 1968), Gurness (Hedges 1987), Bu (ibid.) and Skaill (personal communication, Gelling) would suggest that there is little real similarity between the assemblages of the two areas. The Iron Age pottery of the rest of Scotland and Ireland is either non-existent or depressingly undiagnostic.

In 2000 MacKie published a list of the major artefacts types excavated from brochs in Orkney and on the north-east tip of mainland Scotland (Caithness and Sutherland) and, similar to Lane, he concluded that 'although it must be admitted that reliable archaeological evidence for the Iron Age cultures of the far north-east mainland is still woefully inadequate…it can be seen that there are several independent strands of evidence which point to the broch province there as being fundamentally different in several ways from those in the island areas of Atlantic Scotland' (MacKie 2000b, 108–9; see table).[4]

Part of the problem is the lack of synthesis of the Northern Isles and Northern mainland material, due to the perceived difficulty of working with the material, particularly the perceived characteristics (or lack of) of the pottery. That said Harding (2004, 133) agrees with Lane and MacKie contrasting the wealth of decorated pottery in the west with the pottery of Shetland and Orkney that has never shown itself to possess much in the way of decoration. Thus, the key difference to scholars such as Harding, MacKie and Lane is the differences in decoration between the zones.

Thus, given the lack of excavated Sutherland mainland sites, particularly on the north-west, a central research question of this study was to understand whether the Clachtoll pottery (and other material culture) was more aligned with the 'Western Isles and Skye Settlement Sequence' or the 'Northern Settlement Sequence'.

THE WESTERN ISLES

The most extensive research in Scottish Iron Age pottery has been carried out on assemblages from sites in the Western Isles, the first recognisable typology being produced in 1948 by Sir Lindsay Scott at Clettraval wheelhouse. In this report he tried to define stylistic changes within an Iron Age sequence, and to date the beginning of the sequence to the 1st century BC by comparisons with pottery from England and France. Scott's work provided the basis for subsequent typologies (*e.g.*, Young 1956; 1966; MacKie 1974; Campbell 2002). Young's (1966) work presented an account of Hebridean pottery from the Iron Age to the pre-Viking period. Young outlined a sequence of pottery development from 'weak rimmed' incised vessels, sometimes with pin-stamp decoration, through the emergence of more sharply everted rims forms, sometimes decorated with fluted rims, cordons and arcades, followed by a decline in decoration and the emergence of long flaring rims (Young 1966, 53, fig. 4). Some of these later flaring-rim vessels had cordoned decoration, but a final bucket-shaped form of undecorated pottery was seen as the last pre-Norse type. As Lane (1990, 110–11) reminds us Young's paper was essentially a 'pre-radiocarbon' paper written in a time when the Iron Age of northern Britain was defined as short and predetermined by immigrants reaching Scotland in the 2nd to 1st centuries BC. Both Scott (1948) and Young (1966) both hinted at a sequence in which applied ornament outlived incised ornament on Iron Age pottery, with plain wares coming at the end of the sequence (see Harding 2000, 24).

The next two decades of research were led by MacKie (1963; 1965b; 1974), particularly his work at Dun Mor Vaul and his publication of Balevullin, and the subsequent publication of the first radiocarbon dates for the Scottish Iron Age (MacKie 1969). MacKie identified six or seven 'wares' plus additional types and traits with the Iron Age assemblages including *Dunagoil Ware, Vaul Ware, Balevullin Vases, Everted Rim Ware, Clettraval Ware* and *Dun Cuier Ware*. The 14C dates from Dun Mor Vaul allowed many of these types to be sequentially dated from as early as the 7th/6th century BC to the 3rd/4th century AD. Although Lane (1987; 1990) was critical of Dun Mor Vaul he nonetheless (1990, 113) acknowledges the stratigraphic evidence from Dun Mor Vaul does support the earlier views and sequences of Scott and Young, particularly that incised decoration began earlier than channelled decoration of the Clettraval Style. It also supports Young's suggestion that everted-rim vessels, decorated with cordons and decoration and sometimes with internal fluting of the rim gave way to plain wares in the later Iron Age.

Since the publication of Dun Mor Vaul MacKie's analysis has been severely challenged, particularly by Lane (1990) and Topping (1985b; 1987). Topping's work (1985b; 1987) re-examined the typology and chronology of past studies and, after considering the problems of calibration of the 14C dates and the dating of small finds, he concluded that previously suggested typologies – based on form and decoration – were over-simplistic and offered a more structured framework of chronological horizons and wares than really existed in the archaeological record. Topping also highlighted that the pottery assemblages used to construct narratives were still dramatically small and that without the uniformity of commercial or specialist production the relevance of classification may be limited (Topping 1987, 82–3). Armit (1991) suggested that the pottery typology was not chronologically sensitive as certain decorative traits seemed to be in use over a very long time. Lane (2012, 21) suggests that Topping's and Armit's pessimistic views of the potential to recognise a chronologically sensitive pottery sequence were driven, at least partly, by what Lane (*ibid.*) termed 'the Edinburgh School' of thought which was critical of MacKie's diffusionist views on broch origins and Hebridean material culture but wished to maintain the long chronology offered by the early dates at Dun Mor Vaul.

This is a slightly peculiar statement given that one of the leading Iron Age figures of the 'Edinburgh School' – Dennis Harding – argued in numerous publications that MacKie's work did actually allow a general framework for placing some pottery types within *Early, Middle* and *Late* Iron Age brackets. As Harding (2000, 24) reminds us, MacKie identified 'Dunagoil Ware', 'Vaul Ware' (together with Balevullin vases) and internally-decorated bases as potentially Early Iron Age; 'Everted-rim ware' (with or without cordons), and 'Clettraval Ware' – with cordons of arcaded ornament – as essentially Middle Iron Age; and 'Degenerate Clettraval Ware' and 'Dun Cuier Ware' beginning around the 3rd and 4th centuries AD, that is around the beginning of the Late Iron Age and that 'more recent work may nonetheless vindicate the basic sequence which it [MacKie's suggested pottery sequence]' proposed'. Further, as Harding (2005, 40) states 'in the pre-occupation with dating the origins of complex Atlantic roundhouses it is easy to overlook the fact that MacKie identified at Dun Mor Vaul a pottery assemblage for which he acknowledged an early dating, starting from the middle of the first millennium BC. Incised geometric ornament was present…along with 'Vaul' ware, that is plain, coarse ware jars and vessels on harder fabric with incurving rims'.

Since Topping's and Lane's critiques the dataset has improved dramatically due to the excavation and publication of a range of better-stratified and dated site assemblages, for example from Sollas (Campbell 1991); Dun Vulan (Parker Pearson and Sharples 1999); Beirgh (Harding and Gilmour 2000); Dun Bharabhat (Harding and Dixon 2000); Balelone; Baleshare; Hornish Point (Barber 2003); Eilean Olabhat (Armit, Campbell and Dunwell 2008); Cnip (MacSween 2006); Bornais (Sharples 2012); Cladh Hallan (Parker Pearson *et al.* 2021); Gob Eirer (Nesbitt, Church and Gilmour 2011) and An Dunan (Church, Nesbitt and Gilmour 2013).

Campbell's work at Sollas is particularly important, providing a well-dated pottery sequence around the 1st millennium BC/AD boundary, similar to that at Clachtoll. As Campbell (2002, 141) states the Sollas sequence confirmed Young's sequence with weak-rimmed vessels with incised decoration moving to everted rims with channelled and arcaded decoration. Form A consists of tall, heavy bucket-shaped vessels with upright or slightly incurving rims – they are generally undecorated except for finger tipping in the rim area; MacKie (2007b, 1165) notes that this form seems equivalent to Vaul Ware urns. Form B are smaller, lighter vessels of the same general bucket-shaped form (and often decorated); MacKie (2007b, 1165) notes that one (no. 350) looks like a decorated Vaul Ware vase. Form C has slightly everted rims with either a bucket-form or more rounded profile (again, often decorated); again MacKie (2007b, 1165) sees the type as related to Vaul vases. Form D is a single vessel with a high shoulders and distinctive decoration. Form E vessels have distinctive everted rims, often decorated and with cordons; MacKie (2007, 1165) states that many Form E are classic Clettraval sub-types of Everted Rim Ware. Importantly, the four variations of everted-rim pottery – plain, cordoned, incised and channelled – are all found in the same 1st/2nd century AD deposits at Sollas. They are clearly all contemporaneous variations of a single class of vessel rather than different wares (Campbell 1991, 154), the same broad situation as at Clachtoll.

Subsequent work has also supported Young, MacKie and Campbell's broad sequence; the Middle Iron Age pottery (phases 1a to 4) from Dun Vulan a good example. Phase 1a (1st century BC/AD) is defined by *Dunagoil Ware*; Phases 1b to 3 (1st to 3rd centuries AD) are defined as *Balevullin Ware* (Phase 1b); *Vaul Ware*/pottery similar to Sollas Form A1 (Phase 2) and *Vaul Ware*/pottery similar to Sollas Form A2. Phase 4 (2nd to 4th centuries AD) *Clettraval Ware/Sollas Form B1* pottery (see Parker Pearson 1999, 210).

Armit's work at Cnip (2006, 221) defined three broad phases: Phase 1 (? BC–AD 1); Phase 2 (AD 1–100; and Phase 3 (AD 100–250). MacSween's (2006) analysis of the pottery showed that during these 3 periods a range of rim types (8) were in use: plain, flat, everted, internally bevelled, inverted, necked, T-shaped and rounded. In all phases everted rims were the dominant type with only a handful or fewer examples of internally bevelled, necked, t-shaped and rounded forms (*ibid.*, 91–2, tabs 3.9–10). In terms of decoration the overall impression is of a few standard designs, such as an applied straight or zigzag cordon around the shoulder or neck of the vessel, and outwith this a fairly wide range of motifs. Where determinable decoration seems to be restricted to the upper part of the vessel, above the shoulder or around the neck. The general sequence indicates that in all phases the most common type of decoration was applied, followed by incised decoration; by far the most common motif was the zigzag cordon (*ibid.*, 93–5, tabs 3.13–14). By phase 3, applied decoration accounts for almost 60% of the assemblage (*ibid.*, 94, tab. 3.13). MacSween (2006, 101) concludes that, 'it appears that pottery gradually declines both in quality and quantity, with less variety of form and motif and thicker, less accomplished vessels. The near total dominance of applied decoration in Phase 3 seems to result largely from the loss of variety in decorative techniques, rather than any innovation or the adoption of new motifs'.

More recently, the assemblage from An Dunan (MacSween and Johnson 2013) finds ready parallels with many other Hebridean assemblages. For example, flat, everted and plain rims were used throughout the life of the site and smoothing and wiping of the vessel surface were the most common surface finishing techniques. There are also close similarities in the use of some decorative features such as fingertip impressions below the rim, applied roundels and wavy cordons.

Recent years have also seen new dating programmes of actual residues which date the usage of pottery types directly (*e.g.*, Campbell 2002). This new work certainly answered Lane's 1990 clarion call for a re-examination of the Hebridean Iron Age sequence using a number of site sequences and several sets of C-14 dates; his belief that 'the full publication of all these sites will go a long way towards establishing if chronological variation does exist in the pottery sequence' (*ibid.*, 113).

Using this new and emerging evidence numerous scholars have offered updated synthetic narratives for Hebridean pottery with the publications by Harding (2000; 2004); Campbell (2002); Armit, Campbell and Dunwell (2008) and Lane (2012) of particular importance. All of this recent work is tremendously important but we must also acknowledge MacKie's (1997; 2007b) work which relates much of the new pottery from the Hebridean sequences to established pottery nomenclature. If the 'Edinburgh School' can be accused of being too pessimistic many recent scholars can be accused of being reluctant to relate their individual site assemblage 'forms' and 'types' to wider parallels and nomenclature.

Reviewing this new emerging evidence Lane (2012, 21) now sees the Middle Iron Age as being defined by three major themes: the emergence of more elaborate decoration perhaps in the 1st century BC/AD, and its combination with everted rims and channelled decoration in the 1st or 2nd century AD, and the decline of incised decoration perhaps by the 3rd century AD. Arguably, this general sequence, although better dated, is not much different from the basic sequences outlined by Young and MacKie half a century ago. Campbell (2002) and MacSween (2006, 101) largely concur, highlighting that there is now a generally accepted relative Iron Age Hebridean sequence:

1. Undecorated pottery with flat, rounded or slightly inverted rims (MacKie's Dunagoil Ware).
2. The addition of pottery with slightly everted rims and decoration, mainly impressed and incised.
3. An increase in the variety of decoration with the applied decoration and channelled decoration and sharply everted rims.
4. A decrease in the range of decorative motifs, with applied cordons being most common, and a lengthening of the neck.

As highlighted above, the Clachtoll pottery shows many similarities with other Hebridean assemblages (old and new) and arguably fits into stage 3 of the above sequence. As the above narrative has highlighted, almost every sherd of decorated pottery from Clachtoll can be paralleled in the Western Isles, Skye, Argyll and Inner Hebridean assemblages and would fit easily within the general western pottery sequence.

However, in order to answer the research question of what the closest links to the Clachtoll pottery are, it is necessary to look beyond the Western Isles, Skye and Inner Hebridean area. Given the proximity to Caithness and the Northern Isles are there similarities with these areas too? This task is far from easy as these areas have seen little, if any, published synthetic papers that rival the aforementioned Hebridean synthesis.

Shetland

In any discussion of pottery, particularly from the Northern Isles, one has to acknowledge the work of Ann MacSween. With a few exceptions, MacSween has written almost all of the most recent pottery assemblage reports. Further, in outlining a broad pottery typology for Kebister (Dalland and MacSween 1999, 189, tab. 38) her publication is arguably the closest to a published sequence from the Bronze Age to the Late Iron Age and is a sound basis for discussion here; MacSween is one of the few pottery specialists who has actually attempted to place the individual site assemblages into a wider Atlantic Scottish

narrative; many of the other published site reports are mere descriptive catalogues.

As Downes (2000, 60) highlighted there is still a lack of a published prehistoric ceramic sequence for Shetland. Discussions are still largely site based with particular importance given to the pottery sequences recovered from Jarlshof and Clickhimin (Hamilton 1956; 1968). However, excavations over the last three decades, particularly at Mavis Grind, Scalloway, Kebister, Scatness, Bayanne and Sumburgh Airport, allow broader patterns to be deduced.

Our understanding of the Shetland Early Iron Age sequence is aided by work at Mavis Grind (Cracknell and Smith 1983), Kebister (Dalland and MacSween 1999), Bayanne (MacSween 2014) and Sumburgh (Downes 2000). The latter site, particularly the Early Iron Age phase (Phase 8), is of particular importance as it produced a variety of jars (carinated, straight-sided, open and ovoid) and bowls (deep, open or ovoid) that allowed for the first time stratigraphically secure and dated types to be analysed. With this new type-site as a reference, other Shetland sites can now be placed within a broader scheme.

More relevant to this study are a handful of sites that relate to the Middle Iron Age Shetland sequence, particularly Jarlshof, Clickhimin, Kebister, Scalloway, Scatness and Bayonne. Over half a century ago, despite the problems with the general sequence, the Jarlshof Iron Age settlement laid the foundations for our understandings of the general Middle Iron Age types including a variety of everted rim types (including various form of decoration), rounded and beaded rims, flat topped rims (square of oblique) and ovoid. Recent excavations, for example at Scatness (Brown 2015, 335) generally support the Jarlshof typology with Middle Iron Age pottery including: everted rims (plain); everted rims with internal fluting; everted rims with applied cordon below the rims; ovoid (inverted forms) and beaded.

Critically, aside from applied pinched banding decoration and fluting on the rim decoration on Middle Iron Age Shetland pottery is a rarity (see also above). For example, of the 3000 sherds recovered from the Iron Age fort at Clickhimin only a few sherds had decoration on the shoulder or body of the pots (Hamilton 1968, 91). In the later periods the pattern broadly continued – Hamilton (1968, 144) notes that the pottery from Clickhimin wheelhouse was 'predominantly plain'. The same is true at Jarlshof where the handful of decorated sherds were recovered from later wheelhouse phases (Hamilton 1956, 77–8). Similarly, MacSween (1998b, 121) noted that very few of the Scalloway vessels were decorated.

Taking all of these known traits together, particularly the decoration (or lack of), the Clachtoll pottery appears to have little in common with Shetland pottery.

ORKNEY

Like her near neighbour, there is still no general published sequence for Orkney, with discussions again largely site based with analysis of varying quality. Writing in 1987 Hedges (1987, 27–8) noted that the only notable assemblages to work with were Stromness Cemetery, Midhowe, Gurness and Bu and those were not without their difficulties. Hedges *(ibid.)* stated, 'twenty-four of the fifty-two known Orkney brochs have produced pottery, though in the case of fourteen this either does not survive or there are three sherds or fewer. Of the remaining ten reasonably sized collections half are completely unstratified'. Excavations and publications over the last three decades of sites such as Tofts Ness, Pierowall, Pool, St Boniface, Skaill and Howe allow greater insight than previous excavations.

Analysis of this material shows, again, that decoration on Middle Iron Age Orcadian pottery is rare. When discussing the pottery from Midhowe Callander and Grant (1934, 511–12) noted 'fragments of pottery were found in great numbers…this constitutes the finest collection of clay pots recovered so far from a broch…[but]…it is remarkable that there was practically no ornamentation on the vessels; only one or two small pieces showed an attempt at decoration, and this consisted of simple incised lines'. Half a century later Hedges (1987, 28–9) pointed out the apparent disjuncture between some Middle Iron Age Orcadian sites that had considerable decoration and others that did not. He noted that 'decoration is as rare on the pottery from Bu, Midhowe and Gurness as distinctive rims are – there are just three stratified pieces from the last-named site'. When discussing the wider Iron Age Orcadian assemblages Hedges suggested that the differences in decoration from sites (*e.g.*, Lingro, Ayre) which had plentiful decoration and Midhowe and Gurness that had little pointed to 'two contemporary ceramic traditions in Broch Period Orkney, a situation that can be paralleled by the Grooved Ware and Unstan Ware of the Neolithic (*ibid.*, 28–9). Recent excavations have not helped the percentages much either; decorated pottery from Middle Iron Age levels at the Howe formed less than 1% of the total number of sherds (Ross 1994, 243).

Again, taking all of this together it appears that Clachtoll pottery has little in common with Orkney pottery.

NORTHERN MAINLAND SCOTLAND

There is no published overview of the Northern Mainland pottery sequence with McIlfatrick (2013)'s PhD study the first attempt to produce one. The pottery assemblages from Caithness and Sutherland largely derive from a mixture of excavations and individual bequests from the late 19th and early 20th centuries; frustratingly, many diagnostic types are largely unprovenanced (see above) and we have to accept that many may not even be from the region. As outlined in Heald and Barber (2016) the 19th and early

20th centuries saw a plethora of Atlantic roundhouse excavations taking place across the region, particularly in the north-east of Caithness with key sites including: Kettleburn; Ousdale; Yarrows; Keiss Road, Ness, Skirza, Keiss Harbour; Wester, Everley; Whitegate; and Nybster (see also Heald and Jackson 2001). These sites have been expertly reviewed by MacKie (2007b). As reference to the original reports show and the meagre total of finds in the National Museums Scotland (there are only around 500 sherds from scores of excavations) – it is inconceivable that this small number represents the total sherds once in use, or probably even found during the excavations. Needless to say there is no clear stratigraphic phasing from these sites to help us create a relative chronology, even from the meagre assemblages.

Over the last decade a number of new projects have been undertaken on Iron Age (particularly Middle Iron Age) sites across Caithness. This work has produced new assemblages with many new radiocarbon dates and better stratigraphic sequences. By placing this into wider narratives of other sites excavated in the post-war period (*e.g.*, Crosskirk, Kilpheder and Cnoc Stanger) a broad sequence can begin to be created for northern mainland Scotland (Heald, Cavers and Barber in prep).

Decoration, or lack thereof, is, again, a critical component of the Northern mainland sequence. Although there are examples it is frustrating that of the few known decorated pottery sherds in the National Museum Scotland from the pre-War excavations almost two-thirds are of unknown provenance. However, as many of the unprovenanced examples are associated with the Tress Barry Bequest (and there are almost no recorded examples of decorated pottery from individual site catalogues excavated by Barry (see McIlfatrick 2013, 186, tab. 5.1-27) then we must surely assume that, as with other objects, Tress Barry cherry-picked his favourite (most decorative) examples that he, presumably, found during his numerous excavations of brochs around the north-east of Caithness. Where we have more provenanced examples – Kettleburn (Rhind 1853), Yarrows (Anderson 1890), Skitten (Calder 1948), Wag of Forse (Curle 1948), Crosskirk (Fairhurst 1984), Thrumster (Barber *et al.* in prep), Everley, Nybster and Whitegate (Heald, Cavers and Barber in prep) – decorated pottery has only been recovered in very small numbers. Applied cordons are particularly rare: for example, at Everley they constitute only 2% of the overall pottery assemblage.

Again, the Caithness pottery seems to have little in common with the Clachtoll assemblage.

SUMMARY

Accepting that some non-Hebridean areas did produce decorated pottery with motifs similar to Hebridean assemblages, it must surely be the case that the

Table 4.1.1 Extrapolated capacity and volume by vessel type based on digital reconstruction modelling

Vessel Number	Vessel Type	Capacity (cm³)	Litres
1	A	3150	~3l
2	B	1425	~1.5l
3	C	5190	~5l
8	F	9900	~10l
11	H	5009 – 6516	~5l - ~6.5l

Clachtoll pottery assemblage is best viewed within the geographically closer Western Isles, Skye, Argyll and the Inner Isles than any other area of Atlantic Scotland. Paraphrasing Harding (2005), there is a whole range of ornamental motifs within the incised or impressed range across Atlantic Scotland which can give parallel hunters the occasional success, but the weight of evidence surely suggests that the Clachtoll pottery is not, in general, representative of Northern Isles or Caithness styles.

Whilst we can now see the Clachtoll pottery within the broader Western Isles, Argyll, Inner Hebrides and Skye sequence it is important to stress that there are also many differences within the wider Hebridean region. This probably reflects the preferences of households, selecting from a commonly used pool of surface-finish techniques and decorative techniques and motifs used by a wider community (MacSween 2006, 103). It is also likely that individual local sequences may not have any further validity across wider regions. For example, as Armit, Campbell and Dunwell (2008) state examples similar to Sollas Type A pottery have recently been found in St Kilda on a site with Middle Iron Age dates, but the pottery is much thicker and cruder than on North Uist. As Campbell (2002, 144) states 'the variety of decorative forms, particularly in the Middle Iron Age where some features seem to be peculiar to individual sites, suggests that generalisations about stylistic developments may be difficult to sustain'. Indeed, as Topping (1985a, 208) states 'to search for a single pottery sequence based on chronological criteria without regard to function and ignoring the possibility of local variations changing through time is a misguided approach'. MacKie (2000b, 105) concurs stating it has long been clear that there are local styles within the Atlantic province and it is likely that local populations had their own pottery traditions. It is clear that the comparatively uniform stone buildings do not imply a completely uniform material culture. As Harding (2000, 21) states 'the fact that the ceramic tradition in the Northern Isles is not the same as in the West testifies to regional autonomy of culture, but they stand together in contrast to the rest of mainland Scotland'.

Cooking and consumption

Although we concur with Harding (2000, 21) when he stresses that the limitations of size, quality and design of Iron Age pottery must have limited the utility of the medium and that pottery would probably not have been nearly the all-purpose utility artefact that we sometimes imagine it to be it is still important to try and tease further information from the assemblages. In general, there is a poor understanding of the nature of cooking practices and cuisine in the Scottish Iron Age. Two useful avenues are open to us: analysis of the size, form and function of the pottery and residue analysis.

SIZE, FORM AND FUNCTION

We have seen that at Clachtoll that the number of vessels was small (no more than between 15 and 20) and that the vessels are probably best viewed as the utensils used by one family group. Thus, such a closed group may allow us insight into different forms and functions of the pottery.

Accepting that not enough of the pottery survives to be sure of the exact shape and form the digital reconstructions presented above none-the-less provide a reasonable working model. Table 4.1.1 outlines the suggested capacity of each main vessel type. To put these figures into a modern context an average cup of coffee can hold about 200 ml, a bowl of soup around 400 ml and a pint of milk around 500 ml.

RESIDUE ANALYSIS

A range of scientific approaches have considerable potential for the study of food, cooking practices and cuisine; one such approach is organic residue analysis of pottery.

The full results of the analysis on the Clachtoll pottery has been outlined elsewhere in this volume (Dunne, Gillard and Evershed, Section 4.3). The results, determined from GC, GC-MS and GC-C-IRMS analyses of lipid residue extracts demonstrated that six pots were used to process solely dairy products (milk, butter or cheese). Three further vessels were used to process mainly dairy products but with the addition of some, likely minor, marine resource processing, such as fish or sea mammal fats, evidenced by the presence of aquatic biomarkers (APAAs) and more positive $\delta^{13}C$ values. This data suggests that dairy products were an extremely important commodity during this period. The presence of long-chain fatty acids in a number of these vessels (CLT12, CLT13, CLT15, CLT18 and CLT20) suggests the addition of leafy plants to the foods processed in these vessels. It is interesting that, although all vessels were predominantly used to process dairy products, the majority were multi-use, also being used to process marine and plant resources, whether at the same time or on separate occasions.

This is the first such study of Iron Age potsherds from mainland Scotland. Previous analysis of Late Iron

Table 4.1.2 Summary of Organic Residue Analysis results on selected pottery sherds and sampled encrusted residues (summarised from Dunne, Gillard & Evershed; see section 4.3 for full results). Red = no measurable lipids; green = measurable lipids

SF No.	Context No.	Vessel No.	Type	Sherd Quantity	Description	Weight (g)	ORA Lab number	Attribution
174	78	1	A	n/a	Sample of encrusted carbonised residues removed from interior surface		CLT 11	Dairy product
181	61	8	F	n/a	Sample of encrusted carbonised residues removed from exterior surface adjacent to applied decoration		CLT 12	Dairy product/marine/plant
160	78	Not assigned	H	1	Lower body sherd	19.2	CLT 13	Dairy product/plant
188	67	14	H	1	Rim sherd	5.4	CLT 14	
111	47	Not assigned	H	1	Base sherd	10.7	CLT 15	Dairy product/plant
220	78	11	H	1	Body sherd	18.9	CLT 16	
220	78	11	H	1	Rim sherd	5.4	CLT 17	
174	75	1	A	1	Body sherd - Mid	3.7	CLT 18	Dairy product/plant
29	42	10	G	1	Body sherd	23	CLT 19	
139	62	Not assigned	G	1	Body sherd	5.4	CLT 20	Dairy product/plant
26	42	10	G	1	Base sherd	13.6	CLT 21	
29	42	10	G	1	Body sherd	7.1	CLT 22	
235	145	5	D	1	Body sherd - shoulder	3.8	CLT 23	Dairy product
220	78	7	E	1	Lower body sherd	13.9	CLT24	
41	42	2	B	2	Body sherds - decorated	11.2	CLT 25	
29	42	18	Unclassified	1	Body sherd - shoulder - decorated	7.3	CLT 26	
162	67	8	F	1	Body sherd	24	CLT 27	Dairy product/marine
188	67	8	F	1	Body sherd - upper pot	16.8	CLT 28	Dairy product/marine

Age potsherds from the Northern Isles showed that 64% of lipid yielding sherds contained dairy products (Cramp *et al.* 2014). This is similar to results from previous work on Iron Age pottery residues from sites in southern England. The analysis of 237 vessels from the Iron Age sites of Maiden Castle, Danebury Hillfort, Yarnton Cresswell Field and Stanwick demonstrated that up to 56% of the extracts, (equivalent to 22% of all of the sherds), contained dairy products (Copley *et al.* 2005). This suggests that dairying was an important part of subsistence strategies at these sites but as part of a mixed meat/milk economy.

Beyond typology: symbolism and cognitive meaning in decoration

As Sharples (2012, 330) highlights it is important – as Campbell (1991) did – to try and move beyond merely using pottery as a chronological or typological indicator. One of the principal avenues open to meaningful discussion is decoration. Sharples (2012, 330) reminds us that in the Hebrides pottery was produced and consumed by households and the primary social event where pottery would be observed would be during cooking and food consumption. If one assumes that the presence, absence and nature of decoration were an attempt to convey coded social messages, then the messages were primarily viewed and understood by members of the household. As Boivin (2008) states it is possible that decoration (or art) was as a semiotic code that refers to certain features of the cultural and natural environment. With this in mind let us turn to the main decorative elements on the Clachtoll pottery.

WAVY CORDON

Sharples (2012, 330–1) argues that perhaps the wavy cordon on Hebridean pottery may be representative of the sea:

> The symbolism of the line seems clear in an island context where the sea is the dominant feature of the view from an elevated location and the description of this decorative element as a 'wavy cordon' seems particularly appropriate as it can be interpreted as an accurate representation of the waves.

Sharples also suggests that the positioning of further decoration above the wavy cordon line may represent 'islands rising out of the sea, or more broadly as the terrestrial world' (*op. cit.*). The location of Clachtoll surely lends support to Sharples' theory and perhaps we could view the wavy cordon pottery from the site in a similar way.

CEREAL CORDON

One of the most distinctive vessels from Clachtoll has an applied cordon with associated linear decoration between

Figure 4.1.14 Detail of the impressed barley cordon on Vessel 1

the cordon and the rim (Fig. 4.1.14); the cordon appears to be mimicking cereal, probably barley. Depictions of floral/cereal images (applied or incised) are known from other Hebridean sites such as Dun Borbaidh (Beveridge 1903, NMS X. HD 324), Dun Bharabhat (Harding and Dixon 2000, 86, fig. 43, no. 7) and Dun Mor Vaul (MacKie 1974, fig. 19, nos. 461 and 465), Hornish Point (Barber 2003, 130, fig. 76 c) and Dun Vulan (Parker Pearson and Sharples 1999, 72, fig. 4.13, nos. 1, 3, 9 and 10, 214–17, fig. 9.2 Type 15). Given the agricultural regime of the Clachtoll inhabitants surely the applied cordon is demonstrating the importance of the agricultural environment that surrounds the household on a daily basis.

And we can, perhaps, take the analogy further. Between the rim and the cordon is impressed and incised decoration largely composed of widely spaced pairs of nested inverted V-shaped incised lines. Given Sharple's convincing argument that the cordon may represent the difference between above and below land (in the case of the wavy

Figure 4.1.15 Detail of projecting ring-headed pin head (SF 154) from Clachtoll overlaid with impressed decoration on sherd from Vessel 2

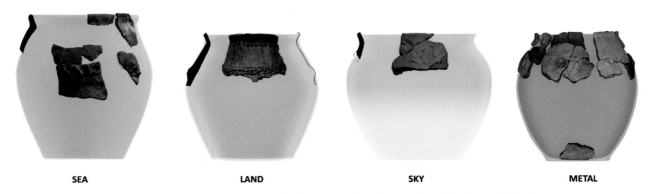

SEA   LAND   SKY   METAL

Figure 4.1.16 Decoration and symbolism: metaphors for Iron Age lifestyles and beliefs

cordon the sea) perhaps the cordon on the Clachtoll vase represents the land and the linear decoration above is mimicking (in vertical form) the actual crops grown from the soil.

RING-HEADED PINS

Type B has been decorated by a projecting ring-headed pin, possibly SF 154 (Figs 4.1.15 and 4.5.1a). Sharples (2012, 331) argues that the stamped circular impressions caused by ring-headed pins may be representations of the sun (or the moon) and there are some supporting analogies as the elaborately decorated pin heads of the Late Bronze Age/Early Iron Age transition are other interpreted as symbols of the sun. To continue the symbolic metaphor it may well be that the V-shapes that inter-disperse the circles on the Clachtoll pottery represents hills and mountains and/or the rising and falling of the sun or moon.

Perhaps there is another symbolic meaning – it is possible that the ring-headed pin impressions represent the importance of other materials to their lives; that is bronze and/or the means of ornamentation. Although some Celtic art objects have been found in Atlantic Scotland the bronze repertoire in Middle Atlantic Scotland is largely limited to pins, ingots and rings. Hunter's (2006a) recent analysis of the massive metalwork of north-east Scotland suggested that non-ferrous objects were made and used within specific, confined localities and, in certain areas, the production and consumption of metalwork was regionally specific, and stimulated by local needs. Further, Hunter (*ibid.*) acknowledges that prestige artefacts played a more significant role in the Atlantic Iron Age than is normally realised. Thus, the pin, for whatever reason, may have had particular local significance to the inhabitants of Clachtoll. That bone, stone and pottery were important to the inhabitants of Atlantic Scotland is shown in the use of these objects within house foundations and other 'ritual' deposits, both within the *domus* and the landscape. These deposits from floor deposits, wall foundations, peat bogs and other wetland deposits are important as they demonstrate that the objects we may

term 'prosaic' (pottery, ards, shares, animals bones) actually had strong utilitarian and ritualistic importance in Atlantic Scotland (see Hingley 1992). Thus, it may well be that any bronze object had symbolic meaning to the household, who felt it appropriate to decorate their everyday belongings with objects that held to them important meaning; either to do with ornamentation or contacts with smiths.

APPLIED BOSSES

Some of the pottery from Clachtoll has applied bosses. On other Atlantic sites, for example the Howe (Ross 1994, 247–8, illus. 147, no. 7114), it has been argued that said decoration is mimicking the components of contemporary metal vessels. This is not a new idea: one of the most diagnostic pottery types from Early Iron Age Shetland are 'carinated vessels'; some scholars (*e.g.*, Downes 2000, 48) suggest that the pottery are skeuomorphs of late Bronze Age bronze buckets.

SUMMARY

By moving beyond typology and chronology we can begin to view the Clachtoll pottery as metaphors for wider Iron Age lifestyles and beliefs (Fig. 4.1.16). It may well be that the decoration on the pottery was chosen to represent the sea; agricultural practices, the sun and moon and bronze objects. All of these aspects would have been critical to the everyday work and practices of the Clachtoll household.

Conclusion

The Clachtoll pottery assemblage is of particular significance for a number of reasons. First, it represents the first securely dated Middle Iron Age pottery assemblage from mainland Scotland and, indeed, from Atlantic Scotland. Second, the catastrophic collapse of the roundhouse suggests that the vessels are part of a 'closed group', and arguably represent a snapshot into the pottery vessels of one family or extended group; the vessels should be viewed as a collective household repertoire. Third, the

3D recording of all finds allows detailed reconstruction of the context of discovery of the pottery which, in turn, allows rare insight into household activities within the roundhouse and, from that, understandings of wider social interactions. Fourth, the assemblage allows one to place Clachtoll, and by inference, west coast mainland Sutherland into wider cultural and geographical landscapes; until now there has been no clarity whether the inhabitants of Clachtoll were more aligned with their west coast neighbours or their more distant neighbours to the north-east and Northern Isles. Fifth, the application of scientific techniques (digital reconstruction and residue analysis) allows better understanding of the form, function and use of the vessels, allowing greater insight into cooking and consumption within the Clachtoll household. Finally, by moving beyond typology and chronology and considering aspects such as symbolism we can begin to glean wider narratives from the pottery that move beyond the functional and relate the assemblage to wider issues of the natural environment, cultural contacts and the wider context of use.

4.2 Heat-affected clay and associated materials

Dawn McLaren

Concentrations of heat-affected clay and a range of associated materials were recovered from the interior of Cell 2 during excavation and as the result of soil sample processing. Although small amorphous agglomerates of peat ash (4.3 g) and desiccated peat (4.2 g) were also recovered from contexts within the broch interior, the recovered fragments heat-affected clay (3359.1 g) and its associated heat-altered hard crust (466.6 g) were confined to Cell 2 with only one exception. The heat-affected condition of these materials is undoubtedly the result of accidental burning during the fire event rather than by intentional firing.

Figure 4.2.2 The fired clay (140) in Cell 2, during excavation

During the excavation of Cell 2, a series of organic and clay-rich floor layers were encountered which had been laid over the basal flag stones (132) of the structure. The majority of the heat-affected clay (141) formed a single thick layer which was spread across the south and east sides of the cell floor. Despite careful excavation and recovery, the material was so friable that the majority of pieces did not retain their original shape on lifting. The largest and best-preserved fragment measures 173.4 mm in length, 131.0 mm in width and is a maximum of 39.1 mm thick (Fig. 4.2.1). It consists of three distinct layers: the upper layer (140) is a thin hard friable crust of a heat-affected beige-pale to grey-blue substance with a fibrous appearance. The margins between it and the fired clay that it sits on are well defined. Only patches of it now survive adhering to the upper surface of the clay layer but the original extent of this vitrified material can clearly be observed on Figure 4.2.2 as a pale-coloured arc, shadowing the curvature of the eastern wall of the cell and respecting the concentration of carbonised processed barley (123) which lay to its immediate west. As it survives, the vitrified crust coats the undulating surface of

Figure 4.2.1 The fired clay from Cell 2

Figure 4.2.3 Carbonised plant stems visible in the fired clay (140)

Figure 4.2.4 SEM image of the carbonised rachis nodes, stems and cereal grains within 140 ((c) NMS)

the clay, apparently settling on to its surface after it was laid down and averages between 2–13 mm in thickness. Under magnification it is clear that this crust is vitrified and glassy and bears traces of a former fibrous plant-based structure which displays elements of patterning in their orientation which is particularly clear on the contact surface with the clay where the organic material is less vitrified and carbonised and the remains of plant stems can clearly be observed (Fig. 4.2.3). ED-SEM analysis undertaken at National Museum Scotland (Troalen 2019) confirms the composition of the material to be rich in silicon, calcium and phosphate with minor traces of iron, magnesium, potassium and aluminium, elements natural to the soil and plant tissues and demonstrates that the crust is made up of the vitrified silicon skeletons of bundles of plant stems, rachis nodes and cereal grains of hulled barley (see Chapter 5) coated in patches with a build-up of salt crystals. This confirms that the hard crust which was seen as a curving spread beside the cache of cereal grains during excavation is the conflated and vitrified remains of a sheaf of barley.

The underlying heat affected clay (141) varies in thickness from *c.* 14 mm to *c.* 26.5 mm and consists of soft-fired fine sandy clay, bright orange-buff to beige in colour implying firing under oxidising conditions and is soft and powdery to the touch. Some layering of the clay can be seen on vertical break edges which suggest it was laid down as lumps of raw boulder clay, packing them together and then smoothing them to form a layer. Below the heat affected clay, is a thin (*c.* 2–3 mm) layer of carbonised plant matter which must have accumulated or been deliberately spread across the sand dusted stone floor of the cell.

Further small quantities of amorphous heat-affected clay fragments (193.8 g) were recovered from (123),

(133), (134), (142) and a single piece of a semi-vitrified organic-based material (1.8 g) similar to that described above from (141) came from (125), also in Cell 2.

The only location beyond Cell 2 where tiny fragments (5.8 g) of heat-affected clay were found was from an accumulation of burnt material within the passageway (041) to Gallery 2. These small fragments were all amorphous in shape and heavily weathered.

Conclusions

The study of the heat-affected clay and the associated vitrified material demonstrates that the floor slabs of Cell 2 had been deliberately covered in a layer of raw boulder clay to create an even, clean and watertight surface to allow the structure to be used as a food storage area. It is only due to the unusual circumstances and conditions created by the fire-event that has enabled such extraordinary preservation of both the cache of processed cereal grains and the vitrified vestiges of what appears to be an unprocessed bundle or sheaf of hulled barley. It is unclear whether the sheaf of grain was stored here awaiting processing or was being kept as seed for the following year's crop but this material has provided important and unusual evidence for the use of at least one of the cells at the broch.

4.3 Organic residue analysis of the ceramics and steatite vessels

Julie Dunne, Toby Gillard and Richard P. Evershed

Introduction

Lipids, the organic solvent soluble components of living organisms, *i.e.* the fats, waxes and resins of the natural world, are the most frequently recovered compounds from archaeological contexts. They are resistant to decay and are likely to endure at their site of deposition, often for thousands of years, because of their inherent hydrophobicity, making them excellent candidates for use as biomarkers in archaeological research (Evershed 1991).

Pottery has become one of the most extensively studied materials for organic residue analysis (Mukherjee *et al.* 2005) as ceramics, once made, are virtually indestructible and thus are one of the most, if not the most, common artefacts recovered from archaeological sites from the Neolithic period onwards (Tite 2008). Survival of these residues occurs in three ways; rarely, actual contents are preserved *in situ* (*e.g.*, Charrié-Duhaut *et al.* 2007) or, more commonly, as surface residues (Evershed 2008). The last, most frequent occurrence, is that of absorbed residues preserved within the vessel wall, which have been found to survive in >80% of domestic cooking pottery assemblages worldwide (Evershed 2008).

The application of modern analytical techniques enables the identification and characterisation of these sometimes highly degraded remnants of natural commodities used in antiquity (Evershed 2008). Often, data obtained from the organic residue analysis of pottery or other organic material provides the only evidence for the processing of animal commodities, aquatic products or plant oils and waxes, particularly at sites exhibiting a paucity of environmental evidence. To date, the use of chemical analyses in the reconstruction of vessel use at sites worldwide has enabled the identification of terrestrial animal fats (Evershed *et al.* 1997a; Mottram *et al.* 1999), marine animal fats (Copley *et al.* 2004; Craig *et al.* 2007), plant waxes (Evershed, Heron and Goad 1991), beeswax (Evershed *et al.* 1997b) and birch bark tar (Charters *et al.* 1993; Urem-Kotsou *et al.* 2002). This has increased our understanding of ancient diet and foodways and has provided insights into herding strategies and early agricultural practices. Organic residue analysis has also considerably enhanced our understanding of the technologies involved in the production, repair and use of ancient ceramics.

Preserved animal fats are by far the most commonly observed constituents of lipid residues recovered from archaeological ceramics. This demonstrates their considerable significance to past cultures, not just for their nutritional value but also for diverse uses such as binding media, illuminants, sealers, lubricants, varnish, adhesives and ritual, medical and cosmetic purposes (Mills and White 1977; Evershed *et al.* 1997a).

Today, the high sensitivities of instrumental methods such as gas chromatography and mass spectrometry allow very small amounts of compounds to be detected and identified. Furthermore, higher sensitivity can be achieved using selected ion monitoring (SIM) methods for the detection of specific marine biomarkers (Evershed *et al.* 2008; Cramp and Evershed 2013). The advent of gas chromatography-combustion-isotope ratio mass spectrometry in the 1990s introduced the possibility of accessing stable isotope information from individual biomarker structures, opening a range of new avenues for the application of organic residue analysis in archaeology (Evershed *et al.* 1994; 1997a).

This stable carbon isotope approach, using GC-C-IRMS, is employed to determine the $\delta^{13}C$ values of the principal fatty acids (C_{16} and C_{18}), ubiquitous in archaeological ceramics. Differences occur in the $\delta^{13}C$ values of these major fatty acids due to the differential routing of dietary carbon and fatty acids during the synthesis of adipose and dairy fats in ruminant animals, thus allowing ruminant milk fatty acids to be distinguished from carcass fats by calculating $\Delta^{13}C$ values ($\delta^{13}C_{18:0} - \delta^{13}C_{16:0}$) and plotting that against the $\delta^{13}C$ value of the $C_{16:0}$ fatty acid. Previous research has shown that by plotting $\Delta^{13}C$ values, variations in C_3 versus C_4 plant consumption are removed, thereby emphasizing biosynthetic and metabolic characteristics of the fat source (Dudd and Evershed 1998; Copley *et al.* 2003).

Aims and objectives

The objective of this investigation was to determine whether absorbed organic residues were preserved in 17 potsherds, two surface or 'burnt-on' residues from potsherds, five fragments of steatite vessels and five surface residues scraped from the surface of steatite vessels. A full list of the pottery sherds submitted for analysis are summarised in Table 4.1.2.

Materials and analytical methods

Lipid analysis and interpretations were performed using established protocols described in detail in earlier publications (Correa-Ascencio and Evershed 2014). Briefly, ~2 g of potsherd and steatite vessels were sampled, and surfaces cleaned with a modelling drill to remove exogenous lipids. Surface residues from the potsherds and steatite vessels were removed using a solvent-washed scalpel. The cleaned powder and encrusted residue were both crushed in a solvent-washed mortar and pestle and weighed into a furnaced culture tube (I). An internal standard was added (20 μg *n*-tetratriacontane; Sigma Aldrich Company Ltd) together with 5 ml of H_2SO_4/MeOH 2–4% ($\delta^{13}C$ value measured) and the culture tubes were placed on a heating block for 1 h at 70°C, mixing every 10 min. Once cooled, the methanolic acid was transferred to test tubes and centrifuged at 2500 rpm for 10 min. The supernatant was then decanted into another furnaced culture tube (II) and 2 ml of DCM extracted double distilled water was added. In order to recover any lipids not fully solubilised by the methanol solution, 2 × 3 ml of *n*-hexane was added to the extracted potsherds contained in the original culture tubes, mixed well and transferred to culture tube II. The extraction was transferred to a clean, furnaced 3.5 ml vial and blown down to dryness. Following this, 2 × 2 ml *n*-hexane was added directly to the H_2SO_4/MeOH solution in culture tube II and whirlimixed to extract the remaining residues, then transferred to the 3.5 ml vials and blown down until a full vial of *n*-hexane remained. Aliquots of the TLE's were derivatised using 20 μl BSTFA (70°C, 1 h), excess BSTFA was removed under nitrogen and the derivatised TLE was dissolved in *n*-hexane prior to GC, GC-MS and GC-C-IRMS. Firstly, the samples underwent high-temperature gas chromatography using a gas chromatograph (GC) fitted with a high temperature non-polar column (DB1-HT; 100% dimethylpolysiloxane, 15 m × 0·32 mm i.d., 0.1 μm film thickness). The carrier gas was helium and the temperature programme comprised a 50°C isothermal followed by an increase to 350°C at a rate of 10°C min⁻¹ followed by a 10 min isothermal. A procedural blank (no sample) was prepared and analysed alongside every batch of samples. Further compound identification was accomplished using gas chromatography-mass spectrometry (GC-MS). FAMEs were then introduced by autosampler onto a GC-MS fitted with a non-polar column (100% dimethyl polysiloxane stationary phase; 60 m × 0.25 mm i.d., 0·1 μm film thickness). The instrument was a ThermoFinnigan single quadrupole TraceMS run in EI mode (electron energy 70 eV, scan time of 0·6 s). Samples were run in full scan mode (*m/z* 50–650) and the temperature programme comprised an isothermal hold at 50°C for 2 min, ramping to 300°C at 10°C min[-1], followed by an isothermal hold at 300°C (15 min). Data acquisition and processing were carried out using the HP Chemstation software (Rev. B.03.02 (341), Agilent Technologies) and Xcalibur software (version 3.0). Peaks were identified on the basis of their mass spectra and gas chromatography (GC) retention times, by comparison with the NIST mass spectral library (version 2.0).

Carbon isotope analyses by GC-C-IRMS were also carried out using a GC Agilent Technologies 7890A coupled to an Isoprime 100 (EI, 70eV, three Faraday cup collectors *m/z* 44, 45 and 46) via an IsoprimeGC5 combustion interface with a CuO and silver wool reactor maintained at 850°C. Instrument accuracy was determined using an external FAME standard mixture (C_{11}, C_{13}, C_{16}, C_{21} and C_{23}) of known isotopic composition. Samples were run in duplicate and an average taken. The $\delta^{13}C$ values are the ratios $^{13}C/^{12}C$ and expressed relative to the Vienna Pee Dee Belemnite, calibrated against a CO_2 reference gas of known isotopic composition. Instrument error was ±0.3‰. Data processing was carried out using Ion Vantage software (version 1.6.1.0, IsoPrime).

Results

Lipid analysis and interpretations were performed using established protocols described in detail in earlier publications (*e.g.*, Dudd and Evershed 1998; Correa-Ascencio and Evershed 2014).

Iron Age potsherds

A total of seven potsherds yielded interpretable lipid profiles (Table 4.3.1) as did the two surface or 'burnt-on' residues. The mean lipid concentration from the potsherds was 0.76 mg g[-1], with a maximum lipid concentration of 3.6 mg g[-1] from vessel CLT23 (V5), demonstrating excellent preservation, and confirming sustained use of the vessel in the processing of high lipid-yielding commodities. The lipid concentration from surface residue CLT11 (V1) was exceptionally high, at 7.2 mg g[-1]. The extracts comprised lipid profiles which demonstrated free fatty acids, palmitic (C_{16}) and stearic (C_{18}), typical of a degraded animal fat (Fig. 4.3.1a–b), were the most abundant components (Evershed *et al.* 1997a; Berstan *et al.* 2008).

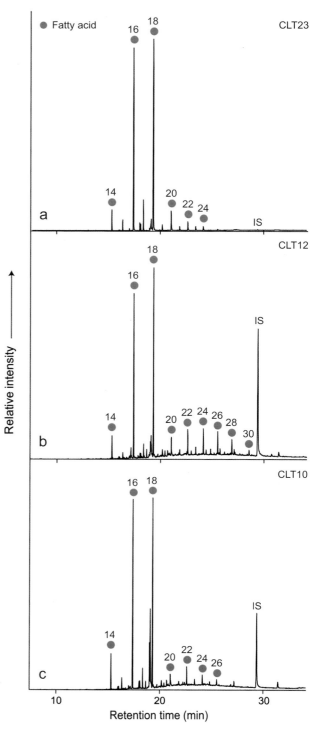

Figure 4.3.1 Gas chromatogram of trimethylsilylated FAMEs from Iron Age pottery and steatite vessel a) CLT23 potsherd b) CLT12 potsherd and c) CLT10, steatite vessel. Circles, n-alkanoic acids (fatty acids, FA); IS, internal standard, C_{34} n-tetratriacontane

Vessels CLT11 (V1), CLT13 (V not assigned, Type H), CLT23 (V5) and CLT28 (V8) include a series of

Table 4.3.1 Summary of the lipid concentrations (µg g⁻¹), total lipid concentration in extract (µg), δ¹³C and Δ¹³C values and attributions of the sampled Clachtoll Broch Iron Age potsherds and steatite vessels

Laboratory Number	Sherd type	Context	SF no.	V no. (pottery)	Lipid concentration ($\mu g\ g^{-1}$)	Total lipid in extract (μg)	$\delta^{13}C_{16:0}$	$\delta^{13}C_{18:0}$	$\Delta^{13}C$	Attribution
Steatite vessel										
CLT04	Surface residue	42	95		391.3	141.1	-27.3	-31	-3.7	Dairy product
CLT10	Lamp fragment	42	60		78.6	116.9	-28.7	-32.8	-4.2	Dairy product/plant
Pottery vessel										
CLT11	Surface residue	78	174	1 (Type A)	7179	2018.7	-28.1	-34.5	-6.4	Dairy product
CLT12	Surface residue	61	181	8 (Type F)	797.3	48.8	-25.6	-29.8	-4.2	Dairy product/marine/plant
CLT13	Lower body	78	160	Not assigned (Type H)	381	365.8	-29.3	-33.6	-4.3	Dairy product/plant
CLT15	Base	47	111	Not assigned (Type H)	48.8	87.4	-27.7	-32.4	-4.7	Dairy product/plant
CLT18	Body (Mid)	75	174	1 (Type A)	178.8	190.5	-28.2	-33.8	-5.6	Dairy product/plant
CLT20	Body	62	139	Not assigned (Type G)	512.6	642.5	-27.6	-32.9	-5.2	Dairy product/plant
CLT23	Body (Shoulder)	145	235	5 (Type D)	3612.8	6349.4	-27	-32.9	-5.9	Dairy product
CLT27	Body	67	162	8 (Type F)	122	223	-24.8	-28.3	-3.5	Dairy product/marine
CLT28	Body (Upper)	67	188	8 (Type F)	507.7	1158.6	-24.5	-28.3	-3.9	Dairy product/marine

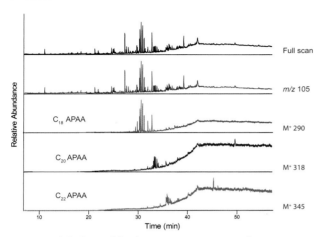

Figure 4.3.2 Partial high-temperature mass chromatogram showing FAME from potsherd CLT12 analysed using GC/MS operated in SIM mode for the detection of C18–C22 APAAs. Components were identified based upon the presence of identical chromatographic peaks for the characteristic fragment ions and molecular ions at the expected retention times

Table 4.3.2 APAAs present in Clachtoll Broch potsherds and steatite vessels

Sample	Sample type	$C_{18}APAA$	$C_{20}APAA$	$C_{22}APAA$
CLT10	Steatite vessel	x	-	-
CLT11	Potsherd	x	x	-
CLT12	Potsherd	x	x	x
CLT15	Potsherd	x	-	-
CLT18	Potsherd	x	-	-
CLT23	Potsherd	x	-	-
CLT27	Potsherd	x	x	x
CLT28	Potsherd	x	x	x

long-chain fatty acids (in low abundance), containing C_{20} to C_{26} carbon atoms. These appear in decreasing abundance from C_{20} onwards (Fig. 4.3.1a). It is thought these LCFAs likely originate directly from animal fats, incorporated via routing from the ruminant animal's plant diet (Halmemies-Beauchet-Filleau *et al.* 2013; 2014).

PLANT PROCESSING

Also present in vessels CLT12 (V8), CLT13 (V not assigned, Type H), CLT15 (V not assigned, Type H), CLT18 (V1) and CLT20 (V not assigned, Type G) are a series of even-numbered long-chain fatty acids ranging from C_{20} to C_{30} carbon atoms (Fig. 4.3.1b). These exhibit a different profile from those discussed above, maximising at C_{22} or C_{24}. These LCFAs are strongly indicative either of an origin in leaf or stem epicuticular waxes (Kolattukudy, Croteau and Buckner 1976; Tulloch 1976; Bianchi 1995; Kunst and Samuels 2003) or, possibly, suberin (Kolattukudy 1980; 1981; Walton 1990; Pollard *et al.* 2008), an aliphatic polyester found in all plants.

Although primarily found on the surface of plant leaves, sheaths, stems and fruits, epicuticular waxes are also found associated with other plant organs, *i.e.* seed oils and coats, flowers, bark and husks (Bianchi 1995). Long-chain fatty acids can also be found in plant oils, for example, groundnut oil comprises 4-7% of C_{20}, C_{22} and C_{24} saturated and monoene acids (Gunstone 2004). However, these LCFAs are not diagnostic to families of plants and so cannot be used as anything other than a general indicator for plant processing.

MARINE BIOMARKERS

As Clachtoll Broch is located very close to the shore, the consumption/use of products from fish and sea mammals in the vessels supplied for analysis should be investigated. Thus, all FAMEs were analysed by GC-MS in SIM mode to check for the presence of aquatic biomarkers, namely ω-(o-alkylphenyl) alkanoic acids (APAAs) and vicinal dihydroxy acid (DHYAs) which originate from the degradation of poly- and monounsaturated fatty acids found in marine or freshwater fats and oils. These are routinely used to detect marine product processing (*e.g.*, Hansel *et al.* 2004; Craig *et al.* 2007; Hansel and Evershed 2009; Cramp *et al.* 2014; Cramp *et al.* 2015). Significantly, CLT12 (V8), CLT27 (V8) and CLT28 (V8) (which contained dairy products, see below) also contained aquatic biomarkers, from C_{18} to C_{22} APAAs (Tables 4.3.1 and 4.3.2 and Fig. 4.3.2). Vessel CLT11 (V1) also contained the C_{18} and C_{20} APAAs. No DHYAs or isoprenoid fatty acids were identified. Generally, the presence of two of the three aquatic biomarkers mentioned above are required for an unambiguous interpretation of fish/marine mammal processing but the enriched $\delta^{13}C$ values of the potsherds (discussed further below) also suggest a marine input.

GC-C-IRMS analyses were carried out on the Iron Age sherds (Table 4.3.1) to determine the $\delta^{13}C$ values of the major fatty acids, $C_{16:0}$ and $C_{18:0}$, and ascertain the source of the lipids extracted, through the use of the $\Delta^{13}C$ proxy. The $\delta^{13}C$ values of the $C_{16:0}$ and $C_{18:0}$ fatty acids from the lipid profiles are plotted onto a scatter plot along with the reference animal fat ellipses (Fig. 4.3.3a). It has been established that when an extract from a vessel plots directly within an ellipse, for example, ruminant dairy, ruminant adipose or non-ruminant adipose, then it can attributed to that particular source. If it plots just outside the ellipse then it can be described as predominantly of that particular origin. However, it should be noted that extracts commonly plot between reference animal fat ellipses and along the theoretical mixing curves, suggesting either the

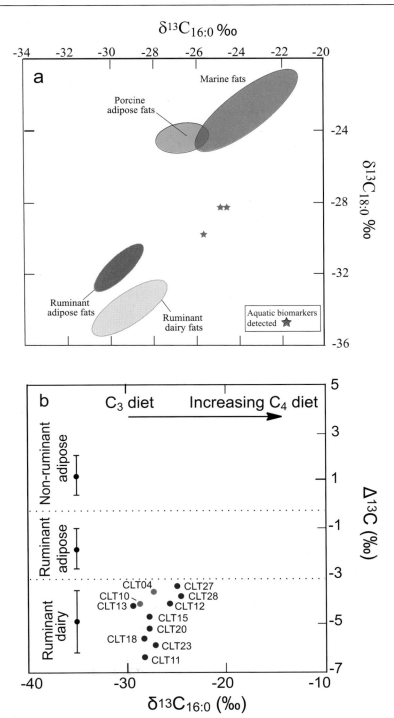

Figure 4.3.3 Graphs showing: **a.** *δ¹³C values for the C₁₆:₀ and C₁₈:₀ fatty acids for archaeological fats extracted from the Clachtoll Broch Iron Age vessels. The three fields correspond to the P = 0.684 confidence ellipses for animals raised on a strict C₃ diet in Britain (Copley et al. 2003). Each data point represents either: blue circles, potsherds and 'burnt-on' residues and red circles, steatite vessels and 'burnt-on' residue.* **b** *shows the Δ¹³C (δ¹³C₁₈:₀ – δ¹³C₁₆:₀) values from the same samples. The ranges shown here represent the mean ± 1 s.d. of the Δ¹³C values for a global database comprising modern reference animal fats from Africa (Dunne, Gillard and Evershed 2012), UK (animals raised on a pure C3 diet) (Dudd and Evershed 1998), Kazakhstan (Outram et al. 2009), Switzerland (Spangenberg et al. 2006) and the Near East (Gregg et al. 2009), published elsewhere*

mixing of animal fats contemporaneously or during the lifetime of use of the vessel (Mukherjee 2004; Mukherjee *et al.* 2005).

Vessels CLT11 (V1), CLT13 (V not assigned, Type H), CLT15 (V not assigned, Type H), CLT18 (V1), CLT20 (V not assigned, Type G) and CLT23 (V5) plot within, or just outside, the dairy reference ellipse (Fig. 3a), suggesting these vessels were solely used to process dairy products. The remaining samples, CLT12 (V8), CLT27 (V8) and CLT28 (V8) plot between the ruminant dairy and non-ruminant ellipse, suggesting use to process mixtures of these products. Significantly, as discussed above, these three samples also contain a series of aquatic biomarkers, namely ω-(o-alkylphenyl) alkanoic acids (APAAs). These vessels do not plot within the marine reference ellipses but do display slightly enriched $\delta^{13}C$ values (Fig. 4.3.3a). It is known that fats and oils of marine origin exhibit higher $\delta^{13}C$ values than terrestrial species arising from the ~7 ‰ enrichment of ocean bicarbonates relative to atmospheric carbon dioxide, which enters the food chain via marine phytoplankton and is passed on to higher trophic level consumers (Chisholm, Nelson and Schwarcz 1982). This suggests that marine products were likely processed in this vessel in low abundance.

Ruminant dairy fats are differentiated from ruminant adipose fats when they display $\Delta^{13}C$ values of less than -3.1 ‰, known as the universal proxy (Dunne *et al.* 2012; Salque 2012). Significantly, all vessels plot within the ruminant dairy region (Fig. 4.3.3b), with $\Delta^{13}C$ values of less than -3.1 ‰ (Table 4.3.1), confirming that all vessels were mainly used to process secondary products, such as milk, butter and/or cheese, although the three vessels mentioned above were also used to process marine products, likely in lower abundances.

Steatite vessels

Five fragments of steatite vessels and five surface residues scraped from the surface of steatite vessels were analysed. Of these, one vessel fragment and one surface residue yielded interpretable lipid profiles (Fig. 4.3.1c). Lipid extract CLT10, a possible lamp fragment, comprised free fatty acids, palmitic (C_{16}) and stearic (C_{18}), typical of a degraded animal fat (Evershed *et al.* 1997a; Berstan *et al.* 2008). Also present are a series of even-numbered long-chain fatty acids ranging from C_{20} to C_{30} carbon atoms, maximising at C_{22} (Fig. 4.3.1c). These LCFAs are strongly indicative either of an origin in leaf or stem epicuticular waxes (Kolattukudy *et al.* 1976; Tulloch 1976; Bianchi 1995; Kunst and Samuels 2003).

Interestingly, the surface residue taken from a steatite vessel yielded a lipid profile which included palmitic (C_{16}) and stearic (C_{18}) fatty acids, typical of a degraded animal fat, together with long-chain even-numbered *n*-alkanoic acids (C_{20} to C_{30}), *n*-alkanols (C_{24} to C_{30}), and *n*-alkanes.

These lipid profiles are generally indicative of the presence of beeswax and will require further analysis by the solvent extraction method to identify higher molecular weight compounds, wax esters, which would confirm the presence of beeswax in this residue.

Both vessels plot within the ruminant dairy region (Fig. 4.3.3b), with $\Delta^{13}C$ values of -3.7 and -4.2 ‰ for CLT04 and CLT10, respectively (Table 4.3.1), confirming that they were mainly used to process secondary products, such as milk, butter and cheese. However, dairy products and leafy plants were likely processed in vessel CLT10 and it is possible that dairy products were mixed with beeswax in the surface residue found on CLT04.

Conclusion

The objective of this investigation was to determine whether organic residues were preserved in Clachtoll Broch Iron Age potsherds, steatite vessels and surface residues from both. The results, determined from GC, GC-MS and GC-C-IRMS analyses of lipid residue extracts, demonstrated that six pots were used to process solely dairy products (milk, butter or cheese). Three further vessels were used to process mainly dairy products but with the addition of some, likely minor, marine resource processing, such as fish or sea mammals, evidenced by the presence of aquatic biomarkers (APAAs) and more positive $\delta^{13}C$ values. Certainly, fish bones, seal and whalebone were found at the site. These data suggest dairy products were an extremely important commodity during this period. It should be noted the faunal assemblage includes cattle and sheep and, if possible, these lipid results should be compared to possible kill-off patterns.

The presence of long-chain fatty acids in a number of these vessels (CLT12, CLT13, CLT15, CLT18 and CLT20) suggests the addition of leafy plants to the foods processed in these vessels. It is interesting that, although all vessels were predominantly used to process dairy products, the majority were multi-use, also being used to process marine and plant resources, whether at the same time or on separate occasions. Analysis of a larger dataset would help to confirm this interesting trend.

Only one of the five steatite vessels yielded a lipid profile, which again demonstrated the processing of dairy products, likely with the addition of leafy plants, in this vessel. It is possible that dairy products were mixed with beeswax in the surface residue found on CLT04.

To our knowledge, this is the first study of Iron Age potsherds and steatite vessels from mainland Scotland. Previous analysis of Late Iron Age potsherds from the Northern Isles showed that 64% of lipid yielding sherds contained dairy products (Cramp *et al.* 2014). This is similar to results from previous work on Iron Age pottery residues from sites in southern England. The analysis of 237 vessels from the Iron Age sites of Maiden Castle,

Danebury Hillfort, Yarnton Cresswell Field and Stanwick demonstrated that up to 56% of the extracts, (equivalent to 22% of all of the sherds), contained dairy products (Copley *et al.* 2005). This suggests that dairying was an important part of subsistence strategies at these sites but as part of a mixed meat/milk economy.

Interestingly, there is no evidence of porcine product processing in vessels at Clachtoll Broch, despite the presence of pig bones in the faunal assemblage, which correlates well with the low levels of absorbed pig fats found in pottery at the Iron Age sites of Maiden Castle, Danebury Hillfort, Yarnton Cresswell Field and Stanwick. This also compares well with the low abundances of pig bones found at Iron Age sites in general (Cunliffe 1991; Hambleton 1999). This suggests pigs may have been processed in other ways, *e.g.*, roasting.

4.4 The iron objects from Clachtoll
Dawn McLaren and Andy Heald

Summary
The iron assemblage from Clachtoll is dominated by tools, particularly those associated with agriculture, food and drink and everyday crafts. Like the other artefacts from Clachtoll the importance of the assemblage derives from the fact that it is a rare, securely dated assemblage from an Atlantic Middle Iron Age site. As Hunter (1998, 365) reminds us there is a dearth of iron from securely dated prehistoric contexts and very few Scottish Iron Age sites have informative ironwork assemblages, with most producing only a few highly corroded fragments (see also Manning 1981, 56). Iron was clearly in use (as seen, for instance, in toolmarks on bone objects, the presence of tool handles and so on) but because it was rarely deposited, presumably because it could be recycled, we are left with only a meagre picture of iron use in the Iron Age. By contrast, Roman sites are rich in iron: it was an abundant and disposable resource; and usually these survive due to rubbish disposal and abandonment, standard taphonomic processes for finds on many Roman fort sites (Hunter and Heald 2008, 205). Analysis of native iron use is also hindered by the fact that when iron objects are found on non-Roman sites they are often difficult to independently date (*ibid.*, 203).

Usually, discussions of iron objects in the Iron Age have revolved around material from Traprain Law (Burley 1956) and the three southern Scottish ironwork hoards (S. Piggott 1953). However, in recent years understandings have been broadened due to the publications of important assemblages from Fairy Knowe (Hunter 1998), Leckie broch (MacKie 2016) and Dun Ardtreck (MacKie 2000a); the iron objects from Clachtoll are a welcome addition to the meagre corpus.

Agricultural tools
Many of the finds from Clachtoll were related to agriculture. During the prehistoric, Roman and medieval periods a range of agricultural tools were used (see Rees 1979; Manning 1985; Goodall 2011). The ard would have been used for preparing the land for crops, the spade for cultivation, the sickle and reaping hook for harvesting the crops. The Clachtoll assemblage is a rare survival of (parts of) an Iron Age agricultural toolkit.

Ard/ploughshare
The ard is the simplest form of plough; it required animals dragging a shaped wooden blade or ploughshare through the ground to lift and break the earth before seed was sown. Ards were sometimes tipped with metal, called a ploughshare. In use they would have been slipped over the front of the wooden foreshare of a bow ard; the shorter examples fitting onto the very tip. Bow ards, similar to an intact example recovered from a peat bog in Døstrup, Denmark consist of five main components: the main curving beak, the foreshare, mainshare, ard-head and stilt (Glob 1951; Fenton 1968, fig. 2). Long linear channels on the upper surface of wooden mainshare heads, such as that from Milton Loch, Kirkcudbrightshire (Fenton 1968, 150–1, fig. 3a) appear to have been created purposefully to allow the wooden foreshare to fit closely on top of the mainshare (Raftery 1996, 270, fig. 393, no. 1). In this configuration the foreshare helps to protect the main share from excessive wear (*ibid.*, 150). Although reinforcement of the foreshare by addition of an iron shoe or tip is not essential, the addition of an iron component would reduce wear to the tip of the shaft and potentially enhance the effectiveness of the share by increasing its ability to withstand stony or hard soils.

Flanged ploughshares and ploughshare tips are well attested in the Iron Age, and more rarely from the Roman period (Manning 1985, 43) and they continue in use into the medieval period (Goodall 2011, 77, 84, fig. 7.2, nos. F3–5) and are usually substantially larger in size than prehistoric and Roman examples. In a review of early and traditional cultivation implements in Scotland, Fenton (1963) usefully summarised later prehistoric and later Scottish examples of iron share components, including wedge-shaped shoes and flanged share tips. These include mostly Roman Iron Age examples, including those from a hoard at Blackburn Mill, Berwickshire (S. Piggott 1953, 47, fig. 12: B31; Fenton 1963, 271–2, fig. 4:1), Traprain Law (Burley 1956, 212, fig. 7, nos. 479–480; Fenton 1963, 272, fig. 4, nos. 2 and 3), Eckford hoard (S. Piggott 1953, 27, fig. 5: E10; Fenton 1963, 272, fig. 14:5) and Falla Farm (Steer 1947). The find from Á Cheardach Bheag wheelhouse, South Uist (Fairhurst 1971, 102, pl. 12) may either be a badly damaged ploughshare or spade blade.

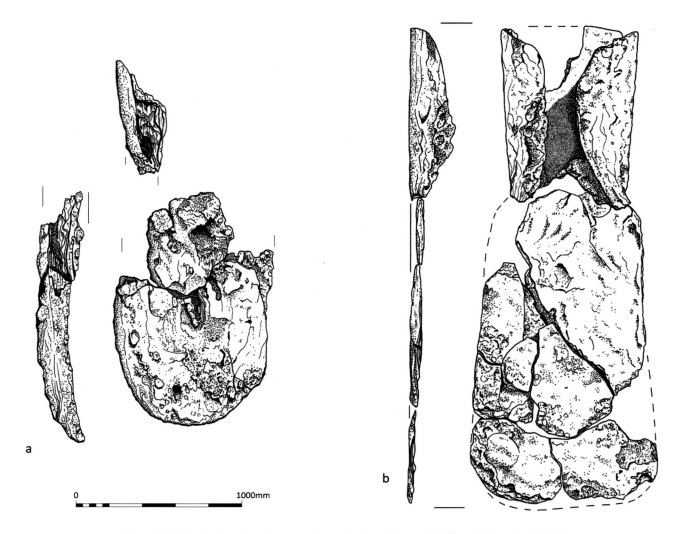

0   1000mm

Figure 4.4.1 Agricultural implements of iron: a) ploughshare (SF 43) and b) spade (SF 69)

Of all the iron share examples cited by Fenton, the Traprain Law ploughshare (1963, 272, fig. 4.3) is among those that bear the most similarity in blade to that from Clachtoll, whilst the example from Drimore (*ibid*, 273, fig. 4.8) also displays many features comparable to SF 43, particularly the surviving flanged edge and the distinctly tapering tip of the blade.

As Fenton (1963, 273) acknowledges, the Scottish group of blades and shares shows considerable diversity in form and further work on more recent finds echoes this assertion (Hunter 2006b, 154). As a result, there exists an element of crossover in terminology between iron ploughshare or ard components and iron fittings or blades for other cultivation implements (see Fenton 1963 and Payne 1947).

Ard points show regional variation according to the availability of raw materials, with stone tips in the Bronze

and Iron Age of the Northern Isles, whalebone tips in the Western Isles, and wood (sometimes tipped in iron, as at Clachtoll) elsewhere (Fenton 1963; Rees 1979, 7–61). The presence of ard marks in excavated layers gives direct evidence for which areas were under cultivation (*e.g.*, Fowler 1983, 113–17, 150–6; Barclay 1985), although these vestigial traces are not always noted in excavation. Some of these may represent the use of a heavy ard to break up ground which had laid fallow.

*SF 43   Socketed ard. Incomplete, large, flat, subrectangular blade surviving in two rejoined fragments (and numerous loose spalls) with long straight parallel edges, one damaged, and a wide, rounded worn end; all breaks are fresh. The tip of the wide blade is distinctly rounded, curving upwards asymmetrically and is worn from abrasion from

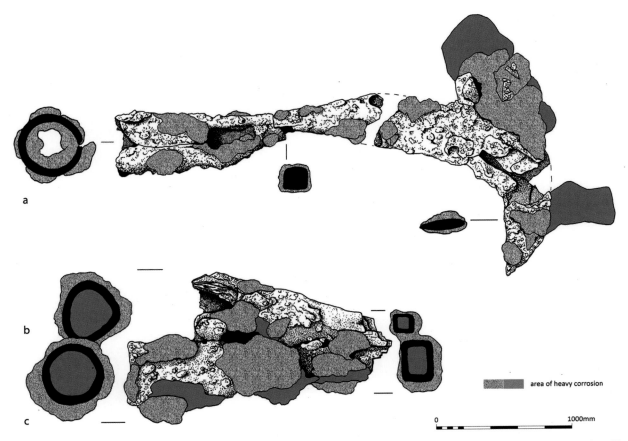

area of heavy corrosion

0   1000mm

Figure 4.4.2 Agricultural implements of iron: a) socketed sickle/scythe (SF 25.3), b) fragments of possible socketed sickles (SF 25.1 and 25.2)

use on one face creating a convex profile at the extreme tip. The opposite end of the blade has deteriorated since deposition and is in poor condition; broken irregularly across the width separating the blade from a single surviving fragment of the tapering rounded flange of a wide, open socket, squat in height, with wood impressions surviving in the interior of the socket; so little of this remains it is impossible to determine its original dimensions. Blade: remaining L 145.5 mm, W (max) 91 mm, T 14.5–18.5 mm; socket (exterior): remaining L 71 mm, W 26 mm, H (min) 25 mm, T 9 mm; socket (interior): H 16 mm, W unknown. Wgt 273.1 g. Context 042 (Fig. 4.4.1a).

Spade blade

In the recent past the spade rather than the plough was the prime cultivating implement in many areas of Atlantic Scotland such as the Hebrides (Cheape 1993, 81) and it is likely that this was the case in the prehistoric period too. As mentioned above (and see Hunter 2006b, 154) identification of such implements is always fraught with

difficulties, as the boundaries between ard, plough and spade shares are not well drawn. The use of whale bone for ards and spades is well attested (Crawford 1967; Rees 1979, 40–1); however Scottish Iron Age spades are very rare (see Fenton 1963) with more recent discoveries known from Leckie broch (MacKie 2016, 83, SF 731, illus. 4.11, no. 2) and Cnip (Hunter 2006b, 154, illus. 3,26c).

*SF 69 Socketed spade. Eight refitting fragments and multiple surface spalls from a substantially complete socketed tool with a long wide subrectangular blade. The open socket is short in proportion to the length of the blade but wide, flattened oval in section, with narrow flanges which curve inwards, the long edges of which are slightly crimped, presumably to secure to the narrow rectangular-sectioned handle. A fragment from the back edge of the socket has been lost. Expanding out from the socket is a shouldered rectangular blade, flat, with long straight edges, gently expanding along its length towards a

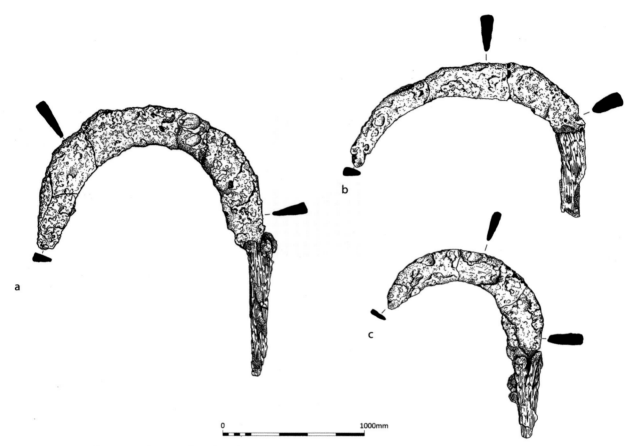

Figure 4.4.3 Agricultural implements of iron: reaping hooks a) SF 44.1, b) SF 44.2, c) SF 44.3

wide rounded cutting edge which is damaged and incomplete. Original (estimated) L 306 mm; socket: L 112.5 mm, W 71–84.5 mm, H (exterior) 24 mm, H (interior) 13.5–25.5 mm, T 9.8 mm; blade: remaining L 188 mm, W 99–117 mm, T 3.5–8 mm. Wgt 415.6 g. Context 042 (Fig. 4.4.1b).

Sickles/scythes/reaping hooks

Sickles and reaping hooks were the main tools used for harvesting cereals and are part of a large group of closely related implements, varying in size but all with hooked or curved blades (Manning 1985, 50). Manning (1985, 51) defines sickles as tools with blades which resemble a question mark in shape; reaping hooks are tools apparently intended for reaping cereals but are not sickles as previously defined. When discussing medieval examples Goodall (2011, 81) defines reaping hooks as having curved blades with their edges entirely to one side of the handle, unlike the sickle with its curved back blade.

Sickles first appear in the late pre-Roman Iron Age, although they are commoner in Roman contexts (Rees 1979, 458; Manning 1985, 51). The earliest known Scottish examples are Roman Iron Age, in the hoards of Carlingwark (Kirkcudbrightshire) and Blackburn Mill (Berwickshire), and from Traprain Law (East Lothian; S. Piggott 1953; Burley 1956, no. 481). One from Tentsmuir (Fife), found with a shouldered bucket urn of later 1st millennium BC type may be earlier (unpublished: East Fife Museum SAAUM 1977.1993), although a Roman Iron Age date cannot be ruled out (Hunter 2007a).

The majority of Iron Age sickles and reaping hooks are of a whittle-tanged or flanged variety and tend to be quite restricted in size, such as the small, flanged example from Dun Laith, Skye which although damaged at the blade tip and handle flange, is only around 80 mm in length (MacKie 1965a; G Cruickshanks, pers. comm.). This contrasts with the more robust form of the set of three reaping hooks (SF 44.1–3) from context (042) (Fig. 4.4.3). The graduating size of the Clachtoll reaping hooks and the variation in the curvature and angle of the blade to the tang is of interest but it is unclear whether these variations in form are suggestive of slight differences in function or the personal preferences of the maker or user.

The socketed sickles or scythes (SF 25.1–3) from context (042) also form an intriguing set of tools, clearly stored together in the broch, similar to the reaping hooks. It is unfortunate that the blades of two of these implements (SF 25.1 and SF 25.2) have been lost to a mass of iron corrosion but the similarity in the size and the form of the sockets suggest that they derive from the same or similar type of tool to the complete but broken example (SF 25.3). At over 320 mm in length, this tool was a substantial size with a long gently curving blade extending out from a robust conical socket which would have held a wooden handle. The angle of the blade to the socket of SF 25.3 suggests that the handle may have been long and set at an obtuse angle to the blade, similar to modern day scythes but this is purely conjectural. An alternative possibility of the function of these implements are billhooks, employed for tasks such as coppicing, lopping the stems and branches of young trees and for laying hedges (Goodall 2011, 80).

*SF 25.1 Possible socketed sickle fragment. Three joining fragments consisting of a conical socket, possibly from a socketed sickle (see SF 25.3), corroded on to edge of SF 25.2, broken across robust rectangular-sectioned stem between the socket and the tool, blade lost and original form and size of implement is unknown. The socket is long and conical in form, closed, with a squared end; the abutting long parallel edges obscured by adhering remains of SF 25.2. X-radiography demonstrates the interior of the socket to consist of a fairly short circular-sectioned socket tapering along length to a rounded base. A small sub-circular perforation (D 5.5 mm) is present, 32 mm from squared open end of the socket. Beyond the socket, the tool continues to taper in width and thickness forming a solid rectangular-sectioned stem, broken across the width and the rest of the implement lost in a mass of amorphous corrosion. Remaining L 280 mm; socket (exterior) L 168 mm, diam 45.5 mm, T 7 mm; socket (interior): L 133 mm, diam 11–33 mm; stem: W 23 mm, T 15 mm. Wgt 1284.1 g (including adhering stone). Found corroded together in group with SF 25.2 and SF 25.3. Context 042 (Fig. 4.4.2b). (Please note: this was found as a huge, corroded mass comprising remains of three individual tools. Conservation have done all they can to release the individual items from the mass of solid corrosion but it has not been possible to fully expose and the blades are lost in a mass of amorphous corrosion product.)

*SF 25.2 Possible socketed sickle fragment. Two joining fragments consisting of a conical socket, possibly from a socketed sickle (see SF 25.3), corroded on to edge of SF 25.1, broken across robust square-sectioned stem between the socket and the tool, blade lost and original form and size of implement is unknown. The socket is long and conical in form, partially closed, with a damaged but presumably originally squared end; the partially abutting long parallel edges obscured by adhering remains of SF 25.1. X-radiography demonstrates the interior of the socket to consist of a fairly short circular-sectioned socket tapering along length to a rounded base. Hints of a small rectangular perforation (diam 7 mm) is visible on x-ray, 12 mm from damaged open end of the socket. Beyond the socket, the tool continues to taper in width and thickness forming a solid narrow square-sectioned stem, broken across the width and the rest of the implement lost in a mass of amorphous corrosion. Remaining L 180 mm; socket (exterior) L 129 mm, diam 49 mm, T 6.5 mm; socket (interior): L 121 mm, diam 8–40 mm; stem: W 16 mm, T 14.5 mm. Wgt 180 g. Found corroded together in group with SF 25.1 and SF 25.3. Context 042 (Fig. 4.4.2b). (Note: this was found as a huge, corroded mass comprising remains of three individual tools. Conservation have done all they can to release the individual items from the mass of solid corrosion but it has not been possible to fully expose and the blades are lost in a mass of amorphous corrosion product.)

*SF 25.3 Socketed sickle or scythe. Five refitting fragments (G, H, I, J, K) comprising a substantially complete socketed sickle with a long conical closed socket tapering smoothly into a long curving hooked blade, wedge-shaped in cross section, the tip of which is bent at right-angles to the socket. Fragments cleaned and removed from encasing corrosion during conservation but not re-joined. Found corroded together in group with SF 25.2 and SF 25.3. Original L (est.) 322 mm; socket: L 121.5 mm, diam (exterior) 22.5–47.5 mm, diam (interior) 11–38 mm, T 5–6.5 mm; blade: L (back) 291.2 mm; W (max) 46 mm, W (tip- min) 7 mm, T 4–8 mm; shoulder with socket: W 17 mm, T 17 mm. Wgt 852.9 g (including adhering stone). Context 042 (Fig. 4.4.2a).

*SF 44.1 Reaping hook, intact. Moderately long iron blade distinctly hooked in form; curvature is so pronounced that the tip of the blade is almost at the same height as the blades' junction with the tang (distance from cutting edge of blade tip and junction of tang/blade: W 128 mm). Blade has a wedge-shaped profile with a strong back which curves in parallel to the cutting edge, blade narrowing towards a blunt rounded tip. A rectangular tapering tang extends from the base of the blade, positioned slightly off-centre, in line with the back of the blade but stepped back from the cutting edge creating a rounded choil. Surviving traces of the original wooden handle (birch (cf. Betula); A Crone, pers. comm.) remain in a mineralised condition on the surfaces of the tang. This is the largest hook of the group (SF 44). Blade: L (back) 270.6 mm, W (max) 30.8 mm, W (min, at tip) 12 mm, T (back) 4.5–6.2 mm, T (cutting edge) 1.5–2 mm; tang: remaining L 102.3 mm, W 7.5–13.5 mm, T (min) 2.5 mm; handle: remaining L 102.3 mm, W 12.6–18.2mm, T 13.4–14mm. Wgt 125.4 g. Context 042 (Fig. 4.4.3a).

*SF 44.2 Reaping hook, substantially intact. Moderately long blade, slightly hooked, set at almost right-angles to the whittle tang which is broken; the tip of the tang is lost and its original length is unknown. The blade is wedge-shaped in profile with a strong, thick back and much narrower cutting edge and tapers strongly along its length to a narrow, rounded tip. The tang is central to the base of the blade, tapers along its surviving length and the surfaces are obscured by mineralised wood (not identified, possibly birch; A Crone, pers. comm.). Blade: L (back) 207.5 mm, W (max) 28.3 mm, W (min, at tip) 9.5 mm, T (back) 5–7.8 mm, T (cutting edge) 2–3 mm; tang: remaining L 62 mm, W 8.5–14 mm, T (min) 4.5 mm; handle: remaining L 62 mm, W 18–20.8 mm, T 12.8–21.2 mm. Distance from cutting edge of blade tip and junction of tang/blade: W 137 mm. Wgt 100.9 g. Context 042 (Fig. 4.4.3b).

*SF 44.3 Reaping hook, intact. Gently curving iron blade of roughly semicircular form, lentoid in cross-section with a strongly rounded back, curving in parallel to the cutting edge, the blade narrowing towards the rounded tip. Centrally positioned whittle tang, square in cross-section and tapering along length towards squared tip. The surfaces of the tang are obscured by the mineralised wood of the handle, identified as birch (cf. Betula; A Crone, pers. comm.). This example is the smallest of the three hooks that comprise the group SF 44.

Blade: L (back) 165.8 mm, W (max) 28.2 mm, W (min, at tip) 11 mm, T (max) 3–5.7mm, T (cutting edge) 2–4 mm; tang: L 64.3 mm, W 8–14 mm, T (min) 3.5 mm; handle: remaining L 64.3 mm, W 15–23.4 mm, T 11.3–23.4 mm. Distance from cutting edge of blade tip and junction of tang/blade: W 83 mm. Wgt 57.3 g. Context 042 (Fig. 4.4.3c).

Tools

Pick

Picks from the Roman Iron Age and medieval periods are usually discussed as tools of a stonemason (*e.g.*, Manning 1985, 30; Goodall 2011, 43). Picks are known from the Eckford Hoard and Blackburn Mill (S. Piggott 1953, 27, fig. 6, E13 and E14, 48, fig. 13, B37).

*SF 58 Pickhead fragment. Small, short tapering pick head broken across a short ring-shaped socket; *c.* 45% of circumference of socket survives. Socket has pronounced internal angles indicating use with a trimmed, square-sectioned handle. Pick formed by forging together the tapering terminals of the strip used to produce the socket. Remaining L 78 mm; pick: L 49 mm, W 6–18 mm, T 5–8 mm; socket: remaining L 29 mm, W 26 mm, T 3–5 mm, internal diam *c.* 25 mm. Wgt 20.9 g. Context 042 (Fig. 4.4.4a).

Knives

Numerous different types of iron knives were used throughout the prehistoric, Roman and medieval periods across Britain (see Manning 1985, 108; Ottoway 1992, 558; Cowgill *et al.* 1987 and Goodall 2011, 105). Indeed, particularly in the later periods blades from knives and shears are among the most common and varied metal finds on sites, reflecting their importance and versatility as tools for work and home (see Cowgill, Neergaard and Griffiths 1987, viii). Aside from nails knives are usually the most common iron finds on Hebridean and Skye Iron Age sites with examples known from, for example, Garry Iochdrach (Beveridge and Callander 1932, 41), Dun Vulan (*cf.* Parker Pearson and Sharples 1999, 126), Dun Ardtreck (MacKie 2000a, 329), Dun Leccamore (Ritchie 1971, 110), Dun Beag (Callander 1921, 125), and Applecross (Peteranna 2012, 78). And they are, of course, well-attested on other Scottish Iron Age sites, including Carlingwark (S. Piggott 1953, 35–6, fig. 9, C24 and C25), Traprain Law (Burley 1956, 205–7, fig. 7), Fairy Knowe (Hunter 1998, 357–8, illus. 27, no. 84) and Leckie (MacKie 2016, 101, fig. 4.10, nos. 4 and 8).

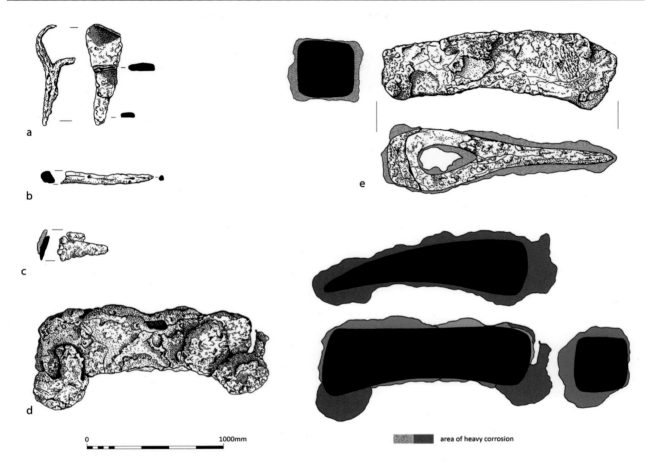

Figure 4.4.4 Iron tools: a) pick (SF 58), b) tang (SF 31), c) tang (SF 76), d) axe-head (SF 67), e) axe-head (SF 219)

*SF 31 Tool tang (possibly from a knife or similar) or nail shank. Broken fine square-sectioned bar, tapering along length to blunt rounded damaged tip, fresh break at opposite end. Distorted along length. Remaining L 66 mm, Diam 3.5–5.5 mm. Wgt 5.5 g. Context 042 (Fig. 4.4.4b).

*SF 76 Knife tang fragment. Short, flat, rectangular tang, tapering along length towards rounded tip, broken forward of the junction with the blade; original length and form unknown. Angular spall of iron corroded to one face. Remaining L 35.5 mm, W 3.7–4.3 mm, T 1–2.5 mm. Wgt 2.6 g. Context 048 (Fig. 4.4.4c).

SF 288 Tool tang fragment. Fine bar-shaped tang, square in cross-section, possibly from a knife or similar. Tang has squared terminal but has broken forward of the junction with the blade. Surfaces are encased in amorphous mineralised wood (not possible to identify to species; A. Crone, *pers comm*). Remaining L 38.2 mm, W 16.5 mm, T 13 mm. Wgt 5 g. Context 042. (Extracted from animal bone SF 113, new number assigned post-excavation.)

Miscellaneous tools

SF 290 Ferrule fragment. Fragment of a short cylindrical ring-shaped ferrule/collar, possibly part of the socket of a tool. Remaining L 30 mm, H 21.3 mm, T 5 mm. Wgt 17 g. Context 078. (Extracted from animal bone SF 210, new number assigned post-excavation.)

Woodworking

Two types of iron tools from Clachtoll – axes and adzes – were associated with woodworking.

Axes

Although the number of finds of axes from native Iron Age sites across Scotland is small the limited corpus suggest that various types of axes were used: including socketed and shaft hole. Iron socketed axes have been discussed by Childe (1935, 249–50; 1946, 80–96), Stevenson (1966, 20, fig. 1) and Manning and Saunders (1972). Both socketed and shaft hole axes were recovered from Traprain Law (Burley 1956, 210–11); the latter type formed part of the

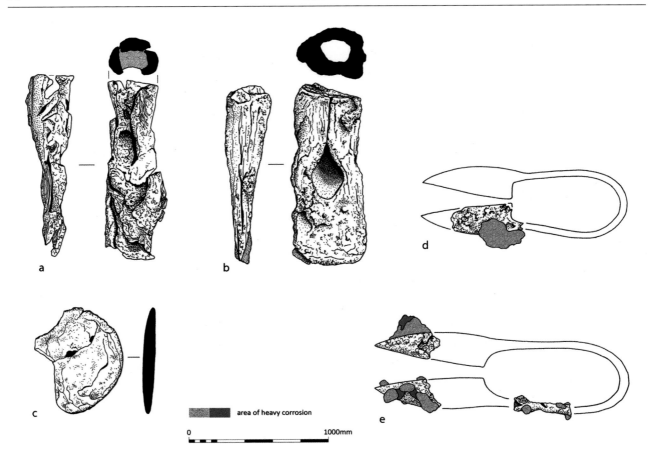

Figure 4.4.5 Iron tools: a) adze (SF 42), b) adze (SF 52.1), c) lunate scraper (SF 52.2); shears d) SF 157, e) SF 105

Carlingwark Hoard (S. Piggott 1953, 36–7, fig. 9, C 51). A possible axe or adze was found at Fairy Knowe (Hunter 1998, 359, 361, illus. 29, no. 441). Examples from Atlantic Middle Iron Age are rare, with examples from Dun Vulan (Parker Pearson and Sharples 1999, 228) and Dun Ard-treck (MacKie 2000a, 331, 388, illus. 25, no. 24). MacKie (*ibid.*) argues that the Dun Ardtreck axe is a much-worn Roman Army tool that ended up on a native site.

*SF 67   Axe-head, intact. Tool surfaces remain heavily deformed and obscured by corrosion. Identification relies heavily on x-radiography which demonstrates an axe-head with a heavy, robust, square butt, the blade tapering in depth and thickness towards mid-length, beyond which the blade transitions asymmetrically towards the cutting edge. The back of the axe-head remains straight along its length but beyond mid-length, the blade expands in depth, curving on its lower edge towards the cutting edge which is gently rounded. Traces of an ?oval socket are visible on the upper surface but distortion though corrosion is so severe it has

not been possible to reveal this feature more fully. The axe blade has a distinct curvature to it which is either the result of post-depositional damage or use. L 143 mm; butt: W 39 mm, H 41.5 mm; cutting edge: H 50.5 mm, T 5.5 mm. Wgt 605 g. Context 042 (Fig. 4.4.4d).

*SF 219 Axe-head, intact. Heavy, robust, squared butt, perforated transversely by a tear-drop-shaped socket (L 43 mm; W 22.5 mm) widest towards the butt and tapering towards the cutting edge. Forward of the socket, the blade tapers in thickness and expands in width steadily along the length curving slightly downwards towards a squared cutting edge. Convex/concave long cross-section. Similar to SF 67 but larger. L 166 mm; butt: W 42 mm, H 43 mm; cutting edge: H 46 mm, T 5 mm; max H of blade: 51.5 mm. Wgt 1337.4 g. Context 125 (Fig. 4.4.4e).

Adzes

Adzes, which differ from axes by having their blades set at right angles to the handle, are used for removing heavy waste, levelling, shaping or trimming the surfaces of timber (Goodall 2011, 22). Such implements have been found in Early Iron Age and Roman contexts across the UK. In terms of Scotland they are rare with examples again found at Traprain Law (Burley 1956, 211–12), and the three hoards at Eckford, Blackburn Mill and Carlingwark (S. Piggott 1953, 27, 48). A possible axe or adze was found at Fairy Knowe (Hunter 1998, 359, 361, illus. 29, no. 441). The authors do not know of any definitive examples from nearby sites to Clachtoll (*e.g.*, the Inner and Outer Hebrides and Skye).

*SF 42 Adze. Substantially intact socketed adze with short rectangular blade surviving in an extremely friable and damaged condition. The blade tapers in thickness but gently expands in width to form a slightly curving cutting edge, damaged at both corners due to corrosion. The hand-forged socket is oval in section, open, with slightly lopsided long flanges which may have originally abutted but one of which is broken resulting in the loss of the long edge. Small circular perforation (Diam 5.5 mm), broken, present at the end of the socket on the edge with the surviving flange. Traces of amorphous mineralised wood are present in the socket (not identifiable to species, A. Crone, *pers comm*). Remaining L 129 mm; blade: L 74 mm, W 43 mm, T 11–14.5 mm; junction of blade with socket: W 33.5 mm, T 15 mm; socket: L 55 mm, W 36 mm, T 29.5 mm, diam (interior) 26 mm. Wgt 120.9 g. Context 042 (Fig. 4.4.5a).

*SF 52.1 Adze, intact. Robust socketed adze, fairly squat in form, with short rectangular blade, tapering in thickness but expanding slightly in width towards a robust squared cutting edge, one corner of which is distorted probably during use. The socket is short, cylindrical and closed with an oval cross-section. No obvious organics survive within socket. L 126 mm; blade: L 70 mm, W 14–15.5 mm, T 3–15.5 mm; junction between blade and socket: W 16.5 mm, T (no obvious shoulder) 19 mm; socket: L 48 mm, W 39–42.5 mm, T 29–33.5 mm, interior diam 17.5–22.5 mm. Wgt 270.5 g. Context 042 (Fig. 4.4.5 b).

Hide-working

One find was associated with leatherworking, a lunate scraper.

Lunate scraper

*SF 52.2 Lunate scraper. Robust lunulate blade fragment, rejoined during conservation from two fragments, broken across width, possibly across a perforation (hints observed on x-ray; D 2.5–3 mm) for suspension when not in use but this may just be damage from breakage; one rounded corner of thick V-shaped concave back is lost. Blade is wide and convex, the extreme tip of which is plano-convex in section suggesting use as a scraper rather than cutting tool. L 63 mm; remaining W 73.5 mm; T (back) 7.4 mm; T (blade edge) 4.5 mm. Wgt 50.9 g. Context 042 (Fig. 4.4.5c).

Textile working

Shears

Shears were used in prehistory for almost all of the tasks for which scissors would be used today. Various types of shears are known from Romano-British contexts but rarely can they be assigned a precise function. Smaller shears, like the ones from Clachtoll, would have been used for shearing sheep, cutting cloth or domestic and personal use (Manning 1985, 34). Shears have been recovered from Newstead (Curle 1911, 291 pl. lxviii, 5); Traprain Law (Burley 1956, 213–14), Lochlee (Munro 1882, fig. 138), Blackburn Mill hoard (S. Piggott 1953, 45–7, fig. 12, no. B29) and Leckie (MacKie 2016, 82–3, 102, illus. 4.11, no. 3). The shears from the Ashgrove Loch crannog, Stevenston, are undated, and could be Dark Age or later (Archaeological Collections Relating to Ayrshire and Galloway, vn, 56–61)

*SF 105 Snip shear fragments, incomplete. Three fragments representing portions of a pair of snip shears. The tips of both blades survive (a and b) represented by flat tapering blades, backs curving to the tips and flat (slightly concave) cutting edges. Almost identical in size, shape and point of breakage. The third fragment is a thin rectangular bar fragment (c), broken at both ends which may be part of an arm of the shears. Blade (a): remaining L 46 mm, max W 19 mm, T 3.5 mm; blade (b): remaining L 35 mm, max W 18.5 mm, T 3.5 mm; arm fragment (c): remaining L 37 mm, W 5–7 mm, T 5 mm. Wgt 20.3 g. Context 048 (Fig. 4.4.5e).

*SF 157 Shear blade fragment. The blade has a flat cutting edge and a gently curving back, broken just beyond the junction with the fine subrectangular arm, damaged at the choil, and the tip of the blade has been lost. Remaining L 53.5 mm; blade: remaining L 44 mm, W (max)23.5 mm, T (approx.) 4 mm; arm: remaining L 9.5 mm, W 5.5 mm, T (approx.) 4 mm. Wgt 24.2 g. Unstratified (W baulk) (Fig. 4.4.5d).

SF 199 Bar fragments. Two joining fragments of a fine rectangular-sectioned bar or shank, broken at

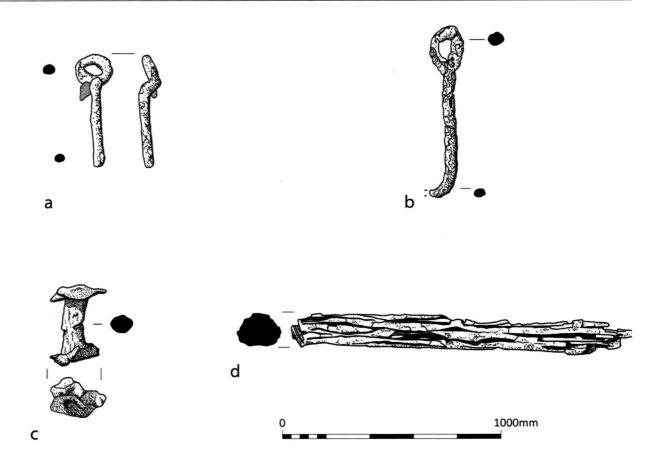

Figure 4.4.6 Iron ornaments and fittings: a) projecting ring-headed pin (SF 73), b) ring-headed pin (SF 49), c) clench bolt (SF 256.1), d) bolt (SF 109)

both ends. Similar to shear arm fragment (see SF 105 and SF 157). Remaining L 49 mm, W 5 mm, T 4 mm. Wgt 4.2 g. Context 078.

Decoration

Pins

Two iron pins were recovered from Clachtoll; the pins would have been worn as an ornament, fastening together cloaks or other garments. Pins remain the chief material expression (in metal) of the Atlantic Province culture. Interest has traditionally been with the examination of stylistic developments through time or as an indicator of cultural traits. Smith (1905; 1913) was the first to endeavour to trace the local development of pins during the Long Iron Age and many have followed since (Dunning 1934; Stevenson 1955; 1966; Kilbride-Jones 1980; Foster 1990). Stevenson (1955) undertook the first systematic study of Iron Age Scottish pins demonstrating that several different

ring-headed pins were prevalent during the first half of the 1st millennium AD. There is now a generally accepted sequence: the ring-headed pin is ancestral to projecting ring-headed pins which could either be wire or cast. The cast projecting series then became more elaborate, perhaps around the 3rd and 4th centuries AD (Kilbride-Jones 1980), resulting in rosette headed pins, ibex-headed pins, and proto-handpins. From this final group emerged the hand pin, probably around the late 5th or 6th century AD, continuing into the 8th and 9th centuries in an altered form (Foster 1990; (see Stevenson 1955, 288–90 for a discussion of the type found at Clachtoll)).

Examples of iron pins are known from, for example, Kilpheder (Lethbridge 1952, 183–4, fig. 4, no. 2) and Sithean a Phiobaire (*ibid.*, 184, fig. 5, no. 6); there is also a possible example from Dun An Fheurain (Ritchie 1971, 108). Other examples are known from Fairy Knowe (Hunter 1998, 356, 358, illus. 27, no. 373) and Leckie (MacKie 2016, 78, 99, fig. 4.8, nos. 20–21).

Figure 4.4.7 Reaping hook group

Figure 4.4.8 Clachtoll iron pins

Food and drink

Vessels

Various fragments of sheet metal were recovered, likely to be parts of metal vessels, perhaps for food storage and/or consumption.

SF 231   Vessel fragment. Nine fragments from the body and the rim of a sheet metal vessel. The rim is folded and rolled (W 2.5–3.5 mm; H 3 mm). Approx. exterior rim diam 98 mm. See also SF 232 and SF 247. Wgt 6.8 g. Context 145.

SF 232   Vessel fragment. Thin flat fragment of sheet metal, square in shape with one corner missing; no original edges survive to confirm form (but see SF 247 – metal is the same). Remaining L 15.5 mm, W 14.5 mm, T 1 mm. Wgt 0.3 g. Context 159.

SF 247   Vessel fragments. Ten fractured angular fragments from a sheet metal vessel with rolled and folded rim. (see also SF 231, SF 232). Wgt 5.3 g. Context 159.

Fixtures and fittings

Although the organic interior decorations do not survive on any broch sites, at Clachtoll we have rare evidence of fixtures and fittings.

*SF 49   Ring-headed pin, intact. Two re-fitting fragments rejoined during conservation. Produced from a subcircular iron rod. Straight shank, bent at one end into a closed and flattened loop-shaped head; the opposite end tapers to a blunt narrow tip which is bent at 90 degrees to the shank, at opposing angle to head. L 80 mm; head: H 19.5 mm, W 13 mm, diam 4 mm; shank: diam 4.5 mm. Wgt 6.6 g. Context 042 (SE quad). (Fig. 4.4.6b).

*SF 73   Projecting ring-headed pin fragment surviving in two rejoining fragments, produced from a very fine oval-sectioned iron rod, short projecting neck with square cross-section, head bent around to form a closed slightly oval ring; shank broken mid-length and tip lost. Under magnification the surfaces have abundant post-depositional organics adhering. Remaining L 52 mm; head: diam 12–14 mm, W 3 mm; shank: diam 3.5 – 3.7 mm. Wgt 3 g. Context 048 (Fig. 4.4.6a).

*SF 109   Tool or large bolt. Robust, thick, circular-sectioned shank with low-domed circular head, damaged and opposite end lost through extensive corrosion effecting all surfaces. Shank is slightly expanded in diameter towards mid-length but unclear if this is result of expansion due to corrosion or original form. Possible drift or chisel? Or just simple bolt? Remaining L 157 mm, head: remaining L 16.5 mm, W 13 mm, T 4 mm; shank: diam 10–13 mm. Wgt 66 g. Context 067 (Fig. 4.4.6d).

SF 227   Nail fragment. Square-sectioned shank bent and broken mid-length. Head is distorted and sits at an angle to the shank. Definitely looks used and distortion is consistent with its removal from timber fixture. Remaining L 35 mm, head: diam 14.5 mm, T 4 mm; shank: diam 4.5 mm. Wgt 7.5 g. Context 082.

*SF 256.1   Clench bolt, intact. Short oval sectioned shank, rectangular head, rove *in situ* but damaged and original shape unclear. L 35 mm; head: L 21.5 mm, W 17.5 mm, T 4.5 mm; rove: L 25.1 mm, W 16 mm, T 4.2 mm. Wgt 12 g. Context 082 (Fig. 4.4.6c).

SF 259.1   Nail. Robust and corroded iron nail, sub-square head, slightly domed with rounded edges, square-sectioned shank. L 111.3 mm; head: diam 18 mm, T 7.6 mm; shank: diam 8.5 mm. Wgt 49.6 g. Context 082.

SF 259.2   Modern nail. Extruded stainless steel 6-inch nail. L 100.5 mm. Wgt 13.8 g. Context 082.

SF 286   Nail or fishhook. Fine shank tapering towards fine pointed tip, bent mid-length at 90 degrees, head lost. Surfaces encased in massive corrosion product. Remaining L 50.5 mm, D 2.5–5 mm. Wgt 7.6 g. Context 062. (Extracted from animal bone SF 170. New number assigned post-excavation.)

SF 289   Probable nail fragment. Tapering tip of a fine rectangular bar or nail, extreme tip lost. Remaining L 15.7 mm, W 5.2 mm, T 2.5 mm. Wgt 1.2 g. Context 121 (entrance). (Extracted from soil samples, new number assigned post-excavation.)

Discussion

Like the other artefacts from Clachtoll the importance of the assemblage derives from the fact that it is a rare, securely dated assemblage from an Atlantic Middle Iron Age site. Usually, discussions of iron objects in the Middle Iron Age have revolved around material from Traprain Law (Burley 1956), the three southern Scottish ironwork hoards (Piggott 1953), Fairy Knowe (Hunter 1998), Leckie (MacKie 2016) and Dun Ardtreck (MacKie 2000a); the iron objects from Clachtoll are a welcoming addition to the meagre Scottish corpus.

The iron assemblage from Clachtoll is dominated by tools, particularly those associated with agriculture, food and drink and everyday crafts. The most striking and important group of finds are the objects associated with agriculture: the ard, spade, sickles and reaping hooks (Fig. 4.4.7). This assemblage gives important insight into the agricultural practices surrounding the broch and, presumably, the everyday activities of the roundhouse inhabitants.

However, we should also, perhaps, view this agricultural toolkit in a manner beyond the functional. Numerous studies of Iron Age Atlantic Scotland have highlighted the importance of various objects within house foundations and other 'ritual' deposits, both within the *domus* and the landscape. Importantly, these suggest a concern with fertility and the agricultural cycle, rather than, as in previous times and/or other areas, the deposition of metalwork (also see Hunter 1997). It has been argued that various items had a particular link with the agricultural cycle and hence concepts of fertility and prosperity (Hingley 1997, 13–15, 23–4, 38–9). As Hunter (2007a) reminds us, such special treatment of agricultural equipment is seen in the tools in the Carlingwark, Blackburn Mill and Eckford (Roxburghshire) hoards (S. Piggott 1953), the sickle from a pit at Albie Hill (Dumfriesshire; Strachan 1999), the ard head from the substructure of Milton Loch crannog (Kirkcudbrightshire; C.M. Piggott 1953, 143–4; Rees 1979, 42–3), and the ard beam from a peat bog near Lochmaben (Dumfriesshire; Rees 1979, 43). The Dryburn Bridge and Tentsmuir sickles may be further examples. The context of the ploughshare from a peripheral area of the wheelhouse at Á Cheardach Beag, South Uist (Fairhurst 1971) may indicate ritual deposition within the house (Hingley 1992, 23) and the numerous pits at Sollas, North Uist (Campbell 1991) can also be seen in this light. The wooden ard from a peat bog at Virdifield, Shetland and the iron ard-share from a wetland deposit in Swordale, Sutherland further demonstrates the ritual deposition of agriculturally associated objects in the landscape (Hingley 1992, 23). The deposition of bog-butter found in a number of mosses in western Scotland (Ritchie 1941; Earwood 1991), was also a long-lived tradition.

These deposits from floor deposits, wall foundations, peat bogs and other wetland deposits are important as they demonstrate that the objects we may term 'prosaic' (*e.g.*, ards, shares, sickles) actually had strong importance across Atlantic Scotland beyond the functional and perhaps the finds from Clachtoll had similar significance.

Away from the agricultural implements the tools from Clachtoll show a range of craft processes being carried out in and around the broch. While attributing tools to crafts is a treacherous task, there seems to be evidence of leatherworking, woodworking and textile working. The typical Middle Iron Age knife is represented as are pins (Fig. 4.4.8), typical for the Scottish Iron Age; the pins remind us that, although copper alloy generally survives better, iron was also used for decorative purposes.

The nails and bolts were probably associated with interior buildings, fixtures or fittings. However, nails are surprisingly rare finds on Iron Age sites. Hunter (1998) recently reminded us Howe has the largest assemblage, with 30 (Ballin Smith 1994, 217–19); Hurly Hawkin produced eight (Taylor 1982, 231), Dun Mor Vaul seven (MacKie 1974, 125), Gurness two (Hedges 1987, 214–15) and Crosskirk one (Fairhurst 1984, 119). They are equally sparse in crannogs (Munro 1882). As Hunter (1998) states one may assume that nails may only survive in quantities in exceptional circumstances (such as destruction by fire, perhaps); but this was not the case at Clachtoll. Either one did not actually need nails to build a broch or, equally likely, they were recycled.

And, of course, organic objects from Clachtoll (see McLaren this volume) show us that other iron objects were used for a range of activities. For example, analysis of various tool marks on bone objects shows the use of axes or cleavers, saws and fine blades. The whale vertebra chopping block is covered with tool marks made during craft activities, the marks formed by at least four different iron tools, ranging from punches to cleavers.

The actual iron objects and the invisible remains of others makes the Clachtoll assemblage one of the most important surviving iron assemblages from northern mainland Scotland. Like the other finds from the site it allows a rare snapshot into the tools used by people working the land and other resources during their every-day routines.

4.5 The copper alloy
Andy Heald

Summary

Five items of copper alloy were recovered from Clach-toll: a 1944 penny (SF 5), a sheet fragment (SF 82), a projecting ring headed pin (SF 154) and a modern nail with a flat oval head and 1967 half-dollar coin (both SF 164). The modern finds are not of note; the coin and the nail being surface finds in the area of cell 4 and the 1944 penny being a modern intrusion within context (034). The sheet and the pin are discussed in more detail below. Both were analysed by qualitative X-ray Fluorescence by Dr Gemma Cruickshanks, National Museums Scotland. Two analyses were undertaken on each object, with the aim of characterising their alloy composition.

Projecting ring-headed pin

SF 154   Almost complete ring-headed pin; oval looped head (12.2 x 13.7 mm), fine circular-sectioned drawn wire shank (Diam 2 mm), missing part of the tip. L: 82.4 mm. Context 049. XRF revealed that the pin is a brass alloy, containing Cu, zinc (Zn) and Sn (Fig. 4.5.1a).

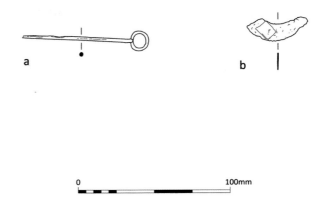

Figure 4.5.1 The copper alloy finds: a) projecting ring-headed pin (SF 154) and b) sheet fragment (SF 82)

Projecting ring-headed pins supposedly derive from ring-headed pins (see Dunning 1934; Stevenson 1955; Foster 1990). There are two types of plain projecting ring-headed pins: those made from wire or those cast. The origin and chronology of both is a matter of debate (Stevenson 1955; MacKie 1969; Clarke 1971). Both MacKie and Stevenson agree that cast pins are of a later date than simple bent wire pins, which MacKie claims are the normal type found on brochs and wheelhouses (MacKie 1974, 129). Few well-dated examples have been found. Although Stevenson (1966, 20–2) suggested a date between the 2nd and 3rd centuries AD excavations at Scalloway, Shetland suggests that the type may have survived into the 5th century AD (Sharples 1998, 185).

Projecting ring-headed pins are common, but not exclusive, to Scotland, where they have been found at many Iron Age sites from Dun Mor Vaul (MacKie 1974) in the west to Crosskirk (Fairhurst 1984) in the east and as far north as Shetland and can be made of iron as well as copper alloy. The type is widespread in the Hebrides (Clarke 1971, fig. 4) and, as at Clachtoll, these pins were commonly used to stamp Hebridean pottery. Moulds for the manufacture of plain projecting ring-headed pins have been found at Sollas, North Uist (Campbell 1991, 163, illus. 22, no. 498), North Uist; Traprain Law, East Lothian (Burley 1956); Gurness, Orkney (Hedges 1987); Berigh, Lewis (Harding and Gilmour 2000, 63) and Mine Howe, Orkney (Heald 2001).

The presence of Zn in objects is usually taken to indicate manufacture during the Roman Iron Age or later; copper alloys containing zinc are almost entirely absent from pre-Roman copper alloys (Dungworth 1995; 1996, 410–11; 1997).

Sheet

SF 82   Curving sheet fragment. Dimensions: remaining L 39.3 mm, W 6.3-10.7 mm, T 1.2 mm. Context

42. XRF revealed the presence of copper (Cu), tin (Sn) and lead (Pb), indicating the object is leaded bronze in composition. Leaded bronzes are less chronologically distinct but typically pre-Roman (Fig. 4.5.1b).

4.6 The ironworking and other residues
Dawn McLaren, David Dungworth and Andy Heald

Introduction
Although no structural evidence of metalworking features was uncovered during excavation at Clachtoll over 3.4 kg of vitrified material was found from the interior floor levels and associated contexts. A programme of visual examination, aided by scientific chemical and microstructural analysis of a sample of pieces has demonstrated that the majority of the vitrified material is waste deriving from ironworking activities and, in particular, indicates very inefficient bloomery smelting practices. The assemblage is almost exclusively composed of ironwork-related bulk slags with very little in the way of micro-residues which would be anticipated in the case of *in situ* ironworking. The implication of this, therefore, is that all of the slags found within the broch are residual and have been brought into the broch, either incidentally or intentionally for a purpose which is not fully understood. No evidence of *in situ* metalworking within the broch itself was indicated, suggesting that although ironworking was taking place in the vicinity prior to or during the occupation of the tower, it must have been located outside the walls of the broch.

The assemblage: macroscopic analysis
The process of producing iron objects is a two stage process (McDonnell 2000, 218). The first stage involves the extraction of iron from the ore using the smelting process to produce an iron bloom and secondly, the working of the metal into artefacts by smithing (McDonnell 1994, 100). Both processes produce waste by-products in the form of a range of vitrified and heat-affected materials, some of which are diagnostic of particular stages in the ironworking process whilst others are more difficult to distinguish and categorise.

The vitrified material from Clachtoll was visually examined and provisionally categorised on the basis of morphology, density, colour, vesicularity and response to a magnet. In general, slag assemblages can be divided into two broad categories. The first group includes material which can be attributed to a particular industrial process such as ironworking; these comprise ores and smelting and smithing slags. Only a few, for example tapped slag and hammerscale, are truly diagnostic

(of smelting and smithing respectively). The second category of vitrified material includes a range of non-diagnostic slags which could have been produced by a number of different activities but show no diagnostic characteristic that can identify the specific process. There is often a significant amount of material within this non-diagnostic category which is unclassifiable making the allocation of individual pieces – particularly small samples – to specific types and processes difficult (Crew and Rehren 2002).

What was immediately apparent from the initial visual examination of the Clachtoll broch slag assemblage was that although ironworking slags were recognised, the assemblage was unusually limited in terms of quantity and the range of slag types present and did not represent the typical suite of waste that would be anticipated from an Iron Age ironworking site.

The individual classifications of slag are discussed in more detail below but to summarise the assemblage comprised a single plano-convex accumulation of slag, a couple of possible similar cake fragments, a very limited quantity of runned slags suggestive of iron smelting and iron-rich unclassified slags, alongside a suite of undiagnostic vitrified material including fuel ash slag. What was unusual was the proportion of the assemblage which had the appearance, morphology, colour and response to a magnet that would typically be anticipated from bloom fragments or smithing debris. Some fragments were so strongly magnetic, but amorphous in shape, that it was initially thought that they were fragments of unprocessed iron bloom, the primary product of iron smelting and the material from which iron objects could then be forged. Other amorphous but clearly iron-rich pieces were entirely obscured in surface corrosion comprising mineralised plant-based organics (including grasses and rushes) some of which had small flakes and spheres embedded in the corrosion product, suggesting that these may be smithing waste, the by-product of bloom- or blacksmithing.

This initial examination confirmed without doubt the presence of ironworking slags and pointed towards the possibility of ironworking taking place within the broch but despite careful processing and scanning of the soil samples collected in the field, a total lack of micro-debris was present and no hammerscale flakes or spheres were recovered. Had bloom or blacksmithing taken place in the broch, significant quantities of such micro-debris would be anticipated and yet none were found.

The assemblage: scientific analysis
The unusual composition of the assemblage in terms of the range of slags represented and the paucity of micro-debris raised a number of questions that could not

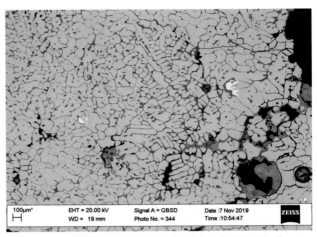

Figure 4.6.2 SEM image of Clachtoll broch SF 129 showing abundant 'blobby' wüstite (very pale grey) with rare metallic droplets and a glassy matrix

Figure 4.6.1 Slag Sample (SF 129 [048])

be answered though visual examination alone. For this reason, a programme of scientific analysis consisting of chemical and microstructural analysis was conducted by Dr David Dungworth on a small but targeted group of samples which were felt, at time of visual examination, to comprise a representative sample of the assemblage including fragments of possible bloom, unclassified iron slag including pieces with possible hammerscale flakes embedded in the surface corrosion products, and a possible edge fragment from a plano-convex cake.

The key questions that the analysis aimed to investigate were: As the proportion of possible bloom fragments amongst the assemblage is unusual for Iron Age assemblages in Scotland, can the identification of the bloom and possible iron-rich smithing slags be confirmed by their chemical composition and microstructure? If these are not consistent with bloom fragments, can another explanation be offered for their strongly magnetic character and iron-rich appearance? Are the small flakes and spheres noted in the corrosion products of a small number of pieces consistent with micro-debris resulting from smithing? And finally, has the conflagration had any discernible effect on the slags that may explain their unusual character and appearance?

The full details of this analysis and the methodology used is presented in the site archive but has been summarised here. The cleaned and dried samples were mounted in low-viscosity epoxy resin and then ground and polished to a 1-micron finish (Vander Voort 1999). The microstructure was recorded using images obtained with a scanning electron microscope (SEM). The chemical composition of the samples was determined using an energy dispersive

spectrometer (EDS) attached to the SEM. All chemical data is expressed as stoichiometric oxides, normalised to 100wt%.

SF 129

This lump of slag (SF 129; [048]) lacks a diagnostic morphology that would allow the definite identification of the process that produced it (Fig. 4.6.1).

The microstructure of SF 129 is dominated by rather 'blobby' wüstite (FeO, Figs 4.6.2 and 3) with occasional metallic droplets, and a glassy matrix (Fig. 4.6.4). The form of the metallic inclusions is perhaps more consistent with the slag having formed during smelting rather than smithing. The wüstite contains a small proportion of a second (darker) phase in the form of laths that have precipitated

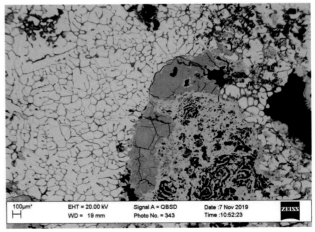

Figure 4.6.3 SEM image of Clachtoll broch SF 129 showing abundant 'blobby' wüstite (very pale grey) with areas of corrosion (bottom and right)

Table 4.6.1 Slag samples selected for scientific analysis

SF	Context	Context description
129	48	Floor deposit composed of peat ash
130a	49	Floor deposit composed of lenses of plant matter and peat ash
131	49	Floor deposit composed of lenses of plant matter and peat ash
132d	49	Floor deposit composed of lenses of plant matter and peat ash
166d	49	Floor deposit composed of lenses of plant matter and peat ash
186	67	Floor deposit below midden material (047)

in two preferred orientations (at 90° to each other). This phase was too small to allow any direct measurement of its chemical composition; however, it is possible that this phase is magnetite. The matrix is entirely glassy, no laths of fayalite (Fe_2SiO_4), or other phases, were observed.

The fact that the matrix of this sample is entirely glassy suggests that the slag lump has not been affected by exposure to excessive heat (which would be expected to have encouraged the devitrification/crystallisation of the glassy matrix). The magnetic properties of this lump of slag could be explained by the presence of magnetite in the wüstite; however, it was not possible to confirm the presence of magnetite by direct observation. It is not immediately clear when the putative magnetite precipitated; this could have been when the slag first cool, but it could also be due to a later heating event.

SF 130a

This lump of slag (SF 130a; [049]) has a dense layered appearance on the break surface but all other surfaces are largely obscured by corrosion products (Fig. 4.6.5).

The microstructure is similar to that seen in SF 129: very abundant blobby wüstite (Figs 4.6.6–8), but in this case some hercynite ($FeAlO_4$) is also present, and the matrix contains fine fayalite laths (Figs 4.6.7 and 8). The presence of hercynite and fayalite suggests that this slag had a slightly different thermal history. While secondary heating could account for the precipitation of hercynite and fayalite, the growth of these phases might reflect a slightly slower primary cooling, compared to SF 129.

SF 131

Macroscopic examination initially classified this fragment (SF 131; (049)) as unclassified iron slag with extensive iron corrosion products on the surface which appear to be mineral-preserved organics of grass or rushes. These are present on all surfaces and are likely to have formed post-deposition. The sample has a typical microstructure for early ironworking slags with wüstite, fayalite and a glassy matrix (Figs 4.6.10–12). The wüstite is mostly

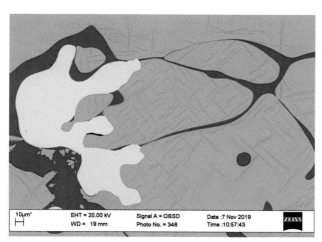

Figure 4.6.4 SEM image of Clachtoll broch SF 129 showing abundant 'blobby' wüstite (very pale grey) with a second (darker) phase precipitated as laths within the wüstite, a metallic droplet (white) and a glassy matrix

Figure 4.6.5 Slag lump (SF 130a, [049])

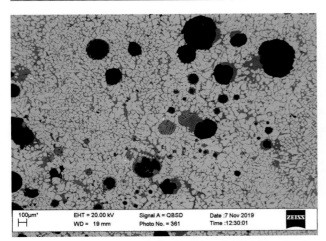

Figure 4.6.6 SEM image of Clachtoll broch SF 130a showing abundant 'blobby' wüstite (very pale grey)

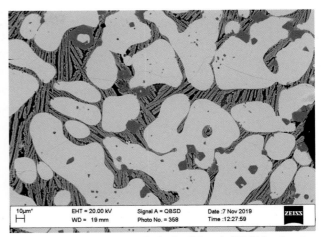

Figure 4.6.7 SEM image of Clachtoll broch SF 130a showing 'blobby' wüstite, and hercynite (small darker euhedral) crystals, with a matrix of fine fayalite laths and glass

present as relatively large (primary) 'blobs' in a vaguely dendritic arrangement (Figs 4.6.10 and 11). A small amount of much finer wüstite (Fig. 4.6.12) is present and appears to be secondary. At very high magnification, the glassy matrix appears to contain some very small crystals (probably fayalite).

SF 132d

A further fragment of unclassified iron slag (SF 132d; (049)) is also almost entirely obscured by post-depositional powdery iron corrosion products which appear to be mineral-preserved organics of grass or rushes (Fig. 4.6.13). The sample has a microstructure which shows extensive post-depositional corrosion (Figs 4.6.14 and 15); however, the original microstructure appears to have comprised blobs of wüstite in a glassy matrix (*cf.* SF 129).

SF 166d

This amorphous fragment (SF 166d; (049)) was initially suspected to be smithing slag due to the presence of small flakes embedded in the extensive corrosion products that coat the surfaces (Fig. 4.6.16). The microstructure comprises very abundant 'blobby' wüstite, occasional metallic droplets and a glassy matrix (Figs 4.6.17 and 18). A few regions showed a lower proportion of wüstite (Fig. 4.6.19); however, these regions appear to have been more susceptible to post-depositional corrosion.

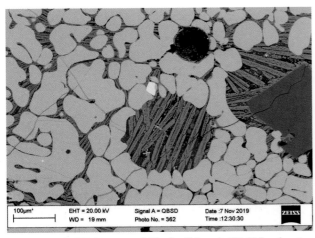

Figure 4.6.8 SEM image of Clachtoll broch SF 130a showing 'blobby' wüstite, and a blob of metallic iron (white), in a matrix of fine fayalite laths and glass

Figure 4.6.9 Slag Sample (SF 131, [049])

Table 4.6.2 Average chemical composition of each slag sample

SF	Na₂O	MgO	Al₂O₃	SiO₂	P₂O₅	K₂O	CaO	TiO₂	MnO	FeO	H
129	0.36	0.38	2.71	6.02	0.19	0.42	0.77	0.07	2	86.2	5.1
130a	0.46	0.52	5.66	7.56	0.48	0.31	0.66	0.27	0.98	82	2.8
131	1.05	0.64	4.16	18.2	0.32	0.66	2.3	0.17	3.64	68	3.6
132d	0.4	0.51	2.69	5.5	0.28	0.33	1.15	0.06	2.77	85.4	2.8
166d	0.4	0.65	3.19	7.18	0.29	0.48	1.48	0.07	3.36	82.1	7.6

Table 4.6.3 Chemical composition of wüstite-rich slags from Birnie and Culduthel (Dungworth unpublished)

Site	Ref	Description	Na₂O	MgO	Al₂O₃	SiO₂	P₂O₅	K₂O	CaO	TiO₂	MnO	FeO
Birnie	50	Unclassified	0.19	<0.1	3.26	5.52	<0.1	0.27	0.68	<0.1	0.82	89.3
Culduthel	1132	Unidentified	0.38	0.15	6.21	9.54	0.42	0.65	1.51	<0.1	2.62	78.1
Culduthel	1142	PCHB frag	0.53	0.28	2.55	10.37	0.19	0.67	1.05	<0.1	0.27	83.9
Culduthel	1153	Bloom frag?	0.41	0.21	2.79	7.46	0.34	0.48	1.7	<0.1	1.71	84.6

SF 186

This fragment was provisionally identified as a possible bloom fragment (partly on the basis of its response to a magnet (Fig. 4.6.20). The microstructure is dominated by corrosion (Fig. 4.6.21) with no areas surviving intact to allow chemical analysis. The surviving microstructure appears to be dominated by fayalite with very little wüstite.

Each sample was analysed (using SEM-EDS) to determine the average chemical composition (using six separate areas for each sample). The average results are displayed in Table 4.6.2 (sample SF 186 was too corroded to allow any reliable chemical analysis). A measure of homogeneity-heterogeneity (H) has been calculated for each sample, which is the sum of the chemical variance (*cf.* Dungworth 2007). Low values <1 are typical for tapped smelting slags, while non-tapped smelting slags and smithing slags usually have higher H values.

The slag composition shows strong links to the microstructures described above. Samples SF 129, SF 130a, SF 132d and SF 166d are all rich in iron (Table 4.6.2) and this is reflected in their microstructures which are dominated by wüstite. SF 131 contains much lower levels of iron and has a typical microstructure for early ironworking slags. The concentrations of a range of other elements in the slag samples (Na, Mg, Al, P, K, Ca and Mn) are broadly similar to other early Scottish ironworking slags.

The samples of slag from Clachtoll broch that have been subjected to scientific analysis have characteristics that are unusual and difficult to explain. Four out of the six samples are rich in iron oxide (82–86wt% FeO) and have microstructures that have anomalously high proportions of wüstite (FeO). The two remaining samples (one of which was too corroded to allow any meaningful chemical

analysis) appear to have more usual microstructures for early ironworking slags.

The wüstite-rich slag samples from Clachtoll broch have parallels among slag samples from Birnie and Culduthel (Table 4.6.3); however, to date such slags have formed a very small proportion of analysed slags and have largely been dismissed as 'outliers'. The form of these slags provides little assistance in determining the process(es) which may have generated them. These slag samples rarely provide any morphologically diagnostic features that would allow them to be certainly identified as either smelting or smithing slags. Bloomery iron smelting and iron smithing often takes place under non-equilibrium conditions and so compositional variation (especially of iron) is to be expected (*cf.* Dungworth 2011). Nevertheless, the wüstite-rich slags appear to represent a particularly inefficient end of this spectrum.

If these wüstite-rich slags were generated during smithing, then they would indicate that the smithing was rather inefficient — a significant proportion of the metallic iron that was being smithing was being lost in the slag. However, the microstructure does not resemble debris formed when iron has been overheated (Dungworth and Wilkes 2009). The samples contain metallic iron inclusions but their form and nature are not what would be expected during the oxidation of metallic iron. Partially oxidised iron should have a metallic core with layers of oxides (wüstite, magnetite and hematite), but the metallic inclusions in these samples have no oxidised outer layers.

If the slags were generated during iron smelting then they would also indicate a rather inefficient process — the iron content of these slags is almost as high as many analysed iron ore samples. If they were formed during smelting, then they represent melting of ore but with little

Table 4.6.4 Summary of the slag assemblage by type and weight

Type	Count	Weight (g)
Indicative of ironworking		
Possible bloom/iron off-cut	1	105.3
Iron-rich smelting slags	10	1148.3
Plano-convex cakes & fragments (PCC)	2	1458.3
Runned slag (RS)	3	107.8
Unclassified Iron Slag (UIS)	17	583.7
Undiagnostic vitrified materials & other		
Fuel ash slag (FAS)	10	14.1
Fuel residues	10	1
Magnetic Vitrified Residues (MVR)	13	11.3
Non-Magnetic Vitrified Residues (NMVR)	7	0.1
Sintered organics	1	2.3
Burnt sand	4	27.9
Total	*78*	*3460.1*

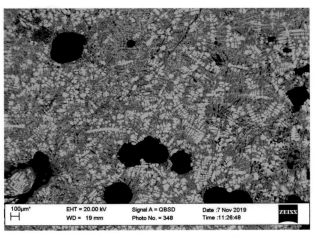

Figure 4.6.10 SEM image of Clachtoll broch SF 131 showing 'blobby' wüstite

reduction of the iron oxide to metallic iron. The presence of small metallic iron inclusions, and in particular the tendency for the larger examples to exhibit dendritic forms, is consistent with the reduction of some iron oxide (ore) to metallic iron (*cf.* Blomgren and Tholander 1986).

On balance, it seems slightly more likely that these wüstite-rich slags were generated by smelting rather than smithing. If they are smelting slags, then they represent the most inefficient, most unsuccessful smelting slags using a bloomery process. Considerable effort must have been expended to heat the ore (and probably melt it) but little or no iron was extracted from these lumps. It is possible that these samples (like their counterparts at Birnie and Culduthel) were just a small proportion of the slag generated, and that the process was overall successful in generating a bloom of metallic iron (or steel).

Crucially the iron-rich smelting slags (wüstite-rich slags) subjected to scientific analysis do not have microstructures that would suggest that they were significantly affected by secondary heating during the conflagration of the broch. If bloomery ironworking slags were subjected to significant heating then it might be expected that the glassy matrix would be transformed into crystalline phases (especially fayalite). These wüstite-rich slags tend to respond to a magnet more than most early ironworking slags. This could be due at least in part due to the presence of metallic iron in these samples. In addition, the wüstite occasionally contains what might be small laths

of magnetite. While the precipitation of magnetite might conceivably be linked to a heating secondary episode (and so linked to the burning down of the broch), the presence of metallic iron inclusions seems unlikely to be a product of conflagration.

In summary, unlike the slag assemblages recovered from other Iron Age sites, such as Applecross, Highland (Cruckshanks, pers. comm.) and Howe, Orkney (McDonnell 1994) where every part of the ironworking process is attested, the slag assemblage from Clachtoll is atypical in composition, representing only parts of what appears to have been a very inefficient smelting process. Typical components of many early ironworking assemblages are missing here including fragments of ore (likely bog ore), ceramic furnace or hearth lining and micro-debris such as hammerscale and slag spheres. None of the slag from the site has been confidently identified as waste deriving from bloom or blacksmithing, a process which would be expected to have occurred considering the number of iron tools recovered which would likely have required occasional repair and maintenance. Overall the composition of the assemblage is atypical and not fully representative of the suite of waste typically encountered from either smelting or smithing activities.

Further, the slag appears to be representative of a very inefficient smelt. The early iron metallurgist needed fuel, iron ore and a furnace structure with bellows to smelt iron and the process itself has been rehearsed elsewhere in detail (McDonnell 1998, 151–4, fig. 27). At Clachtoll, the presence of the ironworking slags, and those that are particularly iron rich, demonstrates that ore and fuel were indeed available and that the technology was there to conduct the smelt and yet all evidence points towards an inefficiency in the process. If the tentative thesis (that these wüstite-rich slags represent unsuccessful smelts, or at least the most unsuccessful parts of otherwise successful

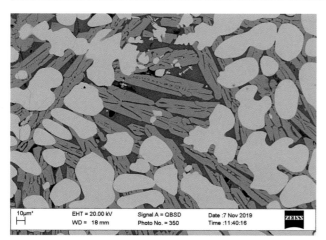

Figure 4.6.11 SEM image of Clachtoll broch SF 131 showing 'blobby' wüstite, fayalite laths and a glassy matrix

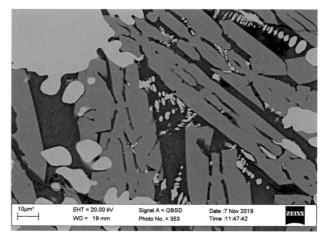

Figure 4.6.12 SEM image of Clachtoll broch SF 131 showing large, 'blobby' (primary) wüstite, small dendrites of (secondary) wüstite, grey laths of fayalite and a glassy matrix (this contains some very small crystalline phases (probably [secondary] fayalite)

smelts) is accepted, then some explanation for their prevalence at Clachtoll broch is required. These slags constitute two-thirds of the analysed slag from Clachtoll broch, while at, for example, Birnie (G. Cruickshanks pers. comm.) and Culduthel (Dungworth and McLaren 2021) they formed less than 10% of the assemblage.

Assessing the scale of iron production at Clachtoll is impossible to determine on the basis of this assemblage, both due to the apparent secondary contexts they were recovered from but more especially due to the clear bias in the selection of pieces which had been selected to be brought into the broch. It can only be assumed that the 3.3 kg of ironworking waste represents a small proportion of the waste produced as the result of a minimum of two smelting episodes.

Classifications

As outlined above, the classification of the slags from Clachtoll relied on a combination of both macroscopic examination and scientific analysis of a targeted samples. Where possible, the categories defined follow established terminology, *e.g.*, McDonnell 1994; Starley 2000; McLaren and Heald 2006. These are summarised in Table 4.6.4.

Ironworking slags

Plano-convex slag cake (PCC): These are plano-convex bowl-shaped accumulations of dense dark red-brown slag which can form in both smelting furnaces and blacksmith's

Figure 4.6.13 Slag sample (SF 132d, [049])

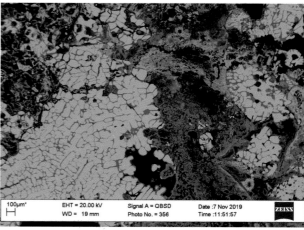

Figure 4.6.14 SEM image of Clachtoll broch sample SF 132d showing islands of wüstite-rich slag surrounded by extensive areas of corrosion

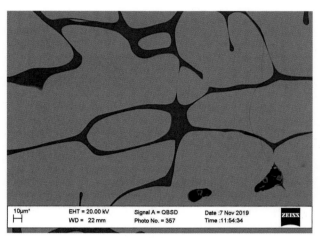

Figure 4.6.15 SEM image of Clachtoll broch sample SF 132d showing wüstite blobs in a glassy matrix

Figure 4.6.16 Slag sample (SF 166d, [049])

hearths. Differentiating between cakes produced during these two processes largely relies on size, weight, density, response to a magnetic as well as the abundance and size of any fuel inclusions (McDonnell 1994, 229). One intact subcircular cake came from (042). It weighs 1426.7 g and has a maximum diameter of 131 mm and depth of 58 mm. On the basis of its size and weight, this has been identified as a furnace base, formed when smelting slag accumulates and cools in the bottom of a furnace. A wedge-shaped fragment (31.6 g) from a second cake came from (049) but it is too small and fractured to allow any further classification.

Iron-rich smelting slags: As described above, the majority of the fragments which fall into this category at Clachtoll were initially classified as possible bloom fragments due to their dense but visibly iron-rich appearance but though analysis of samples has been determined to be inefficient iron rich smelting slags. The indications of the iron-rich composition were macroscopically apparent due to the presence of abundant iron corrosion products (often incorporating mineralised plant matter), distinctive hairline cracking and corrosion blisters common on archaeological iron, the deep red-brown colouration and the strong response when scanned with a magnet. These slags (10 fragments) form an unusually large proportion of the assemblage (1148.3 g; 33%wgt) for early ironworking assemblages.

Runned slag (RS): Three small fragments (107.8 g) of waste have a distinctive 'ropey' flowed appearance and have clearly seeped or flowed in a liquid stage around lumps of charcoal. Such slag flows are commonly found in abundance on smelting sites and in some instances provide clear evidence of where the slag was tapped from the furnace and allowed to flow out, leading to their classification as 'tapped slags' (McDonnell 1994, 100).

However, small, short runs of molten waste can also form in a smithing hearth (Crew and Rehren 2002, 86). The small, fractured pieces from Clachtoll are of a size and form that would be consistent with smelting waste but the quantities are so limited this cannot be certain. None of the fragments are obviously tapped.

Unclassified iron slag (UIS): The remaining bulk slags (17 fragments; 583.7 g) are fractured and small. Such slags are a common component of slag assemblage and can be produced during both iron smelting and smithing. Small fractured amorphous pieces of iron silicate slag are a common component of slag assemblages (Crew and Rehren 2002, 84) and are typically interpreted as rake-out material from a smelting furnace or smithing hearth. Differentiating between the two processes (*e.g.,* smelting and smithing) through visual examination of this material alone is difficult and for this reason such slags are often referred to as undiagnostic ironworking slags. At Clachtoll, this material is quite heterogenous in appearance but is typically vesicular, porous and red-brown in colour, some with distinct impressions or small inclusions of charcoal embedded in the surfaces. Most pieces were magnetic, some strongly so, and it is probable that most of this material is associated with the iron-rich smelting slags previously described.

Undiagnostic vitrified materials

Fuel ash slag (FAS): Fuel ash slags are formed when material such as sand, earth, clay, stones or ceramics are subjected to high temperatures, for example in a hearth. During heating these materials react, melt or fuse with alkali in ash, producing glassy (vitreous) and porous materials (Bayley 1985, 41). These slags can be formed during any high temperature pyrotechnic process and are not necessarily indicative of deliberate industrial activity

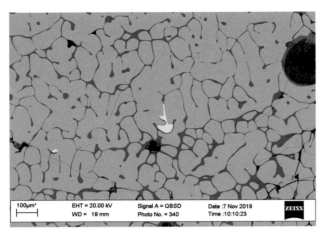

Figure 4.6.17 SEM image of Clachtoll broch SF 166d showing abundant 'blobby' wüstite (very pale grey) with rare metallic droplets and a glassy matrix

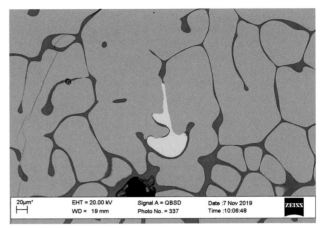

Figure 4.6.18 SEM image of Clachtoll broch SF 166d showing abundant 'blobby' wüstite (very pale grey) a metallic droplet and a glassy matrix

(McDonnell 1994, 230). Only 14.1 g of this material was recognised amongst the assemblage.

Magnetic and non-magnetic vitrified residues (MVR and NMVR): Small quantities of magnetic material (11.3 g) comprise extremely small (typically less than 10 mm in diameter and here often *c.* 2 mm) represent a mixture of small, fractured fragments detached from larger accumulations, small stones and silica. Although these pieces (MVR) are magnetic, they are undiagnostic in form and are not indicative of ironworking. Similarly 0.1 g of small flecks of non-magnetic vitrified material were recognised and may be akin to fuel ash slags.

Fuel residues: Small quantities (1 g) of dark brown-black, porous and brittle vesicular material with a slightly glassy appearance. These include a mixture of desiccated fragments of peat, coal cinders (probably from sea coal) and vitrified charcoal.

Sintered organics and burnt sand: Small amorphous fractured fragments of buff-beige coloured sintered material (2.3 g) were present with a friable and brittle texture and frequent voids which are suggestive of a layered structure. Under magnification the material is comprised of the mineral component (the silicates) of grass, rush and/or straw stems, which have transformed under exposure to intense heat and have become glassy and fused in patches but retain the fibrous detail of the plant material. This is similar in appearance to sintered organics recovered from a burning layer within a roundhouse at Moredun Top hillfort, Perth and Kinross (McLaren in prep). These sintered organics alongside fragments of burnt sand (27.9 g) also bear some broad similarities to sintered sands from Late Iron Age and Norse contexts at Bornish (Sharples 2012; Young 2012, 294–5) and East Mound, Bay of Skaill,

Orkney (McLaren 2019) which are recognised as having a non-metallurgical origin.

Contextual analysis and distribution

Vitrified material was recovered from 16 stratified contexts across the excavated interior and entrance of the broch (contexts 007, 035, 042, 047, 048, 049, 052, 053, 062, 067, 074, 078, 100, 136, 137, 153) and from unstratified deposits (Table 4.6.5). The vast majority of slag derived from deposits within the main floor areas of the broch but material was also recovered from the entrance passage (052) and (153), infill material within the deep area or 'souterrain' (078) and from contexts within Cell 2 (136, 137).

Undiagnostic vitrified material, probably not metalwork related, was encountered as a low-level scatter throughout the floor levels of the broch and from the destruction layers. These include: fuel residues from the burnt remains of the collapsed floor (007), magnetic but undiagnostic vitrified material from a burnt deposit within a wall void, perhaps related to the destruction event (035), fuel ash slags and sintered sand from the destruction deposit (042), fuel ash slag from midden material overlying bedrock (047), fuel ash slag from a sandy yellow clay flooring material (048), magnetic but undiagnostic vitrified material from mixed flooring in the south-west quad of the broch interior (062), further magnetic vitrified material from burnt deposits adjacent to hearth (074), fuel ash slag and sintered organics from the loose rubble infill (078) of the 'deep area' or souterrain, non-magnetic vitrified material from the fill (100) of culvert, vitrified fuel residues from a layer of sandy clay in cell 2 (136), magnetic vitrified residues from charcoal-rich humic clay (137) also in cell 2 and fuel ash slag from fractured rubble at the broch entrance (153).

Metalworking debris was far more restricted in distribution and was associated with nine contexts: from

Table 4.6.5 Summary of the distribution of slag by type and weight

Clachtoll Broch, Assynt (AOC 60094)

Context number	Context	Ironworking						Undiagnostic of process					Total Weight (g)
		Bloom/Fe off-cut	PCC	Fe-rich smelting slag	RS	UIS	FAS	Fuel Residues	MVR	NMVR	Sintered organics	Burnt Sand	
007 I	Burnt remains of collapsed upper floor							<0.1					<0.1
35	Burnt deposit within wall void, may be related to destruction event								<0.1				<0.1
42	Burning event: burnt deposit across entire broch interior		1426.7			6	0.1					27.9	1460.7
47	Midden material overlying bedrock			215.1			6.9						222
48	Deposit of sandy yellow clay, possibly a floor deposit composed of peat ash	105.3		692			0.1						797.4
49	Floor material: lenses of organic rushes/ matting and peat ash		31.6	203.1	107.8	346.3			7.8				696.6
52	natural infill from lintel collapse and water percolation in entrance passage					27.5							27.5
53	Fill of stone tank [052], mix of food waste, hearth debris & fc stone					53.1							53.1
062 (SW quad)	Mixed flooring material in SW quad								3.2				3.2
74	burnt deposits adjacent to hearth, peat ash-rich hearth debris?								0.2				0.2
78	Loose rubble and mixed fill of 'deep area'					15.1	6.9				2.3		24.3
100	Fill of culvert [059]									0.1			0.1
136	Cell 2: light brown silty clay over flag-stone surface (132)							1					1
137	Cell 2: charcoal rich humic clay								0.1				0.1
153	Fractured rubble at broch entrance						0.1						0.1
u/s	unstratified			38.1		10.1							48.2
Total		105.3	1458.3	1148.3	107.8	583.7	14.1	1	11.3	0.1	2.3	27.9	3460.1

the destruction deposit (042), from midden material overlying bedrock (047), from a sandy yellow clay floor (048), from floor material comprising lenses of organic material and peat ash (049), from collapsed material in the entrance passage (052), from the fill of the stone tank (053), from a flooring deposit (067), from loose rubble infiltrating the 'deep' area or souterrain (078) and as unstratified finds.

The largest concentration of waste by weight (1460.7 g; 42%wgt) came from the destruction deposit (042) which overlay the *in situ* floor levels and hearths. This implies two things: a) that at least some of the non-metalworking related vitrified material (*e.g.*, sintered sand and fuel ash slag) were generated as the result of a combination of organic and non-organic materials fusing together under the high temperature of the fire that swept through the broch interior, perhaps specifically elements of the wood/wattle interior structure and/or roof, and that, b) the likelihood is that the metalworking related slags that were recovered from this deposit may have been located on an upper level of the broch.

A total of 17 fragments of metalwork related slags came from flooring material (049). This is the largest concentration of waste by quantity (22% by quantity) and represents the most comprehensive suite of slags from any context across the site, yet it only amounts to 688.8 g in weight (20%wgt). This floor deposit, and that of (048) which also included small quantities of metalworking waste (797.4 g) included layers of peat ash. The assumption is that most of this peat ash was generated and spread across the floors from the central hearth but is there a possibility that some of the ash and charcoal within these layers was brought into the broch from elsewhere as flooring material, including the slag as incidental or accidental inclusions?

Discussion

The association of ironworking with Middle Iron Age sites is well-attested across Atlantic Scotland from a range of sites such as wheelhouses and brochs.

Turning to Clachtoll's near neighbours in the Inner and Outer Hebrides and western Sutherland probable iron slag occurs on a number of Iron Age sites such as Foshigarry (Beveridge and Callander 1931, 326); Á Cheardach Mhor (Young and Richardson 1960, 150); Bac Mhic Connain (Beveridge and Callander 1932, 46); Garry Iochdrach (*ibid.*, 41); Á Cheardach Bheag (Fairhurst 1971, 90); Allasdale (Young 1953, 100), Cnip (McLaren and Heald 2006); Cnip 2 & 3 (Armit and Dunwell 1992, 137); Galson (Edwards 1924, 192), Dun Cuier (Young 1956, 300), Dun Ardtreck (Photos-Jones 2000), Dun Leccamore (Ritchie 1971, 106), Balevullin (MacKie 1963, 163) and Applecross (Peteranna 2012, 22). Although many cannot be independently dated it is likely that most date to the

broad Middle Iron Age period with the finds from Cnip, Cnip 2 and 3, Dun Ardtreck and Applecross attributable to this period.

That said many other broadly contemporary sites either have no ironworking debris (*e.g.*, Sollas (Campbell 1991); Hornish Point (Barber 2003); Kilpheder (Lethbridge 1952)) or only very small traces (*e.g.*, Dun Vulan (Dungworth 1999, 230) and Dunan Ruadh (Mortimer 2000, 270–1)). Thus, the current record appears to suggest that approximately 50% of excavated Hebridean sites have evidence of ironworking to some extent (see also McLaren and Heald 2006, 157).

Thirty years ago we knew little about the role and status of iron and non-ferrous metalworking across Atlantic Scotland. Thus, in his review of Iron Age Scottish society Hingley (1992, 41) could only state that 'there is at present very little comprehension of the function of the household and the community in the context of agricultural and industrial production'. Work over the last 30 years has increased our understanding dramatically particularly through the excellent work of McDonnell (1994; 1998; McDonnell and Dockrill 2005) and Cruickshanks (2017). Arguably, there are two broad interpretations. First, where sound evidence of ironworking has been interpreted as an indicator of the high status of the site and craft alike (McDonnell 1998; McDonnell and Dockrill 2005). Second, a more prosaic view whereby ironworking debris in some form could perhaps be expected on many, if not all, Iron Age sites (*e.g.*, Lethbridge 1952, 182; Armit 1996, 151). The suggestion that ironworking took place in the vicinity of roundhouses and the like is not a new idea. A structure at Seafield West associated with a smithing hearth and debris may conceivably be some form of windbreak (Cressy and Anderson 2011, 11). In later periods, for example at Dunadd, Argyll, there was plentiful evidence that iron smithing was carried out at the site but the focus of this activity was not located within the excavated areas (McDonnell 2000, 220).

That broadly 50% of excavated sites in our study area do not have evidence for ironworking may support the view that it was a restricted activity, its occurrence perhaps suggesting some form of associated status. However, it is arguable that a variety of factors – taphonomy, chronology, preservation and location of metalworking – are creating a misleading picture.

It is the author's belief that when small amounts of slag are recovered from the interior of domestic settings, it is plausible that this may not be evidence of actual ironworking taking place within the building. Where we have good stratigraphic evidence (*e.g.*, Cnip) it appears that the slag from roundhouses is either unstratified and/or recovered from secondary contexts (*e.g.*, middens used as wall fills during construction). Importantly, as argued at

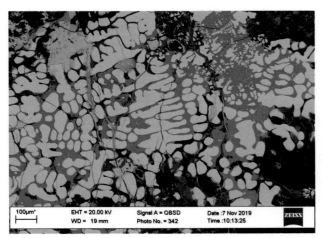

Figure 4.6.19 SEM image of Clachtoll broch SF 166d showing an area with less wüstite but extensive corrosion

Figure 4.6.20 Slag sample (SF186, [067])

Cnip (McLaren and Heald 2006, 157) some slag from 'floor layers' cannot be taken as evidence of *in situ* metalworking as the slag may derive from material deliberately brought in from elsewhere to make floors, particularly if none of the micro-slags are recovered. This may explain why zero or very little slag has been recovered from recent excavations at Hornish Point, Sollas, Dun Vulan and Dunan Ruadh where one may assume the recovery of slag may be more prevalent due to more robust sampling strategies.

If the slag is not secondary then we would argue that the small amounts of slag represent, at best, everyday repair or manufacture of prosaic, functional objects. In a society where a range of iron tools was essential for everyday activity – agriculture, food consumption, the creation of clothes – the maintenance of said tools was a necessity. This is not to suggest that everyone could repair a knife or a plough; but that they knew someone in the local area that did. In summary, we do not accept that every occurrence of slag need be indicative of specialised activity, a smiddy or status. In other words, the slag from roundhouse interiors are as likely to be secondary, brought into the interior as construction material (walls or floors), or if this is not the case, related to local repairs.

These suggestions are supported by the logic that it is entirely likely that large-scale ironworking activity, particularly smelting, took place outwith the wheelhouse and roundhouses. This is entirely in keeping with the rare examples of an area or building which could arguably either have been for occasional, intermittent smithing and/ or a full-time working forge.

Arguably, the best example ironworking site from our study area is from Applecross (Peteranna 2012). During excavation of a broch mound an area of intense slag and a metalworking structure – defined by a setting of horizontal slabs and a bowl structure – was recovered nearby and outwith the broch. Charcoal from the metalworking debris was dated to between the late 3rd and mid-1st centuries BC (*ibid.*, 22–3) and the slag contained both smelting and smithing debris (*ibid.*, 62). Although the 'furnace-like structure' from Á Cheardach Bheag cannot be related to a specific industrial process it may be associated with ironworking (Fairhurst 1971, 90). Although located within the entrance passage to a wheelhouse (*ibid.*, 80, fig. 3) it is, as Fairhurst acknowledged (*ibid.*, 90), 'inconceivable that a glowing furnace should stand across the only entrance to the dwelling'. Fairhurst (*ibid*) argues that it is a primary feature; irrespective it was still outwith the domestic interior. Not enough of the features associated with the bronze- and iron-metalworking evidence at Cnip 3 were uncovered to suggest what the arena for specialised industrial activities looked like (Armit and Dunwell 1992, esp. 147). Thus, it is likely that if we want to find solid evidence of ironworking areas in the Middle Iron Age Atlantic Scotland then we need to either find them outwith roundhouses through serendipity (*e.g.*, Cnip 3) or targeted excavation out with the interior roundhouse domestic settings that we usually focus our attention on. As Armit and Dunwell (*ibid.*, 147) state, the possibility of well-preserved specialist workshops of Iron Age date surviving in their wider landscape gives these sites an importance in a far wider context than Atlantic Scotland. The publication of recently excavated workshop sites (notably Mine Howe and Culduthel) should shed considerable light on manufacturing practice and process

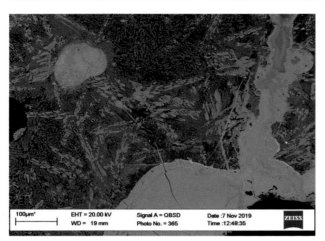

Figure 4.6.21 SEM image of Clachtoll broch SF 186 showing some fayalite laths in an otherwise extensively corroded material

across the wider Iron Age landscape and enable debate on the nature of these unusual specialised sites.

And with these thoughts we return to the Clachtoll assemblage. The absence of any micro-residues from Clachtoll suggests that the slags were generated outside the broch but selected for deposition inside the broch. Given the comments above it is entirely possible that the slag was brought into the broch incidentally alongside turves or other material which could have been spread across the interior space as flooring material. No distributional clustering of ironworking waste was observed during the excavation to suggest that the slags might have been collected and stored as a resource to be utilised at a later date (*e.g.*, collected under the misapprehension that they could be forged due to their iron-rich appearance).

Of course, looking for a practical and pragmatic explanation for the presence of the slags may be the wrong approach. It is possible that the Clachtoll selection and deposition drew on understandings of the significance of these slags as failures or the symbolic connotations of ironworking in general. The symbolism of production has been much-discussed recently with numerous studies suggesting that the symbolic nature of metalworking was as important as the actual object made (*e.g* Hingley 1997; 2006; Giles 2007). Whilst it is plausible that the iron slag from Clachtoll was brought into the household interior as a symbolic gesture it is equally likely that a far more prosaic explanation resulted in its deposition, for example use as building/flooring material. The value in the Clachtoll assemblage lies in the fact that it is rare example of smelting from Middle Iron Age Atlantic Scotland indicating that the inhabitants of the roundhouse had access to, or perhaps even controlled, one of the most important raw materials in the area: iron.

4.7 The coarse stone, pumice and steatite

Dawn McLaren, with lithological identifications by Fiona McGibbon

Introduction

A moderate-sized but wide-ranging assemblage of worked stone, pumice and steatite was recovered during excavation, consisting of 99 individual items. These include a range of food preparation equipment such as rotary querns and a substantial knocking stone, cobble tools produced from locally procured beach cobbles, pumice nodules which were used as abrasives in association with various crafts, as well as a unique and remarkable series of steatite lamps, used to provide light to areas of the broch interior. A further highlight of the assemblage is the large quantity of spindle whorls which attest to textile production and a set of unfinished discs which demonstrate that the whorls were being manufactured on site. Contextual analysis suggests that some of these objects and the associated activities that they represent were in use or in storage within the upper levels of the broch structure which collapsed during the fire which engulfed and destroyed the structure. The assemblage provides valuable insights, not hitherto seen amongst contemporary broch assemblages, into the dating, production and everyday use of items of worked stone in Atlantic Scottish Iron Age assemblages.

In addition to the artefacts recovered during the 2017–18 excavations, a quern stone fragment was found at the broch in 2005 by Euan MacKie and is included in the discussion of the excavated assemblage. Further to this, accounts of the recovery of a steatite cup or lamp found in 1871 are known and will be referred to below.

Catalogue

The catalogue is split into broad functional groups within which typological categories are described and discussed. The discussion section which follows attempts to draw this information together by addressing themes such as resource procurement and manufacture, function, condition and deposition, and to set the assemblage within a broader Atlantic Scottish Iron Age context with reference to contemporary assemblages, specifically those situated in the Western Isles. To aid comparative analysis of the cobble tools, the classification system utilised at the Howe (Ballin Smith 1994, 196) based on wear type, has been followed.

Due to the large quantity of worked stone recovered, particularly the pumice, only a summary catalogue is presented here, whilst a full and detailed catalogue is presented in the archive. Geological identifications by Fiona McGibbon have been incorporated in the catalogue descriptions below but full lithological descriptions based on macroscopic examination are also presented in an archive report. A consideration of the wider implications of resource procurement specific to the talc-rich schist are discussed separately (McGibbon, Section 4.8) and geochemical analysis of a sample of the steatite objects (Jones, Section 4.8) also provides a valuable insight into the possible provenance of this raw material. It is worth noting at the outset that the term 'steatite' has been used as a shorthand throughout this report to describe various talc-rich schist lithologies whilst more precise lithological identification of individual items is presented in the object descriptions.

Abbreviations: L length, W width, T thickness, D diameter, Dpt depth, R remaining dimension. An asterisk beside a number indicates illustrated items.

Food processing and consumption

The querns

A total of eight rotary quern stones were recovered during the 2017 excavations: five disc-quern upper stones with vertical handle sockets, two disc-quern lowers, one of which was unfinished, and fragments of a further disc-quern which lacks distinctive features to allow it to be classified confidently either as an upper or lower stone. A ninth fragmentary quern was recovered prior to the excavation by Euan MacKie during his inspection of the rubble mound in 2005, details of which are included here. It is so heavily damaged it is unclear whether this represents an upper or lower stone.

All of the rotary querns conform to disc-shaped querns; no other type of rotary quern stone (*e.g.*, bun, beehive, etc.) is present amongst the assemblage. Disc-shaped rotary querns are typical for the Atlantic Iron Age (MacKie 1971, 52–5; 1972) and are defined as stones which are thin in proportion to their wide diameter and typically have flat or near flat upper surfaces with D-shaped or vertical edges. The form and quantity of examples found within the broch at Clachtoll is not unexpected, as such querns are common objects to be recovered within broch assemblages in Atlantic Scotland (MacKie 1971). With the exception of a single substantial unfinished lower stone (SF 126), apparently abandoned in the process of manufacture, and the heavily damaged quern fragment found by MacKie, the querns at Clachtoll all display evidence of wear.

UPPER ROTARY QUERN STONES

*SF 125 Upper rotary quern, produced from the convex surface of a garnet and mica-rich biotite schist (?Dalradian) slab or split boulder. Disc-shaped stone is substantially intact but missing a large spall from D-shaped edge (80% circumference

surviving) adjacent to handle sockets. A biconical feeder pipe (max D at upper surface 78 mm, D interior 54 mm, D at grinding face 42 mm) perforates the centre of the stone. Upper face is gently rounded with peckmarks remaining from manufacture. Vertical handle socket has been pecked and gouged 63.5 mm from rounded edge (max D at upper surface 44.5 mm, interior D 30.5 mm), interior surfaces are smoothed and worn at a slight angle from contact with the handle and socket has worn though to the grinding face. A short distance (31 mm) from the edge of this socket is a second shallow (replacement) conical socket with round base (surface D 30 mm, interior D 15.5 mm, Dpt 16 mm). Grinding face appears to exploit a natural layer of quartzite, which is slightly dished towards central feeder, displays signs of extensive use including a concentration of concentric abrasion and polish towards the periphery of the face. Lithology is unlikely to be locally sourced. D 360, T 47.5 mm. Context 062, flooring material in SW quad (same as (049) in the north) (Figs 4.7.1a, 4.7.14).

SF 127 Thick subcircular disc-shaped quern, convex upper surface produced from a slab or split boulder of red Torridonian sandstone with minimal evidence of modification to the shape of the edges which are rounded with some areas of abrasion. Upper surface has been lightly pecked to shape, visible around the vertical handle socket and across *c.* 30% of the surface but dispersed and irregular. At the centre of the face is a circular feeder pipe (max D at upper surface 92.5 mm, inner D 62 mm), pecked on the surface then with clear concentric striations visible on one side of the interior surface, either from boring to shape or from rubbing during use. Worn conical vertical handle socket with smoothed interior, worn though to the grinding surface (Max D at upper surface 51.5 mm, interior D 29 mm, D at grinding face 71 mm. Grinding face evenly pecked (D 4 mm) to dress, well-worn with a band (W 26 mm) of abrasion and polish around periphery of face. Damaged around circumference of handle socket (D 65 × 69 mm), presumably the result of the handle wearing though the thickness of the stone, but the area of damage has been pecked to smooth, presumably to enable the quern to continue in use. L 428, W 401, T 75 mm. Context 067, flooring deposit below midden (047) at the south side of the structure.

*SF 150 Subcircular disc-shaped upper rotary quern produced from Torridonian sandstone. Naturally convex smooth upper face with rounded edges

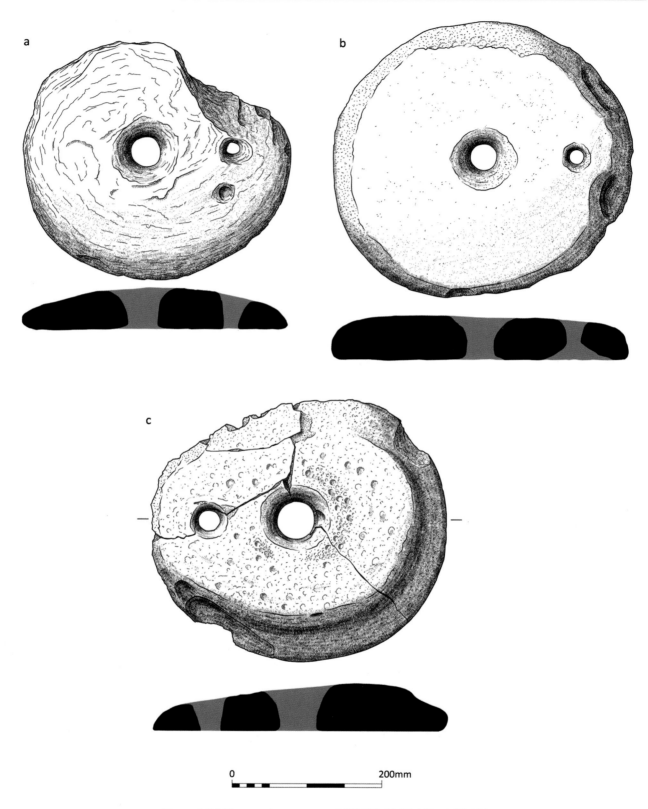

Figure 4.7.1 Upper rotary querns: a) SF 125, b) SF 150, c) SF 194

pecked to shape. Central feeder pipe has been bored and pecked from the upper surface creating wide but shallow conical hole (D 88.5 mm) tapering to a short cylindrical feeder (D 38 mm). Conical vertical handle socket (Max D at surface 37.5 mm, interior D 22.5 mm) placed 64.5 mm from rounded edge, interior is smoothed though wear and is gently angled away from the feeder towards the rounded edge. Socket has worn though to the grinding face causing spalls to detach from the grinding face around the periphery of the handle which has been reworked by pecking to smooth the facet and retain in use. Grinding face is well used with regular pitting from dressing particularly around the periphery of the face associated with areas of smooth from abrasion and polish. L 389, W 375, T 36–53 mm. Context 047, midden deposit (Fig. 4.7.1b).

*SF 192 Approximately 50% of a red Torridonian sandstone disc-shaped upper rotary quern surviving in two rejoining fragments. Only 25% of the original D-shaped rounded edge survives; other areas of the edges are damaged with fresh angular fractured facets. Stone has broken across the central, circular, conical feeder pipe (D 90 mm at upper surface) which tapers in diameter to a short cylindrical pipe (D 50.5 mm). No hopper is present around the central pipe. Concentric striations resulting from manufacture and use are observed in section within the pipe. A vertical conical handle socket (max D 43 mm) has been bored from the upper surface of the quern 59 mm from the rounded edge and has worn though the grinding surface leaving a circular hole (D 10.5 mm) around which the grinding face has been damaged by flakes and chips becoming detached and lost. The grinding face is abraded from use but regularly pitted across the

surface, suggestive of re-dressing; occurred prior to the handle wearing though to the grinding face. Unclear of stone sourced from outcrop or loose drift block due to extent of surface shaping. Original D approx. 378 mm, T 58 mm. Context 082, modern entrance structure (Fig. 4.7.2).

*SF 194 Disc-shaped upper rotary schist quern stone surviving in four joining fragments, a further four small fragments are present but no longer refit. Subcircular in plan rather than truly disc-shaped, irregular cross-section. Well-defined rounded D-shaped edges around *c.* 50% of circumference with a distinct convex bevel or around 40% of the circumference of the grinding face creating a slight lip but this is largely natural and the result of water erosion pre-use. Rounded upper surface is pitted from dressing and from the detachment of dense clasts (spherical garnets?) though weathering. Shallow pitted band (W 33 mm) encircling feeder, poorly defined. Central feeding pipe is a short biconical hollow (max D 88 mm at upper surface, D 61 mm at grinding face, tapers to min D 51 mm), the interior of which preserves distinct gouge and peckmarks from production with metal and stone tools. Wide conical vertical handle socket (D 48 mm at upper surface) has worn though to the thickness of the stone creating a circular hole (D 29 mm) in the grinding face. Grinding face is convex with well-developed wear consisting of concentric abrasion, particularly towards the feeder pipe and handle socket),

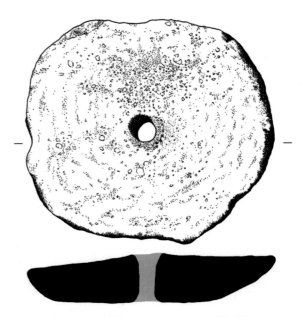

Figure 4.7.2 Upper rotary quern SF 192

Figure 4.7.3 Lower rotary quern SF 208

planed-off garnet clasts and pits where clasts have detached. Band of smoothed abrasion (W 33 mm) around perimeter of grinding face; dished profile indicates use with a lower stone with pronounced dished grinding face. Unlikely lithology to have been sourced in the local area, possibly imported. D 393, T 48.5–64.5 mm. Context 067, flooring deposit below midden (047) at the south side of the structure (Figs 4.7.1c, 4.7.15).

LOWER ROTARY QUERN STONES

SF 126   Large, thick, subcircular disc of coarse grained Torridonian arkosic sandstone, edges gently rounded towards one side whilst the others are vertical as though roughed out but unfinished with two areas of damage to the circumference. An attempt has been made to flatten one face evidenced by numerous large but shallow circular peckmarks dispersed across the face and an off-centre circular concentration of peckmarks forming a shallow dished hollow (D 70.5 × 78.5 mm, Dpt 23 mm). Opposite face also pitted from limited preparatory dressing with a central shallow round-based hollow (D 82.5 × 97 mm, Dpt 19mm), roughly pecked, probably abandoned in the process of trying to perforate the stone. D 481 × 50 mm, T 130–157 mm. Context 062, flooring material in SW quad (same as (049) in the north).

*SF 208   Intact disc-shaped rotary quern produced from coarse grained Torridonian sandstone/conglomerate with central socket which fully perforates the thickness of the stone. The edges are D-shaped in profile but uneven with some area of damage and areas which appear largely unmodified, reflecting the natural shape of the slab used to produce the quern. Central socket is biconical (D (at grinding face) 46.5 mm, D (basal surface) 78.5 mm, min D 39 mm) with distinct pitting from manufacture remaining around the perforation on the basal surface. The grinding face is dished resulting in the area encircling the central socket standing proud but lacks any distinct lip around the periphery of the grinding face. Wear is also evident due to the regular pits across the surface which are the result of natural dense clasts detaching during use. Where similar clasts remain they are planed off though abrasion from use associated with a build-up of polish, which concentrates in a band around the perimeter of the face. Basal surface is convex, undulating and pitted with damage at one area of the rounded edge. D 448 mm, T 55.5–88 mm. Context 078, mixed fill in the 'souterrain' [069] (Fig. 4.7.3).

UNCLASSIFIED ROTARY QUERNS

*SF 193   Fragment of a subcircular disc-shaped quern produced from a silver biotite schist, *c.* 30% of circumference has been lost and approx. 60% of periphery of grinding face is damaged. The surviving edges are irregular and weathered suggests the disc was split from the surface of a natural beach slab or boulder with minimal shaping of edges. Off-centre central circular perforation, pecked or bored from one face (Max D at surface 59 mm, interior D 37 mm, grinding face (sharply defined edges) 34.5 × 27 mm), with a halo of peckmarks (D 42) around feeder on grinding face. Grinding face demonstrates well developed wear in the form of abraded, planed off dense clasts, voids from detached clasts, dispersed peckmarks from dressing and areas of use-polish. No handle socket survives making it unclear if this is an upper or lower stone. Unlikely lithology to have been sourced in the local area, possibly imported. Original D 324, T 13–46 mm. Context 074, burnt remains from the use of the central hearth (Fig. 4.7.16).

*2005   Approx. 45% of circumference of rotary quern of Torridonian Sandstone, broken across central circular perforation, edges severely damaged in places and grinding face lost. One original face survives, being an unmodified surface from a sandstone slab which gently undulates across its surviving length and width; it is unclear if this represents the upper surface of an upper stone (probable) or basal surface of a lower stone. No handle socket remains. The central socket fully perforates the thickness of the stone and can be seen in cross-section to be gently biconical in profile, widest at the upper and lower surfaces (Max D 35.5 mm) and narrowing towards mid-height (Min D 29 mm). Original D min 360, remaining L 346, T 72 mm. Context: found in wall of broch by Euan MacKie 08/08/2005 during examination of unexcavated rubble mound (Fig. 4.7.18).

Knocking stone

A substantial hollowed stone (SF 61) was uncovered set within an intact and *in situ* floor surface (056) within the north-east quadrant of the broch interior (Fig. 4.7.4). Not only does this tool appear to be in its original position, still set within the peat-ash and clay floor that had been built up around it to stabilise it during use, but the large bowl-shaped hollow created in the centre of the upper face was filled with partially processed charred cereal grain providing a snapshot of the activities that were taking place in the broch immediately before the fire engulfed the structure. The stone is a knocking stone, used to dehusk barley (*cf.* Fenton 1978, 396). The barley grains would be placed in the bowl-shaped hollow with a little water and then dehusked with a wooden mallet or mell, similar to that shown in H.B. Curwen's early 20th-century photograph of one in use at Griciegarth, Foula, Shetland (*ibid.*, fig. 190). Part of a stone trough or possible knocking stone was encountered set into the primary broch floor in front of a cell entrance at Crosskirk Broch, Caithness (Fairhurst 1984, 131, no. 452) and similarly, a knocking stone was found embedded in the floor at Galson, Lewis (Edwards 1924, 193, fig. 5). Examples are also known from the brochs at Keiss (Anderson 1901, 127), Nybster (unpublished; NMS: x.GA 680) and Skitten broch (Calder 1948, 138, fig. 5 a, b), Caithness and possible mortars or knocking stones come from Á Cheardach Bheag, Drimore, South Uist (Fairhurst 1971, 100), Ousdale broch, Caithness (Mackay 1892, 354) and Broch of Ayre, Orkney (Graeme 1914, fig. 4), to name a few.

*SF 61 Substantial subrectangular dark grey-green gneiss cobble/boulder, water-rounded and smoothed surfaces suggesting coastal provenance or glacial erratic. Positioned mid-width but off-centre towards one naturally squared end, is a wide and deep (D 270 mm, Dpt 242 mm) conical hollow, the interior carefully pecked to shape, the markings softened and smoothed as the result of use. When discovered, the bowl was filled with charred cereal grain (045) and appears to be *in situ*. L 619 mm, W 534 mm, min T 245 mm. (stone remains *in situ*. Not examined firsthand during analysis). Context 050, set within a solid peat-ash and clay floor surface (056) in NE quad (Fig. 4.7.5).

Household equipment

Lamps

A remarkable set of ten handled steatite cups or lamps (Fig. 4.7.6) were recovered from the broch, the majority of which derive from the burnt deposit (042) which covers the interior area. In addition, a small hemispherical steatite bowl (SF 195) was found. It is sufficiently different in form and size – and therefore, potentially function – to merit individual consideration and is discussed separately below. In published excavation reports these objects are variously described as handled cups and lamps reflecting a long-held ambiguity regarding their potential function or functions. In addition to the assemblage under discussion here, it is worth noting that a small steatite cup was found at Clachtoll in August 1871 (Ordnance Survey Name Book 1848-78, Book 18, 102; CANMORE ID 4501). A further record exists of the discovery of a steatite cup 'found many years ago in a recess of the right-hand guard chamber by the Rev. J.M. Joass of Golspie, in whose possession it still is' (RCAHMS 1911; Canmore ID 4499). It seems likely that the two accounts refer to the same object but this is far from certain.

While the type has a marked concentration in Aberdeenshire (Ralston and Inglis 1984), there are numerous examples from Atlantic sites of Iron Age date

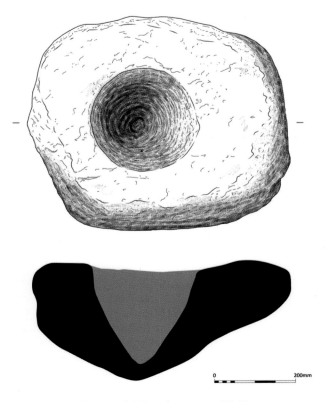

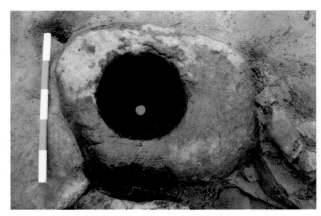

Figure 4.7.4 Knocking stone in-situ

Figure 4.7.5 Knocking stone SF 61

(Close-Brooks 1972; Sharples 1998) and small numbers of examples are known from Ireland and the Isle of Man (Steer 1956, 244). Callander's early study of 'cups of stone with short handles' (1916) noted that they were frequently perforated for suspension by a thong and interpreted their function as drinking cups, 'not to be confused with hollowed stones of less regular shape without handles, which belong to the same period, and seem to have been used as lamps' (*ibid.*, 146–7). Steer's later study (1956) observed their potential use as eating or drinking vessels, representing stone skeuomorphs of contemporary wooden cups and ladles (*e.g.*, Lochlee Crannog; Munro 1882, figs 102 and 104) but also presented an alternative explanation of their function as lamps, as suggested by examples such as that from Nybster broch, Caithness which were blackened by soot and smoke (Steer 1956, 246). Following the latter interpretation, the bowl of the lamp would have been filled with fuel, perhaps an oil, on which a wick would have floated. Steer observed that very few of those examined with National Museum of Antiquities of Scotland (abbreviated here to NMAS, now National Museums Scotland (NMS)) collections were sooted leading to the conclusion that they were principally designed as drinking or eating cups but, in some instances, saw secondary use as lamps. Later comment by Stevenson (1966, 28 and note 67) considered the function of these vessels further, contradicting Steer's observations on the presence of sooting, and confirming that a large proportion of those examined at NMAS did indeed display signs of burning or sooting around the rim. Close-Brooks (1972, 297) later remarked that irrespective of demonstrable signs of heat damage or burning on individual examples, the use of these handled cups as lamps 'is still the most likely interpretation of their function'.

Although the frequent recovery of these handled objects from brochs suggests a broad date range from the last few centuries BC to the early centuries AD (Ralston and Inglis 1984) the stratified example from Scalloway, Shetland demonstrates that the type continued in use until at least the second half of the 1st millennium AD (Sharples 1998, 205). In each instance, these lamps (as they will henceforth be referred to) consist of hemispherical bowls of assorted sizes, depths and shapes, with a short integral handle projecting from one area of the rim or body. At Clachtoll, the handled lamps have all been formed from talc-rich schist, commonly referred to as steatite or soapstone, although examples of schist and sandstone are known elsewhere such as from Dun Telve, Glenelg (Curle 1916) and West Plean, Stirlingshire (Steer 1956), and in some instances, steatite and sandstone (handled and unhandled) examples are found together, such as at Kettleburn and Everley brochs, Caithness (Anon 1892, 237; Anderson 1901; Heald in prep), Clickhimin

wheelhouse, Shetland (Hamilton 1968, 135, fig. 59, pl. xxxii a and b), Fairy Knowe, Buchlyvie, Fife (Clarke 1998, 379) and Carlungie I Souterrain, Angus (Wainwright 1963, 142, nos. 131 and 132), *inter alia*. These handled lamps of steatite and occasional examples in other stones are more complex and accomplished in design and execution than the simple sooted hollowed stones often found in Iron Age settlement contexts such as those from Crosskirk broch, Caithness or Á Cheardach Mhor, South Uist (Young and Richardson 1960). They also differ significantly from the simple crudely hewn stone lamps with asymmetric figure-of-eight hollows in the upper surface, thought to form separate recesses for the fuel and the wick, such as those known from Broch of Kettleburn, Caithness, or Okstrow Broch, Orkney (Anderson 1878, 330–1, figs 1 and 2).

The predominance of the use of steatite examples at Clachtoll is expected based on ready access to local outcrops and is reflective of a national pattern where steatite is the preferred material (due to the ease at which it can be carved but also for its attractive colouration and refractory properties which would allow it to withstand the heat from the flame without cracking) with smaller numbers of sandstone and schist examples known (Steer 1956, 244).

Although steatite and other stone lamps, some handled and some without, are frequently recovered from Iron Age sites across Scotland and are regularly encountered in association with brochs, this group of lamps from Clachtoll is remarkable for several reasons: firstly, the quantity from a single site is unparalleled; secondly, most display evidence of use in the form of sooting, staining and heat discolouration, dispelling any ambiguity of their use as lamps; thirdly, variations in the stone itself could suggest either exploitation of a heterogeneous outcrop or a variety of sources; and finally, the lamps themselves comprise a diverse group in terms of form, size, capacity and decoration.

Aspects of the form, size, condition and function of the lamps is considered further below with reference to lithological studies conducted by Fiona McGibbon (Section 4.8, below); rare earth element (REE) analysis undertaken by Richard Jones (Section 4.8, below) and organic residue analysis from samples recovered from the interior of the bowls by Toby Gillard, Julie Dunne and Richard Evershed (Section 4.3, above).

*SF 27   Well-made and carefully finished small and compact hemispherical tremolite talc-schist bowl with short projecting handle; broken in half across the circular hollow but rejoined during conservation. The hollow is circular and deep (D 64.6–65.7 mm, Dpt 32.4 mm) with steeply sloping interior surfaces and gently rounded base, smoothed and well-finished and stained from

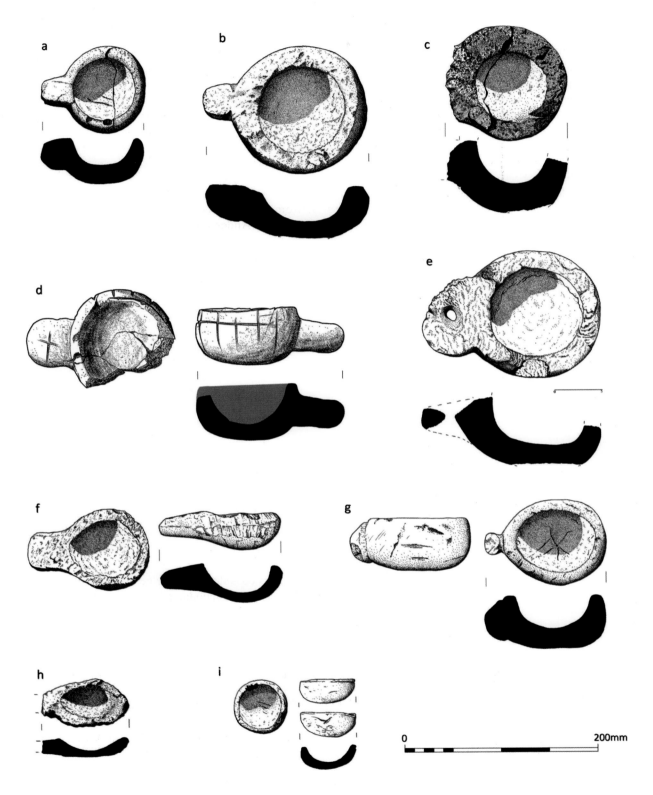

Figure 4.7.6 Steatite lamps and miniature bowl: a) SF 27, b) SF 36, c) SF 59, d) SF 66, e) SF 70, f) SF 95, g) SF 106, h) SF 163, i) SF 195

use. Hollow is surrounded by a narrow plain rounded rim (W 9.5–13 mm), damaged in two areas adjacent to the break. The exterior surfaces are smooth and rounded and carefully finished as is the gently rounded base. Projecting from one end, parallel with the rim, with no shoulder or junction, is a short subrectangular handle (L (from interior of hollow) 31.2 mm, L (projecting beyond rim) 25 mm). The handle gently tapers in width and thickness along its length (W 22.3–33 mm, T 25.3–32.2 mm) terminating in a bipartite tip, damaged at the extreme tip toward one rounded corner. The basal surface of the handle slopes strongly towards base, forming a steeply angled junction with the lower body of the exterior of the bowl. L 106.5 mm, H 46.8 mm. Wgt 305.6 g. Context 042, burnt deposit across entire broch interior (Fig. 4.7.6a).

*SF 36   Shallow circular hemispherical amphibole-talc-schist lamp with intact handle protruding from one edge. The exterior of the bowl (D 140.2–142 mm) is gently rounded with smooth and carefully finished surfaces and a gently rounded but stable base. A wide centrally placed circular hollow has been produced (D 96.5 × 98.5 mm, Dpt 21.5–35.5 mm) with strongly concave edges and a shallow round base and is surrounded by a thick, plain, rim (T 24–27 mm) flattened around much of the circumference becoming slightly thicker (T 27–29.2 mm) on either side of the projecting handle, damaged adjacent to the handle and towards the centre of opposing edges. The handle (L (from interior edge of hollow) 61.8 mm, L (projecting beyond rim) 35.6 mm) is squat, sub-square in plan tapering gently in width from the junction with the bowl (W 43.3 mm) to the blunt rounded tip (W 30.5 mm), flat on the top and rounded on the bottom surface (T 37 mm). Right-angled corners formed between external edge of rim of bowl and long edges of the handle are marked by neat triangular notches (L 11 mm, W 9 mm). Faint vertical gouge marks visible around the inner surface of the rim and peckmarks observed across surfaces implying production with both metal and stone tools. All surfaces, including the stable rounded base and interior of hollow, smoothed and softened by abrasion to finish. L 177 mm, H 43–59.5 mm. Wgt 1438.1 g. Context 042, burnt deposit across entire broch interior (Fig. 4.7.6b).

*SF 59   Substantial portion of the hemispherical bowl of a lamp produced from an antigorite-chlorite-talc schist, very friable, surviving in two rejoined fragments, split across the bowl; a third small fragment derives from the stub of a handle, no longer joining. 80% of the plain rounded rim has been lost and a scar remains on one rounded edge confirming the former presence of a projecting handle, now lost. The exterior of the bowl (D (exterior) 120–122 mm) is plain with smooth rounded edges curving gently to a smooth, gently rounded base, damaged towards to fore, perhaps from impact, resulting in the loss of a large circular spall (D 62–65 mm); sooting survives throughout. Where the rim survives, it is thick and plain, and is markedly thicker on one side of the bowl than the other (T 21–29 mm), particularly towards where the handle would have formerly projected. The narrow circular dished hollow (D 78 mm, Dpt 38 mm) has steeply sloping sides which narrow to a distinctly rounded base which is stained from use. Only one small fragment from the core of the handle survives (submitted for XRF analysis). From the scar that remains on the edge of the bowl (W 56.3 mm, H 33 mm), it appears to have been wide and thick, projecting from the upper surface of the bowl without any shoulder and extends only halfway down the exterior of the bowl. Remaining L 141 mm, H 57.3 mm. Wgt 991.9 g. Context 042, burnt deposit across entire broch interior (Fig. 4.7.6c).

SF 60   Wedge-shaped fragment from the base and lower body of a hemispherical or ovoid lamp produced from talc-schist. Less than 20% of the bowl survives making it impossible to determine the lamps original form with confidence. Lower body appears thick-walled (T 26.2 mm) and fairly steep-sided, upper body and rim lost, interior of hollow curves gently to a flat base which is very thin (T 11.5 mm) towards the centre. Remaining radius (from exterior to approx. centre of interior bowl) 71.5, estimated original D *c.* 142 mm, remaining H 44.5 mm. Wgt 277.9 g. Context 042, burnt deposit across entire broch interior.

SF 65   Fourteen angular and fractured small fragments of a hemispherical or ovoid lamp produced from talc-schist. Less than 33% of the lamp survives comprising non-joining fragments from the base, body and rim, a fragment of the latter preserving the scar from which a handle (min H 20 mm, positioned 17 mm from tip of rim) would once have projected. Exterior of base has been flattened (min T 17.2 mm), the sides gently expanding (max T 27.3 mm) and curving upwards to a pronounced rounded body, exterior surfaces smoothed with no obvious tool marks surviving. The rim is plain (T 14 mm) and slightly inturned. The base of the hollow survives suggesting a fairly wide (min Diam 73.4 mm), shallow bowl.

Min exterior Diam 221 mm, min H 72.5 mm. Wgt 683.7 g. Context 042, burnt deposit across entire broch interior.

*SF 66 Hemispherical bowl-shaped lamp of talc schist with projecting thick lug-shaped handle, broken and degraded across the bowl, surviving in nine rejoined fragments (a further 7 chips were recovered but no longer rejoin); the rim has been lost from one edge with only 60% of the circumference surviving. The bowl is hemispherical in shape with smoothed and rounded exterior surface (D 113.4–115 mm) decorated below the rim with two transverse concentric incised grooves, one (W 2.2 mm) immediately below the rim and c. 8 mm below this, a second groove (W 1.7 mm), slightly less carefully executed. From the upper of the two grooves, extending down the body of the bowl and cutting though the second transverse groove are a series of vertical linear grooves, widely but regularly spaced (ave. 18 mm), which extend down towards the base where they each fade out. This decoration overlies faint diagonal tool marks (fine gouge or chisel) from manufacture, particularly to one side of the projecting handle. The hollow is wide and deep (D 85.3–87 mm, Dpt 50.6 mm) with a smooth rounded base, stained across 50% of the interior; distinct vertical tool marks (W 1.5 mm) present towards the handle from manufacture which has collected soot from use. The rim is narrow (T 6.5–8.7 mm) and slightly inturned. Projecting from one end of the bowl is a short sub-square handle (L (from interior edge of hollow) 69 mm, L (from exterior of rim) 54.5 mm), positioned off-centre with a distinct shoulder (H 5.6 mm) between the tip of the rim and the upper surface of the handle. The long edges of the handle gently contract to form a waisted profile (W 49 mm), terminating in a wide blunt rounded tip (W 51.5 mm) but remaining consistent in thickness along length (T 32.7 mm). The top of handle is decorated with a criss-cross or saltire design produced by two overlapping linear gouges (L 32–34 mm, W 1.2–1.5 mm). The basal surface is smooth and rounded. L 152.4 mm, H 64.5 mm. Wgt 722.4 g. Context 042, burnt deposit across entire broch interior (Fig. 4.7.6d).

*SF 70 Substantially intact shallow hemispherical bowl of coarse-grained talc schist with projecting subrectangular handle with rounded corners, perforated towards the centre and badly degraded at one edge leading to the loss of one corner of the handle; steatite is very friable resulting in lamination and loss of flakes of stone, particularly from the rim and handle. Significant concentric cracking on the interior of the bowl under the rim, concentrated towards one side only. Bowl has D-shaped smoothed exterior surfaces and the base is damaged resulting in spalls detaching from the centre of the basal surface. The interior of the bowl (D 98.6 × 100 mm, Dpt 33.4–38 mm) has steeply sloping sides with a gently concave, almost flat bottom which has been carefully smoothed to create an even surface with no visible tool marks apart from fine striations from abrasion to finish. Surrounding the bowl is a plain thick rim (T c. 19.4–20.5 mm), thinning in places due to post-depositional damage and expanding (T 22.5 mm) on either side of the integral projecting handle. The handle is subrectangular (remaining W 87 mm, L (from bowl interior) 73.5 mm, W (projecting beyond rim) 54.3 mm, T 18.5–37.5 mm) with one rounded short edge surviving, terminating in a blunt squared end with rounded corner; the opposite edge is largely lost due to the friability of the stone. An asymmetric oval perforation (D 11 × 12.6 mm) pierces the handle vertically, its uneven form the result of the upper surface of much of the handle. At the junction with the bowl, the beginning of the handle contracts in width slightly to produce a more rounded appearance. A decorated lamp with a similar handle is known from Farleyer Moor, north of Aberfeldy (Close-Brooks 1972, 296, fig. 4). L 191 mm, bowl (exterior) D 139.4–144.5 mm, max H 74.6 mm. Wgt 1468.9 g Context 042, burnt deposit across entire broch interior (Fig. 4.7.6e).

*SF 95 Small, shallow hemispherical talc-schist bowl with a subrectangular handle projecting from one end. The bowl is circular in plan with a plain narrow rim (T 10.7–12 mm), damaged around 60% of the circumference, with D-shaped rounded edges which are marked with a minimum of three transverse concentric (often overlapping) rows of ? knife cut facets (ave. W 10 mm) and vertical gouge marks (W 2 mm) from manufacture or reshaping. Unlike the interior of the hollow, basal surface and handle, there has been no attempt to smooth or finish the exterior of the bowl. The interior of the bowl is a wide subcircular hollow (D 61 × 72.8 mm, Dpt 30.9 mm), surfaces smoothed but with tool marks remaining. The handle, which is subrectangular in shape (L (from interior edge of bowl) 42.2 mm, W 31.6–43.5 mm, T 12.2–28.5 mm) with parallel straight edges, blunt squared end with rounded corners, sits marginally higher (5.5 mm) the rim, whilst the pitted rounded base slopes strongly upwards to form the bottom of the handle with no shoulder or junction. L 126.3 mm, bowl (exterior) D 86–89 mm, H (at bowl) 37 mm, (at junction between bowl and handle) 40 mm. Wgt 334.6 g. Context 042, burnt deposit across entire broch interior (Fig. 4.7.6f).

*SF 106 Small ovoid bowl of talc schist with vertical rounded edges, small but deep central hollow (D 65 × 83 mm, Dpt 38 mm), plain rounded rim (T 11–13.8 mm) and short, vertical handle projecting from the apex of one narrow rounded end. The handle is narrow (W 23 mm) and short, projecting only 19 mm beyond the edge of the rim, but has a thick 'hogbacked' vertical profile (H 42.5) which extends almost the full height of the bowl. A distinct narrow groove (4–6.5 mm) runs around the circumference of the handle creating a distinct channel between it and the bowl, perhaps to facilitate a binding. Immediately flanking the handle on one near vertical edge are a series of fine linear gouge marks, vertical in orientation, remaining from manufacture and several dispersed shallow grooves are noted on and below the rim in the interior of the bowl. The centre of the interior of the bowl is damaged, from which radiate hairline cracks, perhaps from impact from below. Some damage noted on the base; although not completely flat, the base is stable. A series of three deep and fresh transverse gouges are present on the exterior of the bowl on one side (L 20.2–24 mm, W 3.8–5.5, Dpt 1.5–2.3 mm). On excavation the bowl was infilled with charcoal-stained soils which were removed during conservation to reveal a stained, slightly sooted interior surface. A similar but much smaller lamp to this comes from Kirkhill, west of Inverness (Close-Brooks 1972, 295, fig. 3) and one made of sandstone with a similar lug-shaped handle is known from West Plean, Stirlingshire (Steer 1956, pl. xviii: 1). L 126.2 mm, bowl (exterior) D 102.2 × 91 mm, H 56 mm. Wgt 666.3 g. Context 048, floor deposit composed of concentrated peat-ash (Fig. 4.7.6g).

*SF 163 Small elongated ovoid shallow lamp of talc schist with projecting subrectangular handle (W 26 mm, T 13.5 mm), the tip of which is broken and the original length is unknown. The base of the lamp is convex but quite irregular with no evidence of attempts to smooth or finish; the upper surface has a shallow oval hollow (58.5 × 33–34 mm) curved into the centre of the upper surface with a plain rim (T 7–10 mm) which is damaged towards the rounded tip, at the opposing end to the handle. Shallow concentric abrasion and pitting is present on the interior of the hollow from production but no discolouration or residue noted from use. L 90.5 mm,

W 50 mm, H 17.5–18.5 mm. Wgt 98.8 g. Context 048, floor deposit composed of concentrated peat-ash (Fig. 4.7.6h).

Miniature hemispherical bowl

In addition to the handled bowls already described, is a small unhandled hemispherical bowl produced from talc-schist. Its plain appearance, augmented only by an incomplete and slightly haphazard incised line below the rim on the exterior surface, and the similarity of the colouration of the steatite used to produce the bowl is reminiscent of the lamps just described but here there is no strong indication of function. A similar small hemispherical steatite bowl, with external surfaces bearing two horizontal zones of knife paring marks remaining from production was recovered from a Viking-age midden at Jarlshof, Shetland (Hamilton 1956, 141, pl. XXXI, 2) where the bowl is thought to be a Norwegian import. The date and provenance of the Jarlshof bowl are not considered to be relevant to the Clachtoll example.

*SF 195 Small hemispherical talc-schist bowl. Distinctly rounded base (D 44 × 46 mm, dpt 19.5 mm), interior as scratches/tool marks but these are currently obscured by residual soil. Plain rim (T 5 mm), rounded in parts but damaged in two opposing areas in antiquity. Body (T 9–10 mm) is even and smoothed on both exterior and interior surfaces. Narrow, slightly haphazard V-sectioned line incised below rim on exterior surface around *c.* 45% of the circumference, varies in thickness and depth (W 0.5–1 mm). Ext Rim D 55.5–56.5 mm, H 24.3 mm. Wgt 84.5 g. Context 078, mixed fill in the 'souterrain' [069] (Fig. 4.7.6i).

Weight

A single large, perforated cobble (SF 20, Fig. 4.7.7) of a silver-grey mica-schist was recovered from a layer of windblown sand (028) overlying the rubble of the collapsed broch. Its surfaces are sooted and heat-discoloured in patches suggesting it was exposed to intense heat during the fire. Perforated stones of various shapes and sizes are common components of broch assemblages and could have fulfilled a range of functions such as net-, thatch- or loom weights. The wear around the perforation is pronounced and asymmetrical, concentrating towards the narrowest edge of the stone, which is worn so thin that it is at risk of breaking. The level of wear and its concentration in such a discrete area of the perforation suggests it hung on a narrow suspension that was regularly moved, causing significant softening and shedding of the stone at the point of suspension. Its recovery above or amongst the collapsed rubble of the broch would more readily fit a thatch-weight or similar to hold down roofing materials but it may be some form of counterweight related to an internal hatchway or shutter, lost to the fire. Simple, functional weights such as these are common finds on Iron Age and later sites, including a cache at Jarlshof, Shetland (Hamilton 1956, 183) and individual examples from Everley, (Heald forthcoming) and Crosskirk broch (Fairhurst 1984, 132), for example.

*SF 20 Large flattened ovoid silver-grey mica-schist cobble, surfaces smooth and water-rounded with a naturally wide rounded end tapering along the length towards a slightly narrower blunt rounded tip. Bored from the flatter of the two faces, mid-length along one long straight edge and only 15 mm from the edge is a wide conical perforation (D at surface 68 × 65 mm, D at opposite face 34 mm) and there is extensive wear and thinning of the stone towards this edge in the form of a smooth worn facet which extends from the interior of the perforation (W 6 × 12.5 mm, edge T 12.5 mm) across and around the narrow strip of stone surviving on this edge perhaps from being rubbed against the surface of a rope. Light discolouration on one face from heat damage. Cobble has drift-sourced appearance but is an unlikely lithology in the area. May be imported stone. L 236 mm, W 177 mm, T 62.5 mm. Context 028, deposit of windblown sand/organic growth overlying (042) and underlying rubble (011) (Fig. 4.7.7).

Tools

Cobble tools

The number of cobble tools (Fig. 4.7.8) recovered from the broch is not large (Q=17). This is unusual as cobble tools are often found in large quantities and frequently dominate worked stone assemblages recovered during modern excavations undertaken on Iron Age complex roundhouse structures in Atlantic Scotland (*e.g.*, Crosskirk Broch, Caithness; Fairhurst 1984). This group of tools, which encompass stones with a variety of distinctive wear traces which are understood to reflect a range of functions, form a significant component of most Iron Age stone tool assemblages (Clarke 2006, 1). At Clachtoll, as elsewhere, such cobble tools have been produced from locally-sourced water-rounded pebbles and cobbles and typically display little or no modification prior to use.

In the past, cobble tools were often described simply as 'hammerstones' (*e.g.*, see Á Cheardach Mhor, Drimore, South Uist: Young and Richardson 1960). These hand-held tools were recognised as prosaic, everyday tools and were rarely considered to be of any value in terms of understanding site function or chronology. It was typical for such artefacts to be subject to cursory examination only and to be briefly mentioned within wider excavation reports. Yet recent detailed analysis of the wear patterns present on such stones indicates that a range of use-wear can be identified (including abrasion, smoothing, rubbing, pounding, fracturing as the result of heavy percussion damage, polish, staining and adhering residue) indicating that the generic term 'hammerstone' masks a wide range of distinct functions. The classification of tool types at Clachtoll has been based on the nature of the wear, following the scheme used in the Howe report (Ballin Smith 1994, 196). It should be noted, however, that this approach describes wear rather than function and is complicated by the fact that different stone types will wear differently due to their varying properties. In addition, many tools display combinations of wear patterns indicating a range of functions. These multifunction tools are discussed after consideration of single-function tools.

Hammerstone

A single hammerstone (SF 146) was recognised by the presence of severe pitting and fracturing at both ends indicative of percussive damage with fairly vigorous physical force. Its small size and light weight, however, is not suggestive of heavy-duty use.

SF 146 Flattened subrectangular fine Torridonian sandstone pebble, water-rounded smooth surfaces throughout. Struck on two opposing corners of the same face resulting in wedge-shaped spalls from each contact point to detach and are now lost. Fracture surfaces very fresh but soiled. Opposite face and adjacent edge have patches of dark brow residue adhering. L 78 mm, W 51 mm, T 23.5 mm. Unstratified.

Pounder (see also SF 214)

These tools have pitted and pecked wear formed as the result of pounding to crush or pulverise various materials. Past interpretations of their significance were often based on the assumption that these tools were used exclusively for food processing but they could have been used to prepare a variety of material types and are not necessarily associated to the preparation or consumption of foodstuffs, without precluding this function.

SF 97 Subspherical ?pink techtonised granitoid or quartzite cobble. Surfaces pitted from erosion and uneven in patches, potentially due to leaching from peat. Concentration of surface damage (17 × 27 mm, 25.5 × 46.5 mm) on two opposite

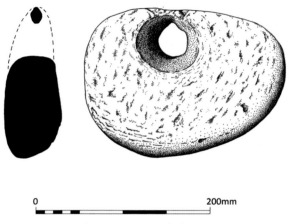

Figure 4.7.7 Weight SF 20

Figure 4.7.8 Selection of cobble tools

convex faces. Difficult to determine whether this is the result of use or natural/incidental damage. L 75 mm, W 65.5 mm, T 62 mm. Context 042, burnt deposit across entire broch interior.

SMOOTHERS (SEE ALSO SF 28 AND SF 257, POSSIBLY SF 309)

Smoothing stones and often whetstones display surface smoothing and staining as the result of use. They are differentiated here by the concavity of the surface as an indication of whetting and by the presence of dark red-brown residue which is typical of those with convex wear formed as the result of rubbing. This follows the criteria adopted at Dunadd, where large numbers of smoothing stones/burnishers were found (Lane and Campbell 2000, 178, 179, 185) and have been interpreted as hide processing tools due to the presence of organic staining from animal fat.

Five probable smoothers have been recognised at Clachtoll, with a further single example represented amongst the combination tools. With such a small group, teasing out broader patterns of use or the mechanisms for the selection of the raw materials to be used as tools is not clear. Both quartzite and sandstone cobbles have been used and a variety of shapes selected including flattened ovoid, ovoid and subrectangular. Traces of wear amongst this group typically concentrate in bands along the long edge of one naturally smooth and often convex face but in instances like (SF 07), wear can be more dispersed, covering more than one surface. Two of the smoothers amongst this group are fire-cracked. Both (SF 08 and SF 304) were recovered from burnt layers affected by the fire suggesting the heat damage in evidence on these examples was not a result of its principal use or secondary use as pot-boilers. The heat-damage on SF 08 makes it difficult to classify its use with confidence. Although consistent

with use as a smoother, a possible function as a rubbing stone for grinding grain is not out of the question.

*SF 07   Flattened ovoid quartzite cobble, both faces smoothed and lightly abraded though rubbing, corresponding with patches of dark staining and high sheen. This staining and sheen cover most of one extensive convex face, extending onto two opposing round edges; the opposite face has a distinct linear band (W 32 mm) of residue across centre of the short axis of the face. L 88.5 mm, W 77.5 mm, T 35 mm. Wgt 359.2 g. Context 028, deposit of windblown sand/organic growth overlying (042) and underlying rubble (011) (Figs 4.7.8 and 4.7.9a).

SF 08   Flattened ovoid water-rounded red Torridonian sandstone cobble, convex/concave in cross-section with naturally rounded ends and edges. Concave face is smoothed with a well-developed sheen from use consistent with a smoother or rubbing stone but unusual in that it is associated with a convex surface. One rounded end and centre of adjacent rounded edge is pitted and chipped resulting in heat damage which has also caused discolouration and hairline fracturing of surfaces. L 161 mm, W 86.5 mm, T 48 mm. Wgt 1055.4 g. Context 028, deposit of windblown sand/organic growth overlying (042) and underlying rubble (011).

SF 225b Ovoid quartzite-rich water-rounded cobble, smooth and even surfaces and naturally rounded ends, plano-convex in cross-section. Surfaces are covered in distinct patches of dark red-brown and brown-black staining, probably from handling. There is a narrow band of red-brown residue (interrupted) which runs around the periphery of the stone, adjacent to the flat smooth face and this face is covered in staining, concentrating towards the centre. Little modification to the stone itself but patterns of staining is suggestive of use as a smoother. L 111.5 mm, W 63.2 mm, T 43 mm. Wgt 247.2 g. Context 082, modern entrance structure.

SF 258 Subrectangular water-rounded fine Torridonian sandstone cobble, plano-convex in section with naturally smooth rounded surfaces, one long convex edge and opposite naturally straight and vertical edge. This vertical edge is stained and has a light sheen that may relate to use from rubbing against a smooth surface. The apex of the convex face and centre of flat face is also smoothed and lightly polished from use. L 83.5 mm, W 58 mm, T 37 mm. Wgt 284.7 g. Context 163, organic material mixed with wind-blown sand overlying bedrock.

SF 304 Fire-cracked angular spall detached from the rounded edge of a water-rounded quartzite-rich sandstone cobble. Two incomplete oval areas (20 × 7.5 mm, 15 × 34.5 mm) of red-brown staining and residue from use are present on the surviving surface. Between the two areas of staining is a band of polish (W 10.5 mm) suggesting use as a smoother/polisher. Remaining L 50 mm, W 30.5 mm, T 10 mm. (Extracted from animal bone SF 137.) Wgt 22.6 g. Context 042, burnt deposit across entire broch interior.

Burnishers

At Clachtoll, a small number of tools categorised as polishers or burnishers have been identified. The wear is typically confined to the extensive smooth faces or the tips of rounded cobbles and these tend to display smoothed and highly polished rubbed facets which are often convex or flattened in plan. These are distinguished from smoothers due to the general lack of dark staining and residue, and due to the high polish that has developed as the result of use. It is unclear what type of materials these tools were used to polish but their concentration in a single area and deposit (context 082) suggests concentrated activity.

SF 236a Small plano-convex ovoid pebble of Torridonian sandstone, water-rounded surfaces. Flat smooth face is polished and smoothed from rubbing. L 35 mm, W 28 mm, T 14.5 mm. Wgt 21.5 g. Context 082, modern entrance structure.

SF 236b Small plano-convex ovoid pebble of Torridonian sandstone with water smoothed surfaces with a light sheen at apex of convex face. L 33 mm, W 30.5 mm, T 14 mm. Wgt 21.6 g. Context 082, modern entrance structure.

SF 303 Flattened ovoid ?granite pebble, water-rounded with formerly smooth surfaces, now irregularly pitted as the result of heat-damage and spalling around mica-rich clasts. This pitting cuts though a smoothed and polished surface which retains a distinct sheen and surface lustre, particularly on one face. L 56.5 mm, W 50.5 mm, T 15 mm. Wgt 71.2 g. Context 082, modern entrance structure. Extracted from faunal remains SF 259.

Strike-a-light (see also possible example SF 309)
Two single-function strike-a-lights (SF 71 and SF 94), were recognised amongst the assemblage (Fig. 4.7.17). These are of a specific type of strike-a-light known as 'tracked stones', which were noted initially by Anderson (1883) with regards to Scottish examples and later Knowles (1889, 497) in discussing Irish finds and defined by Childe as 'natural quartz pebbles, bearing on one or both faces a sharp groove in which traces of a rusty brown powder are often observable' (1936, 233, pl. XLIV). Anderson (1883) initially suggested that the sharp longitudinal grooves on the faces of these stones were used to sharpen bone pins but this was later refuted by Childe who suggested that the V-shaped profile of these score marks implied an alternative function (Childe 1936, 233). Drawing on references to similar Danish and Scandinavian examples, some of which have been found associated with the fire-lighting kits, lead him to conclude that tracked stones were a particular form of strike-a-light (*ibid.*); the longitudinal grooves and associated dark red-brown powder or surface staining the result of repeated scraping or striking with an iron fire-steel or pyrite. These differ from more common types of strike-a-light whose surfaces are marked by sets of fine linear red-brown striations (*e.g.*, Bac Mhic Connain, North Uist (Beveridge and Callander 1932, 49), Broch of Burrian (MacGregor 1974, 93), Gurness (Hedges 1987, 152, 249)) and where a distinctive scored or rubbed groove is absent. During his consideration of this artefact type in Scotland, Childe lists all Scottish examples of tracked stones known at the time of the study which demonstrate an Atlantic Scottish distribution which concentrates in Orkney Islands, the northern highlands (Caithness and Sutherland), Western Isles and Argyll and Galloway with far fewer numbers being found from the southern and eastern mainland (Childe 1936, 236, fig. 1). The corpus of known examples has expanded exponentially since Childe's consideration but the pattern of distribution he noted in 1936 still broadly holds true with numbers concentrating in the north and west of the country. Within the category of tracked stones, Childe also noted a progression over time from simple unmodified pebbles whose working was confined to the sharp linear groove on one or two faces to a more carefully produced, deliberately shaped 'shuttle-shaped' stone with flattened faces and signs of working around the sides to facilitate suspension from a belt when not in use (*ibid.*, 233).

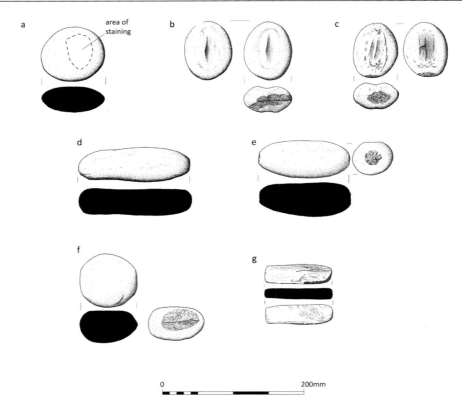

Figure 4.7.9 Cobble Tools: a) smoother SF 07, b) strike-a-light SF 71, c) strike-a-light SF 94; combination tools d) SF 28, e) SF 214, f) SF 257; g) whetstone SF 93

The tracked stones from Clachtoll are both simple examples of this type but both display traces of use-wear from other functions in addition to the distinct grooves that have been scored into the surfaces. Example SF 94 which was recovered from (047) midden deposit has been formed on a water-rounded quartzite pebble with both ends displaying evidence of use as a small pounder and one face has not one but two distinctive grooves cross-cutting the extensive concave face; the concavity of the face being a feature noted on many Irish examples (Knowles 1889, 498). The second tool, SF 71, is more extensively worked with areas of facetted abrasion at both ends, resembling more the 'shuttle-shaped' stones noted by Childe (1936), and both extensive faces appear to have been smoothed in addition to the longitudinal scores being worked into the centre of the faces. The entire surface of this cobble is stained a bright red brown, probably from handling in contact with iron-rich powder produced during use. It was recovered from the burnt layer (042) which covered the broch interior, suggesting that the tool may have been used or stored in the brochs upper levels. Both tools display extensive signs of wear implying that they may have saw regular if not daily use. Similar examples, usually found in ones and twos, are known from broch sites such as The Howe (Ballin Smith 1994, 202, 204, illus. 109: 4321), Dun an Iardhard,

Skye (MacLeod 1915, 67); Garry Iochdrach and Bac Mhic Connain, North Uist (Beveridge and Callander 1932, 41, 49) whilst at Dun Beag, Skye eight examples were recovered, one accompanied by signs of use as a hammerstone (Callander 1921, 121). Although it is not always possible from the original published account to differentiate between forms consistent with Childe's 'Tracked Stones' and those showing signs of more prosaic and expedient use as a strike-a-light but there are accounts that confirm that in occasional circumstances, both forms are found together, such as at Bac Mhic Connain, North Uist (Beveridge and Callander 1932, 49).

*SF 71   Flattened ovoid quartzite cobble, each rounded end has an off-set pair of oval abrasion facets (28 × 15 mm; 25.5 × 5 mm) at the tip; each of the facets is at an obtuse angle indicating prevalence of use towards one face (reflecting the idiosyncrasy of use). Both faces are smoothed and flattened from rubbing and are scored longitudinally at the centre of the face with a wide V-shaped groove (L 45 mm, W 3.5 mm, Dpt 3 mm; L 42 mm, W 4.5 mm, Dpt 2 mm), the interior of which is smoothed and abraded. Area surrounding groove on both faces are stained red-brown associated with a light sheen which

extends onto and concentrates in patches of polish towards the rounded edges. Tiny spalls of ferrous-rich residue adhere to both rounded ends of the stone and on one convex face. L 84 mm, W 38 mm, T 37.5 mm. Wgt 329.2 g. Context 042, burnt deposit across entire broch interior (Fig. 4.7.9b).

*SF 94 Flattened ovoid water-rounded quartzite cobble, one rounded end flattened from use as a pounder (22 × 30 mm); opposite end is also pitted from similar use but wear is more dispersed and more poorly developed. The centre of both oval faces are heavily dished along the long-axis at the centre of each are concentrations of linear abrasions. One face has a single wide linear hollow (max L 14 mm, W 4 mm, Dpt 2.5 mm), u-shaped in cross-section as the result of repeated episodes of concentrated abrasion accompanied by a light sheen and red-brown staining. At each end of the hollow are small shallow pits. Opposite face has two similar linear grooves, side-by-side (ave. L 41 mm, W 3 mm, Dpt 1.5 mm), also corresponding with patch of red-brown staining and with ephemeral areas of pitting at each end. L 77.5 mm, W 61 mm, T 36.5 mm. Wgt 272 g. Context 049, flooring composed of organic material and lenses of peat-ash/clay (Fig. 4.7.9c).

UNCLASSIFIED TOOL

SF 309 Angular fire-cracked fragment detached form the rounded edge of a smooth and water-rounded quartzite-rich beach cobble; opposing long edges of the spall are stained with red-brown linear streaks from use. Insufficient extent of markings survives to confirm identification with certainty but could indicate use as a strike-a-light or smoother. Surviving L 42.3 mm, W 31.7 mm, T 13.3 mm. Wgt 15.4 g. (Extracted from faunal remains SF 221.) Context 047, midden deposit.

COMBINATION TOOLS

Typically, combination tools account for a significant component of any substantial cobble tool assemblage (McLaren and Hunter 2014, 284, 292). These tools display more than one type of distinctive wear suggesting use in a range of tasks. Common combinations seen on other Iron Age sites are tools used for abrading and pounding (*e.g.*, grinder/pounders) or as abrasives used latterly for heavy-duty hammering (*e.g.*, grinder/hammerstones). At Clachtoll, the number of combination tools amongst the stone assemblage is limited to only three examples. Interestingly, all three have seen use as smoothers as indicated by patches of light abrasion resulting from repeated

rubbing against a soft surface associated with areas of dark red-brown staining and a light sheen. Associated use-wear indicates use as a pestle for grinding and pulverising (SF 028), pounding (SF 218) and abrasion from grinding (SF 257). It has not been possible to determine principal and secondary use in these examples as the various use-wear concentrates in distinct areas of each of the stones with little or no overlap.

*SF 28 Smoother/pestle. Elongated ovoid water-rounded Torridonian sandstone cobble, surfaces natural smoothed but cracked and laminated on one long edge. Both rounded ends display circular convex grinding facets (D 23.5 mm, D 19 mm), one with more pronounced wear than the other. One flat smooth face has been abraded as the result of rubbing, corresponding with patches of red brown staining which continues onto the rounded edges. A distinct oval patch (13 × 26 mm) of waxy red-brown residue is present immediately adjacent to the area of lamination on long edge. L 159 mm, W 47–43 mm, T 37.5 mm. Wgt 479.6 g. Context 028, deposit of windblown sand/organic growth overlying (042) and underlying rubble (011) (Figs 4.7.8 and 4.7.9d).

*SF 214 Pounder/smoother. Elongated ovoid fine red Torridonian sandstone water-rounded cobble, damaged at both ends from use in the form of circular peckmarked facets (D 16 mm, D 19 mm). Two opposing extensive faces, one naturally convex and the other concave, are smoothed from rubbing associated with a light sheen and patches of dark staining from use. L 127.5 mm, W 57 mm, T 48.5 mm. Wgt 549.8 g. Context 044, post-fire abandonment deposit, windblown sand and plant growth overlying stairs (048) in Gallery 3 (Fig. 4.7.9e).

*SF 257 Smoother/grinder. Flattened spherical quartzite water-rounded cobble, plano-convex in cross-section. One end flattened from use in the form of a bipartite abraded facet (23 × 49 mm) and the flattened face smoothed and stained from use. In addition, there are some dark brown smears across the surface which may relate to handling during use. L 82 mm, W 78.5 mm, T 49 mm. Wgt 477.3 g. Context 153, fractured rubble in entrance (Figs 4.7.8 and 4.7.9f).

WHETSTONE

Despite the number of bladed implements recognised amongst the iron assemblage (McLaren and Heald, Section 4.4) only a single whetstone was present. It can be expected that any extensively used metal blade will become blunt and inefficient over time, requiring periodic resharpening of the cutting edge, using tools such as whetstones and sharpening stones. The single whetstone (SF 228) has been produced from an off-white limestone giving it a distinctive appearance amongst the rest of the assemblage and care has been taken to abrade the stone to shape prior to use.

*SF 228   Rectangular Durness limestone whetstone, slightly undulating but vertical and parallel long edges, one narrow end deliberately squared, whist the opposite end is blunt and rounded. Both faces are flat and smooth but only one, with a detached chip at one corner of rounded end, is smoothed from abrasion from whetting, accompanied by an oval concentration (19 × 24 mm) of fine parallel oblique sharpening groves across the centre of the face. All edges have been abraded to shape, particularly the short ends. L 94.5 mm, W 22.7–28.7 mm, T 15 mm. Wgt 85.6 g. Context 144, accumulation of windblown sand, post-abandonment, Guard Cell 1 (Fig. 4.7.9g).

Textile processing

Thirty-six discs in various stages of production, finishing and wear were recovered from the broch interior. This group is dominated by spindle whorls displaying evidence of wear and use (Q=14) alongside various discs and whorls in the process of manufacture. Although all examples are part of the same *chaine opératoire* for the ease of discussion these are described under two main groups: the first being finished and worn spindle whorls which provide evidence of textile production and the second, the various discs, whorls, and other objects in the process of manufacture, which are described under the separate heading 'stone working' below. These two groups are considered together in detail within the discussion.

Spindle whorls

A total of 14 whorls are present, most of which are intact and show some evidence of use observed as either softening and abrasion of the circumference of the central perforations or from smoothing and softening of the features on the surface of the whorls as the result of handling (*e.g.*, SF 190, SF 207, SF 218). The latter is often accompanied by a light sheen on the surface of the stone. All of the whorls have been produced from talc-rich lithologies (steatite) although there is considerable variation in the colour and texture between examples which is a direct reflection of the variation in the raw material used. These

whorls were used to hand-spin fibres into yarn to weave into textiles, perhaps for use as garments, amongst other functions (O'Brien 2010). Hand-spinning thread involved the use of a wood or bone spindle or rod with a notch at the bottom or top for to draw out natural fibres and a circular-sectioned stem around which the thread would be wound (*ibid.*, 15). Hand-spinning was typically thought to be carried out using the suspension method where one end of the spindle was weighted (*ibid.*) using a whorl which could be produced from a range of materials including ceramic, bone and stone. At Clachtoll, only stone examples were recognised amongst the artefact assemblage.

Most are discs but more globular examples (*e.g.*, SF 147) are also present. In diameter, the whorls range from 34 mm to 48.8 mm with an average of 36 mm; in thickness they range from 9.2 mm to 25.5 mm, the average being 15.7 mm; and in weight they range from 26.3–70.2 g with the average being 44.2 g. This variation in size and weight is taken as an indication that the materials being spun were not homogeneous, potentially both plant fibres and wool, and that a range of whorls was required to produce yarns of various weights and properties. Five of these whorls are decorated (SF 93, SF 197, SF 212, SF 215, SF 218), comprising 36% of the finished group. In four instances (SF 93, SF 212, SF 215, SF 218) this decoration consists of a series of short, incised lines which radiate out from the edge of the central perforation to the external edge on at least one face. The number of lines, the strength and depth at which they have been executed vary, perhaps reflective of different hands involved in production or individual preferences. SF 197 stands out amongst the decorated examples in having a series of incised concentric grooves incised into the edge of the whorl. SF 215 is also worthy of note in having one face decorated by radial lines whilst the other has two partial arched lines which are concentric to the central perforation and may represent mark-out lines.

In terms of distribution, these whorls were recovered from seven contexts across the excavated area. The majority come from floor surfaces (contexts 048, 049, 062, 067 and 159) whilst a single example (SF 218) came from a midden deposit (context 047) and four whorls were recovered from the fill (context 078) of the souterrain. One of the whorls from the souterrain (SF 147) is heat damaged and fractured, perhaps indicating it was damaged during the fire and may have been infiltrated the fill of the souterrain after falling from a height from the upper levels.

*SF 93   Two thin halves, once joining, of a small thick disc-shaped amphibole talc schist whorl, dark silver-grey in colour with a central cylindrical drilled perforation (D 6 mm). Stone has laminated horizontally resulting in the two halves of the stone to detach and one face has been entirely lost. The surviving face has been flattened and smoothed by abrasion prior to decoration in the form of eight evenly spaced short, incised lines that radiate out from the edges of the central perforation towards the rounded edges. The incisions are U-shaped in profile and fresh in appearance. D 35.7 mm, T 15.1 mm. Wgt 33.4 g. Context 049, flooring composed of organic material and lenses of peat-ash/clay (hearth 051 set into) (Fig. 4.7.10a).

SF 96   Intact disc-shaped whorl of talc-rich schist with crenulated strong foliation forms across both faces. A spall has detached in antiquity near vertical rounded edge and periphery of one face but this has been smoothed over with abrasion suggesting accidental damage during manufacture. Central hour-glass perforation (min D (internal) 7.5 mm, max D (surface) 9 × 9.5 mm, 9 × 9 mm) the edges of which appear smoothed from wear. D 42.1 mm, T 9.8 mm. Wgt 29.33 g. Context 062, flooring material in SW quad (same as (049) in the north).

*SF 104 Disc-shaped whorl of talc-bearing schist, wedge-shaped in profile with D-shaped edges and central biconical perforation (min D 6.5 mm, max D 8.5 mm), the edges of which are softened as the result of use. Both faces are degraded and friable (rejoined during conservation and stabilised). Surfaces have a light sheen which may be result of handling. D 40 × 41 mm, T 11.5–15 mm. Wgt 40.1 g. Context 048, floor deposit composed of concentrated peat-ash (SE quad) (Fig. 4.7.10b).

SF 142 Intact whorl produced from amphibole-talc-schist with smooth flat faces, abraded D-shaped edges and central bored or drilled perforation (min D (internal) 7.5 mm, max D (surface) 7.5–9mm, 8 × 8 mm). D 42.5 mm, T 19.1 mm. Wgt 58.1 g. Context 048, floor deposit composed of concentrated peat-ash.

SF 147 Intact globular whorl, produced from fine-grained amphibole-talc-schist, convex faces and carefully shaped and smoothed D-shaped edges with central drilled perforation (min D (interior) 6 mm, max D (surface) 7 mm). D 37.5 mm, T 19 mm. Wgt 44.5 g. Context 062, flooring deposits in SW quad (same as 049).

SF 189 Heavily heat-fractured fragment of a thick, flattened globular coarse amphibole-talc-schist whorl with D-shaped edges, broken across central perforation (min D (internal) 5 mm, max D (surface) 9-9.5 mm) resulting in the loss of *c.* 45% of circumference with further damage to adjacent edge. Perforation can be seen in section as a slightly misaligned biconical hole bored from both surfaces.

D 48.8 mm, T 25.5 mm. Wgt 43.8 g. Context 078, mixed fill in the 'souterrain' [069].

SF 190 Intact flattened globular whorl of dappled amphibole-talc schist with smoothed, gently convex faces and D-shaped abraded edges, smoothed from handling. Complete hourglass-shaped bored perforation (min D (internal) 7.5 mm, max D (surface) 8.5–9.5 mm). D 43 mm, T 15.9 mm. Wgt 48.2 g. Context 078, mixed fill in the 'souterrain' [069].

*SF 197 Golden mica-amphibole-talc schist whorl, thick disc-shaped with central biconical bored perforation (Max D 10.5 mm, min D 6.5 mm), edges decorated with a series of horizontal grooves around the circumference giving the edges a ridged profile. One face is substantially damaged; a detached spall has removed much of the face and the stone has delaminated and split across the thickness (conserved to stabilise). D 43 mm, T 15.5 mm. Wgt 33.8 g. Context 078, mixed fill in the 'souterrain' [069] (Fig. 4.7.10c).

*SF 212 Thick disc of chlorite/talc-rich rock with abraded flat faces and gently rounded, near-vertical edges. Four short diagonal incised lines (L 2.5 mm, W 0.5mm) radiate out from the edges of the central hour-glass bored perforation (min D (internal) 5 mm, max D (surface) 7 × 7.5 mm, 7.5 × 7.5 mm), slightly off-set. D 45 mm, T 18.6 mm. Wgt 70.2 g. Context 067, flooring deposit below midden (047) at the south side of the structure (Fig. 4.7.10d).

*SF 215 Thin disc-shaped whorl amphibole-talc schist, oval rather than truly circular in shape with a central hour-glass bored perforation (D 5.5 mm). The stone is so shiny that the decoration is not immediately obvious but one face, which is slightly damaged at one edge, has an evenly spaced series of incised lines that radiate out from the edge of the central perforation. The opposite face has two parallel incised arched lines, concentric to the curving edge and perforation; unclear if these are marking out lines or decoration. D 43.2 mm, T 9.2 mm. Wgt 26.3 g. Context 067, flooring deposit below midden (047) at the south side of the structure (Fig. 4.7.10e).

*SF 218 Flattened globular chlorite/talc-rich rock whorl with gently rounded faces and D-shaped edges and central drilled perforation (D 7.5 mm). Three strong, evenly spaced and straight incised lines radiate from the edge of the perforation on each face, the lines extending and wrapping around the rounded edge to join. The surfaces are softened with a light sheen from handling during use. D 41.3 mm, T 19.7 mm. Wgt 54.3 g. Context 047, midden deposit (Fig. 4.7.10f).

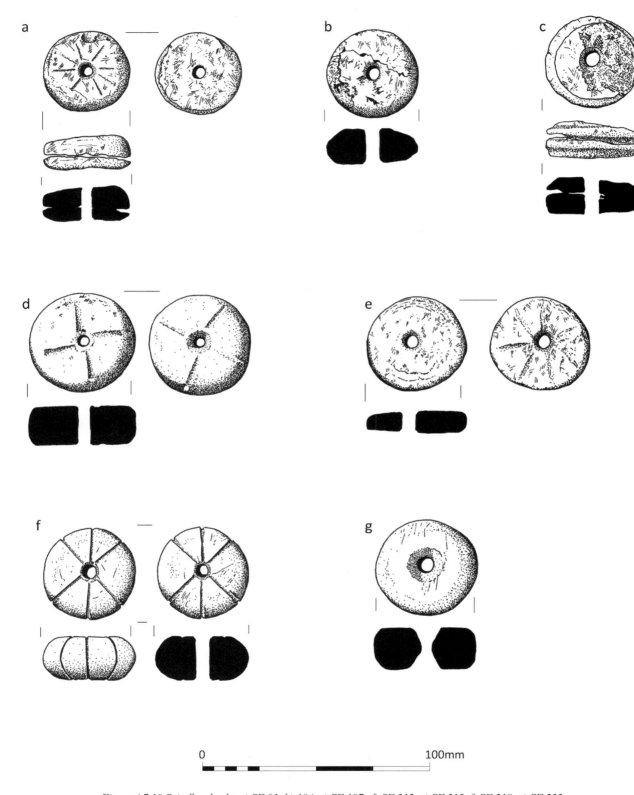

Figure 4.7.10 Spindle whorls: a) SF 93, b) 104, c) SF 197, d) SF 212, e) SF 215, f) SF 218, g) SF 222

*SF 222 Thick disc-shaped amphibole-talc-schist whorl with flat, smoothed, and abraded faces, D-shaped edges, and a bored central hourglass perforation (D min (internal) 7 mm, D max 13.5 × 14 mm). D 43.7 mm, T 16.5 mm. Wgt 63.9 g. Context 078, mixed fill in the 'souterrain' [069] (Fig. 4.7.10g).

SF 243 Flattened ovoid amphibole-talc-schist pebble, surfaces smoothed and rounded due to abrasion with D-shaped edges and a drilled central perforation (D 6 mm). Edges of perforation, on both faces, appear smoothed and softened from use. Surfaces softened, with a light sheen, due to handling. L 34 mm, W 31 mm, T 16 mm. Wgt 26.9 g. Context 159 (upper), deliberate deposits of sand for flooring.

SF 207 Whorl or weight? Flattened globular oval amphibole-talc-schist pebble, surfaces and D-shaped abraded to smooth with an off-centre but narrow drilled perforation (D 5 mm), sheen around perforation suggests use. D 38.5 mm, T 20.1 mm. Wgt 46.2 g. Context 048, floor deposit composed of concentrated peat-ash.

Stone working

Perforated and unperforated discs

A further 22 discs in various stages of production and use are present amongst the assemblage. These are predominantly unfinished whorls but a small number of other discs are present that could have enjoyed a range of alternative functions including as small weights (*e.g.*, SF 141, see also SF 207 above), beads (SF 213) as well as a possible bow-drill pad (SF 038). Distinguishing between small spindle whorls and large beads is a perennial problem as a certain amount of overlap is inevitable. At the Howe, an attempt to differentiate between the two was made on the basis of weight with whorls of 10 g or less being identified as beads (Ballin Smith 1994, 192). One perforated disc from Clachtoll (SF 213) sits outside the main group in terms of size and weight, being only 11 g, and has thus been described below as a possible bead.

The unfinished whorls demonstrate categorically that they were being worked inside the broch and consist of a single possible manuport (SF 198), roughouts in various stages of production from roughly hewn (SF 79) to well developed (SF 180), some displaying the beginnings of a central perforation (SF 10) to those that appear finished but lack any unambiguous evidence of use. This latter category is difficult to separate from the finished and worn whorls described above and there is likely to be considerable overlap between these two rather arbitrary groups. The evidence for the production of whorls will be considered in the discussion that follows, teasing out

patterns in the selection of raw materials, tools and methods of production, as well as aspects of their morphology, decoration and distribution.

POSSIBLE WHORL MANUPORT
SF 198 Flattened subcircular beach pebble of garnet biotite, psammitic schist, strongly layered with differential erosion recessing the middle layer giving it a bipartite profile. No obvious shaping but may have been collected for inherent suitability of shape for whorl manufacture. D 51.6 mm, T 23.5 mm. Wgt 80.9 g. Context 078, mixed fill in the 'souterrain' [069].

WHORL ROUGHOUTS, UNPERFORATED
SF 17 Thick flat unperforated disc of chlorite/talc-rich rock with abraded faces, one flat and the other gently convex, edges with facetted abrasion as the result of shaping. Stone is damaged in several areas around the edges and periphery of the faces, perhaps leading to the abandonment of the piece. D 42.7 mm, T 17.5 mm. Wgt 57.7 g. Context 028, deposit of windblown sand/organic growth overlying (042) and underlying rubble (011).

*SF 33 Thick unperforated talc/tremolite-rich disc, both faces flattened and smoothed by abrasion and the edges gently rounded (near vertical). One flat face is decorated by a fine incised swirl made by a sharp metal point (W 0.5 mm) which encircles two small shallow circular peck marks (D 2 mm) at the centre of the face. The execution of the incised swirl is slightly shaky and a little haphazard in appearance but undoubtedly intentional. A similar thick disc with incised markings on both faces, encompassing a possible stylised bird on one, is known from Keiss Road Broch, Caithness (Anderson 1901, 137, fig. 18) and small discs with curvilinear doodles come from Burland, Shetland (McLaren and Hunter 2014). D 47.6 mm, T 21.1 mm. Wgt 93.5 g. Context 042, burnt deposit across entire broch interior (Figs 4.7.11a and 4.7.27).

SF 79 Actinolite-chlorite schist disc, abandoned at an early stage of manufacture, perhaps using an already water-rounded beach pebble. Edges are partially faceted with abrasion to shape but no other working traces are in evidence. Both faces are naturally pitted. D 58.3 mm, T 20.8 mm. Wgt 90.6 g. Context 042, burnt deposit across entire broch interior.

SF 152 Thick unperforated amphibole-talc-schist disc with smoothed and abraded near-vertical edges and slightly convex faces, appears wedge-shaped in cross-section due to detached spall from the periphery of one face. D 53.1 mm, T 23.8 mm. Wgt 96.8 g. Context 028, deposit of windblown sand/organic growth overlying (042) and underlying rubble (011).

SF 172   Thick subcircular actinolite/tremolite-talc schist disc, edges in the process of being shaped with distinct abrasion facets visible. No shaping or smoothing of faces has occurred. D 56.2 mm, T 23.5 mm. Wgt 131.1 g. Context 048, floor deposit composed of concentrated peat-ash.

*SF 180 Thick, unperforated chlorite-talc-rich disc with smooth flat faces and abraded, near-vertical edges. D 49.6 mm, T 22.8 mm. Wgt 106.3 g. Context 078, mixed fill in the 'souterrain' [069] (Fig. 4.7.11b).

WHORL ROUGHOUTS, INCOMPLETE PERFORATION

SF 02   Thick disc-shaped actinolite-talc schist whorl with flat damaged faces and abraded edges that vary in shape from near vertical to D-shaped; off-centre biconical perforation (min D 5mm, max D 6 × 8.5 mm) bored from both sides creating an oval rather than truly circular, mis-aligned hole. The edges and interior of the perforation are uneven and fresh implying it was abandoned in the process of manufacture. Spalls have detached from both faces (?impact) which are discoloured in patches as the result of exposure to heat. D 40.5 mm, T 20.2 mm. Wgt 52.6 g. Context 011, lower layer of rubble.

*SF 10   Fairly thick amphibole-talc-schist disc, convex faces and partially abraded, facetted D-shaped edges. The beginnings of a small conical depression (min D 2.5 mm, max D 7 mm, Dpt 6.5 mm) present at the centre of one face. Heat damage is in evidence in the form of a pinky-buff discolouration of the stone and pits on the surface that appear to be the result of loss of natural clasts. D 47.2 mm, T 21.5 mm. Wgt 70.3 g. Context 028, deposit of windblown sand/organic growth overlying (042) and underlying rubble (011) (Fig. 4.7.11c).

SF 74   Disc-shaped amphibole-talc-schist whorl with D-shaped edges, abandoned in the process of being shaped and smoothed. One face has been flattened by abrasion but the other is more uneven with minimal evidence of shaping and surface spalling around the periphery of the face. Towards the centre of both faces are the beginnings of an hourglass perforation in the form of a small, shallow, circular hollow

(D 3 mm, Dpt 2–2.5 mm). The hollows are misaligned, perhaps leading to the abandonment of the piece. D 46.7 mm, T 12.8 mm. Wgt 47.5 g. Context 048, floor deposit composed of concentrated peat-ash.

SF 117   Flat oval amphibole schist stone in the process of being shaped into a whorl, edges facetted by abrasion. Both faces are rough and uneven but towards the centre of each is a small, shallow, round-based hollow (D 5 mm, Dpt 1.5 mm; D 3.5 mm, Dpt 3.5 mm) which are slightly misaligned. D 44.2-50.2 mm, T 16.2 mm. Wgt 62.8 g. Context 048, floor deposit composed of concentrated peat-ash.

SF 153   Disc-shaped fragment of amphibole-talc-schist, split horizontally though the thickness of the stone leading to the loss of one face. The surface that survives has been flattened by abrasion and groups of distinct, cross-cutting vertical and horizontal striations are visible from manufacture. Off-centre on surviving face is a small, shallow, round-based hollow (D 3 mm, Dpt 2 mm). Edges are well shaped, near vertical and have been smoothed to finish. D 51.2 mm, T 5.1–14.9 mm. Wgt 55.1 g. Context 048, floor deposit composed of concentrated peat-ash.

SF 177   Heat-affected actinolite-chlorite-talc schist subcircular disc, edges facetted with abrasion to shape and smooth, damage to both surfaces and little of the original faces surviving. Narrow bored hourglass perforation (min D (internal) 4.5 mm, max D (surface) 6 × 7.5 mm, 7.5–9 mm), off-centre towards and steeply angled towards one edge. D 38.1 mm, T 9.6–17.7 mm. Wgt 35.9 g. Context 071, rubble tumbled remains of inner broch structures mixed with (048), ash from the central hearth.

WHORLS, PROBABLY FINISHED BUT UNWORN

SF 40   Disc-shaped spindle whorl of amphibole-talc-schist with vertical abraded edges, gently convex faces and central cylindrical, drilled, perforation (D 6.5 mm), the edges and interior of which is very fresh, probably unused. Striations from abrasion during manufacture are observed across all surfaces. D 37.2 mm, T 14.3 mm. Wgt 33 g. Context 042, burnt deposit across entire broch interior.

SF 47   Whorl, intact, produced from chlorite-amphibole-talc schist with a slight golden hue, pinky-beige in colour perhaps as the result of heat damage. Whorl has D-shaped edges and slightly convex faces, flattened globular in shape with a large biconical

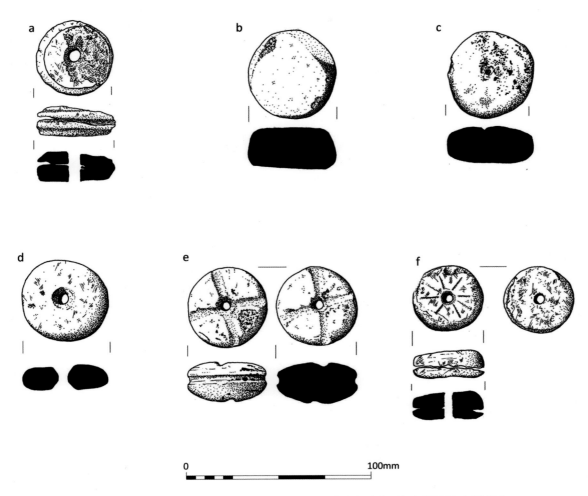

Figure 4.7.11 Spindle whorls: a) SF 33, b) SF 180, c) SF 10, d) SF 88, e) SF 196, f) SF 209

mis-aligned but complete bored perforation (min D (internal) 7.5 mm, max D (surface) 10 × 11 mm, 10.5 × 11 mm). D 35.9 mm, T 17.1 mm. Wgt 31.9 g. Context 042, SE quad, burnt deposit across entire broch interior.

SF 50   Thick disc-shaped whorl intact but possibly unused, produced from amphibole schist, faces flat, edges gently rounded. Very few tool marks from manufacture survive on the surfaces. Central cylindrical, drilled, perforation (D 7 mm), slightly angled so that it appears off-centre on one face. D 38.5 mm, T 17.4 mm. Wgt 47.3 g. Context 042, NW quad, burnt deposit across entire broch interior.

*SF 88   Disc-shaped whorl of amphibole-talc schist with gently convex faces and D-shaped edges which have been abraded and smoothed to shape. Central pecked and bored hour-glass shaped perforation (min D (internal) 5 mm, max D (surface) 12 × 14 mm, 12.5 × 12.5 mm) adjacent

to which are two, possibly three, small shallow circular hollows (D 2 mm) on one face only, drilled as decoration, perhaps intending to form a ring around the central hollow. The opposite face is naturally pitted. D 43.2 mm, T 14.6 mm. Wgt 46.6 g. Context 042, burnt deposit across entire broch interior (Fig.4.7.11d).

*SF 196 Flattened globular chlorite-amphibolite whorl with convex faces and D-shaped edges, decorated on both faces with a slightly haphazard incised equal-armed cross (W 4 mm) which radiates out from the edges of the central bored perforation (min D (internal) 5 mm, max D (surface) 8 × 8.5 mm). A distinct horizontal groove (W 3–4 mm) has been incised around the middle of the rounded edge. D 43.8 mm, T 20.4 mm. Wgt 59.6 g. Context 078, mixed fill in the 'souterrain' [069] (Fig. 4.7.11e).

*SF 209 Thick globular whorl of chlorite/talc-rich rock with convex faces and D-shaped rounded edges.

The flatter of the two faces is decorated with a series of six fine incised lines (W 0.5 mm) radiating out from the edge of the central narrow conical perforation (min D (internal) 5 mm, max D (surface) 5.5 × 5.5 mm) around three-quarters of the face, the fourth quadrant is plain and the whorl may have been abandoned during decoration. The opposite face is undecorated. A narrow groove (W 1.5 mm) has been incised around the middle of the rounded edge, which has been overcut with a series of irregular short oblique grooves, again covering only a portion of the circumference. D 33.6 mm, T 20.7 mm. Wgt 35 g. Context 067, flooring deposit below midden (047) at the south side of the structure (Fig. 4.7.11f).

OTHER

In addition to the unfinished and finished whorls, just described, are three discs which sit outside this group due to their size, weight, shape or form and alternative functions can be postulated. The first, SF 38, is similar to the thick disc-shaped unfinished whorls but is marginally larger and heavier than the group above. On both faces are narrow, shallow, round-bottomed hollows which are slightly misaligned. In contrast to many of the unfinished perforations observed on the whorls, the interior of these hollows and their edges are smoothed and softened as if rubbed and are encircled by a light sheen on the faces surrounding the hollows. Although it is possible that this is another, albeit slightly larger, unfinished whorl, the apparent wear within the hollows is suggestive of an alternative function, perhaps a bow drill pad. A further potential bow drill pad (SF 23) was recognised amongst the assemblage is discussed in more detail below.

At the other end of the scale from the large bow drill pad is a very small, perforated disc (SF 213). This disc is similar to the whorls in every way apart from its size and weight which fall below the group described above. Although it is not impossible that this small, perforated disc could have functioned as a whorl, its weight, at only 11 g, may not have been effective unless used with the finest of fibres and may instead have seen use as a bead or pendant.

A third outlier from the group described above is SF 141 which has been identified here as an unfinished weight or possible whorl. It is a small flattened oval pebble which has seen little modification or shaping to the edges but has broken in antiquity across the width resulting in the loss of one end of the pebble. A narrow perforation has been sunk off-centre and appears to have been made after the breakage of the stone, lacking any evidence of wear or use. It is unclear how such an unbalanced stone in terms of its shape and the position of its perforation could have effectively functioned as a whorl and may instead have been used as a weight.

*SF 38 Bow drill pad? Large, thick talc/tremolite-rich disc, both faces flattened and smoothed, the near vertical edges abraded to shape with distinct striations visible from production. Towards the centre of both faces (one is a little off-centre) is a shallow, round-based, circular hollow; the beginnings of an unfinished bored hour-glass shaped perforation (min D 5.5 × 6 mm (internal), max D (surface) 8.5 mm, Dpt 4.5 mm). A deep irregular linear gouge is immediately adjacent to the hollow on one face. Two bow drill pads are known from Crosskirk Broch (Fairhurst 1984, 126) and a similar example comes from Hillhead broch (unpublished; NMS: X.GA 852), both Caithness. D 58.5 mm, T 21.8 mm. Wgt 136.5 g. Context 042, burnt deposit across entire broch interior (Fig. 4.7.12a).

*SF 141 Unfinished whorl or weight. Fragment of a flat oval amphibole-talc-schist pebble with D-shaped rounded edges, one end of which has broken off cleanly and is now lost. Both faces abraded to flatten and smooth. An off-centre, drilled, cylindrical perforation (D 5 mm) appears to have been made after the breakage of the stone, but the placement may be fortuitous. D 37.6 mm, T 19.6 mm. Wgt 32 g. Context 048, floor deposit composed of concentrated peat-ash (Fig. 4.7.12b).

*SF 213 Disc-shaped bead/pendant/whorl. Small flat slightly oval talc schist disc with central conical perforation (max D 10.3 mm, min D 6 mm). Faces have been abraded to flatten and smooth with fine striation marks remaining from abrasion, distinct on one face especially. Edges have been rounded though abrasion. L 28.5 mm, W 27 mm, T 8 mm. Wgt 11 g. Context 067, flooring deposit below midden (047) at the south side of the structure (Fig. 4.7.12c).

*SF 128 Possible pendant roughout. Flat oval disc of fine-grained, micaceous sandstone, crudely shaped by abrasion around circumference with distinct bevelled grinding facets remaining from production. A small circular round-based hollow (max D 6 mm, min D 3 mm, Dpt 4 mm; max D 7.5 mm, min D 3 mm, T 4.5 mm) is present at the centre of one rounded end of each face, 11.5 mm from the edge, appears bored (?with fine gouge) but are misaligned and do not perforate the thickness of the stone. L 49.5 mm, W 47.5 mm, T 13.5 mm. Wgt 43 g. Context 049, flooring composed of organic material and lenses of peat-ash/clay (north) (Fig. 4.7.12d).

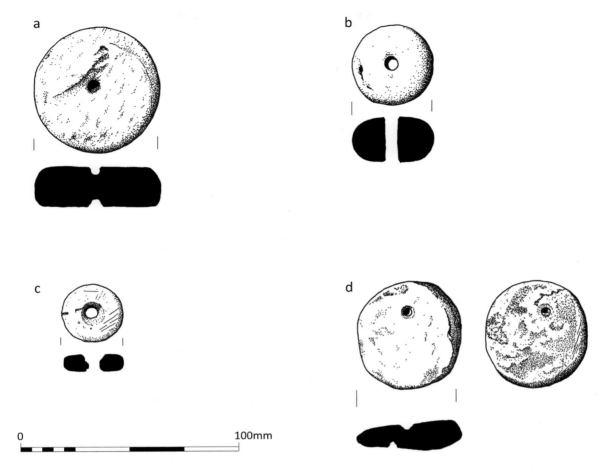

Figure 4.7.12 Other discs: a) possible drill pad SF 038, b) unfinished whorl or weight SF 141, c) bead or pendant SF 213, d) pendant roughout SF 128

Pumice

Pumice has a long history of use in Atlantic Scotland, from the Neolithic to the recent past for a range of functions such as ornaments, floats, burnishers and abrasives for finishing leather-hard pottery, wood, bone or in the treatment and preparation of animal skins (MacGregor 1974, 92; Ballin Smith 1994, 212–13; McLaren and Hunter 2014, 294). At Clachtoll, 18 fragments of dark brown-black basaltic pumice were recovered from five contexts; most show signs of use. A summary catalogue of the pumice is presented in Table 4.7.2 and a selection are illustrated in Figure 4.7.13. The fragments show a range of vesicle sizes and derive from small pebbles to larger cobbles. In most instances, their colour and vesicle sizes are consistent with an Icelandic source (McGibbon, Section 4.8; Newton 2000, 405–6; Newton and Dugmore 2003). One example, SF 32b, recovered from (042) is quite different in appearance, deriving from a larger cobble with much larger vesicles and displaying a more silicate-rich composition. It seems likely that this also derives from an Icelandic source but merits individual

note as its appearance and texture is unlike the rest of the assemblage and may suggest an alternative provenance.

Four fragments (SF 133d, SF 307, SF 308, SF 311), representing 22% by count of the pumice amongst the assemblage, have no obvious signs of working, suggesting the collection and storage of what was a limited and unpredictable resource. Two of these natural pebbles (SF 133d) and (SF 311) from floor deposits (048) and (067) were burnt and may have been incorporated within hearth waste which was then spread out or trampled into the floor. Ten examples (55% by count) were broken or displayed distinctive breaks suggestive of deliberate snapping or cutting – perhaps to make them easier to use or a more suitable size for their particular function – or as an attempt to conserve a valued but limited resource. This is consistent with the findings at Burland, Shetland, where 13% of the large pumice assemblage recovered there had been broken or deliberately cut (McLaren and Hunter 2014, 294). Four of the broken fragments from Clachtoll display evidence of use as an abrasive after breakage (SF 32c, SF 32d, SF 185b, SF 185c) and these were found

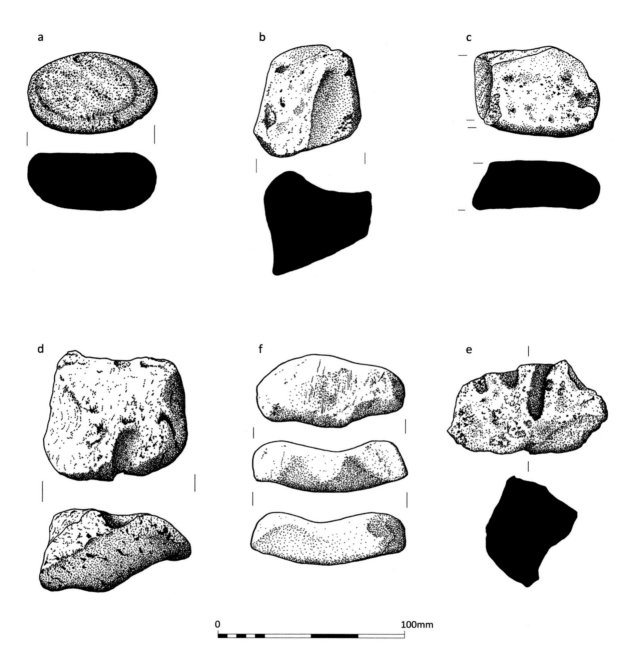

Figure 4.7.13 Pumice: a) SF 32A, b) SF 32C, c) SF 32D, d) SF 32E, e) SF 133A, f) SF 185C

amongst the burnt layer covering the broch interior (042) and the fill (078) of the souterrain [069]. Most of the broken fragments (Q=6) were, however, unmodified, and in one instance (SF 133b) it is unclear whether breakage has been deliberate due to the ragged character of the fracture edges. Apart from the fragments which may have been detached from a larger pebble before use, none of the pumice displayed any modification or shaping prior to use. All worked pieces were used for abrasion. The wear facets can be categorised into four groups: grooved (Q=2; SF 32e, SF 185c), notched (Q=1; SF 32e), flattened (Q=3; SF 32c, SF 133a, SF 185b) and concave or dished

Table 4.7.1 Summary of the Clachtoll worked stone assemblage by broad function group and type

Functional group	Type	Quantity found during excavation	Quantity found prior to excavation
Food preparation and consumption	Upper rotary quern stone	5	
	Lower rotary quern stones	2	
	Unclassified rotary fragment	1	1
	Knocking stone	1	
Household equipment	Steatite Lamps	10	1
	Miniature steatite bowl	1	
	Weight	1	
Cobble tools	Hammerstone	1	
	Pounder	1	
	Smoother/possible smoother	5	
	Burnisher	3	
	Strike-a-light	2	
	Unidentified	1	
	Combination tools	3	
	Whetstone	1	
Textile production	Whorls, finished and worn	14	
Stone working	Whorl manuport	1	
	Whorl roughout, unperforated	6	
	Whorl roughout, incomplete perforation	6	
	Whorls, finished but possibly unworn	6	
Discs (other)	Possible bow drill pads	2	
	Unfinished whorl or weight	1	
	Disc-shaped bead/pendant/small whorl	1	
	Possible pendant roughout	1	
Pumice	Pumice	18	
Miscellaneous	Stained stones	2	
	Fire-cracked stones	3	
Total		99	2

abrasion (Q=5, possibly 6; SF 32a, c–e, SF 133a and possibly SF 133b). The specific functions are unknown but those with flattened and dished abrasion could include the processing of hides or the finishing of items of bone, metal or steatite; abrasion marks on some of the steatite discs and lamps are consistent with being scoured with pumice to smooth and shape prior to final finishing of the surfaces. The grooved pieces are likely to represent the manufacture or maintenance of points of bone, wood or metal (Clarke 2006, 335) which compares well with the abrasion marks from production of several the bone and antler objects (*e.g.* shank of perforated pin SF 275).

Where the pumice pebbles have not been broken or snapped, the natural form is generally water-rounded ovoid or flattened ovoid. One piece, SF 32b, is much larger and heavier than the other pumice pieces from Clachtoll and, as alluded to already, has a different composition and surface texture to the rest of the assemblage. Many of the surfaces are angular as though pieces have been removed from the ends and faces, suggesting the pebble was once larger than it appears today with a remaining length of 116 mm, width of 83 mm and thickness of 82.5 mm. It weighs 374.6 g, significantly more than any other pieces amongst this group. The rest of the pumice pieces (whether intact pebbles or fragments and not including SF 32b) range in length from 31 mm to 86 mm, the average being around 56 mm; in width from 24.5 mm to 92.5 mm, the average being around

Table 4.7.2 Pumice assemblage summarised by wear

SF number	Natural	Broken/cut/ snapped	Grooved	Notched	Flattened abrasion	Dished abrasion	Burnt	Other
SF 32a						x		
SF 32b		x						
SF 32c		x			x	x		
SF 32d		x				x		
SF 32e			x	x		x		
SF 133a					x	x		
SF 133b						? (unclear if natural)		
SF 133c		x					x	
SF 133d	x						x	ferruginous deposit on surfaces?
SF 133e		x						break may be natural
SF 185a		x						
SF 185b		x			x			peat-ash within voids
SF 185c		x	x					
SF 305		x						
SF 307	x							
SF 308	x							
SF 310		x						
SF 311	x						x	

43 mm; in thickness between 15.5 mm to 75 mm, the average being around 32 mm; and in weight between 4.5 g to 170.1 g with the average being 39.5 g.

In terms of distribution, the pumice was recovered from only five contexts across the interior of the broch: the burnt deposit covering the entire interior (042), floor deposit (048), flooring (067) and the mixed fill (078) of the souterrain [069]. Although the quantities are small and the inferences that can be drawn from their distribution are necessarily limited as a result, it is of note that 50% of the abraded pieces (Q=4) were recovered from the burnt deposit (042), perhaps indicating that these fragments had been stored or used on the upper levels of the broch interior. Although no specific matches in wear facets on the pumice to other objects amongst the assemblage could be recognised, the evidence presented above suggesting that at least some of the spindle whorls and unfinished perforated and unperforated discs were being made on the upper floor levels allows a little speculative conjecture that at least some of the pumice pieces could have been used in this process. The remaining abraded or possibly abraded items lack any distinctive patterning but are restricted to contexts (048) and (078).

Miscellaneous

Hollowed stone

A naturally flat water-rounded cobble of sandstone (SF 23) with a narrow and somewhat irregular round-based hollow at the centre of one face was recovered from wind-blown sand and plant-growth (044) overlying the stairs (048) in gallery 3. Its surfaces are softened as the result of weathering consistent with it being exposed to the elements for an extended period prior to being covered over with rubble from the fallen broch walls. How this object came to be incorporated in this deposit is unclear, but it is possible that it was displaced from the upper floor levels of the broch during the fire, similar to the whalebone anvil discussed elsewhere (McLaren, Section 4.9). The extent of weathering on the surfaces of this object makes classification of its wear difficult to assign with confidence.

The hollow appears to have been the result of abrasive wear but is uneven suggesting that that the blunt, rounded implement in contact with the surface of the hollow was repeatedly moved or adjusted so that the position and orientation of use varied. A likely function to explain this wear is that of a bow drill pad, used to cushion the hand during the use of the drill, either for fire-lighting or, in conjunction with a drill bit, used to create perforations in a range of material types. Bow drills typically consist of a wooden spindle or stock, used in conjunction with a bow (of wood and sinew) which induces the rotary motion of the spindle, and a drill-bit of stone or metal (Ilan 2016, 262, fig. 1). Downward pressure would be applied to the top of the spindle, creating friction of the drill bit against the material intended for perforation. A pad, capstone or drill socket of stone could be used at the top of the spindle during use to protect the palm of the hand of the user whilst exerting downward pressure on the spindle (*ibid.*, 264). A second possible example (SF 38) produced from a well-finished disc of talc-rich schist was recognised amongst the burnt deposit (042) covering the broch interior alongside a group of whorl roughouts, unfinished and possibly unworn whorls. It is possible that these pads formed part of the tool kit used in the production of the whorls. Similar examples are known from Crosskirk Broch (Fairhurst 1984, 126), Hillhead broch (unpublished; NMS: X.GA 852), both Caithness, and a possible example is also recognised amongst the worked stone from broch of Burrian, Orkney (MacGregor 1974, 96, fig. 20, no. 275).

SF 23   Flat oval coarse red Torridonian sandstone water-rounded cobble, edges rounded but badly laminating. At centre of one gently convex face is a shallow round-based ?bored circular hollow (D 22 mm, dpt 14 mm), interior edges pitched at an angle as though worked at obtuse rather than vertical angle. All surfaces are eroded due to weathering, including the interior of the hollow. L 128.5 mm, W 108.5 mm, T 33.5 mm. Wgt 619.6 g. Context 044, post-fire abandonment deposit, windblown sand and plant growth overlying stairs (048) in Gallery 3.

Stained stones

Although otherwise unmodified, two pebbles (SF 201 and SF 234) amongst the assemblage are covered in irregular and interrupted patches of dark red-brown to black staining. SF 201 consists of a flattened ovoid water-worn quartzite pebble with staining across all surfaces. It derives from flooring deposit (087). The second example (SF 234) is an asymmetric flattened ovoid red Torridonian sandstone cobble with dark staining on one face which came from the modern entrance structure (context 082). The staining has a similar colour and consistency to that used to apply emblems and decoration on painted pebbles (Ritchie 1972), such as those recovered from various broch sites including examples from Howe, Orkney (Ballin Smith 1994, 82), Broch of Burrian, North Ronaldsay (Traill 1890, 352; MacGregor 1974, 95–6) or Keiss Road Broch in Caithness (Anderson 1901; Heald and Jackson 2001, 134, tab. 1), amongst others. Yet, these stones from Clachtoll display no pattern to the staining and the patches are so irregular that they appear to have been transferred during handling of the pebble or cobble rather than forming any purposeful pattern or design. A combination of scientific analysis on examples of painted pebbles from Old Scatness, Shetland (Ambers 2001, 24; 2010, 322) and experiments conducted to recreate the staining and decorative effect of painted pebbles (Arthur *et al.* 2014) suggest the staining is achieved by the application of soot or pitch, a sticky black bituminous substance which is formed due to the distillation of vapours from the burning of peat in an open hearth (*ibid.*, 8). A similar province for the staining and residue noted on SF 201 and SF 234 can be suggested here but in these instances, the transfer of the pitch to the surfaces of the stones appears incidental rather than by design.

Fire-cracked stone

Three fragments of fire-cracked stone (SF 306, SF 312, SF 313) were extracted from soil sample retents and from the faunal remains assemblage. In each instance, these consist of small angular fractured pieces detached from the surfaces of otherwise natural water-rounded cobbles with no evidence of modification beyond their heat-discoloured and broken condition. It is likely that these cobbles had seen use as pot-boilers for heating water or other substances. This involves placing stones on the fire in a hearth to heat them. Once hot, the stones would be removed from the fire and placed in water with the intention of the heat transferring from the stones to warm the liquid. The transference of hot stones into cold water creates a thermal reaction which can result in the stone cracking or fracturing. The three examples from Clachtoll were recovered from: flooring deposits (062) in the SW quad (SF 306); fractured rubble (153) in the entrance (SF 312); and from a mix of cooking waste (053) within stone tank [052] (SF 313).

Distribution

Context 011, lower layer of stone rubble, overlying (042)

Only one stone artefact was recovered from this layer: talc-rich schist spindle whorl (SF 02), faces damaged. Undecorated and apparently unworn.

Context 028, deposit of windblown sand/organic growth overlying (042) and underlying rubble (011)

Eight stone artefacts derive from this context consisting of a cobble smoother (SF 7), a smoother grinder (SF 28), a heat affected multifunction cobble tool (SF 8), two steatite (talc-rich lithologies) discs (SF 10 and SF 17) which are probably whorl roughouts, a large, perforated mica-schist weight (SF 20) and an unfinished spindle whorl (SF 152).

Context 042, burnt deposit across entire broch interior

Twenty-three items of worked stone were recovered from amongst the burnt layer across the interior of the broch. This has been interpreted as the burnt remains of the collapsed roof and internal structural remains, including possible upper floor levels and it is therefore likely that most, if not all, of these finds were used or stored on the upper levels of the broch. These artefacts include eight talc-rich schist lamps (SF 27, SF 36, SF 59, SF 60, SF 65, SF 70, SF 95) in various conditions, most of which show evidence of use and many of which are damaged or broken as the result of impact. This damage often occurs on the base of the lamp, towards one curving edge or end as though the lamp has fallen and become damaged as the result of the base or sides impacting against a hard surface; a scenario that fits very well with the hypothesis that they fell from an upper level during the collapse of the internal structures. Also present were three undecorated talc-schist and amphibole schist spindle whorls (SF 47, SF 50, SF 88) and four talc-rich schist discs (SF 33, SF 38, SF 40, SF 79): SF 38 has been roughed out and carefully shaped with smooth vertical edges and flat faces, one of which has a shallow spiral doodle scratched into one face, another larger disc, again with vertical edges and flat faces have small, smooth and round based shallow circular hollows at the centre of opposing faces, this may be a disc in the process of manufacture but the smoothness of the hollows is suggestive of use and this may have seen use as a bow-drill pad; SF 40 and SF 79 are likely spindle whorls abandoned in the process of manufacture, the former with an unworn perforation and the latter which is roughed out but remains unperforated. Also present from this context are several cobble tools including a pounder (SF 97), a smoother/pounder fragment (SF 304) which is fire-cracked and a well-used tracked stone (SF 71), as well as five pieces of pumice (SF 32a-e), all of which display evidence of working and may be associated with the production of the whorls, amongst other functions.

Context 044, post-fire abandonment deposit, windblown sand and plant growth overlying stairs (048) in Gallery 3

Two items of worked stone were recovered from this content in the form of a cobble pounder/smoother (SF 214) and an oval flat slab of sandstone with a central uneven subcircular hollow, possibly a bow-drill pad or similar (SF 23).

Context 047, midden deposit

Three items of worked stone were present within the midden deposit including an intact and well-worn upper rotary quern stone (SF 150). The vertical handle socket had worn through the grinding surface creating damage around the area where it broke through. No attempt appears to have been made to create a replacement handle socket so this quern may have been laid down as a stabilising slab within the midden after becoming exhausted. Also present within the midden was a radially decorated spindle whorl (SF 218) and a fire-cracked fragment of a cobble tool (SF 309) perhaps a smoother or a strike-a-light. It is fragmentary and heat-affected condition suggests it had been used as a pot boiler, resulting in it fracturing and subsequently being discarded.

Context 048, floor deposit containing concentrated peat-ash

Sixteen items of worked stone were recovered from this floor deposit. These comprise two talc-schist lamps (SF 106 and SF 163), four spindle whorls (SF 104, SF 141, SF 142, SF 207), four probable unfinished whorls (SF 74, SF 117, SF 153, SF 172) and six fragments of pumice (SF 133a–e; SF 305), which include worked (*e.g.* SF 133a), fractured (*e.g.* SF 305) and unworked pebbles (*e.g.* SF 133d). One of the talc-schist lamps is intact (SF 106) and is oval in shape with a small squat vertical handle; the other (SF 163) is a small shallow lozenge-shaped scoop or lamp, very crudely shaped out and appears unfinished. All of the whorls, both finished and unfinished have been produced from talc- or amphibole-rich schist. Of note, SF 104 and 141 are finished but broken, both likely to have been broken as the result of a blow rather than as the result of heat damage. Two finished whorls (SF 142 and SF 207) undecorated. Amongst the unfinished whorls, two are simple roughed out discs (SF 74 and SF 172), one (SF 117) has an unfinished perforation, whilst another (SF 172) has been shaped and perforated but the surfaces remain unfinished.

Context 049, flooring composed of organic material and lenses of peat-ash/clay (north)

Only three items of worked stone came from this floor surface. These comprise two non-joining fragments (SF 093) of a broken spindle whorl, finished and decorated with a series of incised radial lines on both faces, a well-used tracked stone (SF 094) with evidence of secondary use as a pounder and a flat oval disc of micaceous sandstone (SF 128) with the beginnings of a perforation at one end as though intended for use as a pendant but abandoned during manufacture.

Context 050, knocking stone set within a solid peat-ash and clay floor surface (056) in NE quad

Intact gneiss knocking stone (SF 61) was found set within a peat-ash and clay floor surface (056) to keep it in place during working and was filled with partially processed charred barley grains. This tool appears to be *in situ* and abandoned during use.

Context 053, fill of stone tank or setting [052] associated with Hearth 3

A single fire-cracked spall (SF 313) from the surface of a heat-affected cobble. Probably used as a pot boiler.

Context 062, flooring deposits in SW quad (same as 049)

Four items of worked stone and a fragment of a fire-cracked cobble (SF 306) were recovered from this floor deposit. The worked stone comprises two undecorated talc-schist spindle whorls (SF 96 and SF 147). Also present is a very well-worn upper rotary quern (SF 125) produced from a non-local schist. The quern had been damaged as the result of extensive use, seeing fracturing and chipping to the edges, perhaps damage occurred by it being stored on its edges when not being used, as well as thinning of the stone from wear, resulting in the vertical handle socket wearing though to the grinding surface and causing damage to the working surface. Despite this damage, a second shallow handle socket had been produced to try to keep the quern in service. It is unclear whether the quern would have still been usable in its current condition or whether it had been used to exhaustion and laid down here as a paving slab. The final item is a thick subcircular slab of sandstone (SF 126) which appears to have been abandoned in the process of roughing it out to make a rotary quern, probably a basal stone.

Context 067, flooring deposit below midden (047) at the south side of the structure

Eight items of coarse stone came from this flooring deposit. As this floor surface was covered by a layer of midden (047) it is assumed that the floor surface was no longer in use and all objects incorporated within it had been incidentally, accidentally or purposefully abandoned. These include a small steatite bead or whorl (SF 213), two fractured pumice pebbles (SF 310 and SF 311) displaying no evidence of wear, three amphibole-talc-schist or chlorite-talc whorls, each one complete and decorated with incised radial motifs. Also present was an intact upper sandstone rotary quern (SF 127). It had seen extensive wear resulting in the thinning of the stone which caused the base of the vertical handle socket to be worn away, breaking through and causing damage to the grinding face. Four joining fragments of a second upper rotary quern (SF 194), this time produced from schist, perhaps procured from a source beyond the local area were also recovered. It is likely that the querns had been laid down as paving slabs within the floor surface after breakage to (SF 194) put it out of service and it is possible that SF 194 due to its damage though wear was also considered to have been exhausted.

Context 071, rubble tumbled remains of inner broch structures mixed with (048), ash from the central hearth

A single chlorite-talc-schist spindle whorl (SF 177) was recovered from this rubble deposit. It was damaged on both faces, probably from a blow.

Context 074, burnt remains from the use of the central hearth

A damaged rotary quern stone (SF 193) with a fully perforated central socket, unclear if upper or lower, came from this deposit.

Context 078, Mixed fill in the 'souterrain' [069]

Fourteen items of stone were recovered from the fill of the 'souterrain' feature [069]. It is unclear whether this deposit represents material stored within the feature, collapsed floor levels which infiltrated from above or a deliberate infilling of the feature with midden material. The stone objects include a small intact hemispherical talc-schist cup or bowl (195), an intact rotary quern stone (SF 208), five spindle whorls, one of which was broken (SF 189), two of which were decorated (SF 196 and 197) and two of which were undecorated (SF 190 and SF 222). Whorl (SF 197) is damaged and friable, either as a result of the degradation of the stone or from a blow. A stone disc (SF 180) could be a roughout for a whorl, whilst (SF 198) is a natural heavily weathered disc-shaped pebble of garnet biotite psammitic schist which may have been collected with the intention of working into a whorl but the stone displays no evidence of modification. Also present within this deposit are five pieces of pumice, one (SF 185a) fractured, perhaps deliberately, two worked or possibly worked (SF 185b and c) and two unworked pebbles (SF 307 and SF 308).

Context 082, late/post-abandonment deposits in entrance passage

Five items of worked stone were recovered from this area, including a group of stones with evidence of similar or aligned functions displaying wear resulting from rubbing and have been interpreted variously as burnishers, smoothers and polishers (SF 236a and b, SF 303 and SF 225). Approximately 15% of a broken upper rotary quern stone (SF 192) was found. Also present were three pebbles, all of which lacked evidence of wear but had staining on their surfaces that may be the result of handling (SF 234, SF 236c).

Context 087, subdivision of (049) flooring deposit

Only one item of interest was noted from this context. This was a small water-rounded quartzite pebble with unusual staining (SF 201) on the surfaces. There was no obvious evidence of use as a tool but the patchy and irregular staining could be pitch or a similar substance which has transferred from someone's hands during handling.

Context 144, accumulation of windblown sand, post-abandonment

Amongst this windblown sand deposit is a fine bar-shaped whetstone produced from possible Durness limestone (SF 228).

Context 153, fractured rubble in entrance

Amongst the rubble in the entrance of the structure was a smoother/grinder (SF 257) and a fragment of a fire-cracked cobble (SF 312).

Context 159, deliberate deposits of sand for flooring

Amongst this sand flooring material was an amphibole-talc-schist spindle whorl (SF 243).

Context 163, organic material mixed with windblown sand overlying bedrock

A smoother (SF 258) produced from a water-rounded sandstone cobble was recovered from this deposit.

Unstratified

A small possible hammerstone (SF 146) produced from a water-rounded fine sandstone cobble was recovered from unstratified soils.

Discussion

Coarse stone tools are amongst the most prolific types of material culture recovered from later prehistoric sites in Scotland (Hingley 1992; Pope 2003; Clarke 2006) due to the ready availability of good quality local stone sources and the survival of worked stone because of the natural robust and durable properties of the raw material. Despite the common recovery of cobble tools, querns and other worked stone artefacts on archaeological excavations, their significance is often undervalued and under studied as has been argued elsewhere (Heald and Jackson 2001, 142; Hunter 2007c, 288). Most of the stone tools from Clachtoll are undoubtedly prosaic everyday objects which were locally sourced, easily produced and readily discarded. Yet, they hold the potential to provide information about the day-to-day activities undertaken by the occupants of the site as well as revealing details of Iron Age exploitation of local resources and contacts beyond the immediate locale of the broch.

The following discussion will attempt to tease out patterns of manufacture and use by addressing issues such as the sourcing of the raw materials used, the condition of the stone tools, the crafts and processes they represent as well as decoration. Three of the most significant aspects of the assemblage – the querns, the steatite lamps and the evidence for the production of whorls – will be considered in detail below.

Raw materials

The vast majority of the stone assemblage utilises locally procured rock types, predominantly Torridonian sandstone, which was used for large disc-querns to small hand-held cobble tools. The raw materials used have been carefully selected, choosing stone shapes, sizes and lithologies suited to their intended purpose (Hunter 2015, 229), a pattern that is particularly apparent in the small but varied range of cobble tools from the site. Pumice may also have been collected fairly locally, either as drift, excavated from alluvial deposits or found eroding out of sand dunes. Many of the pumice pebbles appear to have been broken deliberately to detach smaller pieces for use, either for ease of handling or to conserve a valuable resource, which would imply an erratic and unpredictable resource requiring careful management and conservation of collected fragments. This valued material was used for a wide variety of functions at the broch and would have been sought out and collected along the coastline. Rare rock types amongst the assemblage are the whetstone (SF 228) produced from Durness Limestone. Although probably locally procured, it is the only example amongst the assemblage and was undoubtedly favoured due to its fine-grained abrasive properties and striking appearance.

A handful of items stand out from the assemblage due to their non-local rock types and these include two schist quern stones (SF 125, Fig. 4.7.14; SF 194, Fig. 4.7.15) and a further example of biotite schist (SF 193, Fig. 4.7.16) which are unlikely to have been provenanced in the local area and represents a rock type found in the Grampian Highlands and the north and west of Ireland. It has not been possible to provenance this schist more closely, but Dalriadian schists are found in the southern highlands (eastern Sutherland, Ross-shire and Inverness-shire), Argyll, Appin, Grampian and Shetland.

The most challenging items amongst the assemblage to put into context in terms of sourcing of raw material are the discs, whorls and lamps of steatite. Macroscopic examination of the lithology of the steatite artefacts (Section 4.8, below) confirms that this is a heterogenous group implying that the raw material came either from a heterogenous source or a range of different sources. In the past, assumptions were made that steatite objects (or specifically the rock itself) came from Shetland (*e.g.* Young and Richardson 1960, 168). Within the Clachtoll assemblage, the presence of broken and damaged steatite objects presented an opportunity to conduct intrusive scientific analysis with a view to better understanding the provenance of the rock. Samples of steatite were collected at known outcrops near the broch and were subject to lithological examination (Section 4.8, below) alongside the worked stone assemblage. These geological samples were then submitted alongside a selection of fragmentary steatite objects for geochemical analysis using a combination of portable x-ray fluorescence (P-XRF) and rare earth element analysis (REE) (Section 4.8, below) to try to establish whether the modern-day outcrop near the broch may have been the source for the lamps and whorls recovered and to allow comparison to the existing database of Scottish steatite. The analysis indicates that although the source or sources were potentially local to the broch, the finds analysed did not derive from the outcrops of steatite nearest the site and no close match was found on the existing database (Bray 1994). Although the steatite is not consistent with a Shetland source and is chemically closer in comparison to mainland Scottish sources, the location of this outcrop or outcrops could not be identified.

Household and craft activities

The stone assemblage from the broch represents four main categories of artefact: food preparation and consumption (rotary quern stones, knocking stone, at least some of the cobble tools); tools associated with various crafts including textile production (spindle whorls), hide or skin working (smoothers), stone working (unfinished whorls and quern) and general purpose tools which could have seen use in a range of tasks (cobble tools, pumice, bow drill pads); household equipment including a single large weight which may be a thatch-weight or similar whilst a set of steatite lamps demonstrates how light was introduced to the interior of the broch asides from the central hearth; and ornaments, which form a rare element to the assemblage, represented by a single possible bead and unfinished pendant.

General purpose cobble tools and food processing equipment in the form of rotary querns dominate the assemblage but a small number of tools amongst the assemblage hint at more specialist tasks. Smoothers used in the preparation of hides comprise 30% by count of the cobble tool assemblage. The presence of only one whetstone is unusual as they are common finds within broch assemblages but (SF 228) is valuable as it demonstrates that iron knives and bladed instruments were commonplace on the site, perhaps more so than the small iron assemblage recovered would suggest. A small number of strike-a-lights attest to firemaking (Fig. 4.7.17), an everyday task which would have been commonplace but is rarely demonstrable from artefact assemblages.

Fragments of pumice were gathered from the local coastline and many put to use as abrasives. Although it is likely that these saw use in association with a range of materials found at the broch, making it impossible to state with certainty what the use-wear represents in each instance, they were probably employed in hide processing, stone object manufacture (*e.g.* spindle whorls), bone and wood working as well as potentially having a role in scouring the bowls of the lamps and to create texture to some of the pottery vessels.

Graining the grain: the quern stones

The nine rotary quern stones from the broch form an interesting group and close analysis has enabled some significant details to be determined. All five upper stones have been extensively worn; in each instance, the base of the vertical handle sockets have worn through the grinding faces indicating that a substantial thickness of the stone has been lost due to abrasion through use. In four cases (SF 127, SF 150, SF 192, SF 194), the grinding face has worn through and penetrated the base of the handle socket, resulting in spalls detaching from around area of the socket and subsequently causing damage to the grinding face. The damage is not sufficient

Figure 4.7.14 Rotary quern stone SF 125: a) plan view of upper surface of stone, b) detail of handle socket and attempted replacement socket

Figure 4.7.15 Re-assembled rotary quern stone SF 194: a) plan view of upper surface of stone, b) grinding face showing concentric wear

on its own to have put the querns out of use but would probably have made them more difficult to operate and could have had an impact on efficiency. Indeed, in two instances (SF 127 and SF 150) the fracture surfaces on the grinding faces caused by this damage appear to have been pecked and softened suggesting deliberate modification to the grinding face in an attempt to keep the quern in use despite the damage. Further attempts to extend the life of the querns is noted on SF 125 where the handle had also broken through to the grinding face, this time without causing such severe damage and where a second shallow, and apparently expedient, handle socket had been bored into the upper surface. All of the upper stones are substantially intact except for SF 192, where only 50% of the stone survives in two joining fragments. As with the upper stones already described the handle socket on this example had broken through the grinding face causing damage to working face, but in this instance,

no obvious effort appears to have been made to smooth over the damage. Interestingly, the damage appears to cut though a well-used grinding face which had already been redressed, as evidenced by numerous small peckmarks and pits dispersed across the face.

Two of the rotary querns are lower stones (SF 126 and SF 208). Quern SF 126 is an unfinished roughout, abandoned at an early stage of production, whilst SF 208 is intact and has evidence of wear from use. This latter quern is notable due to the fact is appears to be of the adjustable variety of lower quern stones and it is also possible that (due to the presence of hollows marking the intended position of the central socket) SF 126 was also intended to be adjustable. Typically, lower quern stones have a narrow but often fairly deep central circular socket which pierces the grinding face within which a vertical spindle (presumably of wood or iron) would be inserted. The upper quern stone would then be placed over the top of this spindle, inserting it through the central perforation known as a feeder pipe, so that the upper and lower stones were positioned grinding face to grinding face. The upper

Figure 4.7.16 Rotary quern stone SF 193

Figure 4.7.17 Strike-a-lights (SF 71 and SF 94)

stone would then be rotated around the central spindle whilst the lower stone remained stationary. The distance between the grinding faces could be adjusted manually to create finer or coarser flour by adding or removing washers (presumably of wood, antler or bone) over the spindle between the two stones. Adjusting the texture of the flour would require removing the upper stone to add or remove such washers. In contrast, SF 208 appears to derive from an adjustable pair of querns. This means that the upper and lower stones were combined using a more complex mechanism which would enable the distance between the grinding faces to be adjusted without having to remove the upper stone. Adjustable querns remained in use in some parts of Scotland even into the early twentieth century (Fenton 1978). In contrast to non-adjustable querns, the central socket on adjustable querns fully perforates the thickness of the lower stone to enable a long spindle to be inserted through it, held in place by a wooden plug (also known as a bush). The spindle would protrude upwards and be fitted through an iron bar-shaped rind or a wooden *sile* attached to the base of the feeder pipe and grinding surface of the upper stone (*ibid.*). The spindle would also protrude downwards and be attached below the lower stone to a hinged beam known as a lightning tree which would have allowed, using a simple tightening device, the tree and spindle to be raised or lowered, thereby lifting the height of the upper stone and, as a consequence, adjusting the fineness of the flour produced (*ibid.*, 392–3; MacKie 1987, 5–8, pl. 3; 2007, 498). Rather than being turned by hand at ground level, these adjustable querns were often used on a simple wooden bench or table (Fenton 1978, 392, fig. 193).

Dating the inception of the use of adjustable rotary querns in Scotland is currently not well understood. Close-Brooks suggests that the presence of rind sockets on upper disc querns was influenced by Roman military

quern types with their fixed rinds across the top of the upper stone hopper (1983, 218). The recovery a rotary stone with rind recess at Traprain Law, East Lothian (*ibid.*, 218, fig. 97:7), certainly attests to their use in the Roman Iron Age but MacKie (1987, 5–11) has argued that they were in use from at least the 1st century BC, illustrated by the recovery of completely perforated lower stones from Iron Age contexts at the Howe, Orkney, Leckie Broch, Stirling and elsewhere (Ballin Smith 1994; MacKie 2007a, 498). The complete perforated lower quern (SF 208) recovered from the fill (078) of the souterrain [069] at Clachtoll is consistent with the form of adjustable querns and reinforces MacKie's earlier hypothesis that this type of quern was not a Roman introduction and was already in use across many areas of Scotland by the beginning of the 1st century BC. It should be noted, however, that no upper stones with rind sockets were found amongst the Clachtoll assemblage.

The unfinished lower stone (SF 126) is worthy of further comment. Unfinished rotary querns are not common amongst settlement assemblages in Scotland; this stone providing a useful addition to the growing corpus of known examples (McLaren and Hunter 2008, 106–7, tab. 1). Do any surface details provide information on why the example from the broch may have been abandoned? Close examination of the stone confirms that the edges of the stone have been very crudely fractured to form an approximate disc shape, but the thickness of the stone is considerable and working of the faces to thin does not appear to have been attempted. Towards the centre of each extensive face are hollowed areas of pecking, presumably marking the beginnings of an attempt to perforate the stone. The tool marks that survive leave little doubt that these hollows were fashioned using stone tools. Peacock's (2013) study of quern production observed that technical requirements, particularly possession of appropriate iron tools, placed constraints on rotary quern manufacture and that such tools and skill in their use, may not have been accessible to all (*ibid.*, 137–9; Hunter 2015, 229). It is possible that the maker of the quern at Clachtoll did not have the requisite tools to fashion the central socket but this assertion is purely conjectural.

Lithological examination of the querns has demonstrated that three querns have been made on schist, one of biotite schist (SF 193) and the other two (SF 125 and SF 194) possibly Dalriadian and are unlikely to have been sourced in the local area; these likely represent imports into the area from south or west. Both upper quern stones (SF 125 and SF 194) have been extensively used and SF 125 displays evidence of attempts to extend its life by the placement of a second handle socket after the primary socket had worn though, suggesting that this was a prized and valuable household tool. SF 193 is incomplete and insufficient characteristic features survive to allow it to be categorised as an upper or lower stone with confidence. It has a fully perforated central socket which could be a simple feeder pipe or the spindle socket for an adjustable lower quern stone, as already described. Despite the similarity in dimensions of the three schist querns (SF 125 at 360 mm; SF 193 at approx. 324 mm; SF 194 at 393 mm), the fact that the unclassified stone (SF 193) is narrower in diameter than uppers SF 125 and SF 194 and does not match the topography of wear patterns on the corresponding upper stones, argues against these forming upper and lower pairs. The rest of the rotary quern stone examples have been produced with slabs or split boulders of Torridonian sandstone, a rock-type readily available in the area. This includes the unclassified quern fragment found by MacKie in 2005.

The presence of potentially non-local schist quern stones at Clachtoll is not altogether unsurprising considering the evidence amongst the other artefact categories from the site that point towards potential imported goods (*e.g.* the marine ivory dagger pommel; McLaren, Section 4.9). A wider understanding of the implications of such trade and exchange remains difficult to interrogate in the absence of comparable levels of study amongst other broch assemblages. The question of the provenance of the stone used in the production of querns is one that cannot be answered without systematic lithological examination, as argued for elsewhere (McLaren and Hunter 2008, 106–7). Hingley (1992) poses the question of whether access to and supply of querns [and pottery] which may have been brought into regions from elsewhere were perhaps controlled by dominant households, based in substantial houses. At present, it is impossible to elucidate nuanced answers to such a question in the absence of data to support the presence of non-local items of worked stone in Atlantic Scottish broch contexts, but it can be assumed that exchange of these objects at a local level may have been a common occurrence (*ibid.*, 22). The potential importance of high-quality stone and longer-distance transportation of raw materials and finished goods could well have promoted these objects into the category of exotic items, as Hingley has argued (*ibid.*, 23), providing us with a platform to understand the efforts made to keep the non-local schist querns in service for as long as possible and then for them to be reused as paving material within the broch flooring. Alternatively, the importation of querns produced from non-local stones may well reflect the movement of individuals, possibly as part of fostership or marriage patterns (Hunter 2015, 229).

The vast majority of the quern stones do not appear to have been functional at the time of the destruction of the broch. Following the pattern of quern deposition noted widely across Scotland and beyond is the reuse of quern stones as paving or building material. At Clachtoll, none of the quern stones were associated with the earliest floor levels but four (SF 125, SF 126, SF 127, SF 150) were incorporated within flooring and midden (contexts 047, 062, 067) relating to surfaces in use around Hearth 2, whilst SF 193 and SF 194 were recovered from contexts relating to the use of Hearth 3. The broken upper stone (SF 194) is of particular interest as it was found amongst a collection of cobbles and pebbles buttressing a large vertical post-stone [072] at the south end of the hearth. The association of Iron Age quern fragments and hearth features is one that can be widely paralleled across Scotland, including examples from Burland, Shetland (McLaren and Hunter 2014) and Grantown Road, Forres (Engl and McLaren 2016, 39), to name a few. The concentration of querns within flooring in the southern half of the interior is also of interest and although not fully understood, can be paralleled elsewhere within Iron Age structures, such as House 4 at the Later Iron Age (Phase 6) roundhouse at Broxmouth, East Lothian, where a series of rotary quern stones were incorporated into three sequential phases of flooring in the internal area of the structure, directly opposite the entrance (Büster and Armit 2013, 145–9, illus. 7.27, 7.28, 7,29). As noted at Broxmouth, the 'recurrent deposition of rotary quern stones in the same area of paving towards the rear of the structure directly opposite the entrance cannot be the result of chance' (*ibid.*, 151) and this observation was interpreted as the non-random structuring of material within the building (*ibid.*, 152). This non-random placement is demonstrated as a long-held practice with evidence stretching back into the Early–Middle Bronze Age (Pope 2003, 328), as seen at sites such as Lairg, Sutherland where a large, inverted saddle quern was deliberately placed within the flooring to the rear of the building (McCullagh and Tipping 1998, 42–9) whilst Iron Age examples are known from the wheelhouse at Á Cheardach Mhor, Drimore, South Uist (Young and Richardson 1960, 150) as an example.

Looking back to Clachtoll, a further fragmentary upper stone (SF 192) was recovered from the entrance but this deposit (082) is so disturbed it is not possible to determine whether this could have been incorporated in the broch wall itself, becoming mixed up in rubble during its collapse, or whether this may have been used as a paving stone in the entrance passage. A similar interpretation can be given for the fragmentary quern found by MacKie prior to the excavation which came from the collapsed rubble of the tower, implying that it had been built into the super-structure of the broch and was already in a fragmentary condition at the time of its reuse as a building stone. The final quern, an intact lower stone (SF 192), was recovered grinding face down on the stone floor of the 'souterrain' [069] within (078).

A final point of note regarding the Clachtoll quern stones is the condition of the quern found by MacKie in 2005 (Fig. 4.7.18). This represents less than half of the original circumference of the stone, having broken across the central socket, and displays damage to the edges and grinding surface. Due to its recovery from the rubble of the collapsed tower, the assumption is that it was in a broken state prior to its incorporation within the structure suggesting that it likely dates to the earlier phase of activity on the site and is, therefore, one of the few objects which may relate to activity pre-dating the extant broch structure. The damage that is observed to the edges and grinding face of this quern fragment could well be the result of crushing during the collapse of the structure. Alternatively, the complete removal of the grinding face could have been deliberate, similar to that seen at Broxmouth, East Lothian (McLaren 2013, 317) and further afield (Heslop 2008, 68–72). Larger synthetic studies of quern deposition confirm that not every Iron Age quern was subject to special treatment after it had come to the end of its use but the deliberate destruction, fragmentation and defacing of quern stones is a practice that re-occurs widely across Iron Age assemblages in Britain (Hingley 1992; Pope 2003, 267; Heslop 2008, 69; McLaren 2013). This pattern of special treatment prior to and during deposition of some querns, arguably including this particular example from Clachtoll, attests to the special significance in which such tools were held in society, not just as functional household implements but as symbols embodying concepts of fertility, the agricultural cycle and the life-cycles of individuals, communities and households (Williams 2003; Heslop 2008).

Lighting the way: stone lamps
All the lamps from the site consist of a hollowed bowl with a handle projecting from one edge (Fig. 4.7.19). Each lamp has been carved from a rock type generally described as 'steatite' (also known as soapstone or talc-rich schist) however the colour and texture of each varies,

reflecting differences in the lithology (McGibbon, Section 4.8). This is confirmed during lithological inspection determining that although all are talc-bearing there is a range of lithologies present dominated by talc-rich schist (fine and coarse-grained) as well as examples produced from amphibole-talc-schist (SF 36), antigonite-chlo-rite-talc-schist (SF 59) and tremolite-talc-schist (SF 27). Although the most abundant sources of steatite are known at outcrops such as Catpund and Clibberswick, Shetland (Forster and Turner 2009) and more distant, sources in Norway, it is understood that steatite lamps from Iron Age contexts in mainland Scotland are not manufactured from Shetland stone (Bray 1994, 22; Forster 2009, 50; Hunter 2015, 230, illus. 13.2) contrary to past assumptions (*e.g.* Á Cheardach Mhor, Drimore, South Uist: Young and Richardson 1960, 168). This is confirmed by analysis undertaken on a selection of the lamps from Clachtoll (Jones, Section 4.8) but interestingly, samples of stea-tite collected locally to the broch did not provide close chemical compositional matches to the artefacts analysed.

A significant aspect of this group is the variability and diversity in the design and size of the lamps. Although there are similarities between examples, each lamp is unique. Most examples consist of a hemispherical bowl (*e.g.* SF 27, SF 36, SF 59, SF 66, SF 70), whilst others (*e.g.* SF 106 and SF 163) are distinctly more ovoid in form. SF 95 is hemispherical externally, but the hollow is asymmetric and extends in length toward the handle, however, this shape may be a distortion the working evi-dence observed on the exterior surfaces of the bowl. SF 60 and SF 65 are too fragmentary to be confident of their original shape, however, SF 65 could have been similar in style to SF 70.

Although each lamp from Clachtoll is of the handled variety, the forms of the handles are also diverse in shape and size. These include wide subrectangular or sub-square projections in line with the top of the rim of the bowl, with a wedge-shaped profile (*e.g.* SF 70); a slightly longer rectangular handle with rounded terminal extending from just below the rim of the bowl with no junction or sharp transition from bowl to handle (*e.g.* SF 95); wide, square handle, with pronounced rounded corners which is stepped down below the rim of the bowl (*e.g.* SF 66); short and narrow vertical lug-shaped handle (SF 106), similar to examples such as that from Kirkhill (Close-Brooks 1972, 295, fig. 3); and short, thick, sub-square handles (*e.g.* SF 27 and SF 36).

As already outlined, the shape of the lamps and the form of their bowls and handles display great variation amongst intact examples. The same can be said in terms of the relative size of examples amongst the group, as summarised in Table 4.7.3. The Clachtoll group can be crudely divided into three categories: small, under 110 mm in length (*e.g.* SF 27 and SF 163); medium, between

Figure 4.7.18 Rotary quern fragment found by Euan MacKie prior to the commencement of the excavations

Figure 4.7.19 Stone lamps Group

110 and 130 mm in length (*e.g.* SF 95 and SF 106); and large, 130 mm to 190 mm (*e.g.* SF 36, SF 59, SF 66, SF 70). Of note is example SF 163 which is significantly smaller than the rest of the group with a remaining length of only 90.5 mm. This example consists of a very small shallow ovoid lamp with a lentoid shaped shallow bowl, broken across a projecting subrectangular handle which extends from one narrow end. This example this has been very crudely produced and appears unfinished. A small number of particularly diminutive lamps are known amongst the Scottish corpus including that from Kirkhill, west of Inverness (Close Brooks 1972, 295, fig. 3) which has a maximum length of only 66 mm and resembles very closely example SF 106 amongst the current assemblage. Close-Brooks observes during the discussion of the Kirkhill example that most lamps are at least 76 mm in width and that few are smaller although singular examples from Dun Telve Broch, Glenelg (NMS: X.GA 979; Curle 1916, 251, fig. 9), Bellrannoch Quarry, Broxburn, West Lothian (NMS: X.AQ 111) and an unprovenanced example in the collections of Hawick Museum are known (Close-Brooks 1972, 295). Close-Brooks defines these examples as miniatures and considers whether they may be regarded as toys (*ibid.*, 296), an assertion worthy of future detailed consideration. The possibly unfinished lamp, SF 163, at only 90.5 mm in length, although small, seems to sit comfortably at the smaller end of the broad spectrum of sizes of lamps and is not truly a miniature, unlike the examples identified from Kirkhill, Dun Telve etc (*ibid.*).

A previous study of stone lamps (Steer 1956) demonstrated that only 15% of the 75 examples examined in the collections of NMAS had long handles, defined as those being over 50.8 mm in length. An example from Woodside Croft, Cusalmond, Aberdeenshire is a particularly extreme example of a long-handled cup (Callander 1916, fig. 2). The vast majority (85%) of those examined by Steer had short handles. Although this observation is valuable,

the definition of 'short' and 'long' based simply on size is a little unsatisfactory as it is the proportion in size and length to the diameter of the bowl which ultimately predicates whether a handle can be described as short or long, as SF 70 amongst the Clachtoll assemblage amply demonstrates. Also, no mention was made in this earlier study of the shape of the handles which makes it difficult to compare the Clachtoll lamps to this wider data set in a meaningful way. Based on the proportion of size and length of the handle to the exterior diameter of the bowl and the overall length of the lamp, rather than Steer's arbitrary measurement criteria, all of the examples from Clachtoll are of the short-handled variety. It is of interest that amongst this current group, it is the handle, and more specifically the junction between the bowl and the handle of the lamps, which tend to be the focus for any form of embellishment although SF 66 is a notable exception.

As Callander previously noted, the decoration, when such exists, is invariably done in geometric patterns formed by straight lines incised on the exterior wall and handle of the vessel (1916, 149). At Clachtoll, two examples show simple ornamentation around the handle: in SF 106, a groove has been carved around the root of the projecting lug-shaped handle creating a division between the external edge of the bowl and the handle. It is unclear if this is purely for aesthetic purposes as it may have been intended to facilitate a binding, for example a string or sinew, to enable the lamp to be suspended whilst unused. SF 36 has a short thick subrectangular square handle, with two short incised triangular indentations at the angle between the external edge of the bowl and the beginnings of the handle. Like SF 106 it is likely that this embellishment fulfilled both aesthetic and practical purposes, the indentations providing recesses which could have been intended to keep a binding or suspension cord in place to facilitate storage when not in use. Only one lamp amongst the group was heavily decorated. This lamp (SF 66) is decorated on the exterior rounded surfaces of the hemispherical bowl by a two of horizontal incised grooves, widely spaced below the rim, cut through by widely and slightly haphazardly executed incised vertical lines, similar to an example recovered from a cairn near Woodside Croft, Culsalmond, Aberdeenshire (Callander 1916, 146, fig. 1). The handle of this lamp is sub-square in shape with rounded edges and the upper surface of the handle is slightly concave. This surface is decorated with a simple incised saltire or equal armed cross. The concavity of the handle noted on this example is a feature highlighted by Steer (1956) who suggests that such shallow concavities were intended as thumb grips to help hold the lamps during use, although the weight when filled would make it difficult to hold the lamp in a balanced way in one hand. Three handled lamps made of schist from the broch of Dun Telve, Glenelg illustrate these concave handles (Curle 1916, 125, fig. 9) more effectively. Only one lamp (SF 70) amongst the Clachtoll assemblage was perforated through the handle. Steer's previous study indicated 60% of lamps examined within NMAS collections had perforated handles (Steer 1956, 244). It is unclear if this high proportion reflects a bias in collection strategy which favoured retention of examples displaying unusual or significant features or if this is a true reflection of a preference in Iron Age design. It is thought that the perforation of the handle was to facilitate suspension of the lamp while not in use, allowing it to be stored away from harm (Close-Brooks 1972, 297). This assertion is bolstered by a heavily ornamented example from Farleyer Moor, near Aberfeldy, which displays a band of geometric incised motifs which run diagonally across the convex base which would only have been visible when the lamp was suspended and not in use (*ibid.*, fig. 4) and a fragmentary lamp from Fairy Knowe, Buchlyvie which displayed polish through wear on the interior surfaces of the perforation (Clarke 1998, 379, illus. 37).

Although rarely stated in press, there has been a general assumption (as with many other artefact categories) that variations in design of such objects from site-to-site is likely to be a reflection of individual or community preferences, or particular makers favouring particular shapes and sizes, or chronology, seeing changes to shape and form though time with anticipated style drifts from generation to generation. The diversity of form in the examples observed at Clachtoll, however, suggests that individual preferences and the quirks of the maker may well be the defining element structuring their design, and that variability in form is not a reflection, at Clachtoll at least, of any significant time span.

In most instances the lamps from Clachtoll have been carefully shaped and well finished with smooth, abraded, and rounded surfaces, not just on the exterior surfaces of the bowl and handle but within the concavity of the bowl itself. Careful examination of the surfaces, however, reveal evidence of the tools used in the production process as well as the finishing stages of manufacture. Lamp SF 106 (Fig. 4.7.20a) is very well finished on the exterior but has a series of regular, closely spaced, vertical, linear tool marks (gouge or narrow-bladed chisel) which are present on the concave surface of the bowl running from the interior lip of the rim down towards the rounded base of the hollow. These incised gouge-marks are thought to be from the initial stage of hollowing out the lamp and are overlain by a series of finer horizontal and diagonal

Table 4.7.3 Summary of condition and dimensions of the steatite lamps. 'R' denotes remaining dimension

SF number	Condition	Max L (mm) including handle	Max ext D (mm) bowl	Max interior D (mm) bowl	Dpt bowl (mm)	H bowl (mm)	Handle L (mm)	Handle T max (mm)
SF 27	Intact	106.5	89.5	65.7	32.4	46.8	25	32.2
SF 36	Intact	177	142	96.5	35.5	59.5	35.6	37
SF 59	Substantial portion but damaged	R 141	122	78	38	57.3	unknown	33
SF 60	Fragment	unknown	est. 142	unknown	unknown	R 44.5	unknown	unknown
SF 65	Fragmentary	unknown	Min 221	Min 73.4	unknown	Min 72.5	unknown	Min 20
SF 66	Substantial portion but damaged	152.4	115	87	50.6	64.5	54.5	32.7
SF 70	Substantially intact but damaged	191	144.5	100	38	74.6	54.3	37.5
SF 95	Intact	126.3	89	72.8	30.9	37	42.2	28.5
SF 106	Intact	126.2	102.2	83	38	56	19	42.5
SF 163	Unfinished?	R 90.5	76	58.5	12.5	18.5	R 12	13.5

gouge- or chisel marks (Fig. 4.7.20b) made when evening out the surfaces of the hollow. All of these marks have been softened as the result of abrasion to smooth, perhaps using pumice or sand. Although less clear on SF 27, similar fine but shallow incised gouge marks overlain by fine striations are visible on the interior of the hollow. Fine tool marks, obscured by later smoothing to finish are also present on the interior of the miniature bowl (Fig. 4.7.21).

Lamp SF 95 also displays significant traces of working across the surface, particularly around the exterior of the bowl on one side consisting of a minimum of three transverse concentric (often overlapping) rows of cut facets probably made with a narrow square tipped chisel (ave. W 10 mm) and vertical gouge marks (W 2 mm) from initial manufacture or reshaping of the bowl after damage. Unlike the interior of the hollow, basal surface and handle, there has been no attempt to smooth away the tool marks or finish the exterior of the bowl. The position and direction of these chisel marks suggest working when the bowl was set in an inverted position. The interior of the bowl displays a series of fine concentric striations towards the rounded base may be the result of abrasion either with pumice or sand. The unfinished appearance of the exterior of the bowl is in direct contrast to the condition of the rest of the surfaces of the object, suggesting that these working traces may be the result of later modification or repair rather than initial working. Evidence for repair and modification of steatite lamps is rare but other examples are known such as the fragment of steatite lamp from Carlungie Souterrain I, Angus (Wainwright 1963) which had a projecting lug-shaped handle which had broken off in antiquity and the stump had been rubbed down, leaving the vertical perforation though the handle as a long exterior groove (Stevenson 1963, 148, fig. 41, pl. xxxvi, no. 131).

The lack of any evidence of steatite chips, flakes, or other waste from the process of manufacture suggest that the bowls were, at least, roughed out elsewhere and were not produced within the broch itself. The presence of crude working traces on the surfaces of SF 95 and the potentially unfinished example SF 163 cannot rule out on-site working but these may be the exception rather than the rule. An intriguing reference is made to a 'hollowed stone of flattened spheroidal shale with a projection on one side, like a stone cup in the making' from Midhowe broch, Orkney (Callander and Grant 1934, 498) but it is unclear if this is in anyway similar to the Clachtoll objects.

Turning to consideration of the condition of the lamps, a remarkable number were intact or substantially intact on discovery. These include SF 36, SF 95 and SF 107 and SF 27, the latter of which had broken cleanly across the width of the bowl post-deposition, probably due to the pressure exerted from the collapsed rubble above. Lamp SF 70 is substantially intact but there is significant

damage to the bowl in the form of a hairline crack which runs around the circumference as well as the loss of a large proportion of the rim and handle, mainly due to extreme friability of the stone. Decorated lamp (SF 66) is missing half of its bowl and was found in a fragmentary condition suggesting breakage of the object on one edge during the collapse of the structure during the fire. The other lamps are heavily damaged (SF 59), fragmentary (SF 65) or are represented by only a single piece (SF 60). A number of the lamps display damage to the base (*e.g.* SF 59), lower surface of the handles (*e.g.* SF 95) or to one particular area of the edge object (*e.g.* SF 66) and in each instance, these appear to be the result of a heavy blow or impact, perhaps the result of the object falling from a height. It is significant that eight of the ten lamps (SF 27, SF 36, SF 59, SF 60, SF 65, SF 66, SF 70, SF 95) were recovered from the burnt deposit (042) which covers the broch interior suggesting that the majority of the lamps were used or stored in the upper levels of the broch. Only two (SF 106 and SF 163) were recovered from the floor deposits (context 048). An account of the lamp found in 1871 records that this came from a recess in the guard cell wall and may have been *in situ* and undisturbed at the time of recovery. This accords well with the recovery of a cup-shaped lamp of micaceous sandstone with a short

Figure 4.7.20 Steatite lamp SF 106: a) photograph of stone lamp, b) detail of tool marks in the interior of the bowl

projecting rounded lug which was recovered from a niche in the broch wall at Crosskirk broch, Caithness (Fairhurst 1984, 125, no. 366, illus. 75).

Prior to conservation work to stabilise and clean the lamps, it was difficult to distinguish between blackened soot-based deposits on the surfaces which may have resulted from use, and the charcoal-stained soils in which many of the lamps were found. After careful cleaning during conservation, five of the Clachtoll lamps display clear evidence of sooting and staining consistent with use as a lamp (Q=5; SF 56, SF 66, SF 95, SF 106, SF 127); in some instances, little macroscopic staining/sooting was evidence but heat-discolouration of the stone was present (*e.g.* SF 65 and SF 70); whilst others remained relatively unsoiled (SF 35 and SF 163). In order to try and resolve the ambiguity about their function, organic residue analysis was undertaken on samples of carbonised encrusted residues or sooting removed from the interior surface of the bowl and in some instances on loose sherds of the bowls with the aim of detecting and identifying surviving lipids from the original contents. This is the first occasion that this form of analysis has been conducted on Iron Age steatite handled lamps although X-ray defraction (XRD) and X-ray fluorescence (XRF) analysis was undertaken on two sandstone mortars or lamps from Fairy Knowe, Buchlyvie (Davidson 1998) to try to better characterise the use of these objects. The analysis of the Fairy Knowe objects was not conclusive but detected residues of potash alum, suggesting a possible role in preparing alum as a preservative for curing hides amongst other potential uses (*ibid.*, 390). Analyses of the Clachtoll lamps was conducted on scrapings of residue from the interior of six bowls (SF 27, SF 59, SF 65, SF 70, SF 95, SF 106) and in four instances involved analyses of detached sherds of the bowls themselves (SF 59, SF 60, SF 65, SF 66); full details of this analysis, the methods used and the subsequent results are presented in Section 4.3, above. Surviving lipids were detected in only two examples. The lipids recognised in association with SF 60 (laboratory number CLT 10) comprised free fatty acids typical of degraded animal fat and long-chain fatty acids indicative of leaf or stem plant matter, the animal fat plotting with the ruminant dairy region suggesting a link with dairy products. Similarly free fatty acids deriving from degraded ruminant dairy fat were noted on SF 95 (laboratory number CLT 04) mixed with a lipid profile suggestive of the presence of beeswax (Dunne, Gillard and Evershed, Section 4.3).

How should this organic residue evidence be interpreted against the previous studies of this object type in Scotland? There is little doubt from the sooting and staining of the surfaces of the bowls that many, but perhaps not all, saw use as lamps. A perfectly reasonable assumption has existed in the published literature that had these objects seen use as lamps, the fuel was likely to be oil deriving from cetaceans or seabirds such as gannets, and fish (Sharman 1998, 149). Could the dairy signature detected suggest that these handled lamps were not designed principally as lighting equipment but rather as scoops or ladles used in processing dairy products such as milk, cheese or butter only to be used at a later stage as lamps, as suggested by Steer (1956, 246)? This cannot be ruled out on the basis of the organic residue results from only two of the objects at Clachtoll. The presence of beeswax in conjunction with SF 95 provides very rare evidence of the use of this valuable resource in the Iron Age and also bolsters the interpretation of these items as lamps. Can an alternative explanation be presented which might explain the presence of dairy lipids within the bowls? Rather than interpreting this evidence as the result of use in the production or consumption of dairy-based foodstuffs, it is entirely possible that the dairy signature from two of the Clachtoll examples indicates that the dairy product itself was the source of fuel, in the form of butter lamps (Pope 2003, 262). Butter lamps appear rarely as the subject of academic investigation, particularly in an archaeological setting, and yet this is a traditional lighting fuel in many areas of the globe even today, such as in Tibet where lamps within Buddhist temples and monasteries traditionally use yak butter as fuel and give off a smoky, flickering light. The use of butter as a lighting fuel in an archaeological context is bolstered by a recent study of organic residues preserved on three Iron Age ceramic lamps at Sahib, Jordon, which found lipids which indicate that the fuel used was derived from animal fat, possibly of ruminant origin (Mayyas *et al.* 2017).

During the Clachtoll project, a similar study of residues sampled from the surface of a steatite lamp fragment from recent excavations by at the Iron Age settlement at East Barns, Dunbar (AOC unpublished) was conducted and gleaned similar results to SF 60 from Clachtoll – free fatty acids typical of degraded animal fat and long-chain fatty acids indicative of leaf or stem epicuticular waxes. Like Clachtoll the fatty acids detected plot firmly within ruminant dairy fats suggestive of the production or use in conjunction with dairy products (Dunne, Gillard and Evershed 2019). This certainly bolsters the view that despite their disparate provenances (Assynt, Sutherland and Dunbar, East Lothian) that there was a consistency, or at least, similarity in the function of these steatite objects.

The quantity of lamps recovered from Clachtoll is exceptional in an Atlantic Scottish context. Handled examples come from Crosskirk, Everley, Kettleburn, Keiss Road and Nybster, Caithness (Fairhurst 1984, 125; Anderson 1901; Anon 1892, 239–40; Steer 1956, 245), Carn Laith, Gospie, Cinn Trolla, Kintradwell, Stoer Head broch, Sutherland (Curle 1916, 251), Dun Beag, Skye (Callander 1921, 120, fig. 6) and Galson, Lewis (Edwards

Figure 4.7.21 Detail of tool marks on miniature bowl SF 195

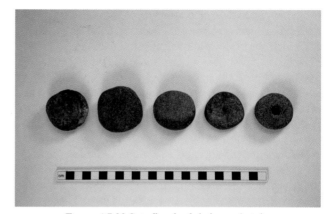

Figure 4.7.22 Spindle whorl chaine opératoire

1924, 198; Steer 1956, 245). Recovery of lamps, either handled or unhandled, of steatite or other stone, are typically limited to one or two examples. The closest parallel to the assemblage under discussion here in terms of form and number of lamps comes from Dun Telve, Glenelg (Curle 1916). Curle remarks that "vessels of stone have here been much in vogue" (*ibid.*, 252) in reference to the three intact handled examples produced from mica schist and three fragments of a further two examples, also of schist, one of which was decorated on the exterior of the bowl with a convex moulding below the rim, below which was a band of ornamentation consisting of a series of incised chevrons (*ibid.*, 250–1, fig. 9). At least two stone lamps or cups are known from Keiss Road broch (NMS: X.GA 575, 576), a minimum of four lamps/cups from Keiss broch (NMS: X.GA 528, 526, 525, 527) and a minimum of three lamps/cups from Everley broch (NMS: X.GA 698, 699, 700, 701).

Evidence for whorl production

Perforated and unperforated discs attest to the production of spindle whorls on the site. Although whorls are often thought of as ubiquitous finds on Iron Age sites, a study of their occurrence amongst 450 Iron Age assemblages in Scotland has demonstrated that they are found on only 30% of sites (Hunter 2015, 228). A far greater proportion of site assemblages examined in the north and west mainland, Northern Isles and Western Isles are associated with whorls (*ibid.*, tab. 13.3) than in the south, suggesting subtle differences in their use and deposition circumstances.

At Clachtoll most of the key stages of the supposed *chaine opératoire* are represented (Fig. 4.7.22): from a single possible manuport (SF 198), roughouts in various stages of production from roughly hewn (SF 79) to well developed (SF 180), some displaying the beginnings of a central perforation (SF 10) to those that appear

finished. Amongst those that appear finished, some have been decoration (*i.e.* SF 93) but so fresh in appearance it is difficult to establish whether these are only lightly used or unworn examples. In contrast, a small number of whorls (*e.g.* SF 197) display evidence of wear in the form of softening of the tools marks of the surfaces and particularly the edges of the perforation, associated with a light sheen from handling during use. The vast majority of these whorls, either in a complete or unfinished condition, have been produced from talc-rich rocks, predominantly amphibole-talc schists and chlorite-talc-schists which range in colour from a pale to dark silvery blue-grey to a deep bronze. These rock types would have been favoured not just due to their durability and relative ease at which they can be carved, but also due to the aesthetic qualities of the stone itself, many of which would have shimmered in the fire-light during use.

Only one possible manuport was recognised amongst the group in the form of a water-rounded and eroded biotite garnet psammite schist pebble (SF 198). Portions of the rounded edges of this natural pebble have witnessed differential water erosion giving it a stepped profile that makes it appear at first glance to have been partially worked but the shape and profile is entirely natural (F. McGibbon, pers. comm.). It may have been picked up from the shoreline for its inherent suitability of shape, size and weight for production of a whorl or simply due to is natural aesthetic properties. Although roughouts are present amongst the assemblage in varying stages of working, it appears that the most basic roughing out stage – where the overall desired shape is fractured, chipped or chiselled from a larger pebble, cobble or outcrop – was not undertaken elsewhere and not inside the broch as, with the exception of the possible manuport just described, no talc-schist blocks, pebbles or partially roughed out discs were recognised amongst the assemblage. Nor were any concentrations of large to medium-sized chips, flakes or other forms of debitage recovered. This implies that the basic shaping and preparation of the stones was largely undertaken at the source; the roughouts brought back to the broch for perforation and finishing. Six broad shapes of whorl (finished and unfinished) were recognised amongst this group and summarised in Table 4.7.4 below. Thin and thick disc-shaped roughouts and whorls dominate the assemblage but globular, flattened globular, flattened ovoid and thick flattened globular examples were also in evidence. Whether this difference in shape was related to subtle differences in the intended function of the whorl or to the preferences of those individuals producing them is unclear but this variety in shape at Clachtoll is not related to chronological distinctions.

The dimensions of these whorls can also be seen to form a fairly tight group. In terms of diameter, the whorls (both unfinished and finished) range from 33.6 mm to 58.3 mm, and in thickness from 9.2 to 25.5 mm. As Figures 4.7.23 and 4.7.24 demonstrate, the largest proportion of whorls (Q=18, 55% by count) cluster between 40–49 mm in diameter and the majority (26, 79% by count) are between 15–24 mm in thickness.

In addition to the importance of the size and relative proportion of the whorls from the broch, the weight of individual examples is also significant (Fig. 4.7.25) as this is largely determined by the strength of the yarn desired from a given fibre (MacGregor 1974, 88). Unlike the large groups from Broch of Burrian which display an almost continuous spectrum of weights with no particular tendency to cluster around any specific weight, the Clachtoll whorls, including those unfinished and those that appear finished, cluster between 30 g to 59 g, accounting for 61% of examples from the broch. Perhaps unsurprisingly, the unfinished whorls tend to be heavier than those that are intact, presumably reflecting the reduction of mass during the final shaping and finishing process. It is possible that the range of weights (and sizes) of whorls amongst the Clachtoll assemblage represents different materials being processed, such as plant fibres or wool, and as suggested

at Burrian, the heavier whorls may have been used for doubling or plying yarns to give them greater strength (*ibid.*, 89).

Nine of the whorls are decorated (summarised in Table 4.7.5) and consist of examples embellished with series of bored dots, incised radial lines, and concentric lines surrounding the perforation on one or both faces, as well as a small number being decorated on the edges. In general, the decoration is geometric and incised radial lines are the most common amongst the group. Two examples (SF 196 and SF 209) are 'pulley whorl' type (MacGregor 1974, 92, fig. 18, no. 249) having a continuous groove around their edge, a type occasionally encountered on broch sites including that from Dun Mor Vaul, Tiree (MacKie 1974, fig. 16, no. 300).

The embellishment of stone artefacts in the Iron Age is rare (Evans 1989) but is occasionally noted on rotary quern stones and spindle whorls (Fig. 4.5.26) where there is a general correlation and similarity in the motifs used between the two artefacts (McLaren and Hunter 2008, 114–19). Decoration consisting of combinations of simple incised radial lines is the most common decorative style for stone whorls in Iron Age Scotland. Similar examples have a wide distribution and frequently associated with broch sites such as the Keiss Road Broch, Caithness (unpublished; NMS: X.GA 591); Broch of Burrian, Orkney (MacGregor 1974, 92, fig. 18:249); Dun Telve, Glenelg (Curle 1916, 254, fig. 10) and Dun an Iardhard and Dun Ardtreck, Skye (MacLeod 1915, 67; MacKie 2000a, illus. 25:65), to name a few. The whorl (SF 88) decorated by bored dots surrounding the perforation is more unusual but can be paralleled amongst assemblages from the brochs of Ousdale, Wester, and Yarhouse, as well as one from Freswick Sands, all Caithness (unpublished; NMS: X.GA 353, X.GA 648; X.GK 30; X.GA 774).

One spindle whorl roughout (SF 33), if that is what it was originally intended to be, is more unusual and is decorated with a fine spiral line carved into one face

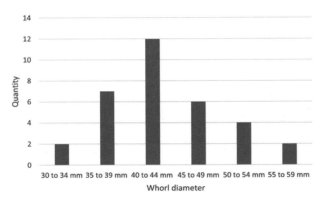

Figure 4.7.23 The diameter of whorls (unfinished and finished) from Clachtoll

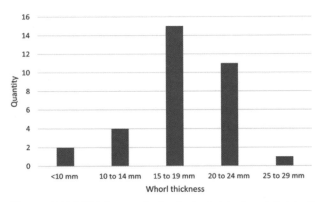

Figure 4.7.24 Thickness of whorls (unfinished and finished) from Clachtoll

Table 4.7.4 Summary of whorl shape (unfinished and finished)

Shape	Quantity
Disc	10
Thick disc	13
Globular	2
Flattened globular	5
Thick flattened globular	1
Flattened ovoid	2
Total	33

Table 4.7.5 Range of decoration displayed on the spindle whorls from Clachtoll

SF no.	Condition	Flat face(s)				Edges			
		Spiral	Dots	Radial lines	Concentric lines	Groove	Multiple grooves	Radial lines	Short oblique incised lines
SF 33	Unfinished (unperforated)	*							
SF 88	Finished. ?worn		*						
SF 93	Finished. ?worn			*					
SF 196	Finished. ?worn			*		*			
SF 197	Finished. Worn						*		
SF 209	Finished. ?worn			*		*			*
SF 212	Finished. Worn			*					
SF 215	Finished. Worn			*	*				
SF 218	Finished. Worn			*				*	

(Fig. 4.7.27), perhaps a simple doodle or personalised decoration. Small stone discs with ephemeral scratched doodles are known from Burland, Shetland (McLaren and Hunter 2014, 291). The incised decoration on SF 128 from Burland is a particularly close example to SF 33 from Clachtoll, which has a series of curvilinear, concentric and spiral scratched lines covering one face (*ibid.*, fig 4.37, no. 128). Like that from Clachtoll, the Burland disc decoration is shallow and irregular, and has the appearance of doodles rather than formal decoration. The appearance of such simple curvilinear designs is important as it demonstrates as Evan's earlier argues (1989), that the general lack of motifs incorporating curvilinear design on Iron Age worked stone is a choice rather than a restriction imposed by the inherent properties of the material type.

The quantity of unfinished whorls and discs amongst the Clachtoll assemblage is unparalleled amongst published broch assemblages in the Western Isles, Inner Hebrides and north-west mainland. Occasional unfinished examples in amongst larger assemblages are fairly frequently encountered (*e.g.* Clatchard Craig, Fife: Close-Brooks 1986, 175, no. 175; Dun an Iardhard, Skye: MacLeod 1915, 67; Nybster, Caithness: Heald in prep; Garry Iochdrach, North Uist: Beveridge and Callander

1932, 41; Midhowe Broch, Orkney: Callander and Grant 1934, 497, to name a few) but their numbers are small and tend to suggest episodic, expedient production when demand required it rather than production on masse. For example, amongst the 25 stone whorls from Broch of Burrian, Orkney (MacGregor 1974, 112), only one (SF 253) was unfinished consisting of a roughed out blank with the beginnings of a perforation on both faces whilst a second example (SF 233) displayed signs of possible reworking in the form of an attempted expansion to the perforation using a tubular drill. The general paucity of evidence of whorl production is likely to be biased by problems of recognition where unfinished or roughed out discs have, quite reasonably, been ascribed to a variety of possible functions or intended use. An excellent example of this is found at Hurly Hawkin, Angus where around 50 small stone discs were recovered in varying stages of production from crudely flaked to finely ground. Henshall (1982, 233–5) reasonably argued the abrasion noted on the faces and edges of many of these discs could be the by-product of their use as rubbing or grinding tools, becoming better "finished" from the resulting wear. The majority of these are unperforated and were classed as a distinct category of tool by Henshall. Only five of these

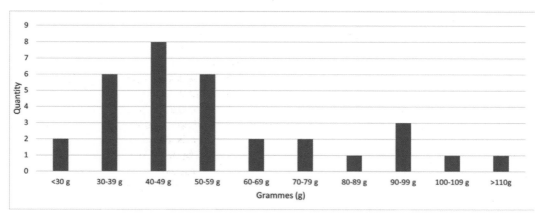

Figure 4.7.25 Weight of whorls (unfinished and finished) from Clachtoll

discs were perforated but these were considered to be secondary modifications unrelated to an intended use a whorls (*ibid.*, 235). A similar assemblage to that at Hurly Hawkin comes from Crosskirk broch, Caithness (Fairhurst 1984, 126–8) where 35 discs were recovered. These were split into three main groups: counters, small discs and pot lids. The second group, small discs, are very similar in shape and size to those found at Clachtoll, but examples with unfinished perforations or the beginnings of a perforation were entirely absent, leading to their rather unsatisfactory classification. These two examples amply demonstrate that the distinction between unfinished whorls and small discs used or intended for use in a range of other crafts and functions is not always possible to distinguish with confidence. The evidence of whorl production at Clachtoll is less ambiguous and provides a very valuable case of organised production albeit on a small scale. Were the whorls being made at Clachtoll to satisfy the needs of the occupants of the broch itself and, if so, what does this inform us about the scale of textile production at the site? Or were the people of Clachtoll producing whorls for trade?

Looking in closer detail at the distribution of the unfinished and finished whorls amongst the broch interior deposits is instructive and leads to significant insights. Eleven whorls (33% by count) came from rubble and deposits relating to the collapsed superstructure and upper internal levels of the broch (contexts 011, 028, 042, 071), including six (SF 33, 40, 47, 50, 55, 79, 88) which were recovered from the burnt deposit (context 042) which covered the entire broch interior. Importantly, none of the whorls from these upper layers displayed evidence of wear and appear to represent a group of whorls in the process of production, with examples which have been roughed out but are unperforated, those where the perforation has begun but has not been completed to those which appear largely finished but are so fresh in their condition there is significant doubt whether they ever saw any use. Most of the whorls found during the early stages of the excavation

in these upper layers come from the north-west and south-east quadrants, implying that the manufacture of whorls was either carried out in the broch's upper interior levels and/or whorls in the process of production were stored on the upper floors.

The rest of the whorls came from various floor levels and deposits within the broch interior. A single decorated and worn whorl (SF 218) came from midden (context 047) whilst seven (SF 180, 189, 190, 196, 197, 198, 222) were recovered from the mixed fill (078) of the souterrain [069]. The group from the souterrain also form an interesting collection as they include a possible manuport (SF 198), an unperforated roughout (SF 180), two whorls which are complete but display an absence of observable wear (SF 196 and 189) and four which display clear signs of use-wear, two of which are decorated (SF 190, 197). From the surrounding floor levels, seven examples came from context (048). These include four unfinished examples (SF 74, 117, 153, 172), one with possible light use only (SF 142), and two which display signs of wear (SF 104, 207). One example, SF 93, decorated but showing evidence of light use only came from organic flooring material (049) whilst two whorls (SF 147, 209), both worn from use, were recovered from the same flooring (062) in the SW quadrant. Below midden (047), flooring (067) in the southern half of the broch incorporated three whorls, two of which (SF 212 and SF 215) were decorated and worn, and a third example (SF 209) was finished but displayed little evidence of use-wear. The final example (SF 243) which was finished and worn, came from a deliberate deposit of sand (159) which had been laid down as flooring.

In summary, we have examples of whorls from both floor-level deposits and from collapsed material that are likely to have derived from the upper flooring levels within the broch tower. Roughouts and unfinished examples come from deposits suggestive of working or storage on the upper flooring levels of the tower, from floor deposit (048) and from within the fill (078) of the souterrain [069], concentrating towards the south-east

Figure 4.7.26 A selection of the decorated spindle whorls

Figure 4.7.27 Stone disc with incised spiral design (SF 33)

quadrants of the interior. Examples which display extensive wear are entirely lacking from the deposits that may relate to the upper flooring levels within the tower. Although unfinished, unworn or lightly worn examples are not exclusive to these deposits and are found within the various floor levels, the whorls that display convincing evidence of wear are more widely dispersed across the floor levels, concentrating in contexts 062, 067 and 078.

Condition of the stone tools

The worked stone from Clachtoll survives in a wide range of conditions reflecting the various states of use of individual objects at the time of the fire: material abandoned in the process of manufacture (whorls, possibly the lower rotary quern); objects which were in use at the time of the fire (knocking stone, thatch weight, at least some of the lamps); and artefacts which had already gone out of use and been incorporated into floor surfaces or walling (querns).

Looking more closely at the lamps, although most are intact, some display damage to the base or one edge that is suggestive of breakage as the result of an impact from below and are likely to have occurred by the lamps falling from a height. The position and context of recovery suggests that these may have been in use or in storage in the upper levels of the broch, the damage occurring when the internal structure collapsed during the fire. Mirroring this, some of the unfinished whorls show similar fracturing as though damaged by impact. The majority of cobble tools are intact and many could well have still been functional in their recovered condition. Here the context of recovery is instructive as they derive from a variety of contexts including the burnt layer (042), flooring deposits (049) and, interestingly, there is a cluster of burnishers situated at the entrance (082). Could these have been abandoned in the process of use, as can be argued for the knocking stone?

In contrast, the quern stones are mostly intact but appear damaged as the result of extensive use. As considered earlier, it can be argued that attempts were made to keep the querns in service as long as possible which attests to their value in the household as key food processing tools and potentially in a more symbolic role as objects which embody concepts of fertility with links to the agricultural cycle. Even those quern stones which were imported from further distances were eventually exhausted with use despite attempts to extend their lives and reused within the flooring rather than suffering a more casual discard. No obvious pairs were identified amongst the assemblage suggesting that some of these querns may have been rescued and removed before the tower collapsed or else stored outside the broch walls.

Beyond the broch walls: worked stone from Clachtoll in context

The worked stone assemblage from the site is not large in comparison to many broch assemblages in the Northern Isles where a ready supply of workable stone and multi-period occupation lead to the accumulation of significant and wide-ranging assemblages. At only 101 items (including the two objects found prior to excavation) the size of the Clachtoll broch assemblage is more comparable to sites such as Crosskirk, Caithness from which a minimum of 113 items were recovered (Fairhurst 1984) or Dun Vulan where a minimum of 80 items of stone and pumice were recognised (Parker Pearson and Sharples 1999) but falls somewhat short of the *c.* 180 items from Dun Mor Vaul, Tiree (MacKie 1974). Accurate comparison with broch and wheelhouse assemblages in the Atlantic province is hampered by a lack of quantification and detail in past excavation reports, particularly when describing the discovery of items such as hammerstones and cobble tools which tend to be brushed over and given only the most cursory of mentions.

To allow the stone assemblage from Clachtoll to be put into its wider context, a survey of the published excavation records of 40 sites in Caithness and the Inner and Outer Hebrides was conducted and the results presented in Table 4.7.6. This survey is not intended to be comprehensive but simply to allow broad comparisons to be made between the Clachtoll worked stone assemblage and those of comparable date and/or character. Rather than focussing on the quantity of worked stone recovered for the reasons set out above, focus has been placed on the functions and classifications of stone objects, under the same broad classifications already discussed for Clachtoll. A caveat must be stated in that where possible, published identifications have been followed but where identifications are ambiguous or fall outside of the broad classifications, they are noted under the miscellaneous category. It is likely that this will mask subtleties in the analysis but is intended simply as a framework for discussion. It is notable that worked stone in Caithness tends to be more varied in terms of range represented as opposed to assemblages from North and South Uist which, in the main, are far more limited with some notable exceptions including Foshigarry, Bac Mhic Connain and Garry Iochdrach, North Uist (Beveridge and Callander 1931; 1932) and Galson, Lewis (Edwards 1924).

As anticipated, items associated with food processing and consumption, and tools dominate most assemblages. Rotary querns are found on 26 sites (65%) whist saddle querns, a type entirely absent from Clachtoll, are found on 14 (35%). Pot lids are amongst the most consistent object found across the sites (42.5%) and yet, again, are intriguingly absent from Clachtoll. The absence may be explained by the use of a different material, such as skin covers or wooden lids, but this is conjectural. Cobble tools are ubiquitous, appearing on 97% of sites surveyed. Where they appear to be absent this may be a reflection of a lack of recognition rather than a genuine absence. In terms of the types of crafts represented by surviving tools, spindle whorls, whetstones and pumice dominate the group. Twenty-one assemblages (52.5%) include spindle whorls attesting to textile production but intriguingly appear to be more frequently encountered on broch sites in Caithness and Skye as opposed to broch, wheelhouse and other sites in Lewis and North and South Uist. Stone whorls also appear to share a stronger association with brochs than any other type of structure. Could this suggest specialisation of textile production in discrete areas of the north and west? The current survey is not nuanced enough to answer this question with confidence, particularly as it fails to consider whorls produced from bone or ceramic, but this is an interesting pattern which would benefit from closer study. Whetstones are found on 22 sites (55%), again with stronger representation in Caithness, Skye and also South Uist. The same number of assemblages include pumice but here the spread across

the areas surveyed is more balanced. Polishers, burnishers and smoothers are difficult to distinguish in some earlier excavation accounts meaning that it is difficult to tease apart function. As displayed on Table 4.7.6, this is almost certainly a conflation of tools associated with hide-processing, metalworking and pottery production. They are also probably under-represented here as there are likely to be examples amongst the cobble tools and those described under the shorthand of 'hammerstone'.

Household items present amongst this group include socket stones or pivot stones which are recorded on ten sites (25%) and weights on only seven sites (17.5%). This category is very broad and masks a range of possible functions including thatch-weights, door-weights but also potentially loom weights or net-weights. Lamps – so prominent amongst the Clachtoll assemblage – are found on 12 of the sites surveyed (32.5%) and, like the spindle whorls already mentioned, appear to cluster in Caithness and are absent from the sites surveyed in North Uist. This pattern is unlikely to be the result of relative proximity to viable sources of steatite, in which case a similar proportion of sites in Skye (due to proximity to Glenelg source) would surely also include examples. Ornaments are the least well represented category of stone as is expected, bolstered here by the inclusion of items of shale, jet (and other black organic stones) and amber.

Despite the close correlation of the Clachtoll pottery assemblage to contemporary assemblages in the Western Isles, the worked stone assemblage from the broch finds closer correlations in terms of range of objects present, with broch sites in Caithness.

Conclusions

The recovery of a comprehensive range and quantity of worked stone objects at Clachtoll is significant due to the excellent preservation of the items recovered but also due to the close dating of the short-lived activity within the structure; a picture which can often be muddied on other broch sites due to evidence of long-lived sequential phases of activity which frequently rework, redeposit and mix together finds across various episodes of use. This factor has proven to often complicate attempts to synthesise artefact assemblages, particularly those of coarse stone, steatite and pumice, which often comprise types which are not particularly chronologically sensitive when dealing with short-lived episodes (McLaren and Hunter 2014, 284). The assemblage from Clachtoll is one of the rare few instances uncovered using modern excavation techniques that provide us with a momentary snapshot of a home, presenting the opportunity to better quantify and characterise what in many ways appears to be a fairly typical and prosaic Iron Age broch in use between the 1st century BC and 1st century AD.

Table 4.7.6 Summary survey of 40 Iron Age sites from Caithness, the Inner and Outer Hebrides, etc. by range of worked stone present with a comparison to Clachtoll

Site	Region	Site type	References	Food Production/consumption							Household			Craft and tools							
				Vessel	Vessel stopper?	Pot lids or discs	Rotary quern	Saddle quern	Rubbing stone (for use with saddle quern)	Knocking stone and/or mortar	Socket stone	Lamp	Weight	Loomweight	Spindle whorls	Cobble tool ('hammerstone'/grinder/pounder/combination tools)	Sharpening stone	Whetstones	Strike-a-light	Polishers or rubbers	Pumice
Clachtoll	Assynt	Broch	This paper				X			X		x (handled)	X		X	X		X	X	X	X
Allasdale (Tigh Talamhanta I)	Barra	Wheelhouse and souterran	Young 1953						X		X					x		x	x	x	x
Dun Cuier	Barra	Broch	Young 1956			x	x	x			x				x	x		x	x	x	x
Skitten, Kilminster	Caithness	Broch	Calder 1948			x	x	x		x					x	x				x	
Kettleburn	Caithness	Broch	Rhind 1853; Anon 1892			x		x		? (re-used saddle quern)		x (handled & unhandled)			x	x		x	x	x	
Keiss Harbour	Caithness	Broch	Anderson 1901; Heald & Jackson 2001			x	x	x				x (handled & unhandled)			x	x		x		x	
Keiss Road	Caithness	Broch	Anderson 1901; Heald & Jackson 2001			x	x	x				x (handled & unhandled)			x	x		x	x		
Whitegate	Caithness	Broch	Anderson 1901; Heald & Jackson 2001			x	x	x							x	x					
Everley	Caithness	Broch	Anderson 1901; Heald & Jackson 2001; Heald forthcoming			?						x (handled & unhandled)	x		x	x		x	x	x	
Nybster	Caithness	Broch	Anderson 1901; Heald in prep			?	x	x		x	x	x			x	x		x	x	x	x

(Continued)

Table 4.7.6 (Continued)

Site	Region	Site type	References	Food Production/consumption							Household			Craft and tools							
				Vessel	Vessel stopper?	Pot lids or discs	Rotary quern	Saddle quern	Rubbing stone (for use with saddle quern)	Knocking stone and/or mortar	Socket stone	Lamp	Weight	Loomweight	Spindle whorls	Cobble tool ('hammerstone'/grinder/pounder/ combination tools)	Sharpening stone	Whetstones	Strike-a-light	Polishers or rubbers	Pumice
Thrumster	Caithness	Broch	Barber in prep			x						x	x		x	x		x		x	x
Crosskirk	Caithness	Broch	Fairhurst 1984			x		x		x	x	x (handled & unhandled)	x		x	x		x			
Dun Telve, near Glenelg	Highland	Broch	Curle 1916			x						x (handled)			x	x	x	x			
An Dunan	Lewis	Cellular	Church, Nesbit & Gilmour 2013			x										x					
Dun Bharabhat	Lewis	Broch	Harding & Dixon 2000			x									x	x		x	x	x	
Galson	Lewis	Cellular	Edwards 1924			x		x		x		x (handled)	x	?x		x			x		x
Gob Eirer	Lewis	Promontory enclosure	Nesbitt, Church & Gilmour 2011													x				x	x
Gress Lodge, Stornoway	Lewis	Settlement	MacKie 1966							x						x					
Cnip	Lewis	Wheelhouse	Armit 2006													x					
Dun Carloway	Lewis	Broch	Tabraham 1977													x					
Clattraval	North Uist	Broch/Fort overlying chambered cairn	Scott 1935													x					x
Eilean Maleit	North Uist	Wheelhouse	Armit 1998												x	x					x
Eilean Olabhat	North Uist	Cellular	Armit, Campbell & Dunwell 2008												x	x		x			x

(Continued)

Table 4.7.6 Summary survey of 40 Iron Age sites from Caithness, the Inner and Outer Hebrides, etc. by range of worked stone present with a comparison to Clachtoll (Continued)

Site	Region	Site type	References	Vessel	Vessel stopper?	Pot lids or discs	Rotary quern	Saddle quern	Rubbing stone (for use with saddle quern)	Knocking stone and/or mortar	Socket stone	Lamp	Weight	Loomweight	Spindle whorls	Cobble tool ('hammerstone'/ grinder/pounder/ combination tools)	Sharpening stone	Whetstones	Strike-a-light	Polishers or rubbers	Pumice
				Food Production/consumption							Household			Craft and tools							
Foshgarry	North Uist	Wheelhouse and cellular	Beveridge & Callander 1931		x	x	x	x			x				x	x	x	x	x	x	x
Dun Thomaidh	North Uist	Broch	Beveridge 1911					x	x		x					x		x	x		x
Garry Iochdrach	North Uist	Wheelhouse	Beveridge & Callander 1932	x		x	?	?	x	x	x				x	x		x	x	x	x
Bac Mhic Connain	North Uist	Wheelhouse	Beveridge & Callander 1932			x	x	x			x					x	x		x	x	x
Baleshare	North Uist	Wheelhouse	Beveridge 1911; Barber 2003				x									x					x
Sollas	North Uist	Wheelhouse	Campbell 1991			x	x								x	x					
Dun an Iardhard, Uiginish	Skye	Broch	MacLeod 1915				x								x	x		x	x		
Dun Ardtreck	Skye	Broch	MacKie 2000a				x								x	x		x	x	x	x
Dun Beag	Skye	Broch	Callander 1921			x	x					x (handled)			x	x		x	x	x	x
Dún Mór, Dornie	Skye	Artificial platforms	Neighbour 2000													x					
Á Cheardach Bheag, South Uist	South Uist	Wheelhouse and cellular	Fairhurst 1971				X			X	X					X		x			X
Á Cheardach Mhor	South Uist	Wheelhouse	Young & Richardson 1960			x	x	x				x				x		x			x

(Continued)

Table 4.7.6 (Continued)

Site	Region	Site type	References	Vessel	Vessel stopper?	Pot lids or discs	Rotary quern	Saddle quern	Rubbing stone (for use with saddle quern)	Knocking stone and/or mortar	Socket stone	Lamp	Weight	Loomweight	Spindle whorls	Cobble tool	Hammerstone / grinder/pounder/ combination tools	Sharpening stone	Whetstones	Strike-a-light	Polishers or rubbers	Pumice
Dun Vulan	South Uist	Broch	Parker Pearson & Sharples 1999				x										x		x			x
Kilpheder	South Uist	Wheelhouse	Lethbridge 1952			x	x										x					
Cill Donnain (phases 4-8)	South Uist	Wheelhouse	Parker Pearson & Zvelebil 2014								x						x					
Dun Mor Vaul	Tiree	Broch	MacKie 1974			x	x								x		x		x	x	?x	x
Balevullin	Tiree	Settlement	MacKie 1963				x										x			x		
Loch Bhasapoll, Cornaig	Tiree	Settlement	MacKie 1963												x		x				x	

Table 4.7.6 Summary survey of 40 Iron Age sites from Caithness, the Inner and Outer Hebrides, etc. by range of worked stone present with a comparison to Clachtoll (Continued)

Site	Region	Site type	References	Ornament			Other					FC stone	Range of worked stone present
				Ring	Bead	Pendant	Discs	Balls	Axe	Pebbles (misc)	Misc		
Clachtoll	Assynt	Broch	This volume			?X	X					x	13
Allasdale (Tigh Talamhanta 1)	Barra	Wheelhouse and souterran	Young 1953			?x					x		7
Dun Cuier	Barra	Broch	Young 1956							X	x Sinker?; stone mould frag.	x	13
Skitten, Kilminster	Caithness	Broch	Calder 1948				x (?counter/gaming piece)				x tether stones, ashets (?saddle querns), anvil stones		13
Kettleburn	Caithness	Broch	Rhind 1853; Anon 1892		x		x						13
Keiss Harbour	Caithness	Broch	Anderson 1901; Heald & Jackson 2001			x				x	x decorated slate, knife, painted pebble, steatite object, stone mould	x	13
Keiss Road	Caithness	Broch	Anderson 1901; Heald & Jackson 2001							x	x Gaming counter; stone mould		11

(Continued)

Table 4.7.6 (Continued)

Site	Region	Site type	References	Ornament			Other					FC stone	Range of worked stone present
				Ring	Bead	Pendant	Discs	Balls	Axe	Pebbles (misc)	Misc		
Whitegate	Caithness	Broch	Anderson 1901; Heald & Jackson 2001							x			5
Everley	Caithness	Broch	Anderson 1901; Heald & Jackson 2001; Heald in prep				x (jet)			x	x anvil stone/ mortar	x	12
Nybster	Caithness	Broch	Anderson 1901; Heald in prep				x (counter?)				x haematite	x	14
Thrumster	Caithness	Broch	Barber in prep		x		x (counter/ gaming pieces)				x stone mould		10
Crosskirk	Caithness	Broch	Fairhurst 1984				x	x			x painted pebble; tank lid; grooved slab		15
Dun Telve, near Glenelg	Highland	Broch	Curle 1916										6
An Dunan	Lewis	Cellular	Church, Nesbit & Gilmour 2013		x (amber)						x intact shale armlet	x	5
Dun Bharabhat	Lewis	Broch	Harding & Dixon 2000										6
Galson	Lewis	Cellular	Edwards 1924		x								10
Gob Eirer	Lewis	Promontory enclosure	Nesbitt, Church & Gilmour 2011								x anvil stone		4
Gress Lodge, Stornoway	Lewis	Settlement	MacKie 1966										2
Cnip	Lewis	Wheelhouse	Armit 2006										2

(Continued)

Table 4.7.6 Summary survey of 40 Iron Age sites from Caithness, the Inner and Outer Hebrides, etc. by range of worked stone present with a comparison to Clachtoll (Continued)

Site	Region	Site type	References	Ornament			Other						Range of worked stone present
				Ring	Bead	Pendant	Discs	Balls	Axe	Pebbles (misc)	Misc	FC stone	
Dun Carloway	Lewis	Broch	Tabraham 1977										1
Clattraval	North Uist	Broch/Fort overlying chambered cairn	Scott 1935										2
Eilean Maleit	North Uist	Wheelhouse	Armit 1998								x (?maul/weight)		3
Eilean Olabhat	North Uist	Cellular	Armit, Campbell & Dunwell 2008								x haematite		5
Foshigarry	North Uist	Wheelhouse and cellular	Beveridge & Callander 1931	x				x	x	x		x	18
Dun Thomaidh	North Uist	Broch	Beveridge 1911										7
Garry Iochdrach	North Uist	Wheelhouse	Beveridge & Callander 1932		x (jet/shale)		x	x	x	x			17
Bac Mhic Connain	North Uist	Wheelhouse	Beveridge & Callander 1932								x stone mould		10
Baleshare	North Uist	Wheelhouse	Beveridge 1911; Barber 2003										3
Sollas	North Uist	Wheelhouse	Campbell 1991										4
Dun an Iardhard, Uiginish	Skye	Broch	MacLeod 1915		x (amber)						x steatite armlet fragment		7
Dun Ardtreck	Skye	Broch	MacKie 2000	x (jet/shale)	x (amber)		x				x palette & counters	x	10
Dun Beag	Skye	Broch	Callander 1921	x		x	x	x			x stone moulds		14
Dùn Mór, Dornie	Skye	Artificial platforms	Neighbour 2000										1

(Continued)

Table 4.7.6 (Continued)

Site	Region	Site type	References	Ornament			Other					FC stone	Range of worked stone present
				Ring	Bead	Pendant	Discs	Balls	Axe	Pebbles (misc)	Misc		
Á Cheardach Bheag, South Uist	South Uist	Wheelhouse and cellular	Fairhurst 1971										6
Á Cheardach Mhor	South Uist	Wheelhouse	Young & Richardson 1959										6
Dun Vulan	South Uist	Broch	Parker Pearson & Sharples 1999				x				x cup-marked stone		6
Kilpheder	South Uist	Wheelhouse	Lethbridge 1952										4
Cill Donnain (phases 4-8)	South Uist	Wheelhouse	Parker Pearson & Zvelebil 2014							x (?sling stones)			1
Dun Mor Vaul	Tiree	Broch	MacKie 1974	x (jet/ shale)	x (jet/ shale)		x			x	x includes anvil stone, poss pot smoothers and ingot mould		16
Balevullin	Tiree	Settlement	MacKie 1963										2
Loch Bhasapoll, Cornaig	Tiree	Settlement	MacKie 1963								x 'anvil stone'		4

4.8 The talc-rich schist objects

Fiona McGibbon and Richard Jones

A note on the talc-rich schists amongst the Clachtoll assemblage

Fiona McGibbon

Talc schist is a name applied to a range of alteration products of rocks formed during volatile-rich metamorphism. As such it does not form extensive sheets or layers and is not a mappable unit. It is likely to exist as small pockets and lenses which only form in suitable protolith rock types which tend to be magnesium-rich, mafic compositions (in the Assynt area protolith rocks could be mafic gneiss, or Scourie dykes). It is a hydrous rock type and so forms when chemically active waters interact with pre-existing rocks often associated with shear zones. As such it can form a range of grainsizes, textures and mineralogies depending on several variables – the pre-existing rock type, the nature of the hydrous fluids, and the exact environment of metamorphism. Most of the talc 'schist' artefacts are not particularly schistose which makes an alteration source rather than a regional metamorphism source more likely. This can explain the diversity of talc bearing lithologies seen in the artefact assemblage at Clachtoll which are varied but all essentially variations on a theme, their heterogeneity probably reflecting the heterogeneity of the local source. They are all dominated by talc, an amphibole (which may be actinolite, tremolite or anthophyllite – but impossible to say without further data), and chlorite in varying proportions, grainsizes and textural types. Some show regular iron-stained pits where a ferruginous mineral (only examined macroscopically) seems to have been leached or oxidized out, and interstitial dolomite/magnesite. Many show an almost porous texture suggestive of the hydrous alteration mechanism likely to have formed them.

Two samples of talc-bearing rocks were collected from local outcrops. The sample from (NGR) NC 04305 26805 shares many petrographic similarities with several artefacts examined. It shares the following features: green-grey resinous bladed mineral (most likely an amphibole from the actinolite-tremolite series); interstitial white, powdery, soft material (probably talc); a coppery-brown mineral (possibly rutile) and the presence of equant pits. The other local sample (from NC 05476 26305) is more schistose and is almost pure talc with small black specks of another mineral (too small to identify) and limonite lined equant pits which is seen on the broken surface showing this to be a pervasive rather than a surface feature. Both local samples share petrographic features with the objects examined and show that hydrous alteration of magnesium rich local rocks is occurring. Whether the actual localities represent the source of the worked material would be harder to prove, and it should be kept in mind that given

the mode of occurrence numerous other local sources are likely.

Chemical analysis of 'serpentine' artefacts

Richard Jones

Introduction

Four samples of stone from fragmentary stone lamps (SF 59, SF 60, SF 65, SF 66) recovered during the excavation were selected and submitted for geochemical analysis. In each instance, the fragments selected derived from fractured and damaged or incomplete lamps where detached pieces of stone were readily available or, in the case of SF 60, where the presence of fractured edges of a sherd were exposed. All of which were identified macroscopically by Fiona McGibbon (above) as variations on talc-bearing schists, also known as steatite.

The purpose of the chemical analysis of the artefacts was two-fold: to explore whether they all shared the same or similar source, and if so whether that source lay close to the broch. Two rock samples were collected from an outcrop at NC 04775 26997, roughly 1.4 km from the broch as the crow flies (Fig. 1.2), to compare with the artefacts.

Chemical analysis involved the determination of the elemental composition, primarily the rare earth elements which, since the pioneering work on steatite from Scottish contexts by Ian Bray (1994) and subsequently by Jones *et al.* (2007) and Forster and Jones (2017), have been shown to be sensitive to origin. The major, minor and trace elements can provide supplementary information on origin.

Artefacts and geological material

The four artefacts and two geological samples are identified as serpentinite.[5] The former can be judged from the appearance of SF 60: hard, crystalline stone but with a smoothed worked surface with almost a soft feel to it, light grey in colour. The texture varies: SF 65 and SF 66 are finer grained than SF 59 which is itself coarser than SF 60. SF 59 is notably crumbly owing to the effects of use wear or burning. The two geological specimens are hard and crystalline, lacking any soft surface feel. They were collected from within the large area of Scourian gneiss (Fig. 1.2); an igneous dyke of metamicrogabbro and amphibolite lies just to the north of the sampling location. In their study of the layered intrusive rocks in the region, Bowes *et al.* (1964) make frequent reference to the presence of serpentinite (*ibid.*, 165). The broch itself lies in an area of sandstone and windblown sand.

Methods

The artefacts were sampled by drilling into the fabric which had been cleaned of weathering or surface contamination, using an electric drill with a tungsten carbide drill head yielding *c.* 500 mg of powder. In the case

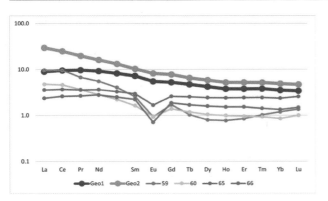

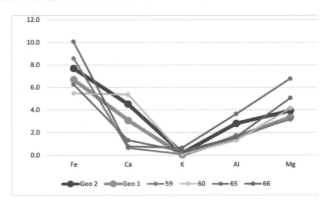

Figure 4.8.1 The chondrite corrected REE concentrations in the geological samples and artefacts. The vertical scale is logarithmic.

Figure 4.8.2 The concentrations (in % weight) of Fe, Ca, K, Al and Mg in the geological samples (thick line) and the artefacts. Concentration values normalised to the Si content.

of geological samples, a fragment was detached and crushed, yielding *c.* 1 g of powder. The sample were analysed at the Scottish Universities Environmental Research Centre, East Kilbride by ICP-MS (inductively coupled plasma mass spectrometry) using an Agilent 7500ce instrument. The concentrations (in ppm) of 14 rare earth elements (REE), which are given in Table 4.8.2, were assessed by displaying them graphically, as is conventionally done, in chondrite-normalised form and examining the REE pattern and concentration ranges. This is in effect a visually-based pattern recognition process. Portable X-ray fluorescence (pXRF) was then applied to the cleaned surface of the artefacts providing semiquantitative determinations of at least 20 elements, from major to trace. The instrument was an energy-dispersive Thermo Niton XL3t with a 50 kV silver X-ray tube and a Geometrically Optimized Large Drift Detector, and the instrument's calibration algorithm was TestallGeo with a count time of 60 seconds. At least four separate spots on each artefact were analysed. No great claims of accuracy can be made: most element determinations of USGS BCR, DNC, AGV and GSP

(powdered) standards were found to be up to 20% lower than the certified compositions, and for chromium at low concentration (<200 ppm) the discrepancy was much larger (Forster and Jones 2017, 236); for this reason the semi-quantitative nature of the analysis is emphasised.

Results

The REE patterns of both artefacts and geological samples are broadly similar (Fig. 4.8.1), featuring either a gradually decreasing concentration from La to Lu or a flattish plateau from La to Nd followed by a very gradual decline from Sm to Lu. The REE concentrations are relatively high, ranging from *c.* 1 to 29.6. But closer examination reveals some differences: first, the geological samples have higher concentrations than do the artefacts; second the latter, but not the former, display a Eu anomaly, although this feature is unlikely to be significant in terms of origin; third, SF 65 and SF 66 form a pair, as do, if less closely, SF 59 and SF 60. These results would suggest that the type of stone selected for the artefacts is broadly similar in geological terms to the samples collected at NC04775 26997, but the match is imperfect. Furthermore, the artefacts appear to be represented by a single stone source within which there are (natural) textural differences which would account for the observation above about the contrast between SF 59/60 on the one hand and SF 65/66 on the other. Alternatively, there was more than one source, perhaps neighbouring each other. Although directly comparable REE data is not readily available, it is noted that the REE pattern at least resembles those of Scouriemore ultramafics and gabbros, analysed by Sills *et al.* (1982, fig. 7) as part of their study of these Lewisian rocks' geochemistry and petrogenesis.

Turning to the pXRF data (Table 4.8.3), the broad similarity in REE content between artefacts and geological samples is borne out in the corresponding plot of the major-minor elements (Fig. 4.8.2). Their concentration ranges are quite wide, especially so in Ca, K and Mg,

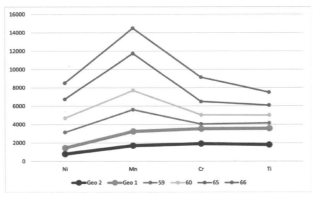

Figure 4.8.3 The concentrations (in parts per million) of Ni, Mn and Cr in the geological samples (thick line) and the artefacts. Concentration values normalised to the Si content.

Table 4.8.1 The serpentinite samples from Clachtoll Broch analysed chemically

Small Find Number	Description
59	Handle fragment detached from bowl of serpentine lamp
60	Serpentine lamp fragment
65	Serpentine lamp fragment near base
66	Serpentine lamp, detached fragments
Geological specimen 1 from NC04775 26997	Serpentine
Geological specimen 2 from NC04775 26997	Serpentine

Table 4.8.2 Chondrite corrected concentrations of rare earth elements expressed in parts per million, determined by ICP-MS

	La	Ce	Pr	Nd	Sm	Eu	Gd	Tb	Dy	Ho	Er	Tm	Yb	Lu
Geo1	8.928	9.502	9.654	9.227	7.205	5.509	5.233	4.726	4.211	3.760	3.758	3.770	3.505	3.390
Geo2	29.560	24.813	19.702	16.094	10.270	8.172	7.757	6.504	5.801	5.166	5.150	5.129	4.841	4.633
59	9.633	9.598	6.717	5.500	2.578	0.931	1.706	1.032	0.793	0.765	0.843	1.017	1.184	1.347
60	4.729	4.561	3.615	2.792	1.623	0.943	1.373	1.172	1.035	0.981	0.949	0.921	0.841	0.990
65	3.580	3.669	3.579	3.637	2.968	1.678	2.600	2.538	2.425	2.400	2.428	2.435	2.357	2.563
66	2.366	2.596	2.657	2.791	2.222	0.709	1.869	1.693	1.584	1.519	1.524	1.411	1.330	1.479

Table 4.8.3 Concentrations of twelve elements expressed in parts per million, determined by pXRF. <LoD denotes below limit of detection

	Ni	Fe	Mn	Cr	Ti	Ca	K	S	Al	P	Si	Mg
Geo 1	798	76854	1713	1917	1809	45296	1863	1175	28035	<LoD	183889	39266
Geo 2	704	70852	1631	1725	1875	32486	253	978	16860	<LoD	194658	35398
59	1659	84710	2328	501	567	6351	914	1404	17279	3314	181386	30989
60	1409	49549	1893	895	772	48579	771	1390	11789	6385	166712	37599
65	1796	54858	3533	1277	953	11637	3036	1680	14145	5300	160818	44244
66	1546	88708	2425	2334	1234	6854	5739	3358	32097	5695	161978	59645

reflecting natural variation. The trace elements are more informative (Fig. 4.8.3) in the way they show the geological samples standing somewhat apart from the artefacts in terms of both pattern and concentration. The artefacts share the same pattern, but it is reassuring to find SF 59 and SF 60 separating slightly from SF 65 and SF 66. The high Mg and Cr contents, in particular, in both the artefacts and geological samples are consistent with what would be expected in serpentiniferous material.

Discussion

The results are reasonably clear. The artefacts are composed of a stone – serpentinite – that occurs at many locations inland from the broch. The one location that was sampled matches the artefacts in REE composition in broad terms, but closer inspection of the full range of elements suggests it was not the source; in addition, its physical properties indicate that it would be hard to work into shape, let alone be capable of taking a soft polished surface.

Unfortunately, the combination of the widespread occurrence of the base rock, gneiss, from which the serpentinite has associated, coupled with an absence of archaeologically relevant reference data for serpentinite in NW Scotland means that in principle the task of confidently locating the source(s) would be a major task in terms of fieldwork and analysis. But in practice, this task would benefit from petrographic (thin section) characterisation of the artefacts as well as newly obtained geological samples; mineralogical analysis would also provide useful supporting information.

For the moment we can be content that the present chemical data, bearing in mind it is very limited in quantity, points to the exploitation of either a single source that displays some natural variation in its texture or to more than one source – these may be close to each other, need not lie far from the broch but would share the essential property that the stone was workable.

One interesting observation on the pXRF data is that the artefacts contain measurable amounts of phosphorus (P) whereas the geological samples do not (Tables 4.8.2 and 4.8.3). This is not the result of contamination with say animal bone at the broch because, as apatite, the Ca content would be proportionately higher which is not the case. Rather, it could somehow reflect either the higher than average phosphorus content in the soils around the broch resulting from the use of (modern) fertiliser or the artefacts' function.

4.9 The worked bone

Dawn McLaren, with a contribution by Helen Chittock (osteological identifications by Jackaline Robertson)

Introduction

The worked bone and antler assemblage discussed here is surprisingly limited in quantity (51 items in 243 fragments, including pieces of working debris, partially worked items and unfinished objects) and also in the range of objects identified considering the abundance of faunal remains recovered from the series of deposits within the broch interior and also in comparison to other Iron Age broch assemblages in Atlantic Scotland. These objects include common types, such as simple pins, which are readily paralleled amongst contemporary assemblages but also include more enigmatic and perhaps expediently made objects whose purpose and function is a matter of some debate. Most items are well preserved but often fragmentary, preserving good evidence of manufacturing traces and wear. Overall, this group of objects (Fig. 4.9.1) is dominated by tools associated with textile and hide-working but small numbers of ornaments, tools of a variety of functions, handles and unfinished items as well as working waste have been recognised. Of particular note is a small dagger or sword pommel produced from cetacean tooth/ivory and a number of long-handled bone comb fragments which attest to networks of contacts and exchange beyond the locale of the broch.

The worked bone has been classified according to broad functional categories following the approach adopted by Ballin Smith (1994) in the discussion of the bone from Howe, Orkney and are summarised in Table 4.9.1. An overarching consideration of these classifications seeks to synthesise the material from the catalogue in terms of raw materials, technology, function and decoration, together with broader comparisons following Hunter *et al.* (2013) regarding the unusually large assemblage of worked bone from Broxmouth Hillfort, East Lothian. Where the function can reasonably be inferred, a discussion of each type precedes the respective catalogue.

Sources of the raw materials

In conjunction with examining the worked bone and antler to identify wear and possible function, the items were also examined by faunal remains specialist Jackaline Robertson to attempt to identify the species and skeletal element used. As with most assemblages of worked bone, it was not possible to identify heavily worked material to species and element in all instances (Hunter, Gibson and Gerken 2013, 251). Where identification was possible (Table 4.9.2), it is clear that the community at Clachtoll took advantage of both domestic and locally available wild resources including: cattle, red deer (bone and antler), sheep/goat, pig and bird bone as well as cetacean bone deriving from a minimum of two individuals (an adult and juvenile). The properties of each of these categories of bone for working have been considered in full elsewhere (*e.g.*, MacGregor 1985; Hallén 1994, 197–200) and will not be discussed in detail here.

The quantity of animal bone recovered from the interior of the broch suggests that selection of suitable material for working would not have been unduly restricted by availability. At Howe, bone-working and implement production was seen as a direct by-product of meat consumption and the gaining of pelts and hides (Ballin Smith 1994, 183) and a broadly similar narrative can be argued for the Clachtoll assemblage.

Dominating the assemblage by virtue of the quantity of unfinished and unworked pieces is red deer antler. This total includes antler fragments with no surviving working traces, but their discovery on site implies that were deliberately gathered after shedding or retained from butchered carcasses with the intention of future use, although like the cetacean bone, this quantity could well have been quite small and was undoubtedly seasonal. Only two burr fragments, possibly from the same antler but no longer conjoining, were recognised. These derive from a shed antler or antlers and were found in a blackened and charred condition amongst (042).

The preference for the use of red deer antler is probably due to its size which allows a great variety in working possibilities (MacGregor 1985; Hunter, Gibson and Gerken 2013, 254) and is also known as an excellent shock absorbing material which is ideal for use as handles as well as chopping and cutting tools (Hallén 1994, 197). It is likely that the cast antlers would have been a predictable and potentially abundant resource which could be gathered annually in the spring (Tuohy 1999, 10–12, tab. 2.1; Hunter, Gibson and Gerken 2013, 254). The large proportion of antler amongst this assemblage suggests that the community at Clachtoll understood the seasonal movements of the stag populations, being familiar with the areas where they habitually shed their antlers each spring, allowing access and collection to be organised when required (*ibid.*). Yet the frequency of antler finds in the assemblage is not significantly out of proportion with the quantities of red deer bone, in contrast with other Iron Age broch assemblages such as that from Fairy Knowe, Buchlyvie (Smith and Young 1998, 319).

Items of mammal bone include elements procured from both large mammals (cattle and deer) and medium-sized mammals (sheep/goat and pig). Most of the identifiable bones derive from the long bones of the animal carcass; as the limb bones are typically discarded during the primary butchery process (Hunter, Gibson and Gerken 2013, 253), they would have been readily available as a source of raw material for working. The lower limbs have limited food value and could thus be made available immediately after butchery. This preference shown for the use of long bones for production of tools is widely comparable amongst assemblages from Atlantic Scotland and beyond (*e.g.*, Hallén 1994; Hunter, Gibson and Gerken 2013, 253). At Clachtoll there is no suggestion that the bones of a particular species were favoured for working as the result of broader cosmological or cultural choices. Rather, the inherent properties of the bone, its size, shape and density, appear to be the principal concerns structuring the choices of the raw material used.

Cetacean bone forms a small but significant proportion of the worked bone assemblage. Like the mammal bone already discussed, the extent of modification to the cetacean bone has often made it difficult to determine the particular element used which limits what can be said about the species of cetacean mammal involved and how many individuals are represented amongst the assemblage. The presence of fragments of unfused vertebral epiphyses and at least two fused vertebrae indicate the use of bone from both an immature and mature animal suggesting a minimum number of two individuals but little more can be said than this. The quantity of cetacean bone present is insufficient to suggest regular

culling of whales but rather are likely to result from episodic strandings and scavenging of beached carcasses (MacGregor 1974, 106; Hallén 1994, 199). Overall, a similar pattern of resource utilisation has been recognised amongst Iron Age assemblages elsewhere such as at Nybster (Heald *et al.* in prep) and Crosskirk Broch (Fairhurst 1984) both in Caithness, Bac Mhic Connain (Hallén 1994, 199) and Sollas (Campbell 1991) on North Uist, and Howe, Orkney (Ballin Smith 1994, 183) to name a few. Interestingly, although in situ weathering or erosion of the bone surfaces prior to incorporation into floor levels and midden material at Clachtoll could account for the degraded surfaces noted on some pieces, the extent of weathering and the pitting of the surfaces observed on a fragment of worked cetacean bone (SF 284) suggests that the bone had been exposed for some time, evidenced by marine worm activity, prior to the bone being collected and worked.

A small dagger or sword pommel (SF 274) was produced from cetacean ivory (S. O'Connor, pers. comm.) but is so heavily modified that it cannot be identified to species.[6] A single shank fragment from a pin or point (SF 275) was the only object recognised amongst the assemblage to be produced from bird bone. The unworked bird bone assemblage from the site was also limited, restricted to only 12 fragments including guillemot and puffin (J. Robertson, Section 5.4b).

Table 4.9.1 Summary of the worked bone and antler by functional group and type. The numbers shown in (brackets) denote quantity of fragments as opposed to object/group

Functional group	Type	Quantity
Ornaments	Splayed-head pin	2
	Perforated pin	1 (3)
Weaponry	Pommel	1
Tools: textile- and hide-working	Long-handled bone combs	4
	Needles	2
	Hide-rubber	4 (5)
Tools: other	Spatulate tool	1
	Points	2
	Working Surface	1 (16)
Handles	Handles	4 (6)
Miscellaneous	Cetacean bars	3 (44)
	Fitting or handle	1
Working evidence	Unfinished items	3 (8)
	Roughout	1 (3)
	Working waste	5 (9)
	Unworked?	16 (136)
Total		51 (243)

Figure 4.9.1 Selection of the worked bone from Clachtoll

Table 4.9.2 Summary of species of bone used by broad classification of artefact type. The numbers shown in (brackets) denote quantity of fragments as opposed to object/group

Type	Species of bone				
	Antler	Terrestrial mammal bone	Cetacean	Bird	Unidentified
Object	10 (in 13 fragments)	7	7 (63 fragments)	1	1 (in 3 fragments)
Unfinished/working waste	5 (in 14 fragments)	2	2 (4 fragments)		
Unworked	8 (in 13 fragments)		8 (123 fragments)		
Total	23 (in 40 fragments)	9	17 (190 pieces)	1	1 (in 3 fragments)

Working evidence

Unlike many other Iron Age worked bone and antler assemblages, such as Sollas and Cnip, North Uist (Campbell 1991; Hunter 2007b), the quantity of unfinished objects and working waste was limited (Table 4.9.3). Large numbers of individual fragments of antler and cetacean bone were recognised and may represent pieces of degraded objects or debris from working but the lack of tool marks on these make it impossible to discuss them in detail. An attempt has been made below to summarise the artefact types recognised by animal bone used, yet the group is so limited in quantity that it is difficult to tease out meaningful patterns in resource exploitation and the utlilsation of bone and antler for working.

Three fragments of a roughly shaped cetacean bone bar or baton (SF 285) is the only unambiguous roughout (Fig. 4.9.2). Potentially unfinished items are also rare amongst the assemblage comprising two items of bone (SF 267 and SF 268) and two partially worked or unfinished antler objects (SF 263 and SF 264). In addition, a burnt fragment of a long-handled bone comb (SF 140, Fig. 4.9.13a) displays remarkably little wear leading to the suggestion that it may have been re-cut or was abandoned in the process of manufacture. Small quantities of working waste were noted amongst the antler and cetacean bone alongside fragments, some burnt or charred, which lacked any obvious evidence of modification.

Figure 4.9.2 Cetacean bone roughout of a squared bar or baton (SF 285)

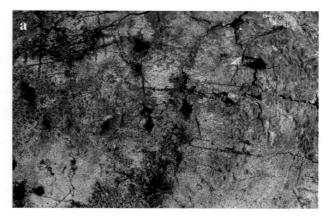

Figure 4.9.3 The marine ivory pommel (SF 274)

Figure 4.9.4 Detail of tool marks on the working face of the whalebone working surface (SF 024): a) diamond-tipped punch, b) circular-tipped punch

Figure 4.9.5 Detail of striations from abrasion of surface of pin (SF 275) made during production

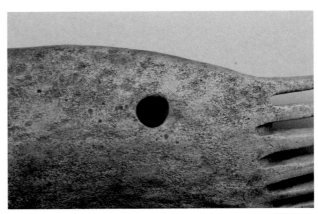

Figure 4.9.6 Detail of the drilled perforation on comb SF 148

The assumption is that the vast majority of the working of bone and antler took place in and around the broch; although the working of bone and antler at Clachtoll was likely a site-based activity, the working may have been largely focused outside of the broch itself, or else such waste was regularly cleared out, as suggested by the generally small quantities of antler working debris, particularly burr fragments, in proportion to the quantity of antler objects and partially worked items recognised. One exception to this local production model could possibly be the cetacean tooth/ivory dagger pommel (SF 274, Fig. 4.9.3) which may have been manufactured elsewhere or represent local copy of an Atlantic Scottish and Irish Iron Age type (Rynne 1983) although on-site production cannot be ruled out.

In all, 29 antler items were noted amongst the assemblage in 40 fragments. A third of these fragments (13; 33% of antler fragments) display no obvious signs of working and consist of angular spalls from the surface of antlers, broken tine fragments and two burr fragments, some of which are burnt and others with weathered surfaces. A further four items in eight fragments (20% of the antler fragments) consist of working waste. These include knife cut (*e.g.*, SF 278) and snapped splinters (*e.g.*, SF 283) which are likely to be debris discarded during working and ten fragments, many of which fit together, from worked but probably unfinished or abandoned crown and beam fragments (SF 263 and SF 264). Bone in its fresh state is more easily worked than fresh antler, which is extremely resilient and more resistant to impact (MacGregor 1985, 23–29). Carving antler is much easier when it has been soaked (*ibid.*, 64; Tuohy 1999, 15) and it is likely that the antler was subjected to some form of pre-treatment prior to working.

The finished antler objects total ten, collected in 13 fragments. Often the material is too highly worked to be sure what part of the antler it derives from but where

it is possible to distinguish, beam sections, particularly from mature stags which grow large and robust antlers, were used to make combs (SF 148 and SF 206) and larger handles (*e.g.*, SF 269), as well as various tools and fittings (*e.g.*, SF 279), while tines were used as smaller handles, for various small fittings and occasionally for points and rubbers (*e.g.*, SF 281).

Working evidence of terrestrial mammal bone was less well represented amongst the worked bone assemblage but this results from difficulties in distinguishing working waste from butchered bone (J. Robertson, pers. comm.), an issue that can be paralleled amongst many bone working sites (Foxon 1991, 190; Hallén 1994, 193). Only nine items of worked mammal bone were recognised; the majority of these (7; 78% of mammal bone fragments) constitute finished and used objects, whilst two objects (SF 267 and SF 268), using a cow phalanx and a sheep/goat tibia respectively, appear unfinished and abandoned in the process of manufacture. Teasing further patterns out of such a small group is difficult but it is worth noting that both pins (SF 103 and SF 216) amongst this group were produced from pig fibulas consistent with Iron Age pin manufacture across Scotland (MacGregor 1985, 120–1), whilst long bones and metatarsals from cattle and deer saw use for the larger and more robust items (*e.g.*, blunt nosed instrument SF 265).

As already described, the cetacean bone utilised amongst the assemblage is likely to have been an episodic and unpredictable resource. Evidence of worked bone in the form of finished products and working waste is present amongst the assemblage alongside fragments which display no obvious working but, in many instances, the eroded, charred or burnt condition of the surfaces makes recognition of working traces difficult to detect. In total there are seven objects made from cetacean bone including an anvil or working surface (SF 24) which has been made on an unmodified adult vertebra,

Table 4.9.3 Summary of the worked bone/antler assemblage by function, object type and bone species used. The numbers shown in (brackets) denote quantity of fragments as opposed to object/group

Functional group	Type	Antler	Mammal	Whale	Bird	Indeterm.	Quantity
Ornaments	Splayed-head pin		2				2
	Perforated pin					1 (3)	1
Weaponry	Pommel			1			1
Tools: textile- and hide-working	Long-handled bone combs	3		1			4
	Needles		2				2
	Hide-rubber	2 (3)	1	1			4
Tools: other	Spatulate tool		1				1
	Points	1			1		2
	Working Surface			1 (16)			1
Handles	Handles	3 (5)	1				4
Miscellaneous	Cetacean bars			3 (44)			3
	Fitting or handle	1					1
Working evidence	Unfinished items	1 (6)	2				3
	Roughout			1 (3)			1
	Working waste	4 (8)		1			5
	Unworked?	8 (13)		8 (123)			16
Total		*23 (40)*	*9*	*17 (190)*	*1*	*1 (3)*	*51 (243)*

bars, batons and hide rubbers (*e.g.*, SF 75) which may have been produced from the dense cortical bone of the rib and, finally, a dagger pommel (SF 274) which was made of marine ivory but cannot be more closely identified to species. Items such as the decorated bone comb fragment (SF 271, Fig. 4.9.13d) are extremely dense suggesting utilisation of cetacean bone but the species and skeletal element used cannot be identified (J. Robertson, pers. comm.).

Fresh whalebone is notoriously unpleasant to work with due to the rich natural oils which saturate the bone. Rather than utilising bone from a fresh whale carcass it is likely that the skeleton was left to weather and dry out for some time prior to working (J. Robertson, pers. comm.). Yet, as many of the implements of cetacean bone appear to have seen use as hide-rubbers, it is possible that the use of fresh whalebones was seen as advantageous: the natural oils in the whalebone aiding the processing and preparation of animal hides, but this has yet to be established. At Bac Mhic Connain, North Uist the presence of charred and burnt whalebone fragments lead to the suggestion that such items may have been sawn to use the fats within the bone as fuel in fires, particularly the cancellous tissue (Hallén 1994, 197, *e.g.*, GNB 114). The lack of tool marks on many of the cetacean bone fragments from Clachtoll makes it difficult to be confident about a similar use but a significant proportion are charred, adding weight to this particular hypothesis.

A single pin or point shaft of worked bird bone (SF 272) was also recognised amongst the assemblage but no working waste could be identified.

Toolmarks and working traces

The worked bone objects display clear evidence of the manufacturing techniques employed including a wide range of toolmarks and wear patterns. These are described in detail in the catalogue. Although very few metal tools were recognised amongst the assemblage (Heald and McLaren, Section 4.4) either because they have not survived post-deposition or as a result of them being removed from the site prior to the fire that engulfed it, the worked bone and antler assemblage provides a useful proxy record of the range of tools which were originally present and employed. Examination of the surfaces of the worked bone indicate the use of a range of iron tools, including heavy chopping implements (axes or cleavers), fine blades for whittling and paring, saws, and a range of punches (Fig. 4.9.4). Antler in particular also appears to have been worked by snapping and splitting to detach tines for discard and to shape out the necessary material very roughly prior to more detailed working. Wedges of bone or iron could be employed to split the bone and to hammer into the cancellous tissue of the antler to hollow it out (MacGregor 1985, 57, fig. 58). No such wedges (in either bone or metal) survive amongst the Clachtoll artefact assemblage but

Figure 4.9.7 Detail of the bored perforation on handle SF 286

Figure 4.9.8 Detail of punched peforation on SF 268

have been recognised elsewhere, such as within the Iron Age assemblages from Bac Mhic Connain (Hallén 1994, 194) and Sollas (Campbell 1991, 158, illus. 20), North Uist, where examples produced from both bone and antler were recognised.

Irregular scratches on the surfaces of some items such as perforated pin (SF 275, Fig. 4.9.5) suggest that much of the abrading of objects to shape was done with pumice or sandstone rather than metal files (MacGregor 1974; 1985, 58; Hallén 1994, 194–5). The recovery of abraded pumice amongst the stone assemblage (D. McLaren, Section 4.7) testifies to its collection and use as a tool for the production of artefacts, including those of bone and antler but very few pieces displayed the characteristic notched appearance of use in conjunction with pin/point manufacture.

The presence of circular drilled perforations (Fig. 4.9.6) on some items (*e.g.*, SF 148 and SF 273) attest to the use of a bow drill despite no trace of one being present amongst the metal or wood assemblages. The use of a bow drill would not only have been less labour intensive than biconical boring (Fig. 4.9.7) with the tip of a knife (*e.g.*, SF 121 and SF 267) or punching (*e.g.*, SF 262) to create a piercing (Fig. 4.9.8) but it was also preferred when a neater finish was designed (Hallén 1994, 195; Hunter, Gibson and Gerken 2013, 256). The presence of biconical and punched holes demonstrates that a range of techniques were performed to create perforations and piercings, perhaps decided upon by the material being worked, what the item was intended for or who was working the material.

Object range

The range of artefact types present in the Clachtoll worked bone and antler assemblage is limited in comparison to most Atlantic Iron Age broch sites both in the variety of categories present and in quantity. In this respect it bears similarities to assemblages such as that from Crosskirk

Broch, Caithness (Fairhurst 1984, 120) which although not rich or large when compared to assemblages from other brochs and wheelhouse sites such as Broch of Burrian, and the Howe, Orkney (MacGregor 1974; Ballin Smith 1994), is probably a representative one for the period, reflecting a short episode of occupation and one not confused or inflated by subsequent, later periods of activity. Overall, the objects are fairly mundane, consisting of prosaic tools and simple ornaments, many of which are fairly expedient in character.

A variety of crafts and activities are indicated by the implements recognised. A large number of these objects, including the needles (Fig. 4.9.15a and b) and the long-handled combs (Fig. 4.9.13) attest to weaving and other aspects of textile production and probably hide processing as suggested also by the cetacean bone and antler hide-rubbers (Fig. 4.9.15c–f). Points and awls may also have seen use for the working of hides whilst the spatulate-ended tool (Fig. 4.9.15h) has been interpreted here as a possible potting tool. The small quantities of handles (Fig. 4.9.18) attest to the presence of composite tools, including a possible saw blade or similar, whilst the whalebone vertebrae working surface (Fig. 4.9.17) serves as a valuable proxy record of many types of metal tool (punches, saw, knife blades) which have not survived. Further evidence of on-site craft activities comes in the form of roughouts, unfinished items and working waste (Figs 4.9.2, 4.9.19, 4.9.20) which attest to the working of antler, bone and cetacean bone yet the quantities of waste remain small enough to suggest that the production of items was to meet the demands of the household rather than a large-scale level of manufacture (Ballin Smith 1994, 184). This includes at least one antler long-handled comb which was either modified and recut to prolong its life and efficiency during use or was in the process of primary production.

Ornaments are rare amongst the assemblage and consist of only three pins (Fig. 4.9.9), all of a simple form that can be widely paralleled amongst contemporary

Figure 4.9.9 The bone pins from Clachtoll Broch

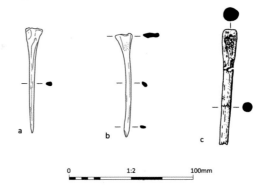

Figure 4.9.10 The bone pins: a) SF 103, b) SF 216, c) SF 275

assemblages in Atlantic Scotland. One stand-out object, for both the fineness of its production and its form, is the cetacean bone dagger or sword pommel (SF 274, Figs 4.9.3 and 4.9.11), a recognisable type with a distribution across Atlantic Scotland and Ireland (Rynne 1983). This example is extremely small, suggesting use with a dagger or a miniature implement, rather than a sword as most examples of these distinctive decorated pommels are attributed to (*ibid.*). Despite the diminutive size, it has been finely produced from cetacean ivory and ornamented in a simple but distinctive style, decorated on both faces with a carved semi-ring-shaped motif. The fineness of the manufacture of this item stands out against the rest of the assemblage. Unlike the rather expedient looking tools and ornaments, this is a very elegant example of the type. There is no trace of the blade that it was originally associated with. The pommel was recovered from within the souterrain after completion of excavation, perhaps having washed out from behind the walling of the feature after heavy rains. Although its context of deposition is not certain and its association with the souterrain tentative, it undoubtedly derives from the deposits in the broch interior and its burnt condition suggests it was either damaged during the fire or burnt in an earlier event and incorporated within midden or flooring. Other examples of this type of pommel from Scotland derive from brochs and wheelhouses in the Northern and Western Isles but a recent example found alongside other plainer pommels and one in the midst of manufacture were recovered from Mine Howe, Orkney and may be associated with a workshop specialising in the production of high-status composite objects, including weaponry (F. Hunter, pers. comm.). Whether this type of pommel saw production in a single locale or were locally produced copies of an existing type, they are undoubtedly prestige objects which signal an awareness and understanding of broader stylistic traditions and points towards a wide network of contacts beyond the region.

Although Clachtoll Broch has produced a range of worked bone and antler objects which are broadly consistent with other Atlantic Scottish Iron Age sites, many typical categories of worked bone are remarkable by their absence here. The omission of commonplace and regularly encountered object types including femur-head spindle whorls, antler picks, notched implements including mattocks and blades, heavy-duty hafted implements such as mallets and hammerheads, cetacean vessels, perforated antler rings and fish gouges and the restricted quantity of pins. In contrast to the Howe (Ballin Smith 1994) where heavy-duty agricultural tools such as picks, shovels and mattocks produced from antler and bone made up a significant component of the assemblage, no agricultural tools were recognised amongst the worked bone from Clachtoll. This pattern is in contrast to the iron assemblage from the broch which is dominated by agricultural tools. This absence within the bone assemblage can hardly be a matter of a lack of access to suitable resources and is either a cultural choice or a result of a distinction in where such items were stored and disposed of outside of the broch itself.

Decoration

Decoration is rare amongst the assemblage, implying that it was perceived to have had particular, restricted values and meanings (Hunter *et al.* 2013, 260). Only three items are decorated and is limited to singular simple cross-cross or saltire mark on the exterior shaft of two long-handled bone combs (SF 140 and SF 271, Fig. 4.9.13 a and d). Both are incomplete, one burnt, but appear to have been made with a saw blade. The third decorated item is the small cetacean tooth/ivory dagger or sword pommel (SF 274, Fig. 4.9.3) which is ornamented on both faces with semi-ring-shaped grooves incised into the bone. In both instances, the motifs employed follow wider regional or national decorative traditions (Rynne 1983; Tuohy 1999).

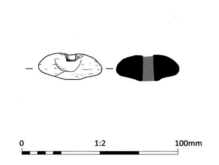

0   1:2   100mm

Figure 4.9.11 The marine ivory pommel (SF 274)

Figure 4.9.12 The long-handled combs

Distribution

Items of worked bone and antler, including unfinished items and possible working waste, were recovered from 13 contexts within the broch as well as a number of unstratified finds and are summarised in Table 4.9.4. The majority come from deposits within the broch interior, some of which may have been brought down into the interior space from the intramural stairwells or galleries when the tower collapsed (028), from the burning layer itself (042) representing a conflated mass of roofing material and upper floor levels suggesting that artefacts from within this layer may have been stored or used on the upper levels of the broch, as well as a number of ground-floor level floor and midden deposits (*e.g.*, (044), (047), (048), (049), (062), (067), (077) and (078)). Particularly rich contexts for worked bone include the burning layer (042), midden material south of hearth 2 (047) and the loose rubble fill (078) of the deep 'souterrain' area [069]. Much more restricted quantities of worked bone were found in the intramural structures including Cell 1 (145), Cell 2 (123) and the entrance passage (082).

Burning layer (042) and possible upper-story material
The first notable concentration of worked bone comes from (042), a thick layer of burnt debris covering the occupation surfaces and hearth sequences and interpreted as a burnt layer representing collapsed internal organic features and/or roofing material. This layer was rich in artefactual material including the head of a bone needle (SF 068), an intact pin (SF 103), an intact possible hide-rubber (SF 265), the tip of a cetacean bar/baton which may be a hide-processing tool (SF 266) and a fragment of a facetted point (SF 281), all unburnt. Also present were fragments of worked antler possibly representing unfinished items or working waste and a number of burnt and unburnt antler and cetacean bone fragments with no obvious evidence of modification. What is surprising about the bone present within this deposit is both the number of intact or

substantially intact objects and the unburnt condition of many of these suggesting that some were protected somehow from the worst of the blaze despite their recovery from this burnt collapsed deposit. The presence of both finished and used objects, as well as possible unfinished or unworked pieces, within this collapsed material implies the use or storage of these artefacts in the upper levels of the broch, hinting at the possibility that textile and hide-processing may have taken place on these upper levels as well as around the hearth.

Another item, a whalebone vertebra working surface (SF 24), may also have been displaced during the collapse of the structure being pushed from the internal area to the south-west and into the mouth of the passage of cell 3 (044). The working surface is substantially complete but is damaged around the edges and has been charred as the result of the fire. It is not possible to determine whether it also fell from an upper level, as argued for the material from (042), but its stratigraphic position argues against it being in its working location.

From a layer of brown-pink sand (028) overlying (042) representing a combination of material eroded from the still-standing broch walls without a roof, wind-blown sands and natural soil development came two fragments of antler: one (SF 282) is an irregular splinter of antler tine with cut mark demonstrating tine was deliberately removed from the beam, the other (SF 282) is an irregular spall detached from the surface of antler tine and displays no obvious evidence of working.

Flooring deposits

A number of the items of worked bone were associated with the internal floor levels, particularly in the southern half of the broch interior. Two fragments of the shank of large burnt perforated bone pin (SF 275), a robust cetacean bone point (SF 75), a substantially complete cetacean bone bar or baton (SF 108/123) interpreted as a hide or textile processing tool, and a burnt and broken fragment of a

Table 4.9.4 Distribution of worked bone/antler by context

Tool: textile/hide working	Points	Spatulate tool	Working Surface	Handles	Miscellaneous	Working waste/unfinished	Other
SF 68 needle fragment; SF 265 blunt nosed point, poss. hide rubber;	SF 281 fragment of faceted antler point				SF 266 tip of cetacean bar/baton	SF 282 cut splinter of antler; SF 263 & SF 264: unfinished antler objects/working debris; SF 283 two heat affected fragments of antler, one with knife cut and second has been snapped	SF 292 irregular spall of antler, no signs of working; SF 276 & SF 277 burnt antler, no signs of working; SF 293 weathered antler fragment, no signs of working; SF 294 four burnt splinters of antler (no obvious signs of working), SF 295 two blacked burr fragments (shed), SF 299 unworked cetacean bone fragment; SF 301 15 fragments of unfused whale vertebra, unworked.
SF 121 needle, broken; SF 280 antler hide-rubber			SF 024: cetacean vertebra working surface (charred)	SF 262 hollowed long bone pierced at both ends (or fitting?)		SF 284 Weathered cetacean bone, chopped at one end	SF 300 c.30 angular fragments of cetacean bone, weathered. SF 302 61 fragments of cetacean bone, no obvious use or modification.
SF 75 robust cetacean bone point, poss. hide rubber; SF 140 burnt fragment of decorated long-handled comb (recut?)					SF 108/123 cetacean bone bar/baton, poss. hide rubber;		

(Continued)

Table 4.9.4 Distribution of worked bone/antler by context (Continued)

Tool: textile/hide working	Points	Spatulate tool	Working Surface	Handles	Miscellaneous	Working waste/unfinished	Other
		SF 149 Spatulate-ended tool fragment (?potting)				SF 267 unfinished bone object, partially perforated; SF 268 perforated phalanx, possibly unfinished	SF 297 burnt fragment of whalebone, no original surfaces survive
SF 206 Long handled comb, only 1 worn tooth surviving						SF 285 3 fragments of whalebone batton roughout, 2 conjoin.	
SF 148 Intact and used long-handled bone comb, perforated for suspension							
SF 175 socketed antler tip, poss. hide scraper; SF 271 fragment of decorated long-handled comb				SF 182 two fragments of perforated antler-time handle	SF 270 tip of cetacean bone bar/baton, poss. hide-rubber;	SF 278 splinter of antler, cut;	SF 296 Burnt fragment of antler, no signs of working; SF 298 11 splinters of cetacean bone, unworked
							SF 286 Four joining fragments of cetecean vertebra, weathered and charred but with no obvious use/modification SF 223 2 fragments of antler, heat-affected, ?cancellous tissue lost or hollowed out

(Continued)

Table 4.9.4 (Continued)

Tool: textile/hide working	Points	Spatulate tool	Working Surface	Handles	Miscellaneous	Working waste/ unfinished	Other
	SF 272 shank fragment			SF 273 Handle plate fragment with double perforation at one end	SF 279 Y-shaped antler handle or fitting		
				SF 269 Refitting fragments of incomplete robust socketed handle or ferrule			

decorated long-handled bone comb (SF 140) came from peat-ash-rich floor surface (048). The burnt long-handled bone comb fragment (SF 140) appears to have been in the process of manufacture or modification before being abandoned, perhaps thrown into the fire to dispose of it, and its surviving fragments subsequently incorporated in the floor levels during the deliberate spreading of hearth debris in the area surrounding it.

From the flooring material (049) in the northern half of the broch interior came two items of worked bone consisting of an intact plain pin (SF 216) and a spatulate-ended tool fragment (SF 149). Both were unburnt and both display evidence of polish from use prior to their incorporation in the lenses of organic-rich and ash-rich deposits which make up this floor surface. This flooring material continued in the south-west quadrant of the interior (062), from which two unfinished items of bone (SF 267 and 268) were recovered from the organic- and ash-rich deposits which make up flooring material (062). The ultimate design and function of these unfinished items is not readily apparent. Within flooring material (049) in the west quadrant was a deposit of sand (077), supposed to have been laid down to stabilise clay floors in response to wet conditions. Within this layer was recovered an intact long-handled bone comb (SF 148), perforated for suspension and displaying evidence of extensive use but which would still have been serviceable at the time of its deposition.

Below midden material (047), discussed below, in the southern half of the interior was a humic-rich flooring deposit (067) which was associated with two items of worked bone consisting of a damaged and incomplete long-handled comb, surfaces darkly stained and missing all but one tooth (SF 206), extensively used, and three fragments (2 conjoining) of a squared baton (SF 285) of dense cetacean bone. Also present was a heat-discoloured surface spall of cetacean bone.

Midden

The significant proportion of the worked bone came from midden material (047) which was found to overly floor deposit (067) and bedrock. These items include a needle fragment (SF 121) broken across the eye, possibly during use, a possible handle or fitting (SF 262) in the form of a long bone fragment pierced at both ends but damaged across both, a possible antler hide-rubber (SF 280) and large numbers of angular but apparently unworked fragments of whalebone. The surfaces of these objects are degraded implying some degree of weathering/erosion prior to disposal or final incorporation, particularly a heavily weathered chopped bar of cetacean bone (SF 284) which appears to have seen considerable erosion of the surfaces prior to it being worked. Here, the mixture of intact, substantially intact and incomplete, as well as burnt and unburnt objects is not well understood, and implies that various episodes of accumulation led to the formation of these layers rather than them representing discrete deposits.

'Souterrain' [069]

A further artefact-rich context was the loose rubble and mixed fill (078) of the 'souterrain' [069]. Four worked bone objects, dominated by tools relating to textile and hide-working were recovered, consisting of a socketed antler tip (SF 175), possibly a hide-scraper; rubbed tip of a cetacean bone bar or baton (SF 270) possibly a hide-rubber; a fragment of a decorated cetacean bone long-handled comb (SF 271) with short, stained, polished teeth and two refitting fragments of a perforated antler tine handle (SF 182), with a thin recess for receiving a thin blade, such as a saw or cleaver, or similar. All four items were broken and incomplete but all displayed evidence of use. Only the rubbed tip of the cetacean bone bar (SF 270) displayed any charring or burning which need not relate to the fire-event. Also present was a fragment of antler tine, cut from the beam and possibly hollowed out (SF 278) representing possible antler working waste, 11 angular splinters of unburnt cetacean bone, probably all from the same bone but no longer conjoin and may be further fragments of (SF 270) and a burnt splinter of antler. It is unclear if this represents deliberate episodes of dumping of detritus within [069] during the lifetime of the broch occupation, or the debris of overlying flooring (*e.g.*, (047)) into [069] during the collapse of the structure; it is impossible to distinguish between items that may have been stored or dumped in this feature and those which derive from the overlying floor layers. In addition to the objects already described from this feature is a small marine ivory pommel (SF 274) which was found in the interior space after the completion of the excavations, having likely washed out from behind the walling. It almost certainly derives from *in situ* deposits within the broch but its association with this particular feature is tentative.

Entrance passage

From the upper fill of the entrance passage (082) consisting of compressed and reworked material due to regular footfall were four joining fragments (SF 286) of a whalebone vertebra; no obvious evidence of use or modification of these pieces were noted but the edges are heavily weathered and spine has been lost or removed.

Cells 1, 2 and 3

The whalebone vertebra working surface (SF 24) found in Cell 3 has already been considered above but further worked bone fragments were recovered from Cell 1 and 2. These consist of a Y-shaped antler handle or fitting fragment (SF 279) which came from a black-brown organic deposit (145) within Cell 1. Amongst a thick deposit of burnt cereal grain (123) within Cell 2, was recovered two conjoining irregular splinters of antler tine (SF 223), charred but not completely burnt and lacking obvious evidence of modification.

Evidence of deliberate deposition?

Teasing apart patterns in distribution with such a small group of objects poses a challenge and any suggestions must be considered with a modicum of caution as a result. The various flooring deposits and layers encountered during excavation probably give us the best insight into the activities undertaken within the broch if we assume that the majority of this material was the product of activity within the broch, but this is not assured and it is entirely possible that midden deposits could have been imported into the interior spaces from outside the structure itself as has been suggested on other broch and wheelhouse sites (*e.g.*, Armit 2006; McLaren and Heald 2006, 157). Within these floor levels, a mixture of intact and fragmentary items is encountered, variously in burnt, charred and unburnt conditions. No particular artefact type concentrates in any particular layer type to suggest the prevalence of specific crafts or activities at different stages of the broch's occupation. We do, however, see tools relating to textile production and hide working occurring around the hearths, particularly to the south. Some items are charred or burnt, including a fragment of decorated bone comb (SF 140) which may have been abandoned during manufacture or modification and discarded into the fire, later to be spread amongst the hearth debris across the interior as a floor surface. What is intriguing is the small number of intact or substantially intact fine objects, particularly the pins and the long-handled combs and their re-occurrence within flooring material. An intact pin (SF 216), fine and delicate and vulnerable to breakage, came from flooring material (049); an incomplete but extensively worn long-handled comb (SF 206) came from (067), despite its broken state – all of the teeth had been lost except for one – no detached teeth were recovered from this context during soil sample processing, implying that the teeth were already lost at the time it was incorporated within this floor layer; an intact long-handled comb (SF 148) perforated for suspension and displaying evidence of extensive use, came from deposit (077) laid down to stabilise the floor surface. Were these items accidentally or incidentally incorporated in the floor levels? Or could they have been deliberately deposited to mark the refurbishment of the interior space? The quantity of objects involved is so small that it is not possible to argue the latter confidently but deliberate

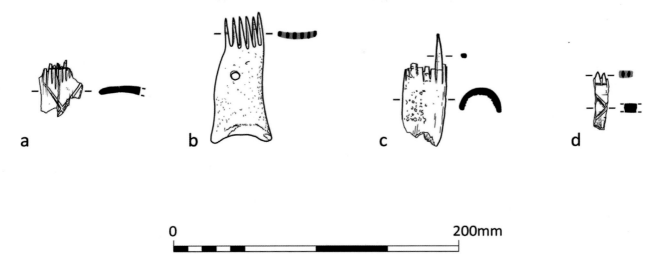

Figure 4.9.13 The long-handled combs: a) SF 140, b) SF 148, c) SF 206, d) SF 271

deposition of intact objects during such refurbishments cannot be ruled out in this instance.

Object lives

As can be argued for many of the artefact groups from Clachtoll Broch, the relatively short duration of use of the structure prior to its abandonment by fire in the 1st century AD places great value on the close contextual dating of the items of worked bone, an aspect often complicated in broch excavations by the use and reuse of the structures over centuries. This typically results in the mixing and moving of internal floor deposits, the removal of earlier deposits and reworking of midden layers, to the wholesale refurbishment of the internal spaces, which in turn results in the reworking and mixing of artefactual material from various phases. Teasing apart the phasing or dating of individual items can be problematic for this reason and very few amongst the wide array of worked bone objects in use during the Iron Age, particularly those amongst settlement assemblages, are closely datable. This has often hindered attempts to conduct detailed comparative analysis of the composition and range of similar assemblages between sites in Atlantic Scotland and places significant limitations on attempts to create overarching syntheses of bone working and the refinement of bone and antler use patterns beyond a site-specific level (although see Foxon 1991; Hallén 1994; Hunter, Gibson and Gerken 2013).

At Clachtoll, the range of radiocarbon dates obtained from the various floor deposits, middens and burning layers indicate that the *in situ* deposits built up over decades rather than centuries, suggesting that the bulk of the worked bone assemblage relates to activity between the 1st century BC to 1st century AD. Despite the structural evidence of substantial rebuilding of the broch and pockets of early deposits overlying the bedrock that probably relate to episodes of use centuries earlier, none of the items of worked bone are of closely datable types that can be definitively assigned to this early phase. The worked bone assemblage as a whole is consistent with the 1st-century BC/AD date indicated by the radiocarbon analysis and associated material culture.

Like many other Iron Age worked bone and antler assemblages in the region, the items represented in this group consist of simple dress fasteners, tools and working waste. Many of these appear well used and relate to day-to-day crafts and activities which would have been commonplace during this period, such as textile production and hide processing. The points and handles point to a wide range of roles and tools, while the working of bone and antler is ubiquitous on Iron Age sites where bone preservation is good. Despite their often-simple form, considerable effort has been put to their manufacture, particularly in the case of the long-handled combs. Others are more expedient in character, such as the splayed head pins which take their form from the raw material and require only basic modification to achieve the desired shape.

In a few instances, such as comb (SF 148), the objects have seen extensive use, whist others, such as comb (SF 140) appear to have been in the process of production or modification. Many of the tools appear to have broken during use, including needle (SF 121), leading to their discard and incorporation within floor and midden layers. Others were in working order at the time of the abandonment of the broch. Unusually, there is little evidence of the repair of damaged or broken objects which bolsters

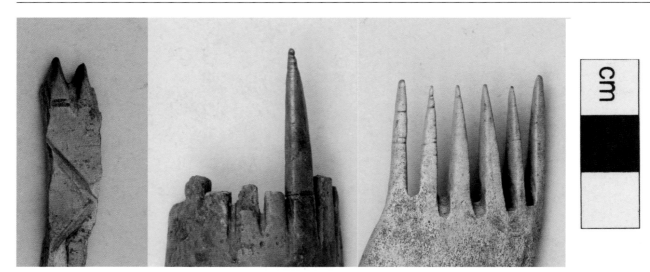

Figure 4.9.14 Detail of the variation in use-wear observed on the long-handled bone combs

the suggestion that there was a ready source of raw material from which replacement tools and implements could be fashioned. Of wider significance is the range of tool marks in evidence on these pieces which attests to a varied toolkit which is no longer in evidence amongst the surviving metals assemblage, including circular and diamond-tipped punches or awls, saws and a possible cleaver. Were these items considered of particular value and salvaged from the fire or were they stored and used outside of the broch itself? The answer to this question is something we can only speculate on.

Catalogue

The catalogue of the worked bone and antler has been organised into functional categories, as far as possible, with a summary of the classification and relevant comparanda followed by the detailed descriptions. Due to the small quantities involved, the catalogue describes terrestrial mammal bone, cetacean bone and antler together under functional groupings. Abbreviations used: D diameter, H height, L length, W width, T thickness.

Personal ornaments

Only three unambiguous ornaments of worked bone were identified amongst the assemblage consisting of two plain pins with splayed heads (SF 103 and SF 216) and large perforated pin with bulbous head (SF 275) broken mid-length along shank and the tip lost. The latter had been heavily burnt. A third shank fragment catalogued below as a pin/point fragment (SF 272) could well derive from a further pin but so little survives it is not possible to be confident about the identification. Pin (SF 216) was recovered intact from floor surface (049) and the second

intact example (SF 103) came from the burnt layer (042) which overlies the floor levels inside the broch. The fragments of the large burnt perforated pin (SF 275) were extracted from animal bone collected from a floor deposit (context 048).

Pins (see also SF 272)

A variety of bone pin types are current throughout the Iron Age and these have been considered and reviewed in detail by a number of authors (Stevenson 1955; MacGregor 1974; 1985; Foster 1990) who have attempted to ascribe broad date ranges based on form. Only three pins (Fig. 4.9.9) were recognised amongst the Clachtoll assemblage. Two (SF 103 and SF 216, Fig. 4.9.10 a and b) are plain with intact splayed heads formed by retaining the natural proximal articular end of the bone for decorative effect and conform to MacGregor's (1985, 120–1) 'pig fibula' form or Hunter, Gibson and Gerken's (2013) plain splayed head pins. These are a typical pin form observed throughout Scotland and have a long currency of use from the Late Bronze Age (*e.g.*, LBA levels of Sculptor's Cave, Covesea, Moray (Benton 1931, fig. 8.8; also fig. 18.5, from later levels; Cruickshanks and Hunter 2020, 108, illus. 5.15, SF 814) throughout the Iron Age and into the Viking-age (*e.g.*, Freswick, Caithness (Curle 1939, pl. LXXIII), Birsay, Orkney (Curle 1982, 73–4, illus. 48; see MacGregor 1985, 121 for other Viking examples).

The trend favouring the use of pig fibula to produce pins of this type is widely noted across Iron Age assemblages from Scotland as the natural shape of the bone 'immediately recommends itself as a pin' (MacGregor 1985, 120). The proximal end of the pig fibula naturally expands forming a head which is retained to prevent the

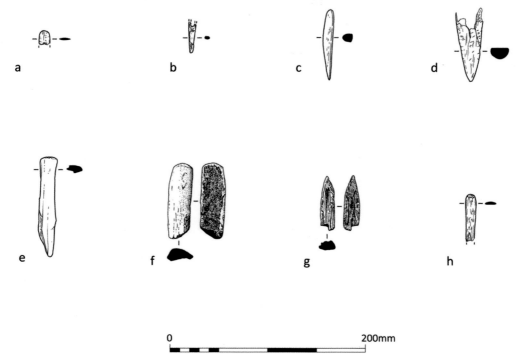

Figure 4.9.15 The worked bone and antler tools: a) needle SF 068, b) needle SF 121, c) hide rubber SF 075, d) hide rubber SF 175, e) hide rubber SF 265, f) hide-rubber SF 280, g) point SF 281, h) spatulate-ended tool SF 149

pin from slipping out of place during use; the shaft of the fibula is naturally fine and narrow in diameter making it easy to trim down or slice off to create a pointed tip (*ibid.*, 120–1). Their common recognition amongst Iron Age assemblages from Atlantic Scotland and beyond attests to them being everyday ornaments and the Clachtoll examples can be readily paralleled including those from Crosskirk and Nybster broch, Caithness (Fairhurst, 1984, 122 illus. 72, eg. no. 655; Heald *et al.* in prep), Foshigarry, North Uist (Hallén 1994, illus. 10, GNA 75); Broch of Ayre, Burrian, Gurness, Howe, Pool, Sanday, all Orkney (Graeme 1913, 44, fig. 11; MacGregor 1974, 71–6, figs 7 and 8, nos. 80–100; Hedges 1987, fig. 2.24; Ballin Smith 1994, 171; Scalloway, Shetland (Smith 1998, 171, fig. 109) as further afield including as Keil Cave (Ritchie 1967, fig. 2) and Dun an Fheurian, Argyll (Ritchie 1971, fig. 2), Lochspouts, Ayrshire (Munro 1882, 175, fig. 171), and Broxmouth, East Lothian (Hunter, Gibson and Gerken 2013, 269, illus. 10.15).

The third pin (SF 275, Fig. 4.9.10c) is incomplete but represents a much larger and robust example with a swollen rounded head and robust, tapering, circular-sectioned shank which is perforated below the head. Despite the charred and heat-discoloured condition of the surfaces, striations from abrasion or filing to smooth and finish the surfaces are still observable and hints of a polish remain.

SF 103   Plain pin with splayed head, intact. Flared head formed by natural proximal articular end of pig fibula; distal end removed and shaft shaped to a point. Oval-sectioned shank tapers strongly towards a fine point which is facetted by abrasion to shape. The head and upper shank are largely unmodified but dark stained. Below the head the surface is abraded to shape, the striations softened and polished from use. L 87.2 mm; head: 13.2 × 4.2 mm; shank D: 3.2 × 4.3 mm. Wgt 2.3 g. Context 042, burnt deposit across entire broch interior (Fig. 4.9.10a).

SF 216   Plain pin with splayed head, intact. Flared head formed by unmodified proximal articular head of pig fibula, distal end removed and shaft modified to a point. Oval-sectioned shank tapers gently, curving slightly along length, towards damaged slightly rounded tip. Surfaces abraded to shape with a light sheen from use. Surface is irregularly stained. A very close parallel comes from Scalloway, Shetland (Smith 1998, 171, fig. 109, no. 6). L 86.5 mm; head: 13.2 × 4.4 mm; shank D: 4.5 mm. Wgt 2.2 g. Context 049, floor material (Fig. 4.9.10b).

SF 275   Perforated pin. Three conjoining fragments of a substantial bone pin with flattened pear- or barrel-shaped head produced from a dense long-bone fragment of a large mammal. Articular head of

Figure 4.9.16 Photograph of the whalebone working surface (SF 024)

bone removed and shaped to form a flat-topped swollen bulbous head which tapers strongly into an oval-sectioned robust shank, broken across a drilled biconical perforation (D 4.5 mm) immediately below the head, with a further break across the shank mid-length; the tip has been lost and the original length is unknown. Articular tissue of bone visible on dorsal face of bone. Fine striations from abrasion to shape and smooth the surfaces are observed across all surfaces, particularly the shank, the surfaces of which have been burnt to a pale grey to peachy-pink colour whilst the core of the bone is dark grey/brown; the head appears to have been protected from the intensity of the fire. Surviving L 97.4 mm (conjoining fragments); head: L 30 mm; W 12.1 mm; T 10.4 mm; shank: W 7.1–8.2 mm, T 6.8–8 mm. Wgt 9 g. The two shank fragments were extracted from animal bone (SF 98) from context 048, floor deposit, whilst the head was recovered from spoil (Fig. 4.9.10c).

Weaponry

POMMEL

The most significant individual item amongst the worked bone is a small decorative pommel (SF 274, Figs 4.9.2 and 4.9.11) from the terminal of the handle of a bladed weapon. The possession of a weapon such as a sword or dagger during the Iron Age would have identified the owner as a person of substance in the community, reflecting perhaps their status or role, and would have marked them out as someone of wealth and influence in the community (Sharples 1991). The weapons and their associated scabbards and fittings can be elaborate pieces of craftsmanship which often incorporate personalised features (Sharples 2003, 157) as well decorative motifs that are not only for aesthetic embellishment but are also symbols to be read and understood, probably by only a select few amongst the community (Giles 2008). For others, they were impressive objects to be admired. Both the blade itself, whether a sword or dagger, and its elaborate fittings, such as pommels and hilt guards made of rare cetacean tooth and ivory, would be regarded as prestige items. Even when separated from the blade, an item such as the Clachtoll pommel would have been a recognisable component from a weapon and it is possible that pommels and hilt guards may have retained in circulation despite being separated from the blade itself. In Scotland, many similar Iron Age cetacean tooth and ivory pommels and hilt guards are known but these are typically no longer associated with their weapon.

The pommel has been produced from a piece of cetacean tooth/ivory but the surfaces are so heavily modified it has not been possible to determine the species. It is small and slender and has been very carefully shaped and finished. A semi-ring-shaped decorative indentation on both faces identifies it as an example of a well-known type found across Atlantic Scotland and Ireland. Although by no means common, this particular type with the ring-shaped carving embellishing the faces, was subject to a detailed study by Etienne Rynne (1983) who investigated examples made out of wood and bone from both Scotland and Ireland in an attempt to better understand their decoration, distribution and chronology. Rynne argued that they represent stylised skeuomorphs of La Tène metal pommels (*ibid.*, 189) and formed a distinctive type of organic sword hilt decoration in Ireland and Highland Scotland (*ibid.*, 195). Subsequent study of more recent excavated examples suggested a floruit of use during the 1st to 2nd centuries AD (Sharples 2003, 157). The Clachtoll pommel is an important addition to the known corpus due to its close dating; its recovery from the broch interior providing a secure date for its deposition to the second half of the 1st century BC or the early years of the 1st century AD (see Chapter 3). This stretches back the known chronology of its type and provides a useful benchmark from which less closely dated or stratigraphically insecure examples from elsewhere can be compared.

Similar examples are known from Broch of Burrian, Orkney (MacGregor 1974, 76–8, fig. 9:127; Rynne 1983, 189–90, fig. 85:2); North Uist (Close-Brooks and Maxwell 1974, 290; Rynne 1983, 190, fig. 85:3) and a small bone quillon of a similar style comes from Wheelhouse II at Á Cheardach Bheag, South Uist (Fairhurst 1971, 100, fig. 10:1). Since Rynne's study, several more examples have been discovered including an identically decorated pommel and a plain sword guard or quillon from Scalloway, Shetland (Smith 1998, 158, fig. 101, 3759 and 2587). The Scalloway pommel was found in the rubble infill of the abandoned building outside the broch, in a

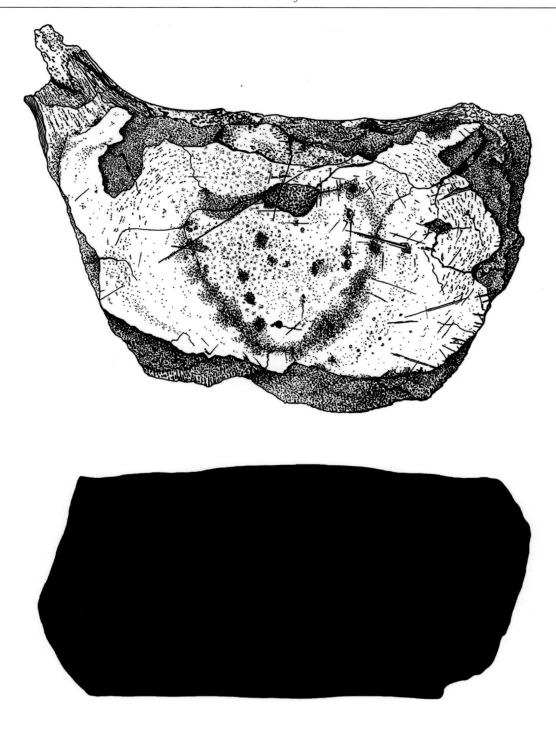

Figure 4.9.17 The whalebone working surface (SF 024)

context that dated to the 3rd or 4th centuries AD (Sharples 2003, 157) suggesting that these pommels and presumably their associated blades were still circulating in Atlantic Scotland slightly later than Rynne anticipated. More recently, several hilt guards and pommels produced from cetacean ivory and teeth have been recognised amongst the assemblage from Mine Howe, Orkney including at least one unfinished example (F. Hunter, pers. comm.). This group includes a heavily degraded pommel made out of a cetacean tooth with a flattened ovoid shape and a semi-ring shaped covering the centre of the faces, similar in form to those already described. Although the pommel was once well finished with highly polished surfaces, the ivory has deteriorated and split resulting in at least one episode of repair with metal rivets.

Other broadly similar pommels and hilt guards are also widely known but these are plain and lack the distinctive semi-ring carved decoration of the examples under discussion here. These include an pommel from Gurness, Orkney (Hedges 1987, fig. 2.37, no. 202) rivetted perhaps to repair, a possible pommel or tool handle of whalebone from Hurly Hawkin, Angus (Henshall 1982, 232, fig. 8:61), a plain hilt-guard from Keiss Road broch, Caithness (Heald and Jackson, 2001, 134), a plain pommel and hilt guard from Lingro Broch, St Ola, Orkney (Rynne 1983, 194, fig. 90:3 and 4) and a fragment of a small plain oval ivory item with a countersunk rectangular slot perforating the height of the object from Cill Donnain wheelhouse, South Uist which was interpreted as a decorative toggle (Parker Pearson 2014, 147, 153, fig. 12.1, no.145). Although lacking the distinctive decorative embellishment it is closely similar in shape to a quillon from Á Cheardach Bheag and is, like the pommel under discussion here, very small in size, only being 29 mm in length.

Although very similar in form to the examples with semi-ring-shaped embellishment considered by Rynne, the Clachtoll pommel is more delicate and elegant in shape, tapering strongly towards its flattened base through which the tip of the tang of the blade would have been inserted. At only 45 mm in width and 16.2 mm in height, it is a diminutive example of the type, perhaps suited to association with a dagger rather than a sword.

SF 274 Dagger or sword pommel. Small but elegantly carved cetacean bone pommel, squat lentoid in shape with slender rounded tips and a rounded but damaged humped back. Carefully shaped flattened oval facet (9.7 × 16.6 mm) at the base surrounding a rectangular socket which perforates full height; perforation wider at flattened base (5.3 × 8.7 mm) than at rounded back (4.5 × 7.3 mm) where a spall has detached post-deposition. Semi-ring-shaped groove carved into both faces, creating a sub-circular boss. Burnt. W 45 mm; H 16.2 mm; max T 10.1 mm. Wgt 5.8 g. Context: recovered from within the 'souterrain' structure after the completion of the excavations, having likely washed out from behind the walling (Figs 4.9.2 and 4.9.11).

Tools: textile and hide-working tools

Tools relating to various aspects of textile manufacture and skin or hide processing are the most prominent group of implements amongst the worked bone and antler objects from the site, complimenting the array of stone whorls recovered from the broch (McLaren, Section 4.7). The most recognisable of these tools are a group of long-handled combs, surviving in various conditions, and displaying a range of use-wear patterns that indicate differences in function between individual items amongst the group. Also recognised are needles and a variety of bone, antler and cetacean bone implements which each display smoothing and polishing as the result of being rubbed against a soft surface, and probably saw use in skin or hide processing.

LONG-HANDLED COMBS (BY HELEN CHITTOCK AND DAWN MCLAREN)

The four combs from Clachtoll (Figs 4.9.12 and 4.9.13) represent a small, but significant, group of readily recognisable implements, representing a well-known Iron Age tool type found across Britain in areas of good bone preservation (Henshall 1950; Hunter, Gibson and Gerken 2013, 273). Although only one comb (SF 148) is complete, the remains of all four provide important information on the use of these enigmatic objects and the wider traditions they were part of. The function of the combs has been much debated and is still contested (*e.g.*, Coughtrey 1872, Henshall 1950; Hodder and Hedges 1977, 17; Coles 1987, 105–6; Tuohy 1999; Hunter, Gibson and Gerken 2013, 274; Stirling and Milek 2015). They were traditionally accepted as being used primarily for beating down the horizontal weft threads on a warp-weighted loom (Henshall 1950, 146). Claims that they will not have been effective in this process led to suggestions that they were used as hair ornaments (Hodder and Hedges 1977, 99), with alternative theories including uses in defleshing hides and preparing fibres for fabric production. Following experimental work and use-wear analysis (Tuohy 1995; 1999; 2000), it has been suggested instead that they may have been used in braiding or in the weaving of decorative borders, or potentially other forms of craft, such as wool combing, forming multi-functional textile production tools (Tuohy 1999, 97). Recent research has examined the aesthetic properties and functions of the combs, as an unusually high proportion are decorated (Chittock 2013; 2014) and ongoing experimental work (Beamer 2019) aims to explore the viability of previously postulated functions in comparison with use-wear evidence.

In Tuohy's examination of 144 combs from northern Britain, all were made from either whalebone or antler (1999, 38), as opposed to those from southern Britain, which tend to use either antler or the long bones of livestock animals. Antler is generally the more common material used at Scottish sites (*ibid.*), although those from the Northern Isles trend towards the use of cetacean bone (MacGregor 1985, 189) but with many caveats (Hallén 1994, 222). The selection of materials for making combs will have been based partly on the availability of materials, but may also have been governed by other factors, such as the varying properties of these materials (Chittock 2014). Of the examples from Clachtoll, three combs (SF 140, SF 148 and SF 206) have been produced from beam or thick tine fragments of antler, whilst the small, fractured fragment of a fourth example, represented by (SF 271) has been made from a thick, dense, piece of cetacean bone. The patterns of material selection for the antler combs can be teased out a little further: the extreme curvature of SF 206 has been made of fairly narrow beam fragment (presumably from a young adult); in contrast, the width and density of both (SF 140) and (SF 147) imply the utilisation of beam fragments from a large antler, presumably that of a mature stag.

Only one of the four combs from Clachtoll broch, (SF 148), is complete, although (SF 206) may be a near-complete example with a short handle. SF 148 probably falls into what Tuohy describes as a specifically northern type, possibly used for wool combing, which has a much shorter handle than most southern combs and fits neatly into the palm of the hand (Tuohy 1999, 40).

The butt type of SF 148 is either Tuohy's Type N or R, following the contours of the antler to form a slightly concave end but one which lacks the distinctive concavity or profile to align this with 'fish-tail'-type butts, common in broch and wheelhouse assemblages in Atlantic Scotland such as those from Crosskirk Broch, Caithness (Fairhurst 1984, 120–1, illus. 71:481) but thought to be a trait of early broch assemblages (Smith 1998, 156). This example is distinctly polished at the butt, which, according to Tuohy, is also a northern trait (1999, 38) but in this instance, also represents a build-up of polish as the result of rubbing against the hand during use suggesting the implement was well used at the time of its discard or abandonment. This comb is also perforated, where the comb has been suspended on a cord or string, possibly carried on the person or hung for storage. Only seven of Tuohy's 144 combs from northern Britain were perforated (1999), making this example unusual but not unprecedented. Other perforated

examples come from Foshigarry, North Uist (Hallén 1994, 222, illus. 14, GNA 150), Midhowe Broch (Callander and Grant 1934, 485, illus. 26:6) and Gurness Broch (Hedges 1987, 93, fig. 2.19: 19b) Orkney, and Broxmouth, East Lothian (Hunter, Gibson and Gerken 2013, illus. 10:17, SF 184) to name a few. This perforation is unusual its positioning, instead of being located towards the butt, it is off-center on the shaft of the comb: a trait only recorded by Tuohy on four examples in the very south of England (Tuohy 1999). The reason behind the choice to perforate it in such a manner is unclear but the build-up of use-wear around the edges of the perforation (Fig. 4.9.6) attest to it being frequently being suspended.

Tuohy (1999) identifies two broad comb types in northern Britain. One type has fine teeth and a longer handle and is part of the British-wide tradition of comb making and use, which she interprets as possibly having been involved in making braids or borders. The second is a specifically northern type with a shorter handle and more robust teeth. Tuohy suggests this type was used for wool combing (1999, 40). At Clachtoll broch, SF 148 falls into the northern type by virtue of its short handle and moderately fine teeth, the shaft waisted on one long edge only. The other three are more difficult to categorise to Tuohy's classification due to their incomplete condition: the surviving tooth of SF 206 is of similar moderately fine proportions to SF 148 although the butt of the comb is missing and the length of the shaft is unknown, the shaft certainly looks narrower than SF 148 with straight parallel edges but not enough survives to suggest it had a long handle; SF 271 has two distinctly short and broad teeth surviving but this fragment cannot be classified further; SF 140 is heavily fragmented and burnt, also making classification uncertain but the remaining long edge is concave suggesting a comb with a waisted shaft. The use-wear recorded on the surviving teeth of the combs imply that they were used in varied and diverse ways, a pattern noted on the large assemblage of combs from Broch of Burrian (MacGregor 1974, 84), examples from Howe, Orkney (Ballin Smith 1994, 222) and in the recent examination of examples from Broxmouth in south-east Scotland (Hunter, Gibson and Gerken 2013, 274).

At Danebury, Hampshire, large groups of long-handled combs were recovered (Sellwood 1984; Cunliffe and Poole 1991, 354–7). Twenty-one examples from the 1979–1988 excavations had teeth surviving which allowed use-wear analysis to be conducted. The most frequent pattern of use was the breakage of the teeth themselves which are susceptible and vulnerable to damage as the result of use. Most of the combs from the site displayed signs of general wear, such as a polished surface and teeth which have become rounded in section and pointed towards the apices (Sellwood 1984, 375–8; Cunliffe and Poole 1991,

357). Another form of wear observed was the breakage and subsequent wearing smooth of the extreme left-hand tooth or two teeth (Cunliffe and Poole 1991, 357), a pattern noted on (SF 148) amongst the Clachtoll combs.

Turning to the examples amongst the current assemblage, three of the combs from Clachtoll have intact teeth surviving, all of which display use-wear (Fig. 4.9.14). Only SF 148 has a complete set of teeth. The breakage of teeth on the other examples may have occurred during use; accidentally or deliberately; during the collapse of the broch; or during subsequent site processes. It is significant, however, that none of the missing teeth were recovered from the broch deposits during on-site sieving or post-excavation soil sample processing, as might have been expected had the breakage of the teeth occurred post-deposition.

Comb fragment SF 271 stands out amongst the group due to its short but broad teeth which are highly polished, and darker in colour than the rest of the comb fragment. The polish may be a result of smoothing the teeth prior to use but is more likely to represent use-wear. It is unclear whether the shortness of the teeth of SF 271 are the result of extensive use or design, but they are sufficiently different from the teeth surviving on the other three combs from the site to allow speculation of a different purpose and function: unlike SF 148 and SF 206, the use-wear is not asymmetrical and although polished there is no grooving from fibres whist the tips of teeth of SF 271 are stained dark brown. A similar comb with irregular short, broad and blunt teeth like that just described was noted amongst the Foshigarry assemblage (Hallén 1994, 224, illus. 14, GNA 5) where it was noted that it was unlikely to have seen the same use as the longer toothed examples, but no alternative function was offered. It may not be a coincidence that the disparity of use-wear on the Clachtoll blunt toothed comb concords with the use of cetacean bone as the raw material rather than antler, which would have provided the comb with flat rather than curved profile.

The teeth of SF 148 and SF 206 show a different kind of wear to that just considered, displaying a build-up of polish on the tips and between the teeth but also observed in the form of distinctive transverse grooving of the teeth tips from abrasion from threads, a pattern noted on an example from Broxmouth (Hunter, Gibson and Gerken 2013, 274, no. SF 185) which was interpreted as being used consistently and habitually at an angle in the same direction to straighten and separate fibers rather than to bead down a weft. A similar pattern of wear was noted on an unusual, decorated comb from Gurness, Orkney (Hedges 1987, fig. 2.21, no. 53) and was recognised on a large number of the combs where teeth were extant at Danebury, Hampshire (Cunliffe and Poole 1991, 375, fig. 7.29).

In contrast, the stumps of the teeth of SF 140 appear to have been freshly cut when they broke, displaying sharp, angular edges and no distinct polishing or wear. It is possible this comb has been recut or abandoned in the process of manufacture. The process of recutting is identified by Tuohy (1999), who considers incised decorative bands cut through by the teeth of the combs as an indicator of secondary modification, although there are other processes that could also result in this. What remains of the edges of the teeth and the spaces between them on SF 140 appear remarkably unworn with no trace of primary wear later obliterated by recutting. The burnt condition of this example may be significant in this context. It was recovered from (048), a deposit that contained other burnt material, suggesting the comb fragments may have been incorporated into the hearth, and were then discarded along with the other burnt debris. It is worth speculating that this could be a comb abandoned in the process of manufacture or re-working, thrown into the hearth out of frustration, and later raked out with the hearth debris and spread across the floor. Recut combs are rarely recognised amongst Scottish assemblages but roughouts and unfinished examples are present amongst many assemblages such as that from Keiss Road broch, Caithness (Heald and Jackson 2001, 134), Midhowe Broch, Orkney (Callander and Grant 1934, 486, fig. 26:9 and 10) and possibly from Scalloway, Shetland (Smith 1998, 156, fig. 100:5).

Despite the limited number of combs within the assemblage, use-wear evidence from the Clachtoll examples lends weight to the argument that combs are not a homogenous group and the various forms and types in use in northern Britain saw differences in function but that these categories may not have been well-defined and may have overlapped; those from Clachtoll certainly argue for at least two different purposes. Significantly, similar patterns of variable use use-wear have been identified in other assemblages of combs, such as those from Glastonbury and Meare Lake Villages in Somerset (Chittock 2013, 38–40) and at Broxmouth in south-east Scotland (Hunter, Gibson and Gerken 2013, 274). At Glastonbury and Meare, for example, combs were identified as bearing three different types of use-wear, which were present in differing intensities on each object, suggesting they were not a single category of objects serving a single purpose (Chittock 2013, 38–40).

Two of the four combs from Clachtoll broch are decorated. SF 140 and SF 271 both show the remains of incised criss-cross or saltire decoration on the shaft, immediately below the teeth falling into Tuohy's Type 2 decoration. SF 271 has the addition of an incised line at the base of the teeth, whilst SF 140 has a similar lateral line, incised further up the teeth; a feature fairly commonly recorded on Scottish examples such as a single long-handled comb from Broxmouth, East Lothian (Hunter, Gibson and Gerken 2013, 275, fig. 184) and Crosskirk Broch, Caithness (Fairhurst 1984, 120, illus. 71:414), amongst others. The part that remains of SF 206 is plain, as is SF 148. As both decorated combs from Clachtoll are incomplete, it is unclear whether the decoration will have continued down the whole length of the combs or just consisted of one cross, but the latter is more consistent with the Scottish corpus which includes examples from Crosskirk Broch, Caithness (Fairhurst 1984, 120 illus. 71:280 and 414); Midhowe (Callander and Grant 1934, 485, fig. 26:7), Gurness (Hedges 1987, fig. 2.21: nos. 52, 57) Orkney, at Hilswick in Shetland (Tuohy 1999) and at Bac Mhic Connain, North Uist (Hallén 1994, 222, illus. 14, GNB 5), to name a few. A miniature comb, decorated with a slightly off-set saltire towards the teeth from Cill Donnain wheelhouse, South Uist (Parker Pearson 2014b, 146, fig. 12.1, no. 142), has been interpreted as a child's toy but could equally be a potting tool.

All four combs were found within occupation layers in the broch. Comb SF 271 was found in a rubbly occupation layer (078) inside the 'souterrain' structure, along with a range of other objects including stone lamps, spindle whorls and ceramic sherds. This layer was overlain by a clay midden deposit containing frequent animal bone (047), which was, in turn, overlain by (048), a clay/peat ash deposit, which contained burnt comb SF 140, along with other varied finds.

SF 140 Incomplete and burnt comb in two refitting pieces and associated fragments, likely produced from a longitudinally split shard of antler, the rubicose exterior surface removed and smoothed and the cancellous tissue from the interior also shaved off to produce a thin plate. The surviving refitting pieces represent the toothed end of the comb; tips are lost and none of the teeth are complete but the stubs of seven broken teeth remain. They are very fine, with narrow spaces between them, and there is no evidence that the comb was used after the breakage of any of the teeth. Traces of Type 2 decoration are present (Tuohy 1999), forming part of an incised saltire cross at the toothed end of the comb. An incised line crosses the cuts of the teeth, or vice versa, suggesting the teeth may have been recut or were relatively unused, although this may have been an intended design feature. What remains of the edged of the teeth and the spaces between them appear very unworn. L 38.9 mm; W 28.6 mm. Wgt 4.6 g. Context 048, floor deposit (Fig. 4.9.13a).

SF 148 Intact comb, unburnt, produced from beam fragment of large mature red deer antler with a short irregularly concave handle and six robust teeth with wide spaces (ave. W 2.3 mm) between them; consistent with Tuohy (1999) Type N or R butt which is polished. The teeth of the comb (L 18.8–20.2 mm) are also curved across the short axis following the natural curvature of the raw material. Drilled circular perforation (D 5.1 mm) present off-centre towards the toothed end and is worn around the edges indicating suspension by a cord or string. The six teeth are worn, as are the gaps between them. They are slightly polished under magnification and also have very pronounced lateral concentric striations, particularly towards the tips, which are visible with the naked eye. L 92.4mm; W 41.5mm. Wt: 28.37 g. Context 077, floor stabilising deposit (Fig. 4.9.13b).

SF 206 Incomplete toothed end of a bone comb produced from a split and hollowed fragment of antler tine or beam. Only one tooth survives intact (detached but refitted; L 26.4 mm), but the stumps of a further eight teeth are visible. The surviving tooth is highly polished and lateral striations are visible under magnification, in addition to a series of deeper, polished concentric grooves at the tip of the tooth, which are visible with the naked eye. Body is plain and quite degraded, particularly at the edges; butt end is lost. Surfaces are dark in colour and black in places. L 81.2 mm; W 29.7 mm. Wgt 10.3 g. Context 067, floor deposit (Fig. 4.9.13c).

SF 271 Narrow, flat, subrectangular fragment of an incomplete bone comb produced from a plate of dense cetacean bone, two short pointed teeth surviving, no original edges remain and the butt has been lost. Traces of incised saltire cross decoration conforming to Tuohy's (1999) Type 2 decoration present below the teeth; a transverse incision also cuts the bases of the teeth, or vice versa, suggesting the comb might have been recut although this could have been a deliberate design feature. Surviving teeth (L 3.0–3.6 mm) are wide and thick, widely spaced (gap: W 2.3 mm) but worn down to short stumps with well-developed polish and staining as a result of use. Remaining L 41.6 mm; W 8.3 mm. Wgt 2.0 g. Extracted from animal bone SF 210. Context 078, loose rubble and mixed fill of deep area, possible tumble after roof collapse (Fig. 4.9.13d).

NEEDLES

Two needles (SF 68 and SF 121, Fig. 4.9.15a and b) in the form of elongated tapering bone points, perforated towards the widest end were recognised. These are sometimes referred to elsewhere as perforated points to take into consideration the potential variable role that such implements may have performed, particularly in some instances (such as SF 68) where so little survives, it is difficult to distinguish a needle head from a perforated pin head or other type of perforated tool. For example, a fine elongated point with a flattened perforated head from Hurly Hawkin, Angus (Henshall 1982, 232, fig. 8, no. 59) was interpreted as a finely made needle whilst a similar object in both size and form found at Midhowe Broch, Orkney was interpreted as a perforated pin (MacGregor 1974, 71, fig. 8, no. 95).

At Howe, Orkney and Keiss Road Broch, Caithness similar examples to those recovered at Clachtoll have been interpreted as sewing needles and all have been formed from pig fibula (Ballin Smith 1994, 171; Heald and Jackson 2001, 134). Both examples from Clachtoll are incomplete and are broken across the eye. The form of the break on SF 121 is consistent with breakage during use. The degradation of the surfaces of the shank and its recovery from midden deposit (047) suggest it was deliberately discarded and incorporated into this deposit. In contrast, SF 68 is quite fresh but worn from use. It was recovered from the layer of burning covering the broch interior (042).

SF 68 Needle fragment. Flat rounded spatulate-head, lentoid cross-section, broken across a small biconical perforation (D 2.9 mm). Closely spaced fine lateral striations from production cover both faces which are softened but not obscured by wear and a light surface sheen from use or handling. Series of fine longitudinal scratch marks extend from the edge of the perforation towards the rounded end on both sides. Both surfaces are stained. Produced from mammal long bone but species/element not identifiable. A more complete example with a flattened perforated head comes from Hurly Hawkin, Angus (Henshall 1982, 232, fig. 8, no.59). Remaining L 15.3 mm; W 11.3 mm; T 2.4 mm. Wgt 0.3 g. Context 042, burnt deposit across entire broch interior (Fig 4.9.15a).

SF 121 Needle fragment. Very short tapering shank produced from mammal bone, oval in section, broken across the slightly asymmetrically worn biconical bored perforation (Diam: 3.3 mm min). Tip is blunt, 2.2 mm in diameter, and polished from use. Fine diagonal striations on surviving surfaces from manufacture, softened with a light sheen from wear. Modification to surfaces too severe to allow identification of species/element. Similar short needles known from Crosskirk broch, Caithness (Fairhurst 1984, 121, illus.

72, no. 46), Howe (Ballin Smith 1994, 171, illus. 95, no. 2850) and Gurness and Midhowe brochs, Orkney (Hedges 1987, fig. 2.25, no. 83) (MacGregor 1974, 73, fig. 6, no. 46). L 32.3 mm; head W 26 mm; shank D 2.7-4.7 mm. Wgt 0.7 g. Context 047, midden material (Fig. 4.9.15b).

HIDE-RUBBERS

Four possible hide-rubbers (SF 75, SF 175, SF 265 and SF 280; Fig. 4.9.15) have been recognised amongst the assemblage. This classification of tool has been described variously in the literature as hide-rubbers (Hunter *et al.* 2013, 276) and polishers (Hallén 1994, 207). Although encompassing items of various shapes, sizes and forms, a study of examples from Foshigarry and Bac Mhic Connain in North Uist allowed the definition of this classification of tools as those of a convenient size for holding, with rounded ends, carefully shaped and showing signs of rubbing and polished from wear, which may have been used for leatherworking (Hallén 1994, 207). Several types of bone from cattle and red deer were used as scrapers probably for skin and leather working (Ballin Smith 1994, 176–7). A series of robust but irregular splinters of bone with rubbed and polished surfaces come from Midhowe Broch, Orkney (Callander and Grant 1934, 488, fig. 31). These are very similar to SF 75 and SF 265 described below.

SF 75 Short robust point produced from an irregular splinter of dense cetacean bone, sub-square in cross-section mid-length, tapering in both directions to a narrow flattened lentoid-sectioned point at one end (W 1.7 mm; T 2.7 mm) and to a triangular-sectioned blunt rounded tip (W 8 mm; T 5.5 mm) at the other. Surfaces are facetted and abraded but worn smooth, suggesting use as a rubber. No polish. Surfaces stained. L 74.5 mm; max W 10.6 mm; max T 8.4 mm. Wgt 5.8 g. Context 048, floor deposit (Fig. 4.9.15c).

SF 175 Antler tine fragment, split obliquely down length to create point at one end, rubicose surfaces pared with a knife leaving clear longitudinal cut facets and chatter marks; the cancellous tissue at the core of the tine hollowed out to create a conical open socket across which the implement has broken leaving a ragged and irregular edge. Tine split or worn obliquely from the tip to the open socket, exposing the cancellous core and creating a flat face to the socket which has been rubbed to smooth or though use. Tool marks on all other surfaces are fresh. Remaining L 78 mm; open socket: exterior D 18.5 × 27 mm, interior L 39.5 mm, D 13.5 mm; tip: D 4.8 mm; T 19–27 mm. Wgt 10.5 g. Context 078, rubble in-fill of 'souterrain' within broch (Fig. 4.9.15d).

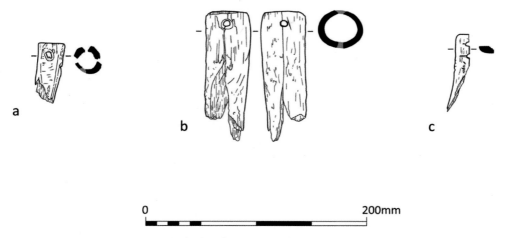

Figure 4.9.18 The handles: a) SF 182, b) SF 269, c) SF 273

SF 265 Robust spatulate-ended, blunt nosed implement produced from a splinter of dense long
bone shaft of large mammal (cow/deer) split
longitudinally and distal and proximal articular
ends removed. Flatter broad end rounded off,
surfaces smoothed and softened as the result of
rubbing and handling; the opposite end roughly
split and abraded into an irregular blunt rounded
point, also smoothed and rounded from wear.
Light sheen over all surfaces. L 105.3 mm; W
7.8–17.3 mm; T 5–12 mm. Wgt 19 g. Extracted
from animal bone SF 99. Context 042, burnt
deposit across broch interior (Fig. 4.9.15e).

SF 280 Elongated subrectangular slice removed from the
rubicose surface of an antler tine, parallel long
edges smoothed towards one blunt rounded end,
bevelled at the tip (W 19 mm; T 5.5 mm) from
abrasion from rubbing; opposite end has been
roughly chopped at oblique angle, may also have
seen working but is now damaged. Cancellous
tissue of interior of tine roughly removed. L
80 mm; W 22.5 mm; T 11 mm. Wgt 9.9 g.
Extracted from animal bone SF 62. Context 047,
Floor deposit composed of concentrated peat ash,
SE quad (Fig. 4.9.15f).

Points

This category follows that defined for examples from
Midhowe Broch, Orkney (Foxon 1991, 194) which
describes them as pointed implements with a build-up of
wear and polish at the tapering tip but are perhaps less
well finished and lack the elaboration of pins (Hallén
1994, 215). There are inevitably examples which display
characteristics of both and could either be simple pins or
piercing tools (*ibid.*, 215). One certain robust and rather

crude point fashioned from a splinter of antler (SF 281)
was recognised from context 042. It appears to have been
split and chopped to shape but is now incomplete and
damaged. The identification of a second item (SF 272) is
less certain as it is a small fragment of a fine shank which
has broken at both ends. It is possible that this represents
a further dress accessory or ornamental pin but the loss
of the head and tip makes this impossible to demonstrate.

SF 272 Pin/point fragment. Short length of a cylindrical
shank produced from a hollow bird bone shaft,
broken at both ends, longitudinally cracked. No
obvious tool marks from production but surfaces
display a high sheen suggestive of polish though
wear. Remaining L 32.6 mm; D 4.1–5.1 mm. Wgt
0.6 g. Context unstratified (otter holt/corbelled
chamber experiment). (Not illustrated.)

SF 281 Antler point. Irregular and angular splinter
detached from the tip of a facetted antler tine
point, one end chopped crudely into a tapering
tip, the opposite end lost. The tine has been split
longitudinally after use resulting in the loss of
one face and opposing end. Surviving L 57.4 mm;
W 15.7 mm; T 9.2 mm. Wgt 4.4 g. extracted from
animal bone SF 39. Context 042, burnt deposit
across entire broch interior (Fig. 4.9.15g).

Spatulate tool

A single spatulate-ended tool fragment (SF 149;
Fig. 4.9.15h) came from the floor material (049). The
fragment is in moderate condition with a light sheen to
the surfaces which has developed as the result of handling
and use but this has degraded post-deposition. Similar
but more substantially intact examples are known from
Crosskirk, Keiss Harbour and Nybster brochs, Caithness

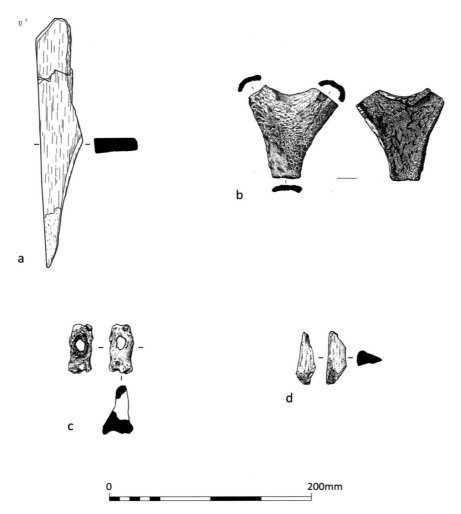

Figure 4.9.19 Miscellaneous objects of worked bone: a) cetacean bar SF 108/123, b) antler fitting or handle SF 279, c) unfinished toggle or bobbin SF 268, d) working waste SF 282

(Fairhurst 1984, 122; Heald and Jackson 2001, 134; Heald *et al.* in prep), Midhowe (Callander and Grant 1934, 487, fig. 27), Broch of Burrian (MacGregor 1974, 79, fig. 10, no. 143), Howe (Ballin Smith 1994, 174, illus. 98: nos. 4532 and 2281), Gurness (Hedges 1987, fig. 2.29), Orkney; Sollas (Campbell 1991, 158, illus. 21) and Foshigarry (Hallén 1994, 205, 207, illus. 6), North Uist; Scalloway, Shetland (Smith 1998, 153, fig. 99, no. 3162). At Scalloway, Sollas and Foshigarry, these spatulate points have been interpreted as modelling tools for potting (Campbell 1991, 158; Hallén 1994, 207; Smith 1998, 153) and an example with an asymmetric bevelled tip observed at Scalloway was noted as being particularly well suited to scraping and smoothing the inside of coil-built vessels (Smith 1998, 153).

SF 149 Spatulate-ended tool, broken mid-length and one end lost. Flat, thin, rectangular-sectioned blunt rounded tip tapering gently into narrow plano-convex sectioned shank. Series of oblique striations, cross-cutting and overlapping from production or use concentrate towards the wide blunt tip. Where original surfaces survive, they retain a light sheen from use and handling but much of the surface is pitted from post-depositional erosion. Produced from mammal long bone but modification to surfaces too severe to allow identification of species/element. Remaining L 50.2 mm; W 8.2–11 mm; T 1.8–3.5 mm. Wgt 2.3 g. Context 049, floor material (Fig. 4.9.15h).

Working surface

A large but damaged vertebra of an adult whale (SF 24; Figs 4.9.16 and 4.9.17) was recovered from context (044) in Cell 3. The epiphyseal surfaces of the vertebra are flat and fully fused indicating it derives from an adult whale but the species has not been identified (J. Robertson, pers. comm.). One of these surfaces has been extensively worked as a chopping block and working surface, and analysis of the tool marks suggest at least four separate tools (likely iron) can be distinguished from the markings, some of which are not represented in the surviving artefact assemblage (*e.g.*, diamond and circular tipped punches, possible cleaver). An unusual ring-shaped concentration of wear which is present, slightly off-centre on this same face, cannot be closely paralleled elsewhere. Rather than being made with a sharp-edged implement, the marks are shallow and diffuse and appear to have been the result of crushing or pounding with a softer implement, perhaps a wood or bone hammerhead, in a repetitive fashion resulting in the almost total obliteration of individual marks and the development of a more defuse ring-shaped pattern. It is unknown what items or materials were being worked on this surface to cause this distinctive wear pattern but a possible association with the secondary stages of roughing out and shaping stone spindle whorls seems likely based on the presence of unfinished discs amongst the stone assemblage.

Cetacean bone working surfaces, chopping blocks and anvils are frequently recovered amongst Iron Age and later bone assemblages from coastal sites in Scotland, from Clickhimin, Shetland (Hamilton 1968, 79) to sites in south-east Scotland such as Broxmouth, Fishers Road East, Castle Park, North Berwick Law and Muirfield (Hunter, Gibson and Gerken 2013, 254; Lowther 2000; Cox 2000; NMS: X.HD 1855 and X.HR 881), all East Lothian. A whale vertebra chopping block (SF 2523) from the Howe (Ballin Smith 1994, 182–3, illus. 105a), has more limited traces of use than the example under discussion here; a series of linear chop marks made with a cleaver or axe cross the face of the vertebra from various angles suggesting that it was freestanding and the user moved around it. In contrast, the wear on the Clachtoll example is more concentrated suggesting it was principally used with the broad edge facing the user. At Cnip, Lewis, several cetacean bone-working surfaces and chopping boards saw use in association with axes leaving deep, heavy chop marks, crush marks whilst others were scattered with fine knife cuts (Hunter 2006b, 144–5, illus. 3.24). At Scalloway, Shetland, a small, flattened fragment of whalebone with numerous knife cut marks and chopmarks was recognised (Smith 1998, 153, fig. 98, no. 3985). The variety and range of toolmarks used in conjunction with these working surfaces appears, in the main, to be more restrictive than the example from Clachtoll, although published examples from early excavations rarely detail the extent of wear observed making it difficult to set out useful comparisons.

SF 24   Whalebone working surface. Damaged but substantially complete fused vertebra deriving from an unidentified adult cetacean, missing most of the original edges, wings and spine though post-depositional erosion and charring. One extensive face (consolidated during conservation) extensively used as working surface, covered in dispersed series and sets of closely set tool marks from at least four distinct tools including deep angular possible axe or cleaver chop marks (ave. L 36 mm; W 2 mm); diamond-shaped punch marks (D 4 mm; max Dpt 5.5 mm); circular punch marks (D 3 mm; max Dpt 5 mm) and fine peck marks/pits (D 1–2 mm). At centre of same face, tool marks concentrate in distinct ring-shaped pattern (D 98.5 × 103.5 mm; W 7–8 mm) implying repeated working of specific object/material. The diffuse and shallow character of these marks is suggestive of repeated crushing, perhaps in association with a soft-headed (?wooden/bone) hammer or mallet. Remaining L 283 mm; W 149 mm; H 141 mm. Wgt 2382.6 g Context 044, wind-blown sand within stairwell gallery 3 (Fig. 4.9.17).

Handles

Four socketed antler/bone handles are present (Fig. 4.9.18), typically formed by hollowing out large antler tine or beam fragments to form conical sockets within which tools, perhaps of metal, could be affixed. Although antler appears to be the material type favoured for this purpose at Clachtoll and elsewhere, due both to its durability and its shock-absorbing capabilities (MacGregor 1985, 23–9), one perforated deer or cow metatarsal (SF 262) is present that could have seen use either as a handle or some form of fitting. Unlike examples elsewhere, such as at Foshigarry and Bac Mhic Connain, North Uist (Hallén 1994, 219), none of the handles had convincing traces of iron or copper staining, which might be observed, where preservation factors are right, from transfer from a metal tool head. The substantial size of some of the handles themselves, and the diameter and length of the sockets, imply use with large and robust tools. Probably the most interesting handle is (SF 273) which has a double perforation at the head (Fig. 4.9.18c), similar to an example Midhowe Broch, Orkney (Callander and Grant 1934, 494, fig. 37) where it was affixed to a single edged serrated saw blade.

SF 182 Handle fragments. Two fragments of a possible handle or handles produced from a sawn, split and hollowed antler tine. The fragments are both subrectangular in shape with concentric cross-sections where the cancellous interior of the antler has been removed and represent two joining halves of a hollowed cylindrical handle or socket, the full dimensions of which are unknown. One end of each fragment has been sawn squarely across the width; the opposite ends are broken and ragged. On both pieces, one edge is broken but these can be refitted and may have split during use; the opposite long edge on both has been knife-cut down its length leaving a narrow-bevelled edge. The thin narrow gap between the two cut long edges may have housed the thin tang of a blade (now lost), fixed in position by a peg or rivet inserted through a conical hole (max D 9.3 mm; min D 5.3 mm) bored at the squared end adjacent to the cut edge on both halves of the socket. Remaining L 55.5 mm; external D (refitted) 23 × 29.5 mm; internal D (refitted) 16 x 20 mm; T 4.5 mm. Wgt 12.4 g. Context 078, Possible midden material (Fig. 4.9.18a).

SF 262 Handle or fitting. Substantially intact metatarsal of deer or cow, proximal articular head trimmed and hollowed; the distal end is lost, broken across a possible bored perforation, original form and dimensions unknown. The damaged proximal end of the shaft has been perforated by a small splayed conical hole (D 6.4 mm at surface; D 2.4 × 3.7 mm interior) which is angled gently upwards towards the end of the bone. Surfaces are pitted and badly rotted. Surviving L 142.2 mm; W 22.4–27.2 mm; T 17.4–22.7 mm. Wgt 42.9 g. Extracted from animal bone SF 62. Context 047, midden material. (Not illustrated.)

SF 269 Socketed handle or ferrule. Damaged robust conical socketed handle or ferrule produced from an antler beam, broad end chopped and cancellous tissue hollowed out from this end. Split down length into two joining halves though a transverse drilled perforation (surface D 8.4 × 9.3 mm; interior D 6.1 × 6.8 mm) which completely perforates the thickness of the beam, set slightly back from the open end, the rim of which is internally bevelled with distinct knife cuts visible from production. Opposite end of handle has been lost. Flattened knife-pared facet with occasional fine chatter marks is present immediately below the transverse perforation, the tool marks softened and polished from rubbing though wear. A similar example comes from Broxmouth, E Lothian (Hunter 2013,

287, SF 190, illus. 10.23). Surviving L 119.2 mm; socket: external D 31.2 × 39.7 mm, interior D 22.3 × 31 mm, interior Dpt 79 mm; broken end: D 25.6 × 33.6 mm. Wgt 89.1 g. Extracted from animal bone SF 171. Unstratified (west) (Fig. 4.9.18b).

SF 273 Perforated handle. Fragment of a flat sub-rectangular plate chopped from split antler tine, broken across two closely set drilled perforations (D 4 mm; D 4.3 mm) set back from squared (?sawn) end; opposite end lost and irregularly broken. Squared end carefully cut, surfaces smoothed and corner rounded. Exterior surface abraded and smoothed to remove naturally irregular rubicose surface with sheen from handling. Short lateral incised lines (L 4 mm × W 05 mm; L 6.2 × 0.8 mm) project from the edges of both transverse perforations. A similar substantially intact but less well finished example of a double pegged handle comes from Midhowe Broch, Orkney (Callander and Grant 1934, 494, fig. 37). Remaining L 74.4 mm; r W 12.6 mm; T 6–7.3 mm. Wgt 4.3 g. Context unstratified, recovered from spoil heap (Fig. 4.9.18c).

Miscellaneous

CETACEAN BARS

In addition to the hide-rubbers already described, three fragmentary robust bar-like objects produced from dense cetacean bone were recognised amongst Clachtoll assemblage: one (SF 108/123; Fig. 4.9.19a) is substantially complete and has been shaped from a large cetacean bone into a rectangular-sectioned bar which tapers asymmetrically in width from mid-length in both directions forming a bevel-ended blunt point at one end and a much wider blunt rounded end at the other. Both ends are smoothed due to rubbing and both extensive faces have a light sheen from use or handling. This item is superficially similar in shape to a large cetacean bone item from Scalloway (Smith 1998, 158, fig. 101, 1) which was interpreted as a bridle cheek-piece but the Clachtoll example lacks any sign of perforation and has clear signs of abrasion and wear on the tips from rubbing. SF 266 and SF 270 are sufficiently similar in shape and wear to the wider blunt end of SF 108/133 for them to be classified here as similar tools but in both instances, the remaining fragments are too fractured and small to confirm this with certainty. The function of these tools is difficult to pin down as the wear observed could be the result of a variety of uses. Similar bar or baton-like cetacean implements were recognised amongst the assemblages from Foshigary, North Uist (Hallén 1994, 207, illus. 7, *e.g.* GNA 81 and GNA 82), Broch of Burrian, North Ronaldsay (MacGregor 1974, 86, fig. 14, no. 185, fig. 15, nos. 202 and 203) and two rubbed and polished bars came from Gurness broch, Orkney (Hedges 1987, fig 2.29, nos. 154 and 161). At Burrian and Foshigarry they were interpreted as smoothing or burnishing tools, perhaps used in hide processing (MacGregor 1974, 86; Hallén 1994, 207).

SF 108/123 Elongated subrectangular bar of dense cetacean bone, probably produced from a rib fragment, substantially complete but broken along one long edge towards widest end where the bar swells in width; found in two fragments but re-joined during conservation. Bar is rectangular in cross-section, fairly consistent in thickness across its length. Widest at mid-length (W 42.8 mm), tapering strongly but asymmetrically in width in one direction towards a thick blunt point, terminating in a facetted blunt tip and less strongly in the opposite direction to form a wide blunt rounded end. The flatter of the two faces is smooth with a light sheen. All edges, except the fractured section on one long edge are smooth from wear. L 253 mm; W 4–35 mm; T 12.4–13 mm. Wgt 138.8 g. Context 048, floor deposit (Fig. 4.9.19a).

SF 266 Bevelled rounded tip of a flat rectangular cetacean bone bar in three joining fragments, broken irregularly across width resulting in the loss of all but the tip of the bar or baton. Bone is charred towards one edge of this broken end. The surviving tip is asymmetrical, and one surface is noticeably convex as the result of rubbing and smoothing. Remaining L 73.7 mm; W 20 mm; T 19–20 mm. Wgt 43.8 g. Extracted from animal bone SF 99. Context 042, burnt deposit across broch interior. (Not illustrated.)

SF 270 Forty-one fractured and angular fragments from a completely disintegrated subrectangular bar or baton produced from dense cetacean bone, perhaps rib. Refitting fragments identified from one cut asymmetrical, bevelled rounded end which is smoothed from rubbing similar to SF 99b, SF 108 and SF 123. Surviving areas of original surface marked with fine linear striations, overlapping and in variety of orientations. Charred and burnt particularly along one edge. Original dimensions not possible to determine: min W 25.5, T 25 mm. Wgt 160.2 g. Extracted from animal bone SF 179. Context 078, rubble in-fill of 'souterrain' within broch. (Not illustrated.)

POSSIBLE FITTING OR HANDLE

A single Y-shaped fitting or possible handle (SF 279) produced from the crown of an antler was recognised from context 145 within Cell 1. It is now incomplete having split in half down its length, probably in use, and the other half now lost, so its full form and function is open to interpretation, but the hollowed-out beam and two tine stubs are clearly a deliberate feature and suggest that this was a tri-socketed item. Parallel to where the split has occurred is a distinct angular cut facet, possibly made with a saw. It is unclear whether this is the vestige of a facet intended to hold in place a thin blade of which there is now no trace or is simply a tool mark remaining from manufacture. The general lack of any wear to the cut edges of the item or to the remaining cancellous tissue in the interior argue against this being some kind of rope or strap junction, whilst the thinness of the walls makes it unlikely to have seen use as a building fixture; a component of bone assemblages recognised on other Iron Age sites such as that from Dun Mor Vaul, Tiree (MacKie 1974, 146, pl. 3). Whatever the function of this item, it is not readily paralleled within the corpus of worked antler objects from Atlantic Scotland. It is possible that worked antler SF 263 and SF 264 are similar items abandoned during production.

SF 279 Fitting or handle? Y-shaped fragment of antler, produced from a the rubicose surface of the junction between the antler beam and pedicle tines, the beam detached by a series of knife cuts and the tines (W 24.5 mm and 30.5 mm) also removed squarely at their base using both a knife and possible saw. The opposite face has been neatly hollowed out; the cancellous tissue deliberately removed. The splayed long edges are rough and ragged as though unintentionally split during use. Parallel to the split edge of the widest antler tine stub is a short (L 16.5 mm) cut facet, made either by chopping with a heavy blade or very roughly sawn. L 96 mm; beam: W 28 mm, T 5 mm; bifurcated end: W 91 mm; T 4–5 mm. Wgt 43.9 g. Extracted from animal bone SF 254. Context 145, black-brown organic silt and animal fat in Cell 1 (Fig. 4.6.19b).

Unfinished/working waste

UNFINISHED OBJECTS

As considered in the discussion above, unfinished objects form only a small component of this assemblage. These comprise a possible unfinished point (SF 267) and a possible unfinished antler object where the intended design or function is unclear (SF 263). Also present is a tentative unfinished toggle (SF 268) consisting of a transversely hollowed out and perforated cattle phalange. The hole that has been made is so large and irregular in execution that it appears unfinished and lacks any evidence of softening or rubbing of the edges to confirm use. The hole perforates the entire thickness of the bone, appearing deliberate rather than attempt to extract the marrow. Four similar perforated phalange toggles were recognised at Sandwick, Unst (Goldberg and Hunter 2019, 109, fig. 6.17) and from an Early Iron Age souterrain at Jarlshof, Shetland (Hamilton 1968, 37). The group of toggles from Sandwick were all found together suggesting a common function, perhaps seeing use in association with bags or nets but the level of wear noted on these examples suggests they were held in a relatively fixed position rather than being regularly moved which would result in far more pronounced smoothing of perforation edges (Goldberg and Hunter 2019, 109). The example from Clachtoll came from floor surface (062). In addition to the objects described here as unfinished is the burnt fragments of a long-handled bone comb (SF 140) which has freshly cut teeth implying that it was either discarded during production (and was therefore unfinished) or was in the process of being recut.

SF 263 Possible unfinished object. Six rejoining fragments representing substantial portion of palmate terminal of antler of mature red deer, two tines surviving in part but tips lost from both. Third tine from crown deliberately removed by cutting then snapping to detach, below which beam (D 48 mm) sawn transversely, snapped to detach and hollowed (D 14.5 × 25.5 mm). All three tines have portions of interior cancellous tissue removed: snapped off stub of tine deliberately hollowed (ext. D 32 mm; inner D 27.5 mm), cancellous tissue exposed and hollowed on other two tines but unclear if this is post-depositional erosion. Series of three fine cut marks (max L 26 mm) on surface of beam below crown and single cut mark (L 13.3 mm) present immediately below detached tine stub. Surviving L 244 mm. Wgt 266.5 g. Extracted from animal bone SF 64. Context 042, burnt deposit across broch interior, NW quad. (Not illustrated.)

SF 267 Possible unfinished perforated point. Articular head from left-hand tibia of sheep/goat (animal older than 1.5 years at death), snapped mid-length along shaft resulting in angular fracture at point of breakage and hairline longitudinal cracks extending towards surviving distal end. Attempt has been made to perforate the articular head from one face of the bone shaft indicated by an unfinished circular hollow (D 6 mm). Ephemeral surface damage in the form of an irregular gouge on the corresponding area of the opposing surface of the shaft confirms an abandoned attempt to perforate. Remaining L 77.4 mm; W 17.5–27.3 mm; T 13.3–20.7 mm. Wgt 16.3 g. Extracted from animal bone SF 170. Context 062, floor material in SW quad of broch interior. (Not illustrated.)

SF 268 Unfinished toggle/bobbin. Cattle phalanx, proximal epiphyses intact, shaft split down ventral face from proximal to distal end of shaft. Irregular and ragged ovoid perforation punched though from dorsal face of the dense bone of shaft (12.6 × 24.3 mm) and naturally hollow cavity to form a more even oval hole (8.6 × 12.9 mm), possibly expanded by a knife, on the opposing ventral face. L 50 mm; W 19.5–24.6 mm; T 11 mm. Wgt 11.5 g. Extracted from animal bone SF 170. Context 062, floor material in SW quad (Fig. 4.9.19c).

Roughout

A single squared bar or baton (SF 285) is the only item confidently identified as a roughout amongst the assemblage. This baton has been chopped and split on all four long faces and cut, perhaps with an axe or heavy-duty cleaver. What the intended function of this item is not certain as it seems to have been abandoned at an early stage of working.

SF 285 Squared baton. Three angular fractured pieces deriving from an elongated squared baton dense cetacean bone, split down the length. Two fragments conjoin across angular and fairly fresh chopped facet. Opposite ends are damaged but also appear cut. Rejoining fragments: surviving L 104 mm; W 23 mm; T 22 mm. Wgt 40.1 g. extracted from animal bone SF 184. Context 067, Flooring deposit under (047) (Fig. 4.9.2).

Figure 4.9.20 Photograph of a worked fragment of eroded ceteacean rib (SF 284)

Table 4.9.5 Unworked antler and cetacean bone recognised amongst the assemblage, by context

Context	Interpretation	Antler	Cetacean Bone
028	brown pink sand (degraded sandstone and windblown sand)	SF 292 irregular spall of antler, no signs of working	
042	Burning layer	SF 276 & SF 277 burnt antler, no signs of working; SF 293 weathered antler fragment, no signs of working; SF 294 four burnt splinters of antler (no obvious signs of working), SF 295 two blacked burr fragments from a min. 1 antler (shed)	SF 299 unworked cetacean bone fragment; SF 301 15 fragments of unfused whale vertebra, unworked.
047	Midden material S of Hearth 2 and within [069]		SF 300 c.30 angular fragments of cetacean bone, weathered. SF 302 61 fragments of cetacean bone, no obvious use or modification.
067	Floor material (S of hearth 2)		SF 297 burnt fragment of whalebone, no original surfaces survive
078	Loose rubble fill of [069]	SF 296. Burnt fragment of antler, no signs of working;	SF 298 11 splinters of cetacean bone, unworked.
082	Upper fill of entrance passage		SF 286 Four joining fragments of cetecean vertebra, weathered and charred but with no obvious use/modification
123	Thick deposit of charred cereal grain and charcoal in cell 2	SF 223 2 fragments of antler, heat-affected, ?cancellous tissue lost or hollowed out	

WORKING WASTE

Five groups of fragments (SF 264, SF 278, SF 282, SF 283, SF 284) comprising nine individual fragments of antler and cetacean bone display tool marks from working but lack any discernible attempt to shape or modify further and are therefore classified here as working waste. The majority of these fragments were extracted from the faunal bone assemblage during analysis implying that there was no separate disposal method for working waste or butchery waste within the broch. Most are splinters of antler showing knife cuts or where the cancellous tissue from the interior of the tine or beam appears to have been deliberately hollowed out. Of particular note is a heavily weathered bar of cetacean bone, possibly a rib segment, which has a distinct bevelled chop mark at one end from being cut with an axe or heavy-duty cleaver.

SF 264 Two refitting fragments and two detached pieces, no longer joining, from the beam of mature red deer antler from the area between the three tines that make up the palmate terminal but tines themselves lost. Deep U-shaped saw cut (L 13 mm) present below break of one tine suggesting it was cut then snapped off to detach and cancellous tissue hollowed out; unclear if other two tines removed deliberately as fracture surfaces worn and eroded. L 92 mm; max W 46.4 mm; T 3.7 mm. Wgt 46.8 g. Extracted from animal bone SF 64. Context 042, burnt deposit across broch interior, NW quad. (Not illustrated.)

SF 278 Subrectangular splinter of antler, probably from tine, cancellous tissue removed or lost, cut transversely across the tine. Tool mark obscured, unclear if chopped or cut. Surfaces covered in patches of dark brown residue, possibly pitch. Remaining L 34 mm, W 16.7 mm, T 8 mm, Wgt 3.1 g. Extracted from animal bone SF 210. Context 078, loose rubble and mixed fill of deep area, possible tumble after roof collapse. (Not illustrated.)

SF 282 Irregular splinter of animal tine, edges fresh and split. Widest and thickest end of the fragment displays vestiges of a knife cut where the tine was detached from the beam. Surviving L 53.2 mm;

W 19 mm; T 7.5–13.7 mm. Wgt 6.9 g. Extracted from animal bone SF 14. Context 028, pink sand (Fig. 4.9.19d).

SF 283 Two fragments of heat-affected antler: one, from tip of antler tine, cut at one end and broken across width and length. L 18.2 mm; W 17.5 mm; T 10.7 mm. Mass 2.1. second fragment is flat sub-square antler tine fragment preserving rubicose surface only, burnt and snapped at one end, opposite end and edges broken. Surviving L 23 mm; W 18 mm; T 7.4 mm. Wgt 1.3 g. Extracted from animal bone SF 39. Context 042, burnt deposit across entire broch interior. (Not illustrated.)

SF 284 Elongated bar of dense whalebone, broken at both ends, surfaces, edges and ends are weathered and eroded, surviving surfaces are soft, friable and pitted. Diagonal facetted chop mark from a large blade cuts though surface at one weathered end. Surviving L 202 mm; W 58.5 mm; T 35 mm. Wgt 211 g. Extracted from animal bone SF 120. Context 047, Possible midden material (Fig. 4.9.20).

UNWORKED?

A moderate quantity of fragments of antler and cetacean bone were extracted from groups of hand-retrieved animal bone. These include 13 fragments from a minimum of eight antler, and 123 fragments from a minimum of eight individual cetacean bones, none of which display any obvious signs of modification or working but merit discussion as they represent materials deliberately brought into the broch. These are summarised in Table 4.9.5 and a full catalogue of these fragments are presented in the site archive.

In some instances, such as SF 277 – a detached and burnt spall from the surface of an antler tine – only one fragment survives but in others, such as SF 300, at least 30 fragments, probably from the same element, are present. Many of these fragments are burnt, particularly those which were recovered from the burning layer (context 042) which covered the floor layers of the broch interior and were presumably burnt during the fire. Their recovery from this layer leads to the conclusion that they might have formed components of the roof or internal upper structures of the broch which collapsed during the fire or that they represent antler and cetacean bone (worked or unworked) which was being stored in the upper levels of the interior. The remainder of the unmodified antler and cetacean bone came from a midden deposit (047), flooring (067), infill material (078) within the 'souter-rain' [069], soils within the entrance passage (082), from deposit (123) within Cell 2 and from degraded wind-blown sand (028) overlying the burning layer. It is entirely feasible that these fragments are pieces of completely degraded objects or working debris but the

absence of any traces of modification to their surfaces makes it impossible to draw further conclusions.

4.10 The organic materials

Penelope Walton Rogers, with a contribution by Dawn McLaren

Leather

SF 256.2 A curled offcut strip of leather, approximately 90 mm long and 2.0 × 2.3 mm in section. No grain surface has survived, but fibres extracted from the end, viewed by transmitted light at ×100–×400 magnification, revealed the translucent brown branching mesh-like structure which is typical of collagen (collagen is the structural protein in animal hides). Context 082, the entrance [recovered during sieving] (Fig. 4.10.1).

Wool

SF 253 A thin wool 4-ply cord, 70 mm long, 2–3 mm thick, twisted Z4S; very matted. The fibres were identified as wool by transmitted light at x400 magnification. Diagnostic features were the presence of fine and medium fibres; continuous medullaa in the coarsest fibres; the absence of pigment granules in most fibres; and a cuticular scale pattern which was waved mosaic with smooth margins. Context 159, cell 1 (Figs 4.10.2 and 4.10.3).

The wool could be identified as a Generalised Medium fleece type within the Ryder system of wool classification, from the following measurements of fibre diameters (in microns). *Range* 11–31, 50, 58; *mode* 20, *mean* 20.8, *Standard Deviation* ±6.5, *Pearson coefficient of skew* +0.42 (skewed to positive); 2% fibres with medullas; 4% fibres with moderate pigmentation. This is a primitive type, relatively common in Iron Age fleeces.

[DM] A further two short lengths of cord (SF 230) were recovered from context 159. These were embedded in amorphous lumps of soil and necessitated careful excision during conservation to separate them from the encasing soil. One fragment is 51.6 mm in length and varies between 2 to 2 mm in thickness. At least two-ply cord is visible macroscopically but is matted and the twist is slightly unravelled which is assumed to have occurred post-excavation. The second fragment is 37.8 mm in length and 2 mm thick; also matted.

Animal hair

[DM] Several accumulations of possible hair or fibres were recognised during excavation of deposit (159) within Cell 1 (SF 229, SF 250, SF 251, SF 256.2). Due to the thick and sticky consistency of the deposit, it was impossible for these fibres to be disaggregated from the encasing soil in the field. During conservation treatment, careful extraction of samples of the fibres from the soil was undertaken enabling closer examination to take place. All four small finds consist of short and narrow tufts of animal hair, similar in appearance, colour but of variable length. One sample (SF 229) was closely identified, and the full detailed description is noted below.

SF 229 Two tufts of animal fibre, one light brown and poorly preserved, 25 mm long; the other dark brown and better preserved, 38 mm long. The fibres are relatively straight. When viewed by transmitted-light microscopy at x400 magnification, the darker fibres proved to be 37–92 microns in diameter; approximately 30% had fragmented medullas; moderate pigmentation was visible in some fibres (indicating a naturally brown coat). The poorly preserved pale sample appeared to be much the same. A sample of the darker tuft was sent to a specialist in animal coat fibres, Dr Philip Greaves at Microtex, who commented as follows: 'Although eroded in most parts, the following features were found in certain areas of these fibres. Regular diameter, oval contour, irregular waved mosaic to rippled crenate scaling. Smooth, near margins. Pigment sparse to dense streaky. Narrow medullae, often interrupted. These features are most consistent with coarse cattle (body) hair.' Context 159 (Fig. 4.10.4).

Figure 4.10.1 Photograph of the offcut strip of leather (SF 256.2) after conservation (© AOC)

Figure 4.10.2 Photograph of the cord (SF 253) after conservation (© AOC)

4.11 The waterlogged wood

Anne Crone

Waterlogged wood was recovered from four contexts, (049), (100), (145) and (159) (Table 4.11.1). Small amounts of wood initially identified as bone and subsequently dried out were also recovered from contexts (049), (078), (087) and (145). The assemblage is dominated by the presence of splinters and slivers of conifer wood, the significance of which is discussed below. Four artefacts were found, a fragment from a vessel roughout, a possible spatula, and two small square pins (Fig. 4.11.1).

The assemblage

Context (049) broch floor

Two small finds of wood were retrieved from this context. SF 202 contained only two thin conifer splinters, while the contents of SF 217 were more varied, including a conifer splinter, a piece of flattened hazel (*Corylus*

avellana) roundwood, two offcuts of oak (*Quercus* sp.) and a fragment of a possible vessel roughout fashioned from alder (*Alnus glutinosa*). SF 165 contained two desiccated splinters of roundwood.

The vessel roughout (Figs 4.11.1a and 4.11.4) consisted of a fragment 70 mm long and 22 mm wide, which curved along its length. In cross-section the fragment is 10 mm at one end and expands to 12 mm at the other. The 'exterior' surface was smooth while the 'inner' surface was corrugated, with ledge-like cuts running across its width. In the cross-section the wood grain can be seen to be aligned at an oblique angle to both faces; this is the alignment found in wooden vessels carved or turned from a half-log. The contrast between the relative smoothness of the outer surface and the corrugated inner surface suggests that this has come from an unfinished vessel, where the outer surface has been axe-dressed to close to its final profile while the interior has been roughly carved out. This is very like other unfinished vessels, such as that from Bracadale (Crone 1993).

SF253 (159) Cell1: Twisted fibres in crowberry rope

Figure 4.10.3 High magnification photograph showing the twisted fibres of the cord ((C) AOC)

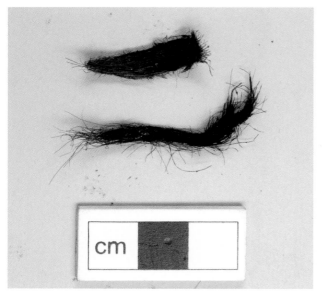

Figure 4.10.4 Post-conservation photograph of two tufts of animal fibre (SF 229) from (159) (© AOC)

Context (078)

SF 210 contained two desiccated splinters of conifer wood.

Context (087)

SF 201 contained six fragments of desiccated wood, all of them charred on the surface. These include two splinters of conifer wood and four flattened fragments of roundwood.

Context (100) fill of a culvert

This context produced five splinters of conifer. Most of them were narrow, thin flake-like slivers which could have exfoliated off a larger splinter. One was larger, 75 mm long, 40 mm wide and 6 mm in thickness, an elongated triangle in cross-section.

Context (145) occupation deposit in Cell 1

Waterlogged wood was retrieved from this context as small finds (SF 226, SF 233 and SF 248), as a special samples (S1) and collected during sieving (Table 4.11.1). Two small pins (Fig. 4.11.1b) were also retrieved from a bag of bone.

The largest piece of wood retrieved was S1, a very poorly preserved length of radially-split Scots pine (*Pinus sylvestris*), 315 mm in length, 67 mm wide and 25 mm thick. Although clearly converted from a larger piece it displayed no evidence of woodworking.

The bulk of the assemblage from this context consisted of conifer splinters; 25–30 splinters were present in SF 233 and 20 were found during sieving. Many of those retrieved during sieving were thin, feathery flakes which had probably exfoliated off larger splinters. A sample of the larger splinters was measured, and their cross-sections recorded (Table 4.11.2). These were also identified as to species and all but one (see below) was Scots pine. They vary in length from 48 mm to 140 mm (av 99 mm), from 8 mm to 24 mm in width (av 17 mm) and from 4 mm to 16 mm in thickness (av 10 mm). On two of the splinters there is charring at one end and these ends also appear to be tapered in shape. Another splinter had a rounded end.

One of the splinters in SF 233 bore small holes *c.* 5 mm in diameter. SF 226 consisted of a single splinter displaying the same holes. These are the holes of the marine wood-boring bivalve *Teredo navalis*, the ship worm. Both the SF 233 splinter and SF 226 were splinters of larch (*Larix* sp.).

SF 248 (Figs 4.11.1c and 4.11.3) has been fashioned from a thin, radially-split splinter of Scots pine and is 65 mm long, 18 mm wide and 5 mm thick. It is shaped like a knife blade and in cross-section it is leaf-shaped. It might be a spatula, but its shape could also be fortuitous (see below).

The two pins (Fig. 4.11.1b) have been fashioned from a conifer wood (their size prohibits further identification without damage). One is 38 mm long and the other is 26 mm long, and they are both square in cross-section, measuring only 2.5 mm by 2.5 mm. Both have been squared off at one end and shaped to a pencil tip at the other. The pins have been carefully fashioned; they are too slight to have been used in structural joinery, but they could have been used in the joinery of small personal items such as storage boxes for example, or in securing textiles.

Context (159) floor surface in Cell 1

Waterlogged wood was retrieved from this context as two small finds, SF 244 and SF 261. Both are dominated by

Table 4.11.1 Summary of the waterlogged wood assemblage

Context	SF	Description	Species	No. frags
49	202	x2 thin splinters of conifer	conifer	2
49	217	Bowl roughout	*Alnus glutinosa*	1
		x1 flattened roundwood	*Corylus avellana*	1
		x1 thin sliver of conifer	conifer	1
		x2 offcuts	*Quercus* sp.	2
100	205	x5 slivers of conifer		5
145	226	frag with teredo beetle holes	*Larix* sp	1
145	233	25-30 conifer splinters	*Pinus sylvestris*	30
		inc 1 splinter with teredo beetle holes	*Larix* sp	1
145	248	thin spatulate object - worked?	*Pinus sylvestris*	1
145	*from sieve*	x20 conifer splinters	*Pinus sylvestris*	20
145	S-1	single piece of wood	*Pinus sylvestris*	1
159	244	x15 conifer splinters	*Pinus sylvestris*	15
		x1 large roundwood offcut	*Betula* sp.	1
		x2 twisted roundwood 6-8 mm diam	*Corylus avellana*	1
		x5 flattened roundwood 4/4/5/10/10 mm diam	*Corylus avellana*	3
		x3 frags of bark - birch?		
159	261	x22 conifer splinters	*Pinus sylvestris*	22
		x1 roundwood	*Corylus avellana*	1
				109

large quantities of conifer splinters, 15 in SF 244 and 22 in SF 261 (Fig. 4.11.4). SF 244 contained some very thin flake-like slivers which may have exfoliated off larger splinters. A sample of the larger splinters was measured, their cross-sections recorded, and a sub-sample identified as to species; they were all Scots pine (Table 4.11.2). They varied in length from 30 mm to 135 mm (av 77 mm), 7 mm to 16 mm in width (av 11 mm) and 3 mm to 13 mm in thickness (av 6 mm).

This context was a little more varied than (145), the other wood-producing context from Cell 1 in that it also contained a large roundwood offcut and eight pieces of roundwood, seven from SF 244 and one from SF 261. The roundwood was all hazel and it was small, from 4 mm to 10 mm in diameter, and in cross-section most pieces had been compressed and flattened. The offcut was a piece of birch (*Betula* sp.) 90 mm long, 42 mm wide and 22 mm thick which had been cleft off a length of roundwood; one end had been chopped off by an axe leaving a sharp, stepped facet.

Discussion

The assemblage is dominated by the conifer splinters (Fig. 4.11.2); some 25% of the splinters were identified and all but two were identified as Scots pine so it is reasonable to assume that the remainder were also pine. They had been chopped from the log so that the growth rings were either parallel to, or perpendicular to the widest face, and all the faces were cleft. The chopping of logs to make kindling could have produced these kinds of short splinters as by-products and they may then have been used in the cell to create flooring. However, the tips of several splinters are burnt, and this raises another possibility, that they were tapers used for lighting. In the early modern period splinters of pine, cut out of the living tree so that they were rich in resin were often used for lighting in peasant homes and were known as 'fir-candles' (Grant 1961, 184). About 50 pine splinters, all burnt at one end, were found on the Iron Age crannog of Oakbank, Loch Tay (Dixon 2004, 154) testifying to the longevity of this

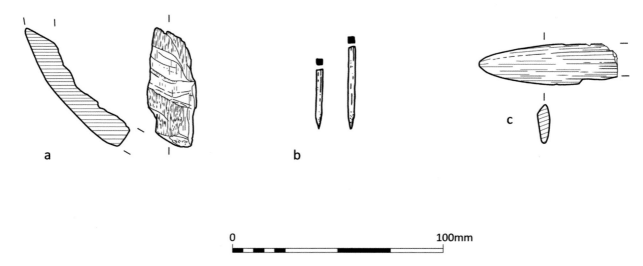

Figure 4.11.1 The worked wooden objects: a) wooden bowl roughout (SF 217), b) two small pins (context 145), c) possible wooden spatula (SF 248)

Figure 4.11.2 Photograph of the wooden tapers (SF 261) pre-conservation

practice. The Oakbank splinters varied in length from 30 mm to 100 mm (*ibid.*) so although smaller overall they fall within the same size range as those from Clachtoll. Similar tapers of firwood were the primary means of lighting the Halstatt salt mines (Reschreiter and Kowarik 2019, 113–114). Experiments have shown that single tapers did not burn well but that they emitted an even light if they were bundled together and moved continuously (*ibid.*) so this might be why there are so many tapers at Clachtoll.

Charring could also have created the tapered, rounded tips seen on other examples, and could also explain the shape of SF 248, the possible spatula (Figs 4.11.1c and 4.11.3). Its lenticular cross-section is similar to some of the other conifer splinters, so it is possible that its shape and appearance are entirely fortuitous.

There were two splinters of larch in the assemblage. The wood was very decayed, so it was not possible to determine which species of larch was present (Taylor 1999), but larch is not native to the British Isles and the

Table 4.11.2 Summary of the waterlogged conifer splinter assemblage. 'Rings' refers to the alignment of the rings with width

Context	SF	L mm	W mm	T mm	Rings*	Species	Comment
145	233	140	22	12	parallel	*Pinus sylvestris*	
		80	20	16	perp	*Pinus sylvestris*	
		65	20	9	perp	*Pinus sylvestris*	
		115	21	13	parallel	*Pinus sylvestris*	
		140	14	11	parallel	*Pinus sylvestris*	charred tip
		132	8	8	perp	*Pinus sylvestris*	tapered & partially charred tip
		50	14	8	parallel	*Larix* sp	*Teredo* holes
		90	9	6	parallel	*Pinus sylvestris*	
		103	11	5	perp	*Pinus sylvestris*	
		94	8	4	perp	*Pinus sylvestris*	
145	from sieve	104	14	8	parallel	*Pinus sylvestris*	rounded tip
		48	19	12	parallel	*Pinus sylvestris*	bark edge present
		65	24	8	perp	*Pinus sylvestris*	
145	266	65	16	11	parallel	*Larix* sp	*Teredo* holes
159	244	135	15	8	parallel	*Pinus sylvestris*	
		70	11	4	perp	*Pinus sylvestris*	
		70	11	7	perp	*Pinus sylvestris*	
		90	7	5	perp		
		90	11	4	perp		
159	261	30	10	5	perp		
		55	8	3	perp		
		63	12	6	perp	*Pinus sylvestris*	
		57	8	4	parallel		
		75	9	6	parallel	*Pinus sylvestris*	
		130	16	13	parallel	*Pinus sylvestris*	
		84	7	5	perp	*Pinus sylvestris*	
		64	8	6	perp	*Pinus sylvestris*	
		75	14	6	perp	*Pinus sylvestris*	
		70	15	8	parallel		

presence of *Teredo* boreholes on both splinters confirms that they represent the use of driftwood. Driftwood is commonly found on archaeological sites throughout the Western and Northern Isles as charcoal (Dickson 1992) but more rarely in a waterlogged condition (Taylor 1999; Church 2000; Crone 2014). A single large fragment of larch was found in the charcoal assemblage (Robertson, Section 5.2). Given the broch's coastal location it is perhaps surprising that more driftwood was not found on the site, because it would have provided a convenient source of fuel and building timber.

Apart from the larch all the other species present in the assemblage would have been available in the local landscape. Some 87% of the waterlogged assemblage is pine and this occurred entirely as splinters. This was also the case at Oakbank crannog where, apart from the

Figure 4.11.3 Photograph of the possible wooden spatula (SF 248) post-conservation

splinters there was only one other piece of pine present (Dixon 2004, 154). Pine is remarkably absent from most prehistoric wood assemblages (Crone 2008, 285–6); it may be because it burns so vigorously that it is fully combusted when used as fuel, but its absence in construction, particularly in areas such as Assynt where it must have been one of the commoner species available, suggests a cultural choice.

Small amounts of hazel, birch and oak were present. The birch and oak were both woodworking offcuts, while the hazel consisted of small roundwood, possibly for use as flooring within the cell.

The bowl roughout (Figs 4.11.1c and 4.11.4) had been carved out of alder which would also have been available locally. Alder has always been a favoured wood for vessel manufacture because it was resistant to splitting once it had been shaped and seasoned and is durable under wet conditions, so it was suitable for containing liquids and food (Morris 2000, 2196). Robertson (Section 5.2) has suggested that a concentration of alder charcoal

Figure 4.11.4 The wooden bowl roughout fragment (SF 217) post-conservation showing chop marks

fragments around a deposit of grain may also represent an alder vessel which contained the grain. The Clachtoll roughout joins a small corpus of 17 Iron Age vessels from Scotland (Crone in prep) but too little of the roughout survives to draw useful comparisons.

4.12 The artefact distribution

Andy Heald, Dawn McLaren and Graeme Cavers

Some methodological considerations

As Armit (2006, 241) reminds us, only in exceptional circumstances should we expect that genuine 'floor deposits', directly representative of the activities carried out in the house, will be preserved *in situ*. That might happen, for example, 'when a building is abandoned or destroyed unexpectedly; perhaps by a fire, through violence, or the sudden death of the inhabitants'. The burning event at Clachtoll appears to preserve such an episode, a rare snapshot of activity during the first centuries BC/AD. As we can see elsewhere in this volume (Chapter 7) analysis of the spatial distribution of the Clachtoll plant macrofossils suggests that the ground floor was divided into separate activity areas and this suggests that comparison of the artefact distribution would be fruitful. Further, as Parker Pearson and Sharples (1999, 350) stress, the domestic domain within roundhouses may have incorporated more than prosaic activities but also ritual and symbolic activities. They suggest that roundhouses may have served not simply as places to live but were embodiments of myth, places of worship, calendars and generally, embodiments of the social and cosmic order. Thus, when we analyse the distribution of artefacts from any structure, we need to try to push the data further than analysis of the mundane. Although at first glance Clachtoll appears to present a rare example of preservation *in situ* – indeed what we might term a 'Pompeii effect' – and a wonderful opportunity to investigate some of the key social, economic and ritual issues describe above, the reality is, of course, much more complicated.

Firstly, the total number of finds from Clachtoll is small. As set out above, there are probably less than 20 ceramic vessels from the site; Armit (2006, 243) suggests that this figure may be indicative of a typical household's use over the course of a single year. Consequently, drawing meaningful, concrete conclusions in terms of activity areas, let alone further leaps into considerations of more ephemeral concepts such as those just described, on such a limited number of finds is likely to be inherently limited, if not statistically and methodologically flawed.

The second issue relates to taphonomy. As Armit (2006, 240) reminds us, it is difficult to identify specific activities

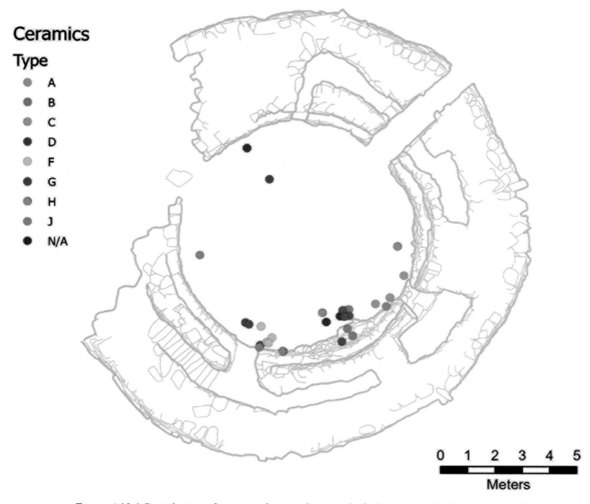

Ceramics

Type

- A
- B
- C
- D
- F
- G
- H
- J
- N/A

0 1 2 3 4 5

Meters

Figure 4.12.1 Distribution of ceramics by vessel type; n.b. findspots include clusters of sherds

within buildings because of uncertainties over the ways in which the various 'floor' deposits may have formed. Indeed, the identification of *in situ*, undisturbed floor deposits in prehistoric buildings has increasingly come to be recognized as a problem. Although the chronological period in which the Clachtoll finds were deposited was limited – probably no more than a handful of decades, and the interior was burned to destruction – the finds undoubtedly relate to different events and flooring phases, broadly categorised as: the creation of floor surface, debris which accumulated or was deposited onto the floor and within features such as the hearth, possible ritual deposition in intentional positions, and the actual conflagration which involved collapse from the upper platforms and the consequent mixing of various contexts. In other words, even at Clachtoll, we must be cautious of conflating find spots into convenient zones for discussion.

A third consideration is whether the finds recovered in roundhouse interiors even represent on-site activity.

For example, it has been suggested elsewhere (*e.g.*, Armit 2006, 243; McLaren and Heald 2006, 157) that metalworking debris recovered from many Iron Age structures and their interiors may be entirely unrelated to the structure (and even the period) in which they were found (see also below). The same is probably true of other finds.

The final consideration is, perhaps, more contentious. Despite the modern preoccupation with finding patterns in artefact distributions, it is important to question whether we should even expect zoning of activities. On a typical Atlantic Iron Age site, the majority of finds relates to crafts and activities associated with the domestic sphere: food production/consumption, bone, stone, textile and leatherworking. It may not be reasonable to expect that these activities were confined to particular interior zones in a regimented fashion, far less that these zones remained static over the course of decades of use. This is partly supported by Armit's (2006, 242)

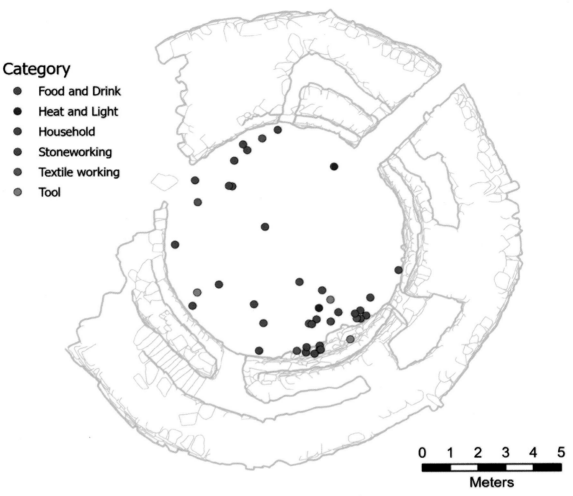

Figure 4.12.2 Distribution of stone objects by category

work at Cnip which demonstrated, unsurprisingly, that food was consumed in most, if not all, excavated parts of the settlement. Most activities within roundhouses – spinning, decorating, leatherworking – do not need fixed locations. Furthermore, adequate light to undertake tasks successfully is perhaps the most important factor. Despite the numerous lamps found within the broch it must be the case that a constraining factor within the confines of the roundhouse interior was lighting: even allowing for an open face on the upper floor galleries (see Chapter 10) that allowed the glow from the hearth to be cast into the compartments, a low fire burning peat and small roundwoods as its primary fuel cannot have provided much light. Thus, the majority of the internal space must have been very dimly lit, and probably very smoky and we have to consider whether such an environment would even have been appropriate for craftworking, etc. requiring fine, detailed work.

Patterns in the finds

Nonetheless, with these caveats in mind, some broad patterns are identifiable in the recovered assemblage. Figures 4.12.1 to 4.12.4 show the distribution of the artefacts from the roundhouse interior by material type; these have been aggregated to their broad class, while Figure 4.12.1 shows ceramics by vessel type (Section 4.1).

The creation of floors and features and associated deposits

The floor surfaces of the broch interior were evidently refurbished on a regular basis, and the process of replenishment and replacement appears to have been ongoing throughout the period of occupation. As we have noted, distinguishing between prepared floor surfaces and debris accumulated during occupation is inherently difficult.

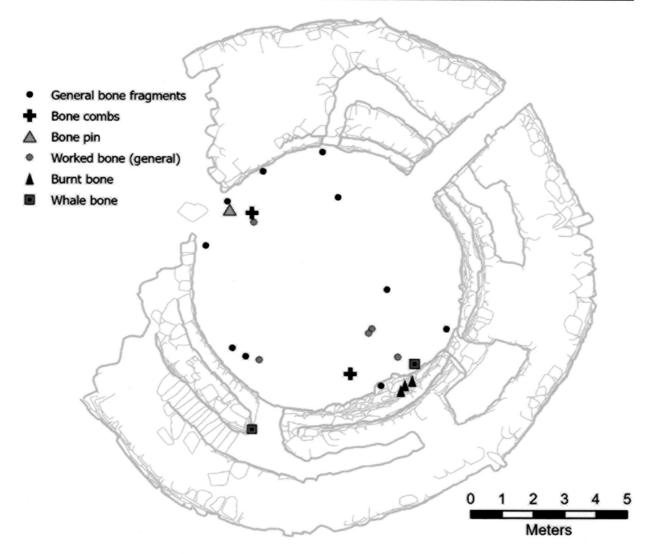

Figure 4.12.3 Distribution of worked bone objects by category

As McLaren (Section 4.7) highlights, the majority of the quern stones from Clachtoll do not appear to have been functional at the time of their subsequent deposition; consequently, analysis of their distribution should not be taken to reliably indicate zones of food preparation within the roundhouse interior. Many of the querns appear to have been incorporated within flooring and discard debris relating to surfaces in use around hearths 2 and 3. A notable concentration of querns within flooring in the southern half of the interior is probably associated with, as McLaren describes, 'non-random structuring' of material within the building. Whilst this process may have involved some structuring principle, it may equally be the case that the querns were simply moved to the rear of the interior space for some mundane purpose, such as storage or for future building or flooring material. Looking in more detail at

the Clachtoll querns, these two factors – the prosaic practicalities of life and the more abstract concepts structuring daily activities – come together and require consideration. It seems to be the case that the exhausted querns were routinely used to refurbish the flooring in the southern half of the structure and that this process can be explained as a practical solution to the active attrition of the soft and friable floor surfaces during use. Yet, this concentration of querns and their position within a specific area of the interior finds parallels across Britain (Pope 2008) and are observed within Iron Age roundhouse structures such as those at Broxmouth, East Lothian (Büster and Armit 2013) *inter alia*, implying that the principals structuring the reuse of the Clachtoll querns went beyond the mundane and can be compared to national depositional patterns. In contrast, the upper quern stone found on the stone

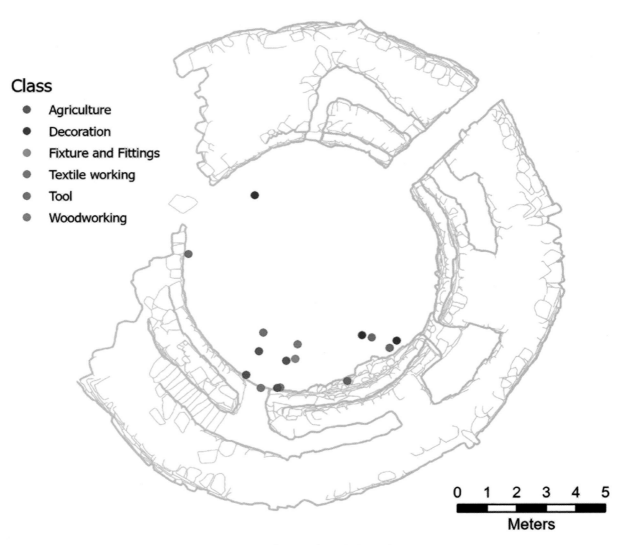

Class

- Agriculture
- Decoration
- Fixture and Fittings
- Textile working
- Tool
- Woodworking

0 1 2 3 4 5

Meters

Figure 4.12.4 Distribution of metal objects by category

floor of the souterrain is probably best viewed as a tool in storage. Although metalworking debris was found in numerous contexts, a comprehensive suite of slags came from flooring material. Again, like the querns, we should not see the distribution of this material as indicative of the working position of a smith, but as the by-product of slag being brought into the interior from elsewhere, probably incorporated into material brought in for use as flooring. This latter point is reinforced by the lack of any evidence of *in situ* metalworking within the broch.

Zones of activity?

As Figures 4.12.1 to 4.12.4 show, no particular artefact type concentrates in any particular area or layer to suggest the prevalence of specific crafts or activities at different stages of the roundhouse's occupation. As noted elsewhere

in this volume, the finds came from a range of context types including middens, the souterrain fill, floor levels and hearth levels, demonstrating that various activities took place in the interior but were apparently not confined to specific zones. We do, however, see tools relating to textile production (bone combs) and hide working occurring around the hearths, particularly to the south. Perhaps important items such as looms were located close to the hearth and main source of light, and it seems probable that spinning was taking place in the NW quadrant of the interior, where bone combs and whorls were found. However, it is likely that these portable items of equipment would then be moved elsewhere when the craft activity was paused or completed, moved away at the end of the day to allow food to be prepared and consumed, and so their ultimate position need not be reliably indicative of a space dedicated to that activity. Some items are charred or burnt, including a fragment of a decorated bone comb which may have been abandoned during manufacture or modification and discarded into the fire, later to be spread amongst the hearth debris across the interior as a floor surface.

Evidence for upper levels

Within the artefact distribution there are patterns which may indicate that some of the objects recovered were originally located on a platform elevated from ground level. In particular, the concentration of artefacts recovered from the south-east quadrant, comprising a range of objects including whorls, lamps and ceramics, seems likely to have accumulated in this area as a result of the collapse of floors located at a higher level, as the structure collapsed.

As McLaren outlines (Section 4.7) many of the whorls come from deposits suggestive of working or storage on the upper flooring. Most of the whorls found in the upper layers come from the north-west and south-east quadrants, implying that the manufacture of whorls was either carried out in the broch's upper interior levels and/or whorls in the process of production were stored on the upper floors. It is surely significant that eight of the ten lamps were recovered from the conflagration layer (042), suggesting that the majority were used or stored in the upper levels of the broch; only two were recovered from within the floor deposits. This argument is bolstered by the damage observed on the base and discrete areas of the edges of some of the lamps which may be the result of impact as they fell from a height during the collapse. Similarly, the largest concentration of metalworking waste by weight came from the destruction layer. This implies two things: a) that at least some of the non-metalworking vitrified material (*e.g.*, sintered sand and fuel ash slag) were generated as the result of a combination of organic and non-organic materials fusing together under the high temperature of the fire that swept through the broch interior, and that, b) the likelihood is that the metalworking slags that were recovered from this deposit may have been located on an upper level of the broch. McLaren (Section 4.9) has shown that much of the worked bone and antler came from deposits which were formed as a result of the collapse of the interior structure, suggesting that these objects were located in upper areas of the building at the time of destruction. Similarly, pot sherd clusters and whalebone anvil recovered from areas such as the stair cell entrance seem likely to have fallen to that position during the destruction event, since their find location seems an improbable and impractical storage area. It is also likely that the sickles and other iron tools, all recovered from the same context and in close proximity to one another, were either stored together on the upper floors or were suspended from the wooden structure.

Ritual deposits and Iron Age cosmologies?

Previous studies (*e.g.*, Hingley 1992; Parker Pearson and Sharples 1999; Armit 2006) have emphasised the ritual and cosmological principles inherent within the Atlantic Iron Age. Such discussions have focussed on structuring principles relating to, for example, the deposition of animal remains, artefacts and human remains, the importance of the sun to roundhouse orientation and the structuring of domestic activities and the importance of the hearth.

The sudden and apparently unplanned abandonment of the Clachtoll broch is both conducive and obstructive to such studies. In one respect, the 'snapshot' effect of the catastrophic destruction presents the real possibility of assessing the layout of the Middle Iron Age building as it operated during occupation, but as noted, the relatively limited quantity of objects recovered allows only limited confidence in the identification of patterns. A small number of items, including the intact projecting ring-headed pin – presumably a valued, if not intrinsically valuable object – and the intact and undamaged antler weaving comb could be considered deliberate or intentional deposits, since both were found within floor deposits protected from the fire and might not be seen as casual losses. However, these are the only examples that cannot be more comfortably explained in more practical terms; in short, while deliberate deposition of artefacts within the floors of the broch interior cannot be discounted, it is difficult to propose that this was a significant factor in the taphonomy of the assemblage. Similarly, the distribution of metalworking waste, as well as stone objects such as the querns, is more easily explainable in mundane terms, most likely in the consolidation of floors during replenishment. A caveat, however, is that the partial sheep carcasses that were evidently buried beneath a floor refurbishment episode are difficult to explain in practical terms, and furthermore find parallels in contemporary Iron Age structures in the Western Isles. This issue is discussed in more detail in Chapter 10.

Conclusion: the constant footfall of daily life

The impression given of the ground floor of the broch during the excavated occupation period is one of practicality, with tasks and crafts taking place across the interior, perhaps focussed around the fire, but perhaps not within pre-determined, fixed, specific locations. We would argue that this is of little surprise and that the identification of zones of craft activity within Atlantic roundhouse interiors is one of hope rather than reality. Given the likelihood that many crafts would probably have taken place outside, coupled with the ongoing process of cleaning and refurbishment of floor levels, archaeologists are in fact left with little to work with. Furthermore, Clachtoll appears to show that many objects now found on the floor levels probably were manufactured/stored/used on higher levels. The implication is that working, craft, storage, sleeping and social quarters were as likely located on the upper levels as they were at ground level. If there were dedicated zones of activity within the building at all, it is likely that these were at a higher level and so difficult to identify within the recovered distribution.

Notes

1   Plain everted rim pottery was widespread across Atlantic Scotland. Said pottery is known from many Hebridean and Skye sites, for example, Cnip (MacSween 2006, 112–14, V62, illus. 3.6(ae), 120–1, V1871, illus. 3.10a, 122–4, V1367, illus. 3.12a), Sollas (Campbell 1991, 154; microfiche 2:c9) and Dun Ardtreck (MacKie 2000a, 325, 377, illus. 22, no. 14). Numerous examples are known from Shetland: Jarlshof (Hamilton 1956, 56–7, fig. 32, 66, fig. 35, 1), Clickhimin – being represented in the Iron Age fort (Hamilton 1968, 94, nos. 11 to 15) and the Wheelhouse phases (*ibid.*, 144–6, fig. 65, nos. 2–5), Kebister (Dalland and MacSween 1999, 184, illus. 162, 1), Scalloway (MacSween 1998b, 134, fig. 80, no. 10), Scatness (Brown 2015, 323–5, figs 7.2.8, SF 40684, SF 40998; fig. 7.2.9, SF 41138) and Bayanne (MacSween 2014, 124, fig. 3.37 no. 315, fig. 3.39, nos. 337, 515). Orcadian examples include the Howe (Ross 1994, 242), Midhowe (Callander and Grant 1934, 501–2, 508; fig. 46; MacKie 2002, 316, 383, no. 8); Oxtrow (MacKie 2002, 379, no. 6); Gurness (Hedges 1987, 168, fig. 2.94; MacKie 2002, 310, 381, illus. 5.76, nos. 4–5). Caithness examples are known from Barioch (unreg), Kilmster (X.GA 1191A; GA1185.2), Ousedale; Road Broch; Wag of Forse; Wester; Yarrows, Everley, Nybster, Thrumster, Whitegate and unprovenanced (see McIlfatrick 2013).

2   Again, such pottery is found over every area of the Atlantic province. Examples from Shetland include Middle Iron Age levels at Clickhimin (Hamilton 1968, 94, 121, 144–6, figs 43, nos. 16–18, 24–7, fig. 52 and fig. 65, nos. 6–26), the Iron Age wheelhouse settlement at Jarlshof (Hamilton 1956, 64–66, fig. 35, 3), Kebister (Dalland and MacSween 1999, 184, illus. 161), Scalloway (MacSween 1998b, 134–6, fig. 80, no. 5), Mousa (MacKie 2002, 155, 378, illus. 4.52, no. 14), Scatness (Brown 2015, 323–30, *e.g.* fig. 7.2.7, SF 19919, 24435, 32172, fig. 7.2.9, SF 39129, 39808), Bayanne (MacSween 2014, 124, fig. 3.39, no. 608) and possibly Clumlie (MacKie 2002, illus. 4.52, no. 9). Everted fluted rims from the corn drier at Scatness show that the type was in use into the first half of the first millennium AD (Brown 2015, 328–9; and see below). Given the preponderance of the type one can only agree with Brown

(2015, 335) who states that, at least in relation to Shetland, 'internal fluting of everted rim sherds is recognised as being characteristic of Middle Iron Age assemblages'. Orcadian examples are known from sites including Lingro (MacKie 2002, 243, 333, illus. 5.113, no. 1), Broch of Ayre (Graeme 1914; MacKie 2002, 384, 330, illus. 5.110. no. 12), Midhowe (see MacKie 2002, 316, illus. 5.82, nos. 7 and 11) and Howe (Ross 1994, 242, SF 7716). As far as the authors are aware there are no definitive everted fluted rims from Caithness. There is often the presumption that fluted rims are more of a Northern Isles tradition but clearly this is not the case. As Young (1966, 55, fig. 5) and MacKie (1965b, 115, fig. 5) highlighted over half a century ago examples of everted fluted rims are found in the Hebrides and Skye. Hebridean examples are known from, for example, Foshigarry (Beveridge & Callander 1931; fig. 25, no. 3; MacKie 2007b, 1153–4, 1262, illus. 9.113, X.NMS GNA 312); Á Cheardach Mhor (Young and Richardson 1960, fig. 6, no. 31; MacKie 2007b, 1140); Clettraval (Scott 1948; NMS.X. EO 510; MacKie 1965b, 115, fig. 5; 2007b; 1258, illus. 9.109, 1315); Cnip (MacSween 2006, 91–2, 124–5, illus. 3.12, I and 3.13, a) and Beirgh (Harding 2000, 23–25; fig. 9; Harding and Gilmour 2000). Examples are also known from Skye, for example from Dun Beag (McIlfatrick 2013, 658); Dun Ardtreck (MacKie 2000a, 325, illus. 22, nos. 19, 23, 24, 29 and 30; 2007b, 828); and Dun Mor Vaul (MacKie 1974, 21, fig. 16, nos. 237, 238 and 305; fig. 18, no. 366; 368–371; fig. 19, nos. 437 and 447).

3   In Shetland such applied neckbands are known from, for example, Jarlshof (Hamilton 1956, 46, fig. 25.1), Clickhimin (Hamilton 1968, 95, 120–4, figs 44, 53 to 54), Kebister (MacSween 1998b, 184, illus. 162, nos. 3 and 4), Scalloway (MacSween 1998b, 122, 134–6, fig. 80, no. 6), Bayanne (MacSween 2014, 124, fig. 3.37, no. 341, fig. 3.39, no. 603) and Scatness (Brown 2015, 323–6, fig. 7.2.7 and pl. 7.2.15); the latter site assemblage suggests that the type may have gone into the Later Pictish periods (*ibid.*, 335). In Orkney applied various applied bands in combination with rims, usually everted, have been found at the brochs of Lingro (Childe 1935, pl. XVI; MacKie 2002, 333, illus. 5.113 and 5114, 1), Ayre (Graeme 1914, 45–6, fig. 12; MacKie 2002, 383–4, nos. 2–5 and 9, 11); Burrian (MacGregor 1974; 98–9, fig. 22, no. 284; MacKie 2002, 351, illus. 5.135, no. 21); Howe (Ross 1994, 244, 250, illus. 144), Midhowe (MacKie 2002, 382, illus. 5.80, no. 5 also has applied cordon) and Gurness (Hedges 1987, fig. 2.98, no. 1260). An unusual example, from St Boniface (MacSween 1998a, 128, 131, illus. 160, no. 12) where pinched decoration was applied just below the lip of the vessel, not at the point of inflection as is usually the case for the majority of applied neckbands – may be part of this group. Definitive examples of applied neckbands from Caithness are rare. However, one sherd from Crosskirk (Fairhurst 1984, 109, illus. 63, no. 740), grouped as Class 1 Pre-Broch, was noted by Fairhurst (*ibid.*, 108–9) as being suggestive of Hamilton's 'neckband ware' from Clickhimin. Another rim example from Caithness (X.GA 888; McIlfatrick 2013, 53, illus. 4; 184, tab. 5.1-250; 685, illus. 10), although unprovenanced and fragmentary, also

has the appearance of an applied neckband. Although McIlfatrick (*ibid.*) classes this as a decorated out-turned rim it may be similar to examples from the Northern Isles, particularly Clickhimin (Hamilton 1968, 95, fig. 44, nos. 3–4).

Although Campbell (1991) has noted that vessels with neck cordons are rare in the Hebrides again, as MacKie (1965b, 115–6, fig. 5) outlined some years ago, neck-band decoration has been found on a number of Hebridean sites such as Clettraval (MacKie 2007b; 1258, illus. 9.109, 1211), Foshigarry (Beveridge and Callander 1931, 348, fig. 23, no. 8; MacKie 2007b, 1154, 1263, illus. 9.114, X.NMS GNA 348, 349); Allasdale (Young 1953, fig. 5, 1; MacKie 1965b, 115, fig. 5; MacKie 2007b, 1113, 1227, illus. 9.76, 1); Garry Iochdrach (Beveridge and Callander 1932, 42; MacKie 2007b, 1156, 1270, 1271, illus. 9.121, nos. 2 and 3, illus. 9.122, no. 33); Á Cheardach Mhor (Young and Richardson 1960, 144, fig. 5, nos. 13–15; Young 1966, 50, pl. 3, no. 3; MacKie 1965b, 115, fig. 5; 2007b, 1140; 1241; illus. 9.91); Buaile Risary (MacKie 2007b, 1156–7, 1259, illus. 9.110, no. 19); Eilean Maleit (MacKie 2007b, 1151); Cnip (MacSween 2006, 104–5, illus. 3.1, d; 118–9, illus. 3.9,a; 122–3, illus. 3.11, g; 126–7, illus. 3.14, f; MacKie 2007b, 1084); Beirgh (Harding 2000, 23–5; fig. 9; Harding and Gilmour 2000); Dun Vulan (Parker Pearson and Sharples 1999, 216); Sollas (Campbell 1991, 154, nos. 210 and 242; microfiche 2:G7–G8); and Eilean Olabhat (Armit, Campbell and Dunwell 2008, 67–71, illus. 25, no. 36). Away from the Outer Hebrides examples have been recovered from Dun Mor Vaul (MacKie 1965b, 115, fig. 5; 1974, fig. 16, no. 241, fig. 18, nos. 363, 379, fig. 19, nos. 435 and 486), Dun an Iardhard, Skye (MacLeod 1915, 68, fig. 13) and Dun Cul Bhuirg, Iona (MacKie 2007b, 1071, illus. 8.266, no. 19).

4 Here is not the place for a detailed critique of MacKie's paper but the author would argue that if certain overlooked non-pottery objects like the Kettleburn tweezers (Rhind 1853), the crucibles from various Caithness broch sites, such as Keiss and Nybster, and the allowance of reuse of Roman metals are added into MacKie's table 1, then the suggested differences between the Northern Isles and Caithness are less apparent; indeed, with the possible exception of a few object types the author would suggest there are not any real differences at all. Quantities are also, in the author's view, irrelevant: it is hardly surprising that larger quantities of material have been uncovered at Gurness and Howe than, for example, many Caithness broch; due to the scale of work and the retrieval recovery bias (see Heald and Jackson 2001; Heald and Barber 2016 for discussion of Tress Barry).

5 There are many differences of opinion amongst contemporary geologists about the appropriate term for serpentinite, the rock consisting of minerals of serpentine and is variously referred to as steatite, soapstone, talc-bearing schists. Although the terms talc-bearing schists and steatite have been used elsewhere to describe the rock used to make numerous handled cups or lamps found at the broch, the term serpentinite and serpentine is preferred here in reference to the associated chemical analysis.

6 A flattened hollow conical bone object (SF 246) was recovered from a deposit (159) within Cell 1. It was thought initially to be the tip of a cetacean tooth artefact but this was later confirmed to be the well-preserved keratinous hoof of a red deer (Sonia O'Connor, pers. comm.) and displays no evidence of working.

5

Environmental evidence

Jackaline Robertson

5.1 The macroplants
Jackaline Robertson

Introduction

This report describes the macroplant assemblage that accumulated during the relatively short occupation of Clachtoll Broch. A total of 98 bulk samples were submitted for analysis along with 52 grid samples. The bulk samples were collected from a series of hearth deposits, floor layers, storage areas and middens from all phases of occupation most of which were archaeologically secure. The grid samples were taken from a single context (042) that covered the entire upper surface of the broch which dated to the final catastrophic burning event. The carbonised macroplant assemblage was large but was concentrated within specific features and the final period of occupation. A small number of waterlogged cereal caryopses and hazelnut shell fragments were noted, but these were a very minor component of the plant remains. This large macroplant assemblage represents an excellent opportunity to study the economic role of a variety of plant resources within an Iron Age broch settlement.

The sampling strategy

Standard bulk samples ranging from 5 to 20 litres were collected from all excavated features. As described above, a single deposit (042), considered to relate to a conflagration that ended the occupation sequence, covered the entire interior of the upper surface. This deposit was an accumulation of material from the final catastrophic burning event which varied in thickness but had sealed all the contexts below. To fully understand the spatial patterning and deposition of ecofacts within this layer, 250 samples were collected from a 50 cm grid. These samples were approximately 0.5 litres in size and 52 were selected for analysis. The results from the grid samples are included within this report but the interpretation of the spatial distribution of the ecofacts within this layer is dealt with in greater detail in Chapter 7.

Methodology

The bulk samples were processed in their entirety by machine in laboratory conditions at Castletown heritage centre, Caithness and at AOC Archaeology, Edinburgh (Kenward, Hall and Jones 1980). The grid samples were processed by hand at AOC archaeology, Edinburgh and at Newcastle University. The sediments were composed mostly of sandy silt although some from Cell 1 and around Hearth 2 were described as damp and greasy. Two samples were waterlogged and are reported separately, in Section 5.3.

The washovers were retained in a 1 mm and 300 mm sieve. The dried washovers were analysed using a low powered microscope at x10–40 magnification. The residues were divided into manageable fractions using a stack system of 4 mm, 2 mm, 1 mm and 0.3 mm sieves. The residue fractions were then scanned by eye and microscope where necessary. The macroplant assemblage was concentrated within a small number of contexts. Due to time constraints the decision was made to study a subsample of the larger deposits. The sub-samples were extracted using a rifle box and 25% of each context was studied. The macrofossils were examined at x10–450 magnifications where necessary to aid identification. Vitrified plant material was extracted from context (140) and was analysed using SEM. All plant identifications were confirmed using modern reference material and seed atlases stored at AOC Archaeology Group (Edinburgh) (Lousley and Kent 1981; Jermy and Tutin 1982; Hubbard 1984; Freethy 1987; Zohary and Hopf 1993; Cappers, Bekker and Jans 2006; Jacomet 2006; Cappers and Neef 2012; Cappers and Bekker 2013; Schulz 2018).

Taphonomy and preservation

The macroplant assemblage was concentrated in specific areas and contexts within the broch and this is directly attributable to the effects of the catastrophic burning event. The macroplant assemblage accumulated through two very distinct mechanisms. The first part of this assemblage was from the earlier occupation and derived from small quantities of small-scale cereal processing, domestic food waste and overspill from hearths, which was overlooked during general cleaning. The second component of the assemblage was created on what was probably the final day the broch was in use. These plants are an accumulation of large-scale processed food, stored crops, building materials and weeds, all burnt *in situ*. This type of evidence of daily life and plant usage rarely survives unless there has been a catastrophic destruction event, as seems to have occurred at Clachtoll. These two preservation pathways have created an excellent opportunity to study how the inhabitants routinely dealt with earlier domestic waste and compare this to their daily life in the final period of occupation.

The preservation of the macroplant assemblage was variable. This was particularly noticeable for the cereal remains which were assessed for morphological damage (Hubbard and al Azm 1990). The cereal from the lower layers were generally classified as distorted. This contrasted with the finds from the final catastrophic burning event where preservation ranged from poor (seeds fused together) to mostly good to excellent (slight puffing to no noticeable distortion). This notable difference in preservation was due to how this assemblage was formed. The plant remains from the lower contexts comprise domestic debris which was directly exposed to heat and then trampled into surfaces, a process which had a derogatory effect. The better preservation of the macroplant remains from the catastrophic burning event was because some material was reduced to ash and this covered the uncharred finds below, including large caches of cereal, creating a protective barrier between them and the fire. The barrier effect of the ash allowed the underlying ecofacts to become safely carbonised while not overly distorted or damaged.

Results

The results from the bulk samples are presented in Table 5.1.1. Macroplant remains were studied from 82 bulk samples and 48 grid samples. The occupation of Clachtoll broch was relatively short and most of the carbonised plant remains were concentrated within the burning event, the knocking stone and from deposits within Cell 2 associated with the final conflagration event. Given the taphonomy of this assemblage it was possible to identify potential changes in agricultural practices within the broch dating from its earliest occupation until its final destruction. The macroplant assemblage was composed of cereals, nuts, fruits, vegetables, building materials, fuel and weeds. As a small number of the richest samples were semi-quantified it is estimated that a minimum of 50,000 plant remains were analysed during this study. The results are discussed below by phase.

Hearth 1 and the earliest floors

Drain (059) contexts (100), (100-N Slot)
From context (100) there were 35 cereal caryopses identified as 25 hulled barley, nine barley, one cereal and one culm fragment. Other edible food included 13 fragments of hazelnut shell. The only find from (100 N Slot) was a small number of charred peat fragments. Preservation of these remains was generally poor. These finds have derived from the reworking of possible crop processing waste, alongside the disposal of food and fuel debris within the stone drain.

Floor contexts (111), (118), (124)
The macroplant assemblage was concentrated within (111) from which one oat, two cereal caryopses, 34 hazelnut shell, one fragment of bracken frond, six stems of heather, one cinquefoils, one common chickweed and one *Cenococcum* spore. In context (118) there were two hulled barley, ten hazelnut shell fragments and from (124) there was one barley caryopsis. Preservation of these remains ranged from poor to adequate and they are considered to represent overspill food and fuel waste from Hearth 1 which was trampled into the floor.

'Souterrain' [069]

Midden contexts (047-SBaulk), (047-SEQuad)
The cereal caryopses from (047 SBaulk) were two hulled barley, six barley and six caryopses. The hazelnut shell totalled four fragments. The weeds were one grass caryopsis, one nipplewort and one knotgrass.

Floor (048-SEQ)
There were 14 cereal caryopses identified as four hulled barley, four barley and six cereals. These are the remains of food residue reworked into the floor.

Loose rubble (078-East)
This deposit was interpreted as an accumulation of loose rubble from a collapse of the superstructure. The

Table 5.1.1 The carbonised macroplant for each of the principal context groups discussed in the text

Context Group			Hearth 1	Hearth 1	Hearth 1	Hearth 1	Sout 069	Sout 069	Sout 069	Sout 069	Sou 069	Hearth 2	Hearth 2	Hearth 2
Context			100	111	118	124	47	47	48	78	104	67	67	76
Species	Name	Plant part	Nslot	Central			Sbaulk	SEQuad	SE Quad	East	Earea	S Baulk	SE Quad	Sbaulk
Crops														
Hordeum Vulgare L.	Six-row hulled barley	Spikelet/s												
Hordeum Vulgare L.	Six-row hulled barley	Caryopsis/es	25		2		2	17	4	15	1	4	7	1
		Caryopsis/es (Waterlogged)												
Hordeum Vulgare L.	Six-row hulled barley	Rachis/Rachides						12						
Hordeum Vulgare L.	Six-row hulled barley	Caryopsis/es												
Hordeum var. Nudum L.	Naked barley	Floret(s)						1		1				
Hordeum sp.	Barley	Caryopsis/es	9			1	6	15	4	9	1	1	2	
Hordeum sp.	Barley	Caryopsis/es (Waterlogged)						4						
Hordeum sp.	Barley	Rachis/Rachides												
Triticum dicoccum L.	Emmer	Caryopsis/es												
Triticum dicoccum L.	Emmer	Glume(s)												
Triticum sp.	Wheat	Caryopsis/es						1						
Avena fatua L.	Wild oat	Caryopsis/es												
Avena fatua L.	Wild oat	Floret(s)												
Avena sp.	Oat	Caryopsis/es		1										
Avena sp.	Oat	Caryopsis/es (Waterlogged)						1						
Avena sp.	Oat	Floret(s)												
Cerealia sp.	Cereal	Caryopsis/es	1	2			6	7	6	24		1	2	
Cerealia sp.	Cereal	Culm(s)	1							1				
Cerealia sp.	Cereal	Straw frag(s)												
Cerealia sp.	Cereal	Straw frag twisted rope(s)												
Cerealia sp.	Cereal	Compacted cereal/straw												
Wild Food														
Corylus avellana L.	Hazel nut	Nutshell frag(s)	13	34	10		4	76			3	19	10	13
Corylus avellana L.	Hazel nut	Nutshell frag(s) (Waterlogged)												
Empetrum nigram L.	Crowberry	Seed(s)												
Prunus spinosa L.	Blackthorn/sloe	Stone(s)												
Building/Flooring/Fuel Material														
Calluna vulgaris L.	Heather	Leaves(s)												
Calluna vulgaris L.	Heather	Seed(s)												
Calluna vulgaris L.	Heather	Flower(s)												
Calluna vulgaris L.	Heather	Stems		6										
Carex sp.	Sedges	Fruit(s)												
Pteridium aquilinum L.	Bracken	Pinnule/Fronds frag(s)		1										
cf. Scirpus sp.	Wood club-rush	Fruit(s)												
Woodland														
Bud(s)	Bud	Buds/bud-scale(s)												
Wood	Wood	Frag(s) (Part charred)		****										
Weed Taxa														
Atriplex sp.	Oraches	Seed(s)												
Brassica nigra L.	Black Mustard	Seed(s)												
Brassica sp.	Cabbage	Seed(s)												
Brassica/sinapis sp.	Cabbage/mustard	Seed(s)												
Bromus sp.	Bromes	Caryopsis/es								1				
cf. Capsella bursa-pastoris L.	Shepherd's-purse	Seed(s)												
cf. Cerastium sp.	Field mouse-ear	Seed(s)												
Chenopodium album L.	Fat hen	Seed(s)								2				
Chenopodium sp.	Goosefoot	Seed(s)												
Danthonia decumbens L.	Heath-grass	Caryopsis/es												
Fallopia convolvulus L.	Black bindweed	Fruits(s)												
Galeopsis Subgenus Galeopsis	Hemp nettle	Nutlet(s)												
Galium aparine L.	Cleavers	Nutlet(s)												

(Continued)

Table 5.1.1 (Continued)

			Hearth 1	Hearth 1	Hearth 1	Hearth 1	Hearth 1	Sout 069	Sout 069	Sout 069	Sout 069	Sou 069	Hearth 2	Hearth 2	Hearth 2
Species	**Name**	**Plant part**	100	100 Nslot	111 Central	118	124	47 Sbaulk	47 SEQuad	48 SE Quad	78 East	104 Earea	67 S Baulk	67 SE Quad	76 Sbaulk
Galium sp.	Bedstraws	Nutlet(s)													
Lapsana communis L.	Nipplewort	Achene(s)							1						
Lycopus europaeus L.	Gypsywort	Nutlet(s)													
persicaria amphibia L.	Amphibious bistort	Fruit(s)													
Persicaria lapathifolium L.	Pale Persicaria	Fruit(s)										1			
Persicaria sp.	Knotweed	Fruit(s)													
Plantago sp.	Plantains	Seed(s)													
Poaceae sp.	Grass	Caryopsis/es							1						
Polygonum aviculare L.	knotgrass	Fruits(s)							1						
Polygonum sp.	Knotgrasses	Fruit(s)													
Potamogeton natans L.	Broad-leaved Pondweed	Fruit(s)													
Potentilla erecta L.	Tormentil	Achene(s)													
Potentilla sp.	Cinquefoils	Achene(s)			1										
Ranunculus sp.	Meadow/creeping/bulbous buttercup	Achene(s)													
Rumex crispus L.	Curled Dock	Fruit(s)													
Rumex longifolius L.	Northern Dock	Fruit(s)													
Rumex longifolius L.	Northern Dock	Perianth(s)													
Rumex sp.	Dock	Fruit(s)													
Spergula arvensis L.	Corn spurrey	Seed(s)													
Stellaria media L.	Common chickweed	Seed(s)			1										
Stellaria sp.	Chickweed	Seed(s)													
	Stems	Frag(s)													
Unknown	Indet	Achene/fruit/seed(s)													
Fuel															
Ash		Frag(s)	*												
Burnt peat		Frag(s)													
Peat/Stem		Compacted material													
Seaweed		Pod frag(s)													
Spores															
Cenococcum sp.		Sclerotia			1				*						
Other															
Animal hair		Frag(s)													

Key:*=<10, **=10-29, ***=29-100, ****=>100-1000, *****=>1000

(Continued)

Table 5.1.1 The carbonised macroplant for each of the principal context groups discussed in the text (Continued)

Context Group			Hearth 2	Hearth 2	Hearth 2	Hearth 3	Hearth 3	Hearth 3	Hearth 3	Hearth 3	Hearth 3	Hearth 3	Hearth 3	Hearth 3	Hearth 3
Context			87 NW	91	94	49 NE & NW Quad	49 NW Q	53 NWQuad	62 SWQ	74 Central	84 NW	85 NW	86 NW	90	93
Species	**Name**	**Plant part**													
Crops															
Hordeum Vulgare L.	Six-row hulled barley	Spikelet/s													
Hordeum Vulgare L.	Six-row hulled barley	Caryopsis/es			1	2	5	161	2	33			1		5
Hordeum Vulgare L.	Six-row hulled barley	Caryopsis/es (Waterlogged)													
Hordeum Vulgare L.	Six-row hulled barley	Rachis/Rachides													
Hordeum var. *Nudum* L.	Naked barley	Caryopsis/es													
Hordeum sp.	Barley	Caryopsis/es		3	3	1	3	33		2		1			1
Hordeum sp.	Barley	Caryopsis/es (Waterlogged)													
Hordeum sp.	Barley	Rachis/Rachides													
Triticum dicoccum L.	Emmer	Caryopsis/es			1										
Triticum dicoccum L.	Emmer	Glume(s)													
Triticum sp.	Wheat	Caryopsis/es													
Avena fatua L.	Wild oat	Caryopsis/es													
Avena fatua L.	Wild oat	Floret(s)													
Avena sp.	Oat	Caryopsis/es							2						
Avena sp.	Oat	Caryopsis/es (Waterlogged)													
Avena sp.	Oat	Floret(s)													
Cerealia sp.	Cereal	Caryopsis/es					3		25						
Cerealia sp.	Cereal	Culm(s)							3		1				
Cerealia sp.	Cereal	Straw frag(s)	1												
Cerealia sp.	Cereal	Straw frag twisted rope(s)													
Cerealia sp.	Cereal	Compacted cereal/straw													
Wild Food															
Corylus avellana L.	Hazel nut	Nutshell frag(s)	1	2	45	3	22	2	2	4	11	3	9	3	4
Corylus avellana L.	Hazel nut	Nutshell frag(s) (Waterlogged)	139							1					
Empetrum nigram L.	Crowberry	Seed(s)								1					
Prunus spinosa L.	Blackthorn/sloe	Stone(s)													
Building/Flooring/Fuel Material															
Calluna vulgaris L.	Heather	Leaves(s)						3							
Calluna vulgaris L.	Heather	Seed(s)													
Calluna vulgaris L.	Heather	Flower(s)					1	1							
Calluna vulgaris L.	Heather	Stems				**		2		2					
Carex sp.	Sedges	Fruit(s)	10												
Pteridium aquilinum L.	Bracken	Pinnule/Fronds frag(s)					1								
cf. *Scirpus* sp.	Wood club-rush	Fruit(s)													
Woodland															
	Bud(s)	Buds/bud-scale(s)													
	Wood	Frag(s) (Part charred)	**												
Weed Taxa															
Atriplex sp.	Oraches	Seed(s)													
Brassica nigra L.	Black Mustard	Seed(s)					1	1							
Brassica sp.	Cabbage	Seed(s)													
Brassica/sinapis sp.	Cabbage/mustard	Seed(s)													
Bromus sp.	Bromes	Caryopsis/es													
cf. *Capsella bursa-pastoris* L.	Shepherd's-purse	Seed(s)						1							
cf. *Cerastium* sp.	Field mouse-ear	Seed(s)													
Chenopodium album L.	Fat hen	Seed(s)													
Chenopodiaceae sp.	Goosefoot	Seed(s)							2						
Danthonia decumbens L.	Heath-grass	Caryopsis/es													
Fallopia convolvulus L.	Black bindweed	Fruit(s)													
Galeopsis Subgenus *Galeopsis* L.	Hemp nettle	Nutlet(s)													
Galium aparine L.	Cleavers	Nutlet(s)													

(Continued)

Table 5.1.1 (Continued)

Context Group			Hearth 2	Hearth 2	Hearth 2	Hearth 3	Hearth 3	Hearth 3	Hearth 3	Hearth 3	Hearth 3	Hearth 3	Hearth 3	Hearth 3	Hearth 3
Context			87 NW	91	94	49 NE & NW Quad	49 NW Q	53 NWQuad	62 SWQ	74 Central	84 NW	85 NW	86 NW	90	93
Species	Name	Plant part													
Galium sp.	Bedstraws	Nutlet(s)													
Lapsana communis L.	Nipplewort	Achene(s)									1				
Lycopus europaeus L.	Gypsywort	Nutlet(s)													
persicaria amphibia L.	Amphibious bistort	Fruit(s)													
Persicaria lapathifolium L.	Pale Persicaria	Fruit(s)											1		
Persicaria sp.	Knotweed	Fruit(s)													
Plantago sp.	Plantains	Seed(s)													
Poaceae sp.	Grass	Caryopsis/es													
Polygonum aviculare L.	knotgrass	Fruits(s)													
Polygonum sp.	Knotgrasses	Fruit(s)													
Potamogeton natans L.	Broad-leaved Pondweed	Fruit(s)													
Potentilla erecta L.	Tormentil	Achene(s)													
Potentilla sp.	Cinquefoils	Achene(s)													
Ranunculus sp.	Meadow/creeping/bulbous buttercup	Achene(s)													
Rumex crispus L.	Curled Dock	Fruit(s)													
Rumex longifolius L.	Northern Dock	Fruit(s)													
Rumex longifolius L.	Northern Dock	Perianth(s)													
Rumex sp.	Dock	Fruit(s)													
Spergula arvensis L.	Corn spurrey	Seed(s)													
Stellaria media L.	Common chickweed	Seed(s)													
Stellaria sp.	Chickweed	Seed(s)													
Stems		Frag(s)													
Unknown	Indet	Achene/fruit/seed(s)													
Fuel															
Ash		Frag(s)													
Burnt peat		Frag(s)	*							*					
Peat/Stem		Compacted material	***												
Seaweed		Pod frag(s)													
Spores															
Cenococcum sp.		Sclerotia					2								
Other															
Animal hair		Frag(s)													

Key:*=<10, **=10-29, ***=29-100, ****=>100-1000, *****=>1000

(Continued)

Table 5.1.1 The carbonised macroplant for each of the principal context groups discussed in the text (Continued)

Species	Name	Plant part	Knocking stone 45 NEQ	Knocking stone 56 NEQuad	Burning 7A	Burning 7B	Burning 7C	Burning 7D	Burning 7E	Burning 7F	Burning 7G	Burning 7H	Burning 71	Burning 71	Burning 10	Burning 17	Burning 18
Crops																	
Hordeum Vulgare L.	Six-row hulled barley	Spikelet/s															
Hordeum Vulgare L.	Six-row hulled barley	Caryopsis/es	*****			12	36	158	56	2	5	>1000	11	9	1	6	332
Hordeum Vulgare L.	Six-row hulled barley	Caryopsis/es (Waterlogged)															
Hordeum Vulgare L.	Six-row hulled barley	Rachis/Rachides		91													
Hordeum var. Nudum L.	Naked barley	Caryopsis/es									53						1
Hordeum sp.	Barley	Caryopsis/es		1		4	8	9	10	2		18	3	7		2	58
Hordeum sp.	Barley	Caryopsis/es (Waterlogged)															
Hordeum sp.	Barley	Rachis/Rachides															
Triticum dicoccum L.	Emmer	Caryopsis/es						1									
Triticum dicoccum L.	Emmer	Glume(s)													2		
Triticum sp.	Wheat	Caryopsis/es															
Avena fatua L.	Wild oat	Caryopsis/es															
Avena fatua L.	Wild oat	Floret(s)															
Avena sp.	Oat	Caryopsis/es		16		1		1		1		11					2
Avena sp.	Oat	Caryopsis/es (Waterlogged)															
Avena sp.	Oat	Floret(s)															
Cerealia sp.	Cereal	Caryopsis/es				2	6	11	47	18	5	10	3	9	1	3	191
Cerealia sp.	Cereal	Culm(s)				3							3				
Cerealia sp.	Cereal	Straw frag(s)		1								2					
Cerealia sp.	Cereal	Straw frag twisted rope(s)															
Cerealia sp.	Cereal	Compacted cereal/straw															
Wild Food																	
Corylus avellana L.	Hazel nut	Nutshell frag(s)				3	2			5	3	4	4		5		
Corylus avellana L.	Hazel nut	Nutshell frag(s) (Waterlogged)															
Empetrum nigrum L.	Crowberry	Seed(s)															
Prunus spinosa L.	Blackthorn/sloe	Stone(s)															
Building/Flooring/Fuel Material																	
Calluna vulgaris L.	Heather	Leaves(s)		2								1	9	**			
Calluna vulgaris L.	Heather	Seed(s)															
Calluna vulgaris L.	Heather	Flower(s)						2				1		**			
Calluna vulgaris L.	Heather	Stems	*						**			1		**			
Carex sp.	Sedges	Fruit(s)					3			1	2	1	1		3		
Pteridium aquilinum L.	Bracken	Pinnule/Fronds frag(s)												***			
cf. *Scirpus* sp.	Wood club-rush	Fruit(s)						1									
Woodland																	
	Bud	Buds/bud-scale(s)															
	Wood	Frag(s) (Part charred)															
Weed Taxa																	
Atriplex sp.	Oraches	Seed(s)															
Brassica nigra L.	Black Mustard	Seed(s)						1				1					
Brassica sp.	Cabbage	Seed(s)															
Brassica/sinapis sp.	Cabbage/mustard	Seed(s)										3			5		
Bromus sp.	Bromes	Caryopsis/es		33													
cf. *Capsella bursa-pastoris* L.	Shepherd's-purse	Seed(s)															
cf. *Cerastium* sp.	Field mouse-ear	Seed(s)															
Chenopodium album L.	Fat hen	Seed(s)								2	2	6	3		10		
Chenopodiaceae sp.	Goosefoot	Seed(s)									2						
Danthonia decumbens L.	Heath-grass	Caryopsis/es															
Fallopia convolvulus L.	Black bindweed	Fruits(s)														1	
Galeopsis Subgenus *Galeopsis*	Hemp nettle	Nutlet(s)													1	1	
Gallium aparine L.	Cleavers	Nutlet(s)															

Table 5.1.1 (Continued)

Context Group			Knocking stone	Knocking stone	Burning	Burning	Burning	Burning	Burning	Burning	Burning	Burning	Burning	Burning	Burning	Burning
Context			45 NEQ	56 NEQuad	7A	7B	7C	7D	7E	7F	7G	7H	7I	10	17	18
Species	**Name**	**Plant part**														
Galium sp.	Bedstraws	Nutlet(s)														
Lapsana communis L.	Nipplewort	Achene(s)												1		
Lycopus europaeus L.	Gypsywort	Nutlet(s)														
persicaria amphibia L.	Amphibious bistort	Fruit(s)	1													
Persicaria lapathifolium L.	Pale Persicaria	Fruit(s)	2	2	2				1	1		1	1	2		
Persicaria sp.	Knotweed	Fruit(s)					1									
Plantago sp.	Plantains	Seed(s)														
Poaceae sp.	Grass	Caryopsis/es				1										
Polygonum aviculare L.	knotgrass	Fruits(s)												7		
Polygonum sp.	Knotgrasses	Fruit(s)												1		
Potamogeton natans L.	Broad-leaved Pondweed	Fruit(s)														
Potentilla erecta L.	Tormentil	Achene(s)														
Potentilla sp.	Cinquefoils	Achene(s)									1					
Ranunculus sp.	Meadow/creeping/bulbous buttercup	Achene(s)				1										
Rumex crispus L.	Curled Dock	Fruit(s)														
Rumex longifolius L.	Northern Dock	Fruit(s)														
Rumex longifolius L.	Northern Dock	Perianth(s)														
Rumex sp.	Dock	Fruit(s)												13		1
Spergula arvensis L.	Corn spurrey	Seed(s)														
Stellaria media L.	Common chickweed	Seed(s)						1						4		
Stellaria sp.	Chickweed	Seed(s)														
Stems	Stems	Frag(s)												1		
Unknown	Indet	Achene/fruit/seed(s)						2	2		3			2		
Fuel																
Ash		Frag(s)														
Burnt peat		Frag(s)										*	**			
Peat/Stem		Compacted material														
Seaweed		Pod frag(s)														
Spores																
Cenococcum sp.		Sclerotia									2	15				
Other																
Animal hair		Frag(s)														

Key: *=<10, **=10-29, ***=29-100, ****=>100-1000, *****=>1000

(Continued)

Table 5.1.1 The carbonised macroplant for each of the principal context groups discussed in the text (Continued)

Context Group	Species	Name	Plant part	Burning 19	Burning 20	Burning 21	Burning 36	Burning 37	Burning 38	Burning 39	Burning 41	Burning 42 NWQ	Burning 42 NEQ	Burning 42 SWQ	Burning 42 SEQ	Burning 61 SWQuad	Post aband
Crops																	
	Hordeum Vulgare L.	Six-row hulled barley	Spikelet/s		2	1											11
	Hordeum Vulgare L.	Six-row hulled barley	Caryopsis/es	61	594	1924	50	7	2420	31	308	*****	*****	*****	*****	49	19
	Hordeum Vulgare L.	Six-row hulled barley	Caryopsis/es (Waterlogged)														
	Hordeum Vulgare L.	Six-row hulled barley	Rachis/Rachides		14	2			66	4	25	2	45	****			
	Hordeum var. *Nudum* L.	Naked barley	Caryopsis/es			1					2						
	Hordeum sp.	Barley	Caryopsis/es	18	71	83	19	4	18	9	15	10	11	13	2	26	8
	Hordeum sp.	Barley	Caryopsis/es (Waterlogged)														
	Hordeum sp.	Barley	Rachis/Rachides														
	Triticum dicoccum L.	Emmer	Caryopsis/es														
	Triticum dicoccum L.	Emmer	Glume(s)											1			
	Triticum sp.	Wheat	Caryopsis/es														
	Avena fatua L.	Wild oat	Caryopsis/es						1								
	Avena fatua L.	Wild oat	Floret(s)														
	Avena sp.	Oat	Caryopsis/es		4	12	1		1		5	3	3	13	1	1	
	Avena sp.	Oat	Caryopsis/es (Waterlogged)														
	Avena sp.	Oat	Floret(s)														
	Cerealia sp.	Cereal	Caryopsis/es	12	53	26	10	2	117	4	7	21	8	***	1	10	5
	Cerealia sp.	Cereal	Culm(s)		6				1	2		***	***	***			1
	Cerealia sp.	Cereal	Straw frag(s)		****	****			63 **	***				**			
	Cerealia sp.	Cereal	Straw frag twisted rope(s)														
	Cerealia sp.	Cereal	Compacted cereal/straw		*				3				**				
Wild Food																	
	Corylus avellana L.	Hazel nut	Nutshell frag(s)					7	1	2	6	6	5	27		38	1
	Corylus avellana L.	Hazel nut	Nutshell frag(s) (Waterlogged)														
	Empetrum nigrum L.	Crowberry	Seed(s)														
	Prunus spinosa L.	Blackthorn/sloe	Stone(s)														
Building/Flooring/Fuel Material																	
	Calluna vulgaris L.	Heather	Leaves(s)		****	****		1	4	5	****	****	****	****			
	Calluna vulgaris L.	Heather	Seed(s)			2			1	*	****						
	Calluna vulgaris L.	Heather	Flower(s)		***	***			3	**	****	***	***	***			
	Calluna vulgaris L.	Heather	Stems		**	**		****		****	****	****	****	****			
	Carex sp.	Sedges	Fruit(s)			3			5		4		2				
	Pteridium aquilinum L.	Bracken	Pinnule/Fronds frag(s)			4			1	***		4					
	cf. *Scirpus* sp.	Wood club-rush	Fruit(s)								4						
Woodland																	
		Bud(s)	Buds/bud-scale(s)									2		2			
		Wood	Frag(s) (Part charred)														
Weed Taxa																	
	Atriplex sp.	Oraches	Seed(s)														
	Brassica nigra L.	Black Mustard	Seed(s)								1	1	1	1			
	Brassica sp.	Cabbage	Seed(s)								3						
	Brassica/sinapis sp.	Cabbage/mustard	Seed(s)		2						5		4	2			
	Bromus sp.	Bromes	Caryopsis/es			7					20						
	cf. *Capsella bursa-pastoris* L.	Shepherd's-purse	Seed(s)			1											
	cf. *Cerastium* sp.	Field mouse-ear	Seed(s)														
	Chenopodium album L.	Fat hen	Seed(s)			31			3		4	4	4	3	1	8	
	Chenopodiaceae sp.	Goosefoot	Seed(s)			3					2					1	
	Danthonia decumbens L.	Heath-grass	Caryopsis/es							1							
	Fallopia convolvulus L.	Black bindweed	Fruit(s)			2					1	2	1				
	Galeopsis Subgenus *Galeopsis* L.	Hemp nettle	Nutlet(s)			2					1	1	1				
	Galium aparine L.	Cleavers	Nutlet(s)		1												

(Continued)

Table 5.1.1 (Continued)

Context Group			Burning	Burning	Burning	Burning	Burning	Burning	Burning	Burning	Burning	Burning	Burning	Burning	Burning	Post aband
Context			19	20	21	36	37	38	39	41	42 NWQ	42 NEQ	42 SWQ	42 SEQ	61 SWQuad	11
Species	**Name**	**Plant part**														
Galium sp.	Bedstraws	Nutlet(s)			3											
Lapsana communis L.	Nipplewort	Achene(s)							1	1						
Lycopus europaeus L.	Gypsywort	Nutlet(s)						1								
persicaria amphibia L.	Amphibious bistort	Fruit(s)			3						1					
Persicaria lapathifolium L.	Pale Persicaria	Fruit(s)		1	2		1	4		5		6	1		1	
Persicaria sp.	Knotweed	Fruit(s)											1			
Plantago sp.	Plantains	Seed(s)								1						
Poaceae sp.	Grass	Caryopsis/es								1			1			
Polygonum aviculare L.	knotgrass	Fruits(s)										2				
Polygonum sp.	Knotgrasses	Fruit(s)								9		2				
Potamogeton natans L.	Broad-leaved Pondweed	Fruit(s)			1											
Potentilla erecta L.	Tormentil	Achene(s)								1						
Potentilla sp.	Cinquefoils	Achene(s)														1
Ranunculus sp.	Meadow/creeping/bulbous buttercup	Achene(s)			1					1		1				
Rumex crispus L.	Curled Dock	Fruit(s)										1				
Rumex longifolius L.	Northern Dock	Fruit(s)						1		2		1				
Rumex longifolius L.	Northern Dock	Perianth(s)						1								
Rumex sp.	Dock	Fruit(s)			2					3						
Spergula arvensis L.	Corn spurrey	Seed(s)		1						1						
Stellaria media L.	Common chickweed	Seed(s)			23											
Stellaria sp.	Chickweed	Seed(s)			1				1	1						
	Stems	Frag(s)				*										
	Unknown	Achene/fruit/seed(s)			2			5	1	4	1	1	2	3	1	
Fuel																
	Ash	Frag(s)										*****				
	Burnt peat	Frag(s)		***	***	**	*	***	****	***	***	****	****			
	Peat/Stem	Compacted material						**								
	Seaweed	Pod frag(s)						*			*					
Spores																
Cenococcum sp.		Sclerotia								3				1		
Other																
	Animal hair	Frag(s)														

Key:*=<10, **=10-29, ***=29-100, ****=>100-1000, *****=>1000

(Continued)

Table 5.1.1 The carbonised macroplant for each of the principal context groups discussed in the text (Continued)

Context Group / Context	Name	Plant part	Post aband 28	Entrance 83	Entrance 106	Entrance 120	Entrance 121	Entrance 129	Entrance 146	Entrance 153	Entrance 158	Entrance 166	Cell 1 155	Cell 1 159	Cell 1 161	Cell 1 163	Cell 1
Crops / Species	**Name**	**Plant part**															
Hordeum Vulgare L.	Six-row hulled barley	Spikelet/s	1														
Hordeum Vulgare L.	Six-row hulled barley	Caryopsis/es	570	10	32	106	4		41	41	108	26			4		
Hordeum Vulgare L.	Six-row hulled barley	Caryopsis/es (Waterlogged)															
Hordeum Vulgare L.	Six-row hulled barley	Rachis/Rachides	5														
Hordeum var. *Nudum* L.	Naked barley	Caryopsis/es															
Hordeum sp.	Barley	Caryopsis/es	150	1	5	26	3	1	12	6	57	14					
Hordeum sp.	Barley	Caryopsis/es (Waterlogged)															
Hordeum sp.	Barley	Rachis/Rachides							1								
Triticum dicoccum L.	Emmer	Caryopsis/es															
Triticum dicoccum L.	Emmer	Glume(s)															
Triticum sp.	Wheat	Caryopsis/es			1												
Avena fatua L.	Wild oat	Caryopsis/es															
Avena fatua L.	Wild oat	Floret(s)															
Avena sp.	Oat	Caryopsis/es									1						
Avena sp.	Oat	Caryopsis/es (Waterlogged)															
Avena sp.	Oat	Floret(s)				9											
Cerealia sp.	Cereal	Caryopsis/es	138	2	3	17	1		1	2	20	2					
Cerealia sp.	Cereal	Culm(s)		1	1				1								
Cerealia sp.	Cereal	Straw frag(s)	2														
Cerealia sp.	Cereal	Straw frag twisted rope(s)															
Cerealia sp.	Cereal	Compacted cereal/straw															
Wild Food																	
Corylus avellana L.	Hazel nut	Nutshell frag(s)	5	7	3	4	2		1	4	2	1	1				
Corylus avellana L.	Hazel nut	Nutshell frag(s) (Waterlogged)															
Empetrum nigrum L.	Crowberry	Seed(s)													1		
Prunus spinosa L.	Blackthorn/sloe	Stone(s)															
Building/Flooring/Fuel Material																	
Calluna vulgaris L.	Heather	Leaves(s)	2														
Calluna vulgaris L.	Heather	Seed(s)															
Calluna vulgaris L.	Heather	Flower(s)															
Calluna vulgaris L.	Heather	Stems				1						•					
Carex sp.	Sedges	Fruit(s)													1	1	
Woodland																	
Pteridium aquilinum L.	Bracken	Pinnule/Fronds frag(s)															
cf. *Scirpus* sp.	Wood club-rush	Fruit(s)															
Bud(s)		Buds/bud-scale(s)															
Wood		Frag(s) (Part charred)												**			*
Weed Taxa																	
Atriplex sp.	Oraches	Seed(s)															
Brassica nigra L.	Black Mustard	Seed(s)															
Brassica sp.	Cabbage	Seed(s)	1														
Brassica /sinapis sp.	Cabbage/mustard	Seed(s)	1														
Bromus sp.	Bromes	Caryopsis/es															
cf. *Capsella bursa-pastoris* L.	Shepherd's-purse	Seed(s)															
cf. *Cerastium* sp.	Field mouse-ear	Seed(s)	1														
Chenopodium album L.	Fat hen	Seed(s)				1											
Chenopodiaceae sp.	Goosefoot	Seed(s)	1														
Danthonia decumbens L.	Heath-grass	Caryopsis/es				1											
Fallopia convolvulus L.	Black bindweed	Fruits(s)															
Galeopsis Subgenus *Galeopsis*	Hemp nettle	Nutlet(s)	1														
Gallium aparine L.	Cleavers	Nutlet(s)															

(Continued)

Table 5.1.1 (Continued)

Context Group			Post aband	Entrance	Entrance	Entrance	Entrance	Entrance	Entrance	Entrance	Entrance	Entrance	Cell 1	Cell 1	Cell 1	Cell 1
Context			28	83	106	120	121	129	146	153	158	166	155	159	161	163
Species	Name	Plant part														
Galium sp.	Bedstraws	Nutlet(s)														
Lapsana communis L.	Nipplewort	Achene(s)														
Lycopus europaeus L.	Gypsywort	Nutlet(s)														
persicaria amphibia L.	Amphibious bistort	Fruit(s)														
Persicaria lapathifolium L.	Pale Persicaria	Fruit(s)	1	1		1					1					
Persicaria sp.	Knotweed	Fruit(s)														
Plantago sp.	Plantains	Seed(s)														
Poaceae sp.	Grass	Caryopsis/es														
Polygonum aviculare L.	knotgrass	Fruits(s)														
Polygonum sp.	Knotgrasses	Fruit(s)														
Potamogeton natans L.	Broad-leaved Pondweed	Fruit(s)														
Potentilla erecta L.	Tormentil	Achene(s)														
Potentilla sp.	Cinquefoils	Achene(s)														
Ranunculus sp.	Meadow/creeping/bulbous buttercup	Achene(s)														
Rumex crispus L.	Curled Dock	Fruit(s)														
Rumex longifolius L.	Northern Dock	Fruit(s)														
Rumex longifolius L.	Northern Dock	Perianth(s)														
Rumex sp.	Dock	Fruit(s)														
Spergula arvensis L.	Corn spurrey	Seed(s)														
Stellaria media L.	Common chickweed	Seed(s)													1	
Stellaria sp.	Chickweed	Seed(s)														
	Stems	Frag(s)		3												
Unknown	Indet	Achene/fruit/seed(s)		1		1			1	1						
Fuel																
	Ash	Frag(s)														
	Burnt peat	Frag(s)								*				*		**
	Peat/Stem	Compacted material														
	Seaweed	Pod frag(s)														
Spores																
Cenococcum sp.		Sclerotia														
Other																
Animal hair		Frag(s)												*		

Key:*=<10, **=10-29, ***=29-100, ****=>100-1000, *****=>1000

(Continued)

Table 5.1.1 The carbonised macroplant for each of the principal context groups discussed in the text (Continued)

Context Group / Species	Name	Plant part	Cell 2 123	Cell 2 125	Cell 2 133	Cell 2 134	Cell 2 135	Cell 2 136	Cell 2 137	Cell 2 140 (SEM)	Cell 2 141	Cell 2 142	Cell 4 81 Upper	Cell 4 81 Lower	Gallery 3 34	Gallery 3 89 SW Quad
Crops																
Hordeum Vulgare L.	Six-row hulled barley	Spikelet/s	122													
Hordeum Vulgare L.	Six-row hulled barley	Caryopsis/es	****	187	3106	1592	39	42	683	**			2	4	2	3
Hordeum Vulgare L.	Six-row hulled barley	Caryopsis/es (Waterlogged)								****						
Hordeum Vulgare L.	Six-row hulled barley	Rachis/Rachides	***		62					***						
Hordeum var. *Nudum* L.	Naked barley	Caryopsis/es				1										
Hordeum sp.	Barley	Caryopsis/es	83	27	19	11	4		78						3	1
Hordeum sp.	Barley	Caryopsis/es (Waterlogged)														
Hordeum sp.	Barley	Rachis/Rachides														
Triticum dicoccum L.	Emmer	Caryopsis/es														
Triticum dicoccum L.	Emmer	Glume(s)														
Triticum sp.	Wheat	Caryopsis/es														
Avena fatua L.	Wild oat	Caryopsis/es											1			
Avena fatua L.	Wild oat	Floret(s)														
Avena sp.	Oat	Caryopsis/es	19	1	98	31			6				32			
Avena sp.	Oat	Caryopsis/es (Waterlogged)														
Avena sp.	Oat	Floret(s)														
Cerealia sp.	Cereal	Caryopsis/es	24	1	30 ****	1	2	3	30		1			1	1	1
Cerealia sp.	Cereal	Culm(s)		6	1											
Cerealia sp.	Cereal	Straw frag(s)			14											
Cerealia sp.	Cereal	Straw frag twisted rope(s)	1	1												
Cerealia sp.	Cereal	Compacted cereal/straw			2											
Wild Food																
Corylus avellana L.	Hazel nut	Nutshell frag(s)	1	1		1			1				4			
Corylus avellana L.	Hazel nut	Nutshell frag(s) (Waterlogged)														
Empetrum nigram L.	Crowberry	Seed(s)														
Prunus spinosa L.	Blackthorn/sloe	Stone(s)														
Building/Flooring/Fuel Material																
Calluna vulgaris L.	Heather	Leaves(s)						1								
Calluna vulgaris L.	Heather	Seed(s)														
Calluna vulgaris L.	Heather	Flower(s)														
Calluna vulgaris L.	Heather	Stems	***			***	*									
Carex sp.	Sedges	Fruit(s)														
Pteridium aquilinum L.	Bracken	Pinnule/Fronds frag(s)	1			2										
cf. *Scirpus* sp.	Wood club-rush	Fruit(s)							1			4				
Woodland																
Bud(s)	Bud	Buds/bud-scale(s)														
Wood	Wood	Frag(s) (Part charred)														
Weed Taxa																
Atriplex sp.	Oraches	Seed(s)														
Brassica nigra L.	Black Mustard	Seed(s)														
Brassica sp.	Cabbage	Seed(s)														
Brassica/sinapis sp.	Cabbage/mustard	Seed(s)		1								1				
Bromus sp.	Bromes	Caryopsis/es		1		1						1				
cf. *Capsella bursa-pastoris* L.	Shepherd's-purse	Seed(s)														
cf. *Cerastium* sp.	Field mouse-ear	Seed(s)														
Chenopodium album L.	Fat hen	Seed(s)		1												
Chenopodiaceae sp.	Goosefoot	Seed(s)									1					
Danthonia decumbens L.	Heath-grass	Caryopsis/es														
Fallopia convolvulus L.	Black bindweed	Fruits(s)	1													
Galeopsis Subgenus *Galeopsis*	Hemp nettle	Nutlet(s)										1				
Galium aparine L.	Cleavers	Nutlet(s)														

(Continued)

Table 5.1.1 (Continued)

Context Group		Cell 2	Cell 2	Cell 2	Cell 2	Cell 2	Cell 2	Cell 2	Cell 2	Cell 2	Cell 2	Cell 4	Cell 4	Gallery 3	Gallery 3
Context	**Plant part**	123	125	133	134	135	136	137	140	141	142	81 Upper	81 Lower	34	89 SW Quad
Name									SEM						
Species															
Galium sp. / Bedstraws	Nutlet(s)														
Lapsana communis L. / Nipplewort	Achene(s)		1												
Lycopus europaeus L. / Gypsywort	Nutlet(s)											2			
persicaria amphibia L. / Amphibious bistort	Fruit(s)											3			
Persicaria lapathifolium L. / Pale Persicaria	Fruit(s)														
Persicaria sp. / Knotweed	Fruit(s)		1												
Plantago sp. / Plantains	Seed(s)														
Poaceae sp. / Grass	Caryopsis/es														
Polygonum aviculare L. / knotgrass	Fruits(s)														
Polygonum sp. / Knotgrasses	Fruit(s)														
Potamogeton natans L. / Broad-leaved Pondweed	Fruit(s)														
Potentilla erecta L. / Tormentil	Achene(s)														
Potentilla sp. / Cinquefoils	Achene(s)														
Ranunculus sp. / Meadow/creeping/bulbous buttercup	Achene(s)														
Rumex crispus L. / Curled Dock	Fruit(s)														
Rumex longifolius L. / Northern Dock	Fruit(s)														
Rumex longifolius L. / Northern Dock	Perianth(s)														
Rumex sp. / Dock	Fruit(s)														
Spergula arvensis L. / Corn spurrey	Seed(s)														
Stellaria media L. / Common chickweed	Seed(s)														
Stellaria sp. / Chickweed	Seed(s)														
Stems	Frag(s)							1							
Unknown / Indet	Achene/fruit/seed(s)	1			1										
Fuel															
Ash	Frag(s)					*									
Burnt peat	Frag(s)														
Peat/Stem	Compacted material														
Seaweed	Pod frag(s)														
Spores															
Cenococcum sp.	Sclerotia									1					
Other															
Animal hair	Frag(s)														

Key; *=<10, **=10-29, ***=29-100, ****=>100-1000, *****=>1000 cereal remains totalled 50, along with three weeds. The cereal numbered 15 hulled caryopses, one rachis, nine barley, 24 cereal and one culm node. The weeds were one bromes caryopsis. Two fat hen and one pale persicaria. These finds are a mix of food and weeds which may have been remixed into this deposit when the roof collapsed.

Levelling material for flagstone floor (103) context (104)

There was one hulled barley, one barley caryopsis and three fragments of hazelnut shell. These are a mix of food remains which were re-worked and trampled into this floor deposit.

Hearth 2

Flooring deposit (067-SBaulk), (067-SEQ)

In (067SBaulk) there were six caryopses identified as four hulled barley, one barley, one cereal. There were also 19 fragments of hazelnut shell. From (067SEQ) the plants numbered 22, composed of seven hulled barley, two barley, two cereal, 10 hazelnut shell and one crowberry seed. This small accumulation of cereal, nuts and wild fruit are food debris which is probably overspill from the hearth that was trampled into the floor surface.

Flooring/levelling material (076-SBaulk)

There was one hulled barley caryopsis and 13 fragments of hazelnut shell. It was believed this area may have been used for storing waste, but given the small quantity of food debris, this material may represent redeposited waste rather than deliberate deposition.

Floor deposit (087-NW)

The carbonised macroplant assemblage was composed of small numbers of cereal straw, one hazelnut shell, heather stems and peat. There were 139 waterlogged hazelnut shell fragments, peat and wood fragments which were partly charred. This material is a mix of food and fuel debris which has been trampled into this surface.

Floor deposit (091)

There were three barley caryopses and two fragments of hazelnut shell. These remains comprise food residue, probably overspill from the hearth which was trampled into this floor surface.

Hearth deposit (095)

There were five cereal caryopses identified as one hulled barley, three barley, one emmer and 45 hazelnut shell fragments. These remains are considered to be domestic food debris.

Hearth 3 and the stone tank

Floor deposit (049-NEQ and NWQ), (049-NWQ)

From (049NEQ and NWQ) there were two hulled barley, one barley and three fragments of hazelnut shell. In (049NWQ) there were five hulled barley, three barley and three cereal caryopses. The hazelnut shell numbered 22 fragments. There were small fragments of bracken and heather along with one orache and some *Cenococcum* spores. The cereal and hazelnut shell are likely food waste whereas the bracken and heather could be building material. The weeds and *Cenococcum* spores are invasive. This material has been reworked into this floor and trampled into the surface.

Stone tank (052) context (053-NWQ)

A total of 221 cereal caryopses and three culm nodes were recovered. The species were hulled barley (73%), barley (15%) and oat (1%). The rest were described as cereal (11%). There were also two fragments of hazelnut shell. There was a small quantity of heather and one Casella bursa-pastoris, two fat hen and one orache. The cereal and hazelnut shell are food waste which were disposed of within this feature. The heather could be the remains of building and fuel waste. The weed seeds are likely invasive.

Floor deposit (062-SWQ)

There were five hazelnut shell fragments of which one was only partly charred. This material is redeposited food remains.

Burnt hearth remains (074-Central)

There were 35 cereal caryopses and three culm nodes. The cereal was 33 hulled barley and two barley. Hazelnut shell numbered 11 fragments. There was a small quantity of heather and charred peat. There was one weed identified as bedstraw. These remains are a mix of food and fuel waste overlooked during the cleaning of this hearth. The weed is probably a contaminant.

Active floor surface (084)

There was one cereal caryopsis and five fragments of hazelnut shell. These remains are food waste.

Peat ash floor (085)

There was one barley caryopsis and five fragments of hazelnut shell. This material is domestic food waste which is probably rake-out from the hearth, used to create an additional floor surface over some underlying decayed organic flooring.

FLOOR DEPOSIT (086-NW)

There was one hulled barley caryopsis, nine fragments of hazelnut shell and one pale persicaria. The cereal and hazelnut shell are food debris which was remixed into this floor layer. The weeds are invasive.

LEVELLING DEPOSIT (090)

There were three fragments of hazelnut shell. This material is redeposited food refuse.

HEARTH SURROUND (093)

There was one barley caryopsis and three fragments of hazelnut shell.

The knocking stone

GRAIN FILL OF KNOCKING STONE (045-NEQ)

The knocking stone was filled with cereal caryopses which were burnt *in situ* (Fig. 5.1.1). The grain from the knocking stone was 100% sampled but given the large number of macroplants only 25% of the sample was analysed. It was noted during excavation that the grains from the lower part of the knocking stone were more complete in that some still had part of the chaff and husks attached. This suggests that the grain within the knocking stone were in the process of being dehusked prior to the final catastrophic burning event. Of the 25% of the sample analysed 5000 hulled barley were counted. There were also 91 hulled barley rachis, 16 oat caryopses, 33 bromes and a small number of straw fragments. The weeds comprised one amphibious bistort and two pale persicaria. There was a small number of heather fragments. Given the small numbers of chaff and weed contaminates present, the barley had undergone the first stages of winnowing and threshing and was awaiting the final stages of processing. The oat and bromes probably grew alongside the hulled barley and were harvested at the same time. The heather was likely an accidental inclusion from some building material that was reworked into the knocking stone during the final conflagration.

SETTING MATERIAL FOR KNOCKING STONE (056-NEQ)

There was one barely and two cereal caryopses which were likely overspill from the knocking stone and became trapped in this deposit in which the stone was set.

The burning event

INTERIOR SUPERSTRUCTURE (007A), (007B), (007C), (007D, (007E), (007F), (007G), (007H), (007I)

Carbonised macroplants were recovered from (007A), (007B), (007C), (007D, (007E), (007F), (007G), (007H) and (007I) which was interpreted in the field as the burnt remains of the interior superstructure. All of these samples except for (007G) were analysed in their entirety.

Figure 5.1.1 General shot of six-row hulled barley from the knocking stone

Deposit (007G) was rich in cereal remains and a 25% subsample was selected for further study. Cereal formed the largest component of this assemblage a minimum of 1535 caryopses and chaff fragments were recovered. The species were six-hulled barley, naked barley, barley, oat and cereal. Small fragments of straw were noted in deposits (007A), (007E) and (007G). The cereal remains, totalling 1094, were concentrated within (007G). The rest of the cereal remains were scattered among the remaining eight contexts in much smaller numbers. It is not possible to establish how the cereals were stored within the broch; they could have been spread out on an upper level for drying or were stored in containers that did not survive the collapse of the broch.

There were also 21 fragments of hazelnut shell present in (007A), (007C), (007E), (007F), (007G) and (007H).

Plants of potential economical use were sedge, wood club-rush and heather which was recorded in small quantities in a number of these deposits. This material could have been used as thatching or as floor covering and was destroyed during the catastrophic burning event.

The weeds were black mustard, cabbage/mustard, fat hen goosefoot, pale persicaria, knotweed, grass, cinquefoils and common chickweed. A number of these species are edible including the black mustard, cabbage/mustered, fat hen, pale persicara and common chickweed. These species could have deliberately collected for use as food. Equally, however, these species are also common contaminants of crops and could have been accidental inclusions of the cereal.

COLLAPSED INTERNAL STRUCTURE (010)

The largest component of this macroplant assemblage was bracken fronds, heather stems, leaves and flowers. The bracken could have been from a floor covering or roof section which was burnt *in situ* along with the heather turf which was possibly part of the roof. The edible food remains were seven cereal remains identified as one six-row hulled barley, two rachis, one caryopsis and three culms and five fragments of hazelnut shell. The weeds were inclusions of ten fat hen, one hemp-nettle, one nipplewort, two pale persicaria, eight knotgrass, 13 dock, four common chickweed, a small number of stems and two poorly preserved seeds. The food and weeds were likely intermixed with the bracken and heather turf when the floor collapsed.

WALL VOID (015) CONTEXT (017)

There were 11 cereal caryopses identified as six six-row hulled barley, two barley and three cereals. The only other find was a single fat hen seed. This material is food waste and weeds that was intermixed within the wall void when the broch was destroyed and provides further evidence of grain storage on in the upper levels of the broch.

BURNT MATERIAL (018)

There was a total of 581 cereal caryopses and one rachis fragments. The species were six-row hulled barley (57%), barley (10%), cereal (33%) and one six-row hulled barley rachis. Preservation of these remains was varied and those described as cereal had suffered significant morphological damage due to heat exposure. The only other find was one dock fruit. The cereal was either being dried or was in storage.

BURNT DEPOSIT (019)

There were 91 cereal caryopses identified as six-row hulled barley (67%), barely (20%) and cereal (13%). These remains were probably redeposited when the fire occurred.

BURNT MATERIAL (020)

The cereal numbered 744 of which two were identified as two spikelets along with 722 caryopses and 20 chaff fragments. The species were six-row hulled barley (82%), barley (9%), oat (1%) and cereal (8%). Of the six-row hulled barley 5% were recorded as being noticeably smaller and more morphologically distorted. This could suggest that some of these grains were not fully ripe when harvested. Other finds were two cabbage/mustard, one corn spurrey, one cleaver and one pale persicaria. The cereal and weeds are a mix of food and invasive contaminates that were destroyed *in situ*.

BURNT MATERIAL (021)

The macroplant assemblage from this deposit was dominated by both cereals and turf material. There was one spikelet, 2048 caryopses and one rachis node identified as six-row hulled barley (94%), one naked barley (0.1%), barley (4%), one wild oat (0.1%), oat (0.6%) and cereal (1.2%). Most of the hulled barley still had

the palea and lemma attached. There was also a large quantity of cereal culm nodes, straw and compacted cereal type material which was semi-quantified rather than counted.

A large quantity of heather and burnt peat was noted and this appeared to have derived from turves that were burnt *in situ*. Among these finds were small inclusions of sedge and wood club rush. These plants could have been accidental inclusions within the turf or were deliberately used as floor or thatching material.

The weeds numbered 88 and were formed of two black bindweed, four cabbage/mustard, seven bromes, one field-mouse ear, 31 fat hen, three goosefoot, two hemp nettle, three bedstraw, three amphibious bistort, two pale persicara, one broad-leaved pondweed, one buttercup, two dock, 23 common chickweed, one chickweed and two poorly preserved seeds which could not be identified further.

The cereal from this deposit had clearly not been fully processed as the paleas and lemmas were still attached. Nor had it been sieved to remove the accompanying weed seeds. This suggests that this part of the broch was reserved for storing grain prior to processing. The presence of turf remains in a context likely to derive from the upper sections of the broch may suggest that turf was used in roofing, or perhaps that peat fuel was used in a hearth located at first floor level or above.

BURNING DEPOSIT (036)

There were 80 cereal caryopses identified as six-row hulled barley (63%), barley (24%), oat (1%) and cereal (12%). These cereal caryopses were probably incorporated into this deposit during the final conflagration.

BURNT DEPOSIT (037)

The edible food was composed of 13 cereal caryopses and seven fragments of hazelnut shell. The cereal was seven six-row hulled barley, four barley and two cereals. The other finds were a small quantity of heather, burnt peat and plant stems. There was one pale persicaria. These remains like those from context (036) represent a small accumulation of redeposited food refuse.

BURNT DEPOSIT (038)

There were 2641 cereal remains composed of 17 spikelets, 66 rachis, one culm and 2557 caryopses. There were also 66 fragments of straw fragments some of which were compacted. The cereal species were six-row hulled barley (95%), barley (1%), cereal (4%) along with one wild oat and one oat. Many the six-row hulled barley still had the rachis attached. There was also one fragment of hazelnut shell. Other finds included a large quantity of heather along with a smaller quantity of sedge, bracken and burnt peat. The weeds totalled 14 and were three fat hen, four pale persicaria, two northern dock and five seeds which could not be identified further. The cereal from this deposit was partly processed and was probably being stored or dried in this location prior to the destruction of the broch. The weeds were likely accidental inclusions within the cereal crop. The peat, heather, bracken and sedge could have been used for building materials or was perhaps intended for fuel.

Burnt deposit (039)

There were 44 cereal caryopses and six chaff fragments. The species were six-row hulled barley (70%), barley (18%) and cereal (12%). Other finds included a small quantity of straw, heather, two fragments of hazelnut shell, one black bindweed, one gypsywort, one chickweed and one poorly preserved seed. There was a large quantity of charred peat and a small number of seaweed fragments within this deposit. These finds represent redeposited food, cereal processing waste, fuel and invasive agricultural weeds. The peat derives from turf used as a structural element or fuel waste.

Burnt deposit (041)

There was 337 cereal caryopses and 25 rachis fragments. The species were six-row hulled barley (92%), naked barley (1%), barley (4%), oat (1%) cereal (2%). There was also a large quantity of straw, bracken, heather, burnt peat along with four sedge fruits. The weed species were varied and numbered 68. The species were one black bindweed, one black mustard, three cabbage, five cabbage/mustard, one corn spurrey, 20 bromes, four fat hen, two goosefoot, one hemp nettle, one nipplewort, five pale persicaria, one plantain, one grass, nine knotgrass, one tormentil, one buttercup, two northern dock, three dock, one common chickweed, one chickweed and four seeds which could not be identified further. There were also three *Cenococcum* spores.

This sample was collected from the passageway to gallery 2 and as such the cereal could be redeposited food or processing waste which was either trampled into this surface or re-deposited after the broch was destroyed. The chaff, straw and weeds are processing waste which was probably trampled into this surface. The heather, peat, bracken and sedge could have been used as a structural element or floor covering.

Burning event (042-NWQ), (042-NEQ), (042-SWQ), (042-SE)

These four samples were rich in cereal caryopses and a subsample of 25% was extracted from each context for analysis. The cereal caryopses were concentrated within this part of the broch and 20000 six-row hulled barley were counted. Over 1000 rachises and culm

nodes were noted within (042NWQ), (042NEQ) and (042SWQ). There was no evidence of chaff fragments within (042SEQ). The other cereal species was one emmer glume recorded in (042SW) and 19 oat caryopses scattered among (042NWQ), (042NEQ) and (042SWQ). Preservation of these cereals ranged from poor to excellent; most were recorded as good to excellent. The cereal from these four deposits had been partly processed and was either being stored in this location to await the final stages of processing or had been left out to dry.

A large quantity of ash was noted within (042NEQ) and this suggests that ecofactual material was permanently removed from the macroplant record.

The only other food was 38 fragments of hazelnut shell scattered among (042NWQ), (042NEQ) and (042SWQ) in small numbers with no evidence of selective or deliberate disposal.

Turves composed of heather and peat were burnt *in situ* within (042NWQ), (042NEQ) and (042SWQ). There were also small numbers of sedge and bracken within (042NEQ) which could have been components within the turves or were used as thatching material.

There were 46 weeds recovered but these were concentrated within (042NEQ) which had 24. The remaining 22 were scattered among (042NWQ), (042SWQ) and (042SEQ) in small numbers with no evidence of selective or deliberate disposal. The species were two black mustard, two cabbage/mustard, four bromes, nine fat hen, three black bindweed, two hemp nettle, one amphibious bistort, seven pale persicaria, one knotweed, one grass, two knotgrass, two knotgrasses, one buttercup, one curled dock, one northern dock, three fragments of plant stem and four poorly preserved seeds. There were a small number of seaweed fragments in (042NEQ) and one *Cenococcum* spore in (042SEQ).

Ash from demolition broch (061-SWQ)

There were 86 cereal caryopses and one piece of straw. The species were six-row hulled barley (57%), barley (30%), oat (1) and cereal (12%). Other edible food finds included 38 fragments of hazelnut shell. The weed was eight fat hen, one goosefoot and one pale persicaria. These remains are cereal which was destroyed *in situ* along with some inclusions of weeds.

Post abandonment and collapse

Demolition deposit (011)

There were 32 cereal caryopses and one culm node. The species were 19 hulled barley, eight barley and five cereals. Other finds included one fragment of hazelnut shell and one cinquefoil. These are redeposited food waste. The weeds are invasive.

DEMOLITION/TUMBLE DEPOSIT (028)

The macroplant assemblage numbered 860 cereal caryopses, five rachis and two fragments of straw. The species were hulled barley (67%), barley (17%) and cereal (16%). There was also one oat caryopsis. There were five fragments of hazelnut shell, one cabbage and one cabbage/mustard seed. There was a small quantity of heather. The weeds were one fat hen, one goosefoot, one hemp nettle and one pale persicaria. This material is redeposited food waste intermixed with some weeds.

The entrance passageway

CLAY DEPOSIT (083)

There were 13 cereal caryopses and one culm node. The caryopses were eight hulled barley, two 2-row hulled barley, one barley and two cereals. There were seven fragments of hazelnut shell. Other finds included one pale persicaria, a small number of stems and one seed which could not be identified further. This material is a mix of food and invasive weeds which were trampled into this surface.

DESTRUCTION EVENT (106)

There were 41 cereal caryopses and one culm node. The species were 32 hulled barley, five barley, one wheat and three cereals. There were three fragments of hazelnut shell. These remains are re-deposited food waste.

ENTRANCE PASSAGE FLOOR (120)

There were 158 cereal caryopses identified as hulled barley (67%), barley (16%), oat (6%) and cereal (11%). There were four fragments of hazelnut shell. There were one caryopsis of heath grass, one piece of heather, one fat hen, one pale persicaria and one seed which could not be identified further. This small assemblage is a mix of redeposited food and weeds.

ENTRANCE PASSAGE FLOOR (121)

There were eight cereal caryopses composed of four hulled barley, three barley and one cereal. There were two fragments of hazelnut shell. These remains are redeposited food debris.

ACCUMULATED MATERIAL (129)

There was one barley caryopsis. This caryopsis was redeposited material that was intermixed within sediment which filled a void created by levelling flags (128).

ORGANIC DEPOSIT (146)

There were 53 cereal caryopses and three chaff fragments. The cereal caryopses were 41 hulled barley, 12 barley and one cereal. The chaff was one barley rachis, one cereal rachis and one culm node. There was one fragment of hazelnut shell. One weed seed could not be identified further. These remains are redeposited food waste.

RUBBLE DEPOSIT (153)

There were 49 cereal caryopses, four fragments of hazelnut shell and one weed seed. The cereal was 41 hulled barley, six barley and two cereals. These remains are redeposited food debris.

ORGANIC DEPOSIT (158)

There were 185 cereal caryopses identified as hulled barley (58%), barley (31%) and cereal (11%). There were two fragments of hazelnut shell, one pale persicaria and a small quantity of burnt peat. These remains are redeposited food, fuel and weeds.

BEDDING DEPOSIT (166)

There were 41 cereal caryopses formed of 24 hulled barley, two 2-row hulled barley, 14 barley, one oat and two cereals. There were small fragments of heather. These finds are a mix of redeposited food and possible building and fuel material.

Cell 1

MIDDEN (155)

There was one fragment of hazelnut shell which is food refuse deposited within the midden.

ORGANIC MIDDEN DEPOSITS (159)

There was a small number of wood fragments and a fragment of rope made from animal hair.

DEPOSIT (161)

There were four hulled barley, one fragment of hazelnut shell, one crowberry, one sedge, one corn spurrey and a piece of heather. This assemblage is composed of mixed remains including food, possible fuel and building materials and weeds.

DEPOSIT (163)

There was a small quantity of burnt peat and partially charred wood fragments. These remains are mixed fuel debris.

Cell 2

DEPOSIT (137)

This context overlay the flagstones (132) in Cell 2. A total of 797 cereal caryopses were recovered identified as 683 hulled barley, 78 barley, six oat, 30 cereal. There were also one hazelnut shell and a piece of plant stem.

DEPOSIT (136)

There were 42 hulled barley and three cereal caryopses.

DEPOSIT (135)

There were 39 hulled barley, of which three still had the awns attached, four barley, two cereal and a small quantity of heather and burnt peat.

DEPOSIT (125)

There were 239 cereal caryopses identified as hulled barley (187), barley (27), oat (1), cereal (24). There was also one piece of twisted cereal straw which had been made into a rope. Other finds were one fragment of hazelnut shell and seven weeds identified as one cabbage/mustard, one bromes, one fat hen, one nipplewort and one poorly preserved seed.

DEPOSITS (140), (141)

During excavation it was noted that a thin crust described as a blue/white fluffy organic residue had survived within deposits (140) and (141). This material was analysed using both a high-power microscope and SEM (Fig. 5.1.2). It became apparent that the texture of this organic material was not fluffy. Instead, this thin crust was highly vitrified and glassy and was the remains of a vitrified sheaf of six-row barley (Figs 5.1.2 and 5.1.3). Underneath this thin crust lay the rest of the sheaf, which was noticeably better preserved, and it was easier to identify spikelets and straw fragments. During the catastrophic burning event the temperature in Cell 2 must have been extremely high, the surface of the barley took the brunt of the fire and was completely vitrified leaving the material underneath better preserved. The presence of sheaves within Cell 2 clearly demonstrate that bundles of barley were transported in their entirety to the broch for processing.

DEPOSITS (123), (133), (134), (142)

The macroplant assemblage from Cell 2 was concentrated in upper contexts (123), (133), (134) and (142). The largest number of cereals were recorded in deposits (123) and (142) of which a subsample of 25% was analysed. The finds from samples (133) and (134) were identified in full. The cereal remains were six-row hulled barley of which a minimum of 15,000 were counted from these four deposits. These were composed of spikelets, caryopses and rachis. The only other cereal noted was 180 oat caryopses of which two were identified as the wild variety. The oat was scattered among contexts (123), (133), (134) and (142) with no evidence of selective or deliberate disposal. Instead, the oat appeared to be an accidental inclusion within the barley grain.

Figure 5.1.2 Close up of the vitrified six-row hulled barley from cell 2

The grain from (123) was of interest as this was a large cache that had been stored in an alder container which was destroyed during the final conflagration (see Section 5.2). The alder vessel took the brunt of the fire and was reduced to fragments which allowed the grain stored within to survive in a carbonised condition and not be reduced to ash or vitrified as in the case of the sheaf stored near the grain. The cereal remains from this upper part of Cell 2 were likely stored in the box and after it was destroyed the grain spilled out onto the floor.

Small quantities of bracken were noted in (123), (133) and (142). Heather was recorded in (134). This material was possibly used to provide packing material for the grain or other foodstuffs and fragile items stored in this location. Small inclusions of weeds normally found in arable fields were also scattered among these four contexts. The presence of barley spikelets, caryopses, chaff, oat and weed seeds all indicate that the grain had undergone

Figure 5.1.3 Close up of the reverse side of the vitrified six-row hulled barley from cell 2

the preliminary stages of processing which would have included winnowing, sieving and drying but was still to be pounded in the knocking stone to separate the remaining spikelets. The barley from Cell 2 represents different stages of food storage in the form of unprocessed bundles stored alongside part processed grain.

CELL 4
FLOOR MATERIAL CONTEXTS (081UPPER), (081LOWER)
There was six hulled barley and one cereal caryopsis scattered among (081Upper) and (081Lower) with no evidence of selective or deliberate disposal of remains in either context. Instead these are a small accumulation of redeposited food remains.

Gallery 3 and the stairs
MODERN INFILL (034)
There were two hulled barley, three barley and two cereal caryopses which represent redeposited food debris.

OCCUPATION DEPOSIT (089-SWQ)
There were three hulled barley, one barley and one cereal caryopsis which represent redeposited food debris.

Discussion
The crops
The largest component of the macroplant assemblage was cereal caryopses which were concentrated within the deposits associated with the final catastrophic burning event. From this final layer many ecofacts including grain were permanently destroyed during the burning event and reduced to ash. Regardless, 47,746 cereal remains were analysed, representing a substantial store of grain within the broch. Similar results have been recorded at Scalloway which also experienced a catastrophic fire which helped preserve a large cache of stored grain (Holden 1998, 126). The cereal assemblage at Clachtoll provides an excellent opportunity to study the crops cultivated, how they were stored and processed over the relatively short duration of the broch's occupation.

HULLED BARLEY
Throughout the occupation of Clachtoll Broch, hulled barley (*Hordeum vulgare* L.) was clearly the dominant cultivated crop, with over 40,000 caryopses and chaff fragments identified. Where preservation allowed it was possible to identify the presence of six-row hulled barley based on the morphology of the rachis internodes and the proportions of symmetric to asymmetric grains. Hulled barley was present throughout the occupation of the broch, but as expected these finds were concentrated within the final phase. The hulled barley from the lower

deposits was composed of relatively small numbers of possible small-scale processing waste alongside food and cooking waste. These finds were over spill from the three sequential heaths that was either trampled accidently into the surrounding floors or deliberately disposed of within the midden. The hulled barley was concentrated in specific deposits within the final conflagration event, the knocking stone and Cell 2. These finds represented material burnt *in situ* during various stages of cereal processing and storage.

NAKED BARLEY
The quantity of naked barley (*Hordeum* var. *Nudum* L.) was small: six caryopses were recovered from five contexts. Identifying naked barley can be somewhat problematic especially if the caryopses are poorly preserved. It has been observed that some hulled barley can mimic the appearance of naked barley if the growing conditions were poor (Holden and Boardman 1998, 99). This is caused by the failure of the grain to adequately fuse to the enclosing lemmas and paleas giving it the misleading appearance of the naked variety (Holden 1988, 99). At Clachtoll most of the grains, especially those from the final catastrophic burning event, had not suffered extensive morphological distortions. It is therefore unlikely that naked barley has been misidentified or significantly overlooked within the surviving assemblage and the number recorded within the assemblage is an accurate representation. The small quantity of naked barley at Clachtoll suggests that this crop was a contaminant of the hulled barley and was not deliberately cultivated.

OAT
The oats (*Avena* sp.) numbered 274 and were composed of both caryopses and floret bases. Those that could be identified all belonged to the wild variety (*Avena fatua* L.). Oats were present throughout the occupation of the broch but were concentrated within the burning event, Cell 2 and within the knocking stone. The oat in all instances was intermixed within larger quantities of hulled barley. There was no evidence to suggest oats were stored separately from barley in any part of the broch. This suggests that the oat was a weed contaminant of the hulled barley crop and was not deliberately cultivated at Clachtoll. Undoubtedly, the 16 oat caryopses from the knocking stone were accidental inclusions intermixed with thousands of hulled barley grains which were in the process of being de-husked when the broch burnt down.

WHEAT
Four wheat (*Triticum* sp.) caryopses and three emmer (*Triticum dicoccum* L.) glumes were scattered throughout the occupation levels. Wheat has previously been

noted on Atlantic Iron Age settlements at Old Scatness (Summers and Bond 2015, 269), Cnip (Church and Cressey 2006, 188), Dun Vulan (Smith 1999, 298), Hornish Point (Jones 2003, 153), Nybster (Robertson in prep) and Thrumster (Robertson in prep). At these sites, where identifications could be verified, emmer was the recognised species. The standard interpretation is that during the Iron Age, growing conditions prohibited the successful cultivation of this species on any significant scale. It has been suggested that wheat could have been imported as a luxury item along with other exotic artefacts which have been recovered from several sites in this region (Summers and Bond 2015, 270). Wheat, including emmer, was present at more southerly Scottish Iron Age sites including Oakbank crannog, Cults Loch crannog and Black Loch crannog where either the growing conditions were more suitable or trade links were more accessible (Miller 2002 35; Robertson 2018; Crone *et al.* 2018). It is possible wheat was traded over long distances, between the north and south. Given the small quantity of wheat at Clachtoll, is also possible this species, like the naked barley and oats, was an invasive weed of the hulled barley crop. Certainly, there was no evidence to suggest that wheat was stored or treated separately form the main hulled barley crop.

CROP STAPLES

The cereal assemblage at Clachtoll clearly demonstrates that six-row hulled barley was the dominant cereal cultivated for the duration of the site's existence and that naked barley, oat and wheat were probably all weed contaminants. This pattern of crop exploitation is expected as barley is better adapted to growing in the marginal soil and climate conditions of the highland and islands of Scotland (Dickson and Dickson 2000). Certainly the importance of barley has been recorded at Old Scatness (Summers and Bond 2015, 252), Howe (Dickson 1994, 134), Cnip (Church and Cressey 2006, 188), Dun Vulan (Smith 1999, 298), Baleshare and Hornish Point (Jones 2003, 153), Pool (Bond 2007a, 182), Tofts Ness (Bond 2007c, 157), Crosskirk (Dickson and Dickson 1984a, 155), Scalloway (Holden and Boardman 1998, 99), Nybster (Robertson in prep) and Thrumster (Robertson in prep). Where sites differed was usually in the species of barley that was cultivated. At Clachtoll six-row hulled barley was the dominant variety throughout its occupation, whereas at Howe naked barley was favoured (Dickson 1994, 134) and sites such as Tofts Ness and Old Scatness reported the deliberate cultivation of both varieties (Bond 2007c, 157; Summers and Bond 2015, 263).

Naked barley is a free-threshing cereal which makes it easier to process. This may explain why other sites such as Howe cultivated this species as it was not as time consuming to render it edible compared to the hulled variety

(Dickson 1994, 135). Hulled barley requires additional processing to de-husk the grains and this demands specific agricultural tools such as a knocking stone. At Clachtoll a knocking stone was employed to de-husk the hulled barley and was in use when the broch was destroyed in the final conflagration event. No such implement was recovered at Howe as their economy was based primarily on the exploitation of naked barley that does not require this process (Dickson 1994, 135). When a variety of barley species are cultivated within the same site, they tend to have different dietary roles. In such circumstances naked barely is normally preferred for human consumption whereas hulled barley is set aside for brewing and animal feed (Summers and Bond 2015, 264). At Clachtoll hulled barley as the only staple crop was used for both human and possibly animal feed.

The presence of oat in small numbers at sites including Old Scatness (Summers and Bond 2015, 267) and Scalloway (Holden and Boardman 1998, 99) was interpreted as the small-scale cultivation of this crop which expanded during later periods in the northern isles (Bond 2002, 183). Certainly, while oat is not native to Scotland, the soil and climate were suitable for either the deliberate cultivation of this species or for it to thrive in the wild. The oat at Clachtoll is likely a weed rather than a deliberate attempt to cultivate a second, if more minor crop. There is no evidence that the population of Clachtoll attempted to cultivate a second crop variety which would potentially have acted as a replacement if the first failed for any reason.

The absence of a secondary crop at Clachtoll could be due to the short occupation of the site which prevented the occupants from expanding their agricultural economy or that any evidence of changes within crop exploitation did not register within the cereal assemblage. Given the size of the cereal assemblage it is unlikely that evidence of a second if more minor crop would have escaped notice. There could have been a cultural preference for six-row barley as the broch occupants were clearly familiar with this species and had all the requisite tools to successfully cultivate and process it, thereby negating the need to experiment with new, possibly unfamiliar crops.

It is also possible that hulled barley was preferred as it stores better in damp conditions (Summers and Bond 2015, 264; Bond 2007c, 157). Certainly, sheaves of barley were transported to the broch for storage in Cell 2 along with large caches of semi de-husked cereal. Regardless of the reason, hulled barley was the favoured cereal species throughout the occupation of Clachtoll and it appears a secondary crop was not cultivated. Nor was there evidence to suggest that the growing conditions of the barley were so poor as to require risk management strategies where the crops were harvested early (Bond 2003, 106).

Harvesting, storage and crop processing

The presence of barley sheaves in Cell 2 coupled with the recovery of culm nodes, straw fragments and arable weeds demonstrate that hulled barley was either uprooted or the stems were cut low to the ground. These were then gathered into bundles for transport. The inhabitants of the broch were deliberately harvesting the barley using these techniques as the straw was a valuable resource used for thatching, flooring, fuel and animal feed (Smith 1999, 332). Some of the sheaves were subsequently stored in Cell 2, where they awaited further processing. Alongside the sheaf was a large cache of spikelets, caryopses, chaff fragments and some weeds. These remains had undergone the preliminary stages of processing in that they had been threshed, raked, winnowed, sieved and dried and were ready for long term storage (Hillman 1981, 132–3). At this stage, the grain is kept in a dry stable condition until needed for pounding. It is also possible that some of the large cache of grain in Cell 2 was being held in reserve as seed for the following year's sowing.

The presence of chaff and weed seeds suggests that some of the earlier stages of processing occurred within the immediate confines of the broch. If processing did occur inside it was likely practised on a small scale as it seems improbable that the broch interior with a single entrance would have proved suitable for this activity on a larger scale, which typically generates significant quantities of dust and requires adequate floor space. Historically, crops were winnowed outside in a breeze or, if it did occur inside, this was in a building with multiple doors or air vents to allow for a cross breeze (Smith 1999, 332). Such ventilation did not exist at Clachtoll so larger quantities of grain were probably winnowed and threshed outside the broch. If outside conditions were wet, it is likely that small quantities of grain were processed inside as and when required.

Grain prior to storage must be dried, as if damp is likely to spoil and be rendered inedible. Barley could also have been dried prior to threshing to make processing easier (Smith 1999, 332). At Clachtoll it is likely the grain was dried using the hearths or was scattered on the upper floors. Certainly, analysis of the grid samples of (042) indicates that cereal caryopses were concentrated within specific areas which suggest that material was either being stored or had been left to dry in selected locations. The agricultural technology at Clachtoll was designed specifically to process hulled barley. The knocking stone was used to pound the spikelets and this implement was evidently in use on the day the broch was destroyed.

The crops grown at Clachtoll remained stable but there was a noticeable shift from the earlier phase which practised a small-scale subsistence economy to the final occupation which had become a storage and processing centre. This interpretation is based on the surviving evidence that the crop assemblage from the early stages of occupation is significantly much smaller with little signs of processing when compared to the much larger accumulation of crops in varying stages of storage and processing during the final occupation. However, it is possible that taphonomic factors such as continual refurbishment and cleaning of the earlier floors has removed much of the ecofactual evidence, and it was only the final conflagration event that preserved evidence of large-scale crop processing. While this interpretation cannot be fully ruled out, if Clachtoll broch had always been employed for processing grain on a significant scale it would still be anticipated that some evidence of this would survive in the earlier phases, especially as the charcoal and animal bone assemblages all suggest that some domestic debris was allowed to build up within the broch throughout its occupation.

Clachtoll Broch may have undergone a similar change in agricultural practises previously observed at Howe, Scalloway, Old Scatness and Pool during the Middle to Late Iron (Bond 2002, 182–3). This was believed to represent the end of small subsistence economies which involved day-to-day processing of food as and when required to bulk processing of grain on a much larger scale (Bond 2002, 183). Direct comparison of the Clachtoll hulled barley crop from the earliest occupation where the cereal derived from domestic food and cooking refuse to the final days of the broch where large-scale storage and processing of grain occurred, signifies that there was a major shift in agricultural practices and how this broch was used in a relatively short period of time. By the time the broch was destroyed it is possible it acted as processing centre for numerous smaller settlements which used this facility to store their crops. The main disadvantage of storing large quantities of crops and processing them on mass in a single enclosed location is the increased probability of fire as the grain must be routinely parched. This change in how the broch was used to store and process crops may have contributed to the final conflagration event, but this must remain speculative.

Flax

A total of 12 flax (*Linum usitatissimum* L.) seeds were recovered from two grid samples (042 C11) and (042 E15) from the final catastrophic burning event (Fig. 5.1.4). These remains were in an area that appears to have been used for storage. There was no sign of this species in any of the lower deposits and its presence in the final phase could signify an addition to the cultivated crops. Alternatively, it is possible that flax was exploited throughout the occupation of the broch, but evidence of it did not survive within the carbonised plant assemblage. Unlike cereal, flax does not have to be routinely exposed to heat prior to storage and if required to produce fibres then the

Figure 5.1.4 The flax recovered from final catastrophic burning event (042 C11)

stems are left to decompose in water (Bond and Hunter 1987, 178; Holden and Boardman 1998, 99). Consequently, flax tends to leave little evidence of its presence within a carbonised macroplant assemblage and the best opportunity for recovering it may be from conflagration events (Holden and Boardman 1998, 99).

Flax in relatively small numbers has previously been noted at Iron Age deposits at Crosskirk (Dickson and Dickson 1984, 152), Scalloway (Holden 1998, 127), Howe (Dickson 1994, 135) and Old Scatness (Summers and Bond 2015, 270). The recovery of flax at multiple sites suggests it was deliberately cultivated but on a small scale. Flax was also present in the Pictish and Viking levels at Old Scatness (Bond and Summers 2010, 193) but cultivation of this species noticeably increased during the Norse period at sites such as Pool (Bond 2007a, 186). While the number of flax seeds at Clachtoll was small this species did have an economic role within the final phase although what role it had in the earlier stages of occupation is unclear.

Flax can be processed to produce food, linseed oil, preservatives, medicine, cattle fodder in the form of linseed cake, cloth used for clothes, rope, sacking, sails along with the chaff and stems used to feed to livestock or a fuel source (Bond and Hunter 1987 178; Dickson and Dickson 2000, 254). The small number of flax seeds at Clachtoll suggests this species probably fulfilled a basic dietary role. Certainly, the recovery of fragments of flax from a human coprolite at Warebeth broch indicates it was consumed by the human population (Dickson 1994, 135). If the crop were large enough, it could have been exploited for more than just food. Certainly, there was evidence that oils extracted from plants were used within several stone lamps at Clachtoll (see Section 4.3). The plant species used was not identified but linseed contains 35–40% oil and unlike animal fats do not become rancid (Dickson and Dickson 2000, 254). Linseed could potentially have provided a source of oil for lighting at Clachtoll.

It has been suggested that pre-Norse use of flax concentrated on exploiting the seeds as processing the fibres was a more complex operation, beyond the capacity of most earlier subsistence economies (Dickson 1994, 135; Dickson and Dickson 2000, 254). Supporting argument for this is offered by the small number of flax seeds and capsules which are usually recovered at most Iron Age sites including Clachtoll. This suggests that the economic role of this species was somewhat basic, rather than representing large-scale processing of fibres (Summers and Bond 2015, 271). Wool processing did occur at Clachtoll and some of the spindle whorls used to prepare this resource are like those required for creating coarse linen (Bond and Hunter 1987, 179; Dickson and Dickson 2000, 254).

It is possible but unlikely that flax fibres were processed on a very small scale at Clachtoll alongside the wool. Several spindle whorls were recovered, and the stone tank situated within the broch may have been used for retting the stems for linen production. Such a procedure would have created an unpleasant environment within the immediate vicinity of the broch as the material had to decompose. If flax was retted, then this probably occurred in an outside location. If wool production met the demands of the broch, then it is unlikely that additional time was invested in processing flax to extract fibres. Certainly, there was no surviving evidence of any material woven from flax, but several worked animal hairs were present in the midden. The available evidence indicates the small flax crop cultivated at Clachtoll was utilised for its dietary and possible oil properties with no conclusive proof it was processed for cloth.

Wild edible species

NUTS

Hazelnut (*Corylus avellana* L.) shells were recovered from throughout the broch in relatively small numbers in both a carbonised and waterlogged condition. The shell fragments were concentrated in the hearth deposits and burning event. Hazelnut is a common find at most prehistoric sites as the shells are often deliberately exposed to heat during roasting and are sometimes recycled as a kindling material or disposed of in fires during cleaning. The shell assemblage was composed of small fragments from discarded domestic food waste rather than representing large-scale food processing, storage or roasting of large caches (Bishop 2019). The absence of any stored hazelnuts or large-scale processing is of note as cereal was both stored and processed in large quantities in the latter occupation of the site. As has been described in the charcoal assemblage (Section 5.2), hazel appears to have grown in the near vicinity and the nuts would have been easily exploited as a seasonal and nutritional food source. The absence of any stored hazel caches within the broch perhaps suggests this resource had only a minor dietary role, where stored elsewhere or were not seasonally available when the structure was destroyed.

Figure 5.1.5 Turf fragment recovered from final catastrophic burning event (042 H15)

FRUITS

The assemblage contained a small number of crowberry (*Empetrum nigrum* L.) seeds; the berries are edible and have been collected as a food resource (Smith 1999, 331). The crowberry from the lower deposits may represent food waste whereas the seeds from the grid samples tended to be recovered alongside large fragments of heather and could have been accidental inclusion within the turf material used for building and fuel. A small quantity of blackthorn/sloe (*Prunus spinosa* L.) was noted in the grid samples; the fruits are edible, if somewhat bitter, but if dried became more palatable (Dickson and Dickson 2000, 281). This plant can also be used to treat a variety of medical conditions including asthma, scabies and sore throats (Dickson and Dickson 2000, 281). The blackthorn/sloe was probably collected for food or medicine and only survived within the archaeobotanical record because it was charred in the final conflagration event.

VEGETABLES

Vegetables due to their fragile structure tend to be underrepresented within most carbonised plant assemblages, especially when compared to cereals and nuts which are much more likely to be deliberately exposed to heat (Zohary and Hopf 1993, 181). This proved true at Clachtoll where there was little definitive evidence for the deliberate collection of wild green plants to supplement the diet. There were a small number of orache (*Atriplex* sp.), fat hen (*Chenopodium album* L.), cabbage/mustard (*Brassica/Sinapis* sp.), hemp nettle (*Galeopsis* sp.), bedstraw (*Galium* sp.), nipplewort (*Lapsana communis* L.), knotgrass (*Polygonum aviculare* L.), black bindweed (*Fallopia convolvulus* L.), pale persicaria (*Persicaria lapathifolium* L.), common chickweed (*Stellaria media* L.) and corn spurrey (*Spergula arvensis* L.) which are all edible (Renfrew 1973; Smith 1999, 331). None of these species were found in large concentrations that signified deliberate collection or storage. However, it is possible these plants were collected directly from the field as and when required for their edible leaves and seeds (Holden and Boardman 1998, 101). Many of these plants have a high food value and could have been used to add some variety to the diet and flavour to cereal pottage (Renfrew 1993, 24).

If these plants were gathered only when needed at Clachtoll, then this would leave little trace of their presence within either the lower deposits or in the final catastrophic burning event as there would have been no need to store them in large numbers. However, these species, while edible, are also common contaminants of agricultural fields and could have been easily transported to the broch not as food but as an accidental inclusion of the hulled barley crop. As the barley was harvested low to the ground this increases the opportunity for agricultural weed species to become entangled within the crop. Some of these weed species have been recorded at Crosskirk and while it is probable some of them were used as a food source, it is just as likely they were accidental inclusions (Dickson and Dickson 1984, 155). The economic role of these species at Clachtoll is therefore subjective as conclusive proof for their deliberate inclusion within the diet has not survived.

Building and fuel materials

Species such as heather (*Calluna vulgaris* L.) and bracken (*Pteridium aquilinum* L.) were deliberately collected and utilised within the broch as flooring, bedding, roofing and later recycled for fuel. The heather and bracken from the lower deposits was typically associated with fuel debris but these remains could originally have been components of building remains later recycled for fuel. These two species from the final conflagration event were destroyed *in situ* and provided surviving evidence of their structural role within the broch. Large concentrations of heather and peat survived in several contexts from the final burning event and may have belonged to roofing material that was destroyed *in situ* (Fig. 5.1.5). The bracken noted in Cell 2 was likely used for packing or flooring to create a waterproof surface to prevent the grain from going mouldy. Grain if it becomes damp is quickly rendered inedible and can encourage the spread of pests such as insects, whereas bracken contains natural insecticides and flavonoids which have antibiotic properties would help act as a barrier (Donnelly, Robertson and Robinson 2002). Both species would have been available in the surrounding landscape.

Small quantities of sedge (*Carex* sp.) and grass (*Poaceae* sp.) were present in the broch and these have historically been used for flooring and thatching (Smith 1999, 331; Johnston and Reilly 2007). These two species have routinely been recovered at several waterlogged crannog sites such as Oakbank crannog, Cults Loch and Black Loch where they were interpreted as forming floor layers (Miller 2002, 41; Robertson 2018, 85; Robertson and Roy 2019, 11–12). These plants probably had similar roles at Clachtoll but due to taphonomic differences between waterlogged wetland and carbonised sites, evidence of their structural role is easily overlooked or under-appreciated in charred macroplant assemblages. Sedge and grass would both have grown locally in the surrounding landscape and provided a useful building and fuel resource.

There were a small number of seaweed fragments and these were probably brought to the site deliberately. This material has been used for fuel, animal feed, manure, medicine and thatching (Holden and Boardman 1998, 102). What role it had at Clachtoll is unclear as none of these fragments were associated with the hearth structures and instead were concentrated within the burning event suggesting that they had been burnt during the final conflagration.

Weeds

The weeds species grow in a range of habits such as arable fields, meadows, moorland, grassland, waste ground and coastal areas. These species were introduced to the site as accidental inclusions of the hulled barley crop, building materials, fuel and introduced on the feet, clothes and hides of both the human and animal inhabitants. As already discussed, many of the weed species may have had a dual role at Clachtoll. Species such as fat hen and common chickweed along with others may have been exploited as a source of vegetables but are also found growing in arable fields and waste ground. The same is true of sedge and grass which grow in grassland and heathland and could be easily introduced accidently to the site or collected deliberately as use for flooring or thatching. Other species such as plantains (*Plantago* sp.), buttercup (*Ranunculus* sp.) and violet (*Viola* sp.) are much more likely to represent weeds which were introduced accidently. The weed plants were concentrated in the final catastrophic burning layer and tended to be localised within specific locations and this is discussed further in Chapter 7.

Conclusion

The two preservation pathways that created the macroplant assemblage produced an excellent opportunity to study the economic importance of agriculture and the role of plants within this economy and diet. The macroplant assemblage prior to the destruction of the broch had formed primarily through the disposal and overspill of small-scale crop processing waste, cooking debris, fuel and invasive weeds from the hearths that were subsequently trampled into the floors or disposed of within middens. The macroplant assemblage was concentrated within

the final destruction event from which large numbers of cereal in differing stages of processing and storage were encountered along with evidence of structural elements composed of turves, flooring and thatching material along with a variety of weeds.

The macroplant assemblage from both the early and final occupation clearly demonstrates that six-row hulled barley was the only crop that was deliberately cultivated and harvested throughout the use of the site. The inclusions of naked barley, oat and emmer wheat were accidental, and their economic contribution can be discounted. The only obvious change for crop exploitation was the presence of flax in the final burning event and while it is possible this species was exploited earlier, evidence of this has not survived within the carbonised assemblage. The large concentration of six-row hulled barley in the final burning event suggests that the broch at this time was used as a central storage and processing area for grain from possibly smaller settlements. This could demonstrate a major shift in agricultural practices from what was a small-scale subsistence economy to a large-scale processing site. This represents a major shift in how this broch was fundamentally used but overall, the plant species exploited for food, building materials and fuel along with the invasive weeds remained relatively stable and unchanged throughout its occupation.

5.2 The charcoal
Jackaline Robertson

Introduction

Charcoal was collected from the bulk samples from all phases of occupation and from a series of grid samples from context (042) which covered the entire surface of the broch from the final catastrophic burning event. This report focuses primarily on the charcoal from the bulk samples, but the grid samples are included within the results section. The grid samples are discussed in greater detail in Chapter 7, which concentrates on understanding the spatial deposition of the finds. The charcoal assemblage accumulated during the short time the broch was inhabited and from the final conflagration event. The fragments are composed of fuel debris, structural elements and artefacts.

Methodology

Only those contexts which had charcoal fragments larger than 4 mm were selected for further analysis. A maximum of 20 fragments where possible were selected for species identification from each sample. Species identifications were confirmed by analysing the transverse, tangential and radial sections at ×70–×450 magnification and using keys and texts stored at AOC archaeology group (Schweingruber 1978). A further 74 charcoal which were identified as potential structural elements or artefacts were chosen from ten contexts to be measured. The measurements were taken using digital callipers and the results are recorded in millimetres.

The charcoal assemblage was concentrated within a small number of features. Understanding the taphonomy of this assemblage was complicated by the catastrophic burning event. At times it was difficult to distinguish between fuel debris and material which may have originally formed part of a structural element or artefact. To ensure as much accurate information as possible was obtained, the following criteria were used as a rough guide in interpreting this assemblage: those contexts from the lower phases that had small quantities of mixed wood species were designated as fuel waste, whereas larger concentrations of a single species were interpreted as a structural component or artefact.

Understanding the charcoal assemblage from the upper layers was more complicated as many contexts contained larger concentrations of mixed wood species, but these remains were not necessarily fuel debris. As the upper floors and roof burned it is probable that fuel debris, structural material and artefacts became intermixed, and to overcome this difficulty the samples from the final burning event were analysed closely for the presence of charcoal deriving from multiple sources.

Results

The charcoal assemblage weighed 2.0 kg and 1,066 fragments were selected for species identification from 81 bulk samples and a further 385 from 36 grid samples. The species present were alder (*Alnus glutinosa* L.), birch (*Betula* sp.), hazel (*Corylus avellana* L.), heather (*Calluna vulgaris* L., larch (*Larix* sp.), rowan (cf. *Sorbus* sp.), pine (*Pinus* sp.), cherry (*Prunus* sp.), oak (*Quercus* sp.), willow (*Salix* sp.) and elm (*Ulmus* sp.). The dominant species was hazel (39%) followed by alder (20%), birch (15%), heather (9%), oak (7%), pine (6%), rowan (3%), willow (0.5%), larch (0.3%) cherry (0.1%) and elm (0.1%) (Fig. 5.2.1). Preservation of the charcoal was varied. Those fragments from the conflagration event were noticeably friable and broke apart more easily than those recovered from the underlying layers. Overall preservation of these fragments ranged from poor to excellent, but most were categorised as adequate to good. The results from the bulk samples are briefly summarised below by phase and context.

Hearth 1 and the earliest floors

DRAIN [059]: CONTEXTS (100-DRAIN) AND (100-NORTH)

The drain fill (100) was sampled in two locations, marked as (100-drain) and (100-north). The charcoal was concentrated within context (100-drain) which had 37.2 g compared to (100-north) which had 2.5 g. The species in (100-drain) were alder (40%), hazel (5%), oak (25%), birch (5%) and willow (5%). Hazel and willow roundwood formed 20% and 5% respectively. Context (100-north) had 2.5 g of charcoal identified as hazel (45%), pine (22%), oak (22%) and birch (11%). The presence of hazel roundwood (33%) was noted. These remains are fuel debris from hearth 1 which has been reworked into culvert (059) during cleaning of this feature.

FLOORS (111), (118-CENTRAL), (124)

The charcoal from the three floor layers was small (5.8 g) and was scattered among the contexts with no evidence of elective or deliberate disposal. Context (111) had 3.2 g composed of birch (40%), hazel (30%), alder (10%), heather roundwood (10%) and pine (10%). The charcoal (1.2 g) from (118Central) was hazel (60%), alder (10%), birch (10%) and pine (20%). Hazel roundwood formed 50% of the identified fragments. In context (124) there was 1.4 g composed of oak (90%) and hazel roundwood (10%). This small accumulation of charcoal has derived from redeposited fuel debris.

The souterrain [069]

MIXED DEPOSITS (047-SBAULK), (047-SE QUAD)

The mixed, midden-like deposit (047) was sampled in two locations, labelled (047-SBaulk) and (047-SEQuad). From deposit (047SBaulk) the charcoal (10.5 g) was hazel (65%), birch (15%), rowan (10%), alder (5%) and cherry (5%). This was the only part of the site from which cherry was recovered. In context (047SE Quad) the charcoal (15.2 g) was hazel (60%), alder (20%), willow (10%) and oak (10%). Roundwood was composed of hazel (55%) and willow (5%). These deposits were described as used for the disposal of midden refuse such as cooking and hearth waste or for short-term storage of materials. Given the presence of mixed wood species and roundwood it appears that this area was utilised for the disposal of hearth waste which included some fuel debris.

FLOORING (048-SEQUAD)

The charcoal (4.6 g) from this floor layer was composed entirely of oak splinters. The oak from this context could be part of a timber frame from the wall or other structural element which was burnt *in situ*.

RUBBLY DEPOSIT (078-EAST)

The charcoal (2.0 g) was pine (50%), oak (15%), oak roundwood (5%), hazel roundwood (15%), birch (10%) and rowan roundwood (5%). This deposit was described as loose rubble with a sandy matrix. The charcoal assemblage

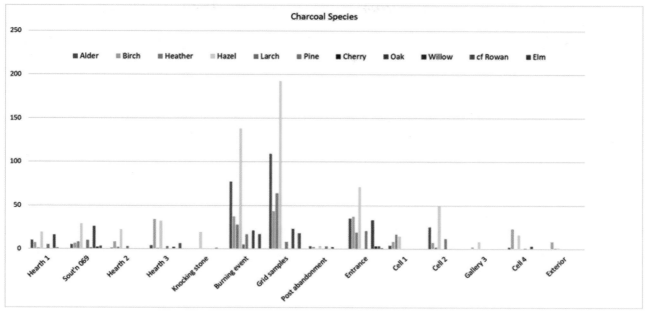

Figure 5.2.1 The charcoal species for both the principal context groups and grid samples context (042) discussed in the text

was small and composed of mixed species but there is evidence that structural or artefactual elements were present in this context. One piece of hazel roundwood had been worked and the tip of a stake was visible. Given the small size of the roundwood it is possible this belonged to an artefact such as a basket. It is possible that some fuel debris was reworked into this context after the collapse, but the hazel is likely from a structural element. It is also possible that the pine and oak originally had a structural role in this part of the broch before the floor collapsed.

LEVELLING DEPOSIT (104)

A small quantity of charcoal (0.2 g) was identified as heather roundwood (80%), birch (10%) and hazel roundwood (10%). This material is considered to be redeposited fuel debris.

Hearth 2

FLOORING (067-S BAULK), (067-SE)

The charcoal (3.1 g) from (067S Baulk) was hazel (60%) and birch (40%). The roundwood was composed of hazel (40%) and birch (30%). There were three fragments of charcoal (0.7 g) formed of two pieces of heather roundwood and one fragment of alder. These remains are redeposited fuel waste.

FLOOR/LEVELLING MATERIAL (076-SBAULK)

The charcoal (1.0 g) was hazel (60%) and birch (40%). Hazel roundwood accounted for 40% of the identified fragments. This deposit was described a dump of material and the charcoal is representative of redeposited fuel waste.

FLOOR (087-NW)

The charcoal (1.7 g) was composed entirely of hazel. Given the small size of this assemblage it was not possible to establish if these fragments formed part of a structural element or if it is from redeposited fuel waste.

FLOOR (091)

The charcoal (0.8 g) was birch (40%), hazel (40%) and pine (20%). There was one single piece of hazel roundwood. These fragments are fuel waste which were trampled into the surrounding floor.

HEARTH WASTE (094)

There was a small quantity of charcoal (0.2 g) identified as two pine and one fragment of hazel. These fragments are redeposited fuel waste.

Hearth 3 and the stone tank

FLOOR CONTEXTS (049-NE/NW), (049-NW)

In context (049NE/NW) there was 0.7 g of charcoal identified as birch (80%) and hazel (20%). A larger concentration of charcoal (14.8 g) was noted in (049NW). The species were birch (60%), hazel (20%), alder (15%) and pine (5%). Alder and hazel roundwood both formed 5% of the assemblage. The charcoal is an accumulation of fuel debris which has been trampled into these surfaces when the hearth was cleaned.

STONE TANK [052] CONTEXT (053)

A small quantity of charcoal (2.2 g) was hazel (60%), rowan (20%), alder (10%) and birch (10%). The stone tank was deliberately filled with cooking and hearth waste which included this small accumulation of fuel debris from the hearth.

FLOOR (062-SW)

The charcoal (0.7 g) was hazel (57%) and birch (43%). There was one piece of hazel roundwood. A fragment of birch had what appeared have a hole drilled through the surface. It is possible that the birch and perhaps the hazel had been worked and then later recycled as fuel debris which was reworked into this deposit. Given the small size of this assemblage it is impossible to prove if the birch was part of structural element which was destroyed *in situ*, or if it was a piece of worked wood which was recycled for fuel.

HEARTH DEPOSIT (074)

The charcoal (12.0 g) was a mix of hazel (35%), birch (30%), rowan (20%), oak (10%) and heather (5%). Roundwood was present and was composed of hazel (20%), rowan (20%) and heather (5%). These remains are fuel debris from the hearth.

FLOOR (086-NW)

The charcoal (3.3 g) was birch (50%), hazel (30%) and pine (20%). Birch roundwood formed 10%. These fragments are redeposited fuel debris.

HEARTH SURROUND (092) CONTEXT (093)

The charcoal (3.1 g) was hazel (70%) and birch (30%). The hazel roundwood was formed of 20%. This material was redeposited fuel debris.

Area around the knocking stone

DEPOSIT (045-NE QUAD)

The charcoal (17.3 g) from context (045NE Quad), around the knocking stone, was composed entirely of roundwood identified as hazel (95%) and willow (5%). It is the excavators' interpretation that the knocking stone was located within an internal compartment within the broch but that any associated superstructure had not survived. The homogeneity of the charcoal assemblage from this context suggests makes it likely that it represents a wattle screen of hazel and willow withies that was used to separate this area from the rest of the interior space.

The burning event

BURNT DEPOSITS (007A), (007C), (007E), (007F), (007G), (007H), (007I)

These samples were all collected from the scarcement ledge and were interpreted as the remains of internal fittings or structure that had carbonised *in situ*. The sampling strategy involved taking grid samples designed to identify any spatial differences in wood use or if the flooring material remained consistent within this area. The charcoal assemblage, however, was relatively small and only 100 fragments (21.2 g) were identified from across the samples. The dominant species was hazel (78%) followed by birch (12%), heather (4%), rowan (3%), alder (2%) and pine (1%).

In context (007A) the charcoal (2.1 g) was composed of hazel (70%), birch (20%) and alder (10%). Hazel roundwood formed 10%. In context (007C) the charcoal (1.2 g) was hazel (80%) and heather (20%). Hazel and heather roundwood formed 10% and 20% respectively. It was noted that these fragments were very friable and broke apart easily. The charcoal (10.3 g) was concentrated within (007E) which had hazel (80%), rowan (15%) and alder (5%). Hazel roundwood accounted for 45%. The charcoal (1.2 g) from (007F) was composed entirely of hazel. In deposit (007G) the charcoal (3.6 g) was birch (50%) and hazel (50%). Hazel roundwood formed 25%. The charcoal (2.7 g) in (007H) was formed of hazel roundwood (90%) and heather roundwood (10%). The charcoal (0.1 g) from (007I) was composed of small fragments identified as hazel (90%) and pine (10%).

These samples do contain small concentrations of mixed species, but it is unlikely they have derived from fuel debris. Instead the hazel appears to have been a major structural component in the internal superstructure of the broch. It is possible other species such as birch, heather and rowan were also used to construct this structure, though probably with a lesser role and perhaps for specific functions. Only single fragments of alder and pine were observed and these species could have had only a minimal role in the structure.

BURNT DEPOSIT (010)

The charcoal (2.9 g) was alder (90%) and hazel (10%). These fragments were noticeable friable and broke apart easily. A small hole made by a tool was observed along the edge of a piece of alder. Given the small size of the hole it is possible this was designed to hold a small pin and that the alder was part of a box or wooden container.

BURNT DEPOSIT (017)

The charcoal (7.8 g) was composed of oak splinters. This deposit of oak charcoal was sampled from wall void (015) so it seems most likely that these remains were part of a small structural element such as a post or stake which was burnt *in situ*.

BURNT DEPOSITS (020), (021)

The charcoal (5.5 g) from (020) was rowan (55%), hazel (40%) and alder (5%). Roundwood was identified as rowan (30%) and hazel (25%). In context (021) the charcoal (38.0 g) was alder (55%), hazel (35%), heather (5%) and pine (5%). Roundwood comprised hazel (30%), alder (5%), heather (5%) and pine (5%). Both spreads of charcoal were recovered from the middle of the garth along with hearth debris. Given the presence of hearth debris it is possible these charcoal fragments are fuel waste rather than remnants of structural material.

CHARCOAL DEPOSIT AGAINST INNER WALL (022) CONTEXTS (037), (038), (039)
The charcoal (0.5 g) from (037) was heather roundwood (90%) and birch (10%). In context (038) the charcoal (3.9 g) was hazel (60%) and heather (40%). Roundwood was identified as heather (40%) and hazel (35%). The charcoal (84.9 g) was concentrated in (039) and the species were alder (95%) and hazel roundwood (5%). Understanding the role of the charcoal within these deposits was complicated given the presence of large quantities of ash which indicates that much organic material was irretrievably destroyed. It is possible that some of this material is redeposited fuel waste in contexts (037) and (038) but there is evidence to suggest that the remains of wattle and turves were possibly destroyed in contexts (037) and (038) and an alder timber in (039).

BURNING DEPOSIT (041), (042-NEQ), (042-NWQ), (042-SEQ), (042-SWQ)
In context (041) the charcoal (22.6 g) was pine (75%), alder (15%), hazel (5%) and oak (5%). The pine was formed of large fragments which could have been used for lighting tapers. It is unclear if the other wood species from this context are fuel debris or structural remains. There was a single fragment of hazel (0.1 g) recovered from context (042 SEQ).

The charcoal (433.2 g) from (42-NEQ) was composed of large fragments of hazel (55%), larch (25%) and alder (20%). Roundwood was identified as hazel (55%), larch (10%) and alder (5%). The hazel and alder could be part of wattle structure. The pine could be from a structural element such as a timber, post or used as a taper.

Context (042-NWQ) had a large quantity of charcoal (773.3 g) of which 85% was identified as roundwood. The roundwood fragments were hazel (35%), alder (20%), heather (15%), rowan (10%) and birch (5%). The non-roundwood fragments were composed of alder (15%). The roundwood fragments – except for the heather – were formed of large pieces of wood. Although composed of mixed species this material is more likely to have formed a wattle screen or similar structure which was burnt *in situ* as opposed to being fuel residue.

The charcoal (185.9 g) from context (042SWQ) was dominated by roundwood which formed 90% of the assemblage. The roundwood was alder (35%), birch (35%), hazel (10%) and heather (10%). The non-roundwood pieces were alder (10%). The alder and birch were formed of large pieces or roundwood. These remains are likely from a wattle structure rather than fuel material.

ACTIVE FLOOR SURFACE (084-NW)
The charcoal (13.2 g) was birch (65%), hazel (15%), alder (10%), heather (5%) and rowan (5%). Roundwood was identified as hazel (10%) and heather (5%). There was no obvious evidence of any surviving structural elements but some fragments, such as the birch, could have been from a timber burnt *in situ*. Equally, however, these remains could have derived from fuel residue.

Post abandonment and collapse
RUBBLE DEPOSITS (005), (011) AND ABANDONMENT DEPOSIT (028)
Thirteen fragments of charcoal (1.2 g) were recovered from contexts (005), (011) and (028) relating to post-abandonment debris and the collapse of the broch. There were three fragments of alder, two birch, three hazel roundwood, three pine and two oak. The charcoal was scattered among these three contexts with no evidence of selective or deliberate disposal. Instead, these fragments are likely to be representative of redeposition of debris when the broch finally collapsed. Certainly, there is no evidence to suggest these remains were part of the structure damaged in the final conflagration or eventual collapse of the broch.

The entrance passage
CLAY DEPOSIT (083)
The charcoal (11.2 g) was hazel (50%), birch (35%) and alder (15%). The roundwood was hazel (45%) and birch (5%). There is no evidence of any structural remains, instead these are likely redeposited fuel debris which was trampled into this clay surface.

CHARCOAL DEPOSIT WITHIN ENTRANCE FROM BURNING EVENT (106)
The charcoal (53.3 g) was hazel (85%), birch (10%) and alder (5%). Roundwood was composed of hazel (40%) and alder (5%). One piece of hazel appeared to be part of a stake tip or given its small size was part of basket. It is possible that a hazel stake or basket was destroyed in this location during the burning event. The alder and birch were probably re-worked into this surface either before or after the burning event.

DESTRUCTION EVENT (113)
The charcoal (17.8 g) was hazel (55%), pine (35%) and willow (10%). This sample was collected from the

entrance to gallery 4. It is possible the hazel and willow formed part of a wattle screen used as a partition or floor section, or as a screen across the cell entrance. The pine could have derived from a structural element or a taper.

DESTRUCTION EVENT (120)

The charcoal was a mix of alder (45%), oak (30%), hazel (15%), birch (5%) and pine (5%). Roundwood was composed of hazel (10%) and birch (5%). It is possible the alder and oak were structural elements such as timbers or posts burnt during the final conflagration.

ENTRANCE PASSAGE FLOOR (121)

From the floor deposit (121) the charcoal (5.2 g) was alder (55%), hazel (35%), birch (10%) and oak (10%). There was no evidence of any structural remains within this deposit. Instead, these fragments are likely fuel debris that was trampled into this surface.

RUBBLE LAYER (153)

The charcoal assemblage (11.7 g) was a mix of heather (35%), birch (20%), hazel (20%), alder (15%), elm (5%) and pine (5%). Heather and hand hazel roundwood formed 35% and 10% of the identified fragments. This was the only part of the site from which elm was recovered. There was no evidence of any structural material. These fragments were re-worked into this rubble layer when the broch collapsed.

DEPOSIT (158)

The species (32.7 g) were oak (85%), alder (5%), birch (5%) and hazel roundwood (5%). The oak may form part of a small stake or post which was destroyed *in situ*. The other species are likely redeposited material from the above rubble layer.

DEPOSIT (161)

The charcoal (1.2 g) was heather (60%), hazel (20%), pine (15%) and birch (5%). This deposit was believed to be archaeologically secure and therefore these fragments are probably fuel debris which were trampled into this surface.

Cell 1

MIDDEN DEPOSITS (155), (159) AND (163)

From deposit (155) the charcoal (5.9 g) was composed of hazel (60%), birch (35%) and alder (5%). Hazel roundwood formed (45%) of the identified fragments. In context (159) there were two fragments of hazel along with one piece of roundwood (0.4 g). In deposit (163) the charcoal (1.1 g) was heather roundwood (85%), hazel roundwood (10%) and birch (5%). This small accumulation of charcoal is fuel debris. The heather could indicate that peat turves were selected as a fuel source. Cell 1

was evidently a designated receptacle for midden waste including food and other domestic debris. It is therefore of note that the charcoal assemblage from this area of the broch is so small. This could suggest that hearth material was not routinely disposed of within this area. However, analysis of the waterlogged samples from Cell 1 revealed the presence of large quantities of carbonised peat. It is likely that peat was a primary source of fuel with wood species having only a more marginal role.

Cell 2

The charcoal assemblage from Cell 2 was concentrated within two deposits and these are discussed in greater detail below. The rest of the charcoal fragments were scattered among the cell with no evidence of selective or deliberate disposal.

DEPOSIT (123)

The charcoal (14.6 g) from (123) was recovered alongside a large cache of cereal grain. The species were alder fragments (90%) and hazel roundwood (10%). During excavation it was hypothesised that the processed grain had been kept in some type of container to keep it in a dry condition and safe from rodent activity and other pest activities. The predominance of alder fragments around the grain raises the possibility that the caryopses were stored in an alder container until it was destroyed during the final burning event.

DEPOSIT (134)

The charcoal (25.5 g) from (134) was composed of hazel (90%) and alder (10%). Hazel and alder roundwood formed 95% of the identified fragments and these were in the north end of Cell 2. The hazel roundwood included large pieces some of which still had the bark attached and had a residue burnt on the surface. Black crispy material was noted during excavation which was localised in only this part of the cell could be the same residue adhering to some of the charcoal fragments. The charcoal could have been part of a wattle screen used to partition off sections of the cell or create shelves for additional storage.

DEPOSITS (125), (135). (136), (137), (142)

In context (135) there was a small quantity of charcoal (2.1 g) identified as pine (40%), hazel (30%), alder (20%), and birch (10%). Hazel and alder roundwood formed 30% and 10%. Context (135) had a small number of charcoal (1.5 g) fragments identified as hazel roundwood (60%), birch roundwood (20%) and pine (20%). The charcoal (0.6 g) in (136) was hazel (50%), pine (40%) and birch (10%). There was hazel roundwood (20%). In context (137) the species (4.4 g) were hazel (50%), alder (15%), birch (15%), heather (10%) and pine (10%). There was hazel (10%) and heather (10%) roundwood. In context (142) the charcoal (0.9 g) there was hazel (80%), birch (10%) and pine (10%). There was hazel roundwood (20%). The charcoal fragments in these five contexts were material introduced accidentally as components of new floor layers that were used to resurface Cell 2 or were trampled in on the feet of individuals. There is no evidence that domestic waste such as fuel debris was deliberately disposed of within this area which appears to have been kept relatively clean and well organised.

Gallery 3: the stair cell

OCCUPATION DEPOSIT (089-SW GALLERY)
A small quantity of charcoal (0.6 g) was noted in occupation deposit (089) associated with gallery 3. The species were hazel (80%) and birch (20%). These remains have derived from redeposited fuel debris.

Cell 4

FLOOR (081)
From these three contexts the charcoal totalled 7.8 g and was identified as birch (51%), hazel (36%), oak (7%), alder (4%), and pine (2%). This deposit was described as having banded, visible layers of organic material that were interpreted as flooring layers which had been continually refurbished. The charcoal could represent either fuel debris that was accidently incorporated within the flooring material or it could have been deliberately added along with the other plant material as a floor component. There is no evidence to suggest that Cell 4 was ever deliberately used to dispose of hearth waste.

The external areas

CONTEXTS (333), (335) AND (337)
The charcoal (1.8 g) totalled ten fragments that were scattered among three contexts (333), (335) and (337). The species were birch (80%), hazel (10%) and heather (10%). There was one piece of birch and heather roundwood. There was no evidence of selective or deliberate disposal, and these are redeposited fuel debris.

Discussion

Formation of the charcoal assemblage

The size of the charcoal assemblage collected from Clachtoll has been influenced by several taphonomic factors that reduced the number of fragments available for analysis. The charcoal assemblage was formed through two very distinct pathways. The first is from fragments which accumulated during the short lifetime of the broch and was dominated by fuel debris from the three successive hearths and associated floors. Regular cleaning of these

surfaces, coupled with disposal of midden material outside the broch has reduced the amount of charcoal available for study from this earlier period. The formation of the second part of the assemblage occurred during the final catastrophic burning event. The charcoal was concentrated within this final layer, but much of the organic material was reduced to ash. The charcoal from the burning event was distinct from the internal fuel debris in the presence of evidence for structural remains such as wattle, timbers, post and stakes along with a small number of artefacts, which were all destroyed *in situ*.

Species

The woodland species at Clachtoll was dominated by hazel followed by alder, birch, heather, oak, pine along with much smaller numbers of rowan, willow, larch, cherry and elm. These species, except for larch, which must represent driftwood, are native to Scotland and most would have grown in the vicinity to the broch. Hazel grows in scrub, hedgerows and woodland, alder and birch normally prefer damp habitats, oak will grow wherever the soil and climate will allow, pine is adaptable, surviving in sandy soil conditions not normally favourable for other species, while rowan is present in rocky habitats and heather is found in bogs, heaths and open woodland (Linford 2009; Stace 2010; Martynoga 2012). The recovery of only single fragments of cherry, which typically grows in hedges and woods and elm, which prefers limestone such would be found further inland, suggests that these species were either not readily available within the surrounding landscape or were not favoured for fuel or construction.

Hazel, and to a lesser extent alder, birch, heather and oak were the most economically important species used throughout the occupation of the broch. This stability within the wood economy is not surprising as the excavated deposits evidently represent a relatively short period, perhaps less than 50 years. As such, any major changes in either cultural preferences in wood selection or in the surrounding landscape are unlikely to register in this charcoal assemblage, which accumulated too rapidly.

The composition of the charcoal assemblages from Clachtoll, and from Spilt Rock, Clashnessie Dun and from Loch na Clais crannog (see Chapter 9) are similar to those previously reported from broch excavations at Nybster, Thrumster, Pool, Cnip, Howe and Crosskirk (Robertson in prep; Bond 2007a, 200–1; Church and Cressey 2006, 185; Dickson 1994, 133; Dickson and Dickson 1984, 150). At these sites, particularly at the island communities, wood was generally in limited supply. When it was available, it was a useful resource and was used in multiple roles such as for fuel, building and making artefacts. The recurrence of the same wood species from the mainland sites indicates that the character of woodland cover in the north-east and north-west of Iron Age Scotland did not significantly differ. Certainly, mainland communities had access to a wide range of wood resources which either grew in the surrounding landscape or were gathered as drift or bog wood.

Spatial deposition

The charcoal assemblage collected from the hearths and surrounding floors mostly represents fuel debris. The charcoal component of these deposits was relatively small, probably because the hearths were regularly cleaned and the debris disposed of outside the broch, leaving behind only trace amounts that were subsequently trampled into the surrounding floors. It is also possible that wood was not the most important source of fuel utilised by the Clachtoll population. In the hearth deposits fragments of charred peat along with some heather roundwood were observed. It is probable that turves were used within the hearths as a fuel source.

The largest concentration of charcoal was recovered from the burning event and entrance samples. The presence of a fine ash in many of the bulk samples suggests that some organic material was reduced to ash during the final conflagration. Nonetheless, it is clear from the surviving charcoal that the wood species used in the final occupation of the broch and from the entranceway remained consistent with the earlier phases. In both the burning event and from the entrance deposits there is evidence for both the presence of fuel debris and structural elements that were destroyed *in situ*.

Structural elements

Those species favoured for construction were alder, birch, heather, hazel, willow, rowan, oak and possibly larch. The structural elements comprised wattle screens and possible roofing sections, timbers, posts and stakes that were mostly preserved in the final burning event layers, although a smaller number were noted in the lower phases.

The strongest evidence for the presence of wattle/flooring/roofing sections was observed in the final catastrophic burning layers (042NE), (042NW) and (042SW) that contained large pieces of hazel roundwood. The wattle from the final burning event belonged to floor or roof sections destroyed *in situ* that appear to have crashed down onto the floor below. Analysis of the charcoal assemblage also indicated that specific areas within the broch had been sectioned off using wood partitions. From around the knocking stone used to process cereal grain a small quantity of hazel and willow roundwood was recovered. These roundwood pieces were possibly used to construct a wattle screen to separate this cereal processing area

from other parts of the broch. Within Cell 2 there was evidence of a hazel wattle screen that had been used either to subdivide this area into multiple sections or was employed as a shelf for additional storage. Other sources of wood such as alder, birch, heather, willow and rowan were incorporated into some of these wattle floor/roofs/screens but only ever as a minor component.

Species such as alder, oak and possibly larch tended to be reserved for larger building items such as timbers and posts. The remains of oak posts or stakes were recovered from the souterrain [069] floor deposit (048SEQ), burning deposit (017) and context (158) from the entrance passageway. An alder structural element from the final catastrophic burning event was observed in context (039) that was sampled from the inner wall deposit (022). There was also a large fragment of larch noted in burning deposit (042NE) which may have belonged to a structural element rather than from a taper.

It is likely that heather was a component of turves used for roof and wall construction. Heather is known to have been used to create baskets (Dickson 1994, 137) but there was no surviving evidence at Clachtoll that the heather had been woven.

The carbonised artefacts

A possible artefact was noted in context (123) in Cell 2. A large cache of loose cereal had been stored in this location and during excavation it was surmised that the grain was originally stored in some form of container or bag which would have prevented dispersal. The grain was also noticeably well-preserved, further suggesting that a container took the initial brunt of the fire which consumed it. Surrounding the grain was a concentration of alder charcoal fragments, many of them with smooth flat surfaces. It is possible that the barley was stored in an alder container, possibly a bowl or box. The remains of a carbonised alder container (possibly stave-built) were found in similar circumstances in the broch at Howe, amidst a deposit of barley grain on the floor of the broch tower (Dickson 1994, 127, 133). A waterlogged fragment of an unfinished bowl of alder wood was also found in context (049) (Crone, Section 4.11).

There were two small hazel stake tips disposed of within souterrain [069] context (078 East) and context (106) from the entrance. Given the very small dimension of the withy, these two pieces may have come from baskets rather than structural elements. In context (010) from the final burning event there was a piece of alder which had a small circular hole through the surface. This hole is very small and would have been large enough to hold a pin but nothing more structurally substantial. The presence of a small pin hole is more suggestive of an artefact such as a box or container rather than a larger structural element.

Tapers

The charred pine fragments may well be the remains of the pine tapers which dominate the waterlogged wood assemblage, several of which are partially charred. All the charred fragments fall within the size range of the water-logged tapers (see Table 5.3.1). Two splinters of larch were also identified within the waterlogged wood assemblage and both had signs of *teredo* boreholes confirming the presence of driftwood (Crone, Section 4.11). The single piece of larch charcoal was much larger than the tapers, but it might have been gathered from the shore, either to make tapers or for structural purposes.

Wood fuel

Analysis of the assemblage indicates that all wood species were used for fuel throughout the existence of the broch. Hazel, alder, birch, heather and, to a much lesser extent, the other species were all employed as a fuel source. This pattern of wood usage remained constant with no evidence of change. Species such as oak and larch were probably selected primarily for construction whereas pine was preferred for tapers and only later recycled for fuel when no longer required.

Other fuel materials

The presence of heather indicates that turves were brought to the broch and it is likely they were used in multiple roles, one of which was for fuel. It was not uncommon for turves used as a building material to be later recycled as a fuel source or scattered on agricultural fields as a fertilizer (Dickson 1994, 134). Small pieces of carbonised peat were recovered from all phases of occupation particularly from the contexts surrounding the hearths and from the midden in Cell 1. This suggests turves and peat were routinely burnt as a fuel source. Peat tends to reduce more readily to ash and may be underrepresented within the carbonised fuel assemblage. Given the available evidence it appears that turves alongside wood were burnt as a fuel source throughout the use of this site. One of the advantages of peat fires to the inhabitants of Clachtoll broch would be to smoke food items such as fish and meat over a slow burning fire which could then be stored over winter (Dickson 1994, 137).

Other potential sources of fuel were seaweed, animal dung, byre and crop processing waste. A small number of seaweed fragments were noted in the carbonised macroplant assemblage, but these were only a minor component. There was no conclusive evidence for the presence of charred animal dung or byre waste in any of the hearths, associated floor and midden deposits. Small numbers of cereal and processing waste were collected from the lower deposits but not in significant numbers. Instead, the macroplant assemblage was concentrated in the upper occupation contexts. Based on the available evidence it appears that seaweed may have been used on occasion as a fuel source, but it was never an important resource. There was no evidence to suggest that animal dung or byre waste was routinely burnt in the hearths. The presence of the cereal waste probably derived from cooking debris, but if this was burnt deliberately its role as a fuel or kindling material was minimal. This contrasts with many island Iron Age settlements such as Pool, Sanday where seaweed and dung were regularly employed as fuel (Bond 2007, 200–1). An explanation is that Clachtoll, situated on the mainland, had greater access to woodland resources not easily available to the island communities who were more dependent on recycling other burnable materials including dung and byre waste.

Conclusion

The charcoal assemblage demonstrates that the wood species used at Clachtoll remained constant throughout the history of this site. Wood had several economic roles within this economy which included providing material for fuel, building, artefacts and as a light source. Throughout the use of this broch, hazel was the most popular wood species followed by alder, birch, heather, oak, pine with rowan, willow, larch, cherry and elm having a much more secondary role. Woodland when available was an important resource within this economy and was accessible from the surrounding landscape and shore. Clachtoll broch was in use for a relatively short period of time but during its existence there were no significant changes in how woodland resources were exploited.

5.3 Waterlogged macroplant remains

Jackaline Robertson

Introduction

During excavation two contexts (145) and (159) were recorded as waterlogged. These were both collected from Cell 1 where the presence of wood fragments and animal hair were noted. Cell 1 was used as a midden during the later occupation of the broch and the sediments within were damp and greasy; these conditions allowed for the survival of some ecofacts preserved in anaerobic conditions.

Methodology

A subsample of 2.5 kg was extracted from each context and processed by hand (*cf.* Kenward, Hall and Jones 1980). After an initial assessment of the washovers it became obvious that the upper context (145) had mostly dried out prior to excavation and to maximise recovery of ecofact remains the sample volume was increased to 5 kg. The sediments collected from Cell 1 were noticeably dark and oily in texture which differed from the other bulk samples collected from the rest of the broch. All plant macrofossils were examined at magnifications of ×10 and up to ×450 where necessary to aid identification. All identifications were confirmed using modern reference material and seed atlases stored at AOC Archaeology Group Edinburgh (Cappers, Bekker and Jans 2006; Jacomet 2006).

Results

The waterlogged macroplant assemblage is summarised in Table 5.3.1. The assemblage from context (145) was composed of a small quantity of waterlogged and carbonised macroplants. Context (145) which overlay (159) had dried out to a much greater extent probably because it was exposed for longer. Preservation of these remains ranged from mostly poor to adequate. This is probably because the upper deposit has been undermined by fluctuations in the moisture content of Cell

Table 5.3.1 The waterlogged macroplant from Cell 1

Phase			Cell 1	Cell 1
Context			145	159
Sample Vol (Kg)			5	2.5
% Sorted			100	100
Species	Name	Plant part		
Hordeum vulgare L.	Hulled barley	Charred caryopsis/es	1	
Cerealia sp.	Cereal	Charred caryopsis/es	1	
Wild Food				
Corylus avellana L.	Hazel nut	Nutshell frg(s)	*	**
Economically useful plants				
Calluna vulgaris L.	Heather	Leaves(s)		**
Pteridium aquilinum L.	Bracken	Pinnule/Fronds frg(s)		***
Woodland				
Bark	Bark	Bark frags	*	
Bud	Bud	Bud(s) and/or bud-scale(s)		*
Leaf	Leaf	Leaf frags		*
Wood	Wood	Fragment(s)	*	***
Weed Taxa				
Polygonum sp.	Knotweed	Fruit(s)		*
Potentilla erecta L.	Tormentil	Fruit(s)		*
Potentilla sp.	Cinquefoils	Fruits(s)		*
Sonchus asper L.	Prickly Sowthistle	Fruits(s)		*
Stem	Stem	Stem(s)		***
Unknown	Indet	Fruit/Seed		*
Moss				
Sphagnum sp.		Leaves/stems	*	***
Moss sp.		Leaves/stems	*	***
Fuel				
Charcoal		Frag(s)	***	*
Peat		Charred frag(s)	****	***
Peat		Compact peat type material		**
Peat		Frag(s)	***	****
Other				
Animal hair		Fiber(s)		*

Key: *=<10, **=10-29, ***=29-100, ****=>100, unless stated in table all plant parts are preserved through waterlogging

1 which has allowed material to dry out and ultimately decompose. The waterlogged plant taxa were formed of a small number of hazelnut shell, pieces of wood, bark and *sphagnum* sp moss. There were also large inclusions of unburnt peat. The carbonised remains were two cereal caryopses of which one was identified as hulled barley. The only other charred remains were fragments of peat and charcoal.

From the lower deposit (159) a much larger number and variety of waterlogged plants were recorded. Preservation of the waterlogged species was noticeably better when compared to the finds from the upper context (145). Deposit (159) was sealed by the upper layers and changes in the environmental changes within Cell 1 would not have had such an adverse impact on the ecofact material present in the lower deposit. The only edible species were a small number of hazelnut shells. Woodland material was composed of large inclusions of wood fragments alongside a much smaller quantity of leaves and buds. There were also large concentrations of bracken, heather, plant stems, peat and moss some of which was identified as *Sphagnum* sp. The weeds were smaller in number and were knotweed, tormentil, cinquefoils and prickly sowthistle. A few fragments of animal hair were also noted. The only carbonised remains were a small quantity of charcoal.

Discussion

Food remains

The food remains were composed of cereal and hazelnut shell which were disposed of in small quantities within the midden in Cell 1.

Building material

The uncharred fragments of peat could have been intended for fuel or were used as building components. The turves were composed primarily of peat and heather and it is probable these were used to construct roofing and flooring layers. When these were no longer required or needed to be replaced at least some of them were disposed of within Cell 1 and allowed to decompose *in situ*.

Given the large quantity of bracken it is probable this material was deliberately collected for use as flooring, bedding, insulation or roofing. None of the bracken fragments were carbonized so it is unlikely they have derived from fuel debris.

Fuel

Given the large quantity of burnt peat along with some charcoal it appears that both these resources were regularly used to fuel the three hearths which were constructed during the lifetime of this broch. Turves that were imported to Clachtoll to be used as a building material were likely recycled for fuel then later disposed of within Cell 1 alongside other hearth and midden waste.

Woodland material

The wood fragments, while not obviously worked or burnt were disposed of in the midden along with other domestic debris. None of the leaves, bark and buds were charred so this material is unlikely to have been used for fuel. Instead, these remains were an accidental inclusion of the wood which was deliberately transported to the broch to be used in construction and for fuel. The leaves, bark and buds would have been stripped from the wood and disposed of within Cell 1.

Weeds

The weed species are intrusive and there are several routes by which they could have accumulated within Cell 1. These species are unlikely to be food waste and it is more probable they were growing in the surrounding landscape and were introduced to the broch as contaminants of the cultivated crops, peat turves and woodland taxa.

Moss

Moss could have been imported to Clachtoll as a component of the turves or was growing on tree bark. Moss can also have a variety of economic purposes. It can be used as toilet paper, packing, insulation or as medicine. There is no substantial evidence to claim that moss had any specific role within this economy. It is also possible that the damp environmental conditions in Cell 1 encouraged the presence of this species within Cell 1.

Conclusion

The ecofacts recovered from Cell 1 have accumulated through the deliberate disposal of domestic food waste, fuel debris and building materials. The weeds are an accidental inclusion brought to the site as a byproduct of other economically important plant resources. The waterlogged plant assemblage while small provided some evidence for both the use and disposal of food, building resources and fuel at Clachtoll.

5.4 Animal bone

Jackaline Robertson

Introduction

A total of 7,763 animal bone fragments were analysed from the excavation at Clachtoll Broch. While the assemblage is small when compared other contemporary sites in the Highlands and Islands, it still provided an excellent opportunity to understand the economic role of both the domestic and wild species at the site. The bone was recovered from context groups sampled from throughout the short period of occupation, most of which are believed to be archaeologically secure. The assemblage had accumulated through a variety of taphonomic pathways such as from the disposal of butchery waste, domestic food debris, animal carcasses buried in a semi-articulated condition and bone that was damaged in the final conflagration event. The main aim of this study was to analyse the subsistence strategies practised at Clachtoll through the management of animal resources and how this compares to other similar sites in the Highlands and Islands of Scotland.

Methodology

The animal bone was collected both by hand and from the bulk samples. Given the small size of the assemblage all contexts from which bone was recovered were analysed. Some bone fragments extracted from the processed bulk samples were smaller than 10 mm and these were semi-quantified rather than fully counted. The faunal remains were washed then air dried prior to analysis. The assemblage was identified to element and species with the aid of skeletal atlases and the reference collection stored at AOC Archaeology Group, Edinburgh (Schmid 1972; Hillson 1986; Hillson 1992).

Where an element could not be identified it was instead described as large mammal (horse/cattle/red deer), medium mammal (sheep/goat/pig) or small mammal (dog/cat/rodent). No attempt was made to identify the bulk of the ribs and vertebrae to species; instead, these were described as L/M, M/M or S/M where appropriate. Separating sheep and goat bones followed Boessneck (1969) and Payne (1985). When analysing the assemblage, the following criteria were recorded: context group, context, feature, element, species, side, fusion, age, fragmentation, size and evidence of staining on the bone surface. These results are reported in full in the animal bone catalogue, which is stored in the site archive.

Epiphyseal fusion, tooth eruption and wear were assessed to establish the age of the individual. The proximal, distal and shaft areas of each fragment were recorded to determine the level of fragmentation within the assemblage (Dobney and Rielly 1988). Assessing the level of staining used the following method: no staining was rated "0"; some staining affecting less than 25% of the bone surface was designated as "1"; 25–50% surface staining was "2"; while 50–75% was described as 3" and greater than 75% was rated as "4". A four-point system was used to assess preservation with excellent, good, adequate and

poor recorded where appropriate. The assemblage was also examined for butchery marks, pathologies, bone working, burning and carnivore gnawing. Any bone found to be worked was not included in this report and catalogue but was instead given to the finds specialist to be included within the relevant artefact analysis. Only those bones found to be intact were measured (Von Den Driesch 1976).

The assemblage was quantified using number of identifiable specimens (NISP), minimum number of individuals (MNI) and minimum number of elements (MNE). It is noted that all three systems have recognised drawbacks as there is no standardised methodology for calculating these figures and the results can vary accordingly within the same assemblage (Grayson 1984; Lambacher *et al.* 2016). It is however hoped that by using these techniques in conjunction with each other a more accurate interpretation of the assemblage and how species were exploited at Clachtoll broch may emerge.

The NISP was a count of all the fragments from each taxon from all context groups. These calculations include the counts for the large, medium, small and indeterminate mammals. The NISP was recorded by context group to help identify any surviving patterns in deposition of material.

Accurately formulating the MNI figures proved problematic. The archaeological stratigraphy of the three hearths and the surrounding floors are relatively secure but the accumulation of animal remains was a rapid process and it is probable that midden waste especially within Cell 1 accrued over a longer period of occupation. To not artificially inflate these figures, the MNI was analysed as a single-phase assemblage. When calculating MNI the state of fusion and presence of neonates was considered and were calculated separately.

The MNE was recorded for the main domesticates cattle, sheep/goat and pig. The results were tabulated by context group to identify any surviving patterns in how bone was disposed of. Skeletal elements included within these calculations was based on those with surviving diagnostic zones such as the proximal and distal epiphysis and excluded multiple fragments that may have derived from a single bone. In a small number of instances long bone shafts minus the epiphyses were included, but only if it was obvious that they represented single entities.

The sheep/goat burial from Cell 1 was not identified to skeletal element and these results are not included within the NISP or MNE but were added to the MNI.

Preservation and taphonomy

Preservation of the animal bone was variable due to several taphonomic factors, the main two being soil conditions and exposure to heat. The sediments within the broch were mostly described as sandy whereas others, specifically from around Hearth 2 and in Cell 1, were noticeably damp or greasy, resulting in a semi-anaerobic environment. The damp soil conditions which existed around Hearth 2 proved to be generally beneficial for the recovery of bone. In Cell 1, the greasy soil conditions were more detrimental, and several skeletal elements were badly degraded, which at times hindered further analysis.

Burnt bone was present in all context groups but the majority derived from two different sources of activity, which affected the level of preservation. The burnt bone from the lower contexts tended to originate from the hearths. These represented food and cooking debris not fully removed during cleaning of the three hearths that was subsequently trampled into the surrounding floor surfaces. The bone burnt during the final conflagration event was generally better preserved but only where it had been protected from structural detritus crashing directly on top of it during the final collapse of the broch.

The small size of the surviving animal bone assemblage was likely influenced by how refuse was primarily disposed of. It is logical to assume that some domestic debris including butchered carcasses, cooking and hearth waste were permanently disposed of by throwing them directly over the cliff edge, or into middens located outside the vicinity of the excavated area. It is also possible that cuts of meat were either transported to the broch or were removed to a separate location to be consumed elsewhere. This would have an adverse effect on the size of the surviving assemblage since the material left could represent only a small percentage of the actual activities that took place in this location. The one major advantage the animal bone assemblage from Clachtoll broch has, is that these deposits were largely left undisturbed since the final conflagration event and, while small, is archaeologically secure.

Results

A total of 7,763 fragments (22.5 kg) were analysed from 94 samples. The bone was collected from all context groups within the broch described as floors associated with Hearth 1, Hearth 2, Hearth 3, as well as from the souterrain, the knocking stone, the burning event, the post abandonment and collapse layers, the entrance passageway, Cell 1, Cell 2, cell 3 and Cell 4. A small number of bone fragments were also collected from unstratified contexts.

The domestic species were cattle (*Bos taurus*), sheep (*Ovis aries*), sheep/goat (*Ovis aries/Capra*) and pig (*Sus domesticus*). The wild species were red deer (*Cervus elaphus*), whale/dolphin/porpoise (*Cetaceans*), grey seal (*Halichoerus grypus*) and seal (*Phocidae*). These remains mostly accumulated through the disposal of butchery and food waste in the middens and floor deposits which surrounded the three sequential hearths and from the final burning event. There were also several animal carcasses, of which two had been deliberately buried in a semi-articulated condition. It is unclear if the remains of the third individual within Cell 1 derived from a deliberate burial or represented the remains of an animal that died *in situ*.

A small number of rabbit (*Oryctolagus cuniculus*) and rodent (*Rattus/Mus* sp) bones were observed. The rabbit bones are intrusive as this species was believed to have first been introduced to England by the Normans before later colonising the rest of the British Isles (Kitchener 1998, 83). It was noted during excavation that several recent rabbit burrows were in close proximity to the broch and it is logical to assume that some of these individuals burrowed into the archaeological deposits.

Understanding the taphonomy of the rodent bones was more complex. A number of these individuals are potentially modern as they too tend to burrow into archaeological deposits. However, a small number of the rodent bones from the burning event and earlier deposits were burnt, suggesting that they were contemporary with the inhabitation of the site. The absence of any rodent skulls and well-preserved mandibles made it impossible to identify the rodents to species.

The results are summarised below by context group.

Hearth 1 and the early floors

The bone assemblage from Hearth 1 was small and totalled 235 fragments (52.7 g) recovered entirely from five bulk samples. Two deposits were described as a drain (100-Drain) and (100-North) and three from floor layers (111), (118 central) and (124). There was no evidence of any butchery, pathologies' or animal gnawing in this context group.

STONE DRAIN [059] CONTEXTS (100 DRAIN), (100 NORTH)

A total of 33 burnt bone fragments (3.9 g) all described as I/M were noted in (100 Drain) along with one rodent molar (0.01 g) in (100 North). The burnt fragments are food refuse which have been reworked into this feature when the hearth was cleaned. Given the archaeological security of these deposits it is likely the rodent molar is contemporary with the occupation of the broch.

FLOORS (111), (118 CENTRAL) AND (124)

Context (111) had the largest concentration of bone recovered from the earliest deposits. The bone was composed of 173 fragments (17.8 g) of which only a rodent rib was identifiable. The rest of the assemblage was described as L/M (2), M/M (8) and I/M (162). Preservation of these remains was mostly poor to adequate; none were larger than 50 mm and 131 fragments had been burnt. The rodent rib that was unburnt is likely from an animal that died within the broch and was subsequently incorporated into the flooring.

From context (118) there were 24 fragments (30.0 g) and the species were cattle (1), L/M (5), M/M (3) and I/M (15). Preservation of these fragments ranged from mostly poor to adequate and eight had been burnt. There were four fragments (1.0 g) noted in (124) identified as L/M (1), M/M (1) and I/M (2). All four fragments had been calcified and preservation was generally poor except for the M/M foot bone which was noticeably better preserved.

The bone from the three floor deposits had accumulated from the overspill of debris from the hearth which was subsequently trampled into the floor. The absence of larger skeletal elements in these contexts suggests that hearth and cooking waste was routinely removed whereas smaller fragments were overlooked and were frequently reworked into these surfaces.

The souterrain [069]

The assemblage from the souterrain structure numbered 1,393 fragments (4.4 kg) and was retrieved from contexts described as a midden (047), floor deposit (048), and loose rubble from a possible structural collapse (078).

Midden (047)

A total of 849 (3,489.6 g) fragments were recovered from three deposits located within the midden. A total of 160 fragments (1,769.2 g) were noted in (047), with a further 138 (53.8 g) in (047SBaulk) and 551 (1,666.6 g) in (047SE). The species were cattle (47), sheep/goat (17), pig (5), rabbit (4), rodent (7), cetacean (90), seal (1), L/M (326), M/M (106), S/M (4) and I/M (242). Preservation of these remains ranged from mostly poor to adequate with a smaller number recorded as good to excellent. Cattle were present in all three samples whereas sheep/goat and pig were recorded in (047) and (047SE). The cetacean bones were concentrated in (047SE) which had 60 fragments compared to 30 in (047). A single seal bone was present in (047SE).

Rabbit was recovered from (047) and (047SE) and rodent from (047SBaulk), indicating some level of post-abandonment disturbance by burrowing animals. Four bones from (047) and five from (047SE) had been butchered. The butchery marks were composed of marrow cracking and skinning marks. There was no evidence of any pathologies or animal gnawing. A total of 322 fragments had been burnt which included 68 pieces of cetacean bone. This material accumulated through the deliberate disposal of butchery waste, food refuse and possible fuel debris. It is likely that given the high oil content present in cetacean bones these could have been used firstly as a food source, then recycled

as a fuel source within the hearths. The rabbit bones are intrusive whereas the rodents may be contemporary with the occupation of the broch.

Floor (048)

Two samples from flooring (048) were assessed. The bone from this floor was concentrated within (048) which had 162 fragments (342.3 g) compared to 118 fragments (7.7 g) in (048SEQ). The species from (048) were cattle (20), sheep/goat (5), pig (1), L/M (74), M/M (42) and I/M (20). Preservation ranged from mostly poor to excellent. The identifiable elements were dominated by loose teeth and foot bones along with a smaller number of ribs and long bone shafts. This material is probably butchery waste along with some domestic food residue. The finds from (048SEQ) were all poorly preserved and described as cattle tooth fragments (9), rodent incisor (1) and I/M (108). From this deposit 117 fragments had been burnt at a relatively low temperature suggesting that these remains are likely food waste from the hearth which were accidently trampled into the surrounding surface. The only fragment which was not burnt was the rodent incisor.

Rubble from collapse (078)

A total of 163 fragments (560.6 g) were recovered from (078). The species from (078) were cattle (12), sheep/goat (3), pig (3), cetacean (11), seal (9), L/M (32), M/M (90), S/M (2) and I/M (1). The skeletal elements were a mix of loose teeth, foot bones along with a smaller number of skull fragments, ribs and vertebrae. Of note was the presence of several seal phalanges which appear to have been deposited in a semi-articulated condition. A single shallow skinning mark was observed on a M/M rib. Burnt bone formed 114 fragments which included some of the cattle, sheep/goat, pig and seal bones. The cetacean bones were all charred.

From (078East) there were 101 fragments (9.0 g) identified as rodent (11), L/M (2), M/M (2) and I/M (86). Of these 71 fragments had been burnt including a rodent mandible. There was no evidence of any pathologies or animal gnawing on any of the fragments from these two contexts. These remains likely represent a mix of butchery waste, food debris, hearth material and possible fuel residue.

Deposits associated with Hearth 2

There were 530 bones (1027.6 g) present in nine contexts described as floors (067), (067Sbaulk), (067SE), (076Sbaulk), (087), (087NW), (091 Central) and hearth deposits (094) and (094 Central).

Floor (067)

Three samples were analysed from this floor recorded as (064), (67SBaulk) and (067SE) and 184 fragments of bone

(238.7 g) were noted. The species in (064) were cattle (7), sheep/goat (1), pig (4), cetacean (2), seal (2), L/M (11), M/M (41), S/M (1) and I/M (8). Preservation ranged from mostly poor to good. The pig remains included the first and second phalanges which appear to be articulated. A total of 43 fragments were burnt and this included a cattle molar, the pig phalanges, the cetacean fragments, and seal canines. In (67SBaulk) there were 31 rodent bones from a semi-articulated individual along with 38 fragments described as I/M of which 26 had been burnt. Preservation of the rodent remains was typically good whereas the other fragments were recorded as poor. From (067SE) the species were cattle (12), sheep/goat (1), rodent (1), L/M (4) and I/M (20). Preservation of these fragments was mostly poor; 21 fragments had been burnt including one of the cattle molars. There was no evidence of any butchery marks or pathologies. These remains are interpreted as food refuse and hearth waste spilled during cleaning that was subsequently trampled into the floor surface.

Floor (087) and (087NW)
A total of 83 fragments (739.3 g) were noted in (087) and a further 45 (11.4 g) in (87NW). The species were sheep (81), M/M (43), S/M (3) and I/M (1). Preservation ranged from poor to excellent. During excavation of this floor layer the semi-articulated remains of a single sheep were recorded and these two samples were excavated in the belief that one individual was present. Analysis of these remains in laboratory conditions revealed that there were two individuals of which one survived in a more articulated condition. The individual that was recognised in the field was composed of a fragmented skull, maxilla, mandible, hyoid, vertebra, ribs, scapula, humeri, radius, ulna, pelvis, femur, tibia, metapodials, calcaneum and a carpal. The axis and atlas were missing but these could have been overlooked during excavation. There were no phalanges present and it is likely these were removed prior to the carcass being deposited. The surviving skeletal elements from the second animal were composed of humeri, pelvis, femur and tibia. Butchery marks were noted on 13 bones belonging to the sheep burials; five ribs, two thoracic vertebrae, one lumbar vertebra, a radius/ulna and the pelvis. The butchery marks were mostly formed of shallow cut marks which are consistent with skinning although there is evidence of a deeper chop mark on the pelvis. There were signs of possible pathologies noted on a femur and metacarpal. Four sheep bones had been partly burnt but only at a low temperature and a further 49 fragments described as M/M were also charred. A single sheep rib appeared to have been gnawed by a small mammal such as a cat or a rodent. Several skeletal elements had evidence of a black pitch substance adhering to their surfaces. The nature of this substance was not clear, but it is likely

to have been spilled or splashed from the hearth rather than being deliberately applied. These two animals were deliberately deposited in this area within the broch.

Floor (091 Central)
There were 100 I/M poorly preserved fragments (6.5 g) from floor (091), of which 50 had been burnt. There was no other evidence of bone modification. These fragments are likely overspill from the hearth which was trampled into the surrounding floor surface.

Deposit (094)
There were two burnt fragments (1.9 g) from context (094), of which one was identified as a pig canine and the other was a L/M carpal that was chopped in two. The bone from (094Central) totalled 104 burnt fragments (19.1g) recorded M/M (4) and I/M (100). This material is interpreted as food debris, over spilling from the hearth.

Hearth 3 and the stone tank
A total of 1383 fragments (3,128.6 g) were recovered from floor (049), stone tank (053), floor (062), hearth (074), peat ash (085), floor (086), levelling deposit (090) and hearth surface (093).

Floor (049)
The bone numbered 446 fragments (1,469.9 g) and was concentrated within context (049) which had 240 (1450.5g) with a further 31 (0.7 g) in (49 NE/NW) and 175 (18.7 g) in (049NW). The species in context (049) were cattle (30), sheep/goat (7), pig (3), red deer (1), seal (5), L/M (127), M/M (65) and S/M (2). Preservation ranged from poor to excellent. There were nine butchered bones which consisted mostly of skinning marks except for a cattle hyoid which had been cut multiple times to remove it. A M/M rib had been fractured but there was evidence of healing. The bone in (049 NE/NW) was identified as L/M (1) and I/M (30) and 18 of the I/M fragments were burnt. In context (049NW) the species were M/M (4) and I/M (171) of which 79 I/M fragments were burnt. The bone is a mix of butchered and domestic food waste disposed of within this floor surface.

Stone tank (053)
A total of 350 fragments (491 g) were recovered from context (053). From (053) there were 98 fragments (453.1g) and the species were cattle (11), sheep/goat (6), pig (1), grey seal (1), L/M (67), M/M (10) and S/M (2). Preservation ranged from poor to good. A sheep/goat metatarsal had been marrow cracked and three M/M ribs were burnt. There were 252 fragments (37.9 g) in context (053NWQ). The species were pig (1), rodent

(10), L/M (9), M/M (25) and I/M (207). The burnt bone was composed of 120 fragments including the pig molar. The bone from the stone tank is a dump of redeposited butchery and food waste.

FLOOR (062)

From context (062) the bone numbered 155 fragments (1,092.1 g) were identified as cattle (12), sheep/goat (2), pig (1), red deer (2), rodent (1), cetacean (1), seal (3), L/M (80), M/M (52) and I/M (1). Preservation of these fragments ranged from poor to good. Six bones had been butchered. These were two red deer metapodials and a L/M long bone which were marrow cracked and three ribs with shallow skinning marks. One seal rib appeared to have suffered a break but there was some evidence of healing. Another L/M rib had signs of animal gnawing. A total of 19 bones had been burnt. A further nine fragments of I/M bone (1.8 g) were recovered from (062SW) of which six had been burnt. These remains derived from butchery waste along with inclusions of domestic food debris that were reworked into this floor layer.

HEARTH DEBRIS (074)

The bone from (074) totalled eight fragments (33.1 g) and preservation ranged from mostly poor to adequate. The species were sheep/goat (2), L/M (5) and M/M (1). The sheep/goat metatarsal and two L/M fragments had been burnt. From (074Central) there were 212 fragments (23.2 g) identified as cattle (9), M/M (3) and I/M (200). Preservation of these fragments was generally poor and 100 fragments had been burnt. These remains are domestic food debris which is overspill from the hearth surfaces.

PEAT ASH (085)

The bone totalled 22 burnt fragments (0.6 g) recorded as I/M which were all smaller than 10 mm and poorly preserved. These remains were disposed of alongside the peat ash.

FLOOR (086)

There were 26 fragments of poorly preserved I/M burnt bone (1.0 g). These fragments are redeposited food refuse which were trampled into this surface.

LEVELLING DEPOSIT (090)

The bone accounted for 24 poorly preserved I/M burnt fragments (0.6 g) which had been trampled into this levelling deposit.

HEARTH SURFACE (093)

There were 131 fragments (15.3 g) identified as cattle (1), L/M (3), M/M (4) and I/M (123). The cattle molar

preservation was excellent whereas the rest of the assemblage were recorded as poor. A total of 33 fragments had been burnt. This material is considered to represent food and cooking debris, some of which is overspill from the hearth surface.

The knocking stone

The long bone shaft of a rodent (0.1 g) was retrieved from the carbonised grain deposit (045), found within the knocking stone. The shaft was poorly preserved and had been completely calcified. This bone was likely burnt during the final conflagration event along with the cereal caryopses which were also stored within the knocking stone. The rodent bone was probably from an animal that died in proximity to the stored grain and was accidently incorporated into the cereal caryopses.

The burning event

The greatest concentration of animal bone was recovered from the features associated with the burning event. The assemblage totalled 2,290 fragments (3,574.3 g) collected from 19 contexts. These were the sub-contexts of the burning event (042) (see above): (007D), (007E), (007F), (007G), (007I), (010), burnt material (018), (019), (035), (037), (038), burnt deposits (041), (042), (042NEQ), (042NWQ), (042SEQ), (042SWQ) and ash from the destruction of the broch (061SWQ).

BURNING LAYERS (007) AND (010)

These deposits are believed to belong to internal structures within the broch that were destroyed during the major conflagration event. A total of 319 fragments (14.2 g) were scattered among deposits (007) and (010) with no evidence of selective or deliberate disposal. Only two fragments were identified and these were a fragmented cattle molar (4) from context (007G) and a M/M rib (1) in (007D).

The rest of the fragments were designated as M/M (17) and I/M (298) which were scattered among (007D), (007E), (007F), (007G), (007I) and (010). Apart from the M/M rib which was adequately preserved the rest were all poor. This was due to taphonomic issues including exposure to heat and the effects of crushing as the broch walls collapsed. The burnt fragments numbered 301 and none of these exceeded 50 mm in size. There was no evidence of any butchery marks, pathologies or animal gnawing.

BURNT LAYERS (018), (019), (035), (037) AND (038)

A total of 116 fragments (37.7 g) were present in contexts (018), (019), (035), (037) and (038). From context (018) there were nine I/M burnt fragments (0.2 g) all poorly preserved. In deposits (019) and (037) there was one burnt M/M fragment (0.8 g) and one L/M (3.7 g) in each context respectively. In (035) there were 55 burnt fragments (15.2 g) described as L/M (9) and I/M (46). From context (038) there were 50 fragments (17.8 g) and preservation ranged from poor to good. The species were sheep/goat (5), L/M (2), M/M (4) and I/M (39). Forty-one fragments were burnt and these were L/M (2) and I/M (39). The sheep/goat skeletal elements were composed of a scapula, humerus, ulna, tibia and metacarpal. None of these fragments were fused at time of death. Given the condition of these elements it is possible these belong a semi-articulated sheep/goat foetus. The relatively good preservation of these finds suggests that this deposit was somewhat protected from the burning event and later collapse of the broch.

Burnt deposit (041) and (042)
A total of 1603 fragments (3,478.7 g) were recovered from these deposits and preservation ranged from poor to excellent. The animal bone had accumulated through a variety of disposal methods. These fragments are a mix of butchery and domestic food waste some of which was burnt *in situ* during the final catastrophic burning event and then damaged further when the broch later collapsed. There were also the remains of what appeared to a semi-articulated pig and foetal remains from a pig and sheep/goat.

Three fragments of burnt bone (0.1 g) described as I/M were recovered from (041). A total of 311 fragments (1,869.5 g) were noted in (042) and the species were cattle (31), sheep/goat (8), pig (1), grey seal (1), cetacean (16), L/M (181), M/M (64), S/M (3) and I/M (6). Butchery marks were observed on seven bones. These were composed of marrow cracking on two cattle metacarpals along with skinning marks on three L/M ribs, one M/M rib and one L/M fragment. Burning affected 129 fragments.

From (042NEQ) there were 55 burnt fragments (15.5 g) described as L/M (3) and I/M (52). In context [042NWQ] the animal bone totalled 482 fragments (1,076.1 g) composed of cattle (24), sheep/goat (18), pig (4), seal (1), L/M (91), M/M (328) and I/M (16). Three fragments were butchered and 318 had been burnt. A cattle axis had two deep chop marks along with a meta-tarsal that was marrow cracked and a M/M rib had been cut. A sheep/goat pelvis had signs of a pathology composed of a small hole which had penetrated through the centre of the acetabular region. This could have caused an inflammatory infection. The bone from (042SEQ) numbered 603 of which 526 were burnt. The species were cattle (18), sheep/goat (3), pig (2), rodent (8), L/M (115), M/M (106) and I/M (351). Several rodent bones were burnt suggesting they were contemporary with the occupation and final catastrophic burning event. In context (042SWQ) there were 149 fragments (64.2 g).

These were formed of cattle (1), pig (1), L/M (4), M/M (21) and I/M (122). A L/M rib had been butchered and gnawed by a S/M. A total of 89 fragments were burnt.

Ash deposit (061)
This context was described as a deposit of peat ash located within the destruction layer of (042). The bone numbered 141 fragments (32.0 g) were identified as cattle (1), pig (2), rodent (1), L/M (5), M/M (13) and I/M (119). The cattle and pig skeletal elements were composed of tooth fragments. Preservation of these fragments ranged from mostly poor to good. A total of 103 fragments had been burnt. This material is likely domestic waste scattered on the floor which was burnt *in situ* during the final catastrophic burning event.

Active floor surface (084)
From this active floor surface 111 fragments of bone (11.6 g) were collected. The species were M/M (11) and I/M (100). Preservation of these fragments ranged from mostly poor to adequate. A total of 101 fragments were calcified. These remains were likely domestic refuse which was incorporated within this active floor surface which was further damaged during the final catastrophic burning event.

Post abandonment and collapse
A total of 102 fragments (289.2 g) was recovered from three deposits (005), (011) and (028) associated with the post abandonment and collapse of the broch. Contexts (005) and (011) relate to more modern activity whereas (028) could date to a period of abandonment after the fire event but prior to any major collapse of the structure. The archaeological security of deposits (005) and (011) is somewhat suspect and the bone likely represents later redeposition.

Rubble deposit (005)
The only bones recovered from this context were the remains of a semi-articulated rabbit mandible. These are intrusive and belong to an individual that postdates the broch that burrowed into this deposit at a much later date.

Destruction material (011)
There were four fragments of poorly preserved bone (4.9 g) which were noticeably weathered suggesting they had been exposed to the elements for a prolonged period. The species were rodent (1), L/M (2) and I/M (1). This material was of little archaeological value and is more likely to represent redeposited finds.

Destruction deposit (028)
The bone was composed of 96 fragments (283.7 g) identified as cattle (3), L/M (76), M/M (5) and I/M (12).

Preservation of these fragments was mostly poor with only a smaller number described as adequate to good. The poor preservation was a result of burning which occurred during the final burning event and from the later collapse of the broch which has resulted in a high level of fragmentation within this part of the assemblage. A total of 36 fragments had been burnt and most were completely calcified. There was no evidence of any butchery, pathologies or animal gnawing. At least some of this material has been mixed into this deposit from the underlying destruction event when the walls eventually collapsed, perhaps during the collapse itself or by later burrowing animals.

The entrance passage

A small quantity of bone numbering 318 fragments (99.0 g) were recovered from contexts (082), (083), (106), (120), (121), (146), (153), (158), (165) and (166). There was no evidence of butchery marks, pathologies or animal gnawing. These remains were scattered throughout these deposits with no evidence of selective or deliberate disposal.

CLAY DEPOSIT (083)

There were 38 fragments of burnt bone (7.4 g) recorded as L/M (3) and I/M (35). These finds are food residue trampled into this surface as domestic refuse was removed from the broch for disposal during cleaning of the heaths. Alternatively, this domestic food waste could have been reworked into the clay used to create this surface.

DESTRUCTION EVENT (106)

This context was described as a discrete patch of charcoal located within the entrance passageway from which 23 fragments of I/M burnt bone (0.6 g) all smaller than 10 mm were recovered. This material is likely an inclusion within the charcoal as hearth waste or was just general refuse which was trampled into the surface.

ENTRANCE PASSAGEWAY (120) AND (121)

There were 45 burnt fragments (1.1 g) identified as S/M (1) and the rest were described as I/M (44). From (121) there were 17 burnt I/M fragments (0.8 g). These remains are redeposited food waste trampled into this surface or debris from the burning event.

SOIL DEPOSIT WITHIN BROCH ENTRANCE WALLS (146)

There were 24 fragments of bone (1.4 g) of which four formed a fragmented cattle molar along with 20 I/M burnt fragments. This material is probably from the burning event which was reworked into this deposit when the broch collapsed.

RUBBLE DEPOSITS (153), (154)

From deposit (153) there were 54 fragments (15.8 g) identified as cattle (8), rabbit (1), L/M (4) and I/M (41). The cattle remains were composed of fragmented molars. Preservation of this material was poor except for the rabbit pelvis which was described as good. A total of 32 fragments had been burnt. The bone from context (154) numbered 43 burnt fragments described as I/M and poorly preserved. This material has probably derived from the final burning event which was reworked into these contexts during the burning event and final collapse. The rabbit remains are intrusive.

Cell 1

The bone from Cell 1 totalled 912 fragments (7,327.8 g) and was present in contexts (144), (145), (155), (159) and (163). Preservation of these remains was variable and ranged from poor to excellent and was somewhat influenced by their location within the midden. The exception was the semi-articulated sheep/goat skeleton which was badly degraded. This cell was evidently employed as a midden and the animal bone accumulated through the disposal of both butchery and domestic food waste.

CONTEXT (144)

There were 69 fragments (1,544.6 g) of bone recorded as cattle (15), sheep/goat (4), pig (1), red deer (1), seal (3), L/M (34), M/M (9) and S/M (2). Eight bones including cattle and pig skeletal elements had evidence of marrow cracking and skinning. Thirty bones had suffered from some burning, but this generally consisted of small patches of black discolouration on the surface. This suggests the bone was not burnt during the structural conflagration but instead during cooking and food preparation.

CONTEXT (145)

A semi-articulated sheep skeleton was noted within deposit (145). These remains were excavated but preservation was such that analysis was not possible as the fragments were so poorly preserved they fell apart and disintegrated. Although the remains of this animal could not be studied it appears from the photographs taken during excavation that this individual was deliberately deposited within Cell 1 in a semi-articulated condition which indicates that it had not been completely de fleshed or butchered.

A further 435 bones (3,661.0 g) were collected from this context and the species were cattle (48), sheep/goat (9), pig (3), red deer (1), seal (9), L/M (287), M/M (60), S/M (3) and I/M (15). Six bones had been butchered and these included a cattle radius and two metatarsals which had been marrow cracked. A total of 24 fragments were burnt but these were not damaged during the catastrophic burning event but likely during the cooking process.

CONTEXT (155)

There were 235 fragments (864.7 g) identified as cattle (13), sheep/goat (40), seal (1), rodent (1), L/M (54), M/M (8), S/M (1) and I/M (116). The only evidence of bone modification was burning and this affected only small sections of the bone surface in the form of black discolouration.

CONTEXT (159)

In context (159) there were 170 fragments (1,257.4 g) formed of cattle (8), sheep/goat (7), pig (1), red deer (7), seal (3), rodent (3), L/M (115) and M/M (26). Eight bones including one cattle metatarsal had been marrow cracked. One L/M and one M/M fragment had been partly charred at a low temperature.

CONTEXT (163)

From context (163) there were three poorly preserved fragments (0.1 g) described as I/M.

Cell 2

The bone from Cell 2 numbered 254 fragments (85.6 g) from seven contexts (123), (133), (134), (135), (136), (137) and (142). Cell 2 was deliberately used for the long-term storage of both unprocessed crops and large caches of processed grain (See Robertson, *Section 5.1*). Therefore, it is highly unlikely that butchery or domestic food waste would be deliberately deposited in this location as it could potentially contaminate the grain.

DESTRUCTION BURNING (123, (133), (134), (142)

A total of 212 bone fragments (80.7 g) were recovered from contexts (123), (133), (134), (142). There were 83 fragments (33.9 g) in (123) and the species were L/M (82) and M/M (1). A total of 82 fragments had been burnt. The bone from (133) numbered 199 fragments (40.5 g) and the species were rodent (8), M/M (100) and I/M (11). Preservation of these fragments ranged from poor to excellent. A total of 116 fragments had been burnt including six rodent bones. In context (134) there were two burnt sheep/goat foetal metatarsals. In (142) there were eight fragments (0.7 g) identified as rodent (2), M/M (3) and I/M (3). The M/M and I/M fragments were all burnt. Most of these fragments except for the rodent bones and the sheep/goat foetal remains likely accumulated accidently as redeposited food debris. The sheep/goat metatarsals may have been deliberately stored in this location whereas the rodents derived from scavengers that exploited the grain stored in this locality.

SANDY DEPOSIT (135)

Two fragments of poorly preserved M/M bone (4.0 g) were recovered from this sandy deposit. This material was probably an accidental contaminant of the sand that was deliberately laid in the cell to create a floor surface.

DEPOSIT (136) AND (137)

From context (136) a single I/M fragment of poorly preserved bone (0.1 g) was noted. A total of 39 fragments (0.8 g) were recorded in (137) and the species were rodent (8) and I/M (31). The preservation of the rodent ranged from poor to excellent whereas the I/M fragments were all burnt. The rodent and I/M fragments have been deposited at different times. It is likely the burnt fragments are redeposited food and hearth waste remixed into the floor surface either by pieces of bone being trampled into the surface or was an accidental contaminate of the sediment which was used to resurface this cell. The rodent remains could be contemporary with the broch and represent individuals which infested the grain stored in this vicinity.

Cell 4

There were ten fragments of bone (0.5 g) from context (081). All ten fragments were burnt, smaller than 10 mm and poorly preserved. This material is redeposited food waste.

Gallery 3: the stair cell

A small assemblage of animal bone (1.7 g) was present in two contexts (034) and (089SW). In (034) the bone (0.3 g) was identified as a rabbit scapula and a rodent incisor. In context (089SW) the bone (1.4 g) was composed of a poorly preserved cattle tooth, two rodent bones and nine I/M fragments of which two were burnt. Context (034) was described as recent infill which explains the presence of the rabbit. Excluding the rodent bones found in (089SW) the remainder are likely domestic food waste from an occupation deposit which was later reworked into the gallery stairwell deposits. The rodents in (089SW) would appear to be intrusive.

The exterior areas

A small quantity of 25 fragments (596.9 g) were recovered from six deposits (320), (330), (333), (335), (336) and (337). The only fragments which could be identified were a whale vertebra and three cetacean fragments (591.7 g) in (320). The other 21 fragments were scattered among the remaining five contexts with no evidence of selective or deliberate disposal. A total of 23 fragments had been burnt but there was no evidence of any butchery or pathologies.

Unstratified

There were 292 fragments (1,916.2 g) identified as cattle (31), sheep/goat (11), red deer (1), seal (1), rodent (1), L/M (130), M/M (105), S/M (4) and (8) recovered from spoil or other unstratified contexts. Preservation of these fragments ranged from poor to excellent. Butchery marks were recorded on ten bones consisting of a cattle atlas which had been chopped in two, a calcaneum with a chop mark and a series of skinning marks on a M/M scapula, vertebra and ribs. Evidence of a pathology was observed on a cattle metatarsal in the form of three depressions which could have been due to a lesion. A total of 56 fragments had been burnt. Four fragments (9.0 g) of poorly preserved bone identified as L/M were collected from the spoil heap.

Discussion

Species present

The NISP was calculated for both the domesticated and wild species and the results are presented in Table 5.4.1 which is recorded by context group. The MNI for both the domesticated and wild species were calculated as a single-phase assemblage and are illustrated in Figure 5.4.1.

Domestic species

The NISP for the domestic species was cattle (383) followed by sheep (81), sheep/goat (151) and pig (35) (Fig. 5.4.2). Cattle were present in ten context groups, sheep in one, sheep/goat in seven and pig in five. In all context groups except for Hearth 2, cattle were more numerically abundant than sheep/goat. Only in deposits associated with Hearth 2 did the number of sheep exceed cattle and this was due to the burial of two semi-articulated individuals. Throughout the occupation of the broch, pig was only ever present in small quantities. The numerical importance of cattle within the NISP is perhaps misleading as 246 of these fragments were a mix of loose incisors, premolars and molars. Teeth, given their cellular structure, tend to survive well in most environmental conditions especially in the sandy deposits encountered within most of the broch. This interpretation may however also be misleading as given the poor preservation of much of the faunal assemblage it is possible that many of the L/M skeletal elements are in fact cattle.

Analysis of the MNI identified seven cattle, two sheep, six sheep/goat, and three pig. The neonate remains were composed of one sheep/goat and one pig. The small size of the assemblage made accurately interpreting the relative economic importance of the three main domesticates difficult. Nor given the short period of occupation was it possible to accurately identify

any trends and changes in animal husbandry practices between specific context groups within the broch. A more generic interpretation is that both cattle and sheep/goat were the two main domesticates exploited throughout the short occupation of Clachtoll. If either species was the more important and if this changed over time, this is impossible to identify given the current available evidence. What is clear is that pig, as the other domesticated species had only a very minor role as expressed within both the NISP and MNI figures.

The wild species

The NISP for the wild species were red deer (13), whale (1), grey seal (2), seal (35) and cetacean (126) (Fig. 5.4.3). The MNI was calculated as follows: red deer (1), whale (1) and grey seal (2). The red deer bones were scattered among deposits surrounding Hearth 3, the midden in Cell 1 and in unstratified deposits. There was one whale vertebrae which could not be identified further and was collected from a deposit outside the broch entrance. The rest of the cetacean fragments, given their size, were more likely whale rather than dolphin or porpoise but this could not be confirmed. These were concentrated in the souterrain, with smaller numbers in Hearth 2, Hearth 3, the burning event, Cell 1 and the exterior deposits. The grey seal and seal fragments derived from multiple individuals deposited among the souterrain fill, Hearth 2, Hearth 3, the burning event, Cell 1 and from unstratified deposits. The fragments described as seal are probably grey seal, but again this could not be confirmed. The absence of any wild species from Hearth 1 and the earlier floors is not proof these animals were not exploited during this period, but instead likely reflects the poor condition of the bone which prohibited more accurate identifications from this earlier deposit.

There were nine rabbit fragments, which were scattered among deposits within the souterrain, the post abandonment and collapse, the entrance passageway and Gallery 3. The rodent bones numbered 102 and were noted within most of the context groups except for the entrance passageway, Cell 4 and the exterior.

Body part representation

Given the small size of this assemblage figures representing skeletal body parts were produced only for the three main domesticates which were cattle, sheep/goat and pig.

Domestic species

Cattle

The cattle assemblage was composed of large numbers of loose teeth followed by pieces of horn, skull fragments, hyoids, scapulae, long bones, pelvis and foot bones (Table 5.4.2). The skeletal elements are clearly

Table 5.4.1 NNumber of individual specimens (NISP) for each of the principal context groups discussed in the text

Phase	Cattle	Sheep	Sheep/goat	Pig	Red Deer	Rodent	Rabbit	L/M	M/M	S/M	I/M	Whale	Ceta-cean	Grey seal	Seal	Total
Hearth 1	1					2		8	12		212					235
The souterrain	88		25	9		19	4	434	240	6	457		101		10	1393
Hearth 2	19		2	5		32		17	88	4	277		3		2	530
Hearth 3	63		17	6	3	11		292	164	4	813		1	1	8	1383
The knocking stone						1										1
The burning event	79		34	10		9		411	565	3	1161		16	1	1	2290
Post aban-donment and collapse	3					1	2	78	5		13					102
The entrance passageway	14						2	21	3	1	277					318
Cell 1	84		60	5	9	5		490	103	6	134				16	912
Cell 2			2			18		82	106		46					254
Cell 4											10					10
Gallery 3 the stairs	1					3	1				9					14
The exterior								1			20	1	3			25
Unstratified	31		11		1	1		134	105	4	8				1	296
Sheep		81														
Total	383	81	151	35	13	102	9	1968	1391	28	3437	1	124	2	38	7763

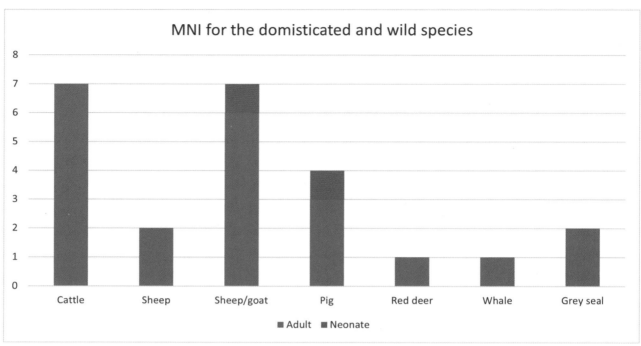

Figure 5.4.1 MNI for the domesticated and wild species

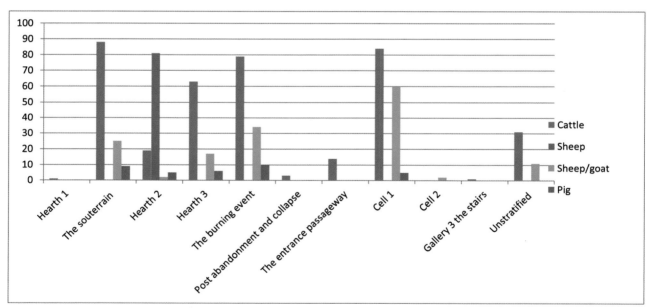

Figure 5.4.2 NISP for the domesticated species

dominated by loose teeth, but the relatively low numbers of other identified fragments are probably due to taphonomic factors. There are many fragmented long bone shafts which, due to poor preservation, could not be conclusively identified to species but were probably cattle. The loose teeth included a fourth deciduous premolar and it has been argued that the presence of this shed tooth in midden material is a good indicator for the stalling of cattle (Mulville 1999, 271). Asides from this single tooth there is no evidence that the cattle were housed in byres long term within the site. This assemblage, while small, is still representative of animals that were transported on the hoof, slaughtered, butchered and consumed at the broch.

SHEEP/GOAT

Most of the sheep/goat skeletal elements were present with the exceptions of the axis and some of the smaller foot bones such as the tarsals (Table 5.4.3). This is probably due to taphonomic factors within the broch rather than as a result of the sampling strategy which was designed to recover these smaller elements. The recovery of three semi-articulated individuals coupled with the presence of most of the skeletal elements indicates that live animals were brought to the broch. There is no evidence to suggest that cuts of meat were either imported or exported to and from other locations. The presence of neonate bones also demonstrates that pregnant ewes were transported to the site and lambing occurred in the vicinity. The sheep/goat body parts have derived from animals that were brought to Clachtoll on the hoof and were subsequently slaughtered, butchered and disposed of in this location.

PIG

The pig bones were composed of maxilla, mandibles, loose teeth, atlas, axis, radii, ulnas and foot bones (Table 5.4.4). The radii and ulna are typically high meat bearing bones, and these were concentred within the souterrain, Hearth 3 and Cell 1. There were no other signs of high-status cuts of pork so the radii and ulnas could have been imported to the broch as joints of meat. However, the presence of maxilla, mandible and foot bones, which usually derive from primary butchery waste were present in the same context groups. This suggests that a small number of pigs in the early occupation of the broch did arrive on the hoof. The near absence of quality cuts of pork in the form of high meat bearing bones such as long bones is of note. As with the cattle it could be that some of the medium mammal long bones not identified to species were in fact pig. It is also likely pig bones including the remains of high-quality cuts of meat were disposed of away from the broch. It is also possible that as this species are usually slaughtered at a younger age the bones are more fragile and susceptible to destruction. Consequently, they are less likely to survive cooking or damage from scavengers and this could have contributed to the small number of surviving skeletal elements. Nor can it be ruled out that joints of pork were transported to other locations and consumed elsewhere.

From the final catastrophic burning event the possible remains of a semi-articulated adult pig and neonate were observed. These fragments were badly burnt and had suffered further damage when the broch collapsed and consequently many could not be confidently identified as pig. If these remains do represent semi-articulated individuals, then pigs while only ever a minor part of the diet arrived on the hoof, were slaughtered, consumed and at least a small number of the skeletal elements were disposed of in the immediate vicinity. The presence of the neonate bones indicates that some animals were bred locally.

WILD SPECIES

RED DEER

The 13 fragments were composed of molars (2), scapula (1), long bones (2), metapodials (3), foot bones (4) and part of a hoof (1). These finds were concentred within the midden in Cell 1 which had nine bones compared to three in Hearth 3 and one in unstratified contexts. These remains are considered to represent butchery and food waste. In Cell 1 the food waste was identified as a scapula and tibia. There was evidence for butchery waste in the form of a possible semi-articulated foot that included an astragalus, phalanges and hoof. The two metapodials from Hearth 3 had both been butchered to extract marrow and it is also possible they were retained for later bone working. A metatarsal was recovered from an unstratified context but there was no evidence of butchery or bone working.

It is possible that a deer carcass was transported to the broch and then butchered. Subsequently a small number of skeletal elements were disposed of within the site and the rest transported elsewhere. Alternatively given the small range of skeletal elements present, it is feasible that deer were butchered elsewhere, perhaps at the kill site, with joints of meat imported to the broch.

WHALE

There was one whale vertebra from context (320) which could not be identified to species. There were also several fragments described as cetacean that could not be identified to element or species but given their size were assumed to be more likely whale. These fragments were probably scavenged from beached individuals, or potentially from small animals that were hunted at sea. It is likely that the carcasses of cetaceans were occasionally washed ashore nor is it uncommon for whales to deliberately beach themselves thereby becoming trapped. The smaller whale species which live in the waters off the Highlands and Islands tend to live in schools and if one can be separated it can be hunted by being driven to shore where the other animals sometimes followed (Mulville 1999, 267). These are all relatively common methods by which the community at Clachtoll could potentially have acquired access to whale as a resource.

SEAL

The skeletal elements were composed of a skull fragment (1), canines (6), premolar (1), maxilla (1), mandibles (4), scapula (2), humerus (3), ulna (3), femur (3), long bone shaft (1), phalanges (7) and fragments (5). Two mandibles were identified as grey seal and it is probable the rest belonged to the same species. The skeletal representation profile indicates that intact seal carcasses were carried to the broch where they were butchered and later disposed of.

Table 5.4.2 Skeletal elements of cattle remains

Element	Hearth 1	The souterrain	Hearth 2	Hearth 3	The burning event	Post abandonment and collapse	The entrance passageway	Cell 1	Gallery	Unstratified	Total
Horn		2			2	1		1		1	7
Horn/skull								1			1
Atlas										1	1
Axis					2			3			5
Mandible		6			2						8
Maxilla					1						1
Loose teeth		64	19	44	53	1	12	33	1	19	246
Hyoid				1							1
Scapula								3		1	4
Humerus p		1		1				1			3
Humerus d		1		1				3			5
Humerus shaft	1						1			1	3
Radius p					1			4			5
Radius d					1						1
Radius/ulna p								1			1
Radius/ulna d								1			1
Ulna					2						2
Pelvis		1		1	1			3			6
Femur shaft						1					1
Tibia p								1			1
Tibia d				1				2			3
Patella		1									1
Carpals		2		4	1			5		1	13
Tarsal		1			3			6		1	11
Astragalus					1			4			5
Calcaneum		4		5	1			3		1	14
Metacarpal p		1		1	2			1			5
Metacarpal d					1						1
Metacarpal p/d								1			1
Metatarsal p		1						3			4
Metatarsal d				1				1		1	3
Metatarsal p/d				1							1
Metapodial					1			2			3
Phalanx 1		1		3			1	1		2	8
Phalanx 2					2					2	4
Phalanx 3		2			1						3
Total	1	88	19	63	79	3	14	84	1	31	383

Table 5.4.3 Skeletal elements of sheep/goat remains

Element	The souterrain	Hearth 2 Sheep	Hearth 2	Hearth 3	The burning event	Cell 1	Cell 2	Unstratified	Total
Horn					2				2
Horn/skull (fragments)		2			1				3
Skull (fragments)	1	14							15
Atlas	1								1
Mandible		3			2			1	6
Maxilla		2			1				3
Loose teeth	6		1	2	4	53			66
Hyoid		2			1				3
Rib		24							24
Thoracic vertebra		2							2
Lumber vertebra		4							4
Vertebra		2							2
Scapula	1	2		2	3	1			9
Humerus p		1						1	3
Humerus d		3	1		2	2			7
Humerus shaft	2								2
Radius p	1							2	3
Radius d	1	1			1				3
Radius shaft	1			2					3
Radius/ulna p/d		1							1
Ulna					2				2
Pelvis		3			3				5
Femur p	1	1			2				4
Femur d		2		2	1	1			6
Femur shaft		2							2
Tibia p	2	1		1		1			5
Tibia d					1	1			2
Tibia p/d		2			1	1			4
Astragalus	2				2			1	5
Calcaneum		1		1	1			1	4
Carpal		2							2
Metacarpal p	1	1						1	3
Metacarpal p/d		1			1				2
Metatarsal p		1		2	1				4
Metatarsal p/d		1		1				1	3
Metapodial	1						2		3
Phalanx 1	2			2	1			2	7
Phalanx 2				1	1			1	3
Phalanx 3	2			1					3
Total	25	81	2	17	34	60	2	11	232

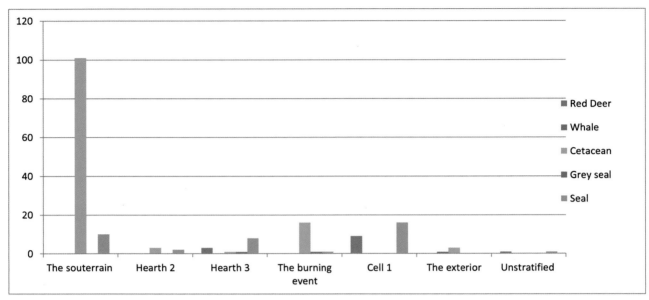

Figure 5.4.3 NISP for the wild species, by context group

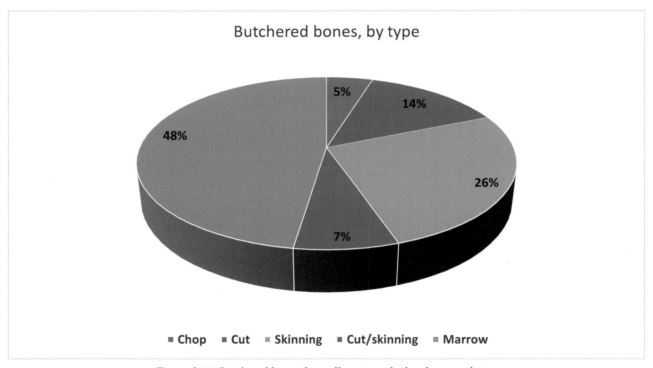

Figure 5.4.4 Butchered bones from all contexts, by butchery-mark type

Ageing

To determine the age of the main domesticates at time of death the following criteria were analysed: tooth eruption, tooth wear and epiphyseal fusion (Silver 1969; Payne 1973; 1987; Grant 1982). An attempt was made to separate the juvenile and adult grey seal and seal bones (Stora

2001). Suitable material for aging the three main domesticates was based on very small datasets. This made calculating accurate kill-off patterns difficult. It is therefore recognised that the conclusions presented are somewhat arbitrary. Given the small number of suitable mandibles it was deemed unnecessary to produce mandibular wear

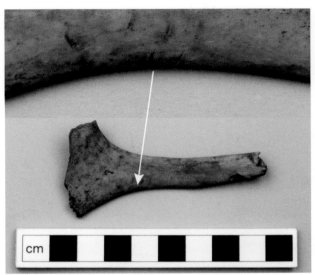

Figure 5.4.5 A cattle hyoid from context (049) displaying a series of small shallow cut marks to surface

stage graphs. However, the fusion stages for the cattle, sheep/goat and pig which record if the skeletal element was unfused or fused at time of death are available in the site archive.

CATTLE

There were six mandibles suitable for study; four were recovered from the souterrain [069] and two from the burning event. The youngest individual was found to have died between the ages of 15–18 months with four slaughtered between 24–36 months. From the sixth mandible only the M2 and M3 were present and both teeth had suffered some damage. Analysis of the surviving tooth surface indicates that the wear was extremely advanced suggesting it belonged to an individual older than 40 months. Analysis of the intact mandibles demonstrates that younger cattle were absent from this assemblage. When the loose teeth are accounted for, the presence of a deciduous premolar alongside permanent molars which displayed little to no wear to the occlusal surface suggests that there is a potential bias towards recognising older individuals, although this is impossible to confirm given the small number of available mandibles.

Evidence for epiphyseal fusion was available for 50 cattle bones, of which two were unfused, one was in the process of fusing and 47 had completely fused at time of death. The two unfused bones were a metatarsal from the burning event and a calcaneum from Cell 1 which belonged to an animal or animals younger than 36 months and 42 months respectively. It was noted that the distal epiphysis of a tibia was in the process of fusing indicating this individual died between the ages of 24–30 months. The rest of the fused bones belonged to animals all older

than seven months with evidence to suggest a number were still potentially alive after 36 months. The kill-off pattern from the surviving cattle assemblage suggests that younger animals were absent, or if not absent only a minor component of the population and their remains have not survived.

SHEEP/GOAT

A total of four mandibles were studied for tooth eruption and wear. Two mandibles were collected from the sheep burial in context (087) both from the same individual, one from the burning event (042) and the other from an unstratified context. The mandibles from the sheep burial and from the unstratified context belonged to animals approximately 36–42 months old at time of death. The mandible from the burning event was from a younger individual that died between the ages of 9–12 months.

Epiphyseal fusion for the sheep/goat was calculated from 72 skeletal elements that included both foetal and adult remains. There were four foetal metapodials and in each instance the proximal epiphysis was unfused. Ten bones were in the process of fusing of which there where two distinct age categories of between 13–16 months and 30–42 months. There were two phalanges which belonged to the younger age group and a mix of long bones which derived from animals killed between the ages of 30–42 months. The remaining 58 fragments were completely fused, and all belonged to animals older than six months. There was no evidence to suggest that any animal survived beyond the age of 48 months.

There were three identifiable peaks at which animals died. There were the remains of one neonate which indicates that stillborn animals were disposed of on site. A further animal was culled between the ages of 9–16 months whereas the majority were slaughtered in their prime between 30–42 months.

PIG

There were four mandibles scattered among the souterrain (069), Hearth 2 and the burning event deposits. Analysis of tooth eruption and wear revealed that the youngest animal died between 7–13 months whereas the rest were slaughtered between the ages of 17–22 months.

There were ten pig bones suitable for studying epiphyseal fusion, of which three were unfused at time of death and six were fused. The three unfused foot bones were one metacarpal and two first phalanges that all belonged to animals younger than 24 months. The fused bones were two radii, one pelvis, one metatarsal and two second phalanges from animals older than 12 months. Evidence of foetal remains were noted within the burning event in the form of a single metatarsal where the proximal epiphysis remained unfused.

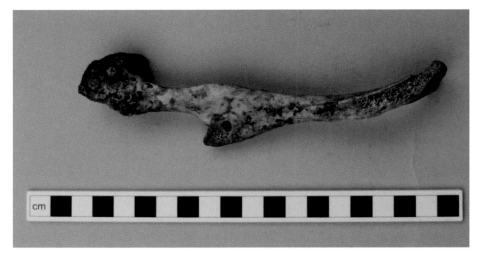

Figure 5.4.6 A sheep/goat pelvis from context (042) with evidence of a pathology affecting the acetabular region of the bone

The age at which most of these pigs were culled was consistent and suggests that they were deliberately fattened for slaughter.

WILD SPECIES

The red deer elements were composed of fused bones from an adult and there was no evidence of any juveniles. The seal bones were a mix of both unfused and fused skeletal elements that belonged to both juveniles and adults.

Sexing

THE MAIN DOMESTICATES

Establishing the sex for cattle and sheep/goat is normally determined by analysing specific skeletal elements such as horn cores, pelvis and metapodials (Boessneck 1969; West 1990; Greenfield 2006). Sex determination in pigs is normally assessed by comparing male and female canines which have sexually dimorphic characteristics. Given the small size of the cattle and sheep/goat assemblages it was not possible to extract any reliable information. Nor were any of the surviving pig canines well enough preserved to allow for an accurate identification of sex.

WILD SPECIES

Two grey seal canines were analysed and given their size and shape were both identified as female (Hewer 1974, 58).

Measurement

Given the high degree of fragmentation within the assemblage the number of bones suitable for measurement for the three main domesticates was small and those that could be measured are recorded in the site archive. From the limited information available it is difficult to draw

any useful comparisons but the skeletal elements from Clachtoll are all within the range of results reported from Crosskirk, Scalloway, Dun Vulan, Cnip, Howe, Tofts Ness and Á Cheardach Mhor and Dun Cul Bhuirg (Macartney 1984, 145–6; O'Sullivan 1998, 107–8; Mulville 1999, 255–7; McCormick 2006, 166–71; Smith *et al.* 1994 144–5; Nicholson and Davis 2007, 192–4; Clarke 1960, 171; Noddle 1980, 227).

While only a small number of sheep bones were measured from the semi-articulated burial they were mostly comparable with those from Á Cheardach Mhor and Sollas, where it was noted that the animals were similar in size to the Shetland and Mouflon breeds rather than the Soay or blackface sheep (Clarke 1960, 171; Finlay 1991, 148). This contrasts with the results from Crosskirk where the character of the assemblage was more in keeping with the modern Soay (Macartney 1984, 140). It is possible the Clachtoll sheep were of a similar stature and breed to other sites on the west coast although this interpretation must be treated with some caution given the relatively small number of bones available for analysis. The same caveats must be applied to the interpretation of the cattle assemblage, but the available evidence suggests the Clachtoll cattle belonged to the short and stocky variety. As only three pig bones were measured, they had little pertinent information to offer. The small size of the assemblage coupled with the short occupation of Clachtoll made it impossible to establish if the size of the main domesticates changed significantly over time as animal husbandry techniques evolved.

Animal husbandry and subsistence strategies

DOMESTIC SPECIES

Cattle: The cattle assemblage is very small so only tentative conclusions can be drawn from the evidence. The animals analysed were culled in their prime with only one identified as being older. It cannot, however, be ruled out that all evidence of more fragile neonates or calf bones were destroyed or not preserved, thereby creating a bias within the data.

Most of the cattle were slaughtered either just before or just as they reached skeletal maturity and were at their optimum meat bearing size. This pattern is similar to that reported at Scalloway, which was interpreted as in keeping with a dairying economy (O'Sullivan 1998, 128). Both young and older animals were present at Old Scatness, Howe and Crosskirk, indicating a more mixed economy where both dairying produce and beef were exploited (Cussans and Bond 2015, 214; Smith *et al.* 1994, 151; Macartney 1984, 142). The cattle from Clachtoll probably had a similar role, in that they were deliberately kept alive long enough to be exploited for dairying and traction and were only later slaughtered for their meat and leather once they were of a suitable size.

Settlements like Clachtoll were probably able to sustain older animals as they must have had access to enough fodder and winter feed (Macartney 1984, 142). Therefore, the pressure to cull larger numbers of calves was not as immediate. The Clachtoll macroplant assemblage demonstrates that there was access to suitable agricultural land which, if managed correctly, would have provided additional fodder and grazing for livestock. The absence of neonates and calves may therefore accurately represent the animal husbandry practised at Clachtoll. The occupants of the broch were therefore able to sustain this small herd for longer periods of time until the animals were deemed ready for slaughter.

This kill-off pattern contrasts with those reported at some of other Western Scottish Iron Age settlements, particularly those in the Western Isles. At sites such as Baleshare, Cnip and Dun Vulan large proportions of calf mortality were recorded (Halstead 2003 145; McCormick 2006; Mulville 1999). High infant mortality was also noted at Pool and Tofts Ness, Sanday (Bond 2007c, 216–19; Nicholson and Davis 2007, 191). Large numbers of young animals within a death assemblage are typically interpreted as characteristic of a dairying economy (Bond 2002, 181). If this model is accurate then the absence of calves at Clachtoll perhaps suggests that dairying was not as important at this site.

However, studies suggest that early dairy cows did not produce milk unless their calves or the stuffed skins of their young were present (Halstead 1998, 14; Bond 2002, 180; Balasse 2003, 8). Therefore, the high mortality of young at the Western Isles and Sanday sites may not be truly representative of a dairying economy. Instead, these animals could have died for other reasons; perhaps they were unneeded for breeding and were deliberately culled to preserve limited food stocks

for the main herd (McCormick 2006, 167). Access to regular fodder and extensive grazing was undoubtedly more difficult to source on most of the islands, especially those on the west coast. Consequently, the absence of neonates and calves at Clachtoll does not automatically exclude the possibility that milk production was important at the site. Certainly, analysis of the pottery and steatite assemblage indicates that a number of these vessels were used to store dairy products (see McLaren, *Sections 4.1 and 4.7*). The small cattle herd at Clachtoll had an important and varied role within this economy and they provided a range of resources before and after death.

There was no supporting evidence that these animals were housed for extensive periods or even entire seasons on the site. Certainly, there is little evidence of dung or burnt dung within the macroplant assemblage (see Robertson, Section 5.1). Traditionally livestock such as cattle are stalled from the autumn to the spring (Smith *et al.* 1994, 149). The absence of any stabling waste suggests that the Clachtoll animals were housed in byres outside the excavated area and animals were brought to the site on the hoof where they were rapidly slaughtered.

Sheep/goat: As with the cattle, understanding the economic role of the sheep/goat was based on a very small assemblage. From the available evidence the sheep/goat had a very mixed role within the economy of Clachtoll. The recovery of foetal remains indicates that pregnant ewes were brought to the site and that stillborn lambs were disposed of within the settlement. The kill-off pattern for the sheep/goat assemblage demonstrates that most of these animals were routinely culled once they had reached their prime. There was no evidence of any elderly individuals within the assemblage. This indicates that the sheep/goat were exploited for a multitude of products such as milk, wool, skins and meat.

The presence of one younger individual alongside older animals indicates that the inhabitants ate both lamb and mutton. Sheep/goat had an important role within most Iron Age societies in the Highlands and Islands of Scotland and similar results to those recorded at Clachtoll have previously been noted at Tofts Ness (Nicholson and Davis 2007, 189), Old Scatness (Cussans and Bond 2015, 227), Dun Vulan (Mulville 1999, 236), Howe (Smith *et al.* 1994, 139), Scalloway (O'Sullivan 1998, 109) and Pool (Bond 2007c, 212). The most obvious exception is Cnip, where sheep had a much-reduced role, which has been argued was possibly due to insufficient grazing to maintain a larger herd (McCormick 2006, 168). Poor grazing or lack of fodder was unlikely to have been problem at Clachtoll; the large carbonised macroplant assemblage indicates the populace had access to land and grazing in the vicinity of the broch.

The semi-articulated condition of the two sheep skeletons is of note as these individuals were deliberately deposited within the broch with some of the flesh, tendons and muscle still attached, which were then allowed to decompose *in situ*. Unless there was a specific reason for not butchering these animals for their flesh, such as they were deemed unfit for human consumption then the primary objective was probably to recover the skins. This perhaps suggests that sheep/goat meat, while consumed at Clachtoll, may not have been as highly valued as the milk, wool and skins from the same animals.

Pig: Throughout the occupation of Clachtoll, pig only ever had a marginal role within this economy. The presence of foetal remains along with adults indicates that pigs were bred in the vicinity. There is no evidence of older individuals within this assemblage. This pattern suggests that pigs were butchered once they had reached their optimum weight size if not before. Pigs which have no secondary products were routinely exploited for their meat, fat manure and bristles (Smith *et al.* 1994, 151). This pattern of animal husbandry is consistent with most other Iron Age sites such as at Old Scatness (Cussans and Bond 2015, 227), Dun Vulan (Mulville 1999, 236), Howe (Smith *et al.* 1994, 139) Scalloway (O'Sullivan 1998, 109), Pool (Bond 2007b, 212), Dun Vulan (Mulville 1999, 272), Nybster (Robertson in prep) and Thrumster (Robertson in prep) where pigs generally had a more minor role in the economy than other domesticated species. An exception was noted at Crosskirk were slightly larger numbers of pig in comparison to sheep were recorded (Macartney 1984, 142). Large numbers of pig within a domesticated assemblage have been interpreted as evidence of possible high status (Bond 2002, 181). However, this interpretation of pork consumption is not beyond dispute (Gilmour and Cook 1998; Parker Pearson and Sharples 1999), and the limited assemblage at Clachtoll may not assist in settling the debate.

WILD SPECIES

Red deer: Of note is the small number of red deer bones in comparison to the much larger quantities of antler, suggesting that venison had a very minor dietary role. The antler appears to have been scavenged from shed remains and was used for tool working at the broch (see McLaren, Section 4.9). Deer lived on the mainland, but it is possible the herd was not easily accessible or that hunting of this species was not a priority. Either scenario is likely and would help explain the small number of deer bones recorded at Clachtoll. It is also possible deer bone unlike antler has not survived within the assemblage. Given the small size of the bone assemblage it is possible that some of the long bones described as large mammal are in fact deer and that poor preservation of the bone has obscured the full dietary role of this species at Clachtoll.

Deer was noted at Crosskirk (Macartney 1984, 136), Howe (Smith *et al.* 1994, 49) Pool (Bond 2007c, 211) Tofts Ness (Nicholson and Davis 2007, 187–8) Dun Vulan (Mulville 1999, 261), Sollas (Finlay 1991, 147), Á Cheardach Mhor (Clarke 1960, 170), Baleshare and Hornish Point (Halstead 2003, 143–4), Cnip (McCormick 2006, 169–71) and Old Scatness (Cussans and Bond 2015, 208). It has been speculated that many Iron Age societies controlled access to this resource dependent on the supposed social status or cultural preferences of the settlements (Mulville 1999, 273). If this interpretation is accurate, it is possible Clachtoll either did not enjoy sufficient status to fully exploit this resource to its full potential or choose not to. Instead, it appears this community focused on collecting shed antler and supplementing their diet with occasional access to venison. If this scenario is correct, it explains why so few red deer bones were recovered, but this interpretation must be tempered with the possibility that deer due to taphonomic factors may be accidently underrepresented within the death assemblage.

Whale: Cetaceans have played an important role in many prehistoric settlements in Atlantic Scotland, raising speculation on how these animals were sourced whether by hunting or scavenging (Mulville 2002, 34). Whales have been routinely hunted throughout the historic period using small boats and there is no reason to suppose this would have been beyond the skills of Iron Age communities (Clark 1947, 87). Smaller whales could be driven ashore where they were then butchered (Mulville 1999, 267; 2002, 37). It is just as likely whales were exploited after being beached or washed onto shore after death. The carcasses were normally butchered directly on the beach making it easier to transport products such as meat, bone, blubber and oil to the settlements (Mulville 2002, 40). Nor can it be ruled out that items such as whale bone were traded between communities as valuable resource. Given the available evidence it is not possible to identify the method by which they obtained access to this resource but the surviving evidence demonstrates it did have an important and varied role within the broch.

Whale bones were utilised for tools at Clachtoll and a second whale vertebra was employed as a chopping block (see McLaren, Section 4.9). Whale bones, given their oil content, were used as a fuel source at other sites (Clark 1947, 100; Mulville 1999, 267; 2002, 40). It was noted that many cetacean bones from the earlier deposits were burnt prior to the final catastrophic burning event and they could easily have been used as a fuel source. Fresh cetacean bones were used in historic times as an alternative fuel when wood and peat were not readily available (Clark 1947, 100). Whale, therefore, did have a significant role within this economy and was exploited for a variety of resources including food, blubber, oil, fuel and for tool working.

Seal: Seals were an important resource at Clachtoll and would have been exploited for meat, blubber, blood, skin and sinew (Mulville 1999, 267). These animals would have been especially vulnerable to hunting when they come ashore to moult in the spring and breed and give birth in autumn (Hewer 1974; Mulville 1999, 267). Grey seal pups normally do not enter the sea for three weeks and as they and the adults are slow moving on land, this makes them particularly vulnerable to attack (Mulville 1999, 267). The seal bones were composed of both unfused and fused skeletal elements and this gives credence to both juveniles and adults being successfully hunted when they came ashore to pup. The hunting of seals during the birthing season is perhaps confirmed by the presence of two female canines. It is not uncommon for seal carcasses to be washed ashore and these too could have been processed by the occupants of the broch as opportunistic finds. Seal has been recovered at Dun Vulan (Mulville 1999, 266), Howe (Smith *et al.* 1994, 147), Scalloway (O'Sullivan 1998, 111–112), Pool (Bond 2007b, 210) Cnip (McCormick 2006, 171–172), Baleshare and Hornish Point (Halstead 2003, 143) and Á Cheardach Mhor (Clarke 1960, 169) and was evidently an economically important resource during this period, whenever available.

Spatial deposition and discard patterns

Analysis of the spatial distribution of the bone made it possible to identify patterns in the ways in which butchery and domestic food waste was disposed of within the broch. From Hearth 1, Hearth 2 and Hearth 3 the bone was mostly composed of domestic food debris some of which was burnt and showed signs of butchery. There were also burnt cetacean fragments in the hearth deposits which could potentially have been utilised first as food and later recycled as a fuel source within the hearths. The relatively small quantity of bone present in these surfaces indicates that they were kept relatively clean of domestic debris. This contrasts with the souterrain fill, which contains a mix of butchery and domestic food waste.

It is unclear at what stage in the occupation of the broch that Cell 1 was deliberately employed as a midden. The bone in this area was composed of both butchery and cooking debris which was deposited alongside other midden material. This demonstrates that there was no attempt to differentiate between these two sources of bone waste and instead they were routinely intermixed with other refuse in Cell 1. The remains of a semi-articulated sheep/goat were also noted within the midden, but how it came to be in this location is somewhat unclear.

The bone from the final burning event was a mix of food and butchery waste that was burned *in situ*. The remains of a semi-articulated pig and a neonate were also present in this final layer.

The bone from Cell 2 was composed of sheep/goat foetal metatarsals, rodent bones and small fragments. The sheep/goat metatarsals must have been deliberately deposited in Cell 2 for later reuse. This area of the broch was used for the storage of food items and it is unlikely that refuse would be deliberately deposited in this location. The rodents were contemporary with the inhabitation of the broch and were probably vermin invading the grain stored in areas such as Cell 2. The smaller bone fragments were likely accidental inclusions that were components of the new floor surfaces which were routinely laid in this cell.

The animal burials

A group of bones from context (087) was identified as the burial of two semi-articulated sheep. The first individual was more articulated, and the only elements missing were the atlas, axis and the phalanges. This animal died between the ages of 36–42 months. The skeletal elements which belonged to the second animal were the two humeri, part of the pelvis, one femur and one tibia. This animal was younger and was approximately 30–36 months at time of death. The semi-articulated condition of the two carcasses indicates they were deliberately deposited in this location and left to decompose *in situ*. Butchery marks were observed on several skeletal elements and this, combined with the missing foot bones, strongly implies that these carcasses were skinned and partly defleshed. There was also some evidence of burning and residue adhering to a small number of the bones. This burning and residue staining probably occurred when the hearth was in use and those fragments in closer proximity to the hearth became partly charred.

The two animals left to decompose *in situ* would have created an unhygienic environment within the broch especially around the hearth which was warm and used for cooking and heating. Clearly, the unpleasantness of smells from such remains is a value judgement not easily assessed by modern standards, but the presence of decomposing animals in such an important part of the broch would have had some impact on living conditions. One possibility that must be considered is that these animals were left to decompose beside Hearth 2 during a short hiatus in the occupation of the broch. When the population returned the carcasses were not removed. Instead, a new floor surface was laid and Hearth 3 was constructed. Alternatively, if the broch was not actually abandoned even for a short period, the sheep were deliberately interred in this area. This could have been undertaken to mark the end of Hearth 2 and form the base for Hearth 3. Given the excellent level of preservation, burial of these two semi-articulated carcasses must have been a rapid process, so that deliberate burial seems most probable.

It is not uncommon for animal carcasses to be entombed within the structures of brochs and wheelhouses. Two sheep burials were noted beneath the floors at Cnip and in both instances the toes were missing, and some skeletal elements were butchered (McCormick 2006, 169). This pattern of sheep inhumation was also recorded at Sollas, North Uist (Campbell 2000, 189). The animal burials at both sites were like those at Clachtoll in that the individuals were skinned but not fully consumed. Several animal burials were also recorded at Howe (Smith *et al.* 1994, 151). These included sheep which, although not butchered for their flesh, had their horns deliberately removed (Smith *et al.* 1994, 151). This pattern of disposal of sheep during the Iron Age in the Highlands and Islands of Scotland indicates that this species perhaps had a ritual role within these societies beyond just providing the traditional primary and secondary products such as wool, meat and milk (Campbell 2000, 194).

In Cell 1, context (155), the remains of a semi-articulated sheep/goat were observed during excavation. This animal was not analysed in laboratory conditions but was photographed *in situ*. On-site observations concluded that these remains derived from a single sheep/goat carcass which was badly burnt and heavily degraded. It was considered during excavation that this individual may have been trapped during the final conflagration event and died in this location to escape the fire. Given the presence of two other semi-articulated sheep within the interior which had been deliberately skinned, however, it is equally possible the animal from Cell 1 was also slaughtered, skinned and deliberately deposited in the midden as butchery waste. The skeleton from Cell 1 did appear to be partly covered by some midden waste. This may suggest it is more likely to represent a butchered carcass rather than an animal that died accidently during the final conflagration event. If this animal did derive from a butchered carcass, then its presence within the midden indicates its disposal did not have the same significance to the community as the sheep recovered from the hearth. This is because the sheep from the hearth potentially represent animals deliberately buried for a specific purpose whereas the individual from the midden was disposed of alongside other general refuse.

The remains of a possible semi-articulated adult pig were observed in context (042), from the final burning event. The skeletal elements that could be confidently identified were the maxilla, atlas, axis, molars, pelvis, a metatarsal with the rest described as medium mammal. This was because preservation was variable, as some had been badly burned and then damaged further when the broch collapsed. Regardless, these skeletal elements do appear to belong to a single individual. It is possible this animal was trapped alive when the broch burnt down, or it had already been slaughtered and was awaiting butchery.

Butchery

A total of 107 fragments had recognisable signs of butchery (Fig. 5.4.4). While the number of butchered bones was small it was possible to identify a range of primary, secondary and tertiary marks which belong to different stages at which the carcass is processed (Rixson 1989, 49). The butchery was undertaken using a variety of tools including knives and choppers. Possible saw marks were observed on red deer antler, but these marks were consistent with bone working rather than butchery. Given the level of fragmentation within this assemblage it was impossible to identify precisely how any of these animals were slaughtered.

The primary stage of butchery is described as the slaughter and dressing of the carcass which includes the removal of the head, skinning and removal of the feet. One cattle atlas was chopped in two and an axis had two deep chop marks. This indicates that the head of this animal was removed by chopping through the neck area. Several bones also had shallow cut marks consistent with the skinning of the carcass.

Secondary butchery typically involves splitting the carcass into manageable joints. Several vertebrae had been butchered but none had been obviously chopped in two as normally occurs in modern butchery when the carcass is suspended in the air. Instead, the vertebrae tended to have their lateral edges sliced off which suggests that the carcasses were laid flat on a surface or on the ground while joints were detached. The ribs had cut marks typically around the head indicating that they were detached from the vertebral column at this stage of processing. A cattle hyoid bone had a series of small, shallow cut marks made when it was removed from the mandible. The butchery practices employed at Clachtoll are comparable to those reported at Scalloway and Howe (O'Sullivan 1998, 129; Smith *et al.* 1994, 150).

The final stage of tertiary butchery normally involves reducing the carcass into cuts of meat suitable for domestic consumption and this includes marrow cracking. This final stage of butchery was noted on a series of long bones and metapodials. There was evidence of shallow cut marks on the long bones which occurred when meat was stripped from the surface. Many of the metapodials had been deliberately marrow cracked using a chopper. Given the large number of fragmented long bones in this assemblage it is likely that most of these were also deliberately broken to extract marrow.

Pathology

Very few bones were affected by obvious signs of injuries and disease. This was probably due to the small size of the assemblage rather than an accurate reflection of the health and nutritional status of the domestic livestock or wild animals.

Table 5.4.4 Skeletal elements of pig remains

Element	The souterrain	Hearth 2	Hearth 3	The burning event	Cell 1	Total
Loose teeth		2	3	4	4	13
Maxilla				1		1
Mandible	1		2	1		4
Atlas				1		1
Axis				1		1
Radius p	1					1
Radius/ulna p	1				1	2
Ulna shaft	1		1			2
Pelvis				1		1
Fibula	1					1
Calcaneum	1					1
MTC		1				1
MT4	1			1		2
Phalanx 1	1	1				2
Phalanx 2	1	1				2
Total	9	5	6	10	5	35

Table 5.4.5 Proportion of burnt to unburnt bone in each context group

Phase	Unburnt%	Burnt%	Number
Hearth 1	25	75	235
The souterrain	46	54	1393
Hearth 2	45	55	530
Hearth 3	67	33	1383
The knocking stone		100	1
The burning event	24	76	2290
Post abandonment and collapse	64	36	102
The entrance passageway	11	89	318
Cell 1	88	12	912
Cell 2	6	94	254
Cell 4		100	10
Gallery 3 the stairs	86	14	14
The exterior	8	92	25
Unstratified	81	19	296
Total fragment count	3586	4177	7763
Total %	46	54	100

Table 5.4.6 Total number of bird bones (identified and unidentified) by principal context groups discussed in the text

Species	Name	Hearth 2	The burning event	Post abandonment and collapse	The entrance passageway	Cell 1	Total
Fratercula arctica	Puffin	1				4	5
Uria aalge	Guillemot					1	1
Bird	Bird	1	1	1	1	1	5
Total		2	1	1	1	6	11

The older individual from the two semi-articulated sheep burial in context (087) had two bones with evidence of pathologies. There was some slight bone growth surrounding the medial condyle and epicondyle of the right femur. This could be the beginnings of arthritis but there was no other contributary evidence to confirm this diagnosis. There was also some damage to the shaft of the metacarpal along with several perforations at both the proximal and distal epiphyses. The damage to the metacarpal was difficult to fully identify as the anaerobic conditions in this deposit had some detrimental effect on the preservation of this bone.

From the contexts associated with the burning event a sheep/goat pelvis had a small hole which had penetrated through the centre of the acetabular. Surrounding this hole on the dorsal side of the pelvis was noticeable bone growth. The damage to the pelvis is unlikely to be an age-related condition, a traumatic break or inherited disorder. Instead, it is more likely this damage was caused by some type of inflammatory infection which was able to penetrate the bone (Bartosiewicz and Gal 2013, 93–5).

Two ribs had evidence of fractures, of which one was tentatively identified as seal and the other was from a medium mammal. Both the seal rib and medium mammal rib were fractured at some stage but in both instances, there was some excess bone growth suggesting they had healed prior to death.

The burnt bone

Of the 7,763 fragments a total of 4,177 were burnt (54%) (Table 5.4.5). Burnt bone was present in all context groups but was concentrated in the final catastrophic burning event which contained 2,290 fragments, of which 76% were burnt. The burnt bone assemblage had accumulated through a variety of methods. Those fragments collected from around the hearths and the souterrain were typically cooking refuse which is interpreted as overspill that was trampled into the surrounding floor surfaces. The bone from the midden in Cell 1 was again food and cooking refuse deliberately disposed of within this location. The material from Cell 2 appeared to be intrusive and was either incorporated accidently when additional floor layers were resurfaced with sediment which had small quantities of domestic debris or were trampled in on the feet of the broch inhabitants. The finds from the other context groups were burnt food and cooking refuse which experienced some level of redeposition. This was particularly true of the fragments present in Gallery 3 and from the post-abandonment and collapse deposits.

Scavengers

Four bones were identified as having marks attributable to animal gnawing. Three of these were ribs from two contexts associated with Hearth 3. Two ribs from context (062) were identified as large mammal and medium mammal. The large mammal rib had small puncture marks located on the edge of the blade and the medium mammal rib had a series of scratch marks along the edge. A sheep rib from the burial (087) had two small puncture holes and scratch marks. From context (042) a rib had five small punctures holes along the blade. These marks were consistent with the teeth of a small mammal such as a dog or cat. Although no dogs or cats were identified within the assemblage several skeletal elements were described as small mammal and possibly belonged to one or both species. The contemporary rodents probably also scavenged for food among both the stored food supplies and midden refuse.

Conclusion

The animal bone assemblage from Clachtoll Broch was relatively small especially when compared to other similar sites in the Highlands and Islands but nonetheless provides valuable evidence for the economic basis of the occupants. The small size of the assemblage was probably due to the relatively short occupation of the broch coupled with the likely disposal of waste outside the excavated area. Regardless important evidence for how animals were used at Clachtoll broch has emerged. This economy throughout its short history was dependent on domestic animal species with a focus on cattle and sheep/goat. Which species – if either – was the more economically important is unclear but what is obvious is that they were utilised for a range of resources before and after death. Pig had only a very minor dietary role. Exploitation of wild resources did occur, but the dietary role of red deer appears to have been marginal, which may have been due to either the perceived status or the short duration of occupation of the site. Marine resources were also utilised in the form of whale and grey seal and these too were used in a variety of capacities. Analysis of the surviving assemblage revealed that the animal husbandry regime practised at Clachtoll Broch was consistent and stable throughout its short occupation until its final destruction during the catastrophic burning event.

Bird bone

Introduction

The bird bone assemblage from Clachtoll Broch was composed of 11 fragments (10.5 g). The bone was recovered both by hand and from the bulk samples which were processed using a 1 mm mesh. The small size of the assemblage is therefore not a reflection of the sampling strategy that was designed to recover both large and small skeletal elements.

Methodology

The bird bone assemblage was identified to element and species using the modern reference collection, keys and texts stored at AOC Archaeology Group Edinburgh (Serjeantson 2009; Cohen and Serjeantson 2015). The results are recorded in full in catalogue 1 which is stored within the site archive. The bird bone was analysed for evidence of epiphyseal fusion, butchery marks, pathologies, bone working and carnivore gnawing. Given the small size of this assemblage no attempt was made to calculate minimum number of individuals and instead the material was quantified by number of identified specimens (NISP).

Taphonomy

The small number of birds recovered from the broch could be due to several taphonomic factors. These include poor preservation of bone, particularly smaller fragments that may not have survived within the sandy soil conditions. It is also probable some bird remains were routinely disposed in middens or dumps located outside the perimeter of the excavated site. Equally likely is that the small number of birds reflects their relatively minor importance to the economy of the occupants, or that these bird species were only available seasonally.

Results

The species and number of identified specimens (NISP) were puffin (*Fratercula arctica*) (5), guillemot (*Uria aalge*) (1) and bird (5) (Table 5.4.6). Preservation of the bird bone ranged from poor to good. The puffin skeletal elements were composed of a tarso-metatarsal recorded in Hearth 1 and a humerus, radius, ulna and tibia-tarsus from Cell 1. The guillemot ulna was recovered from Cell 1. The remaining five bird bones were scattered among Hearth 2 debris, the burning event, the postabandonment and collapse, the entrance passageway and Cell 1. Eight long bones were fused, but as most bird skeletons tend to fuse shortly after hatching this evidence can only demonstrate that there were no juveniles present and these remains belonged to adults (O'Connor 2004, 139). There was no evidence of any butchery marks, pathologies, bone working or animal gnawing.

Discussion

The two species from Clachtoll are both seabirds that have been noted at other broch sites including Howe, Cnip, Sanday, Tofts Ness, Scalloway and Scatness (Bramwell 1994, 153; Hamilton-Dyer 2006, 172; Serjeantson 2007a, 280–1; 2007b, 219; O'Sullivan 1988, 116; Nicholson 2015b, 240). It is probable these birds were hunted at Clachtoll to provide an additional food source to add variety to the diet. Certainly, both puffins and guillemots

have routinely been hunted as a wild food resource in the highlands and islands of Scotland using ropes made from heather simmens, snares and nets to catch them when they flew close to their nests located on cliffs (Bramwell 1994, 154; Serjeanston 2009, 243–5). Puffins and guillemot are also particularly vulnerable to exploitation during the mating season in summer where they breed in large colonies (O'Sullivan 1988, 116; Smith *et al.* 1994, 154; Serjeanston 2009, 237; Sterry and Cleave 2012, 326).

Species such as puffin and guillemot were valued for their meat, which could be eaten fresh or prepared for long term storage by salting, air drying or smoking it in the rafters of the broch over the hearths (Smith *et al.* 1994, 154). Sea birds were important not only for their meat but also for their eggs and feathers (Renfrew 1993, 18). The fat and oil from boiled bird carcasses was routinely reused for cooking, lighting and medicine (Bramwell 1994, 154). While there was no conclusive evidence that eggs, feathers, oil and fat were exploited this probably did occur, and the evidence did not survive within the ecofact assemblage.

The presence of bird bone in Cell 1, which became a midden for domestic debris, indicates birds were consumed and later disposed of along with other food waste. There is no surviving evidence of any butchery marks, but it has been noted it is possible to dismember puffins without tools by pulling them apart manually (Serjeanston 2009, 144). The puffin wing joint in Cell 1 could have been prepared using this method.

Conclusion

The bird bone accumulated from small-scale seasonal hunting of wild seabirds which were brought to site to supplement and vary the diet of the broch inhabitants. Given the size of this assemblage it is not possible to assess how exploitation of seabirds developed or changed during the period that the broch was occupied. The small number of surviving bones, however, suggests that birds had only a very minor dietary role. This accords with the findings from Pool and Old Scatness where bird flesh formed a very causal part of the diet while still providing some variety (Serjeanston 2007a, 284; Nicholson 2015b, 243). Based on the available evidence it appears that seabirds were a relatively unimportant resource at Clachtoll Broch.

5.5 Fish bone

Jen Harland

Introduction

Fish remains were recovered from a variety of areas and phases, with most originating from the occupation phases associated with the sequence of three hearths, the entrance passage, and the burning event that ended occupation of the broch.

The fish remains were entirely recovered by sieving. All bulk samples were sieved using a 1 mm mesh and the flots were captured in a 1 mm and 0.3 mm mesh. The retents were sorted using a stack system of 4 mm/ 2 mm/1 mm/0.3 mm sieves. Fish bone was recovered from both the retents and flots. Evidence of burning was widespread – consistent with the contexts – and bones tended to be very friable as a consequence. However, the rate of identification was excellent suggesting very good survival of this material. Some scales were even recovered from a few contexts. Scales are rarely found because they decay readily, although they are difficult to identify and quantify.

Fish remains from the Iron Age are generally rare compared to the Viking Age and Late Norse period, and their relative absence from the archaeological record led to questions of fish avoidance in cultures around the North Sea (Dobney and Ervynck 2007). Recent work on Scottish material has produced increasing quantities of fish remains from sites that are excavated with full sieving, including some contemporary with Clachtoll, and reanalysis of old excavations has shown that deeper water fishing was occasionally undertaken (*e.g.*, Russ *et al.* 2012).

Methods

The fish remains were received in two batches, with all bags labelled accordingly. Some bone material was identified as frog or toad and is noted below. Three fragments of calcined sea urchin were noted from (042), grid square R4 – either kept as a pretty object, or perhaps eaten.

All material was scanned for the presence of otter spraint, because otters are very fond of living in abandoned archaeological sites both in the present and in the past. They have a preference for eating small, inshore fish, but their characteristic chewing marks and choice of species marks these remains as non-anthropogenic. Spraints are a dense accumulation of very small fish remains, the excreted remains of food, mixed with glandular secretions. Otters deliberately and repeatedly spraint in selected locations including near or at the entrances to their 'holts', the tunnel-like burrows used for sheltering and for raising their young (Kruuk *et al.* 1998, 124). Otters will also spraint within their holts, when young are being fed (Nicholson 2000, 56), and thus spraints can build up over long periods outside of and within otter holts (Kruuk 2006, 78–82). They are relatively common finds at archaeological sites in the Northern and Western Isles with good sampling practices, but they are rare from mainland sites. Otters are known to populate the area around Clachtoll in the present day; no otter bones were recovered from the excavated assemblage.

This assemblage was recorded using the York System, an Access database utility designed for recording zooarchaeological assemblages. The author's own reference collection was used for identification purposes, supplemented by manuals including Watt, Pierce and Boyle (1997), Watson (1986), and Patterson *et al.* (2002). The recording protocol is fully detailed in Harland *et al.* (2003). Briefly, this entails the detailed recording of the 18 most commonly occurring and easily identified cranial elements, termed quantification code (QC) 1. For each of these, the element, species, approximate size, side, fragmentation, texture, and any modifications are recorded in detail. Fish vertebrae (QC2) are recorded in more limited fashion, with counts, element, species and approximate size recorded. Some elements are unusual and particularly diagnostic, like otoliths, and are fully recorded (QC4). The final category of material (QC0), includes elements not routinely identified as well as unidentifiable material. Elements that are from very unusual species, or that are butchered or pathological, are recorded in detail even if not from the QC1, 2 or 4 category. Data analysis involved structured database queries, as well as manipulation using Excel. The full dataset is included in the site archive.

Results

A total of 922 bones were identified to species or taxonomic grouping (like family level), or to element, with a further 608 fragments not identified (Table 5.5.1). This shows an excellent rate of identification, because unidentified fragments usually outnumber those that can be identified by a factor of ×2 or ×3.

Taphonomy

Fragment completeness and surface texture scores were recorded for all QC1 (cranial) and QC4 (unusual) elements. Together with observations of burning and other modifications, these indicate the taphonomic processes that acted upon the assemblage. Only 34 QC1 and QC4 elements were identified, an unusually small proportion compared to the number of vertebrae.

Most fragments had a 'good' surface texture recorded, with some being 'fair' (Table 5.5.2). Percent completeness varied, with most bones showing some degree of fragmentation. Quantities were too small to look at variation between areas or phases. Burning was common throughout most phases, with 16% of all fish remains noted as burnt (Table 5.5.3). This varied through the broch deposits; almost half of the bones contemporary with the Hearth 1 deposits were burnt, but only 10 to 15% of those contemporary with Hearths 2 and 3 were burnt. About a third of the bones from (042), the final burning event, were burnt, perhaps a little lower than might have been expected here. The

Table 5.5.1 Total number of bones identified, and unidentified, by area/phase and element type

Area/phase	Cranial	Vertebral	Other	Total identified	Unidentified	TNB
Cell 1	2	32		34	40	74
Cell 2		2		2	5	7
Entrance passage	4	20		24	86	110
Souterrain	1	35		36	7	43
Hearth 1	2	126		128	35	163
Hearth 2	7	401		408	267	675
Hearth 3		193		193	49	242
Burning event	10	65	2	77	62	139
Post abandonment/collapse	6	5		11	41	52
Modern	2	5		7	16	23
Total	34	886	2	922	608	1530

Table 5.5.2 Percent completeness and surface textures for all QC1 and QC4 elements

Area/Phase	Percent Completeness					Surface Texture	
	<20%	20-40%	40-60%	60-80%	>80%	Fair	Good
Cell 1		1	1			1	1
Entrance passage	1	1		1	1	1	3
Souterrain					1		1
Hearth 1		1		1			2
Hearth 2		2	1	1	3	1	6
Burning event		5	3	1	1	2	8
Post abandonment/collapse		2	3		1	1	5
Modern					2		2
Total	1	12	8	4	9	6	28

Table 5.5.3 Burning and other modifications for all elements, showing percentage of TNB

Area/Phase	Crushed		Burnt: calcined		Burnt: charred		Burnt: all	
Cell 1	5	7%			2	3%	2	3%
Cell 2			1	14%			1	14%
Entrance passage	4	4%	1	1%			1	1%
Souterrain			7	16%	6	14%	13	30%
Hearth 1	1	1%	1	1%	73	45%	74	45%
Hearth 2	7	1%	37	5%	33	5%	70	10%
Hearth 3	3	1%			37	15%	37	15%
Burning event	8	6%	13	9%	32	23%	45	32%
Post abandonment/collapse								
Modern			2	9%	1	4%	3	13%
Total	28	2%	62	4%	184	12%	246	16%

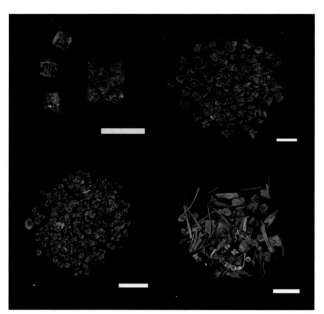

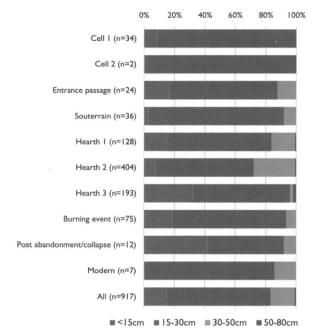

Figure 5.5.1 Images of fish remains from Clachtoll. Top left: (047), SE Quadrant; includes large salmon/trout family vertebrae. Top right: (049), NW Quadrant; entirely 15-30 cm and 30-50 cm total length cod family vertebrae. Bottom left: (093), Central Hearth; entirely <15 cm and 15-30 cm total length cod family vertebrae. Bottom right: (047), SE Quadrant (a different sample from top left); comprises a mix of cranial, vertebral and unidentified material from a variety of sizes of cod family fish. Scale bars all 1 cm.

Figure 5.5.2 Fish sizes for all taxa

colour of the burnt bone can indicate the intensity of the heat; calcined bones that are white have been burnt at a hotter temperature than those that are charred black. Only 4% of the bones were calcined. The bones associated with Hearths 1 and 3 tended to be charred, while those associated with Hearth 2, the souterrain, and the burning event showed higher rates of calcining, suggesting hotter fires. Some contexts had higher rates of burning than others. Context (111), a floor deposit contemporary with Hearth 1, produced only charred fish remains, while context (074), a hearth deposit contemporary with Hearth 3, had 35 out of 36 bones charred. These examples probably indicate fish waste was often discarded in the hearths, probably after consumption; this will be discussed further below.

Crushing can be an indication that bones were chewed (by humans or animals) or trampled. There was no note of cess identified during excavation, a common source of crushed bones. Here, only 2% of all bones were crushed. These tended to be associated with Cell 1, and the burning event, and not with the hearth phases. The Cell 1 assemblage was dominated by the cottids and the rocklings, small inshore fish which are frequently eaten by otters (discussed further below), and the relatively

high rate of crushing and low rate of burning would confirm this. It is therefore likely that otters were present and sprainting in this area, but the main phases associated with the sequence of hearths and the burning only contained anthropogenic material. The relatively high rate of crushing associated with the burning event (6%) could result from the subsequent collapse of the broch impacting the remains.

Concretions were noted adhering to the bones from three contexts: five from (047) SE Quadrant, and three from (067) S Baulk, all of which were associated with Hearth 2. A single bone from (082), the entrance, also had concretions. No carnivore gnawing was noted, suggesting scavengers had no access to the fish remains. No fresh breakage was noted either, indicating the post-excavation processing and packaging was exemplary.

Species

A total of 20 species or taxonomic groupings were identified (see Fig. 5.5.1). Where possible, every attempt was made to identify fragments to species level, but this is not always easy; for example, the rocklings, salmon/trout family, and the flatfish are generally difficult to identify to species. Saithe and pollack can be differentiated when larger or when there are plenty of cranial elements, but here the preponderance of small vertebrae made identification difficult.

Saithe/pollack was the most commonly identified taxa, at 81% of the entire assemblage. The cod family was the most dominant family, at 90% of the entire assemblage.

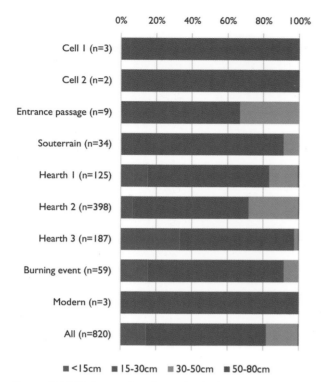

■ <15cm ■ 15-30cm ■ 30-50cm ■ 50-80cm

Figure 5.5.3 Fish sizes for all cod family fish, including saithe, pollack, and saithe/pollack as well as gadid NFI

This including cod family NFI (not further identified) at 6%, saithe at 2%, and pollack at 0.2%. Most of these were probably small saithe, with the occasional pollack. A variety of other taxa were also observed, including sea scorpion at 0.4% and the sea scorpion family NFI at 4%. Rocklings comprised 1% of the assemblage. Other taxa generally represented less than 1% each; these included eel, Perciformes Order NFI, salmon and trout family NFI, wrasse family NFI, the flatfish, ray family NFI, herring, and butterfish/viviparous eelpout. Finally, four frog/toad bones were recovered, all from the entrance passage area.

The species present at Clachtoll broch were almost entirely marine, which is to be expected given the location of the settlement on the Atlantic coast. A few of the species are migratory, including the six eel fragments and the four salmon/trout family identifications. The eels were most likely caught in a local freshwater stream or river, while the salmon/trout family could have been salmon or sea trout caught near the mouth of a river, or salmon, trout or charr all caught in the lochs or rivers. Numerous small lochs are found within a few kilometres of the broch, all of which would be suitable habitats for eels. The area immediately around the broch is a good venue for sport fishing today, including coastal fishing for pollack, mackerel and sea bass from the beach at Clachtoll. The sea bass are likely the result of subtle variations in

fish populations as a response to modern overfishing and climate change, while pollack is a common term used to refer to both saithe and pollack.

There was some variation between areas and phases. Cell 1 has a much higher proportion of sea scorpion family fish and rocklings, and a corresponding low proportion of saithe, pollack or cod family fish. These species are suggestive of otter spraint, thus correlating with the higher proportion of crushing noted in this area. It is possible that some non-anthropogenic deposits were also found in the entrance passage, given that there were four amphibian bones found there. The slightly higher proportion of sea scorpion family fish in the burning event could suggest some otter spraint infilling once the broch was abandoned, but there one of these fish was charred. This could mean that humans were deliberately catching and consuming these fish on occasion, perhaps as accidental by-catch when targeting small saithe.

The souterrain, Hearths 1, 2 and 3, and the burning event all focus on cod family fish, specifically the ubiquitous saithe and saithe/pollack. These will be discussed further below.

Fish sizes and habitats

All cranial and vertebral elements were assigned a broad size category based on comparison with reference material, from tiny (<15 cm total length) up to large (50–80 cm total length). Selected elements like quadrates, dentaries, premaxillae, and basioccipitals were also measured for detailed size reconstruction, but the small size of the assemblage meant few conclusions could be drawn from these; the raw measurements are in the project archive.

Fish sizes are graphically summarised for all taxa (Fig. 5.5.2). Fish of less than 30 cm dominate the assemblage. The high proportions of tiny fish of <15 cm total length in Hearth 3 and the post abandonment/collapse are curious, because this small size is generally too small for humans to bother eating. While there are only a few fish of 50–80 cm total length, their food contributions could well outweigh many smaller fish.

Fish sizes for the major species indicate some variation between areas and phases (Table 5.5.6). The salmon/trout family fish are all of large size, 50–80 cm total length, which may suggest they are salmon (but this could only be confirmed using biomolecular methods). The saithe/pollack show some variation, further explored graphically in Figure 5.5.3. These small fish are mostly 15–30 cm total length, with some even smaller found in a few area/phases. The Hearth 3 phase contains the highest proportion of these tiny fish, and there they account for almost a quarter of all the cod family fish found. These were, for the most part, only just under 15 cm total length. The food value of these is small; a 14 cm saithe weighs 23 g, a 20 cm one weighs

Table 5.5.4 Species counts for all areas/phases (NFI is not further identified)

Taxa	Cell 1		Cell 2	Entrance passage		Souterrain		Hearth 1		Hearth 2		Hearth 3		Burning event		Post abandonment/collapse	Modern	Total	
	NISP	%	NISP	NISP	%	NISP	%	NISP	%	NISP	%	NISP	%	NISP	%	NISP	NISP	NISP	%
Ray Family														2	3%			2	0.2%
Eel	1	3%		4	15%									1	1%			6	0.7%
Atlantic Herring	1	3%				1	3%											2	0.2%
Salmon & Trout Family NFI										1	0%	3	2%					4	0.4%
Pollack								1	1%	1	0%							2	0.2%
Saithe						5	14%			12	3%	1	1%	1	1%			19	2.1%
Saithe/ Pollack	2	6%		4	15%	26	72%	92	72%	380	93%	184	95%	56	75%		3	747	81.4%
Cod Family NFI	1	3%	2	5	19%	3	8%	32	25%	10	2%	2	1%	2	3%			57	6.2%
Gadid/Lotid Families NFI	3	9%		1	4%					1	0%	3	2%	2	3%			10	1.1%
Rockling	8	24%		1	4%											1		10	1.1%
Three-bearded Rockling?	1	3%																1	0.1%
Sea Scorpion								1	1%							3		4	0.4%
Sea Scorpion Family NFI	16	47%		4	15%	1	3%	1	1%	1	0%			8	11%	3		34	3.7%
Scorpaeniformes Order NFI				2	8%													2	0.2%
Wrasse Family NFI														2	3%		2	4	0.4%
Butterfish/Viviparous Eelpout	1	3%																1	0.1%
Perciformes Order NFI										1	0%			1	1%	4		6	0.7%
Halibut Family NFI				1	4%												1	2	0.2%
Flatfish Order NFI																1		1	0.1%
Common frog/Common toad				4	15%													4	0.4%
NISP	34	100%	2	26	100%	36	100%	127	100%	407	100%	193	100%	75	100%	12	6	918	100%
Unidentified Fish	40		5	84		7		36		268		49		64		40	17	610	
TNB	74		7	110		43		163		675		242		139		52	23	1528	

Table 5.5.5 Order, family, Latin binomials and common names

Order	Family	Common name	Latin binomial
Rajiformes	Rajidae	Ray Family	Rajidae
Anguilliformes	Anguillidae	Eel	*Anguilla anguilla*
Clupeiformes	Clupeidae	Atlantic Herring	*Clupea harengus*
Salmoniformes	Salmonidae	Salmon & Trout Family	Salmonidae
Gadiformes	Gadidae	Cod Family	Gadidae
		Pollack	*Pollachius pollachius*
		Saithe	*Pollachius virens*
		Saithe/ Pollack	*Pollachius* sp.
	Gadidae/Lotidae	Gadid/lotid families	Gadidae/Lotidae
	Lotidae	Rockling	Ciliata/Gaidropsarus
		Three-bearded Rockling?	*Gaidropsaurus vulgaris?*
Scorpaeniformes	Cottidae	Sea Scorpion	*Taurulus bubalis*
		Sea Scorpion Family	Cottidae
	Scorpaeniformes	Scorpaeniformes Order	Scorpaeniformes
Perciformes	Labridae	Wrasse Family	Labridae
	Pholidae/Zoarcidae	Butterfish/Viviparous Eelpout	*Pholis gunnellus/Zoarces viviparus*
	Perciformes	Perciformes Order	Perciformes
Pleuronectiformes	Pleuronectidae	Halibut Family	Pleuronectidae
Heterosomata (Pleuronectiformes)	Heterosomata (Pleuronectiformes)	Flatfish Order	Heterosomata (Pleuronectiformes)
Aruna	Bufonidae/Ranidae	Common frog/Common toad	*Rana temporaria/Bufo bufo*

67 g, a 30 cm individual weighs 229 g, and a 40 cm one weighs 549 g. In contrast, a 70 cm saithe weighs 3,008 g, the same as 130 14 cm fish – and a 70 cm salmon weighs 4,116 g, a very considerable quantity of food (Froese and Pauly 2019). Allowing for guts, the cranium and the vertebrae, the food value of the tiniest of these fish is very small indeed. A few larger cod family fish of 30–50 cm were found in the Hearth 1, 2 and 3 phases.

An examination of individual contexts within the larger phases shows a high degree of spatial variation (Table 5.5.9). For example, the Hearth 2 deposits show that some contexts were associated with slightly larger cod family fish (like (049) NW Quadrant), and some only with smaller (like (091) Central Hearth). Within the Hearth 1 deposits, (111) Central has no cod family fish of <15 cm total length, but plenty of 15–30 cm and 30–50 cm cod family fish; in contrast, 100 Culvert has lots of <15 cm and 15–30 cm cod family fish but none larger. The same holds true for Hearth 3: (074) has cod family fish of 15 to 80 cm total length, but (093) Central Hearth has only cod family fish of <15 cm and 15–30 cm total length. The burning event contexts all display a similar range of sizes, without a preference for larger or smaller. This could indicate the Hearth 1, 2, and 3

contexts show the remains of individual consumption events, based either on what was left in the stores, or on whatever cod family fish were available locally at the time.

The small saithe and other members of the cod family would all have been caught either in inland waters or from the shore (and indeed all other taxa, barring the eel and salmon/trout family, could also be caught in the same waters) (Froese and Pauly 2019). These juveniles are found in profusion at certain times of the year, and they can be useful to fill the 'hunger gap' of early spring. They can be used both for their food value, and for their oil: saithe livers can be boiled and the resulting oil used for lighting, culinary purposes, and as an industrial product (Armit 1842, 122; Grant 1842, 88; Naismith 1962, 531). The Old Statistical Account for Assynt describes the plentiful salmon fisheries, the recently developed herring fisheries, and attempts at creating a commercial cod and ling fishery (Mackenzie 1795). The small inshore saithe fishery was not mentioned, but both the statistical accounts and ethnographic sources for the Northern Isles describe the value of these fish to the local inhabitants in recent centuries: they were a staple part of the diet for the poor until the later 19th century (Barry 1805, 293; Low 1813,

Table 5.5.6 Fish sizes for major taxa

Common name	Total length	Cell 1	Cell 2	Entrance passage	Souterrain	Hearth 1	Hearth 2	Hearth 3	Burning event	Post abandonment/collapse	Modern
Eel	15-30cm	1		4					1		
Salmon & Trout Family	50-80cm						1	3			
Cod Family	<15cm						1				
	15-30cm	1	2	3	3	23	7	2	1		
	30-50cm			2		9	1		1		
Pollack	15-30cm						1				
	50-80cm					1					
Saithe	15-30cm				5		4		1		
	30-50cm						7	1			
	50-80cm						1				
Saithe/ Pollack	<15cm					19	26	62	9		
	15-30cm	2		3	23	62	246	118	43		3
	30-50cm			1	3	11	103	3	4		
	50-80cm						1	1			
Gadid/lotid Families	15-30cm	3		1			1	3	2		
Rockling	15-30cm	8		1						1	
Three-bearded Rockling?	15-30cm	1									
Scorpaeniformes Order	15-30cm			2							
Sea Scorpion	<15cm					1				3	
Sea Scorpion Family	<15cm	2		2	1		1		4	1	
	15-30cm	14		2		1			4	2	
Halibut Family	15-30cm			1						1	
	30-50cm										1
Flatfish Order	30-50cm									1	

Table 5.5.7 Element summary by size for all cod family fish (including saithe, pollack, saithe/pollack, and cod family NFI)

Size	Anatomy	Cell 1	Cell 2	Entrance passage	Souterrain	Hearth 1	Hearth 2	Hearth 3	Burning event	Modern	All
<15cm	Cranial								2		2
	Vertebral					19	27	62	7		115
15-30cm	Cranial			1		1	5		5	1	13
	Vertebral	3	2	5	31	84	253	120	40	2	540
30-50cm	Cranial			1							1
	Vertebral			2	3	20	111	4	5		145
50-80cm	Cranial						1				1
	Vertebral					1	1	1			3

Table 5.5.8 Element quantification by size for the major areas/phases, for all cod family fish (including saithe, pollack, saithe/pollack, and cod family NFI)

Total length	Element	Souterrain	Hearth 1	Hearth 2	Hearth 3	Burning event	Total
<15cm	Basioccipital					1	1
	Cleithrum					1	1
	Abdominal Vertebra Group 1			3	5	1	9
	Abdominal Vertebra Group 2		2	2	6	1	11
	Abdominal Vertebra Group 3		4	6	21	3	34
	Caudal Vertebra Group 1		12	9	14		35
	Caudal Vertebra Group 2		1	7	16	2	26
	Total		19	27	62	9	117
15-30cm	Ceratohyal					1	1
	Cleithrum			1			1
	Dentary					1	1
	Hyomandibular			1		1	2
	Infrapharyngeal			1			1
	Maxilla			1			1
	Parasphenoid					1	1
	Preopercular		1				1
	Quadrate			1		1	2
	First Vertebra				2		2
	Abdominal Vertebra Group 1	4	8	23	10	2	47
	Abdominal Vertebra Group 2	7	10	15	10	5	47
	Abdominal Vertebra Group 3	10	23	93	35	12	173
	Caudal Vertebra Group 1	7	14	51	40	12	124
	Caudal Vertebra Group 2	3	29	71	23	9	135
	Total	31	85	258	120	45	539
30-50cm	Abdominal Vertebra Group 1		1	9			10
	Abdominal Vertebra Group 2		2	9	1		12
	Abdominal Vertebra Group 3		4	46	2	2	54
	Caudal Vertebra Group 1	2	3	23		2	30
	Caudal Vertebra Group 2	1	10	24	1	1	37
	Total	3	20	111	4	5	143
50-80cm	Cleithrum			1			1
	Abdominal Vertebra Group 3	1					1
	Caudal Vertebra Group 1			1	1		2
	Total	1		2	1		4

Table 5.5.9 Cod family fish sizes by context, for the major areas/phases

Phase	Context	<15cm	15-30cm	30-50cm	50-80cm
Hearth 1	053 NW Quad		9		1
	100 Culvert	19	36		
	111 Central		40	20	
Hearth 2	047	1	19	6	
	047 SE Quad	1	49	5	
	049 NE+NW Quads	4	23	1	
	049 NW Quad		26	87	
	049 Quad		1		1
	086 NW		1		
	091 Central Hearth	16	98	6	
	094 Central Hearth		16	1	
	62				1
	62 SW Quad		1		
	67 S Baulk	4	18	4	
	76 S Baulk	1	6	1	
Hearth 3	074		18	4	1
	093 Central Hearth	62	102		
Burning event	007		1	1	
	007E		1		
	010		1		
	041 Gallery 2	1			
	042 SE Quad Nr Find 20		8	1	
	042 SW Quad	1	6	1	
	061 SW Quad	5	9	1	
	42	2	19	1	

193). These small, inshore fish could be caught using low-risk fishing strategies, using either small nets or hook-and-line fishing. These small fish were commonly caught from rocky shorelines without having to take a boat out, but equally a small dingy could be used in shallow water to catch these. Were these fish eaten only when fresh, or were they preserved? An examination of element patterning will help to explore these questions.

Element patterning

The small size of the assemblage makes it difficult to examine element patterning in detail, but during identification it quickly became apparent that there was an over-abundance of vertebrae. This was confirmed by quantification (Tables 5.5.7 and 5.5.8). Within most size categories of cod family fish, cranial elements were very under-represented: two cranial bones and 115 vertebral in the <15 cm category, 13 cranial and 540 vertebral in the 15–30 cm category, and one cranial and 145 vertebral in the 30–50 cm category. Only in

the largest category, the 50–80 cm fish, was there a more even balance of one cranial and three vertebral fragments. Since recovery was comprehensive, the lack of cranial elements was not a result of bias. The preservation was generally good and many tiny elements were recovered, so there is every reason to expect that a lack of cranial elements reflects a real pattern.

There is a real absence of fish heads among the small cod family fish that were caught in profusion here. These heads were probably removed when the fish were freshly caught. The food value of these small heads is minor, but they could be used to add flavour to foods. Even if thoroughly cooked they would still be unpalatable to modern tastes, but in the past they may have been eaten. Their remains would be expected to appear in cess deposits, but none of this was recovered at Clachtoll. Alternatively, the fish heads could have been disposed of at sea or outside of the broch. We are left with the bodies, complete with all vertebrae from the most anterior to the end of the tail.

No butchery marks were noted, but these small fish could easily have heads removed by twisting, thus not leaving a record on the bones. These headless fish could have been consumed either fresh, or they may have been preserved by lightly smoking. They could have been hung up to dry and smoke in the rafters of the broch, the smoke from the hearths lightly preserving them. Ethnographic sources indicate this was undertaken recently in the Northern Isles – albeit with the heads still on. An evening's fishing could easily produce hundreds of fish, enough to maintain several families for a few days (Towsey 2002, 41), so they were routinely eaten both fresh and preserved. Excess small saithe not needed for immediate consumption would be cleaned immediately; in recent centuries they were salted at this stage, but it is unlikely that salt in sufficient quantities would have been accessible in the Iron Age. The fish could then be hung to dry outside or indoors (Towsey 2002, 41–2). The fish could be put on wooden spits for hanging over a fire or in a windy place outside (Fenton 1973, 12). Pictures of late 19th- and early 20th-century fish drying in the Northern Isles sometimes show the fish threaded on spits, with the spit entering through the throat region where the gills would have been, and exiting through the open mouth (Orkney Photographic Archive). The dried product was prepared by soaking, boiling, peeling, or could even be eaten 'raw' as a chewy snack (Fenton 1973, 12).

Many of the vertebrae were found burnt, perhaps because bones were disposed of in the hearths in the broch. A dried or smoked and dried saithe would provide a small meal, probably only for one person, and with skill it would be possible to slide the preserved flesh off the vertebral column during eating (like eating a whole smoked mackerel or whole smoked herring today). The lack of rib bones probably means these were eaten, in a similar way to those in anchovies today. These vertebrae could then be tossed into a convenient fire to remove the smell and mess.

Six scales were identified, none of which were inconsistent with the cod family. Scales are difficult to identify to species, and they are also extremely rare in archaeological assemblages. The few known examples are from well-preserved urban deposits, and an unusual layer at Rosemarkie Cave comprising thousands of herring scales. Here, five of these were associated with Hearth 2 and one from the entrance area. Fish would normally be de-scaled during gutting, but it is common to miss a few scales. The five could be from the bodies of preserved cod family fish, discarded during consumption.

Pathologies

Two examples of pathological fish were noted, neither of which was anthropogenic. Both were examples of Type 4, compressed and splayed anterior vertebrae (Harland and Van Neer 2018), one from Hearth 1 and one from the entrance passage. Both were in poor condition.

Discussion

This small assemblage of fish remains from Clachtoll Broch provides an unprecedented insight into Middle Iron Age fish consumption in the centuries either side of the year 1. The assemblage is dominated by cod family fish, particularly saithe and pollack. These are difficult to differentiate, but most appear to be saithe. This species is found around Scotland's coasts in seasonal abundance, and in recent centuries, they were a staple food for the poor in springtime when other food sources were not available.

The inhabitants of Clachtoll were part of an Iron Age world that included sea-based travelling and communication around the coasts, and to the Western and Northern Isles. Despite this, there is little evidence that Iron Age subsistence strategies involved much fish. Further to the south, the lack of fish consumption has led to questions of widespread fish avoidance. In Scotland, recent work on well excavated sites with good sampling strategies has started to reveal sites with fish remains. In Orkney, Berst Ness Knowe of Skea has produced an assemblage of Early Iron Age deep sea fish, showing a sophisticated and consistent use of the sea's abundant resources. By the Middle Iron Age – approximately contemporary with Clachtoll – the inhabitants had largely abandoned deep water fishing and had turned to inshore fishing for small cod family fish (Harland 2016). Parallels can be observed at Old Scatness, Shetland (Nicholson 2015a), and at the ongoing excavations at The Cairns, Orkney. However, the recent re-excavation of Dunbeath Broch, on the east coast of Scotland, suggests a fishery for large cod found in deep water at some distance from the shore (Harland 2019).

The small, inshore cod family fish consumed at Clachtoll and other contemporary sites were fished either from the shore, or using small boats in the relative safety of inshore waters. These did not require skilled maritime knowledge. Other fish were found too, some perhaps fished in local freshwater river systems or lochs – like eels and salmon/trout. The few salmon bones found here were all large and would have provided a welcome variety to the diet, not to mention a considerable amount of food. A few of the species found were unusual and not generally preferred by humans, and these may represent small deposits of otter spraint. These were primarily located in Cell 1.

The small cod family fish remains found at Clachtoll comprised bodies, mostly without the heads. In several contexts, only vertebrae were found. This prompts interesting questions about fish processing and preservation. The heads were probably discarded soon after the fish were caught, perhaps along with the guts and most of the scales. The bodies could then be hung up in the rafters of the broch to lightly smoke, as was done until recently in the Northern Isles. Or, perhaps the fish were eaten immediately, used to fill the gap in the spring after most of the stored food has been used up. Spatial sampling within the broch's floor deposits shows considerable variation even within the same contexts: in some, only tiny fish vertebrae were deposited, and in others only larger fish vertebrae were discarded. These could suggest that these patterns represent the remains of individual meals.

5.6 Shellfish

Jackaline Robertson

Introduction phasing

The excavation from Clachtoll Broch produced only a small assemblage of shellfish. These were collected from 29 contexts described as rubble/roof collapse, floors, midden, entrance way, wall deposits and stairwell. The main objective of this analysis was to establish the economic role of shellfish at the broch and compare these results with other sites in this area.

Methodology

The shells were collected both by hand and from the bulk samples in an effort to maximise recovery of these finds.

These were identified to species using reference material and guides stored at AOC Archaeology Group (Hayward, Nelson-Smith and Shields 1996; Sterry and Cleave 2012). Whole shells were recorded by counting the shell apices for gastropods and valve umbos for bivalve species. Given the large number of fragmented shells, no attempt was made to calculate minimum number of individuals (MNI) figures. Instead, this assemblage was quantified by number of identified specimens (NISP) and as a consequence certain shell species such as bivalves may be overrepresented within the final results. The assemblage was scanned for any evidence of artefactual working, but none was observed. The full results are recorded in the site archive.

Results

The assemblage is summarised in Figure 5.6.1. The species were common periwinkle (*Littorina littorea*), common mussel (*Mytilus edulis*), common limpet (*Patella vulgata*) and Common oyster (*Ostrea edulis*) (Fig. 5.6.1). Preservation of these finds ranged from poor to excellent, but most were described as adequate to good. Shell fragments were recovered from the souterrain [069], Hearth 2, Hearth 3, the burning event, the post abandonment and collapse, the entrance passageway, Cell 2, Gallery 3 the stairs and from an unstratified deposit. The assemblage was dominated by common limpet (55.1%) closely followed by common periwinkle (44.4%). Both common mussel (0.4%) and common oyster (0.1%) were only ever marginal inclusions. While this assemblage was small the

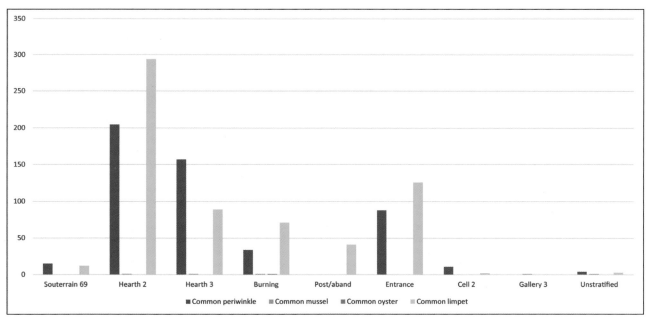

Figure 5.6.1 The shellfish for each of the principal context groups discussed in the text

economic importance of common limpet and periwinkle remained constant throughout the use of the broch.

Discussion

The shell species are all edible and would to some extent have been accessible from the rocky seashore surrounding the broch (Hayward *et al.* 1996). The presence of shell mixed with other midden material and from the occupation floor surfaces strongly suggests these remains represent food debris. It is also possible that the shellfish, in particular limpets, were used as fish bait (Renfrew 1993, 18; Nicholson 2007, 228). Given the small size of the Clachtoll assemblage it is impossible to determine if the shellfish were exploited solely for human consumption or if they had a dual role within this economy. At Scatness it was believed the shellfish were exploited both for food and fish bait (Cussans 2010, 178; 2015, 250). Molluscs have also been employed as a fertiliser but there is no evidence to suggest shellfish were routinely collected or stored for this purpose at Clachtoll (Ceron-Carrasco 2006, 180).

The shellfish assemblages from Tofts Ness, Cnip and Nybster are similar to that from Clachtoll in that only a small number of taxa were observed and common limpet and periwinkle tended to be favoured (Nicholson 2007, 228; Ceron-Carrasco 2006, 180; Robertson unpublished). This contrasts with Crosskirk, Scatness and Howe which all had a larger number of shellfish taxa (Macartney 1984, 135; Cussans 2015, 249–50; Howard 1994, 160). The lack of species diversity at Clachtoll could be due to a number of factors. The most obvious explanation is that the surrounding seashore could not support a larger variety of shellfish species. This theory is supported by the dominance of both common periwinkle and common limpet that tend to favour rocky beaches which are not always suitable habitats for other shellfish (Macartney 1984, 135). Certainly, the beaches surrounding the broch are predominately rocky.

The small number of common mussels at Clachtoll suggests that easy access to mussel beds was restricted (Macartney 1984, 135). Alternatively, it is possible that some bivalve species including mussels were viewed as a potential hazard to human health during certain seasons and therefore were deliberately not gathered as a regular food resource (Cussans 2010, 178). The recovery of a single oyster shell clearly demonstrates that this species was not routinely available in this locality.

The small number of shellfish at Clachtoll could also reflect its low economic importance as a food resource or that collecting it was viewed as too labour intensive for the dietary rewards it provided (Renfrew 1993, 18). Species such as common limpet are traditionally viewed as famine food. This is because the flesh which

Table 5.7.1 Clachtoll Broch: Insects and other invertebrates recorded from context [159]

Feature	Cell 1
Context	159
Sample volume	5L
INSECTA	
HEMIPTERA: HETEROPTERA (true bugs)	
Lygaeidae (ground bugs)	
Lygaeidae spp. [oa-p]	2
HEMIPTERA: HOMOPTERA	
Cicadellidae (planthoppers)	
Ulopa reticulata (Fabricius) [oa-p-m]	1
COLEOPTERA (beetles)	
Carabidae (ground beetles)	
Calathus fuscipes (Goeze) [oa]	1
Staphylinidae (rove beetles)	
Xylodromus concinnus (Marsham) [rt-st-h]	18
Olophrum sp. [oa]	1
Omaliinae sp. [u]	2
Aleochariinae spp. [u]	3
Stenus sp. [u]	1
Staphylininae sp. [u]	1
Ptinidae (spider and woodworm beetles)	
Ptinus fur (Linnaeus) [rd-sf-h]	7
Anobium punctatum (De Geer) [l-sf]	1
Cryptophagidae (silken fungus beetles)	
Cryptophagus spp. [rd-sf-h]	3
Atomaria spp. [rd-sf]	1
Latridiidae (minute brown scavenger beetles)	
Latridius minutus group [rd-st-h]	2
Corticariinae spp. [rt]	2
Salpingidae	
Aglenus brunneus (Gyllenhal) [rt-ss-h]	38
Curculionidae (weevils)	
Rhinoncus sp. [oa-p]	1
Curculionidae sp. [oa-p]	1
Coleoptera sp. and sp. indet. [u]	2
HYMENOPTERA (bees, wasps and ants)	
Formicidae sp. (ant)	+
Hymenoptera Parasitica sp. (parasitic wasp)	+

(Continued)

Table 5.7.1 Clachtoll Broch: Insects and other invertebrates recorded from context [159] (Continued)

Feature	Cell 1
Context	159
Sample volume	5L
SIPHONAPTERA (fleas)	
Pulex irritans Linnaeus [ss] (human flea)	++
Siphonaptera sp. indet. body segments (probably human flea)	+
ARACHNIDA	
Acarina spp. (mites)	C
Pseudoscorpiones sp. (pseudoscorpions)	P
Total adult beetles and bugs	88
Concentration beetles and bugs per litre of sediment	18/L

Ecological codes shown in square brackets are: h – house/building, l – wood/timber, m – moor/heathland; oa – outdoor taxa not usually found within buildings or in accumulations of decomposing matter; ob – probable outdoor taxa, p – plant–associated, sf – facultative synanthropes; ss – strong synanthropes; st – typical synanthrope;, u – uncoded.

Abundance of insects other than adult beetles and bugs has been estimated as follows: + 1–3 individuals, ++ 4–10. Abundance of other invertebrates has been recorded as present (P) or common (C)

is described as rubbery is not traditionally regarded as desirable and is usually only gathered when easily accessible in large quantities or when access to other food resources was limited (Ceron-Carrasco 2006, 180; Nicholson 2007, 228). Given the large quantities of other food items within the broch in the form of both meat and grain it is unlikely the inhabitants needed to gather shellfish for extra nutrients to survive in times of hardship, but instead these were an additional supplement to add some variety to the diet. It is also feasible that the small size of this assemblage has contributed to an unintentional bias. It is probable some domestic debris was disposed of directly into the sea and into middens located outside the perimeters of the excavated area, thereby permanently removing this evidence from the ecofactual record.

Conclusion

The evidence demonstrates that shellfish in particular common periwinkle and common limpet were deliberately harvested from the surrounding rocky seashore and brought to site to be used as a food resource and perhaps also as fish bait. These two species were consistently favoured throughout the history of the broch whereas common mussel and common oyster had only a very marginal role if any. Shellfish did have an economic role at Clachtoll but how important this resource actually was to the community is somewhat unclear given the small size of the surviving assemblage.

5.7 Insects from Cell 1

Enid Allison

Introduction

Two deposits within Cell 1 which is situated on the north-east side of the entrance passage, were described as waterlogged during the excavation. Wood fragments and animal hair were noted in both contexts. They were overlain by a thick layer of windblown sand and rubble. A sample from (159), the lower of the two deposits, was submitted for examination of insect remains.

Methods

The sample had a volume of 5 litres and processing broadly followed the methods of Kenward, Hall and Jones (1980). Wet-sieving was carried out using 0.3 mm mesh, and organic material was separated from the rest of the sediment using the 'washover' method. Paraffin flotation to extract insect remains was then carried out on the washover fraction, with recovery also on 0.3 mm mesh.

Beetle (Coleoptera) and bug (Hemiptera) sclerites were removed from the paraffin flot onto moist filter paper for identification using a low-power stereoscopic zoom microscope (×10–×45). Identification was by comparison with modern insect material and reference to standard published works. Nomenclature for Coleoptera follows Duff (2018). Minimum numbers of beetles and bugs were recorded, and taxa were divided into broad ecological groups for interpretation based on Kenward, Hall and Jones (1986), Kenward (1997) and Smith *et al.* (2020). The groups used are given in Table 5.7.1. The diversity (species richness) of the whole assemblage and of the decomposer component, were measured using the index of diversity (alpha) of Fisher, Corbet and Williams *et al.* (1943). This was calculated using a purpose-written computer program created at the University of York in 1992 by Harry Kenward, that was subsequently adapted to run on a personal computer by John Carrott.

The extracted insect material is currently stored in industrial methylated spirits in glass vials. Abbreviations used in the description of the insect assemblage are: α – alpha for the whole assemblage; αRT – alpha for the decomposer component; SE – standard error of alpha.

The insect assemblage

Context (159), the lower deposit within Cell 1, was described as a greasy organic silt, with lenses of charcoal and multiple deliberate deposits of sand that appeared to have been used as a base for a renewable floor surface (information from the context register). The character of the artefacts suggests a midden-type deposit.

An estimated 88 beetles and bugs of 23 taxa were recovered. A full list of taxa is shown in Table 5.7.1. Fragmentation of sclerites was very low but the entire assemblage was affected by chemical erosion, with all sclerites showing varying degrees of colour loss and thinning.

The low diversity of the assemblage indicated that it was dominated by a breeding community, and that there had been little ecological mixing (α = 10, SE = 2). Decomposers were by far the most abundant ecological group (81% of the assemblage), and their diversity was particularly low suggesting a very pure community that exploited a narrow range of conditions (αRT = 2, SE = 1). An assemblage derived from midden material would typically have a higher diversity, unless only a very restricted range of material contributed to the midden.

The assemblage is consistent with an origin in a floor deposit in an enclosed internal space. Almost all the beetles making up the decomposer group are members of a 'house fauna' (77% of the assemblage). The best represented species were *Aglenus brunneus* (38 individuals), *Xylodromus concinnus* (18 individuals) and white-marked spider beetle (*Ptinus fur*; 7 individuals). White-marked spider beetles scavenge on a wide variety of dry organic debris, either of animal or vegetable origin, while *Xylodromus concinnus*, *Latridius minutus* group, *Cryptophagus*, and *Atomaria* would have colonised any relatively dry mouldering plant debris within the building, such as floor litter or stored cut vegetation. Woodworm beetle (*Anobium punctatum*) may have attacked structural wood or could have been imported with firewood. Six human fleas (*Pulex irritans*) were also recorded.

Aglenus brunneus is a blind, flightless beetle that is strongly synanthropic, (*i.e.*, it is essentially dependent on human activity and settlement for survival). It appears to be associated with deep layers of decomposing material, and in Roman to pre-Norman archaeological deposits it is associated with house floors, although in some cases it may be a post-depositional burrower in the deposits (*e.g.*, Kenward 1975; Kenward and Hall 1995; Carrott and Kenward 2001; Kenward *et al.* 2011). It is very unlikely to have existed in the wild in the vicinity of the broch and, being flightless, was almost certainly introduced onto the site by human agency, probably in materials transported to the broch from settlement elsewhere. The records from this site add to the existing evidence for the presence of the species in Iron Age Britain (Lambrick and Robinson 1979; Smith *et al.* 2000).

The limited range of outdoor taxa (8% of the assemblage) were all represented by single individuals and some of these probably represent the importation of materials. *Ulopa reticulata*, a planthopper (Homoptera: Cicadellidae) found on heathers (*Calluna* and *Erica*; LeQuesne 1965, 18), and a very poorly preserved *Olophrum* typically found in moss, were probably introduced in peat. *Calathus fuscipes*, a ground beetle (Carabidae) typically found in relatively dry, open grassland, may provide an indication of the outside environment.

6

The floors and internal deposits: soil micromorphology

Lynne Roy

Introduction

The exceptional preservation and taphonomic conditions of deep floor deposits at Clachtoll Broch present an unprecedented opportunity for microscopic investigation of the floors of an Iron Age broch unmodified by reuse in later centuries. This chapter reports on the results of micromorphological analysis of floor sediments from the broch interior and discusses how it has been used to indicate the function and changing intensity of use of occupation horizons. Micromorphological analysis of floors can provide insights into construction material deposition and the use of space (Macphail *et al.* 2004; Milek 2012a) and identify events not observable at the macro scale, such as hearth rake-out (Shillito and Matthews 2013), *in situ* burning (Courty, Goldberg and Macphail 1989) and flooring refurbishment (Cavers and Crone 2017; Robertson and Roy 2019).

During the excavation, floors were characterised as being comprised of highly decomposed organic silts and clays, typically containing frequent charcoal flecks and fragments of burnt bone as well as patches of inorganic sand, clay and lenses of orange/yellow peat ash. Undisturbed kubiena samples were collected from the floor sequences in several locations, with a view to analysis of microstratigraphy and resolution of refurbishment episodes that were not identifiable at macro scale. The location of the sections from which the samples were taken is shown on Figures 2B.2, 2B.8 and 2B.12 and the section drawings showing the locations of the samples are depicted on Figures 2B.Sect-04, 2B.Sect-06, 2B.Sect-11, 2B.Sect-12, 2B.Sect-19 and 2B.Sect-23.

Eighteen samples were prepared for analysis using the methods of Murphy (1986) at the University of Stirling in the Department of Environmental Sciences. Samples were observed in plane polarized light (PPL) and cross polarized light (XPL) at magnifications of ×50, ×100, ×200 and ×400. Thin section description was conducted using the identification and quantification criteria set out by Bullock *et al.* (1985) and Stoops (2003), with reference to Mackenzie and Adams (1994) for rock and mineral identification. Plant remains were identified with reference to Schweingruber (1978) and with the assistance of AOC's archaeobotanist Jackaline Robertson. A coarse/fine (c/f) limit of 25 μm was used for both the mineral and organic components.

Results

Entrance passage: context (130)

Context (130) was hypothesised as a natural sand deposit of glacial origin. It comprises a single unit at the base of sample K33 which was taken from the north-facing section of the entrance. The deposit is highly heterogeneous with a mixed moderately sorted mineral composition interleaved with weakly banded organic plant tissue remains. Organic material is generally disaggregated and dominated by clusters of individual cells, unidentifiable reddened tissue and organ fragments, phytoliths (2–3%) and amorphous black material (10%). The unit has a platy microstructure with rare polyconcave planar voids and channels. Anthropic inclusions were limited to non-cellular possibly charred organic material. Observed pedofeatures include faint microlaminations (2000 μm thick), clay lenses (1–2%) and clay coatings to voids (<1%).

The banded and microlaminated nature of this deposit indicates that it is not of glacial origin. The moderate sorting of the coarse mineral component is consistent with natural (aeolian or alluvial) deposition, however,

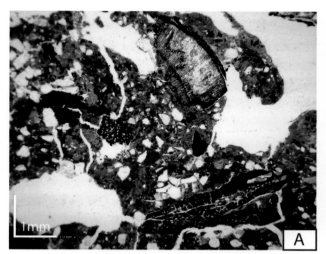

Figure 6.1a Channel and chamber voids within (130)

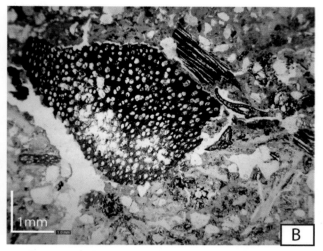

Figure 6.1b Coarse organic components within (121)

the heterogeneous nature of the deposit, its compaction and location within the entrance to a building suggest that it is not a wholly natural deposit. Considering both the mineralogy and the organic component it is likely that (130) is an incipient A horizon/weak soil developed on glacial material which incorporates evidence for initial occupation of the broch. The micromorphological evidence is consistent with a trampled occupation horizon incorporating material from a diverse range of sources subsequently trampled, fragmented and compressed. The observed clay lenses are reminiscent of slaking crusts and are indicative of areas of standing water or puddling suggesting that the deposit was somewhat damp. The observed clay coatings to voids are indicative of clay mobilisation through the profile which would be consistent with trampling in a damp environment. It is thus suggested that (130) represents gradual accumulation of occupation debris onto an incipient A horizon which in turn had developed on the underlying natural sand (not represented in the sample sequence).

Entrance passage: context (129)

(129) was hypothesised as a mix of natural and occupational debris and found infilling the fissures in the bedrock in the entrance passage. It is represented within Unit 2 of Sample K33 where it has a clear horizontal boundary with the underlying (130). The deposit has a randomly distributed and unsorted coarse mineral component, consistent with a dumped deposit although the coarse organic component, specifically coarse cellular charcoal, is banded and is more typical of sequential deposition. Cellular charcoal comprises 10% of the unit and is frequently >1000 μm in size. Patches of grey ash (2–3%), rounded aggregates of reddish brown to black sediment (soil) (2–3%) and phytoliths (<1%) were also observed. Pedofeatures include clay coatings (<1%), welded faecal aggregates

and faecal pellets (2–3%). These pedofeatures alongside channel and chamber voids (15%) (Fig. 6.1a) suggest post-depositional reworking of the deposit which may have blurred boundaries between an earlier lower dumped deposit and an upper charcoal-rich dumped deposit which is now only distinguishable by a difference in the quantity and distribution of coarse charcoal. The source of the dumped material is not clear and contains natural glacial mineral material intermixed with hearth waste. The location of this deposit infilling fissures in the bedrock indicates that it may have been deliberately dumped in order to create a more even surface although this event took place after the initial trampling and build-up of occupation debris represented by (130).

Entrance passage: context (121)

Context (121) was hypothesised as degraded flooring material. It is represented within Unit 3 of K33 and Unit 1 of K34 where it comprises the whole sample. The deposit is heterogenous with randomly sorted and arranged coarse mineral components (60%) made up of rock fragments of sandstone and schists. The coarse organic component includes blackened sub-angular charred fragments (10%), cellular charcoal (5%) weathered/degraded bone (2–3%) and anorthic sediments clasts (1–2%) (Fig. 6.1b). In K33, (121) has a diffuse boundary with the underlying (129) and is largely distinguished by its coarse nature and higher frequency of faecal pellets (5%) the by-products of soil microfauna which have, in places, created a crumb microstructure indicative of substantial levels of post-depositional reworking. The context is relatively porous (15%) and has a channel and chamber microstructure.

Post-depositional reworking has removed the majority of sedimentary signatures which might confirm site formation processes and there is no micromorphological evidence of deliberately constructed surfaces such as

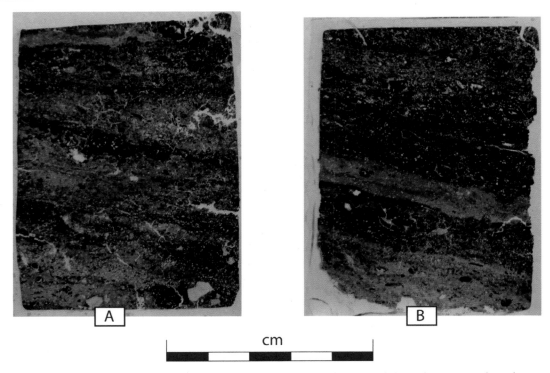

cm

Figure 6.2 Scan of thin section slides showing laminated nature of (091) and sharp discontinuity boundaries

ash deposition or peat covering as appears to be the case within the broch interior. However, the fragmented organic inclusions are similar to the components of floor surface within the broch interior and thus consistent with trampled floors which have accumulated through the gradual build-up of geologically and anthropically derived materials. It is unlikely that materials were deliberately imported into the entrance passage to create floors as appears to have been the case within the broch interior. This is consistent with the confined entrance space where importation of material for floor coverings would likely have resulted in the proximity of the roof becoming problematic and necessitating digging out and removal of floor strata, a process which has likely occurred elsewhere within the structure. Furthermore, the insulation of floors in the entrance would likely been less essential than in the interior and removal of accumulated floor strata within the confined space of the entrance would not have been practical.

Phase 2: context (091)

Context (091) was identified to the south of the hearth and described as a deep deposit of organic flooring deposits from which a sequence of six thin section samples (K25–30) have been studied. The samples were derived from the east-facing section of the central hearth complex as shown on Figure 2B.Sect-12. (091) contains a superimposition of 36 micro-stratigraphical contexts of horizontal layers

deformed by compaction and trampling. Their thickness ranges from less than 2 mm to up to 30 mm (Fig. 6.2). The layers are characterised by microlaminated ferruginous plant remains, fuel residues and banded coarse mineral material. Fuel residues are mixed, comprising peat/turf, charcoal, charred plant (derived from heath-like plants), vesicular char and peat ash (Fig. 6.3a). Bone fragments (Fig. 6.3b) are also present in varying quantities. Micro-structures are complex but predominantly massive por-phyric to moderately lenticular. Pedofeatures throughout the sequence comprise occasional to rare dusty silt and clay coatings to voids and mineral grains with occasional to rare infillings of voids and pore spaces.

The lowermost deposits are some of the best preserved and comprise discrete sedimentary units of micro-lam-inated plant material separated by sharp discontinuity boundaries (Fig. 6.3). Unit 1 of K25, the earliest sampled deposit of (091), is a heterogeneous deposit with a coarse to fine (c/f) ratio of 65/35. The coarse mineral fraction comprises 40–50% of the unit approximately 50% of which is quartz with the remaining 50% comprising a mix of feldspars, chlorite and intrusive igneous fragments with high order interference colours. The mineral material is moderately horizontally banded. The coarse organic material is rich in evidence for anthropic activity includ-ing charred peat fragments (5–10%), cellular charcoal (5%), bone fragments (burnt and unburnt) (1–2%) and reddened and rounded pottery or clay daub fragments

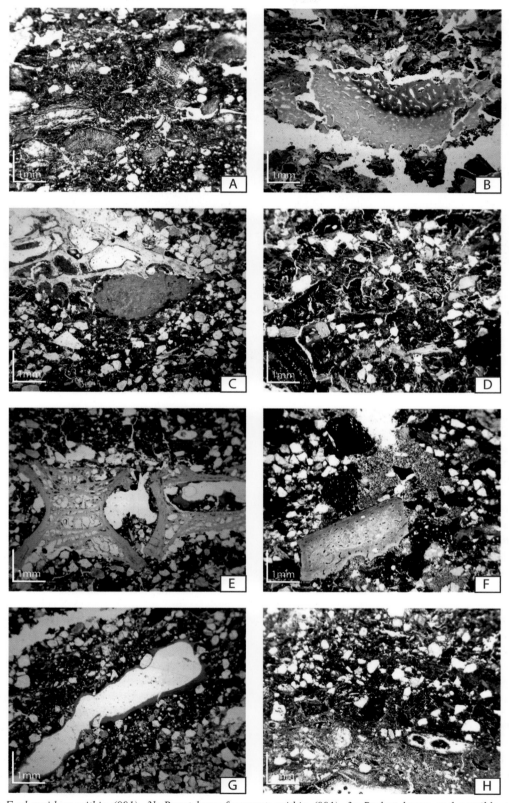

Figure 6.3a Fuel residues within (091), 3b Burnt bone fragments within (091), 3c Rodent bones and possible coprolite (091), 3d Banding of fuel residues within (091), 3e Semi-articulated vertebrae (091), 3f Fuel residues and burnt bone within (091), 3g Strongly oriented crescentic clay coatings (091), 3h Alternate bands of mineral rich material interspersed with charred material (091)

(<1%). The unit is compact with a porphyric c/f related distribution and massive to moderately lenticular microstructure. There is a sharp boundary between Unit 1 and the overlying Unit 2.

The base unit of (091) (Unit 1, K25) is most likely a sub-floor levelling deposit. It has a greater frequency of rock fragment inclusions, quartz, feldspars and chlorite minerals than in the overlying units. Anomalous and exotic volcanic rock clasts likely reflect the deliberate use/importation of a different source material to level/construct the floor. By contrast, the laminated sequence of floor occupation deposits overlying Unit 1 and comprising the majority of (091) are characterised by fine particles of charcoal, charred peat and bone rich domestic hearth rake out and spreads of sand as well as by the sub-horizontal orientation of the elongated components. These are all characteristics consistent with periodic accumulation and compaction (Goldberg and Macphail 2006, 221) and thus typical of occupation floor surfaces.

Unit 2 (K25) is finer than the underlying unit with very fine sands and silts dominating the matrix; coarse mineral material accounts for only 20% of the unit. The b-fabric is weakly crystallitic which may indicate the presence of ash. Anthropic indicators are common and varied and include charred peat (20%), bone (5%), charred plant remains (1–2%), phytoliths (1–2%) and charred seeds (<1%). The organic material has a preferred horizontal alignment and a moderately banded distribution. Anthropic indicators are yet more frequent in Unit 3 and include charred peat (10–15%), charcoal (10%) and bone (including semi-articulated bones of a likely rodent) (10%). Probable rodent bones were also observed within Unit 4 alongside a probable omnivore coprolite (Fig. 6.3c). Unit 1 of sample K26 correlates stratigraphically with the aforementioned Unit 4 of K25, it is moderately banded (Fig. 6.3d) and also contains evidence for probable rodent activity in the form of a cluster of molars and incisors at the base of the slide. Evidence of food preparation/consumption is also present in Unit 1 of K26 as burnt and unburnt seeds and caryopses and common fuel residues (peat and charcoal). Semi-articulated vertebrae of a small mammal (probable rodent) were observed within Unit 1 of K28 (Fig. 6.3e). The presence of minute, chemically weathered bone fragments and the yellowish/pale brown colour of the fine organo-mineral matrix in which they were embedded, suggest that this unit also contains a mixture of omnivore and herbivore dung. A general increase in fuel residues (Fig. 6.3f) upwards is notable up to Unit 4 (K26) which contains a smaller proportion of food residues. This unit also has a higher proportion of dusty clay coatings to voids and is more porous than underlying layers.

Higher up in the sequence (specifically within K27 and K30), strongly oriented crescentic clay coatings (Fig. 6.3g) and slaking crusts were identified sub-parallel to the surface. Such features are typically indicative of exposure to rain and thus often interpreted as evidence for unroofed structures. However, as demonstrated by French (2003) chemical alterations in oxidation and reduction processes can lead to the dispersal of silt and clay particles within localised areas, in occupation deposits within roofed spaces. Experimental micromorphological studies at Butser and Lejre revealed moderately or strongly oriented silty clay coatings in accumulation deposits and found these to be associated with areas of organic decay and turbulent conditions of trampling which caused the mobilisation of silty clay particles (Banerjea *et al.* 2015). The deep floor sequence (091) was also associated with a narrow stone drainage channel [059] and subsequently with large stone flags ((053) and (068)) indicating that water accumulation within the broch interior was sufficiently severe as to require structural water management solutions. Thus, the strongly oriented clay coatings crusts likely derive from a combination of puddling, trampling and organic decay which was notably more prevalent in the upper layers of this context.

The floor layers identified are typical of beaten floor layers identified elsewhere within the broch (*e.g.*, (062), (086)) and characterised by a wide variety of anthropic inclusions (burnt peat, soil allochthonous soil, coprolites, amorphous organic matter, bone and ash crystal). The beaten floor accumulations are compact with weak to well-developed laminae composed of moderately sorted sand silt, charcoal, burnt peat, organic bones and rare coprolites. There is a general trend towards a more loosely consolidated fabric within units which are richest in charred fuel remains (charcoal and peat). These layers occasionally contain burnt microartefacts, but lack evidence of *in situ* burning. After charcoal and burnt peat, bone and charred seeds were the most common microartefacts observed.

The individual units/floor layers identified within (091) have the appearance of cyclical trample spreads, tentatively interpreted as a record of regular (seasonal?) activity raking out and laying down trample material and organic materials. Alternate bands of mineral rich material interspersed with charred material (Fig. 6.3h) may reflect replenishment of floors, or perhaps changes in use with more heavily charred layers representing winter months when more fuel was consumed. Changing proportions of fuel residues with burnt peat and charcoal varying in the overall proportion present may also be indicative of changing fuel use according to season with more efficient and hotter wood fuels being used in the winter, or perhaps changes in hearth function, *i.e.* periods of use for cooking which require efficient quick burning fuels as opposed to a reduced use for heating and light from a low burning peat fire. The floors lower in the sequence appear to have

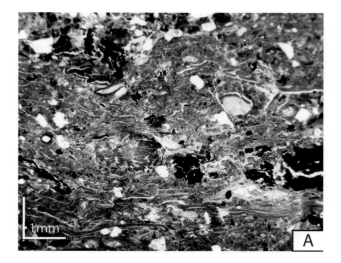

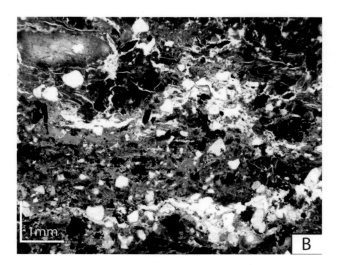

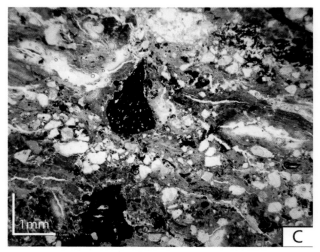

Figure 6.4a Elongate fibrous plant tissues (087), 4b Microlamination (087), 4c Vesicular char and peat ash (087)

formed in relatively dry conditions perhaps reflecting their proximity to the hearth whilst in use. The upper floors appear to have accumulated to become level with the central hearth surface, effectively making its continued use unsustainable and marking the end of the second phase of occupation/hearth use.

Phase 2: context (087)

Context (087) is represented in thin section sample K12 (Units 1–5) and at the base of sample K13 (Unit 1) and derived from flooring contexts adjacent to the hearth (Fig. 2B.Sect-04). Six stratigraphic units were identified, all of which are compact with porosity ranging from 5–10%, excepting Unit 4 where it was observed to be less than 5%. The coarse material across all units displays a preferred horizontal orientation and units are distinguished from one another primarily by differences in proportions of mineral and organic materials and in particular the relative dominance of elongate fibrous plant tissue remains (Fig. 6.4a). Platy to lenticular microstructures dominate and are typical of occupational floor layers (Courty *et al.* 1989; Milek 2012a). The lowest unit contains a high proportion (40%) of herbaceous epidermal and vascular plant tissues arranged in horizontal layers with very few fragments of secondarily thickened woody tissue. Anthropic indicators within the lowest unit (Unit 1, K12) comprise fuel residues in the form of charcoal (3–5%) and burnt peat (3–5%) with relatively high proportions of charred bone (3–5%) and phytoliths (1–2%). The overlying layer (Unit 2, K12) has a higher proportion of mineral material (40%) and a lower (10%) corresponding coarse organic component. The coarse mineral material is weakly banded and includes 40% coarse sand-sized rock fragments and rare (<1%) vivianite crystals. Organic material is similar in overall composition to the underlying layer although overall proportions of organics are lower. A vesicular glassy fragment is likely slag. Both burnt and unburnt peat fragments are present along with aggregates of anorthic sediment.

Units 3 and 5 of Sample K12 are similar to Unit 1, both having high proportions of organic material including well preserved horizontally lain elongate plant tissues and plant stems (5–10%) and mixed fuel residues (3–5% charcoal, 3–5% peat, 5–10% fine black material) as well as burnt and unburnt bone (3–5%), ash (1–2%) and phytoliths (1–2%). There are trace amounts of Fe/Mn accumulation, hypocoatings and depletions (<1% each) and limpid silty clay coatings of voids (<1%). The intervening unit (Unit 4) is much finer in nature with a c/f ratio of 50/50 compared with the 70/30 ratio observed through the rest of the context. Unit 4 is also remarkable in its absence of elongated plant tissue observed elsewhere throughout the context as well as absence of charcoal and bone. Reddish/black charred peat fragments

cm

Figure 6.5 Scan of thin section slides showing microlaminations (086)

constitute 10% of the unit. A single heated clay fragment was also observed. Unit 1 of Sample K13 is broadly similar to Units 1, 3 and 5 of K12 but was observed to contain a lower overall proportion of plant tissue fragments (3–5%). Fuel residues comprise a mix of charcoal and charred peat and crystallitic ash in similar proportions to those observed in Units 1, 3 and 5 of K12.

Preservation of organic material indicates damp, semi-waterlogged preserving conditions. The presence of elongated horizontal cellular plant tissues suggests importation of heath-like plant materials, most likely as a deliberate act to cover and insulate the floor. The higher proportion of plant materials within the lowermost unit (Unit 1; Fig. 6.4a) suggests that this may have acted as foundation or insulating layer in which larger quantities of plant materials were imported as a preparation surface over the underlying irregular bedrock surface.

Microlamination (Fig. 6.4b) and weak striation of birefringent fabric within Units 2 and 4 of K12 supports the interpretation of a 'beaten floor' (Macphail and Goldberg 2010) similar to that observed in (062) and developed upon the underlying preparation surface of plant material and fuel residues. Fuel residues are mixed, comprising peat/turf, charcoal, charred plant (derived from heath-like plants), vesicular char and peat ash (Fig. 6.4c). Bone fragments are also present throughout (087) (excepting Unit 4 of K12). Burnt bone is fragmented and generally exhibits indicators of medium to high intensity burning (Hanson and Cain 2007) with partial loss of histology, carbon deposits and

calcination observed at edges of fragments. Amorphous black material and punctuations are also present across the context and occasionally intermixed with Fe/Mn pedofeatures indicating a reducing environment typical of compacted sediments (Lindbo, Stolt and Vepraskas 2010). Laminated silty and dusty clay pedofeatures characteristic of floor surfaces (Courty *et al.* 1989) were also observed

Unit 4 is both finer and less porous than other units within the context. It contains a different range of anthropic indicators, including anorthic sediment fragments and a small fragment of heat altered clay but is remarkable in the absence of plant tissues, charcoal and burnt bone. The compacted, banded, nature of the deposit combined with the presence of sediment inclusions that likely originate from outside of the structure combine to suggest a deliberately compacted/trampled deposit possibly following an occupation hiatus. Unit 4 thus likely represents a single episode of compaction to create a 'cleaner' floor surface onto which the daily living activities responsible for the formation of Unit 5 were then played out.

The microstructure of Unit 3 is predominantly massive with occasional channels and chambers observed. These channels and chambers along with evidence for some limited soil faunal faecal matter suggest bioturbation within the context. The consistently high levels of organic material present within the unit would have been conducive to soil fauna activity and may also indicate organic floor coverings which have been comminuted, or the importation of peaty turves for flooring.

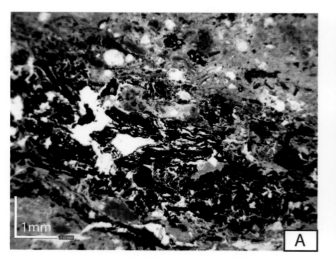 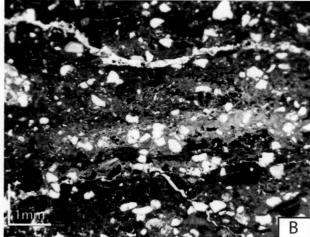

Figure 6.6a Vesicular char (086), 6b Fuel residues (086)

Phase 3: context (086)

Context (086) is represented in thin section sample K13 (Units 2–5), K14 (Units 1–7) and at the base of sample K15 (Units 1–4). The samples were derived from flooring contexts adjacent to the hearth overlying context (087). It was described as a deposit of flooring material comprised of organic reeds/rushes and dense grey silt/clay. Fifteen stratigraphic units were identified, each made up of lenses of microartefacts and microaggregates superimposed upon one another to create a laminated bedding structure (Fig. 6.5). All units are compact (porosity 5–10%) with massive to platy microstructures and a porphyric distribution of coarse grains.

The boundary between units within (086) is generally diffuse although the boundary with the underlying (087) is sharp and indicative of a change in use. Unit 2 of K13 is a coarsely banded deposit comprising a mix of fuel residues (charcoal (3–5%), bone (3–5%), and ash (3–5%)) as well as unburnt organic plant tissues and woody fragments (5–10%). Two fragments of pottery or heated clay were also observed. Coarse components are horizontally banded and generally arranged parallel to the base of the slide. Coarse mineral material comprises a mix of quartz and feldspars with sandstone and schist rock fragments (10–15%); vivianite was also observed. Observed pedofeatures are limited to a trace of silty clay coatings and partial infillings to channel voids. Unit 3 is more compact in nature and has a massive microstructure. Coarse components are similar in composition to the underlying unit with the exception of cellular charcoal which was not observed within Unit 3. A small area of grey vesicular char is likely rendered animal fat and a by-product of food/animal processing. Unit 4 of K13 is broadly similar to Unit 3 and includes a mix of fuel residues including charred peat or animal dung (15–20%), charcoal (5–10%)

and phytolith rich grass (or dung) ash (3–5%) as well as heat affected clay fragments indicative of earth rake out. Fuel residues make up a lower proportion of Unit 5 compared with Unit 4 which has a higher c/f ratio. However, Units 4 and 5 are broadly similar in terms of microstratigraphy, compaction and composition. Vesicular char was also observed within Unit 4 (Fig. 6.6a) and may have formed during cooking and/or may represent the remains of rendered fat burnt for lighting. The presence of fatty residues and dung in this floor surface suggest a level of background detritus not observed in other contexts reflecting perhaps the location of this context adjacent to the hearth where greater quantities of debris accumulated and were tolerated.

Evidence for partial reworking of (086) is present within Unit 1 of K14 which has a high proportion of organic matter, including horizontal parallel layers of herbaceous epidermal and vascular plant tissues. The unit includes a range of fuel residues (peat/dung char 10%, cellular charcoal 2–3%) although in much lower proportions than observed within the units within K14 (Fig. 6.6b). Food processing residues are present in the form of both burnt and unburnt bone fragments (2–3%). The bone fragments are smaller than 5 mm and highly weathered, with abundant pits and cracks and weathering rims (*cf.* Bullock *et al.* 1985). Marine shell fragments (1–2%) are poorly sorted but several sand sized particles could be aeolian in origin. Unit 2 of K14 contains a similar range of fuel residues to the underlying unit but has lower proportions of unburnt fresh plant material (plant tissues and peat fragments) when compared with Unit 1. Coarse material within Unit 2 has a stronger preferred horizontal alignment and weakly striated crystallitic birefringence fabric likely reflecting the presence of peat ash. Units 3–7 were found to be broadly similar to Unit 1 with similar pro-portions of herbaceous plant tissues and fuel residues. However, no bone was observed within Units 3 and 6. A single charred seed was recorded within Units 3 and 5. A large (10 × 15 mm) fragment of unburnt peat or turf was recorded within Unit 4. Lenses of grey calcitic ash become more frequent upwards and correspond with a decreasing frequency of cellular charcoal.

The lower Units (1 and 2) of sample K15 are similar in composition to those observed within K13 but are generally more fragmented in nature with most inclusions being coarse sand sized or smaller and moderately aligned parallel to the base of the slide. The proportion of coarse organic material within Units 1 and 2 of K15 is generally lower than in K14 (25% of Unit 1 and 15% of Unit 2) with Unit 2 in particular containing a substantially higher pro-portion of coarse mineral material. The boundary between Units 1 and 2 is diffuse. The coarse mineral arrangement of both units is poorly sorted but weakly banded and the b-fabric exhibits weak striations which suggests this unit is a discrete surface lens which has been subject to compaction or trampling (Simpson *et al.* 1999).

Fuel residues observed in the finely stratified layers within each unit are comprised of fine woody charcoal and charred plant material. These fuel rich layers typ-ically have a low porosity and as such it is likely that fuel ash was dumped and then trampled on the floor surface, a process that was hypothesised in (062) and also on floor layers within House 2 at the Iron Age set-tlement of Bornais, South Uist (Milek 2012b, 59), where more delicate fragments of charcoal and burnt bone are frequently seen to have been broken up, forming layers of moderately sorted deposits. The associated moderate levels of amorphous red and black fine material present within these layers indicates either strongly humified or charred organic material consistent with peat or herbivore dung. The sequence repeats several times within each unit although post-depositional reworking has somewhat blurred the boundaries within and between units which are diffuse. The sequence also bears resemblance to deposits described from Links of Noltland (Hamlett 2014) which in turn were likened to 'layer cake' deposits from Bronze Age layers in Grotta Cotariova, Italy, where periodical burning of dried and trampled dung deposits formed alter-nating layers (Mlekuž 2009 cited by Hamlett 2014). The apparent absence of charcoal within Unit 4 and differing proportions of fuel residues observed across the sediment sequence within (086) is key to understanding the differ-ences between the finely stratified layers identified. There is also a broad negative correlation between the proportion of phytoliths present and charcoal. Since the abundance of opal phytoliths is low in wood ash (Karkanas *et al.* 2002) this can tentatively be suggested as evidence of a change in activity in the vicinity of the hearth which required

different fuel types. Given that wood, peat and animal dung have different burning properties, the use of differ-ent fuels within the fire may indicate a change in activity requiring either a higher level of light or heat or more consistent temperature. Peat and dung are more efficient fuels compared to wood and generate a more consistent temperature; thus, their fires are easy to maintain over longer periods of time and useful for food preparation (Bradbaart, Poole and Hiusman 2012). Seasonal availa-bility of fuels may have made wood preferable at certain times of year. Alternatively, the undertaking of tasks that required more light may have resulted in preferred use of wood over peat or dung.

Phase 3: context (085)

Context (085) is represented within Units 5–7 of Sample K15 and Units 1–3 of Sample K16. It was hypothesised that this layer represents a resurfacing layer of peat ash used to cover over decaying floor material prior to relaying of the floor. Unit 5 of K15 has a diffuse boundary with the overlying (086) from which it is distinguished primarily by its finer nature and lower proportion of coarse organic materials. It has a low porosity (5–10%) and massive to platy microstructure consistent with trampling. It contains microlaminations comprising thin lenses (200 µm) of fine blackened material which contain a mixture of both wood and peat ashes interleaved between thicker lenses (1000 µm) of matrix material with rubified iron nodules characteristic of peat and turf ash (Fig. 6.7a). The organic fraction comprises a mix of burnt and unburnt material including reddish brown herbaceous plant tissue which may be unburnt peat or dung. The overlying Unit 6 has a higher coarse organic component and a weakly striated crystallitic b-fabric indicative of the presence of ash. A fragment of smooth vesicular mineral material was interpreted as ashy slag. Unit 7 of K15 and Unit 1 of K16 are broadly similar and have striated appearance as result of thin laminations of fine orange to black likely charred material interleaved within the sediment matrix. Patches of crystallitic ash (3–5%) were also observed. Approximately 10% of both units is comprised of unburnt plant tissues remains which are generally horizontally aligned and may represent the remains of floor coverings or unburnt peat. Unit 2 of Sample K16 is broadly similar to the underlying unit in terms of organic composition but is coarser and has a more varied mineral composition. The mineral component is moderately sorted and arranged parallel with the base of the slide. The microlaminations observed in the underlying units of this context were not noted within Unit 2 and it has a massive microstructure with no natural peds visible. The boundary between Unit 2 and the overlying Unit 3 is sharp at macro scale and clear at magnifications greater than x100. Unit 3 is a relatively

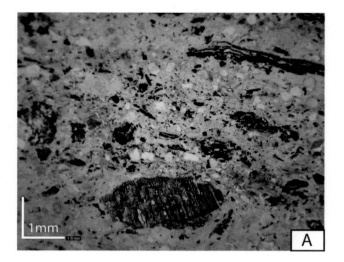

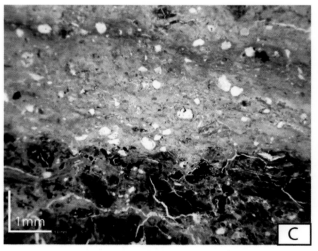

Figure 6.7a Wood and peat ashes in (085), 7b High clay content (085), 7c Sharp discontinuity boundaries (085)

fine deposit with higher proportion of clay (405) than observed elsewhere throughout the site. In contrast to the underlying unit both the coarse mineral and organic components are randomly arranged. The unit also contains a relatively high proportion of vesicular slag (1–2%) and rounded anorthic sediment or soil fragments (3–5%).

Context (085) was hypothesised as a deliberate preparation of compacted fuel residues used to recover the floor. The evidence in thin section suggests that this process was perhaps a little more sporadic than hypothesised. Distinct layers observed within the context are indicative of sequential deposition over several episodes of rake out/fuel residue dumping rather than a single deliberately recovering event. The presence of herbaceous epidermal and vascular tissues within Unit 6 of Sample K16 is indicative of incorporation of some unburnt fresh material during this process and thus this context does not appear to represent a single 'clean' relaying episode but a sequence of events or perhaps installation of sub-floor levelling deposits. The greater compaction of this context and general higher proportions of ash demonstrate that this floor had a different composition to the non-constructed earthen floors identified elsewhere in the broch. The floor is consistent with deliberate and periodic deposition as opposed to the gradual accumulation observed in underlying layers. Units 3 (K16) and 5 (K17) have an unusually high clay content (40%) (Fig. 6.7b) which suggests deliberate importation of sediments for construction from outside of the broch. Unit 2 of Sample K16, has a different rock and mineral composition than the underlying layers, specifically the inclusion of angular rock fragments which are also indicative of a different source material. Coarse sand and rock aggregates such as those observed within Unit 2 of K16 can increase the strength of an earthen building material (Berge 2000). Thus, it seems that at least two external sources of construction material were deliberately imported into the broch to repair and strengthen the floor. The observed sharp boundary between Units 2 and 3 (Fig. 6.7c) are consistent with the rapid deposition of Unit 3 on top of a prepared or repaired surface. The coarse components are randomly oriented and arranged which suggests that this deposit may have been deliberately imported and dumped. In this sense the units within (085) are not dissimilar to floors at the Iron Age site of Cnip in Lewis where floors were periodically removed and new floors of clean sand laid down (Armit 2006). The source of the material used to construct the floor at Clachtoll is not known but given the high clay content was likely derived from an area off site and deliberately imported which would have required a significant effort.

The subsequent hypothesised 'relaying' of the floor likely comprised little more than recommencement of normal activity (or reoccupation following a period of hiatus) with perhaps some importation of floor coverings in the form of peaty turves or rushes visible in the upper layer of (085) and lower layers of (084).

Phase 3: context (062)

Context (062) was hypothesised as comprising mixed flooring material and was observed to comprise six units within Sample K8. The sample was removed from the south-facing section of the south-west quadrant (Fig. 2B. Sect-06). The context is compact with microstructures typical of occupational floor layers (Courty *et al.* 1989, Milek 2012a) ranging from massive (Units 1 and 3) to platy/lenticular (Units 2 and 4–6). Coarse minerals are weakly banded and moderately to poorly sorted within a porphyric (closed to open) coarse fine related distribution. Units 1 and 3 share a stipple speckled microcrystallitic birefringent fabric related to coarse mineral weathering. The birefringent fabric of Units 2 and 4–6 is masked by fine amorphous organic matter and thus is undifferentiated in each case. Unburnt turf/peat fragments are present within Unit 4 (1–5%).

Anthropic inclusions are present in greater amounts in Units 1 and 3, while Units 2 and 4 contain more and better-preserved organic residues and pedofeatures related to Fe/Mn movement. Clay (<1%) and silty clay (2–5%) infill pedofeatures occur with greater frequency in Unit 3. Anthropic inclusions of vesicular char (<1%), charcoal (1–5%), charred plant material (1–5%), bone (1–2%) and burnt peat (<1%) are fragmented (likely from trampling) within Unit 1. Quantities are generally higher in Units 2 and 3 with burnt peat accounting for up to 10%. Boundaries between sedimentary units are clear to sharp in each case and are particularly sharp both above and below Unit 2. Within Unit 4, prismatic calcite crystals are typical of wood ash (Wattez and Courty, 1987).

The observed sharp boundaries above and below Unit 2 and to a lesser degree Unit 4 appear to have formed where a layer of peat fuel (Unit 2) or grass ash (Unit 4) residue formed a layer resting upon the surface of the unit. This indicates that fuel residues were spread over the surface of the floors. The units within (062) thus appear to represent a series of 'beaten floors' (Macphail and Goldberg 2010) representing distinct activity episodes separated by, and developed upon, a prepared surface of fuel residues.

Silty and limpid clay pedofeatures are present in varied quantities across all units of (062) indicating low energy down profile movement of fine material, this has filled pore spaces within the microstructure and within and around anthropic inclusions but appears unrelated to cracks. This together with orthic Fe/Mn nodules indicates that the floor was damp throughout its use and formation allowing the precipitation of Fe and movement of clay particles.

Phase 3: context (084)

Context (084) is represented within Units 4–6 of K16 and 1–4 of K17 and was a hypothesised as the active floor surface at the time of the fire. It survives as a series of stratified layers separated by clear to sharp boundaries within which microlaminations (1,000 μm thick) are commonly observed. Microstructures are typically massive to platy and the context is very compact with <5% porosity

Unit 4 of K16 is composed of herbaceous plant tissue remains (10%), reddish brown amorphous organic matter (10%) charred peat (10%), 3–5% charcoal, 3–5% rubified iron nodules and 1–2% phytoliths. Coarse materials are moderately banded and aligned horizontal with the base of the slide creating a microlaminated appearance. Unit 4 has a clear boundary with the overlying Unit 4 which is much finer in nature as a consequence of greater proportions of amorphous yellow, orange and black fine organic material. The coarse organic material is comprised primarily of subrounded blackened organic matter (10%) plant tissues (5%) and woody organ fragments (1–2%). No food or fuel residues were observed. Unit 5 has a clear boundary with the overlying Unit 6 but is coarser and has a relatively high proportion of anthropic indicators including fuels residues of charcoal (10%) and ash (1–2%). Units 1 and 2 of K17 are broadly similar to Unit 6 of K16 and are distinguished by slight variations in coarse organic components. In particular Unit 1 of K17 contains 10% reddish brown peaty fragments which may be unburnt peat fuel or dung. Unit 2 of K17 was more compact than the overlying unit and also displayed stronger horizontal banding. It also contained a more diverse range of coarse organic anthropic components including charred peat fragments (10%) bone (1–2%) and ash (2–3%)

(084) thus appears to represent a series of occupation horizons. Minimal indicators of anthropic activity were identified within Unit 5 of K16 and this unit is interpreted as deliberately lain plant material as matting or to form a floor surface with the high proportion of fine organic matter representative of comminuted plant material. (084) is generally more compact than other floors within the broch and porosity is commonly <5%. This compaction may reflect the location of (084) beneath (042) which represents the remains of a catastrophic fire. It likely that this fire burnt to sufficiently high temperatures to draw up some moisture from underlying layers resulting in partial collapse of sediment structure thus creating the massive microstructure and low porosity observed here. However, the preservation of unburnt plant tissue fragments throughout (084) suggests that despite the heat of the fire it did not spread so far down this sequence so as to result in charring of underlying layers and the

charred residues observed in this context most likely result as a consequence of activity at the time of use rather than post-depositional charring of previously fresh deposited material.

Burning event: context (042)

(042) is represented within the Units 3 and 4 of sample K17 and in the upper units (Units 6 and 7) of Sample K8 (south-west quadrant) (Fig. 2B.Sect-06). It was hypothesised to have formed as a result of a single event that marked the end of the occupation although queries remained as to whether this represented burnt flooring or the collapsed remains of upper floors or a roof.

Within K17 both units retain characteristics similar to the underlying (084) being moderately banded and preserving microlaminations *c.* 1,000 µm thick. However, Units 3 and 4 contrast with the underlying units due to their darker colour and dominance of charred residues. The dark brown to dark reddish-brown colours of the matrices suggests that they have been reddened by heat. The majority of organic components in both units are charred or burnt although some unburnt plant tissue remains (5%) were identified towards the base of Unit 3. Unit 4 has a higher coarse mineral component and is more porous in nature with channels and chamber voids observed. The mineral fraction of Units 6 and 7 of K8 accounts for 50–70% of the context and includes a diverse mix of mineral types including numerous rock fragments in the lower unit with high interference colours indicative of an igneous origin. Anthropic indicators in the lower unit include charred residues (charcoal (1–2%) and burnt peat (1–2%)) and phytolith rich possible ash patches (1–2%). Anthropic inclusions in the upper unit (Unit 7) of (042) are comparatively more varied and abundant and comprise vesicular char (<1%), woody charcoal (1–2%), charred plant remains (1–2%) and burnt peat (1–2%). Anorthic patches of sediment (1–2%) with clear boundaries with the surrounding matrix were noted in Unit 7. Dusty clay coatings to mineral grains and partial infillings between mineral grains were also observed.

The base unit in both samples appears to represent the remains of a fire. Given the laminated appearance of the sediment and its similarities with the underlying (084), Unit 3 of K17 is interpreted as the remains of a burnt floor surface. Here the temperature of the fire was sufficient to redden the substrate but was not so high as to entirely burn off all organic matter as evidenced by preservation of charcoal and plant tissue remains. However, the base layer of (042) within sample K8 (Unit 6) is dominated by coarse mineral material suggesting a higher temperature fire which has burnt away the majority of organic material. This indicates that the temperature of the fire varied locally within the broch with some areas reaching higher temperatures than others. The similarities between the burnt deposits of (042) and underlying (084) are useful in defining the lower units of (042) as remains of organic flooring material representative of the final period of occupation of the broch. Micromorphological analysis of a 'red ash layer' at Scalloway broch originally thought to represent the remains of collapsed roofing material also found it to represent the remains of organic flooring (Carter 1998, 31).

The upper units of (042) within both K8 and K17 have a higher porosity than the majority of sedimentary units within the broch. These upper units represent the period following the fire and thus also incorporate sedimentary signatures of abandonment including channels and chambers indicative of reworking by soil fauna which has somewhat blurred the sedimentary signal. Soil faunal activity has been observed to begin following exposure to sunlight (Milek 2012a), thus indicating that the broch became unroofed allowing for partial reworking of the upper deposit shortly after its deposition. However, while many excremental pedofeatures were found infilling faunal channels that had been created post-deposition, the presence of a patchy and localised crumb microstructure appears to have existed within this deposit prior to its burning. This evidence along with the more diverse mineralogy of the upper units may indicate that the upper layers of (042) comprise the remains of roofing material formed, at least in part, from turf brought onto the site from the surrounding landscape. The clear to sharp boundary between the sedimentary units also supports an interpretation of collapsed roofing material or flooring from the upper storeys which has fallen on to the lower burnt floor surface shortly after the fire.

Micromorphological evidence thus indicates that (042) was formed as a consequence of three primary formation processes; a fire on the floor surface, collapse of roofing/flooring material from above and subsequent exposure to the elements and partial reworking.

Cell 4: context (081)

Context (081) was hypothesised as decomposed flooring material that had been repeatedly refurbished in a similar manner to the floors encountered within the central broch interior. (081) is represented within Units 1–3 of K21, 1–3 of K22 and 1–2 of K24. The samples were all derived from the east-facing section on Cell 4 as shown on Figure 2B.Sect-23. The boundaries between the units are diffuse and they are distinguished primarily by variations in the coarse organic component. The coarse mineral component typically comprises 30% of each unit and has a mixed mineral composition dominated by quartz (15%) with very few feldspars (2–3%). The coarse mineral component is weakly banded and in some cases randomly oriented and arranged. The coarse organic component comprises a mix of fuel (charcoal, ash, peat) and food (bone) residues as well as common to frequent plant tissue remains. The frequency of plant tissues varies between units from 2–3% within Unit 1 of K21 to 50% within Unit 2 of K22.

The microstructure across the context is lenticular with channels and chambers increasing in frequency upwards. Pedofeatures also generally increase in frequency upwards and largely relate to reworking by soil fauna although some features indicative of illuviation (*e.g.*, 2% clay coatings in Unit 1 of K22) and Fe/Mn nodule formation (Unit 1 of K22) are also present. Microlaminations were also observed in each unit but were too diffuse and indistinct to classify (Fig. 6.8a–c).

Micromorphological analysis of the Cell 4 deposits demonstrated that occupation surfaces have been subject to post-depositional reworking. The primary mode of formation of these deposits appears to be trampling which has caused coarse materials to align in bands horizontal with the base of the slide. Preservation of the plant material increases upwards and upper layers of the deposits are generally better preserved despite greater evidence for reworking upwards. Fine anthropic materials, including burnt and unburnt bone, charcoal, charred plant remains and possibly herbivore dung became incorporated into the floor through occupation. Micro-inclusions were on average fairly light. Macro remains included charcoal, burnt bone and peat ash. At least one 'prepared' floor surface (Unit 2 of K22) was recognised. This involved spreading plant material across the floor as observed at Eilean Domnhuill (Dixon 1988).

Discussion and conclusions

Site formation processes

Floors at the point of occupation are rarely found in archaeological contexts (Hunter and Carruthers 2012, 52; Friesem *et al.* 2014). The floor sequences at Clachtoll are exceptionally well preserved and are intact from the truncation, later intrusive deposition or major bioturbation observed at other contemporary sites on the Atlantic seaboard such as Cnip (Armit 2006, 240–1). Bioturbation has been limited by the fact that the broch was also almost certainly roofed throughout occupation and thus protected from weathering and also by the reduction in pore space in floor deposits caused by their heavy trampling (Milek 2012a). The catastrophic burning event which ended occupation at Clachtoll effectively sealed the floors from further disturbance, thus providing an excellent opportunity for study of Iron Age floor deposits at the point of abandonment.

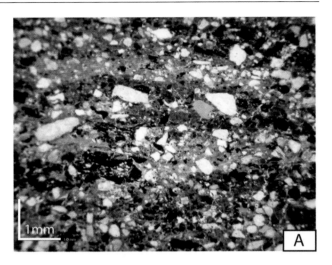

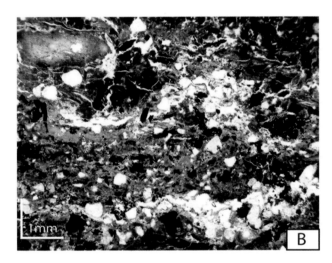

Figure 6.8 Microlaminated microstructures (081)

Mineralogy of the sand grains and lithology of the rock fragments throughout the sample sequence represent a soil parent material (peaty podsols derived from sandstones (Futty and Towers 1982)) typical of the surrounding area. Rock fragments are predominantly sandstones and most are classified as lithic greywackes or arkose (Mackenzie and Adams 1994, 109) although mica schists and gneiss are also present and are consistent with natural geological deposits relating to the sedimentary Bay of Stoer Formation (BGS 2018).

Larger artefacts and ecofacts are absent from flooring units within the broch interior and thus have been removed either by sweeping or by levelling activities during refurbishment. The refuse that has accumulated on the floor during primary deposition thus tends to consist of objects small enough to escape cleaning. Activities and practices inferred from floor deposits within the broch must therefore be viewed within the context of constantly used, reused and cleaned floors.

The boundaries observed within the deep floor sequences comprise of two broad types: diffuse horizontal boundaries with differences in units largely distinguished by change in composition and or concentration of inclusions and sharp horizontal boundaries visible even at higher magnifications. Reasons for the differences in these boundaries are numerous, however, it is hypothesised here that layers separated by diffuse boundaries most frequently reflect a gradual build-up of occupation debris with individual units reflecting seasonal availability of raw materials available for flooring and perhaps variation in activity. It is assumed that floors which were in use over long periods of time were probably maintained in some form. It is also assumed that given the high sedimentation rate indicated by high quantities of fuel and food residues that some form of cleaning would have taken place. A level of basic cleaning is assumed whereby it is envisaged that larger items would have been cleared off the floor on a regular basis (Banerjea *et al.* 2015). Despite compaction of floor surfaces from daily use it is likely that continuous build-up of floors and hearths would eventually have led to reduction in relative ceiling height and necessitated a more organised clear out. Within each floor sequence there are several incidences of very sharp boundaries which it is argued here represent concerted efforts to clean and refurbish the floors. Thus, the deep sequences studied have likely been truncated on numerous occasions through the act of floor maintenance and cleaning. The length of discontinuity that these breaks in floor sequences represent is not possible to quantify.

Deeply stratified organic rich floor layers within the broch interior range in thickness from less than 2 mm to up to 30 mm. Each unit of the deeply stratified organic floor layers identified at the wetland site of Black Loch of Myrton (BLM) is generally between 10 mm and 40 mm in thickness (Robertson and Roy 2019) whereas deeply stratified floor sequences with vegetation mats from the Early medieval floors at Gien, France are between 20 μm and 15 mm in thickness (Borderie *et al.* 2020). The thickness of any given floor unit is dependent upon a wide range of factors one of which is the level of moisture within the sediment. At BLM higher moisture levels have created spongey, thicker floors whereas at Gien a dry roofed interior with little evidence for moisture ingress has created thin, compacted floors. The floors at Clachtoll fall between these two ranges with some evidence for water ingress and localised puddling. Amorphous black material, Ferruginous (Fe) and Manganese (Mn) punctuations and pseudomorphic ferruginous pedofeatures are present across the sediment units and indicate damp reducing environments typical of compacted sediments (Lindbo, Stolt and Vepraskas 2010). Manganese neomineral formation also has a strong association with decaying organic matter; as organic matter is lost by oxidation, black precipitated Mn oxide forms (Bartlett 1988).

Floor construction and composition

The occupation levels are characterised by the superposition of constructed floors and compaction of occupation debris with the compacted deposits being the most dominant. The compacted floors are characterised by an accumulation of stratified plant fragments and debris including peat ash, charred peat fragments and fragmented bone embedded within microlaminations characteristic of trampling (Gé *et al.* 1993; Banerjea *et al.* 2015). The thicker floor units also contain coarse sands, charcoal and small gravels which may have been deliberately added to harden the floors (Banerjea *et al.* 2015).

The constructed floors feature some deliberately imported materials such as clays and coarse sands intermixed with organic material in (085). Importation of heath-like plant materials and peaty turves as a deliberate act to level and insulate the floor is evidenced within (087) and indicates that peat may have been spread on the floor of the broch. Large concentrations of heather and peat were recovered from several contexts from the final burning event and hypothesised as roofing material that was destroyed *in situ* (see Chapter 5) but also likely incorporated flooring material from the upper galleries as well as *in situ* flooring. Microlaminated plant material within the deeply stratified floor sequence of (091) and (087) may represent the remains of vegetal mattings or peats. In similar taphonomic circumstances, vegetation, turf and fuel residues in floor surfaces have been found at Links of Noltland (Hamlett 2014) Cladh Hallan and Eilean Domhuill (Tams 2003). The floors at Clachtoll provide further evidence for intentional use of organic materials in prehistoric floor construction on the Scottish North Atlantic seaboard.

Fuel residues also served as an important floor component. Peat ash is the major component of the deliberately constructed floor surfaces within (085). Micromorphological evidence also indicates that ash from the hearth may have been deliberately spread on the floors as a resurfacing layer as evidenced within two distinct episodes within (062) and also sporadically throughout the accumulation of (091). The incorporation of ash within flooring is well documented in historical contexts in Iceland where ash was commonly spread on earth floors in order to absorb dampness and odours (Milek 2012a). Spreads of hearth rake out were also recorded within Iron Age floors in Structure 14 at Old Scatness Broch (Dockrill *et al.* 2015, 114–15).

Activity areas

Assuming that activities within the broch were spatially differentiated, activity areas should be distinguishable through the uneven spatial distribution of artefacts, faunal remains, hearths and other anthropic elements (Malinsky-Buller *et al.* 2011). Spatial differentiation in artefact distribution is discussed in Chapter 7 but there is also a general pattern of variation exemplified by floor composition and compaction. For example, floor units of (087) show high concentrations of domestic waste and are characterised by ash disposal from the nearby hearth. (091) by contrast contains both less waste and less, but more coarse, mineral materials and was also formed in a damp environment as indicated by Fe oxides and rare dusty coatings. However, the various floor deposits studied do not represent the same lengths of time. Comparing densities of material in different floor deposits is therefore made problematic by the fact that higher densities might simply represent floors of longer temporal duration. Given the apparent impossibility of precisely estimating the duration of different floor deposits this severely compromises approaches based upon density. However, broad spatial characterisation is still possible based on general micromorphological characteristics.

The observed differences in porosity were used by Hamlet (2014, 220) to identify activity zones in Structure 9 at Links of Noltland. Similarly, at Clachtoll, the differences in porosity between guard cells, entrances and the central floor indicate that the central floor is more compacted. Porosity is typically less than 10% adjacent to the hearth and within the central floor in the north of the broch compared with 15–20% in the guard cell and 15% in the entrance. Similarly, anthropic inclusions are proportionally higher in the hearth area than the guard cell and entrance indicating that peripheral floors were kept comparatively free from debris.

Variations in proportions and types of charred remains evidence changes in the type and frequency of fuel use. The presence of burnt peat throughout central floors suggest that peat was a significant fuel component. Peat and cattle dung are both excellent and efficient fuels when dried (Braadbaart *et al.* 2012). However, the use of peat and dung as fuel is commonly underrepresented in the archaeological record due to the fact that char from peat and dung is more friable than char from wood and will be easily lost together with the relatively small ash particles (Braadbaart *et al.* 2012; Canti and Brochier 2017). The identification of peat in the micromorphological samples at Clachtoll therefore provide important evidence for its use.

While not providing the high energy of other fuels, peat is relatively accessible and low in cost. Wood is undoubtedly easy to collect and to burn but is a finite resource and needs years to regenerate. Differential use of peat material is well documented in anthropogenic studies of peat use in fires which frequently see the selective use of peats from the top of the drying stack, which have absorbed rain, or the damper grassier cuts from the top layer of peats in order to keep fires burning over night or in winter periods. The drier, less fibrous peats from lower down the profile are used when higher temperatures are required (Crawford 2018, 117). Wood charcoal is also common in several of the layers and indicates that fuel use was adapted according to availability of resources and firing temperature and light required.

Occupation and lifestyle

A typical archaeological floor layer as identified at Clachtoll encompasses several continuous activity episodes that were altered by sporadic changes in human activities, including cleaning and sweeping of floors, temporary abandonment and subsequent refurbishment.

The floors were apparently refurbished repeatedly, with debris from hearth rake-out evident throughout as bands of orange/yellow peat ash interleaved with organic layers. It is probable that this refurbishment took place on an ad hoc basis, as and when the floor surfaces were deemed too wet or foul to be serviceable and involved removal or sweeping of large waste followed by covering up the existing floor with new material.

Banerjea *et al.* (2015) have argued that compacted trampled deposits are often formed in damp conditions and as such they have the potential to be a useful indicator of doorways or pathways in the archaeological record. At Clachtoll, the dampest deposits with micromorphological evidence for dusty clay coatings and crusts are present throughout the entrance passageway (121) and indicate surface slaking (Courty, Goldberg and Macphail 1989) and thus are consistent with this theory and signify the entrance as a much damper area than the broch interior, an issue that probably necessitated the installation of the stone drain. Fungal sclerotia and very rare diatoms both suggest wet, peaty soils and are likely to have been imported from outside the structure. These may have been derived from unburnt fuel residues from peat combustion, or from animal bedding.

Micromorphological evidence has revealed consistent build-up of occupation debris some of which is rich in organic material and fuel residues. Throughout the building the floors are partly made of waste including animal excrement and bones. This gives us an insight into what might have been considered 'dirty' or 'clean' by the broch occupants. Occupation at Clachtoll appears to have necessitated/involved persistent contact with the waste materials which were a by-product of human occupation, particularly food debris and fuel waste. Cleaning efforts are apparent throughout the floor sequences, but nonetheless the rate of rebuilding or resurfacing the floors seems to be very high according to the level of their preservation and the number of visible laminations. Traces of sweeping and or shovelling can also be inferred by the sharp discontinuity boundaries and surface deformation and thus indicates some effort to clean and remove waste. Conversely however, new floors often appear to have been laid directly on top of extant waste. This does not necessarily reflect a disorganised existence where occupants were not concerned with cleanliness or house maintenance. Instead, it may point to episodic or seasonal variation in activity with short periods of inactivity when materials may have been left to decay rather than cleaned out. Alternatively, it may also point to a culture whereby organic material decomposing on the living floor was considered acceptable. However, while the inhabitants of Clachtoll may not have suffered from the aversion of modern society to rotting material the smell associated with the decomposition of the sheep carcass within context (087) must have been overpowering within a small space. This prompts a few possible interpretations, including that an abandonment of the structure may have occurred. However, deposits of articulated butchered carcasses within roundhouse floors is known from contemporary Atlantic settlement contexts, particularly Cnip (Armit 2006, 32; McCormick 2006, 169) and Sollas (Campbell 1991, 144–7) and Hornish Point (Barber 2003), where they are considered likely to be ritual deposits. This may indicate concerns or requirements that overrode practical issues of comfort, as defined by modern concepts. This point is discussed further in Chapter 10.

The burning layer:
spatial analysis of the macroplant assemblage

Jackaline Robertson and Graeme Cavers

Introduction

To understand the final phase of occupation a series of grid samples were collected from the catastrophic burning layer (042) that were archaeologically secure. A large assemblage of carbonised macroplant and charcoal was recovered from this deposit which covered most of the final surface and marked the end of the occupation of the broch. These two assemblages were analysed in conjunction with each other to answer multiple research questions, the most important being to identify spatial activity areas within the interior. This included recognising storage and food processing areas along with the accidental accumulation of collapsed structural material from the upper levels which occurred when the broch was destroyed.

Methodology

Grid samples were collected from context (042) on a 0.5 m grid, covering the entire garth of the broch. The methodology used for processing the grid samples is described in full in Chapter 5. Due to time constraints it was not possible to process all 250 grid samples recovered, and these are retained in the project archive. Instead, to identify spatial patterns of ecofact dispersal within the broch, the catastrophic burning layer (042) was artificially divided into four quadrants and a minimum of 12 samples were selected from each section (Fig. 7.1). The presence of flax was noted in two samples and to maximise recovery of this species an additional four samples from Quadrant 1 were selected for further analysis. In total, 52 grid samples were analysed from the carbonised layer (042). Carbonised macroplants were noted in 49 samples and charcoal in

40. These results are shown in Figures 7.2 and 7.3, and the contents of the samples are tabulated in Table 7.1.

The ecofact assemblage

The ecofact assemblage recovered from the grid samples was composed of cereals, nuts, wild fruit, building materials, fuel and weed taxa. The economic significance of these species has been addressed in full in Chapter 5, where they were described alongside the macroplant and charcoal recovered from the bulk samples. This report concentrates on understanding the spatial distribution of this final layer of ecofacts, in an attempt to identify activities such as food processing, storage and the presence of burnt flooring, collapsed upper floors and roof structures.

Spatial analysis

The crops

SIX-ROW HULLED BARLEY

The major crop at Clachtoll during the final phase of occupation was six-row hulled barley and 12,047 remains composed of six spikelets, 11,385 caryopses and 656 rachides were quantified from 48 grid samples. The presence of both caryopses and chaff fragments indicates that the broch was a large-scale producer, storage and consumer site prior to its destruction.

The six-row hulled barley was concentrated within Quadrant 1 and 10,264 remains were recovered from all 16 samples. Analysis of the 16 deposits revealed that six-row hulled barley totaling 8,283 was concentrated within four samples: [B7], [C1], [D5] and [E5]. The rest of the 1981 finds were scattered among the remaining eight samples in much smaller numbers. This large assemblage of cereal remains is not domestic food refuse. Instead,

Table 7.1 Macroplant remains from the grid samples of context (042), the burning layer

Vernacular name	Common name	Plant part	A1	B2	B7	C1	C6	C11	D5	E2	E5	E9	E15	F1	F8	F12	F14	G10	G17	H2
Grid number			Grid 1	Grid 1	Grid 1	Grid 1	Grid 1	Grid 1	Grid 1	Grid 3	Grid 1	Grid 1	Grid 2	Grid 3	Grid 1	Grid 1	Grid 2	Grid 1	Grid 2	Grid 3
Sample Mass (g)			642.5	420.6	778.3	397.4	367.7	545.2	681.9	745.6	425.8	559.7	416.3	512.8	569.0	597.5	631.1	522.0	343.0	695.4
Crops																				
Hordeum Vulgare L.	Six-row hulled barley	Spikelet(s)							1		2									2
Hordeum Vulgare L.	Six-row hulled barley	Caryopsis/es	39	74	845	1397	490	364	>4000	144	1730	3	16	3	59	16	464	315		4
Hordeum Vulgare L.	Six-row hulled barley	Rachis/rachides			12	4	39		>250	2	40		1	5	1	2	1	2		1
Hordeum var. Nudum L.	Naked barley	Caryopsis/es						1							1					
Hordeum sp.	Barley	Caryopsis/es	7	20	80	32	7	88		26	65	2	7	11	12		4	93		2
Hordeum sp.	Barley	Rachis/rachides					3	63						1						
Triticum sp.	Wheat	Caryopsis/es																1		
	Emmer	Glume(s)																		
Avena fatua L.	Wild oat	Caryopsis/es									1									
Avena fatua L.	Wild oat	Floret(s)			1															
Avena sp.	Oat	Caryopsis/es			2			1	7		5			2		3		2		
Cerealia sp.	Cereal	Caryopsis/es	2	18	13	7	61	31	57	6	27		3	2	9	2	2	32		2
Cerealia sp.	Cereal	Culm node(s)	2		4	1	1		2					**	**		1	3		
Cerealia sp.	Cereal	Straw frag(s)						*	*	*										
Cerealia sp.	Cereal	Compacted cereal/straw																		
Economic plants																				
Linum usitatissimum L.	Flax	Seed(s)						11					1							
Wild Food																				
Corylus avellana L.	Hazel nut	Nutshell frg(s)	6					5	5	2				4			9		1	
Empetrum nigram L.	Crowberry	Seed(s)					2		2											
Prunus spinosa L.	Blackthorn/sloe	Stone(s)																		
Building/Flooring/Fuel Material																				
Calluna vulgaris L.	Heather	Leaves(s)					***	***					**	****	****		***		****	
Calluna vulgaris L.	Heather	Seed(s)					*		*											
Calluna vulgaris L.	Heather	Flower(s)					*	*							*		*		*	
Calluna vulgaris L.	Heather	stem					***	***	*	*		***	***	*	****		****		****	
Carex sp.	Sedges	Fruit(s)	3		1											1				
Pteridium aquilinum L.	Bracken	Pinnule/Fronds frag(s)			4						2				3			1		
Weed Taxa																				
Atriplex sp.	Oraches	Seed(s)					2				1									
Brassica nigra L.	Black Mustard	Seed(s)							1											
Brassica sp.	Cabbage	Seed(s)							1											
Brassica/sinapis sp.	Cabbage/mustard	Seed(s)														1				
Bromus sp.	Bromes	Caryopsis/es				1	3	4	5					4						
Carduus/Cirsium sp.	Thistle	Fruit(s)													1	1				
cf. Cerastium sp.	Field mouse-ear	Seed(s)									1									
Chenopodiaceae sp.	Goosefoot	Seed(s)				1	2		1		6				1	2		1		1
Chenopodium album L.	Fat hen	Seed(s)			5	1	3		1		2				7	6	4			
cf. Danthonia decumbens L.	Heath-grass	Caryopsis/es									3									
Fallopia convolvulus L.	Black bindweed	Fruit(s)					1													
Galeopsis Subgenus Galeopsis	Hemp nettle	Nutlet(s)				1			1											
Galium sp.	Bedstraws	Nutlet(s)			1															

(Continued)

Table 7.1 Macroplant remains from the grid samples of context (042), the burning layer (Continued)

Grid number			Grid 1	Grid 1	Grid 1	Grid 1	Grid 1	Grid 1	Grid 1	Grid 1	Grid 1	Grid 1	Grid 2	Grid 3	Grid 1	Grid 1	Grid 2	Grid 1	Grid 2	Grid 3
Sample number			A1	B2	B7	C1	C6	C11	D5	E2	E5	E9	E15	F1	F8	F12	F14	G10	G17	H2
Sample Mass (g)			642.5	420.6	778.3	397.4	367.7	545.2	681.9	745.6	425.8	559.7	416.3	512.8	569.0	597.5	631.1	522.0	343.0	695.4
Vernacular name	**Common name**	**Plant part**																		
Lapsana communis L.	Nipplewort	Fruit(s)																		
persicaria amphibia	Amphibious bistort	Fruit(s)				2	2	1	4		1	1				2		1		
Persicaria lapathifolium L.	Pale Persicaria	Fruit(s)				6	3	3			1	1				2	1	1		
Persicaria sp.	Knotweed	Fruit(s)				1			1											
Plantago sp.	Plantains	Seed(s)							1											
Poaceae sp.	Grass	Caryopsis/es								1	1									
Polygonum aviculare L.	knotgrass	Fruit(s)					1													
Potentilla erecta L.	Tormentil	Achene(s)													3					
Ranunculus sp.	Meadow/creeping/bulbous buttercup	Achene(s)					1	1												
Rumex acetosella L.	Sheep's sorrel	Fruit(s)																		
Rumex longifolius L.	Northern Dock	Fruit(s)																		
Rumex longifolius L.	Northern Dock	Perianth																		
Rumex sp.	Dock	Fruit(s)							1									1		
Silene sp.	Campions	Seed(s)																		
Sonchus asper L.	Prickly Sowthistle	Fruit(s)																		
Sonchus oleraceus L.	Smooth sowthistle	Fruit(s)																		
Spergula arvensis L.	Corn spurrey	Seed(s)					1													
Stellaria media L.	Common chickweed	Seed(s)				1	21					9			2	14				
Stellaria sp.	Chickweed	Seed(s)				1	3													
cf. Suaeda maritima L.	Annual Sea-blite	Seed(s)																		
cf. Viola sp.	Violet	Seed(s)																		
Stems	Stems	Stems(s)								*										
Unknown	Indet		1		2	18	1	2					2	1	1	1		1		
Other fuel																				
Charcoal			*	*	*	<4mm	*	****	*	*	*	***	***	***	****	****	***	**	****	*
Burnt peat					**	*	**	****		*	*	*		***	****	**	***		*/* unburnt	
Seaweed		Pod (frags)						40								1	1			
Fungal spores																				
Cenococcum sp.		Sclerotia											*							
Bone																				
Rodent			****	*	*	*		*	*	*			*	*			**			*
Fish			*		*					*			*	*						*
Shell																				
Marine shell																				<4mm small frags
Snail shell																				<4mm small frags

(Continued)

Table 7.1 (Continued)

Grid number			Grid 3	Grid 2	Grid 2	Grid 2	Grid 2	Grid 3	Grid 3	Grid 2	Grid 2	Grid 2	Grid 4	Grid 2	Grid 2	Grid 2	Grid 4	Grid 2	Grid 3	Grid 3	Grid 3	Grid 2/4
Sample number			H7	H12	H15	I5	I14	J2	J7	J12	J17	K4	K9	K11	K15	L1	L8	L14	M1	M4	M11	M13
Sample Mass (g)			663.0	406.2	292.0	601.6	374.4	185.5	425.9	418.4	364.5	354.1	733.6	607.2	501.8	223.8	651.3	688.1	129.2	61.5	565.0	408.2
Vernacular name	Common name	Plant part																					
Crops																							
Hordeum Vulgare L.	Six-row hulled barley	Spikelet(s)																					
Hordeum Vulgare L.	Six-row hulled barley	Caryopsis/es	176	3	3	26	21	1	18	2			13	30	7		6	19	1		9	28
Hordeum Vulgare L.	Six-row hulled barley	Rachis/rachides	1		8	5	14	4	1	1				2	2	2						
Hordeum var. Nudum L.	Naked barley	Caryopsis/es																				
Hordeum sp.	Barley	Caryopsis/es	84	1		1		3	7	10		5	1	21	2	2	7	5			1	12
Hordeum sp.	Barley	Rachis/rachides	1				2															1
Triticum sp.	Wheat	Caryopsis/es																				
	Emmer	Glume(s)																				
Avena fatua L.	Wild oat	Caryopsis/es																				
Avena fatua L.	Oat	Floret(s)						1														
Avena sp.	Oat	Caryopsis/es			3			1						1								
Cerealia sp.	Cereal	Caryopsis/es	9	1	1	1	2		6		1	2	2	8			6	2				
Cerealia sp.	Cereal	Culm node(s)	3	1 ***	***	****	****		**			3 **	3 **	2	8		15	1				
Cerealia sp.	Cereal	Straw frag(s)		***	***	***	*		*			8	8 ****		*		1	1				
Cerealia sp.	Cereal	Compacted cereal/straw										*			****							
Economic plants																							
Linum usitatissimum L.	Flax	Seed(s)																				
Wild Food																							
Corylus avellana L.	Hazel nut	Nutshell frg(s)																				
Empetrum nigram L.	Crowberry	Seed(s)									1								5			
Prunus spinosa L.	Blackthorn/sloe	Stone(s)					3															
Building/Flooring/Fuel Material																							
Calluna vulgaris L.	Heather	Leaves(s)	**	***	****	***	*		*	****	***			1 **			*	*				
Calluna vulgaris L.	Heather	Seed(s)																				
Calluna vulgaris L.	Heather	Flower(s)	***	***	****	***	***		***	***	***											
Calluna vulgaris L.	stem	Stems	**	****	****	***	****	****	****	****	****	***		*			**	**	***			
Carex sp.	Sedges	Fruit(s)																				
Pteridium aquilinum L.	Bracken	Pinnule/Fronds frag(s)		**						*					1			1				
Weed Taxa																							
Atriplex sp.	Oraches	Seed(s)			1 cf		1		1					1								
Brassica nigra L.	Black Mustard	Seed(s)				1																
Brassica sp.	Cabbage	Seed(s)			1																	
Brassica Isinapis sp.	Cabbage/mustard	Seed(s)			2							1										
Bromus sp.	Bromes	Caryopsis/es					2															
Carduus/Cirsium sp.	Thistle	Fruit(s)		1																		
cf. *Cerastium* sp.	Field mouse-ear	Seed(s)			1																	
Chenopodiaceae sp.	Goosefoot	Seed(s)	1		12	3	2	2		1				2					3			
Chenopodium album L.	Fat hen	Seed(s)			4	19	9	13			2			1				1				
cf. *Danthonia decumbens* L.	Heath-grass	Caryopsis/es																				
Fallopia convolvulus L.	Black bindweed	Fruits(s)			11	4	2	2			1											
Galeopsis Subgenus Galeopsis	Hemp nettle	Nutlet(s)										1										
Galium sp.	Bedstraws	Nutlet(s)					3								1							

(Continued)

Table 7.1 Macroplant remains from the grid samples of context (042), the burning layer (Continued)

Grid number			Grid 3	Grid 2	Grid 2	Grid 3	Grid 2	Grid 3	Grid 3	Grid 3	Grid 2	Grid 2	Grid 4	Grid 2	Grid 2	Grid 3	Grid 4	Grid 4	Grid 2	Grid 3	Grid 3	Grid 2/4
Sample number			H7	H12	H15	I5	I14	J2	J7	J12	J17	K4	K9	K11	K15	L1	L8	L14	M1	M4	M11	M13
Sample Mass (g)			663.0	406.2	292.0	601.6	374.4	185.5	425.9	418.4	364.5	354.1	733.6	607.2	501.8	223.8	651.3	688.1	129.2	61.5	565.0	408.2
Vernacular name	Common name	Plant part																				
Lapsana communis L.	Nipplewort	Fruit(s)			1																	
persicaria amphibia	Amphibious bistort	Fruit(s)				2	1															
Persicaria lapathifolium L.	Pale Persicaria	Fruit(s)			1	5				1							1					
Persicaria sp.	Knotweed	Fruit(s)			1	1	1			1	1	1										
Plantago sp.	Plantains	Seed(s)										1	1									
Poaceae sp.	Grass	Caryopsis/es												1								
Polygonum aviculare L.	knotgrass	Fruit(s)																				
Potentilla erecta L.	Tormentil	Achene(s)																				
Ranunculus sp.	Meadow/creeping/bulbous buttercup	Achene(s)									1											
Rumex acetosella L.	Sheep's sorrel	Fruit(s)												1								
Rumex longifolius L.	Northern Dock	Fruit(s)																				
Rumex longifolius L.	Northern Dock	Perianth						1														
Rumex sp.	Dock	Fruit(s)																				
Silene sp.	Campions	Seed(s)				1	1	1														
Sonchus asper L.	Prickly Sowthistle	Fruit(s)				1																
Sonchus oleraceus L.	Smooth sowthistle	Fruit(s)					1															
Spergula arvensis L.	Corn spurrey	Seed(s)					1			1												
Stellaria media L.	Common chickweed	Seed(s)			8	10	4	7						3								
Stellaria sp.	Chickweed	Seed(s)			2			3						2								
cf. *Suaeda maritima* L.	Annual Sea-blite	Seed(s)				1																
cf. *Viola* sp.	Violet	Seed(s)			1		1										1					
Stems	Stems	Stems(s)									***											
Unknown	Indet			1			1				2	1					1					1
Other fuel																						
Charcoal			**	***	**	**	****	**	**	***	****	*	****	**	***	**	**	*	<4mm	*	*	<4mm
Burnt peat			*	****	***	***	**	**		**		*	*				*					
Seaweed		Pod (frags)			2	2																
Fungal spores																						
Cenococcum sp.		Sclerotia				1						*	*									
Bone																						
Rodent				*								*	*	*			*		*	*	*	
Fish												*	*									
Shell																						
Marine shell																						
Snail shell																						1

(Continued)

Table 7.1 (Continued)

			Grid 2	Grid 4	Grid 4	Grid 4	Grid 4	Grid 4	Grid 4	Grid 4	Grid 4	Grid 4
Grid number												
Sample number			M16	N7	N9	O6	O7	O9	Q1	Q7	R2	R4
Sample Mass (g)	**Common name**	**Plant part**	703.1	135.8	187.9	375.6	223.0	208.7	193.0	350.1	440.0	542.0
Vernacular name												
Crops												
Hordeum Vulgare L.	Six-row hulled barley	Spikelet(s)										
Hordeum Vulgare L.	Six-row hulled barley	Caryopsis/es	4	4	260		46	35	48	32	47	32
Hordeum Vulgare L.	Six-row hulled barley	Rachis/rachides	1		3				4	216	4	
Hordeum var. *Nudum* L.	Naked barley	Caryopsis/es							1			
Hordeum sp.	Barley	Caryopsis/es		8	41		26	15	31	4		10
Hordeum sp.	Barley	Rachis/rachides	1		2				1		12	
Triticum sp.	Wheat	Caryopsis/es										
	Emmer	Glume(s)							2			
Avena fatua L.	Wild oat	Caryopsis/es										
Avena fatua L.	Oat	Floret(s)										
Avena sp.	Oat	Caryopsis/es						2	2		4	
Cerealia sp.	Cereal	Caryopsis/es		51	3		15	18	11	8	5	5
Cerealia sp.	Cereal	Culm node(s)			1						1	
Cerealia sp.	Cereal	Straw frag(s)									1	
Cerealia sp.	Cereal	Compacted cereal/straw										
Economic plants												
Linum usitatissimum L.	Flax	Seed(s)										
Wild Food												
Corylus avellana L.	Hazel nut	Nutshell frg(s)	32							1	1	
Empetrum nigram L.	Crowberry	Seed(s)							1	1		
Prunus spinosa L.	Blackthorn/sloe	Stone(s)										
Building/Flooring/Fuel Material												
Calluna vulgaris L.	Heather	Leaves(s)								1		
Calluna vulgaris L.	Heather	Seed(s)								1		
Calluna vulgaris L.	Heather	Flower(s)								1		
Calluna vulgaris L.	stem	Stems	*									
Carex sp.	Sedges	Fruit(s)										
Pteridium aquilinum L.	Bracken	Pinnule/Fronds frag(s)								**		
Weed Taxa												
Atriplex sp.	Oraches	Seed(s)										
Brassica nigra L.	Black Mustard	Seed(s)								1		
Brassica sp.	Cabbage	Seed(s)								1		
Brassica Isinapis sp.	Cabbage/mustard	Seed(s)							3	3		
Bromus sp.	Bromes	Caryopsis/es								1		
Carduus/Cirsium sp.	Thistle	Fruit(s)										
cf. *Cerastium* sp.	Field mouse-ear	Seed(s)										
Chenopodiaceae sp.	Goosefoot	Seed(s)								1		
Chenopodium album L.	Fat hen	Seed(s)			1							
cf. *Danthonia decumbens* L.	Heath-grass	Caryopsis/es								3		
Fallopia convolvulus L.	Black bindweed	Fruits(s)								2		
Galeopsis Subgenus *Galeopsis*	Hemp nettle	Nutlet(s)								1		
Galium sp.	Bedstraws	Nutlet(s)										

(Continued)

Table 7.1 Macroplant remains from the grid samples of context (042), the burning layer (Continued)

Grid number			Grid 2	Grid 4	Grid 4	Grid 4	Grid 4	Grid 4	Grid 4	Grid 4	Grid 4	Grid 4
Sample number			M16	N7	N9	O6	O7	O9	Q1	Q7	R2	R4
Sample Mass (g)			703.1	135.8	187.9	375.6	223.0	208.7	193.0	350.1	440.0	542.0
Vernacular name	**Common name**	**Plant part**										
Lapsana communis L.	Nipplewort	Fruit(s)									1	
persicaria amphibia	Amphibious bistort	Fruit(s)										
Persicaria lapathifolium L.	Pale Persicaria	Fruit(s)					1					
Persicaria sp.	Knotweed	Fruit(s)									1	
Plantago sp.	Plantains	Seed(s)									4	
Poaceae sp.	Grass	Caryopsis/es									1	
Polygonum aviculare L.	knotgrass	Fruit(s)										
Potentilla erecta L.	Tormentil	Achene(s)										
Ranunculus sp.	Meadow/creeping/bulbous buttercup	Achene(s)										
Rumex acetosella L.	Sheep's sorrel	Fruit(s)										
Rumex longifolius L.	Northern Dock	Fruit(s)										
Rumex longifolius L.	Northern Dock	Perianth										
Rumex sp.	Dock	Fruit(s)								2		
Silene sp.	Campions	Seed(s)										
Sonchus asper L.	Prickly Sowthistle	Fruit(s)										
Sonchus oleraceus L.	Smooth sowthistle	Fruit(s)										
Spergula arvensis L.	Corn spurrey	Seed(s)										
Stellaria media L.	Common chickweed	Seed(s)								11		
Stellaria sp.	Chickweed	Seed(s)										
cf. *Suaeda maritima* L.	Annual Sea-blite	Seed(s)										
cf. *Viola* sp.	Violet	Seed(s)										
Stems	Stems	Stems(s)					1					
Unknown	Indet							1	1	2		
Other fuel												
Charcoal			*	**	<4mm	<4mm	<4mm	*	<4mm	***	<4mm	*
Burnt peat			**							**		
Seaweed		Pod (frags)							1 ***			
Fungal spores												
Cenococcum sp.		Sclerotia								**	*	
Bone												
Rodent			*		*	**		*	*	***	**	*
Fish			*		*	*		*	*	**	*	*
Shell												
Marine shell												
Snail shell												

analysis of these samples within Quadrant 1 revealed that specific areas in this locality were used for processing and storing crops. It is also possible that some of the grain had been laid out to dry or was stored on the upper floors of the building and subsequently collapsed onto the ground layer when the broch was destroyed. Regardless of whether some of the material may have derived from upper layers, Quadrant 1 was a focal point for cereal processing and storage.

In Quadrant 2, six-row hulled barley totaling 573 caryopses and 31 chaff fragments were present in 11 deposits. The largest number were in deposit [F14] which had 465 remains with the rest scattered among the other ten samples in much smaller numbers. Those samples in Quadrant 2, including [F14] which had larger numbers of six-row hulled barley tended to be in closer proximity to Quadrant 1. The six-row hulled barley in Quadrant 2 is considered to have accumulated from processing and storage of crops.

A total of 393 six-row hulled barley caryopses and 18 chaff fragments were recorded in ten samples analysed from Quadrant 3. These were concentrated within two squares [E2] which had 146 and [H7] with 177. The remains from Quadrant 3 are likely overspill from the dedicated processing and storage areas which tended to be concentrated within Quadrant 1.

Quadrant 4 had 541 six-row hulled caryopses and chaff fragments in 11 squares. These were concentrated within two squares: [N9] which had 263, followed by [Q7] with 248. The rest of the assemblage was scattered in Quadrant 4 in small numbers, with no evidence of selective or deliberate disposal. These remains are interpreted as overspill from the main crop processing and storage area in Quadrant 1.

Naked barley

There were two naked barley caryopses in Quadrant 1 in deposits [C11], [F8] and one in Quadrant 4, sample [Q1]. Given the small size of this assemblage and lack of evidence to suggest it was ever stored separately from other food stuffs, the naked barley has been interpreted as a crop containment of the six-row hulled barley. During the final occupation of Clachtoll, naked barley had no obvious or significant dietary role within the economy of the occupants.

Barley

The barley remains were composed of 755 caryopses recorded in 38 contexts along with 87 rachides noted in ten samples. The barley is likely to belong to the main crop, but due to poor preservation they could not be identified further. These finds were present in all four quadrants but were concentrated in Quadrant 1 which

had 474 followed by 142 in Quadrant 3, 158 in Quadrant 4 and 68 in Quadrant 2. The caryopses tended to be scattered among Quadrant 1 but were more centralised within grids 2, 3 and 4. The rachides were recovered in small numbers in the center of the broch but tended to be concentrated in larger quantities towards to the outer perimeters of the walls.

The concentration within Quadrant 1 and the more central samples from Quadrants 2, 3 and 4 are not unexpected as these are associated with the processing and storage areas in this locality and may also have accrued from accidental overspill from these activities. The chaff fragments in proximity to the wall have derived from processing waste reworked into these locations during cleaning of the ground floor surface.

Emmer

Two emmer glumes were noted in [Q1] in Quadrant 4, near the wall. There is no evidence this species was deliberately cultivated. Instead, it is more likely it was a weed of the barley crop and was reworked into this part of the broch during the final conflagration.

Wheat

A single wheat caryopsis was recovered from [G10] located in Quadrant 1 towards the center of the broch. The presence of wheat is considered a contaminant of the hulled barley crop given its low frequency within the assemblage.

Wild oat

The wild oat was composed of one caryopsis and three floret bases, scattered among [B7], [E5], [H15] and [J2] located in Quadrants 1, 2 and 3. This species was very much a contaminant of the main hulled barley crop. This explains why it was recovered in such small numbers and why there was no evidence that it was ever stored or processed separately from the main barley crop.

Oat

A total of 37 oat caryopses were recovered from 13 contexts in grids 1, 2, 3 and 4. These finds were clearly concentrated within Quadrant 1 which had 24 caryopses compared to four in Quadrant 2, three in Quadrant 3 and six in Quadrant 4. It was not possible to classify these remains as either belonging to the wild or cultivated variety of oat. Regardless, these remains are considered to be contaminants of the main hulled barley crop, as there is no evidence they were ever stored or processed separately. The analysis of the grid samples indicates that oat had no obvious economic role in the final stages of occupation at Clachtoll.

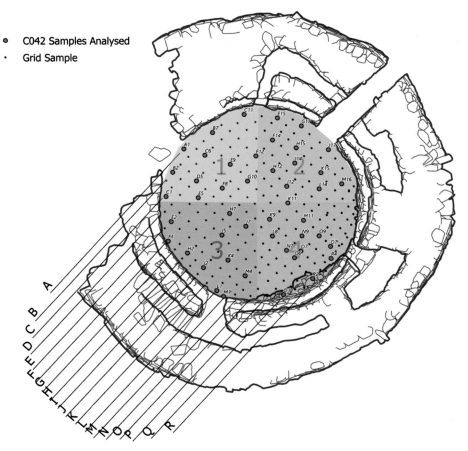

Figure 7.1 Layout of grid samples showing those processed

STRAW AND CULM NODES

Cereal straw and culm nodes were recorded in 27 deposits and this material has derived from crop processing, waste disposal along with the possible storage of hay for animal feed, building material and fuel. Equally, it cannot be ruled out that these straw fragments were incorporated into upper floors or roof sections which subsequently crashed down onto the ground floor layer during the burning event.

Straw fragments were observed in nine samples in Quadrant 1, eight in Quadrant 2, six in Quadrant 3 and four in Quadrant 4. These remains were concentrated within ten specific locations inside the broch interior. The straw and culm nodes from [E5] in Quadrant 1 were recovered alongside large quantities of six-row hulled barley, which is representative of crop processing destroyed *in situ*. The other nine noticeable concentrations of straw were in [E2], [F1], [F8], [H15], [I5], [I14], [J2], [K9] and [K15]. While the presence of small numbers of cereal caryopses were observed in these samples it was obvious that this material had not accrued through the *in situ* destruction of crops being processed, as evidently occurred in [E5]. Analysis of spatial relationships

between these deposits assisted with identifying how this material may have accumulated.

The two samples [E5] and [F8] were near each other and these finds had amassed through both crop processing and overspill from this work area. Deposits [H15], [I5], [I14] and [K15] are closely related and it is possible that the straw is overspill from the processing area. Alternatively, this area could have been a designated disposal location for processing debris or was a storage area for useful plant resources. Samples [E2], [F1] and [J2] were located close to the broch walls and these remains were either deliberately swept into the outer areas during general cleaning, or this too could have been a designated storage area for straw. Deposit [K9] had no obvious connection with any of the other samples containing large quantities of straw, but as few cereal caryopses were recovered it is unlikely this part of the broch was used for cereal processing or storage. Instead, these remains could have accumulated through the random disposal of processing waste, or because this area was being used as a more centralised storage area for hay.

FLAX

Flax was represented by 12 seeds and was recovered only from the final conflagration event. Eleven seeds were concentrated in [C11], Quadrant 1 and one in [E15], Quadrant 2. These remains were both located near each other in Quadrants 1 and 2, in a part of the broch which appears to have been used for storage and processing of other food items. It appears that flax was kept in this location until required. Flax would have been a valuable resource and it follows that it would have been stored in a dry and secure part of the broch.

NUTS

A total of 74 hazelnut shell fragments were present in 13 deposits from [A1], [C10], [C11], [D11], [D12], [D13] in Quadrant 1, [F14], [G17], [M16] in Quadrant 2 [E2], [F1] in Quadrant 3 and [Q1] and [Q7] in Quadrant 4. The shell fragments tended to be recovered from deposits located near the walls of the broch. There was no evidence to suggest these remains represented caches of stored nuts that had been destroyed *in situ,* nor that this was waste from large-scale processing. Instead, the hazelnuts were represented by small fragments more reminiscent of food and or fuel debris that had been trampled or swept into the outer reaches of the floor surface during general cleaning prior to the final conflagration event.

Fruits

Three blackthorn stones were present in context [I14] Quadrant 2 in an area which was used to store and process food.

Eleven crowberry seeds were scattered among six contexts in [C6], [D11] in Quadrant 1, [H15], [J17] in Quadrant 2, [M1] in Quadrant 3 and [Q7] in Quadrant 4. As with the hazelnut shells, the crowberry tended to be concentrated close to the walls of the broch. Crowberry is edible and it is possible these remains along with the hazel represent domestic food debris that was reworked into the deposits surrounding the walls during cleaning. The samples from which the crowberry was recovered also contained fragments of heather that were possibly part of turves used as building material. This evidence raises the possibility that the crowberry from the final phase of occupation may not have been collected for food, but was an incidental component of the turf.

Building materials

HEATHER

The heather was composed of wood fragments, flowers, leaves and seeds recorded in 33 samples from all four Quadrants. Large quantities of heather in the form of compacted turves were noted in six samples in Quadrant 1, eight samples in Quadrant 2, five samples in Quadrant

3 and two in Quadrant 2. These larger concentrations have derived from recognizable turves destroyed *in situ*. These turves may have been a component of internal structures used to line wattle screens, floors and roof sections.

Evidence for agricultural activities and food storage was focused within Quadrant 1 alongside some locations in Quadrant 2 and 3. These activities may have required designated work areas and storage facilities that could have been constructed partly using turf. This may explain why the number of turves is greater in these locations when compared to those in Quadrant 4.

BRACKEN

Small fragments of bracken were noted in nine contexts in Quadrants 1, 2 and 4. In Quadrant 1 there were seven fragments of bracken scattered among [B7] and [F8] in which heather was also noted. From Quadrant 2 bracken was noted in [G17], [J12], [J17], [K15] and [L14] which all had turf fragments. The only sample from Quadrant 4 [Q7] which had bracken also contained a small quantity of heather. While the quantity of bracken is small from the final stage of occupation it tended to be recovered from those areas which also featured heather turves. This suggests that bracken, like turf, was used as a building material within the broch.

OTHER BUILDING MATERIALS

Four sedge were recorded in three samples [B7], [C10], [D13] in Quadrant 1 and one in [E2] in Quadrant 3. Sedge has been used at other prehistoric sites as a building material, but given the small quantity recovered from Clachtoll its importance, if any, was difficult to establish. This may be due to taphonomic issues as the presence of plants such as sedge is more likely to be identified within waterlogged plant assemblages as at Black Loch of Myrton (Robertson in prep). This material may represent accidental inclusions of weeds but it is possible the sedge was used as a flooring and/or roofing material and that the evidence has simply not survived within a carbonised macroplant assemblage.

Weed taxa

It has been speculated that some of the weed species, such as cabbage and fat hen, may have been deliberately collected and stored within the broch for use as an additional food source. Analysis of their deposition within the broch interior reveled the weed taxa tended to be concentrated in those samples which also had large quantities of cereal caryopses, culm nodes and straw fragments. This indicates that the weed seeds were generally agricultural contaminates of the barley crop or building material and were brought accidentally to the broch. There was no evidence to suggest that any weed species was deliberately stored in a specific area within the broch during the final catastrophic burning event. This is not to claim that none of the weed species

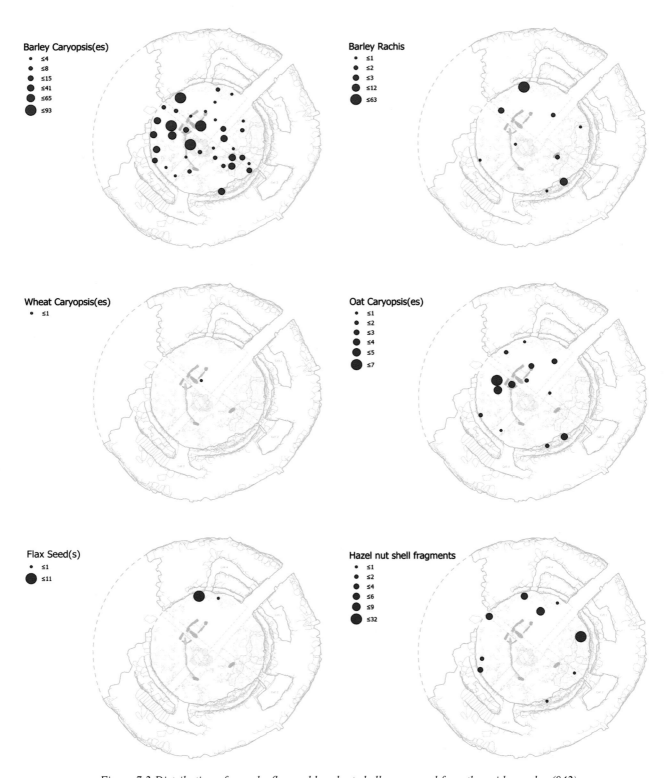

Figure 7.2 Distribution of cereals, flax and hazelnut shells recovered from the grid samples (042)

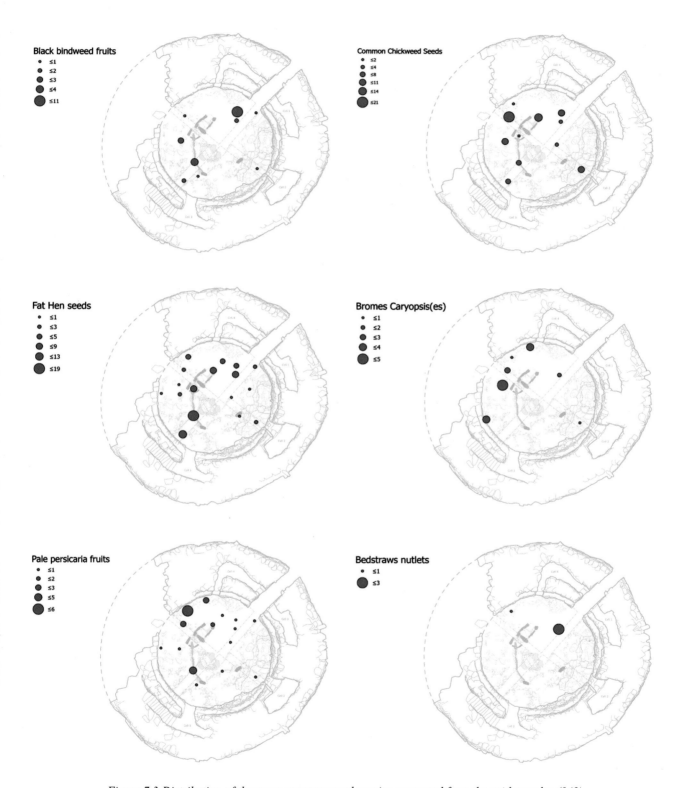

Figure 7.3 Distribution of the more common weed species recovered from the grid samples (042)

had an economic or dietary role within the final stages of occupation, merely that the spatial evidence is more suggestive of an accidental crop contaminant.

Wood

The charcoal assemblage from layer (042) is considered to be an accumulation of wattle screens, floor layers and roofing structures that were burnt and collapsed onto the underlying floor surface when the broch was destroyed. The spatial analysis of this deposit has shown that the wood species favoured for construction was consistent throughout the different areas in the broch and that alder, birch and hazel were preferred for wattle screens and wooden frameworks whereas oak and pine were more likely to be employed for larger components such as planks and posts. Heather also had an import building role within the final phase of occupation as a component of the turves.

The charcoal assemblage (246.7 g) from Quadrant 1 was recovered from 15 contexts and the species was alder, birch, heather, hazel, rowan and oak. The charcoal was concentrated in six deposits in [C10], [C11], [D13], [E9], [F8] and [F12]. The fragments in [C10], [C11], [E9], [F8] and [F12] were composed of mixed species such as alder, birch, hazel and rowan used to construct wattle screens and wooden frameworks. A possible oak post was noted in [D13]. There were also large quantities of heather turves used in construction. While the other nine deposits contained smaller quantities of charcoal there was no evidence of fuel debris and instead these fragments all appear to belong to structural elements. These structural elements were used in the division of internal workspaces on the ground floor of the broch and perhaps also formed part of the upper floor and roof sections which collapsed onto the underlying floor during the burning event.

In Quadrant 2 the charcoal (144.4 g) was recovered from 12 samples and the species were alder, birch, heather, hazel, pine and oak. The charcoal was concentrated in six samples: [E15], [F14], [G17], [H12], [H15] and [J17]. As with Quadrant 1 there was no evidence of any fuel debris and instead these remains have derived from structural elements mostly wattle screens and wooden frameworks.

Quadrant 3 had the smallest charcoal assemblage (18.5 g) noted in six samples and the species were alder, birch, heather and hazel. These fragments were scattered throughout this part of the broch and while it was not possible to conclusively identify the presence of structural elements destroyed *in situ*, this interpretation could not be ruled out.

Charcoal (25.3 g) was recovered from seven samples in Quadrant 4 and the species were alder, heather, hazel, pine and oak. The charcoal was concentrated within [K9] which may have belonged to a wattle screen or wooden framework constructed from alder and hazel. As with the other grid samples there was no obvious evidence for fuel debris.

Conclusion

During the final stage of occupation at Clachtoll the site was used for various activities including processing and storing grain. By analysing the grid samples, areas related to these activities were identifiable within the ecofact assemblage. The deposits in Quadrant 1 and those samples in Quadrants 2, 3 and 4 which either bordered Quadrant 1 or were collected from the center of the broch were generally found to contain larger quantities of cereal remains. The concentration of grain within these locations is indicative of designated areas used for processing or storage of foodstuffs. The smaller number of ecofacts within specific locations in Quadrants 2, 3 and 4 could be due to taphonomic factors which adversely influenced the level of preservation but is more likely an accurate reflection of how this internal space was used.

In the Quadrant 1 and 2 deposits bordering the walls some samples were found to contain valuable resources in the form of flax indicating this area was probably a designated storage area. This contrasts with those samples collected from the outer perimeter in grids 3 and 4 that were mostly found to contain small quantities of reworked domestic cleaning debris.

This was also true of the building material in the form of both turf and wood. The heather turves tended to be accrued within specific samples in Quadrants 1, 2 and 3 with little surviving evidence of this material in Quadrant 4. Structural elements such as wattle screens, floor and roof sections were focused mostly within Quadrants 1 and 2. This may suggest that these areas had additional internal structural partitions, or that some of the upper floor and roof sections had collapsed into this area from above.

By analysing the macroplant and charcoal assemblages in conjunction with each other it has been possible to identify several internal features used for creating defined work areas and storage facilities associated with agricultural practices. This was only made possible as the evidence for this survived within the ecofact assemblage recovered from the final occupation/destruction layer within deposit (042).

The environmental context of Clachtoll and Assynt

Louisa Matthews

Introduction

This chapter summarises the current understanding of the Assynt landscape and environment and gives a brief overview of the how the research in progress aims to address some key questions relating to settlement and economic practice in the Iron Age.

North-west Scotland is in an ideal situation to look at major changes in climatic conditions resulting from shifts in the North Atlantic Oscillation (NAO). It has been shown that in North-West Britain and Norway there is a strong correlation between NAO mode and winter precipitation (Hurrell, Kushnir and Ottersen 2003, 233, fig. 3). The NAO is the most prominent and recurrent pattern of atmospheric variability over the middle and high latitudes of the Northern Hemisphere, especially in the cold months of November to April (Hurrell, Kushnir and Ottersen 2003; Hurrell and Deser 2009). The NAO refers to a redistribution of atmospheric mass between the Arctic and the subtropical Atlantic, and can swing between positive, negative and neutral states. Changes from one phase to another can produce large changes in surface air temperature, winds, storminess and precipitation over the Atlantic as well as the adjacent continents (Hurrell, Kushnir and Ottersen 2003; Hurrell and Deser 2009). These changes can therefore have a pronounced impact on marine, freshwater and terrestrial ecosystems and agricultural activities (Hurrell, Kushnir and Ottersen 2003), which can be detected through environmental proxy records.

The potential of sediment records from Inverpolly, Coigach and Assynt for the reconstruction of past environmental conditions has long been recognised: the area has been the subject of scientific study in regard to late glacial and Holocene environmental change since the

1960s and 70s (Lamb 1964; Moar 1969; Pennington *et al.* 1972). However, much of this early ground-breaking work on environmental reconstruction focussed on major episodes of climate change, inferred from late glacial and post-glacial vegetation successions, and attempts to reconstruct and draw comparisons with established climate models, by comparison with pollen zones detailed by Godwin, Jessen and others (Godwin and Seward 1940; Pennington and Godwin 1947; Jessen 1948; Pennington and Bonny 1970), based on sites across North-West England (Lake Windermere, Blelham Bog), multiple sites in Ireland (Jessen 1948), Loch Droma, Scotland (Kirk, godwin and Charlesworth 1963), and further afield lakes, such as Vågåvatn, Norway (Pennington *et al.* 1972). The original 'Godwin' zones were in turn, based on work done in East Anglia (Godwin and Seward 1940). It was found that for major climate changes, a correlation could be made between the late Weichselian (Late Devensian 14,000–9700 BC) pollen zones from North-West Scotland, Loch Droma and Blelham bog (Pennington *et al.* 1972), but for Holocene (9700 BC onwards) climate changes, synchronous, and/or equivalent proxy signals between England and North-West Scotland could not always be established. For example, there was no discernible change in vegetation where the Boreal-Atlantic transition would expect to be detected in North-West Scotland (Pennington *et al.* 1972).

Establishing the exact timing of vegetation changes from studies conducted in the 1960s–1980s can be difficult. Radiocarbon dates from lake sediment cores required a large volume of sediment, in the case of the North-West Scotland sites examined by Pennington *et al.* (1972) sections spanning several centimetres of sediment were necessary to recover the quantity of organic carbon required, and dates were uncalibrated. In the North-West Scotland examples, dates have cited errors of ± 100 years or more (see dates listed in Harkness and Wilson 1973). When calibrated,[1] the possible range of dates at the 95% confidence level is very wide, meaning that the chronologies can only be constrained at best to a few hundred years. It was therefore impossible to pinpoint switches in vegetation types or ascertain the time period over which these may have occurred with much precision. Later studies have had the advantage of Accelerator Mass Spectrometry (AMS) dating and Bayesian statistical techniques, meaning that better chronologies can be established. Most recently, the focus of study has turned to trying to quantify climate change (in terms of temperature, precipitation, storminess and sea level, from the observed changes in the palaeoenvironmental record), after calls from the Scottish Archaeological Research Framework and other papers (see Hunter and Carruthers 2012; Tipping *et al.* 2012 for details) to disambiguate 'climate coincidences' that can result in overly determinsitic interpretations of the human response to climate change. This work has only just started, so to date it has not been possible to draw quantified or localised conclusions about natural or human impacts on prehistoric climate in Scotland (Tipping *et al.* 2012). There are however, some glimpses into what might be achieved through further study.

Climate in the first millennium BC/AD

The following section provides a summary of the more widely known climatic events in the North Atlantic in the first millennium BC and early centuries AD. The section is split into 'local' and further afield. Scotland has steep climatic gradients (Fig. 8.1; Langdon and Barber 2005), which means that responses to climate changes can be localised and only detectable at locations within a given bioclimatic region. Only very significant climate shifts are detectable across all the bioclimatic regions (Langdon and Barber 2005). Therefore, the splitting of the data into regional and supra-regional aids discussion and interpretation.

Local climate

There are a number of proxy climate records local to North-West Scotland. A high-resolution speleothem proxy record comes from Uamh an Tartair cave, Inchnadamph (Proctor *et al.* 2000; Baker *et al.* 2015), 26 km southeast of Clachtoll. By comparison with historical records, several studies (Proctor *et al.* 2000; Proctor, Baker and Barnes 2002) have been able to demonstrate that annual growth band widths of stalagmites reflect levels of precipitation, with wetter, colder periods producing lower periods of growth and warmer drier periods resulting in higher growth (Proctor *et al.* 2000; Proctor, Baker and

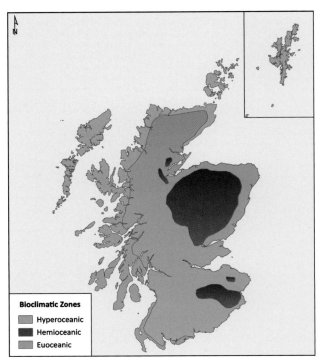

Figure 8.1 Bioclimatic regions in Scotland (Source: Modified from Langdon and Barber 2005, Fig. 1)

Barnes 2002). Precipitation in North-West Scotland is strongly influenced by the winter NAO with higher precipitation in positive NAO winters (Proctor *et al.* 2000). The speleothem record from Uamh an Tartair has been demonstrated to be a good proxy for winter NAO for the period of historic meteorological records (Proctor, Baler and Barnes 2002), and comparison with other climate proxies for NAO allowed this inference to be applied back into the period before written climate records, with the Uamh an Tartair record in agreement with several other records of 1st millennium AD NAO proxies (Baker *et al.* 2015). Periods of low growth in the Uamh an Tartair speleothem record, and thence winter NAO, correspond well with known periods of extra-tropical, northern hemisphere climate warming and cooling in the first and second millennium AD: the Late Iron Age/Early medieval climate downturn of the 3rd—6th centuries (sometimes referred to as the Dark Ages Cold Period), Medieval Climate Anomaly (MCA) *c.* AD 800–1300 and Little Ice Age *c.* AD 1300–1900 (Ljungqvist 2010). This relationship is demonstrated in Figure 8.2. Prolonged periods of low speleothem growth indicating wet winter conditions (Baker *et al.* 2015) and positive NAO occur in the periods AD 290–550 and AD 1080–1430.

The relationship of speleothem growth rates to winter NAO is less clear in the 1st millennium BC. The interpolated NAO conditions in the 1st millennium BC period do not match the comparator NAO record from Greenland

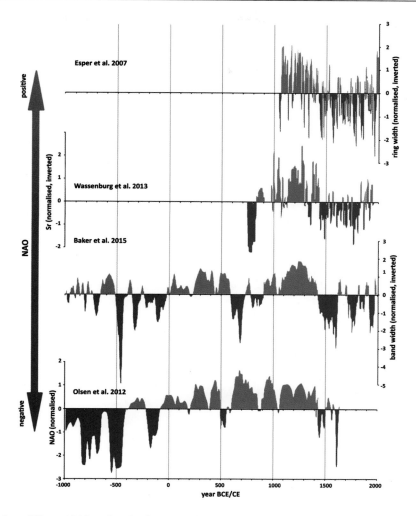

Figure 8.2 The relationship of Winter NAO and speleothem records from Uamh an Tartair cave, Inchnadamph, north-west Scotland. The figure is modified from figure 4 in Baker et al. (2015) which compares the results from Uamh an Tartair with NAO variability: Esper et al.'s (2007) study of a drought-sensitive tree-ring record from Morocco, Wassenberg et al.'s (2013) drought-sensitive Sr stalagmite record from Morocco, and Olsen, anderson and Knudson (2012) West Greenland ice core record. All records were normalised over the period they reflect and values inverted so that positive values reflect positive NAO conditions

(see Olsen, Anderson and Knudson 2012 and Fig. 8.2), and further investigation is required to understand the factors that may be causing this lack of synchronisation. There do not appear to be corresponding periods of prolonged high growth rate at known periods of climatic amelioration, suggesting that in North-West Scotland at least, winter temperature and precipitation are de-coupled: warmer years were not necessarily drier. The Roman Warm Period, where mean terrestrial temperatures in the extra-tropical northern hemisphere were higher than, or as high as, mean 20th-century temperatures (Ljungqvist 2010), is not clearly indicated in the speleothem record.

The normalised growth rate data from the speleothems from Uamh an Tartair (see Fig. 8.3) can be taken as a proxy for local precipitation (water table) conditions

only (and not NAO conditions) in the period 0–1000 BC. When looked at in conjunction with the data from peat humification records from cores taken in the Traligill basin above the Uamh an Tartair cave (Charman *et al.* 2001) the relationship between speleothem growth rate and climate appears more complicated. It should be noted that the number of speleothems that cover this time period (one complete and one intermittent record cover the period) is fewer than in later periods, where the normalised growth rates of five speleothems are examined in Baker *et al.* (2015). Following a period of below normal growth 1000–750 BC there is short-duration peak in growth bands *c.* 700 BC followed by average growth rates for the 3000-year period. This early period coincides with low levels of peat humification in peat cores taken in

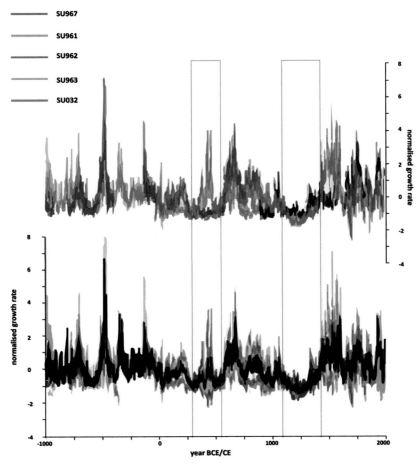

Figure 8.3 Normalised growth rate of the Uamh an Tartair Cave speleothems. Figure modified from Fig. 2 in Baker et al. (2015)

the Traligill Basin above the cave site (Charman *et al.* 2001). Low levels of peat humification are the result of a high water table which reduces organic decay at the peat surface (Chambers *et al.* 2012). A testate-amoeba record from the Traligill basin indicates high water tables before 700 BC followed by a sharp decrease after *c.* 650 BC, when levels of *Empetrum* pollen (a more dry-tolerant ericaceous species) rise considerably (Charman *et al.* 2001). On the Coigach peninsula, Bunting and Tipping (2004) note that in their sediment core from Badentarbat, sediment becomes increasingly fibrous, during the period *c.* 950–650 BC, suggesting a plant community with little or no open standing water, such as a sedge fen. This could suggest drier conditions. The palaeoenvironmental data taken from peat and sediment cores at Assynt and Coigach indicates a dry period that is not categorically shown in the speleothem data,[2] which suggests a brief spike indicating decreased rainfall at 650–500 BC followed by average conditions. This is possibly due to the seasonality of the precipitation that the different proxies detect, or that different proxies have differing sensitives

to climate. Although peatland water table depth (WTD) represents the prevailing balance between precipitation and evapotranspiration across the growing season (Charman *et al.* 2009), it has been argued that in the fringes of Atlantic North-West Europe, bog wetness indicators predominantly indicate summer water levels (Swindles *et al.* 2010) and winter precipitation is thought to be the principal factor determining speleothem growth (Baker *et al.* 2015). It is therefore tentatively suggested that winter precipitation was average/higher during the Early Iron Age, but summers may have been drier.

At *c.* 400–200 BC a period of lower growth (Fig. 8.3) in the Uamh an Tartair speleothems is concomitant with decreased levels of peat humification in peat cores examined by Charman *et al.* (2001), suggesting a period where water availability was higher. Peat humification records from the Traligill Basin suggest further wetness peaks at *c.* AD 150 and 350 (Charman *et al.* 2001). The AD 150 peak is also detected in the record from Ben Gorm Moss (Langdon and Barber 2005), suggesting a more widespread phenomenon (see later section on supra-local climate).

Further north of Assynt and Coigach, an ambitious attempt to get to grips with specifics of climate changes over prehistory uses data from the north coast of Scotland to reconstruct Atlantic storminess over the last 8000 years (Stewart *et al.* 2017). The principal source of bromine in the atmosphere comes from aerosol sea salt, which can travel some miles inland (Stewart *et al.* 2017). When bromine in aerosol form is deposited on ombrotrophic bog surfaces, down-core changes in bromine levels can be used as a proxy for storminess (Stewart *et al.* 2017). The analysis of bromine levels and Bog Surface Wetness (BSW) proxies, from a peat core taken at Shebster, northern Caithness (Stewart *et al.* 2017) was combined with existing climate data (including that from Uamh an Tartair speleothem records), to produce a detailed record of the last 8000 years. This record offers insights into Iron Age climate. The preceding Neolithic and Early Bronze age (to *c.* 1300 cal BC) saw a sustained period of low bromine and BSW, indicating calm and warm conditions. The data indicates that the Early Iron Age may have seen a shift to more stormy conditions, as a result of a more negative NAO, this is coincident with increased BSW, and inferred periods of wet winters at *c.* 950 and 650 BC from the speleothem data (Stewart *et al.* 2017). Indicators of increased summer precipitation and raised water tables at sites in Cumbria (Hughes *et al.* 2000), Ireland (Swindles, Plunkett and Rose 2007a), and multiple proxies indicating increasing wetness from sites across the British Isles (Charman 2010) suggest this increasing wetness is part of a wider trend (Stewart *et al.* 2017) in both summer (BSW records) and winter (speleothem record). In the Early and Middle Iron Age (*c.* 450 BC–AD 350), BSW and bromine levels suggest that storminess continued at previous levels in northern Scotland (just below the 8000-year average), but conditions were warmer (Stewart *et al.* 2017).

Supra-local climate

The speleothem and local palaeohydrology records from Assynt (Charman *et al.* 2001; Proctor, Baker and Barnes 2002; Baker *et al.* 2015) and sediment core from the Coigach peninsula (Bunting and Tipping 2004) give insights into winter NAO conditions and relative levels of precipitation during the Iron Age, but it is necessary to look further afield in order to consider the overall effects of changes to climate in the period.

Reconstruction of summer climate has been examined in Northern Ireland, using testate amoeba as a proxy for water table levels (Swindles *et al.* 2010). As with speleothem data, the relative importance of temperature and precipitation are not easy to disentangle (Swindles *et al.* 2010), however, it is argued that on the Atlantic fringes of North-west Europe, because

unusually warm summers are characterised by dry conditions, peat-based climate reconstructions can be considered records that primarily reflect summer precipitation (Swindles *et al.* 2010). Using chronologically well-constrained peat cores it was possible to infer a wet shift at *c.* 740 BC and periods of widespread summer water deficits at *c.* 1150–800 BC, 320 BC–AD 150, AD 250–470 and AD 1850–2000. Also using bog surface wetness proxies, Langdon and Barber (2005) detected a wet shift *c.* 900–700 BC and dry phases in multiple sites across Scotland between 450 BC–AD 150, and thus broadly coincident with the 320 BC–AD 150 dry shift in the north of Ireland. However, the summer water deficit periods in the north of Ireland detected at 320 BC–AD 470, correspond with higher water tables in northern England and southern Scotland and Ireland (Swindles *et al.* 2010). The evidence to date points towards precipitation records varying geographically, although caution should be exercised given dating uncertainties in records with few absolute dates (the suck-in-and-smear phenomenon described by Christen *et al.* (2007)) and the possibility that the different sensitivities of different proxies may contribute to proxy measures not always being in agreement. It has been suggested that although precipitation appears to be the primary driver of BSW, temperature has some impact at the centennial/millennial scale (Barber and Langdon 2007), at least in northern England, which might explain lower BSW being a feature of the Roman Warm Period. However, Swindles *et al.* (2010) explain that warmer temperatures (such as during the Roman Warm Period), see blocking anticyclones diverting maritime air masses to the north and south resulting in decreased precipitation. There is the further possibility that differences could be accounted for by the positioning of storm tracks in the North Atlantic as suggested by Stewart *et al.* (2017).

Summary

Climate in Assynt varied across the Iron Age due to local and wider climatic changes, and appears to broadly follow the pattern established by Langdon and Barber (2005), where certain changes were cross-regional but at other times, responses appear to be localised. The Bronze Age–Iron Age transition period sees lower than average speleothem growth rates, with short peaks indicating dry conditions at Uamh an Tartair, echoed in the peat humification records from Traligill. This would suggest that Assynt and Coigach sees the same climatic downturn in the Late Bronze Age/Early Iron Age as in other parts of North-West Europe. The summer 'wet shift' *c.* 750 BC observed by Swindles *et al.* (2010) is thought to be part of the widespread climatic deterioration (the Subboreal–Subatlantic transition (Swindles *et al.* 2013)) seen at sites

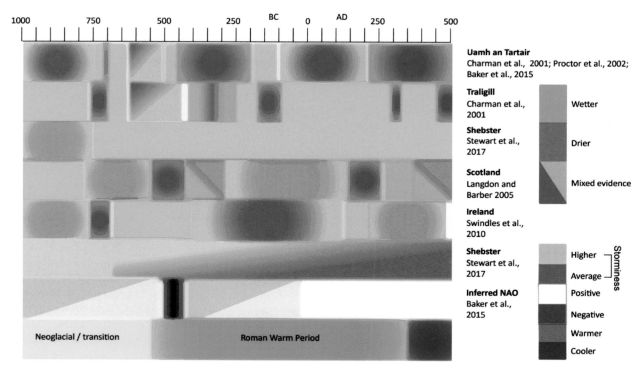

Figure 8.4 Summary diagram of environmental data discussed. The diagram presents simplified representations of proxies for wetness in different studies (rows 1–6). The change in Atlantic storminess recorded at Shebster is represented in row 7, and periods where more than one winter NAO proxy record is in agreement with another (see Baker et al. *2015 and Figure 8.2), is depicted in row 8. Known temperature changes are depicted in row 9, with dates taken from Ljungqvist (2010) and Wang, Surge and Mithen (2012)*

in North Germany (Barber, Chambers and Maddy 2004), Ireland (Swindles, Plunkett and Roe 2007a; 2007b), North England and Denmark (Mauquoy *et al.* 2008; Swindles *et al.* 2010) and again transcends geographical boundaries that usually see highly regional climates in Scotland (Langdon and Barber 2005).

The period 400–200 BC sees increased water availability, with higher water tables at Traligill. The Uamh an Tartair speleothem record also suggests higher precipitation, with a modest low growth (but not long periods of consecutive low growth bands) shown in the speleothem data during this time. The co-occurrence with the Roman Warm Period and summer water deficits in Northern Ireland demonstrates the regional variability of climates and that the relationship between warmer temperatures, precipitation and water table levels is not straightforward.

In the early 1st millennium AD, wet winter conditions in the speleothem record are echoed in the peat humification record above Uamh an Tartair cave, suggesting peaks in wetness *c.* AD 150 and 350 (Charman *et al.* 2001), but otherwise relatively average or stable conditions probably prevailed in North Scotland (Stewart *et al.* 2017). In the 1st millennium AD, the speleothem data unambiguously indicates a strongly positive winter

NAO, indicating a period of wet winters in the Late Iron Age, *c.* AD 290–550, which corresponds with wet shifts in sites across Scotland (Langdon and Barber 2005) and a climate downturn seen in 3rd—6th centuries in northern Europe (Ljungqvist 2010).

Vegetation history

At present there is little specific detail on the vegetation and landscape of prehistoric Assynt. The ambitious programme of multi-proxy study by Pennington *et al.* (1972) focussed research efforts on detecting broad changes in vegetation history and, by inference, in climate, and methods therefore reflected these research questions. Pollen work was often targeted in a way that would have minimised anthropogenic 'signals' (coring towards the deepest sections of large lakes, in order to maximise regional pollen rain capture, would have reduced the chances of capturing the types of pollen that indicate human activity such as cereals and certain herbaceous pollens interpreted as anthropogenic indicators (Behre 1981)) and grain counts were 150 tree pollen grains. Grain counts were high enough to detect the broad patterns of vegetation history that were the focus of the research, but lower than those needed to

Table 8.1 Calibrated radiocarbon dates from Loch Sionascaig (Pennington et al. *1972). Dates listed in Harkness and Wilson (1973) and the European Pollen Database (http://www.europeanpollendatabase.net/fpd-epd/) were calibrated using OxCal v4.3, IntCal13 (Bronk Ramsey 2009)*

Lab Number	Depth From	Depth To	Determination BP	Calibrated date (2 σ) BC	Range in years
Y-2362	250	260	4020±100	2876-2293	583
SRR-12	275	285	4485±100	3498-2906	592
Y-2363	350	360	6250±140	5481-4848	633
SRR-13	400	410	7136±130	6326-5733	593
Y-2364	425	435	7880±160	7242-6432	810
SRR-14	460	470	8523±126	7946-7201	745
SRR-15	500	510	9474±160	9252-8350	902

make detailed interpretations about vegetation cover in even pollen rich sediments (Djamali and Cilleros 2020). In addition, the timing of changes is difficult to determine since radiocarbon dating techniques in the 1970s required large samples, which could represent many years of sediment accumulation. Lastly, efforts to radiocarbon date changes were necessarily focussed around periods of research interest, usually the Neolithic and earlier, meaning that very few radiocarbon dates were taken for sections of core covering later prehistory.

Table 8.1 shows a list of radiocarbon dates from Loch Sionascaig which, when calibrated, return dates that have uncertainties of between 476 and 902 years at the 95% confidence level. When dates are used to construct age-depth models, the possible range of dates between points is considerably larger again (see Fig. 8.5 for graphical representation of this problem). There is a clear need to establish the timing and nature of landscape changes in the prehistoric period more precisely. Using the existing evidence, some general statements and hypotheses can be formed for broad time periods. These are discussed below. With development of AMS radiocarbon dating and chronological modelling techniques (for example, see Blaauw and Heegaard 2012) future studies will be able investigate changes in pollen spectra with greater precision and accuracy in order to define the timing and duration of shifts in vegetation type, the appearance of anthropogenic activity indicators in the record, and generate more nuanced ideas about cause and effect that support interaction between palaeoecology and archaeology.

Woodland and openness

The regional pollen diagrams of Pennington *et al.* (1972; Pennington 1995) and others (see, for example, Moar 1969; Boomer, von Grafenstein and Moss 2012) suggest the birch, pine and hazel wooded landscape of

the Mesolithic–Neolithic Holocene moved to more open conditions from the Neolithic onwards (see Tipping 1994; Froyd 2006; Edwards, Bennett and Davies 2019). There is evidence for a significant 'pine decline' that has been observed at Loch Farlary, east Sutherland (Tipping *et al.* 2008), west Glen Affric (Davies and Tipping 2004; Tipping *et al.* 2006) during the Bronze Age (Tipping *et al.* 2008). Huntley, Daniell and Allen (1997) list further pollen studies and combine this with evidence for pine stumps found in Neolithic peats in numerous locations across the north and north-west highlands demonstrating that the decline was widespread across the region.

Sedges, grasses and bracken and heathland species featured prominently in the more open Neolithic landscape. Blanket peat began to form in upland areas in the Neolithic and into the Bronze Age, although this was not necessarily a continuous progression (Pennington *et al.* 1972), and in other areas peat formation was initiated in the early Holocene (for examples, see Tipping 2008). Increased soil acidity and peat formation are often associated with increased wetness (either precipitation or decreased evapotranspiration), which in turn can cause soil erosion. In Assynt, the increased soil erosion appears not to have been as severe as elsewhere in Britain and Ireland, where lake sediment records see a number of radiocarbon date inversions, where older soils and sediments are washed into lakes on top of younger material (Edwards and Whittington 2001). The degree to which pine (*Pinus sylvestris*) featured in prehistoric woodlands in Assynt is debateable. Assynt lies on the northernmost extent of pine distribution in Scotland at *c.* 3000 BC (see Tipping 1994; Edwards, Bennett and Davies 2019) and a study of pollen from Lochan na h-Inghinn, suggested that 10–20% (total land pollen and spore sum) values of pine were indicative of pine only forming a minor component of the vegetation even at its peak before *c.* 4500 BC (Froyd 2006). So, although Pine pollen remains present in

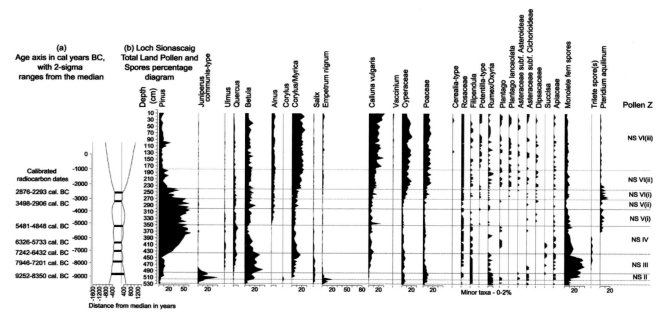

Figure 8.5 Preliminary data from core LNC19, Loch na Claise. Diagram depicts core stratigraphy, age-depth and count data from ITRAX XRF scanning and Loss-on-Ignition data. Age-depth was constructed using rbacon v2.4.2 and IntCal 13Later Holocene Pollen Diagram from Loch Sionascaig and age axis drawn from median values of age-depth model drawn using original radiocarbon dates calibrated and modelled using rbacon v2.4.2 (IntCal13 calibration curve). Part (a) depicts the distance of the minimum and maximum (2-sigma) age-depth model dates from the median date at a given depth. It is not possible to reliably calculate ages into 1st millennium AD due to lack of radiocarbon dates in the upper section of core. Part (b) shows percentage Total Land Pollen and Spores (TLP) using Pennington et al.'s (1972) pollen count data and updated taxanomic names. Diagram shows only selected taxa, herbaceous taxa curves (minor taxa) have been exaggerated by a factor of 10 for legibility. Data retrieved from the European Pollen Database, February 2020

pollen assemblages through the prehistoric period, it may not have formed a significant component of woodlands. Birch (*Betula*) and hazel (*Corylus*) were most likely the predominant taxa, with alder (*Alnus glutinosa*) present on wetter soils, for example around loch edges and stream beds. Willow (*Salix*), elm (*Ulmus*) and oak (*Quercus*) pollen are present through later prehistoric sections of sediment cores, which suggest these trees were present in the landscape, but either at a distance or in low numbers. The species lists from regional pollen diagrams overlap with species found to be in use at Clachtoll Broch, Loch na Claise, Clashnessie Dun and Split Rock with oak, pine, hazel birch and elm all present in pollen diagrams and charcoal/waterlogged wood recovered from the excavations. Rowan, larch and cherry are not recorded in pollen diagrams. Further work would be required to determine if this is the product of low pollen counts and cherry and rowan being low pollen producing species, before assuming that these are not represented in the local woodland. Larch is not native to Britain and only thought to have been introduced in the 17th century.

It should not be assumed that the landscape was near treeless. An analysis on the Coigach peninsula has been able to provide a more nuanced picture of landscape and vegetation history in coastal North-West Scotland. Data from a sediment core at Badentarbat suggests that although the area saw a significant loss of trees prior to 1250 Cal BC (Bunting and Tipping 2004), a low tree pollen signature is not necessarily the product of a treeless landscape, especially where small stands of woodland occur in between other landscape types (for example, see Bunting 2002). In an experiment to model the possible vegetation that would result in a particular pollen signature, a number of the multiple, alternative vegetation-pattern scenarios that were calculated indicated it was plausible for the assemblage to have been the result of a landscape that was nearly one third wooded or more (Bunting, Middleton and Twiddle 2007). At *c.* 50 BC a landscape that was also up to 50% birch-hazel woodland could also have resulted in the pollen signature on the Coigach peninsula (Bunting and Farrell 2018, 233, fig. 3), leading to the warning that: "Assumptions of treelessness in later prehistory, especially those based on pollen records from the centres of medium and large sized basins, probably need to be revisited in many cases. Records from individual sites are often published with caveats, but the nuance of interpretation is easily lost in synthesis or transfer of information" (Bunting and Farrell 2018, 233).

Land use

Direct indicators of land use have been difficult to detect in North-West Scotland. Cereal pollen and other indicators of anthropogenic soil disturbance such as *Plantago lanceolata,* occur in low numbers and/or infrequently. This might suggest little cultivation was taking place, however, given that this inference contrasts with on-site investigations which show the cultivation of barley, wild oats, emmer and (tentatively) flax, it seems more likely that this lack of detection may be due to the heterogenous nature of the landscape with soils capable of supporting agriculture occurring in discontinuous patches. There have been very few published studies of non-pollen palynomorphs, specifically dung fungal spores, that might detect animal grazing activity in Scotland (Edwards, Bennett and Davies 2019) and only one (Davies 2010) from the north-west, which covers the historical period. Where anthropogenic indicators are detected in the pollen record, the evidence suggests humans were present and making an impact on the soils and vegetation through cultivation as far back as the Late Bronze Age. At Duart Bog (Moar 1969) the *Plantago* curve peaks not long after 2457–1776 cal BC,[3] at Badentarbat in zone B4, dated to *c.* 1550 BC–AD 1110, cereal pollen appears in tiny numbers, with a coincident rise in *P. lanceolata* from the start of the zone again indicating Bronze Age/Iron Age activity. In a pollen diagram from Loch Assynt, the appearance of *P. lanceolata* occurs at the same time as the Bronze Age pine decline and increases thereafter (Boomer, van Grafenstein and Moss 2012). The appearance of *P. lanceolata* and cereal pollen also occurs shortly after a late prehistoric pine decline at Loch Borralan (Pennington *et al.* 1972). At Loch Sionascaig (Pennington *et al.* 1972) it is more difficult to determine the date of appearance of anthropogenic indicators. The first appearance of cereal pollen (125 cm) occurs in a section of core not constrained with absolute dates or characteristics (such as the pine decline) that might indicate a date. If a continuous sedimentation rate is assumed from the last known date, then it is likely the first cereal pollen occurrence and more sustained presence of *P. lanceolata* fall in the later prehistoric – most likely during the Iron Age.

In all the examples above, only low numbers of cereal grains and *P. lanceolata* were detected, and there is an almost complete absence of other taxa often associated with arable/disturbance activity such as goldenrod/daisy family (*Solidago virgaurea*-type), cabbage/mustard/charlock family (Brassicaceae), pinks (Caryophyllaceae), chickweeds (*Cerastium*-type), sorrels and docks (*Rumex* species), and goosefoots (Chenopodiaceae) (Edwards *et al.* 2005). This may reflect little cultivation, however, it could also be explained by other factors, such as the proximity of sampling site to soils that support these taxa. The low counts at Loch Borralan and Loch Sionascaig may be the result

of low overall pollen counts (150 tree pollen in the original study (Pennington *et al.* 1972)). Loch Sionascaig and Loch Assynt are both large surface-area lochs. Large basins are known to capture pollen from a wider pollen source area, which can swamp the signal from smaller patches of vegetation, especially for low-growing herbs (Sugita 1994) (for example crop fields) and making them more suited to the detection of regional pollen signals rather than representing smaller-scale heterogeneity (Edwards *et al.* 2019). Loch Sionascaig and Loch Assynt are situated in areas where the underlying geology and topography would be unfavourable to cultivation. It is thought that lower lying coastal zones and/or the Fucoid beds between Ledmore and Loch na Gainmhich, had soils that would have been more amenable to cultivation (Evans, Evans and Rothero 2002). At Badentarbat it was postulated that landscape contained grassy heaths and pasture in more inland areas, which would have been 'shielded' from the sampling point by surrounding vegetation (Bunting and Tipping 2004). Again, this could have an impact on the frequency/quantity of cereal pollens detected.

The lack of cereal and disturbance-indicating taxa requires further investigation, by application of new methods. For example, to more reliably detect (or rule out) the presence of cereal pollen would require a change in methodology – for example, applying rapid scanning used with success to detect cereal cultivation at Clickimin, Shetland (Edwards *et al.* 2005) or, given the relatively low pollen productivity of cereals, to selecting sites that might maximise a cultivation signal, such as those close to occupation sites or known field systems. The deliberate sampling of small basins in different landscape types at Glen Affric (Davies and Tipping 2004) has been used to detect small-scale human activity in a landscape where vegetation was much more heterogenous than that implied by studies that captured regional pollen rain (Davies and Tipping 2004). Similarly, the targeted pollen sampling of a known prehistoric field system has been able to elucidate human responses to local vegetation and environmental change during the Bronze Age at Hobbister, Orkney (Farrell 2015).

Conclusions

At present it is difficult to draw any detailed conclusions regarding vegetation and land use in Assynt during the Iron Age. There is a need to establish clearer and more nuanced narratives about the degree of landscape openness in later prehistory and establish the impact deforestation may have had on soils and vegetation. At the regional scale the indications are that deforestation may not have led to the widespread erosion seen at other locations in Britain (as evidenced by radiocarbon age inversions (Edwards and Whittington 2001)), however, this lack of evidence is not necessarily evidence of absence and could be a result of site selection strategy and a dearth of later Holocene radiocarbon ages in cores taken to date.

Work on vegetation modelling at Badentarbet (Bunting, Middleton and Twiddle 2007; Bunting and Farrell 2018) demonstrated that the application of new methodologies can detect nuances in local vegetation dynamics, which could be fundamental to understanding the landscape and land-use contexts of settlements like Clachtoll and Loch na Claise. Further modelling exercises could well inform discussion about the availability of natural resources, especially wood for building and craft activities.

Further work is also required to investigate the nature and intensity of land use related to agri-pastoral activities. Existing pollen records suggest the presence of cultivation, but cannot accurately identify and pinpoint location, onset and/or change. An effort to detect and identify cereal and pastoral indicator pollen in sediments coupled with the use of faecal sterol biomarkers (and/or non-pollen palynomorphs) to detect the presence of animals at water sources (e.g., D'Anjou *et al.* 2012; Mackay *et al.* 2020; Brown *et al.* 2021), may give insights into landscape-use dynamics.

Future prospects and initial results

Future efforts to investigate the vegetation and climate of North-West Scotland in relation to the Scottish Iron Age should be targeted to answer questions relating to human-environment interactions and establishing chronologies for changes in climate and vegetation conditions. A change of focus in both site selection and methodology should be used to detect both human impact on local environments, and responses to broader climatic conditions. The use multi-proxy analysis on sediment cores taken at or near Iron Age sites, and from locations that maximise the detection of local, as opposed to regional, proxy signals, can address questions relating to the nature and timing of changes to the landscape of Assynt in the later prehistoric period discussed above. The current programme of investigation in Assynt will

apply the method of combing multiple palaeoenvironmental techniques (previously used in South-West Scotland and Ireland to investigate crannog sites as part of the *Celtic Connections and Crannogs* project) to a new geographical area and archaeological context. Examples of how environmental context can be gained from the use of such multi-proxy records can be found in the Iron Age site of Black Loch of Myrton (Crone *et al.* 2018), where faecal steroid biomarkers provided evidence for presence of pigs, ruminants and humans or horses, despite the lack of clear evidence for animal presence on site from excavation and traditional post-excavation approaches. Similarly, multi-proxy evidence from lake sediment records has highlighted the short-term high-intensity impact of human activity on Neolithic pile dwellings on the shore of Lake Zürich, Switzerland (Bleicher *et al.* 2018). The proxies intended for Assynt sites are pollen analysis, loss-on-ignition (LOI), Carbon and Nitrogen isotope and C:N ratio analysis, faecal steroid biomarkers, X-ray Florescence (XRF) and biogenic silica.

The ongoing studies by the present writer aim to approach many of the issues outlined above in greater detail, using analysis of loch sediment cores with the aim of:

- Detecting changes in land-use in and around settlements: for example, using pollen analysis and modelling to determine likely wooded to open ratio of the landscape, refine the chronology for the appearance of cereals, pastoral indicator species and disturbance taxa to detect land use dynamics.
- Changes in lake geochemistry and carbon/nutrient source (XRF, stable isotopes of carbon and nitrogen) to detect direct and indirect effects of human activities on both in-lake ecosystems and introduction of material from erosion and the likely extent/intensiveness of this action.
- Constructing a more tightly constrained chronology for settlement and land-use through use of radiocarbon dates and age-depth modelling of sediment cores.

Table 8.2 *Loch na Claise radiocarbon dates. Dates calibrated using OxCal v4.3, IntCal13 (Bronk Ramsey 2009)*

LabID	Determination BP	Depth (cm)	Calibrated date (2 σ) BC/AD at 95.4% probability
OxA-X-3020-18	11,769±55	231.5	11,784–11,520 cal BC
OxA-X-3020-19	8483±33	183.5	7587–7512 cal BC
OxA-X-3020-20	954±21	32.5	cal AD 1022–1155
OxA-38838	4476±25	143.5	3338–3030 cal BC
OxA-38839	2086±19	93.5	168–50 cal BC

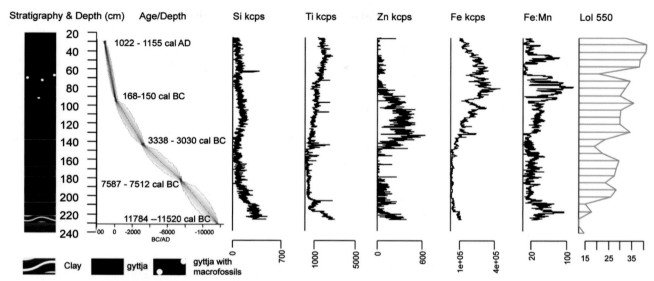

Figure 8.6 Preliminary data from core LNC19, Loch na Claise. Diagram depicts core stratigraphy, age-depth and count data from ITRAX XRF scanning and Loss-on-Ignition data. Age-depth was constructed using rbacon v2.4.2 (IntCal 13 calibration curve)

- Detecting evidence for animal husbandry and agriculture.
- Ascertaining the impact of land-use activities.

The research will take a 'nested' approach to research questions, building up answers from the site-scale to landscape scale and then onto the wider context and implications for research. For instance, what evidence is there for crops being grown in the immediate vicinity of sites? What evidence is there that wood and timber found on sites could have come from the immediate area? Is there evidence for change or differential use across the landscape during the period sites were occupied? What was the nature and extent of this change? Did Iron Age settlement have a lasting impact on lake ecosystems and landscapes?

When results are combined with climate data, such as those detailed above, it should be possible to construct a biography of climatic events (Tipping *et al.* 2012) in North-West Scotland, that explores the complex relationship between landscape and human actions within it.

To date, three sediment cores have been recovered for analysis. One from Loch na Claise adjacent the crannog, one from the now terrestrialised part of a lochan *c.* 500 m south of Clachtoll Broch (hereafter Clachtoll Lochan), and one from Loch an Aigeil *c.* 500 m east of Clachtoll Broch. The Loch na Claise core was chosen to maximise the 'signal' from the crannog site, and is discussed further below. Clachtoll Lochan and Loch an Aigeil were chosen as the closest water bodies to Clachtoll Broch and potentially provide a unique opportunity to detect differential landscape use around the broch. Clachtoll Lochan is shallow, stagnant water and assuming similar conditions

in the past, was possibly more suitable for livestock/agricultural use, whereas Loch an Aigeil is deep with a small inflow and outflow and may have been more suitable for drinking water or processing food/goods.

At the time of writing, analysis of the Loch an Aigeil and Clachtoll Lochan cores is yet to commence. Preliminary results from the Loch na Claise core are encouraging. The core was taken 13 m from the crannog island excavated by AOC and Historic Assynt in 2016. Rangefinder radiocarbon dating of the core indicates the sediments cover the post glacial to modern periods (see Table 8.2). Visual inspection of the core identified layers of sediment containing material of terrestrial origin at 143–7–129.5 cm and 97–92.5 cm. A broken hazelnut shell at 143.5 cm was carbon dated to 3338–3030 cal BC and a charred barley grain recovered at 93.5 cm dated to 168–50 cal BC.[4] Figure 8.6 shows preliminary results from Loss-on-Ignition and ITRAX XRF scanning (1 mm interval) of core LNC19. Loss-on-Ignition was carried out following Heiri, Lotter and Lemcke (2001), after drying for 24 hours at 105°C sample crucibles were placed in a furnace at 550°C for 4 hours.

A full core description is forthcoming; here, only the changes in lake geochemistry relating to later prehistoric sediments are discussed.

The layer at 144–129.5 cm denotes the start of several changes in relative element composition observed from XRF data (Fig. 8.5). The most striking change is a significant change in levels of zinc (Zn) and Iron (Fe). The ratio plot iron/manganese (Fe/Mn) suggests a change in redox conditions in the lake – usually rising Fe/Mn is interpreted as stronger reducing conditions (*i.e.* poor oxygenation of the sediments, Davies, Lamb and Roberts 2015). This can be the result of increased productivity when decaying organic matter in surface sediments uses up oxygen during remineralisation of organic matter by microbial activity (*e.g.*, Schilder *et al.* 2017). In other lochs it has been suggested that raised Fe/Mn was imparted by influx of dissolved iron and manganese from increasingly waterlogged soils in the watershed, and secondarily transmitted to the lake through overland flow (Pennington *et al.* 1972). Zinc will complex with organic compounds and when coincident with increasing levels of organic carbon, can indicate erosion from the catchment when industrial pollution can be ruled out (Cohen 2003; Engstrom and Wright 1984 cited in Smol 2008), although analysis of grain size and carbon content would be required to confirm this (Cohen 2003), the modest rise in levels of silicon (Si) and titanium (Ti), also in this section of the core, suggests erosion could be partly responsible.

A working hypothesis is that the modest increase in Si and Ti and peak spike in Zn from *c*. 144 cm and 94 cm, and LOI from 138–128 cm could be due to increased erosional input, but at low levels, a pattern observed at larger lochs during the Neolithic and Bronze Age and coinciding with the expansion of blanket bog and deforestation in upland areas (Pennington *et al.* 1972) and wetter environmental conditions observed at Badentarbat during the Bronze Age (Bunting and Tipping 2004). However, at this stage, increased productivity of the loch cannot be ruled out as an explanation. Increased productivity may be the result of a rise in lake water temperatures (Smol 2008) allowing increased photosynthesis in the littoral zone (although this relationship is complex (Smol 2008)), cultural eutrophication caused by the introduction of effluent directly to the loch from occupation sites, or from increased nutrients introduced from eroded soils, this latter being caused by anthropogenic action (from increased clearance, ploughing, grazing pressure, etc.), climatic change (increased intensity and frequency of rainfall) or both. Although increased levels of Si may relate to increased introduction of inorganic sediment, they may also be the indicative of the start of anthropogenic eutrophication, because biogenic silica, which is largely produced by algae, can be used as indicator for increased lake productivity.

A significant switch in the relative abundance of elements occurs at 93–94 cm. Above this depth there is a very marked increase in Fe/Mn, but no indication of increasing clastic material (Si begins to decline, Ti remains stable) or erosion indicators – zinc declines markedly from this point. Organic carbon content dips from 36% at 96 cm to 30% at 88 cm before returning to a higher level 32% and 80 cm, suggesting that zinc is not present in high enough quantities to form a complex with organic carbon after this

initial dip, and even after carbon levels rise again. The working hypothesis is that changing Fe/Mn indicates an abrupt change in lake water conditions, again suggesting increased reducing conditions as a result of increased organic decay. The lack of indications that clastic material is entering the lake (low Si, Ti, and potentially Zn) suggests increased nutrients supplied to the loch, perhaps still from erosion, but from organic material that contains higher nutrient levels (*i.e.* with higher levels nitrogen/phosphorus). In other words, although the quantity of material entering the lake (including initially, organic carbon) appears to decrease, the nature of the material is different, and able to make a marked change in lake water conditions. The coincidence with a change in sediment composition and the appearance of the barley caryopsis in the sediment is strongly suggestive of human impact on loch conditions, either direct, from material from the crannog washing into the loch (for example effluent), or from material entering the loch due to increased erosion from land-clearance related to agricultural, pastoral or deforestation activities.

The next phase of work will include analysis of lake productivity using biogenic silica (Schelske 2002), and sediment origin by analysing and plotting $\delta^{13}C$, $\delta^{15}N$ and C/N values (Meyers and Teranes 2001). This aims to determine whether this signal is the result of in-lake processes, or catchment erosion (or both), and whether this may have been the result of anthropogenic action or climate change. The addition of pollen data and faecal biomarker evidence (Mackay *et al.* 2020) may be able to further elucidate the nature of landscape change, especially if this is through human action. Preliminary indications from initial pollen counts are that the first significant levels of disturbance taxa (*Plantago lanceolata*, a biennial that will colonise bare/disturbed ground) appear in the pollen record for the site from *c*. 140 cm onwards and increase in frequency and number up-core as far as 92.5 cm (further sample analysis is currently ongoing). This suggests that anthropogenic disturbances in the catchment were already ongoing before a significant change in lake water conditions occurred.

Notes

1   See Table 8.1: Dates from Loch Sionascaig in Harkness and Wilson (1973) were calibrated using OxCal v4.3 (Bronk Ramsey 2009), IntCal13 (Reimer *et al.* 2013).

2   Although again, it should be noted that the number of speleothems with data suitable for reconstruction purposes during this period is lower than for other periods.

3   Date Q756/7, 3690±110 BP calibrated from Moar (1969), using OxCal v4.3 (Bronk Ramsey 2009), IntCal13 (Reimer *et al.* 2013)

4   Dates were calibrated using OxCal v4.3 (Bronk Ramsey 2009) with IntCal13 (Reimer *et al.* 2013). Figures cited at 95%

The Iron Age landscape of Stoer

Graeme Cavers, Charlotte Douglas and Alex Wood

Evidence for Iron Age settlement activity in the wider landscape around Clachtoll is limited to a handful of sites identified by earlier survey work, including duns or coastal fortifications at Clashnessie, Rubha an Dunain and the Split Rock at Clachtoll beach and a possible crannog or islet settlement at Loch na Claise. Survey of these monuments had been limited to brief descriptions and the measured surveys carried out by Historic Assynt, and no excavation had been carried out at any of them. As such, the chronology of their use was completely unknown, and their bearing on the interpretation of the settlement landscape contemporary with the Clachtoll broch uncertain. In order to provide some context for the excavations carried out at the broch, small-scale evaluation excavations were undertaken at three of these sites, at Loch na Claise, the Split Rock and Clashnessie (Fig. 9.1).

Loch na Claise, islet settlement

The islet in Loch na Claise (NC 0354 3081) had been reported as a possible crannog by the Ordnance Survey's surveyors in 1962, though no close inspection had been carried out and prior to the evaluation in 2016, there was no evidence to confirm this. There was little question that the site was at least in part artificial, however, with rubble visible during periods of low water level and a stone causeway leading to the islet from the north shore (Fig. 9.2). In 2016, when the trial trench was excavated, the islet was visible as a stony mound, covered in juniper bushes and bracken (Fig. 9.3). Traces of structure were visible beneath a thin turf, but the details could not be traced through the thick vegetation.

A trench measuring 3 m by 2m was excavated on the north-eastern quadrant of the islet, constrained by the availability of space above the water level, but ultimately extended to a trapezoidal plan to encompass the stonework encountered (Fig. 9.4). Beneath the turf and topsoil layers, a thin deposit of rubble (102) overlay a stone wall [103], approximately 0.6 m in width and surviving to *c.* 0.4 m in height, although the base of the wall was not excavated owing to waterlogging. The wall formed a rough arc within the trench, approximating the curvature of the islet, although it had clearly been modified from its original line with a lower section [104] – only observed in plan before waterlogging prevented further excavation – taking a different curve and suggesting the wall had originally enclosed a larger area. Within the walling, beneath rubbly deposits were two waterlogged, peaty layers, (106) and (108). The upper, (106), was drier but nonetheless contained woody fragments, charcoal and burnt bone. The lower, (108), was better preserved, with similar inclusions, but excavation was halted before much of this deposit could be excavated, as flooding prevented progress. Bulk samples of both deposits were taken for assessment; these provided the samples from which the C14 determinations were obtained.

Palaeoenvironmental assessment

Charcoal (176.0 g) was recovered from three samples (106), (106 Lower) and (108). The species were alder (56%), hazel (28%), birch (14%) and heather (2%). The charcoal was concentrated within context (106) which had 165.6 g compared to 2.1 g from (106 Lower) and 8.3 g in (108). Small fragments of burnt peat were also observed within contexts (106) and (108). These remains are likely to be representative of fuel debris.

Burnt bone totalling 21.1 g was recovered from contexts (106) and (106 Lower). These remains were poorly preserved due to burning. Most fragments were

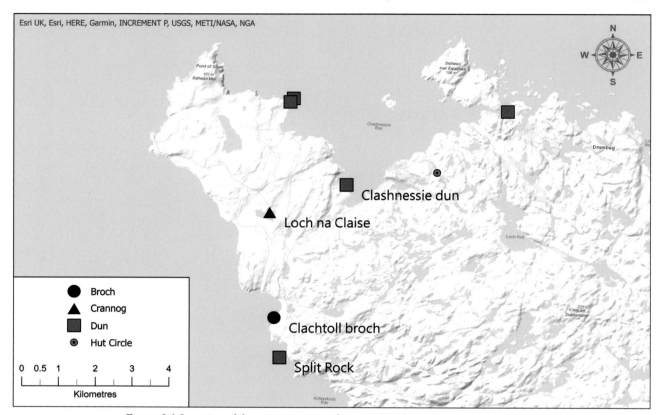

Figure 9.1 Location of the sites investigated across the Clachtoll and Stoer peninsula

unidentifiable although there were a small number of long bone shafts.

Radiocarbon dating

Two radiocarbon dates were obtained, one from each of contexts (106) and (108). The dates indicate occupation in the last two centuries BC at 2 sigma range, and probably in the 1st century BC (Table 9.1).

Loch na Claise: discussion

Although limited in extent, the excavation at Loch na Claise nonetheless provides a valuable contribution to the contextualisation of the Clachtoll settlement, and it is likely that the site was in use at the same time as the broch. With such a limited sample it is difficult to extrapolate further information about the nature or function of the structure, but some inference might be drawn from comparison of the structures' size and complexity. At best, the Loch na Claise islet cannot have provided enough space for a building more than around 9 m in diameter, and there is nothing to suggest that the architecture of the building was in any way sophisticated. Artificial islet settlements are a common feature of the western Scottish Atlantic Iron Age from Galloway to Sutherland (Cavers

2010), and come in a range of formats, including mainly stone built structures and those built entirely in wood; the distinction seems to be of little chronological or cultural significance. It has been argued that in some areas, crannogs perform an equivalent role in the settlement record of Iron Age Scotland as that performed by brochs and other monumental houses: they emphasise defensibility, in appearance if not in practicality, and functioned as productive farmsteads. While these characteristics could apply to the Loch na Claise islet settlement, the structure stands in contrast to the considerably more monumental building at Clachtoll, and while too little evidence is available to allow confident interpretations to be put forward, it seems likely that the site was occupied by a much smaller group, if not one of lower social standing. Future work on the proxy environmental record from Loch na Claise (see Chapter 8), may help to clarify the economic basis of the settlement, and allow more informed comparison with the broch at Clachtoll.

The Split Rock, fortified sea stack

The 'Split Rock' is a prominent sea stack located to the south of Clachtoll beach (NC 0380 2673). The grassy top of the stack is the highest visible point on the rocky

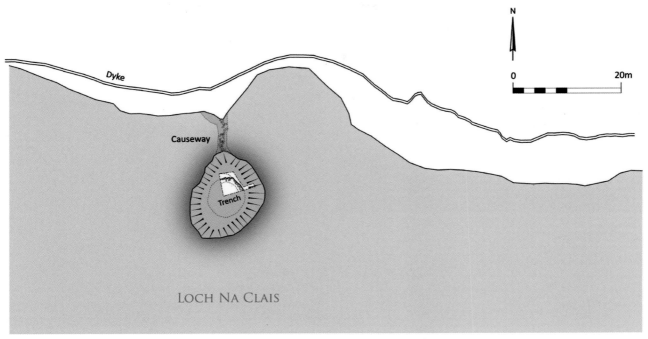

Figure 9.2 Loch na Claise islet, showing the trench location

coast to the south of the broch, and one of the most westerly points, giving panoramic views of the coastal approach from the south, as well as to the west and north (see Figs 9.5 and 9.6). This strategic position is likely to have been of value to the broch occupants, offering a vantage point from which to gain an early warning of the approach of craft from the south and west. Survey during Historic Assynt's work with the Scotland's Rural Past project had identified sections of vitrification within a short length of walling which encloses the crest of the stack. Little remains of this enclosure wall, but it appears that the stack was defended; no internal structures are visible and prior to 2017 there was no further information about the site.

A trial trench measuring 3 m by 1 m, orientated north-west to south-east was excavated on the crest of the stack, west of the visible enclosure wall, in September 2017. The removal of the charcoal rich topsoil, containing debris likely to derive from modern fires, revealed a series of charcoal and organic rich deposits overlying bedrock and abutting the side of a roughly north–south orientated wall (SR-06) (Fig. 9.7)

consisting of a foundation course and a single surviving upper course of subangular sandstone blocks. Rubble was founding lying over and beside the wall indicative of walling material which had subsequently collapsed. One of the lowest organic rich dark grey sandy silt deposits (SR-05) abutting the foundation course of the internal face of the wall produced abundant animal bone (SF4) and sherds of decorated Iron Age pottery (SF5), similar in style to those found at the Clachtoll broch, and is considered to represent an occupation deposit.

Palaeoenvironmental assessment

From Split Rock, charcoal (18.5 g) was present in three contexts (SR-03), (SR-04) and (SR-05). The species were hazel (47%), birch (27%), alder (23%) and rowan (3%). These remains seem likely to be representative of redeposited fuel debris.

The occupation deposit (SR-05) produced numerous fragments of burnt bone, including a cattle incisor and fragments of a metapodial and calcaneum. Numerous other fragments of small and medium mammal bones were

Table 9.1 Radiocarbon dates from the Loch na Claise islet

Context	Lab Code	Determination BP	Calibrated date range, at 1 σ	Calibrated date range, at 2 σ
106	SUERC-70518	2080±29	156–21 BC	190–3 BC
108	SUERC-70522	2031±29	87 BC–AD 17	155 BC–AD 52

Figure 9.3 View of Loch na Claise islet settlement, from the north shore of the loch

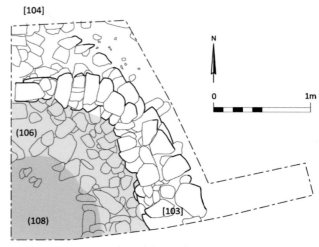

Figure 9.4 Plan of the Loch na Claise trench

present in the burnt bone assemblage, though preservation quality was mostly poor.

Radiocarbon date

A single radiocarbon date was obtained from a hazel charcoal fragment from the possible occupation deposit (SR-05). T his was returned as 2058 ±24 bp (SUERC-87248), calibrating in the range 153 BC to AD 14 at the 2 sigma level.

Ceramics

Andy Heald and Dawn McLaren

Only four sherds of pottery were recovered during the excavations at Split Rock. These derive from three separate pottery vessels (V1–3). The small quantity of surviving sherds and their heavily fractured condition necessarily limits the inferences that can be made regarding their form, function and date. Where possible, the sherds have been compared to the much larger assemblage of pottery found in association with Clachtoll broch. At least two of the vessels represented are very similar in surface finish and decoration to those observed within the broch assemblage and this will be considered in more detail.

Before moving to describing the details of the individual vessels, a few general points can be made about the Split Rock pottery. In each instance the sherds represent less than 5% of the original circumference of the vessel and most, with the exception of V2, are represented by single sherds. All four of the sherds are sooted indicating use of the vessels prior to breakage and discard and they display light to moderate abrasion of the surfaces. All have been produced by coil-construction methods and all are low-fired.

The sherd representing V1, stands out from all the pottery examined from Split Rock and the Clachtoll

broch assemblage due to the fineness of the walls and the smoothed almost burnished exterior surface finish. It is moderately abraded and was recovered from topsoil (context SR/02). Although difficult to state with confidence, it is possible that this sherd derives from a much earlier pottery type and may be early prehistoric in date.

Vessels 2 and 3 are similar to examples observed in Clachtoll broch assemblage and on the basis of their curvature, are potentially fragments of globular jars although not enough survives to confirm this. The exterior surface of V2 has been scraped with a hard-edged implement when still wet to create a smooth and even surface. Into this prepared surface, a narrow horizontal cordon has been produced by the maker pushing their fingernail into the wet clay creating a continuous band of C-shaped divots. This is unparalleled amongst the broch assemblage. Yet, Type A and Type C vessels display narrow horizontal cordons around their shoulders and the style of the cordon seen on Broch V3 and 4 – a narrow pinched up cordon which has been segmented by a regular series of vertical short fingernail impressions – is not dissimilar in design.

Split Rock V3 is represented by a single body sherd. Like V2, the exterior surface has been scraped to smooth, leaving a series of shallow and fine linear impressions on the surface. The scratched surface created during the production process of Split Rock V2 is widely paralleled amongst the Broch assemblage including V8–11. The similarities in surface finish and decoration of the sherds of V2 and V3 are so similar to examples amongst the broch assemblage that a broadly contemporary date for their production and use is invited.

Catalogue

Vessel 1 Body sherd from a thin-walled vessel. Exterior surface is plain but smoothed, almost burnished, broken

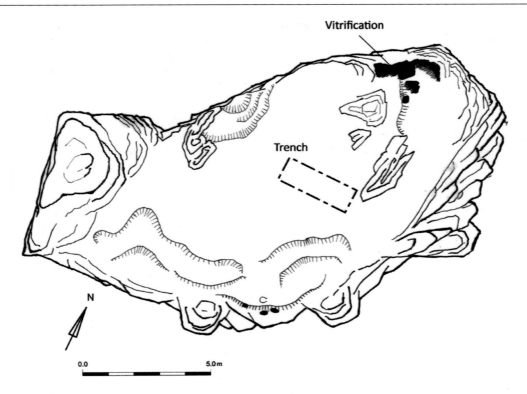

Figure 9.5 The fortification on the Split Rock, showing the position of the trial trench (drawing based on survey by Gordon Sleight)

across coil-junction which is clearly visible on fracture edge of sherd. Fabric is a fine clay, fired moderately hard, oxidised, with no obvious temper. Form of vessel is unknown. Patches of sooting visible on exterior surface. Exterior diameter approx. 125 mm, T 4.5 mm. Wgt 4.1 g. SF 01. Context SR/02, topsoil (not illustrated).

Vessel 2 Two joining body sherds from a variant of Clachtoll Broch Type A and C globular jar. Exterior surface has been scraped in a vertical direction with a hard-edged tool creating a series of closely spaced parallel vertical striations across the surface, visible under raking light. Impressed into this is a narrow (H 9.5 mm) horizontal cordon produced by scraping the fingernail against the clay when wet in a continuous row, creating a band of C-shaped divots in the clay. The fabric is a fine clay, fired hard and incompletely oxidised. Sooting is present on exterior surface. Exterior diameter cannot be assessed with any accuracy but is a minimum of 180 mm, T 6.4 mm. Wgt 11.8 g. SF05. Context SR-05, organic-rich deposit (Fig. 9.8).

Vessel 3 Single body sherd, form likely to be a globular jar but too small a sherd to determine, broken across diagonal coil junction. Exterior surface has been scraped in a vertical direction with a hard-edged tool during production, creating a series of rather haphazard fine linear striations. Fabric is a fine clay, fired hard and incompletely oxidised. Sooting is present on exterior surface and interior surface is stained. Exterior diameter

cannot be assessed with any accuracy but is a minimum of 140 mm, T 6.5 mm. Wgt 22.7 g. SF05. Context SR-05, organic rich deposit (not illustrated).

Stone
Dawn McLaren

Only one item of worked stone was recovered during excavations at Split Rock and consists of a well-used strike-a-light used for fire-lighting. Like the examples used from the broch, this example conforms to Childe's (1936) classification of 'tracked stones' where a long groove or furrow has been abraded into the centre of one or both extensive faces of a water-rounded pebble due to repeatedly being scored or struck with an iron fire-steel or pyrite. The example from Split Rock is also similar to the examples from Clachtoll broch in terms of the type, shape and size of water-rounded pebble selected for use but unlike those from the broch, this example lacks distinctive red-brown staining across the surfaces.

Catalogue

SF 2 Strike-a-light. Flattened ovoid quartzite pebble, circular in plan with D-shaped edges, light pitting observed around circumference (W 7.5 mm) from light use as a pounder and shallow linear groove (L 40.5 mm, W 10 mm) runs longitudinally across centre of face. Edges of groove are not well

Figure 9.6 Excavation on the split rock in 2017

defined and appears abraded. Opposite face also has a distinct linear groove (L 30.5 mm, W 8 mm) across the centre of the face but is angled differently to that just described, interior faces are abraded accompanied by a light sheen and an area of fine haphazard and dispersed pitting is present at one tip of the facet. L 62.5, W 59, T 24.5 mm. SR-02 (Fig. 9.9).

Iron

Dawn McLaren and Andy Heald

Fragments representing the rounded tip of a double-edged blade (SF 003; Fig. 9.10), probably from a sword, were recovered from old topsoil (context 002). The largest fragments that survive have been rejoined during conservation and represent the rounded pointed tip of a fairly wide and flat, lentoid-sectioned blade, broken across the width approximately 106.5 mm from the tip. The original length and form of the blade are unknown. Possible hints of a shallow central fuller are visible by x-radiography but are not observed by visual examination alone making it difficult to be confident about whether these details are the remains of a fuller or seams in the iron relating to the manufacturing process. The edges are heavily damaged as the result of post-deposition corrosion. So little survives that it is not possible to confidently ascribe a date or form to this blade but an Iron Age date cannot be ruled out.

From the same context was recovered a typologically Iron Age stone strike-a-light (SF02) and a sherd of pottery which has very tentatively been identified as early prehistoric in date. The incomplete condition of the blade and how it became incorporated in old topsoil is intriguing but the condition of the surfaces is not sufficiently good enough to distinguish whether the breakage of the blade was likely purposeful.

Catalogue

SF 003 Sword blade fragment. Rounded tip of a double-edged blade, broken cleanly across the width in two

places, refitted during conservation. Edges damaged by corrosion. Hint on x-ray of possible fuller down length of blade (W 6 mm) but not visible macroscopically. A further 3 angular fragments and 4 amorphous spalls no longer join but are almost certainly part of the same object. Remaining L 106.5 mm, W 35.2 mm, T 3.5–4 mm. Wgt 34.6 g. Context SR-02, old topsoil.

Split Rock: discussion

The Split Rock site is small, and the area available for safe excavation is very limited. Consequently, this exploratory excavation cannot offer much more than an indication of the period and manner of the site's use. The identification of a relatively rich archaeological deposit (SR-05) deposit associated with the enclosing wall suggests that the site was probably occupied, while the ceramics recovered along with the strike-a-light suggest similar accoutrements to those that furnished the broch. This evidence, combined with the contemporary radiocarbon date – admittedly only a single determination – strongly suggest that the site was in use at the same time as the broch. Again, the evidence from a limited trial trench cannot be used to extrapolate the details of the function of this structure, but its strategic position suggests that it may have functioned as a look-out or signal post, at least in conjunction with some other purpose.

The presence vitrification in the enclosing wall is intriguing. To achieve vitrification, sustained exposure to temperatures in excess of 1000 degrees is necessary (*e.g.*, latest study, McCloy *et al.* 2021, 12), a scenario that seems improbable unless the wall was timber laced, and even then additional fuel would have been required to sustain the necessary temperatures. This significant – and presumably destructive – burning might find a parallel in the catastrophic fire that ended the occupation of the broch, and it is possible that whatever event caused the destruction of the broch was also inflicted on the Split Rock structure. It should be noted, however, that no vitrification was present at the broch, and the evidence from the destruction layer, context (042), points to the fire having been rapid and fierce, but over quickly (see Chapter 10). An alternative interpretation of the Split Rock vitrification, therefore, might be in relation to signaling or its role as a beacon. Sustained or repeated fires lit and maintained for the purposes of signaling in such a constrained location could account for the vitrification, although this does seem incompatible with the presence of material that would be interpreted as indicative of occupation elsewhere. It is possible that both interpretations are correct, and that the signal or look-out post was occupied as a dwelling, before its abandonment and final use as a beacon.

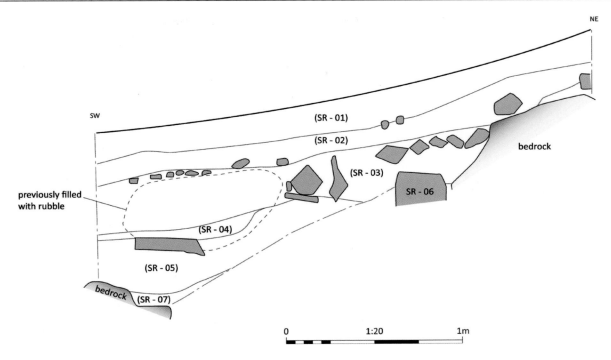

Figure 9.7 Section through deposits excavated in the Split Rock trial trench

Clashnessie Dun

Clashnessie Dun, also known as An Dun (NGR: NC 0563 3157), is situated on an almost detached coastal rocky outcrop in Clashnessie Bay, around 700 m to the north of the settlement of Clashnessie. It is accessed via a steep slope, partially turf-covered, which is connected to the mainland via a rocky causeway. The surrounding landscape is scattered with post-medieval buildings and cultivation remains.

The dun is marked on Roy's map of Assynt (*c.* 1750) which shows it as inhabited (Fig. 9.11), although it is unclear whether this refers to a dwelling there or some other building, such as a fishing bothy, in use at that location. The site appears again on Home's 1774 map of Assynt and is also marked on both the 1st and 2nd edition OS maps, but in the wrong location: it is shown as being on a peninsula some half a mile to the NNE of its actual location.

There is no record of archaeological excavations ever having been carried out at the dun. In 2009, the site was surveyed by Historic Assynt as part of the Scotland's Rural Past Project. The visible remains are very fragmentary (Fig.9.12), but stones interpreted as representing the inner and outer walls were identified at various points around the site's circumference. The probable location of the entrance was identified as being at the south, at the top of the steep slope by which the site can be accessed.

The enclosure formed by the low wall is oval/subcircular in plan, aligned NE–SW, and measuring around 13.0 m

by 10.0 m. The wall, where visible on the ground surface, varies from 1.0 m to 3.0 m in width, surviving to at least three courses high in places. The outcrop on which the dun sits is irregular in plan due to erosion, with an area of the NW section of dun wall having been lost to the sea at some point following the dun's occupation, since there are visible facing stones on either side of the breach.

Trench A

Trench A (Fig. 9.13) aimed to investigate both whether the stones visible to the east of the supposed entrance did indeed represent the wall of a dun, and if so, how this wall was constructed. A trench measuring 4 m x 1 m, aligned NW–SE (Figs 9.13 and 9.14), was excavated, positioned with the intention of crossing the supposed line of the dun wall to the east of the probable entrance.

Wall [602] ran across the lowest, southern end of the trench and comprised large subangular stone blocks up to 0.7 m in diameter representing a wall remaining up to two courses (0.25 m) high. This was interpreted as the outer face of the outer dun wall. Immediately to the north of [602] was [603], a second alignment of subangular stones up to 0.7 m in diameter, surviving up to two courses in height and running east–west across the trench. This was interpreted as the inner wall face of the outer dun wall. [602] and [603] combined are interpreted as forming the outer wall of the dun, which measured around 1.0 m thick. On the shoulder of the slope, further subangular stone blocks up to 1.0 m in diameter [614] were interpreted as

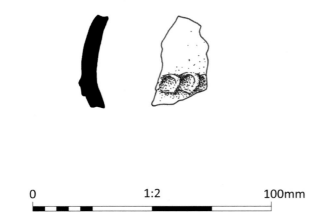

Figure 9.8 Pot sherd recovered from the trial trench on the Split Rock

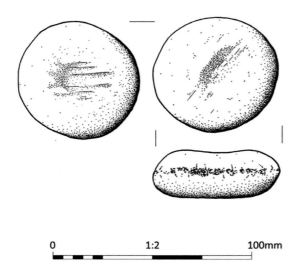

Figure 9.9 Strike-a-light recovered from the trial trench on the Split Rock

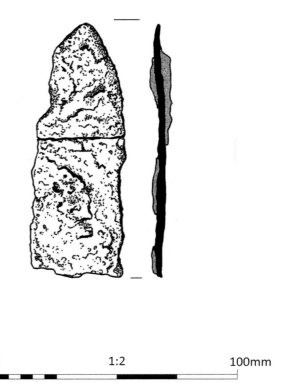

Figure 9.10 Iron sword tip, from the Split Rock

representing the back/inner wall face of the dun. A continuation of [614] was visible in an alignment of stones visible on the ground, running east immediately from the edge of the trench.

Between walls [604] and [614] was deposit (619), a dark orange-brown sandy silt with very few stone inclusions and some charcoal and orange areas suggestive of burning, and occasional heat-cracked stones. This was interpreted as the lower core of the wall of the dun. Both (619) and [614] lay directly on the bedrock, suggesting that the dun structure was built directly onto this surface, either following the removal of turf or because the bedrock was naturally exposed at the time of construction. Overlying (619) was a deposit of dark black-brown sandy silt with numerous inclusions of rounded beach pebbles and charcoal flecks, (618),

interpreted as the upper fill of the earthen core of the wall of the dun. The dun wall was therefore found to be approximately 2.5 m wide, with a thicker (1.0 m) outer wall and rather more slight, single-skinned inner wall. The space between the walls was around 0.6 m wide and was filled with soil with some stone inclusions. Rubble from the collapse of the dun wall was represented by subangular stones up to 0.4 m in diameter, [616], which were contained within a matrix of light brownish-yellow fine, friable sandy silt, (609).

The dun interior contained a handful of features which are interpreted as belonging to a later phase in the dun's usage, since they overlie material interpreted as rubble. They include the remains of a hearth or camp fire, probably of relatively recent date, and beneath the hearth feature was a platform or an area of rough paving. These features cannot be contemporary with the primary occupation of the dun since they overlay deposits associated with the collapse of the dun wall. Similarly, beneath both the hearth and putative platform features was a possible late occupation deposit. However, it was badly disturbed and voided by animal burrowing.

Trench B was placed to examine the probable entrance. Access to the site is gained via a steep scramble up a rocky, turfy slope. During survey of the site, it

Figure 9.11 Clashnessie and Loch na Claise, as depicted on Roy's military map (c. 1750) (Reproduced with kind permission of the Trustees of the National Library of Scotland)

was suggested that the bedrock may have been worked or enhanced to create steps leading up to the dun. A flat area creates a forecourt of sorts immediately to the south of the probable entrance itself, which was interpreted by the SRP survey as having been at the south-west point of the dun's circumference. A small trench, 2.0 m by 0.8 m, aligned NE–SW, was excavated over what was believed to be the southern side of the entrance into the site, encompassing visible stones taken as the edge of the entrance itself, to confirm whether the entrance was in fact located at this point.

Removal of the turf revealed degraded rubble tumble (701) interpreted as being related to the collapse of the entrance area of the dun wall. Beneath (701) were larger subangular stones [702], up to 0.5 m in diameter, spread particularly across the western side of Trench B. This material was interpreted as rubble from the collapse of the dun wall. Removal of the rubble revealed a drystone wallface [704] up to four courses high. The wall was formed of large angular stone blocks up to 0.7 m in diameter, mixed with smaller angular stones up to 0.2 m in diameter. At the southern end of the trench, small stone blocks had been used to even out the bedrock and create a flatter surface onto which the dun wall could be built.

Palaeoenvironmental assessment

The assemblage was limited to a small quantity of charcoal (3.8 g), derived from rubble collapse (617 Lower) and wall core (619). The species were hazel (67%), birch (27%) and oak (6%). These remains are from small roundwoods, and are likely to be redeposited fuel debris. A single cattle molar was recovered from context (617)

and burnt large mammal bone fragments from (617) and (619). Occasional fish vertebrae were also noted in the sample retents from (617).

Radiocarbon dating

Radiocarbon dating was undertaken on cereal caryopses (hulled barley) recovered from a sample of context (619), the lower wall core. The results returned a determination of 1987±30 year BP (SUERC-85842), calibrating in the range 45 BC to AD 117 at 2 sigma, and probably in the range 45 BC to AD 85.

Artefacts

Dawn McLaren

Three fragments of metal objects were recovered from topsoil under a single small finds number (SF 801). All three fragments are heavily corroded to the extent that their surfaces are heavily obscured by rust, making confident identification problematic. Two of the fragments derive from the same object; a hollow subrectangular box (remaining length 43 mm, width 26.6 mm, height 16 mm) composed of iron sheeting with a copper alloy coating, visible across only some of the exterior surface. One intact squared end survives with right angled corners; the opposite end has broken and been lost so the original form and dimensions of the object are unknown. Superimposed on top of the upper exterior surface of the box, parallel to its long edges, is a centrally positioned narrow plano-convex sectioned iron bar (remaining length 35.5 mm, width 13 mm, height 8 mm) which is also broken, just

Figure 9.12 View of Clashnessie Dun, from the south

forward of the break across the width of the hollow box. The method of attachment of the bar to the box is unknown. X-radiography reveals a more complex structure than is apparent from visual examination alone, suggesting layering of iron and copper alloy sheeting (ave. 2.5 mm). The presence of a very fine rivet hole (D 0.5 mm) adjacent to one of the broken edges is also revealed by the x-ray. The original function of this object is unclear and it is likely to be relatively modern in date.

The third fragment is that of a flattened iron ring or hoop; its form revealed through X-radiography. Less than half of the circumference survives but enough remains to suggest a minimum exterior diameter of 44 mm. The curving flattened bar used to produce this is 8.5 mm in width and 4.5 mm in height. Its function is unknown.

Clashnessie: discussion

The excavations at Clashnessie confirmed the presence of a substantial walled structure, with the entrance located at the south. The wall measured around 2.5 m in thickness and survived to a maximum of around four courses, or around 0.25 m. The outer face of the drystone wall was around 1 m thick and so more substantial than the inner face at only 0.7 m. Between the two was a soil core around 0.6 m thick, surviving to a depth of around 0.5 m. The dun wall was built of stones up to 0.7 m in diameter and was constructed directly onto bedrock, with small stones used as chocks to level out the ground surface. Harding's suggested classification (Harding 1984, 218–9) proposed that duns under 50 feet (15.24 m) in diameter are theoretically capable of supporting a roof, while those larger than that can be considered unroofed enclosures, a threshold which has been scrutinised by several later studies (most recently, Strachan 2013, 93–104), but which must be close to an accurate class division between buildings and small forts. The dun at Clashnessie, at around 13 m in diameter, might therefore fall in the a 'dun house' category, and could have been roofed, albeit that such a structure would have had to have been robustly constructed to remain anchored against westerly storms, being in such an exposed location.

The results from the exploratory trenches excavated here do not allow for a detailed assessment of the function of the site, or for any discussion of the economic basis of the occupants; such studies must await further work. However, the radiocarbon date obtained from deposits considered to be contemporary with the primary use – insofar as this can be established based on the limited

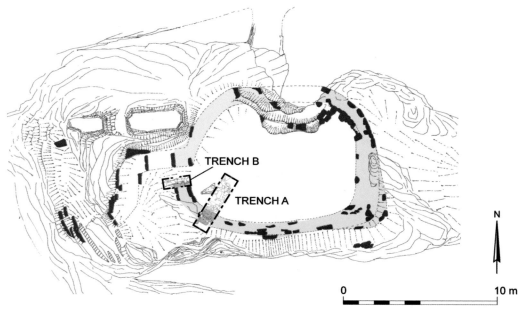

Figure 9.13 Survey of the Clashnessie dun by Gordon Sleight, showing the position of the trial trenches

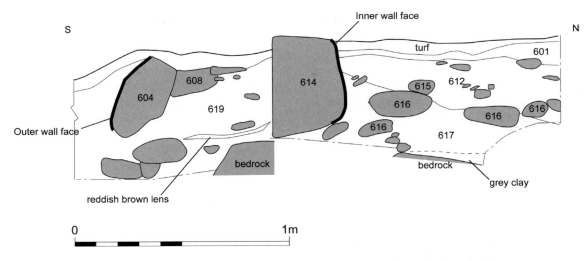

Figure 9.14 Section through deposits in the interior of the Clashnessie dun, Trench A, SE-facing section

excavations – suggest that the site was occupied in the late 1st century BC/early 1st century AD.

Summary: the Iron Age landscape of Stoer and Clachtoll

On the basis of surface survey, the sites targeted for trial excavation might not unreasonably have been expected to produce evidence of occupation from any century from the late Bronze Age (*e.g.*, Nesbitt *et al.* 2011) to the Early medieval period, based on the known chronology of coastal duns, promontory forts and crannogs. This makes the coincidence of the dates obtained from these limited trial excavations, which all calibrate around the turn of the first millennium, all the more remarkable. While isolated dates from trial trenches can only be indicative, on balance, it is likely that all four sites, including the Clachtoll broch, were in use in the final years of the 1st century BC.

This is valuable evidence in the assessment and reconstruction of the community within which the Clachtoll broch functioned. Reconstruction of the contemporary settled landscape has been a source of contention in Atlantic Iron Age studies in Scotland, since in areas such as the Western Isles, evidence for settlements in contemporary use with occupied brochs are very difficult to identify. Where non-broch Iron Age settlement is visible in the Hebrides, this tends to belong to the Middle Iron Age and later, in the form of wheelhouses and cellular settlements that develop as broch towers seem to decline (Armit 2003, 135–40; 2006, 251–3; Harding 2009a), almost certainly in response to a change of social structure and the reduced viability of the monumental tower as a symbol of community authority. From the Middle Iron Age, there is a noticeable increase in the heterogeneity of settlement forms in both the Western and Northern Atlantic sequences, which might indicate increasing stratification in society, contrasting with the relatively homogenous settlement record of the earlier Iron Age when broch towers appear to dominate. As acknowledged throughout, too little of these other sites has been investigated to allow confident interpretations of their function or status in relation to the broch, but the accumulated evidence suggests that they all formed parts of a contemporary settled landscape. Their respective social positions or functions within this system cannot be established at this stage, but on the basis of size alone it is likely that the broch was the major settlement. With the evidence for storage of grain surplus and cereal processing at the broch discussed in Chapter 5, it is perhaps not unreasonable to suggest that this was the administrative centre of the territory, with the outlying settlements functioning as dependant farms held by retainers of the Clachtoll occupants. Discussion of this hypothesis will be returned to in Chapter 10.

10

Interpretation, discussion and conclusion

Graeme Cavers and John Barber

Clachtoll in the traditional paradigm

The evidence from Clachtoll makes some significant contributions to the study and interpretation of brochs and more generally of Iron Age settlement in the north. This has been, and continues to be, a controversial field with conflicting and diverse schools of thought developing over history of Iron Age studies through the 20th and 21st centuries. The developmental trajectory of interpretive frameworks and the key points of dispute have been comprehensively covered in other publications, and we do not intend to rehearse them in full here (for a recent overview, see Dockrill *et al.* 2015, 5–9), and the following discussion involves some paraphrasing of complex arguments, but the crucial lines of enquiry along which the Clachtoll excavation provides some progress is set out before the significance of this evidence can be discussed. The historiography of broch studies is crucial to an understanding of published interpretations that have developed over more than a century, and to a critical assessment of how quite disparate interpretations have arisen in the literature, and this applies as much to our preconceptions of how brochs functioned as buildings as to their interpretation as symbols of their occupants (Baines 2002).

Early writing on the origins of the brochs was produced in the first half of the 20th century in the climate of diffusionist theory that typically opted to attribute innovation and change in the archaeological record to external influence, with the role of independent and spontaneous development treated as the exception rather than the rule (discussed by Harding 2000, 2; Dockrill, Outram and Batt 2006, 5–9). This paradigm culminated in a personally definitive statement on the specific cultural origins of broch culture by Euan MacKie (1965b),

which linked the introduction of monumental tower construction in the north and west of Scotland to the influx of communities from the south-east of England. MacKie's thesis was a development of the earlier 20th-century diffusionist paradigm and based on underlying assumptions about the nature of innovation in pre-Romanised societies that in retrospect look simplistic and ethnocentric. The putative correlation between the displacement of Belgic tribes in southern England as reported by Caesar in the 1st century BC and the appearance of brochs in the north now seems entirely arbitrary. The thesis was based on superficial similarities in certain artefact types (*e.g.*, MacKie 1971, 58), despite the contraindication that Wessex was an unlikely source of broch innovation, not least because stone domestic architecture is alien to the Iron Age settlement record of that area (Harding 2000, 3; 2005). In fact, MacKie himself was later to acknowledge – most explicitly in two review papers of the late 2000s – that the weight of evidence was now in favour of a much earlier origin for complex, broch-type architecture (MacKie 2008, 270–4), undermining the possibility of a 1st-century introduction from the south. Nonetheless, dispute over the correct date for the appearance and rapid spread of brochs has not entirely left the southern migrant paradigm. Parker Pearson and Sharples rejected the requirement for a southern stimulus (Parker Pearson and Sharples 1999) and they retained the conviction that the last two centuries BC is the correct horizon for broch origins, a position recently restated by Sharples in relation to the most sophisticated towers (Sharples 2020, 289). The evidence provided by Bradford University's work at Scatness, however, comprehensively disassociates the origin of broch construction from any late 1st millennium BC stimulus, demonstrating that fully fledged, complex-walled broch towers were being built, in Shetland, within the period 390–200 BC (Dockrill, outram and Batt 2006, 104; Dockrill *et al.* 2015, 474).

The nuances of the ebb and flow of this debate are not usefully repeated here, but it is important to acknowledge the influence of this interpretative trajectory because it will directly affect how the Clachtoll dating evidence, and therefore the evidence in sum, is received by students of Atlantic Iron Age archaeology. Careful scrutiny of the dating evidence is fundamental to our discussion here, partly because of the inherent importance of chronology to the debate (see Dockrill *et al.* 2015, 5–12), but also because it directly influences the interpretation of the status, function and relationship of the site's several forms to with their contemporaneous landscapes.

By definition, the traditional, paradigmatic interpretation of brochs as representative of an implanted elite implies occupants positioned at the pinnacle of a hierarchical society, a status that should be identifiable through material and economic evidence. As such, the interpretive framework through which we assess the significance of this evidence should also be defined and examined. As has most recently been explored in a series of papers specifically considering Iron Age societies (Curras and Sastre 2020), there are alternative interpretations of pre-industrial societies that place less emphasis on wealth and status in the formats familiar to modern, western mindsets, and where the evidence does not fit our preconceptions, we must be prepared to consider alternative explanations.

Through the 1990s and 2000s, some progress was made in the development of an interpretative framework that was more sensitive to the complexities of broch archaeology than the simple equation of 'broch' with 'elite castle'. In the first instance this focussed on reassessment of the definitive architectural features of a 'broch'. Armit's seminal reworking of the classification of brochs and related domestic structures of the Atlantic regions is sometimes misunderstood or misused, but the intention behind his deconstruction of the 'broch' label was to demonstrate that the drystone roundhouses of the north and west encompassed a wide range of variants, of which, the broch towers were only one (Armit 1990a; 1992). By including architecturally related structures within his taxon of 'Atlantic roundhouses', Armit argued that the currency of the dry stone built roundhouse class extended back into the earlier Iron Age, encompassing substantial roundhouses such as Bu (Hedges 1987), Crosskirk (Fairhurst 1984), Calf of Eday (Calder 1939), the early phase of the Howe (Ballin Smith 1994) and more recently investigated sites such as Tofts Ness (Dockrill 2007), allowing a much longer chronology for the monumental roundhouse phenomenon (Armit 2003, 44–50). Armit's new scheme facilitated the incorporation of the related structures that were excluded unnecessarily

by the rigid definition of a 'broch', a concern that had been raised repeatedly since the earliest study of the variability their architecture (*e.g.*, Scott 1947).[1] While not all brochs are equal in scale or complexity (see discussion by Geddes 2006, 3.3.3; Romankiewicz 2009, 381), it is clear that to exclude some on the presence or absence of certain specific architectural features is to beg the question of their original form and function in the first place. However, pointing to the singularity of broch engineering, which required the solution of several complex engineering challenges which are essential to tower building but irrelevant to smaller structures, recognises a canonicity amongst brochs that has been masked by secondary rebuilds, alterations and overbuilding. Broch towers did not evolve from smaller structures in a misapplication of Darwinian stepwise evolution, but were, perhaps exceptionally, the creation of a specific set of cultural circumstances at a specific point in time, around four centuries before Christ.

It is now clear that Atlantic roundhouses account for the majority of the settlement record of the later 1st millennium BC in much of Atlantic Scotland (Fig. 10.1; though *cf.* Cowley 2005, and discussion below), and an interpretative framework is required that accommodates this. Recognition that the Atlantic roundhouse class had much earlier origins than the late 1st millennium BC allowed a new approach to their interpretation and, most importantly, the flexibility to allow brochs and related structures to have functioned very differently at different stages within the societies that built them and, in some instances, reused them, the latter over the greater part of a millennium.

A related consequence of the dismantling of the broch stereotype of the traditional paradigm was the recognition that the role of these monumental buildings may have been more sophisticated than the militaristic, defensive castles of a paranoid and insecure elite, ruling over and controlling a subservient client group. Indeed, this image of brochs and their functions has not really exceeded the scope of Childe's 'Castle Complex' (Childe 1935), a loose categorisation of defensive monuments whose only common trait was their curvilinear stone built enclosing element.

As Armit and others have observed, the geography of broch settlements in areas like Barra, North Uist, Shetland, Orkney and Caithness, where they are present in large numbers and probably associated with relatively restricted tracts of land, does not support their interpretation as the residences of regional kings, however, the title 'king' may be envisaged (Armit 2003, 84; Fojut 2005b). Instead, emphasis has come to be placed on the interpretation of brochs, like other forms of 'monumental roundhouse', as symbols of local autonomy and authority (Hingley 1992, 24; Armit 2005) and latterly as elements in

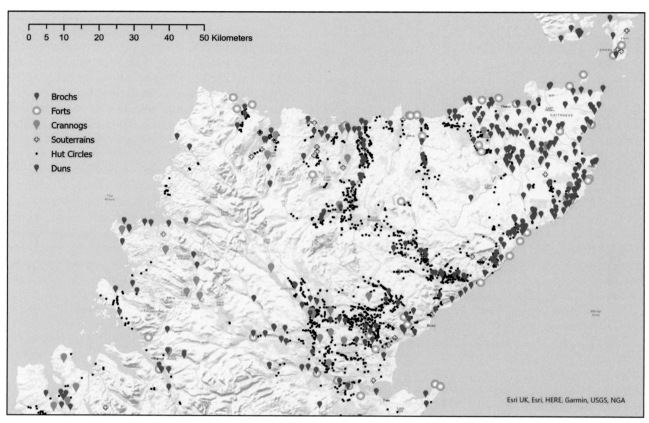

Figure 10.1 Distribution of brochs and other Iron Age settlements in northern Scotland

a House Society (*sensu* Levi-Strauss 1982) as developed by Sharples (2020).

In other areas of Scotland, forts, duns and crannogs may have functioned in similar ways, so that it seems beyond coincidence that excavated evidence increasingly points to the same Early Iron Age origin for a major phase of construction of each of these site types (see for example, Cavers 2006; Crone 2012; Armit and Mackenzie 2013). In Hingley's view, monumental roundhouses of the earlier Iron Age signified the homesteads of productive landowning families, controlling local territories that supported livestock and arable agriculture, an interpretation that aligns more comfortably with the tendency for excavations of Iron Age roundhouses to produce prosaic and mundane material assemblages, common to all contemporary settlements and mostly related to agricultural or domestic-level crafts, regardless of stature or size of the building itself.

In the past two decades broch excavations have been more limited in number than in the 1980s and 1990s, but important results have been published from the long-running excavations at Scatness, where the construction of the broch settlement has been securely dated to between the late 4th and early 3rd centuries BC (Dockrill *et al.*

2015, 458), while similarly early dates have been obtained from construction horizons at Thrumster broch in Caithness (Barber *et al.* in prep). This confirmation of the earlier Iron Age construction date for 'true' brochs has provided a chronological anchor point for the proposal, put forward by the present authors (Barber *et al.* 2021; Cavers, Heald and Barber 2021) and developed most fully by Barber (2017), that the original generation of brochs may have been very short-lived, with the vast majority of true broch towers, featuring all of the architectural and engineering specifications required to attain their height, constructed within a relatively brief horizon which was most likely in the 4th or 3rd century BC (*cf.* MacKie 2010, 92). In this scheme, the stimulus for broch construction may have originated in a highly competitive but highly fragmented social and political climate, where occupant groups sought to legitimise their claims to agricultural territory through displays of architectural prowess and the superficial appearance of defensive power. The source labour for such efforts seems likely to have come from kinship ties and obligations between neighbouring groups, a mechanism that might account for structural similarities observable within broch groups within sub-regions of Atlantic Scotland. As

Figure 10.2 Alan Braby's reconstruction of Carloway (reproduced with kind permission)

cognisance of the debris that choked many brochs or that many others were either built over (*e.g.*, Gurness (Richardson 1948, Hedges 1987), Scatness (Dockrill *et al.* 2015), or The Cairns (pers. comm. Martin Carruthers)) or was simply consolidated at intervals, with the garth floor level migrating up the broch wall, as exemplified at Midhowe (Barber 2017, 203), and the initiation of access stairs at varying levels at Gurness (*ibid.*, 236), and possibly other brochs with apparent mid-level scarcements and other non-canonical features.

These features point to the potential for short term diachrony[2] of settlement within or between structural phases in brochs (Barber 2017, 192–222). The medium-term synchrony of structures was disturbed by collapse or alteration, and restored, or recaptured by consolidation and repair. The meanings of diachrony and synchrony, as used in archaeology, are broadly cognate with their linguistic use (see footnote 2), and in this report the terms are used to distinguish between the statics and dynamics of construction on the one hand, and the not necessarily synchronous sequences of resettlement or other use, on the other. The concept is not as simple or transparent as it may first appear because each construction phase or, for that matter, each demolition phase, results in a static structure but sequential constructions, demolition and rebuilt phases constitute a diachronic construction history. Conversely, the function and use of the structure may have been diachronic even within a single synchronous construction phase, or, as in the case of the final occupation at Clachtoll, in or after a decomposition phase. This was observed by Harding for whom the situation

> invariably has resulted in a long succession of occupational phases and innumerable opportunities for structural alterations (Harding 2009b, 115).

The term 'tectonics' is used in this discussion to try to capture some sense of the social ownership of the variations of occupation and monument, over time, by linking the functional and metaphysical relationships between the structure and its human occupants (see below).

For example, and in the context of Clachtoll, it is not clear how the congestion of the ash-encumbered ground floor at Clachtoll would have facilitated the sort of seating and circulation reflective of the paradigmatic upper-class family seated around their home fires. The putative elite group living in the terminal expression of the Clachtoll monument was certainly not the group who had built or commissioned the primary broch or its Stage 1 succession of constructions; they did not live in a primary nor in a rebuilt, Stage 1, broch tower. Rather, these terminal settlers lived in a wooden structure within the ruined shell of a broch tower some one and a half storeys high, and,

Cavers, Heald and Barber (2021) and Barber *et al.* (2021) suggested, this obsession with ostentatious displays of monumentality may even have subsequently acquired a cult-like status, analogous to the apparent veneration of Nuraghic towers in later Bronze Age Sardinia. In any case, the legitimisation of the occupant group afforded by the presence of a monumental broch tower seems to have allowed land-holding arrangements to remain remarkably stable over many centuries, perhaps ending only in the major reconfigurations of the settlement landscape detectable at the end of the 1st millennium BC and into the following centuries (Armit 2005, 140).

Perhaps the most significant move forward in recent decades, however, has been the recognition that brochs have long and complex histories, often involving wholesale changes in character that could include major changes in form, function, and social status. This recognition is fundamental to the interpretation of the history of the Clachtoll broch.

Synchrony, diachrony and tectonics

The traditional interpretive paradigm envisages a coherent single use for the broch and its interior. It takes no

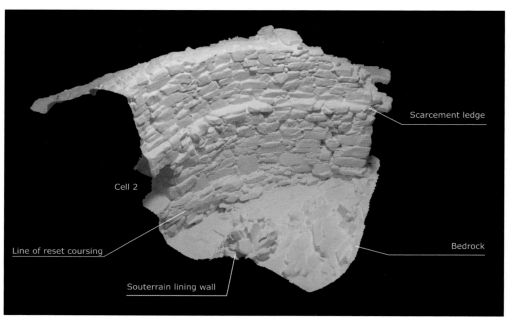

Figure 10.3 SE quadrant of the broch interior, showing the line of reset coursing at the level of the Cell 2 entrance

whilst articulating with its gross, if residual, form they did not experience its primary tectonics.

Chronology of the structure: rebuilding and tectonics

Our good-faith attempt to model the Clachtoll dates suggests that the soft sediments within the garth (the inner void of the broch, contained by the inner wall) were all laid down within the 50-year interval between 50 BC and AD 1 (see Chapter 3). The 'A' value (indicative of the goodness of fit of the model to the data) for this Bayesian analysis is poor but consideration of the fragility of the peat ash deposits and a more general sense arising from the relatively limited artefact assemblage support the idea that this settlement possibly took place within a very short period in that interval and this is how we interpret it.

Two significantly earlier dates are interpreted as residual material from activity on the broch crag in the 4th century BC and, given the abundant evidence for episodic collapse episodes in the fabric of the broch and the presence of the greatly distorted wall foot under and predating the standing inner wall of the surviving ruin, it has been tentatively concluded that the residual material relates to the primary use of the locus. Since the distorted early wall foot curves on the same radius as that of the upstanding broch wall, allowing for its ragged wall-face and is integrated with the primary gallery and, thereby, the outer wall, it is also tentatively concluded that this primary structure has been a broch. Thus, it is argued that the residual wall foot was the primary wall foot of

the very first broch built on this crag. Whilst the standing walls revealed in excavation are parts of a near canonical broch, they are obviously secondary to the fallen, primary broch. To avoid confusion of these wall remnants and walls with the clearly later rebuild, these walls are named as Stage 1 broch remains. Stage 1 comprises the fallen broch, evidenced by the residual wall on the east side of the monument, and the surviving walls built over it.

The secondary Stage 1 wall possesses features essential to the construction of a tower but without functional roles in lesser structures. These include:

i)   Graduated lintels in the entrance passage.
ii) Stacked voids above the entrance, Cell 2, the Stairway Cell, and the very residual indications of a stacked void above the garth entrance to Cell 4 (RHS Guard Cell).
iii) The structural system of the massive walls.
iv) The intramural stairway.

Therefore, it is concluded that the Stage 1 rebuilt broch at Clachtoll was in fact a canonical broch tower exhibiting the tectonics of the 'true' broch tower, in line with the revised standard model (RSM) described by Barber (2017).

The paradigmatic broch tower structure

As we shall shortly discuss, the Alan Braby illustration of an occupied broch, which has become the paradigmatic image for broch towers, illustrates Dun Carloway but is based in some significant part on the broch tower at Mousa, Shetland (Fig. 10.2). It is therefore important to

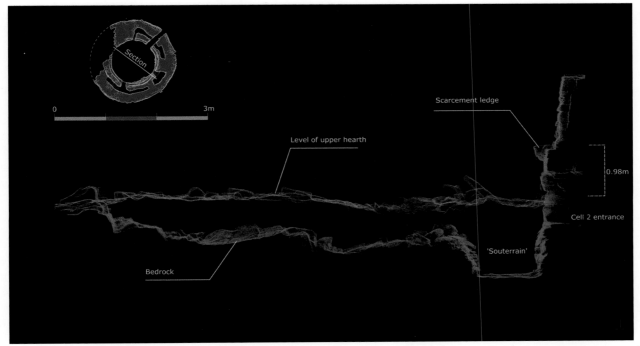

Figure 10.4 East-West section through laser scans of the broch at the level of the uppermost hearth and occupation deposits (orange) and the bedrock following full excavation of the soft deposits (blue). The scarcement ledge is located 0.98 m above the upper occupation surface

note that, uniquely amongst the brochs, Mousa has a helical stairway reaching from just above ground floor level to the wall-head, truncating every gallery floor in its ascent; no other broch tower displays this characteristic. Mousa's external profile is sinuous and the tower is normally represented as a rotationally symmetrical sinuous shape. However, its actual profile changes rather dramatically around the circuit of the monument. This configuration results from masonry creep in the outer wall.[3]

Mousa's helical stairway is truly unique, but the distorted external wall-face has some comparanda, for example at Dun Carloway whose external profile, like Mousa's but to a lesser degree, varies around its perimeter. Midhowe's external profile also shows evidence of slumping, but in this case by the bulging outwards of the outer wall on the east side and the corresponding bulging inwards of the same wall into the ground gallery (Barber 2017, 208–9, figs 87, 95 and 106).

The final forms of Mousa and Midhowe have resulted from large scale deformations of the broch walls, and neither is indicative of its original form. Nonetheless, the form and configuration of the broch at Mousa has come to be considered the norm. Dun Troddan was known to have been complete to wall-head until about 1720 and retains linear outer wall-faces. It does not have a helical stairway (MacKie 2007b, 858–9). Dun Telve, similarly, does not have a helical stairway and, if we exclude the bulge left by the 'conservation' of the secondary door opened above the original entrance, it also has a smooth

linear outer wall-face. Mousa, so frequently cited as the monument-type exemplar, has become the broch form that most people have in mind. Its acceptance as the norm has resulted in the unconscious and unwarranted belief that all brochs were built to its distorted and grossly exaggerated form. Perversely, the acceptance of its form as somehow normal, has made it the paradigm for broch form.

Barber has challenged the Braby paradigm and proposed an alternative broch form, the Revised Standard Model (or RSM) which is illustrated here in Figure 1.11 (after Barber 2017, 106 *et seq.*) and which is compared with the Braby model, and the paradigm it represents, in the following discussion.

Some primary, structural and architectural features of the RSM

In this section we consider just four elements of the RSM for their evidentiary value in interpreting Clachtoll broch; the presence or absence of ground floor hearths, the roofing issue, the related lighting issue and the use and frequency of scarcements.

Ground floor central hearth site

The Braby model does not place the main hearth of the building in the centre of the ground floor, but instead locates it centrally, on the second floor, atop a clay pad. It seems surrounded by radially segmented cells, perhaps

Figure 10.5 Evidence for the rebuilding of the outer wall-face over the collapse of debris of the upper tower. The outer wall-face of the broch on the eastern (landward) side is visible on the left of the image, retaining the loose rubble of the collapsed upper wall to the right. The rubble visible to the right is overlying the capping lintels of the ground floor gallery, close to first-floor level

Casteil Grugaig. Clearly not all were selected to provide a smooth and partitionable floor surface. Thus, if the use of internal spaces for the comfort and convenience of an elite residential group were a desideratum at all, it was certainly not a universal one, and was not one at Clachtoll.

The RSM does not assume a central ground floor hearth, largely because the evidence from excavated sites does not always include one. MacKie has long asserted that a central ground level hearth was a diagnostic of broch towers and in his proposed construction sequence shows a hearth position at ground level (MacKie 2002, 6) but see also Fojut's rejection of the universality of ground floor hearths in broch towers (Fojut 2005a, 192–3). Midhowe, for example, retained some in situ sediments to support secondary structural elements, while Old Scatness was covered by a secondary structure that was not excavated and removed. No example of a wooden structure inside a broch has survived and thus the first-floor hearth site remains an artist's impression, not a piece of archaeological evidence.

The accommodation of the craggy bedrock knoll was an essential constraint on the layout of the building and dictated the layout of the internal space. As discussed above, the 'souterrain' was formed by the sharply quarried bedrock forming a lower 'chamber' within the garth. This structure seems very likely to have been floored over, probably with wicker or lightweight timbers, at the uppermost level of the lining wall, as this would have provided access to Cell 2 at through the elevated entrance. The sub-floor 'souterrain' space would have been rather constricted, perhaps lending weight to the interpretation of subterranean spaces within broch interiors as having significance beyond practical issues of storage. Such below-ground spaces are common in the Caithness and Orkney brochs, where they are often misleadingly referred to as wells, but which seem not to have a practical purpose. It is possible that they functioned as private shrines or had a similar votive function. This is not to suggest that the Clachtoll 'souterrain' was not used simply for storage or another functional purpose – the raised floors of the Phase 6, post-broch aisled roundhouses at Scatness seem to have been designed to separate byre and storage space from living quarters (Dockrill et al. 2015, 153–6). However, to the modern rationale, it would seem there are other, rather easier ways to create storage space within such a large building as Clachtoll, that did not involve the inconvenience of the undulating, craggy bedrock floor.

Souterrains or passages and chambers that performed a very similar function seem to be a recurring feature of the Middle Iron Age use of brochs, often involving the use of original broch wall galleries in ways that were not part of the original broch tower design. This certainly seems to have been the case at Midhowe and probably at Gurness in

Murray's *imdae*, or their equivalent personal spaces (Murray 1979). At Clachtoll, the earliest central hearth was close to the geometric centre of the garth but the mound of ash that buried it accumulated over time and became markedly eccentric, mainly biased westward, and in places discontinuous. As noted above, the spread of the ash mound rather militates against the idea of a cleared annular space suitable for seating and access in an elite residence. The excavators interpret the clay floor around the knocking stone as indicative of a room or compartment, and this, together with the 'souterrain' on the east side, compromise the simple annular arrangement of the paradigmatic model. That said, even if the traditional paradigm were generally applied, the residents would necessarily have made some adjustments to the 'real-world' impediments within individual sites. Several monuments enclose bedrock outcrops, including Dun Carloway and Dun Beag, as well as Clachtoll and, at least putatively,

Orkney, where the secondary 'cellular' buildings, mostly built at first floor level (presumably following the infilling of the garth ground floor with collapse rubble or occupation debris) and featuring orthostatic slab walling overlain by horizontal coursing make use of the intramural galleries as curving subterranean passages. Similar arrangements relating to secondary use have been observed at sites with a similar architectural style such as Dun Mhairtein (Canmore ID: 6840), whereas the Cairns in Orkney is one of several excavated broch settlements where a souterrain was constructed as part of the later Iron Age use of the site (Carruthers 2014). The relevance to Clachtoll is that the use of sub-floor spaces seems to be hallmark of Middle–later Iron Age arrangements, and apparently not a feature of primary broch design. It is even possible that the entrance to the original building was moved from the eastern quadrant, where Cell 2 is now located, to reconfigure the internal space and create the sub-floor space required by Middle Iron Age preferences. In any case, the Clachtoll 'souterrain' made use of an apparently earlier stub of walling, presumably the remnants of an earlier iteration of the structure, to provide the supporting shelf for a timber covering; the walling above this level was reset to respect the curvature of the reconstructed broch and, most likely, the floor level capping the souterrain (See Fig. 10.3).

Roofing issues

As noted above, the question of if, and how broch towers were roofed has been the subject of lengthy and rancorous debate (see Fojut 2005a for good discussion of timber supply). Tanja Romankiewicz acknowledges that:

> The evidence for roof and upper floor constructions of cARs (Complex Atlantic Roundhouses, which includes broch towers) is very sparse and to develop such reconstructions the present work has to rely on the Scottish vernacular record for analogies (Romankiewicz 2011, vol. 1, 151).

Romankiewicz goes on to 'reconstruct on paper' (ROP) broch towers with conical roofs that surmount the stone structures and, in most cases, overhang them and creel roofs that sit inside the towers or inside their upper edges, at wall-head height. Other variants may be discovered elsewhere in her discourse. She seems to eschew the approach of John Hope, who promotes a setting of the roof eaves within the gallery void so that the outer wall-head helpfully acts as a buttress to the roof rafters, albeit at the price of delivering rain water into the outer wall, mainly, but with inevitable water penetration into the inner wall and the garth as well.

In essence, cultural significance can be equated with the information content of the monument (the place)

and in the current context, the creation of an ROP that is not based on evidence from the monument in question simply cannot be relied upon. Given the persistent influence of the Braby model on the current paradigm (below), widespread acceptance of the proposed roofing schemes, derived from single-storied vernacular houses, creates a new set of 'factoids' within the broch mythology. Romankiewicz has very fairly described the sparsity of the evidence, a view which we share, but we question the wisdom of relying on vernacular exemplars to bridge the knowledge gap on the roofing (even if only on paper) of large complex structures. Clachtoll produced no evidence for its roofing, in its broch tower incarnation. Accepting that there is no evidence from other broch remains for the roofing of broch towers we do not propose a roofing structure formulated on evidence from any other monument type.

However, brochs are diachronic monuments and the remains of a burnt wooden structure of MIA date have been recovered at Clachtoll. As noted, the primary broch tower was probably built, and thereafter rebuilt, at Clachtoll in the 4th/3rd centuries BC and while there is no evidence for its roofing some evidence has been preserved for a very different type of roof over the MIA resettlement area within the ruinous broch. Micromorphological analyses at Clachtoll indicate that the interior was extensively roofed, taking the ash and charcoal from the scarcement ledge as evidence for the use of wattle screens, or hurdles, in the formation of a roof. In addition, soil fauna indicative of exposure to open air appears only in the uppermost layers of the internal deposits, presumably colonised very soon after final human abandonment (Roy, see Chapter 6). However, the excavated evidence shows that a major fall of masonry encapsulated the MIA settlement deposits and must have done so during or soon after the fire because the ash and charcoal fragments on the scarcement ledge would have been lost on exposure to even a single shower of rain or a strong gust of wind. It is possible that oxygenation of the upper layers came, tenuously, through this primary, vacuous rubble infill but was later sealed off by at least two further substantial masonry falls.

The ash heap on the garth floor would, similarly, have been washed away in a season's rainfall. The soil micromorphological analyses show that the heap was reworked, through raking out and resurfacing. In consequence there is poor correspondence between the radiocarbon dates and the sedimentary sequence (see Chapter 3) albeit that all the dates from the ash mound, with the exception of the 4th/3rd century BC dates could not be resolved from each other by the radiocarbon method and were, arguably, deposited in a very short interval. During that interval, therefore, it is inevitable that the deposits had been roofed over in some way and thus protected from the weather. This is rare and perhaps the only direct evidence we have for roofing in and of brochs, or broch ruins.

All proposed versions of the roofing of brochs rely on especially large and heavy timbers presumably surmounted with purlins or scarting-board equivalents and finally by heather thatch, possibly over turves. In the absence of any evidence for any of these elements at Clachtoll, it is possible to hypothesise that a substantial roof existed, either at wall-head height (per Romankiewicz 2011 or Fojut 2005a, 792) or at some intermediate level within the broch. For Clachtoll, if such timbers were used, we would have to envisage, however improbably, that all the heavy roof timbers either burned and were reduced to ash or that they all subsequently decomposed without trace following partial burning and collapse, but this would be very special pleading indeed.

Artefacts and structure

Some evidence exists that suggests artefacts and ecofacts were held at a level above the floor. As discussed in Chapter 4, the patterns of recovery indicate that the iron tools fell from a position where they were stored together, for example, while the concentration of objects in the southeast quadrant suggests that these fell here as a higher-level structure collapsed.

As will be discussed further below, the burnt material from the final conflagration event comprises mainly charcoal from small roundwood, such as is used in the manufacture of wattle screens, with a very small proportion of larger carbonised masses, derived from larger and thicker timbers. The significance of this evidence for the interpretation of internal fixings will also be considered further below.

Lighting issues

The use of a full roof, per Romankiewicz's models, or the use of full floors, per the Braby model, would have created difficulties in the provision of light within a broch tower. A full roof covering mezzanine structures could have been a little less problematic. Lighting would have been a constraining factor, even with open mezzanine galleries that allowed the glow from the hearth to be cast into the compartments. A low peat fire, even if augmented with small roundwood cannot have provided much light. Even if we were to allow that all of the stone 'lamps' were used for lighting (which seems unlikely, see Chapter 4) and factor in the use of organic 'butter lamps' and tapers which do not survive, the majority of the internal space must have been very dimly lit, and possibly very smoky. It is perhaps for this reason that the bone weaving combs were recovered

from floor levels, rather than contexts likely to belong to upper floors, suggesting that looms were located close to the hearth, the main source of light.

However, it is possible to provide one element of a solution to the issue by a structural accommodation, viz, the construction of some form of clerestory either at wall-head or in a lower construction and the latter is discussed further below.

Scarcements: roofs and floors

A broch scarcement is a step-like feature created by the use of projecting stones in a level strip around the wall-face or by reduction of the wall thickness at a given horizontal level. They are typically about 35 cm in width. In the traditional paradigm it is assumed that scarcements provided the housing for beam ends of floor or roof structures. The Braby model's apparently completed masonry wall comprises ground level plus two superimposed galleries and there is no observable structural evidence for this configuration in any known broch. The wall-head height of Braby's broch, scaled from the human figures and not from our own preconceived, paradigmatic view, could hardly amount to more than 6 m. Its three galleries are significantly fewer than the seven gallery floors in Mousa (see surveys by Dryden 1890 and Paterson 1922, or Barber 2017, 174), or the five at Dun Telve, or the more than six at Dun Carloway, and so on. In other words, the broch illustrated by Braby has no extant exemplar, not even Mousa, and for structural reasons irrelevant here, probably can never have existed. Despite this, it remains the ideation of our current paradigmatic broch.

Barber argues for a structurally simpler model, omitting all internal wooden fittings, his Revised Standard Model or RSM as illustrated below. This eliminates most of the more egregious structural problems contained in the Braby Model and is consistent with the observable evidence (Barber 2017). The comments offered here on the Braby model are not a reflection on the work of the illustrator who was, in the writers' opinion, completely successful in capturing the then traditional paradigmatic views of the broch model and, to a large extent, these still are the paradigmatic views. That the paradigmatic model was even then incomplete and has subsequently been further superseded, does not reflect poorly on the illustrator.

The scarcement ledge at Clachtoll is positioned at 2.62 m above the internal wall foot within the souterrain, at the lowest point within the garth, and at 1.58 m above the wall foot elsewhere in the broch. The average height of broch scarcements in general seems close to 1.8 m but note that many have been in whole or part, slapped out, built over, or migrated upwards to mid-broch height, as the garth floor level became congested with detritus, masonry collapse and remains of sequential house structures built within them. Clachtoll's uppermost ground-floor deposits and the third and final Clachtoll hearth were encountered 0.98 m below the level of the scarcement (Fig. 10.4).

Armit suggests that the presence of a mid-level scarcement at Mousa is evidence of the presence there of a second floor, which he suggests must have been a mezzanine because of the limited (1.7 m) clearance between the two scarcement levels. However, Mousa, like Midhowe and Dun Telve, has evidence for the slapping through of a secondary entrance above the original primary broch entrance (Barber 2017, 171, 192, 266 resp.) probably because the original entrance passage and the interior had become choked up with settlement debris and masonry collapse. The mid-level scarcement at Midhowe is demonstrably secondary because its masonry context extends across, and blocks a primary stacked void (Barber 2017, 205). The stumps of Midhowe's original entrance passage lintels can be seen at the inner end of the passage, visible as tusking on the right and fractured stumps in their sockets on the left, looking inwards in both cases. Mousa's reconfiguration has traditionally been attributed to 'eloping' Viking visitors (Pálsson and Edwards 1978) and its current form owes relatively little to its original, RSM broch form (Barber 2017, 171–83). Where new entrance passages were forced through brochs, the relocation of the scarcement upwards by about one floor level seems intended to facilitate the continuation of the original tectonic relationship between people and place.

There is no evidence for a mid-level or higher scarcement in the surviving *c.* 7 m height of the remains at Clachtoll (measured between the bottom of the souterrain and the highest point on the wallhead). Indeed, there is no evidence for multiple, contemporaneous scarcements in broch towers in general and reliance on their putative existence to support arguments in favour of multi-storey internal wooden structures in all brochs is vitiated by the observable evidence that these scarcements are all secondary constructions. In addition, the survival at Clachtoll of the intact footings and lowest 60 cm of the stacked void above the entrance passage rules out the possibility that a secondary entrance had been slapped through above the passage lintels. The current lintels, although conserved in 2012 and at an earlier date, are the original lintels, save for two lintels which have been lost.

Thus, there are no grounds for assuming that the scarcement has 'migrated' up the wall to avoid a choked-up ground floor and to form a new level at the lintel height of a new entrance passage. Reuse of Clachtoll broch raised by one floor level in its later tectonics is also ruled out by the presence of carbonised wattles on the scarcement and the continuity of the charcoal deposits of the final conflagration over the whole of the floor both at the same radiocarbon ages. The absence of artefactual materials from within the collapse rubble also militates against the idea of settlement within the garth secondary to the conflagration.

The proximity of the final hearth to the level of a continuous or full floor renders it improbable that the Clachtoll scarcement supported a continuous wooden floor at the time of the final occupation, if it ever did, because, apart from the obvious fire risk to the floor above, the working hearth and the use of its furnishings, like firedogs, pot-stances or spits would have been impractical, so close to the underside of the first floor. Armit hypothesised that at Casteil Grugaig, Lochalsh, the scarcement which in places is only 0.7 m above the current internal ground level (the solum) probably supported a hung, or suspended floor (Armit 2003, 66). Suspended floors are ground-level floors set above the solum over a crawl-way or cellar and their use at Casteil Grugaig would seem appropriate. However, exploration of the gallery anti-clockwise of the entrance of Casteil Grugaig indicates that it continues at its base level (roughly level with the entrance passage's inner end) under the foot of the high surviving wall fragment. Therefore, the supposed high ground level abutting the back wall (roughly 10 to 3 o'clock span) may well be rubble infill, and not, as supposed, a ridge of bedrock. It is possible, or perhaps probable, that the broch at Casteil Grugaig is a canonical broch and that special arrangements for its ground floor were not required.

The ground floor at Clachtoll, in contrast, is a terraced bedrock spur, dropping by about 3 m from west to east, in a series of uneven steps. The exposed bedrock abutting the western internal wall-face has been quarried down by some 40 cm in places. On the east side, the bedrock steps down into a feature that is perhaps inappropriately here termed a 'souterrain' in the context of the EIA Stage 1 primary and Stage 1 secondary brochs, but which may well have served as a souterrain in the functioning of the MIA settlement in the broch for whose occupants it may have had cultural relevance.

It has also been hypothesised that internal floors may have sprung from levels above the scarcement (Armit 2003, 66–7). However, given that we now know the inner floor level was migrated upwards and a new entrance formed above the primary entrance, it is more likely that the mid-level scarcements at Mousa relate to such reorganisations of the monument fabric. Harding argues that a scaffold-like arrangement in wood formed accommodation levels within brochs (Harding 2009, 100–2), but we have no structural or other observable evidence for such an arrangement. Harding (*ibid.*) dismissed Hamilton's lean-to arrangement (Hamilton 1956) because

Not only was this inadequate provision wholly dispropor-tionate to the monumental scale of the stone shell but in practical terms it would have created cramped and drafty living quarters

and Sharples, having postulated that an elite family resided in the broch, further insists that

[While the] precise nature of the timber structures is open to debate, ... it would have required the best quality timber available (Sharples 2020, 299).

The requirement for elaborate structures made from the best timbers available is, arguably, predicated upon the assumption that the broch was a high-status home and could only be furnished in a style that befits a modern conception of high living. The scarcement ledge has the capacity to support a full floor, but at Clachtoll its height relationship with the burgeoning hearth beneath it is contraindicative for the presence of a full floor at this, the ground/first storey, level, in the latest stages of the monument's use. This may the first tangible, if admittedly indirect, support for the presence of a mezzanine floor or, more correctly, for the absence of a full floor in the final occupation configuration of a broch.

Given only an observable ground-floor scarcement, speculation on the existence of extensive and complex carpentry works higher up the tower remains just that, a matter of speculation. The diameter of the garth is a con-stant with height and the challenge of flooring it over at the scarcement level would persist at any higher level. This in turn indicates the need for vertical supports by posts, pillars or, as in the wheelhouses, by masonry pilasters, engaged or otherwise, to support all the upper floors. In the general absence from broch structures of stone-built supports we need to infer that the vertical supports were wooden posts. Above the scarcement level, floor supports carrying the strain of the first floor needed to be suffi-ciently strong to also bear the strain of all higher floor levels, ultimately transmitting the load into the ground. For a broch in the theoretically buildable range of 12 to 20 m height the timber demand would have been high, but of course the posts need not have been continuous from floor to wall-head height, shorter pieces could be superimposed upon each other.

Devices to spread the load at the junctions of pillars and floors would have been required and most reconstruc-tions assume that a simple scaffolding was formed, onto which flooring was lain. The Braby reconstruction does not reveal how the beam ends of the second and higher floors interact with the masonry inner wall, much less how the post heads might support the corduroy floors of separate beams. It will be apparent that the mass of full floors would be hard to manage on simple scaffold-like

structures, most of which would rely on the tensile strength of their bindings rather than that of the wood.

These comments apply to the primary broch tower, but at Clachtoll, evidence survives for a burnt wooden struc-ture that had been erected within the 1½ storey ruinous remains of a once complete RSM broch tower. The nature of that structure is discussed below.

Building and rebuilding within canonical broch tectonics

Structural analysis has indicated major structural failures around the circuit of the Stage 1 broch remains. It is not pos-sible that the collapse episodes recorded above 2 all occurred in a single event, albeit that the majority are explicable as indicative of a major collapse. It is clear, for example, that in the north-east quadrant of the broch the outer wall fell outwards and pulled the inner wall with it, at least locally. Conversely, the damage caused to the surviving upper parts of the stairway complex implies impact from material of the upper, inner wall of the western quadrant, whose lower levels may have folded outwards allowing the wall fabric to fold inwards falling across the garth. Nonetheless, in this instance and in general, most of the infilling material in the garth probably derived from the masonry of the inner wall.

The low numbers of surviving masonry shells of brochs makes it especially difficult to provide reliable estimates of height. In Barber's (2017) modelling two parameters are founded upon to estimate volume and height of the various elements, viz, the internal diameter and the external batter angle (the angle between the slope of the outer wall-face and a vertical raised at its foot). Sadly, both parameters are ambiguous at best in ruinous remains. Brochs cannot be endlessly downscaled, largely because of the constant thickness of the inner wall, and the constant width of the gallery and the need for the outer wall to reduce in thickness and corbel in towards the inner wall (*ibid.*, 136–41). The garth radius of Clachtoll is sufficiently large for downscaling not to have been a constraint on its design and build.

However, as the garth diameter increases, the ground-loading of the inner wall, already at critical levels for smaller brochs using volcanic or metamorphic rock types, exceeds safe loadings for most Scottish rock and soil types. Barber identifies a height range of 12 to 15 m as the probable, and buildable, wall convergence height limits of Clachtoll broch tower. These values should be increased by the height of a masonry collar above the convergence point of the walls, adding perhaps 2 m to the completed wall head height (see Barber 2017, tab. 4.1). However, if the design batter angle was steeper than the ruinous remains indicate, the upper height could theoretically have risen to 20 to 24 m, improbable as this seems.

The broch at Clachtoll, interpreted in the light of Barber's (2017) analysis, indicates the suite of metrics set out below. The critical measurements on which the metrics are founded are the internal diameter/radius and the external batter angle of the outer wall-face. The width of the inner wall and of the gallery are also critical. The diameter was recovered from a best fit circle to the inner wall foot of the inner wall extracted from laser scan data and is set at 8.4 m with radius at 4.2 m. The batter angle of the outermost wall-face varies relatively widely, no doubt in consequence of the several collapse episodes of the monument. The value of this angle is 9.4623 degrees, which corresponds with a slope of 1 in 6, typical of many of the better preserved brochs. The averages for the widths of inner wall and the gallery for all Scottish brochs are 92 and 93 cm respectively. At Clachtoll's distorted remains these values are 99 and 91 cm respectively where they are most easily measured, and although they are quite variable elsewhere in the broch these latter values are used in the calculating the following.

On the basis of these figures, it seems probable that the Clachtoll broch was at least 13.8 m high at the convergence of the inner and outer walls, and may have supported above that level a masonry drum roughly 1.5 m tall giving a minimum completed height of 15.3 m. Its inner radius of 4.2 m, taken with the inner wall and gallery widths, indicates an outer wall that measured 2.3 m in the plane on which it was surveyed.

These parameters indicate a minimum gross built volume of 1323 m^3 and minimum built mass of 3,493 tonnes of Torridonian sandstone with minimum Specific Gravity of 2.64 (tonnes/m^3). This in turn indicates a human energy expenditure of 1720 kWh and with humans rated at 0.6 kwh per diem suggests a total build time of 2,867 days. Employed in teams of 10, 20 or 30 persons, this might have been reduced to 287, 143 or 96 days of project build time, respectively. Again, these are minimum figures and while no claim is made for their accuracy, these values are comparable with similar values suggested on the basis of calculations for other brochs.

Analysis of the rubble and other sediments within the garth at Clachtoll derived from 3D survey suggests that 105.36 m^3 of masonry rubble had fallen into the garth, in three episodes, following the final conflagration of the MIA wooden structure. Calculating how much higher the walls might have been if that masonry were re-erected on the surviving wall-heads is not a simple issue. The first difficulty is that of deciding from which wall the masonry fell. The excavations imply that the outer wall fell outwards and mainly lies outwith the broch. The rump of the inner wall above the scarcement seems similarly to indicate an outwards inclination, but the deposits abutting and overlying the scarcement have come from the inner wall. On

balance, it is assumed that the inner wall is the primary source of the infilling masonry. The surviving inner wall is a two-phase construction: the inner wall-face adjacent to the garth is MIA and, in part, earlier in date, but following a collapse, its outer wall-face was lost and a 'new' backing wall was built against it, propping it in place; this feature was observed during the course of conservation works on the wall head on the eastern side of the broch (Fig. 10.5). The upwards extension of this wall was therefore the source of much of the masonry in the garth.

It is unlikely, however, that the breach in the western (seaward) wall existed in the MIA. Therefore, some of the masonry infill must derive from the inner and perhaps some from the outer wall in this area. For this estimation, only masonry from the inner wall is considered. The area of the inner wall anulus is 29.2 m^2 and the volume required to fill the breach and raise the adjacent wall to the height of the wall-head at the stairway, some 11.6 m^3 of masonry would be required. This would leave sufficient for three 1 m high builds on top of the wall-head of the inner wall. On the basis of the character of the MIA inner wall and its condition this figure seems improbable, and it is more likely that a significant proportion of the internal rubble indeed derives from the outer wall in the western quadrant, implying a collapse inward from the west and outward from the east, south and north of the tower. Nonetheless, these figures would indicate that the structure survived at least 2–3 m higher than the currently surviving wall, a building of imposing proportions, even in its reduced and reconfigured 1st-century BC state.

The wall-head height of the ruined secondary Stage 1 Clachtoll monument before the 1st-century BC reoccupation is unlikely to have risen above the top of the second level gallery. The evidence from the eastern parts of the inner and outer wall prompts the hypothesis that the intention of the builders of the secondary, reduced, Clachtoll was to complete the structure at just above the mid-height of the first-floor gallery, to which level its surviving parts then rose. Included in those parts is the wall core structure revealed in the outer wall adjoining, and anticlockwise of the stairway. It should be noted that the inner wall-face was stabilised with a new backing in lieu of its lost outer wall-face. In addition, the inner wall and the wall core grade down to the outermost wall-face of the outer wall, at an angle of about 40° near the entrance passage and perhaps a little less near the stairwell.

While no evidence for the closure of this breach in the MIA now exists the continuance of charcoal and ash deposits on the scarcement up to the edges of the wall breach rather implies that the scarcement was a closed circuit at the time of the conflagration and that the wall on the west was lost after the Middle Iron Age settlement had been abandoned.

Refurbishment of broch ruins in the MIA to comparable one-and-a-half storey heights, like those at Midhowe, or Gurness, may seem to imply a generally accepted design intention for abandoned and ruinous brochs because the majority of the large surviving brochs have shared a similar fate, thus:

> We have already referred to the evidence from Dun Mor Vaul, Beirgh and elsewhere that indicates that some broch towers were deliberately reduced in height around the 1st or 2nd centuries AD and rebuilt in less monumental style. That was evidently not a universal consequence of secondary occupation, as the surviving remains from Mousa demonstrate (Harding 2009, 116).

However, we hypothesise that dynamic modelling (not yet undertaken) may indicate that the structure is susceptible to masonry failure at about one third of its height. Allt Breac, which now presents as a rather vestigial set of remains, actually survives to a height within the first floor gallery (Cavers, Hudson and Barber. 2013), as does Dun Vulan (Cavers and Barber 2018), Beirgh (Harding and Gilmour 2000) and many more that do not give evidence for secondary reuse of the reduced monument. Although many ruinous brochs are similarly preserved to about this height, the absence of evidence for their reuse at this height weakens the need to invoke an invariable regional design intent for the phenomenon. Thus, where the ruinous broch remains were reused in the MIA, external walls of about this height seem to have been preferred.

However, later trimming-off of some brochs to the top of the then current ground floor level is evidenced at Old Scatness and at The Cairns and it is notable that a secondary aisled house was built within the former's garth, apparently accessed through or across the reduced broch walls. Houses were built over the walls and over the whole of the infilled garth of the The Cairns (Martin Carruthers pers. comm.). These exceptions, like Mousa, in Harding's citation above, should further counsel against any proposal for a universal cultural process of truncation to one and a half storeys whilst accepting a preference of ruins of this size where reuse was practiced. The levelling episode, including trimming off the Old Scatness broch and adjacent houses is attributed to a Norse Period intervention while that of the Cairns probably occurred in the Middle Iron Age.

The evidence for early repair and alteration in the broch masonry in general indicates the work of persons familiar with broch building and anxious to reinstate its tectonics. Thus, their ambitions were cognate with those of the primary broch users, whatever those may have been, and this invites the conclusion that the rebuilders wanted to retain the primary people/place relationship that defines the RSM broch tectonics. Sometimes, however,

the converse is indicated. The imagined preparation of Clachtoll for reuse in the MIA involved building a backing wall to the remnant upper storey of the inner wall. This backing, coincidentally, retained in skeuomorph a residual primary broch feature in the closed-in and skewed stacked void above Cell 2, and thus could be interpreted as implying respect for the forms and tectonics of the primary broch structure. However, this amounted to retention of a fossil feature rather than cognitive construction of a skeuomorph for aesthetic reasons. None of the struts across the stacked void were replaced and the inside of the void was sealed off by the newly built backing wall. The inner wall's masonry leaves on either side of the void are set out of line with each other by 25cm at the wall-head and no attempt was made to correct this. These relict features are residual in their current, and MIA, state and do nothing to indicate a MIA builders' interest in or awareness of the structural function of stacked voids and no attempt was made to recover their functional roles. In short, some features of the rebuilding retained or reconstructed original broch features, but without an understanding of or requirement for the engineering role they were designed to serve.

We have no evidence for the function of the EIA primary and secondary Clachtoll. The interpretations offered in this report are based on the evidence of the domestic refuse from the MIA sediments, around, on and over the primary broch, not from anything contemporary with the primary broch of the EIA, possibly three centuries earlier.

Building and rebuilding outwith primary canonical broch tectonics

Cells 1, 2 and 4 have been rebuilt in forms that are not common to the broch architectural lexicon, *i.e.*, do not lead to canonical broch forms. Arguably, the first broch on the Clachtoll knoll was a ground galleried monument. We suggest that the primary broch was ground galleried and the extant wall cells, except for the apparently unaltered stairfoot cell, are formed by building transverse walls across segments of the ground gallery. The two concentric basal courses for wall-faces, exposed clockwise of the stair head and running thence to the western breach where they peter out, are colinear with the putative ground gallery, but as a result of the topography are one storey above it.

The contorted entrance passage to Cell 1 is strongly indicative of rejoining a damaged or distorted ground gallery cell to the entrance passage following failure of some of its original masonry. The upwards extension of Cell 2 into the first-floor gallery is indicative of non-primary construction and the inclusion therein of large slabs fitted surface-flush onto the transverse wall-faces seems, on the evidence from Clickhimin, Gurness and others to characterise Middle Iron Age building and is alien to primary broch construction. The large dog-legged and somewhat rectilinear plan of Cell 4 (the RHS guard cell) is at odds with generic gallery cells of the original broch builder's *oeuvre*.

The reconstruction or reforming of these elements are all indicative of an intention to retain the appearance of primary broch features by builders who were familiar with their original forms, but who were unaware of their structural functions, and happy to include anachronistic features, like the inset wall-slab panels, within them. They are cognate with the skeuomorphic retention of the stacked void's remains above Cell 2. Their retention did not extend to the retention of their primary structural purpose, nor to realignment of its abutting wall-face leaves into a renewed structurally sound coplanarity. The treatment of the 'lost' stacked void implies that the full circuit of the inner wall was not restored in this episode of rebuilding and this, together with the surface and structural treatments of cells all point to architectural or superficial (*sensu* 'of the surface') restoration of the broch's visual inner environment. It seems safe to assert that these builders were familiar with the forms of brochs but lacked an appreciation of the structural needs of a built tower, in short, they were not tower builders and directed their efforts to recreation of an architectural setting rather than the recreation of a structurally competent three-dimensional monument.

This implies that there is no cultural continuity between the primary builders and the MIA settlers in the broch. Given the up to four centuries of age difference between them, it is not automatically correct to assume that the MIA users of the ruin were ethnically different from the original builders. If, as Barber argues, the primary generation of brochs was created in a spirit of aggrandising monumentalisation and soon abandoned, the context of the creation, like the knowledge of their engineering solutions can have been entirely lost to their own descendants, with all that remains a superficial architectural awareness of the forms of the ancient monuments of perhaps eight or ten generations' earlier date (*cf.* Cavers, Heald and Barber 2021).

Burnt structural remains at Clachtoll

In considering the carbonised remains from the garth and scarcement at Clachtoll, it is helpful first to consider first, the nature of fire damage to wooden material in general and to consider also the fate of unburnt wood buried under soils and masonry for more than 2000 years.

Fire properties of wood[4]

When the temperature of wood rises to 100°C, chemically unbound water begins to evaporate from it. The thermal softening of dry wood begins at a temperature of about 180°C and reaches its maximum between 320°C and 380°C. Then the lignin, cellulose and hemicellulose in the wood begin to disintegrate. The softening of moist wood begins earlier, at about 100°C.

The ignition temperature of wood is affected by how long it is exposed to heat. Wood usually ignites at 250–300°C. After ignition, the wood begins to carbonise at a rate of 0.8 mm per minute of its thickness. Fire progresses slowly in a solid wood product, as the layer of carbon created protects the wood, and slows down the increase in temperature of the wood's inner parts and thus the progress of the fire. For example, at a distance of 15 mm from the carbonisation limit, the temperature of the wood is under 100 °C. In comparison, peat ignition occurs at temperatures between 300–350°C (Usup *et al.* 2004) and results in peak temperature around 600 °C. These values are associated with wildfires but domestic hearths are very unlikely to reach higher peak temperatures.

A test of concept in burning wattle screens

Given the prolific evidence for wattles, and by inference wattle screens, at Clachtoll, a small test-of-concept trial was conducted on five-month-old wattle screens resting in a sapling frame erected against a newly-built segment of broch inner wall (Fig. 10.6). A scarcement was formed on the wall fragment at 0.4 to 0.6 m above the solum. Two woven hurdles were rested, one on the other, on the scarcement's upper surface and were supported by a square framework of small diameter saplings, not more than 5 cm in diameter. About 1.5 m above the scarcement level a single hurdle was lain horizontally on cross members, made from further saplings tied onto the uprights. This was not a viable load-bearing structure and was formed solely to allow observation of the ignition of the fire load. Similarly, this was not an experiment, *sensu stricto*, merely a test of concept.

Various pieces of biscuit fired replicas of prehistoric-type pot were lain onto the hurdle screens and a small fire of brushwood over fire lighters was ignited under the lower screens, which ignited almost immediately. The wattles were quickly consumed and mainly reduced to ash within nine minutes. The fire reached very high temperatures very quickly and the blazing structure was unapproachable after three minutes. The wattle screens were almost fully consumed, but the uprights' charring was restricted to superficial areas adjacent to the blazing screens on the windward side of the construction; the remainder of the uprights appeared unaltered. Once the hurdles had burnt away, the burning of the uprights ceased. The pottery vessels fell more or less vertically from their positions and most of them survived intact.

Post-depositional change

Abandoned to time, the uncarbonised wood would undoubtedly decompose, leaving only a small number of

Figure 10.6 The 'test of concept' burning of replica wattle screens against a 1:1 scale model of the broch's inner wall and scarcement, carried out in a quarry at Stoer. The structure burned to destruction in a matter of minutes

relatively large and relatively formless charcoal masses. Robertson (this volume) has noted that:

> Those …[large charcoal]… fragments from the conflagration event were noticeably friable and broke apart more easily than those recovered from the underlying layers.

This is probably to be expected from the charcoal of carbonised wood that is not fully charred all the way through. After deposition, the cellulose and or lignin which had supported the carbonised volumes but that had not themselves charred, would decay leaving the charcoal patches quite friable. Charred posts observed *in situ* in House 10/1 on Arran were fully reduced to charcoal above their postholes, reduced to friable and then to separated loose fragments of charcoal at a lower level, within the posthole, and had fully decomposed beneath that level (Barber 1997, 7–25). The transition zone of a wooden squared post, from charcoal to solid wood, can be seen in the report on the firing of a reconstructed Anglo Saxon house at West Stow in Feb 2005 (Tipper 2012, pl. 3.40, 66), together with many examples of partly charred timbers. Interestingly, re-excavation of the site of the conflagration at West Stow in 2006, revealed incipient decomposition of the base of the post (*ibid.*, pl. 7.10, 170) although that may have begun before the conflagration. Similar phenomena were encountered after the burning of long houses at Lejre, the report of which is a *tour de force* of the subject (Rasmussen 2007).

Robertson's report, above, lists the species and gives dimensions of a sample of charcoal fragments from the conflagration deposit. This indicates the extensive use of woven wattles and the infrequent occurrence of larger timbers, parts of which had undergone superficial charring. The dimensions of the larger fragments and their frequency are both underestimated by the combined effects of combustion and degradation. However, we shall discuss below further evidence, contingent upon their infrequency and low mass.

Comparanda in wooden house construction

Burnt structural remains from within brochs are rare. It has proved helpful to consider structural remains from other Iron Age and Early medieval structures of similar scale; the former, not least for their relevance to MIA carpentry methods. Roundhouses of the Iron Age are a relatively well understood phenomenon (Pope 2003; Harding 2009) and the many reproductions of roundhouses indicate that a range of scholars have consciously modelled their wooden structures. These models are usually based on excavated evidence for concentric posthole settings and ring ditches with, in some cases, upstanding earthen or earth and stone penannular banks. Actual wooden remains are rare, mainly confined to crannog and crannog-like structures (Crone 2000; Cavers and Crone 2017; Crone *et al.* 2018) and the occasional occurrence of perched water tables, like that at Deerpark Farms, Northern Ireland (Lynn and McDowell 2011).

At Black Loch of Myrton (BLM), a lakeside settlement containing a number of houses one of which, House 2 dates to 435 BC and another, House 3, to the range 400 to 370 BC and thus broadly contemporary with the putative date for primary broch building at Clachtoll. The average

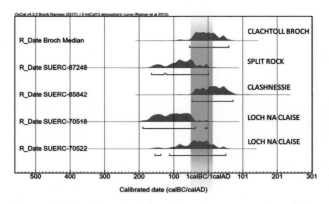

Figure 10.7 Radiocarbon dates from the sites investigated on the Stoer peninsula. The date shown for Clachtoll broch is a calibration of the median of the determinations from the middle Iron Age chronology

Figure 10.8 View of the stair gallery at Kylesku broch, Assynt (photo: G. Cavers)

diameter of the structural posts was just over 19 cm in House 2 and around 16 cm for the smaller exposure of posts in House 3. These houses are circular, House 3 is 9.6 m in diameter and House 2 about 11.9 m in diameter. For comparison, the average diameter of a broch interior is 9.4 m (based on 27 reliably accurate measurements) and of Clachtoll is 8.4 m. The main function of the houses' post rings was to support a roof, it is believed, and, for the outer ring, to resist the unresolved lateral forces of the roof's mass. For the avoidance of doubt, it should be noted that there is no suggestion that either house at BLM was multi-storey. However, the posts must have supported substantial roof structures. At BLM, the sizes of the posts varied between houses and their diameters vary in proportion to the house diameters. The trackway leading through the site is a corduroy path made from tree trunks some 19 cm to 32 cm in diameter. Again, the scale of the timber used is proportional to the use to which it was put and deliberate selection is implied. It seems reasonable, therefore, to argue that Iron Age carpenters could and did consciously gauge their timbers to the tasks and loadings they were designed to support. As noted, the diameters cited here for BLM are broadly indicative of what they perceived as necessary to support a roof over the sorts of spans represented by the broch tower garths.

By a very rough calculation, the mass of the timber required to fully floor Clachtoll with solid timbers is in the region of 7 to 10 tonnes, for softwood and hardwood respectively. These values are highly variable depending, amongst other things, on the wetness of the wood, nonetheless, they are an indication of the order of magnitude of floor mass. The posts would have weighed about 300 kg each and the post ring some 4 tonnes in the aggregate. The use of woven screens as floor panels would greatly reduce this mass. Weighing a little more than 15 kg per hurdle, and each hurdle measuring about 1 m² and hence, some

450 kg per m³, the mass of the floor could be reduced by about 40 %, or somewhat less because a framework of beams would still have been needed.

Lynn excavated a raised rath at Deerpark Farms, Northern Ireland, on top of which, at one phase, two houses had been completely constructed in wattle screening, not as separate panels, but almost as inverted baskets with doubled walls; perhaps the ultimate 'creel houses'. Sufficient of the houses remained, buried in anaerobic conditions under a later stage in the enlargement of the rath, that the Lynn's interpretation cannot be dismissed (Lynn 1988; Lynn and McDowell 2011). No framing timbers were preserved at Deerpark, in contrast with the often-substantial framing of crannog dwellings (above).

It is argued here that the burned structure at Clachtoll was intermediate in its structural scheme between the crannog and Deerpark models. Individual small roundwood stems abound to such an extent at Clachtoll that no credible reconstruction can dismiss their presence in the structure. There is no evidence for larger posts and beams but some larger pieces of charcoal indicate the presence of some larger, probably, roundwood timbers. The maximum cross-sectional dimensions lie between 50 and 64 mm. The latter are so infrequent that their use in formal framing could not be deduced from observation of their distribution in the conflagration layer.

The single storey houses at Deerpark were probably close to the upper limit of what could be achieved with woven walls alone (Lynn 1988; Lynn and McDowell 2011, 602). It is unlikely that a wattle fabric alone could be self-supporting even for the second storey illustrated by Braby, and even less conceivably for multi-storied structures. Perhaps with a more formal and robust wooden framework, firmly affixed to the masonry structure or penned within its circuit, could be constructed to 2 storeys, or more probably 1½ storeys. With a framing provided by infrequent use of larger timbers something like 10 to

Figure 10.9 Aerial view of the Clachtoll broch on completion of the project (image: John Town)

15 cm in diameter, a second storey is credible but higher structures would still probably lack sufficient rigidity and would require the volumes of substantial timbers depicted by Braby and constituting Sharples' 'best timber available'.

Solid wood structures and woven hurdle structures would all have required large masses of wood. For many areas in Highland and Island Scotland the current availability of wood would not suffice to provide this mass locally. In Assynt, there is some woodland even now and provision for some brochs may have been found locally, but in general, the wood required would have to be imported over some distance. Adomnán's *Vita Colombae* (Anderson and Anderson 1961) records a miracle in which monks towing oak trunks from further north to build a church on Iona were saved by the intercession of the saint. Another section of Adomnán's *Vita* records a ship delivering a load of wattles to Iona. No doubt such arrangements could have been made, but the current paradigm does not automatically allow for anything more complex than subsistence farming as the cultural milieu for Iron Age broch builders and as yet we have no means of assessing the possibility of extra-regional timber trade. Increasingly speculative rationalisations have been offered on the procurement of large volumes of wood for the flooring and roofing of broch towers. Most recently, Sharples has suggested that timbers could

have been sequestrated from the local community who then, as now, collected driftwood from the tidelines and stored large timbers as heirlooms (Sharples 2020, 298). The occasional testing of reason in justification of extensive and elaborate wooden lining structures of brochs is eloquent justification for Fojut's *bon mot* that such hypotheses are examples of necessity as the offspring of invention (Fojut 2005a). In setting out our interpretation we shall rely on the observable evidence set out above and noting the constraints imposed by the stone structure while we try to arrive at some suggestions on likely internal fittings. These will, nonetheless, remain an operational hypothesis for testing in future experimental work or field excavation.

Internal fixings – summary

The evidence set out and discussed above points toward a relatively light, perhaps even ephemeral structure erected within the residual garth during the latter half of the 1st century BC. This was a short-lived episode, and accumulated settlement debris of the forms and types evidenced on the east coast and northern brochs. The burnt remains of its internal wooden structure sealed these deposits.

The broch walls in the MIA configuration were unlikely to have been higher than the top of the second floor and in some areas, for example, adjacent to the broch entrance and the stairhead, may not have been significantly, *i.e.*, more than 1 m, higher than they now are. It is likely that the breach on the west side still retained its masonry walling. The interior of the broch had not undergone the raising of its solum and the entrance passage was still the primary access point.

The wooden structure whose existence is confirmed by its carbonised remains, was a mezzanine structure and because charcoal from it has been encountered all round the surviving circuit of the scarcement as well as on the garth floor and there is no reason to doubt that it encircled the whole of the garth. The height of the central hearth, especially in its final phase, was incompatible with a full floor and therefore it is concluded that the first-floor wooden structure was a mezzanine gallery.

The objection to the 'lean-to' mezzanine model based on rainwater ingress could be removed by imagining a mezzanine with a taller cross section inner post ring supporting a roof near second floor level that projected through the mezzanine roof the latter running from the inner post ring to the outer wall-head. The higher central roof would allow for an arrangement similar to a clerestory ring, perhaps shutters were used to allow daylight in and smoke out, while the central roof would overhang the mezzanine roof and similarly move the rainwater to the outside of the structure. Similar solutions have been proposed by Walker and others for related drystone prehistoric settlements (*cf.* Strachan 2013, 100).

The coincident strength of this design lies in the small volume of timbers involved and therefore the small fire load it creates in the structure. All the horizontal and vertical panelling could have been wattle screens and the framing posts and beams could have been of modest scantling, so that the fire load was low. Fire load is calculated as follows:

$$\text{Fire load} = (M \times C) / A$$

Where M is the mass (use weight in kg) multiplied the calorific content, expressed in kilo cals per kg, C, of the material and divide the product by the area of the compartment in m^2 (A). A reasonable estimate of calorific value would be around 7,000 kj/kg. The fire load for Clachtoll, even when substituting wattle screens for most of the panel material represented in the Braby model as solid wood, is extraordinarily high. There is an increased risk factor that a forced-draft inferno could be created with the entrance passage providing the main air inlet, albeit that oxygen for the burning would also pass through the dry-stone walling. The test-of-concept burning described above suggests that the wattles with their high surface area to volume ratio would have flared off with astonishing speed, which may explain why the occupants had no time to collect their equipment and ornaments before fleeing the building.

The speed of combustion and the forced draft would no doubt have created very high temperatures, but it is clear from two evidential sources that it was of short duration. Those sources are the superficial carbonisation of larger timbers (which subsequently decayed) and the absence of fire damage to the stones of the inner wall's inner wall-face. At The Cairns broch, following abandonment of the broch proper fires were ignited within ad hoc hearth sites at various points on the broch floor. Where these abutted the broch wall the stones are crazed and fragmented (Martin Carruthers, pers. comm.). The writers are aware of only one other broch which displays similar damage, at Borwick (Canmore ID 1660), and there it is mostly hidden behind a later lining wall-face.

There is no evidence for fire damage to the stonework at Clachtoll, which supports the evidence of the carbonised remains and implies, like them, that the structure was largely a wattle construction with some formal framing in timbers of greater cross section. If the sort of construction we have imagined had existed, the short but fierce conflagration could have left many useful posts relatively unscathed, and these may have been extracted for further use, despite their envelopment in masonry collapse, simply because good timbers were of such value. Alternatively, they were damaged to some extent but inaccessible because of the masonry collapse and they simply decayed away over the following millennia. The Torridonian sandstone from which the broch is built is massively bedded but some of the beds from which the broch stones were prised loose are comparatively soft and would certainly have suffered as much in a conflagration as the Orkney flagstones of The Cairns broch, albeit in a different way, reducing to sand and gravel rather than fracturing interlaminately. If there had been firing of 200 tonnes or more of dried wood, plus the materials of the roof, including its thatch, it is inconceivable that no sign of that fire would be reflected in the condition of the masonry. Hence we conclude that the structure was slightly built and largely composed of wattle hurdles, in lieu of wooden panelling and were rapidly consumed by the flames.

Use of space, floors and living conditions

There are indications from the spatial distribution of the artefactual material and the plant macrofossils that the ground floor was divided into separate activity areas. Cereal grains were dehusked in the NE quadrant and, if the position of querns is significant, milled into flour in the SW; the storage of grain and unprocessed sheafs in Cell 2 might hint at a circuitous cereal 'production line' within the broch. Other specific activities are less straightforward to demonstrate, although a concentration of spindle whorls in the SE quadrant, probably having been deposited there following the collapse of an upper level, might suggest that spinning took place within one or more of the upper rooms. A constraining factor must have been lighting: even allowing for an open face on the upper floor galleries that allowed the glow from the hearth to be cast into the compartments, a low fire burning peat and small roundwoods as its primary fuel cannot have provided much light. Even if we were to allow that all of the stone 'lamps' were used for lighting (see Chapter 4) and factor in the use of 'butter lamps' and tapers which do not survive, the majority of the internal space must have been very dimly lit, and probably very smoky. It is perhaps for this reason that the bone weaving combs were recovered from floor levels, rather than contexts likely to belong to upper platforms, suggesting that looms were located close to the hearth and main source of light.

There are numerous strands of evidence that the ground floors of the broch were rather dirty, giving the impression that this space was primarily functional. Rodent remains incorporated in the floor materials attest to the presence of vermin, presumably attracted by the large quantities of grain present in the broch as well as the regularly discarded food and cooking debris. There is abundant evidence for the refurbishment of the floors, presumably as they became foul through trampling over organic coverings, and despite the use of peat ash rake-out in an attempt to dry the surfaces the insertion of a soakaway stone drain became inevitable, in addition to the regular shovelling out and replacement of the upper levels.

Cell 1, to the east of the entrance passage, apparently became a refuse dump during the use of the broch. Given the cell was certainly remodelled during the Middle Iron Age reconfiguration of the broch, this suggests that the space within did not serve much practical function during the subsequent occupation phases and became a midden shortly after its construction. It is possible that it was initially used as a latrine, only for continued discard of waste, including food debris and general rubbish, into the interior to nearly fill the space. Similar use of intramural galleries as cesspits and dumping space was recorded by MacKie at Dun Mor Vaul (MacKie 1974, 25) and supports the general impression that the ground-level intramural galleries of brochs were a convenient by-product of the hollow-walled tower design, used for functional purposes, rather than a critical requirement of the arrangement of activities within the building.

More puzzling, however, is the articulated partial sheep skeleton recovered from the floor deposits in the northern interior. This was apparently buried with flesh on the bone, and the smell created as it decomposed must have been overpowering. It is hard to explain this deposit in any practical terms, but it is not unique. Unusual deposits interpreted as votive or 'foundational' beneath floor levels and behind walls are well documented at middle Iron Age settlements at Sollas (Campbell 1991), Cnip (Armit

2006), Cill Donnain (Parker Pearson and Zvelebil 2014) and Hornish Point (Barber 2003) among numerous others. Sheep were a particularly common deposit at Sollas and seem to have been preferentially deposited over other domestic species, whereas wild animals such as red deer were apparently never treated in this way (Mulville and Thoms 2005, 242). Campbell and Finlay suggested that such offerings could relate to ritual feasting, or libations connected with cereal processing and productivity (*ibid.*, 141–7). The precise meaning of this practice is difficult to explain through a modern frame of reference, but the recurrence of similar deposits from contemporary settlements across the Atlantic west strongly suggests it was an important part of the symbolic completion of the house. Perhaps the burial of a sacrificial carcass was intended to promote the health of the larger herd, to protect the productivity of the farm in general, or to provide 'sustenance' to the building in its own right.

While there were undoubtedly structuring principles that governed the arrangements, however, the impression given of the ground floor of the broch is one of practicality, with tasks and crafts indicated by both artefactual and macrofossil evidence and continual trampling indicating the constant footfall of daily use. The implication is that sleeping or social quarters were located on the upper levels, though this cannot be demonstrated from the excavated evidence, and it is perhaps important to remember that social and practical spaces are often not clearly divided in functional farmhouses of any period.

Links, local and distant

Only tantalising evidence has been recovered from the nearby settlements at Clashnessie dun, Loch na Claise islet and the Clachtoll split rock. However, the radiocarbon results from each site indicate that they were all in use broadly contemporaneously with the broch (Fig. 10.7), in the latter half of the 1st century BC, while the ceramics recovered from the Split Rock are a close match to those recovered from the broch. Too little of each site has been excavated to allow any definitive conclusions to be drawn, but it is very likely that these smaller sites were occupied by groups associated with the residents of Clachtoll. All three sites are considerably smaller – none could realistically have accommodated more than a single roundhouse – and it would seem very probable that the residents of each site were clients or retainers of the occupants of Clachtoll, perhaps tied to them through obligations of tribute or through the requirement to supply agricultural produce, cereals, fleece or meat for processing and redistribution at the broch. While this may be seen as stretching the available evidence too far, it is clear that the other contemporary settlements were not on the scale of the Clachtoll broch and at the very least were likely to have been occupied by smaller groups, if not those of lower social standing. In the case of the Split Rock settlement, while there is little doubt that it was occupied as a dwelling, we might wonder whether the choice of this precipitous location was functionally related to the broch. The position is highly visible, while also commanding panoramic views of the coastline to north and south, raising the possibility that the stack could have been a watch post or signal station, positioned to facilitate communication along the western coast, as well as providing early notice of the approach of vessels from the south or west.

The close affinities in the ceramic styles between the Clachtoll assemblage and those from Middle Iron Age sites in the Hebrides must at least indicate close contact between these communities, but might even allow us to speculate at the mechanisms for contact and shared identities across the Atlantic west. If ceramics were generally manufactured locally and, as might be inferred from their primary function as storage jars, primarily a component of the domestic accoutrements of the broch, it is perhaps not unreasonable to suggest that they were primarily made and decorated by women. If this were the case, the movement of women between neighbouring regional groups through marriage alliances might account for the similarity in material culture across relatively distant broch communities. A system of cross-community marriage ties may also have provided the labour and materials required to build and maintain ostentatious structures such as brochs through dowry or reciprocal obligations when families were united. Such inferences will always be speculative, but envisaging an arrangement that both accounts for similarity in domestic material culture and provides the mobilisation of the workforce required to construct a broch has some appeal, and could help to explain how similarity across large areas could arise without relying on external factors.

A model for Iron Age society at Clachtoll

It would be unwise to infer the structure of Middle Iron Age society for the Clachtoll area and its economic basis from the evidence of one fully excavated site and snapshots from its contemporaries, since any calculation or modelling of the significance of this evidence is necessarily predicated on the size of the occupant group. As such, the evidence from Clachtoll for the storage and processing of large quantities of cereals should be treated cautiously, since without any reliable way to estimate the number of people involved in production, processing and consumption, we cannot reliably distinguish between a household-level subsistence economy and the indicators of a more sophisticated system of centralised agricultural production. The economy of the Clachtoll settlement certainly involved a mixed reliance on cultivated crops, wild plants and animals as well as exploitation of marine resources, so that we might infer the control of a wider

territory than the cultivated infield areas immediately associated with the broch. Indeed, given the availability of suitable ground nearby it seems likely that the cultivated ground belonging to the Clachtoll broch occupants was located at some distance from the broch itself, perhaps most likely on the raised ground to the east or on the machair of Stoer and Clachtoll bays, an arrangement that differs from the intense manipulation of soils in the fields immediately adjacent to the brochs of Orkney and Shetland (Dockrill and Bond 2009; Guttmann *et al.* 2008).

Armit envisaged a system of inheritance accounting for the division of land-holding territories in the Atlantic Iron Age and the increasing complexity of wealth distribution within expanding social groups accounting for the fragmentation of Iron Age landscapes over the course of the later 1st millennium BC (Armit 2005). The evidence from the Stoer peninsula might support this trajectory, with expansion into tenant sub-farms, supporting and beholden to the occupants of Clachtoll taking place in the late 1st millennium BC. Where wheelhouses and aisled roundhouses proliferated in the Middle Iron Age of the Western Isles and Shetland and wags and cellular structures were built in Caithness and Orkney (Gilmour 2005; Baines 1999), contemporaneously with the continued use of brochs, and nucleated 'broch villages' developed in Orkney and Caithness, in Assynt this diversification perhaps took the form of coastal duns, islet settlements and probably non-monumental roundhouses. Such structures are beginning to be recognised in numbers in Assynt (*cf.* Cavers *et al.* 2009), largely due to the ongoing survey efforts of Historic Assynt, and this can be expected to continue. Investigation of these structures and their chronological and functional relationship to the Assynt's brochs should be a priority for further research in the area.

If the icon of the broch tower retained some meaning as a symbol of status by the 1st century BC the proximity of the nearby Ardbhair and Kylesku brochs (Fig. 10.8), only a few kilometres away to the east, must suggest that similarly powerful local landholders lived in Assynt alongside those who occupied Clachtoll. The origins for this arrangement may be in the earlier Iron Age, as neighbouring groups built brochs as statements of land tenure within individual territories, though they too may have been elevated to the position of localised centres within a more diverse community by the Middle Iron Age.

In summary, the evidence from Clachtoll aligns with the evidence for the late 1st millennium BC intensification of agriculture and production evidenced at Iron Age settlements in the Western Isles, Orkney and Shetland, and may indicate a similar trajectory of diversification and development of client, satellite settlements located within associated territories. The structural analysis of the building and the occupation C14 chronology, however, reminds us that all of this took place within a secondary phase of activity at the site, probably entirely within the later 1st century BC or the early 1st century AD. While there are indications of the presence of an earlier settlement at the site, there is no surviving evidence for the nature of that occupation, or its economic basis.

A catastrophic end?

There is little doubt that the occupation of the settlement at Clachtoll was brought to a very abrupt end. The fire that swept through the building was followed – if not accompanied – by the collapse of the tower, and the rubble that infilled the interior lay undisturbed thereafter. It is worth reiterating that this is apparently a rare occurrence: almost all other excavated brochs show some evidence for continuity or reoccupation of the site after the end of use of the broch. Gilmour has argued that most brochs that saw Middle and Late Iron Age activity were deliberately dismantled prior to the wheelhouse and cellular phases of their use, a phenomenon he regards as symptomatic of the significant reorganisation of society around the end of the 1st millennium BC (Gilmour 2005, 85–7). As an abnormality in this newly rearranged political landscape, the Clachtoll broch tower may have been too conspicuous as a statement of independence in a region governed by a new regime. Where elsewhere the Middle Iron Age dismantling of brochs and construction of 'inward-facing' wheelhouses allowed these settlements to continue to operate, it is possible that the ostentatious tower at Clachtoll was simply no longer compatible with the current political landscape. While the peripheral buildings adjacent to the broch remain unexplored (Fig. 10.9), it is clear that, whether attacked and deliberately destroyed or lost to a catastrophic structural failure, the fire marked the end of the occupation of the broch tower itself and no attempt was made to re-establish it.

The deliberate downscaling of brochs in the later Middle Iron Age clearly indicates a significant change in the role of these buildings by the early 1st millennium AD. As Harding discusses, at some sites, including Loch na Beirgh and Dun Vulan, a concerted effort was made to construct new buildings within the broch when use of the existing walls, even in a reduced state, could have served just as easily (Harding 2009, 288), so that the disassociation from the earlier broch seems to have been very conscious and deliberate. It is possible that the new arrangements governing the rules of settlement architecture did not suit the Clachtoll broch, so that the settlement had to be effectively 'closed' and abandoned abruptly, perhaps by force.

The wider socio-political circumstances notwithstanding, it appears that the fire at Clachtoll took hold while the building was still in use: the grain overspilling the knocking stone and groups of stored agricultural implements suggest

that the last residents had not planned to leave. Webley's discussion of the ritualisation of abandonment practises might warn us against assuming that the final layers within roundhouse occupation deposits truly reflect the living arrangements (Webley 2007, 139–40), but the end of use of the broch seems to align with the end of Iron Age activity in the wider landscape more generally. Although this can only be tentative evidence based on dates from a few neighbouring sites, it is tempting to suggest that the downfall of the Clachtoll broch also marked the collapse of end of the Iron Age occupation of the Stoer peninsula, a possible rare example of an identifiable political event in the Scottish prehistoric settlement record. While Historic Assynt continue to survey the parish, Late Iron Age and Early medieval archaeology that might throw some light on the form and arrangement of post-broch Iron Age settlement is still conspicuous by its absence. Its identification, perhaps initially through proxy records in sediment cores (see Matthews, Chapter 8), will constitute a key objective for future research in the north-western Highlands.

Conclusion: which Clachtoll broch?

> What is needed is a site like Scalloway broch in Shetland but with signs of a sixth century cataclysm which is of a general rather than a local nature. Clachtoll broch in Assynt might suit; it stands in an exposed position above the rocky shore, overlooking open sea to the west, and the quarter of the wall facing the sea has vanished, presumably due to an unusually violent storm. The broch is above the 8 m contour and the underlying rock is hard and seems not to have given way; the remaining interior is full of rubble and part of the underlying occupation layer should still be there, possibly containing clues about what happened (MacKie 2010, 111).

MacKie (2010) discussed the circumstances of the end of the Middle Iron Age in Atlantic Scotland within his preferred chronological framework that would have brochs continue in use throughout the earlier half of the 1st millennium AD, before an apparent collapse occurring in the 6th century AD. He identified Clachtoll as a suitable candidate for the exploration of the reasons for this catastrophic end, recognising the hallmarks of a catastrophic structural collapse and the absence of any obvious subsequent reuse. In the event, his identification proved insightful, and the results of this project may provide valuable data on the date and nature of the Middle Iron Age collapse of 'broch-centric' society. Where the Clachtoll excavation departs from MacKie's hypothesis is in the chronology: it is clear that this social collapse took place much earlier, by the early decades of the 1st century AD, and provides support for the growing body of evidence for dramatic social change at this period, as the heyday of broch occupation drew to a close.

It is hoped that, through the approach taken throughout this project, the authors have demonstrated the value of critical appraisal of the structural evidence in conjunction with the associated soft-deposit and artefactual archaeology. Dry-stone structures, brochs included, are malleable and fluid in their configuration (Cavers, Barber and Ritchie 2015; Barber 2017), and were repeatedly redesigned to accord with the social requirements of the time. As such, the Clachtoll broch that stood on the day of the fire that ended the occupation was likely one iteration of a much longer-lived settlement. Importantly, the evidence we have reported here provides a vivid snapshot of the waning days of broch use in Atlantic Scotland, but contributes little to the investigation of broch origins. The experience of Clachtoll is a demonstration of how continued or reoccupation can be destructive, leaving only tentative clues to an earlier origin, despite a secure and well-preserved occupation sequence relating to the secondary use. With the lessons of a century of broch archaeology learned, we may be able to place the excavated evidence in its correct context.

Notes

1   Following John Ruskin, we take the view that *structural engineering* – which Ruskin calls 'building' – should be differentiated from *architecture* the latter comprising those elements of a structure not essential for its structural integrity. The former is usually strongly constrained by factors like the available building materials and technologies, whilst the latter is a clearer index of human cultural choice and subsists mainly in ornamentation and display. Archaeologists use the term *architecture* to mean both, and by some obscure extension, to include some element of household, as opposed to house, creating a term whose obscurity, to quote Quiller-Couch, lends it power. This matter is discussed further below in the context of architectural tectonics.

2   Linguists suggest, in terms, that synchronic linguistics describe a language at a specific point of time, usually the present, while diachronic linguistics (from the Greek 'through time') consider the development of a language throughout some or all of its history (Ramat, Mauri and Molinelli 2013, 1–26).

3   A rather more concerning example of masonry creep may be seen inside the broch with alarming cracks in the inner wall and a general tendency for the inner wall to move sideways into the stacked void spaces.

4   Puuinfo, the Finnish Timber Council provides basic design information for the use of timber in modern structures and whilst not a totally disinterested body, they are a not-for-profit organisation whose technical data is freely available, and it has been relied upon here.

References

Ambers, J. 2001 Analysis of the pigment used to produce SF17156 (Pictish painted pebble). In S.J. Dockrill *et al.*, 24.

Ambers, J. 2010 Scientific analysis of painted quartz pebbles. In S.J. Dockrill *et al.*, 322–3.

Anderson, J. 1878 Notes on the structures, distribution and contents of the brochs, with special reference to the question of their Celtic or Norwegian origin. *Proceedings of the Society of Antiquaries of Scotland* 12, 314–55.

Anderson, J. 1883 *Scotland in Pagan Times: The Iron Age.* Edinburgh, David Douglas.

Anderson, J. 1890 Notice of the excavation of the brochs of Yarhouse, Brounaben, Bowermadden, Old Stirkoke and Dunbeath, in Caithness, with remarks on the period of the brochs and an appendix containing a collected list of the brochs of Scotland. *Archaeologia Scotica* 5, 131–98.

Anderson, J. 1901 Notices of nine brochs along the Caithness coast from Keiss Bay to Skirza Head excavated by Sir Francis Tress Barry. *Proceedings of the Society of Antiquaries of Scotland* 35, 112–48.

Anderson, A. O. and M. O. Anderson 1961 *Adomnan's Life of Columba.* Edinburgh, Thomas Nelson and Sons Ltd.

Anon. 1892 *Catalogue of the National Museum of Antiquaries of Scotland.* Edinburgh, Society of Antiquaries of Scotland.

Armit, I. 1990a Brochs and beyond in the Western Isles. In I. Armit (ed.), 41–70.

Armit, I. (ed.) 1990b *Beyond the Brochs: Changing Perspectives on the Atlantic Scottish Iron Age.* Edinburgh, Edinburgh University Press.

Armit, I. 1991 The Atlantic Scottish Iron Age: five levels of chronology, *Proceedings of the Society of Antiquaries of Scotland* 121, 181–214.

Armit, I. 1992 *The Later Prehistory the Western Isles of Scotland.* Oxford, British Archaeological Reports 221.

Armit, I. 1996 *The Archaeology of Skye and the Western Isles.* Edinburgh, Edinburgh University Press.

Armit, I. 1998 Re-excavation of an Iron Age wheelhouse and earlier structure at Eilean Maleit, North Uist. *Proceedings of the Society of Antiquaries of Scotland* 128, 255–71.

Armit, I. 2003 *Towers in the North: the brochs of Scotland.* Stroud, Tempus.

Armit, I. 2005 Land holding and inheritance in the Atlantic Scottish Iron Age. In Turner *et al.* (eds.), 129–43.

Armit, I. 2006 *Anatomy of an Iron Age Roundhouse: The Cnip Wheelhouse Excavations, Lewis.* Edinburgh, Society of Antiquaries of Scotland.

Armit, I. and Dunwell, A. 1992 Excavations at Cnip, Sites 2 & 3, Lewis in 1989. *Proceedings of the Society of Antiquaries of Scotland* 112, 137–49.

Armit, I. and Mackenzie, J. 2013 *An Inherited Place: Broxmouth Hillfort and the South–East Scottish Iron Age.* Edinburgh, Society of Antiquaries of Scotland.

Armit, I., Campbell, E. and Dunwell, A. 2008 Excavation of an Iron Age, Early Historic and medieval settlement and metalworking site at Eilean Olabhat, North Uist. *Proceedings of the Society of Antiquaries of Scotland* 138, 27–104.

Armit, J. 1842 Parish of Westray. In Anon *The Statistical Account of the Orkney Islands*, 114–32. Edinburgh, William Blackwood and Sons.

Arthur, R., Murray, J. and Ritchie, A. 2014 *ARO 12: Painting the Stones Black: Solving the Mystery of Painted Quartz Pebbles.* GUARD Archaeology Reports Online. https://www.archaeologyreportsonline.com/PDF/ARO12_Painted_Pebbles.pdf (accessed 16/01/2021).

Baines, A. 2002 The inherited past of the broch: on antiquarian discourse and contemporary archaeology. *Scottish Archaeological Journal* 24(1), 1–20.

Baker, A., Hellstrom, J.C., Kelly, B.F.J., Mariethoz, G. and Trouet, V. 2015 A composite annual–resolution stalagmite record of North Atlantic climate over the last three millennia. *Scientific Reports* 5(1), 10307.

Balasse, M. 2003 Keeping the young alive to stimulate milk production? Differences between cattle and small stock. *Anthropozoologica* 37, 3–10.

Ballin Smith, B. (ed.) 1994 *Howe: Four Millennia of Orkney Prehistory.* Edinburgh, Society of Antiquaries of Scotland, Monograph 9.

Ballin Smith, B. and Banks, I. 2002 *In the Shadow of the Brochs: the Iron Age in Scotland. A Celebration of the Work of Dr Euan MacKie on the Iron Age of Scotland.* Stroud, Tempus.

Banerjea, R.Y., Bell, M., Matthews, W. and Brown, A. 2015 Applications of micromorphology to understanding activity areas and site formation processes in experimental hut floors. *Archaeological and Anthropological*

Sciences 7, 89–112. Available at: Doi.org/10.1007/s12520–013–0160–5.

Barber, J. 1997 *The Archaeological Investigation Of A Prehistoric Landscape: Excavations On Arran, 1987–81*. Edinburgh, Scottish Trust for Archaeological Research.

Barber, J. 2003 Bronze Age farms and Iron Age farm mounds of the Outer Hebrides. *Scottish Archaeological Internet Reports* 3. Available at: https://doi.org/10.5284/1017938.

Barber, J. 2012 Excavation and Consolidation at Clachtoll Broch. In G. Cavers (ed.) *Life and Death in Assynt's Past (Unpublished report for Historic Assynt)*, 36–65. Edinburgh, AOC Archaeology Group.

Barber, J. 2017 *Approaching the Mind of the Builder: Analysis of the Physical, Structural and Social Constraints on the Construction of the Broch Towers of Iron Age Scotland*. Unpublished PhD Thesis, University of Edinburgh. Available at: http://hdl.handle.net/1842/23430.

Barber, J., Cavers, G., Heald, A. and Theodossopoulos, D. 2021 Memory in practice and the practice of memory in Cathness, NE Scotland, and in Sardinia. In S. Stoddart, E. Aines and C. Malone (eds.) *Gardening Time: Monuments and Landscape from Sardinia, Scotland and Central Europe in the Very Long Iron Age*. Cambridge, Cambridge University Press.

Barber, K.E., Chambers, F.M. and Maddy, D. 2004 Late Holocene climatic history of northern Germany and Denmark: peat macrofossil investigations at Dosenmoor, Schleswig-Holstein, and Svanemose, Jutland *Boreas* 33(2), 132–44.

Barber, K.E. and Langdon, P.G. 2007 What drives the peat–based palaeoclimate record? A critical test using multi–proxy climate records from northern Britain. *Quaternary Science Reviews* 26(25–28), 3318–27.

Barclay, G.J. 1985 Excavations at Upper Suisgill, Sutherland. *Proceedings of the Society of Antiquaries of Scotland* 115, 159–98.

Barry, G. 1805 *History of the Orkney Islands*. Edinburgh, Archibald Constable and Company.

Bartlett, R.J. 1988 Manganese redox reactions and organic interactions in soils. In R.D. Graham, R.J. Hannam and N.C. Uren (eds.) *Manganese in Soils and Plants*, 243–59. Dordrecht, Kluwer Academic.

Bartosiewicz, L. and Gal, E. 2013. *Shuffling Nags, Lame Ducks: the archaeology of animal disease*. Oxford, Oxbow Books.

Bayley, J. 1985 What is ancient technology? An introduction to high–temperature processes. In P. Phillips (ed.) *The Archaeologist and the Laboratory*, 41–4. London: Council for British Archaeology Research Report 58.

Beamer, J. 2019 Archaeological textiles: considering textile production during Iron Age Britain. *Later Prehistoric Finds Group Newsletter* 12, 11–14.

Behre, K.-E. 1981 The interpretation of anthropogenic indicators in pollen diagrams. *Pollen et Spores* 23, 225–45.

Benton, S. 1931 The excavation of the Sculptor's Cave, Covesea, Morayshire. *Proceedings of the Society of Antiquaries of Scotland* 65, 299–357.

Berge, B. 2000 *The Ecology of Building Materials*. London, Routledge.

Berstan, R., Stott, A. W., Minnitt, S., Ramsey, C. B., Hedges, R. E. M. and Evershed, R. P. 2008 Direct dating of pottery from its organic residues: new precision using compound-specific carbon isotopes. *Antiquity* 82, 702–13.

Beveridge, E. 1903 *Coll and Tiree*. Edinburgh, T and A Constable.

Beveridge, E. and Callander, J.G. 1931 Excavation of an earth–house at Foshigarry, and a fort, Dun Thomaidh, in North Uist. *Proceedings of the Society of Antiquaries of Scotland* 65, 299–357.

Beveridge, E. and Callander, J.G. 1932 Earth–houses at Garry Iochdrach and Bac Mhic Connain, in North Uist. *Proceedings of the Society of Antiquaries of Scotland* 66, 32–66.

British Geological Survey (BGS). 2018. *Geology of Britain Viewer*, available at: http://mapapps.bgs.ac.uk/geologyofbritain/home.html, (Accessed 18/03/2018)

Bianchi, G. 1995 Plant waxes. In R.J. Hamilton (ed.) *Waxes: chemistry, molecular biology and functions*, 176–222. Dundee: Oily Press.

Bishop, R.R. 2019. Experiments on the effects of charring on hazelnuts and their representation in the archaeological record. *Journal of Archaeological Science Reports* 26, 101839.

Blaauw, M. and Heegaard, E. 2012 Estimation of age-depth relationships. In H. John, B. Birks, A.F. Lotter, S. Juggins and J.P. Smol (eds.) *Tracking Environmental Change Using Lake Sediments*, 379–413. Dordrecht, Netherlands: Kluwer Academic.

Bleicher, N., Antolin, F., Heiri, O., Haberle, S., Plogmann, H.H., Jacomet, S., Pumpin, C., Rentzel, P., Schafer, M., Schibler, J., Wiemann, P., van Hardenbroek, M., Toth, M. and Zweifel, N. 2018 Middens, currents and shorelines: complex depositional processes of waterlogged prehistoric lakeside settlements based on the example of Zurich-Parkhaus Opera (Switzerland). *Journal of Archaeological Science* 97, 26–41.

Blomgren, S. and Tholander, E. 1986 Influence of the ore smelting course on the slag microstructures at early iron-making, usable as identification basis for the furnace process employed. *Scandinavian Journal of Metallurgy* 15, 151–60.

Boessneck, J. 1969. Osteological differences between sheep (*Ovies aries* Linne) and goat (*Capra capra* Linne). In D. Brothwell and E. Higgs (eds.) *Science in Archaeology*, 331–58. London, Thames and Hudson (2nd edn).

Boivin, N. 2008 *Material Cultures, Material Minds: The Impact of Things on Human Thought, Society and Evolution*. Cambridge, Cambridge University Press.

Bond, J. 2002 Pictish pigs and Celtic cowboys: food and farming in the Atlantic Iron Age. In B. Ballin Smith and I. Banks, 177–84.

Bond, J.M. 2003 A growing success? Agricultural intensification and risk management in Late Iron Age Orkney. In J. Downes and A. Ritchie (eds.), 105–7.

Bond, J.M. 2007a The plant remains. In J. Hunter (ed.), 171–207.

Bond, J.M. 2007b The mammal bone. In J. Hunter (ed.), 207–62.

Bond, J.M. 2007c Plant remains. In S.J. Dockrill, 154–69.

Bond, J.M. and Hunter, J.R. 1987 Flax-growing in Orkney from the Norse period to the eighteenth century. *Proceedings of the Society of Antiquaries of Scotland* 117, 175–81.

Bond, J.M. and Summers, J.R (with contributions from J. Cussans) 2010. In S.J. Dockrill *et al.* 178–96.

Borderie, Q., Ball, T., Banerjea, R., Bizri, M., Lejault, C., Save, S. and Vaughan-Williams, A. 2020 Early Middle Ages houses of Gien (France) from the inside: geoarchaeology and archaeobotany of 9th–11th c. Floors. *Environmental Archaeology* 25(2), 151–69.

Bowes, D.R., Wright, A.E. and Park, R.G. 1964 Layered intrusive rocks in the Lewisian of the North-West Highlands of Scotland. *Journal of the Geological Society* 120, 153–92.

Boyd, J.D. 1967 West Mains of Turin. *Discovery and Excavation in Scotland 1967*, 4.

Braadbaart, F., Poole, I. and Huisman, D.J. 2012 Fuel, fire and heat: an experimental approach to highlight the potential of studying ash and char remains from archaeological contexts. *Journal of Archaeological Science* 39, 836–47.

Braadbaart, F., van Brussel, T., van Os, B. and Eijskoot, Y. 2017 Fuel remains in archaeological contexts: experimental and archaeological evidence for recognizing remains in hearths used by Iron Age farmers who lived in peatlands. *The Holocene* 27(11), 1682–93.

Bramwell, D. and Ballin Smith, B. 1994 The bird remains. In B. Ballin Smith (ed.), 153–7.

Bray, I.S.J. 1994 *Geochemical Methods for Provenance Studies of Steatite*. Unpublished PhD thesis, University of Glasgow.

Brown, L.D. 2015 Prehistoric pottery. In S.J. Dockrill *et al.*, 313–41.

Bullock, P., Fedoroff, N., Jongerius, A., Stoops, G., Tursina, T. and Babel, U. 1985 *Handbook for Soil Thin Section Description*. Wolverhampton, Waine Research Publications.

Bunting, M.J. and Tipping, R. 2004 Complex hydroseral vegetation succession and 'dryland' pollen signals: a case study from northwest Scotland. *The Holocene* 14(1), 3–63.

Bunting, M.J., Middleton, R. and Twiddle, C.L. 2007 Wetland records of a coastal cultural landscape in north-west Scotland: an application of the multiple scenario approach to landscape reconstruction. In C. Green (ed.) *Archaeology from the Wetlands: Recent Perspectives: Proceedings of the 11th WARP Conference, Edinburgh 2005*, 109–17. Edinburgh, Society of Antiquaries of Scotland.

Bunting, M.J., Farrell, M., Bayliss, A., Marshall, P. and Whittle, A. 2018 Maps from mud—using the multiple scenario approach to reconstruct land cover dynamics from pollen records: a case study of two Neolithic landscapes. *Frontiers in Ecology and Evolution* 6(36). https://doi.org/10.3389/fevo.2018.00036.

Burley, E. 1956 A catalogue and survey of the metal-work from Traprain Law. *Proceedings of the Society of Antiquaries of Scotland* 89, 118–226.

Büster, L. and Armit, I. 2013 Phase 6: the Late Iron Age village. In I. Armit and J. McKenzie (eds.), 115–86.

Calder, C.T. 1939 Excavations of Iron-Age dwellings on the Calf of Eday in Orkney. *Proceedings of the Society of Antiquaries of Scotland* 73, 167–85.

Calder, C.S.T. 1948 Report on the excavation of a broch at Skitten, in the Kilmister District of Caithness. *Proceedings of the Society of Antiquaries of Scotland* 82 (1947–48), 124–45.

Callander, J.G. 1916 Notices of (1) three stone cups fund in a cairn in Aberdeenshire, and (2) a short cist containing a beaker urn found at Boglehill Wood, Longniddry, East Lothian. *Proceedings of the Society of Antiquaries of Scotland* 50, 145–51.

Callander, J.G. 1921 Report on the Excavation of Dun Beag, a Broch near Struan, Skye. *Proceedings of the Society of Antiquaries of Scotland* 55, 110–31.

Callander, J.G. and Grant, W.G. 1934 The broch of Midhowe, Rousay, Orkney. *Proceedings of the Society of Antiquaries of Scotland* 68, 444–516.

Campbell, E. 1991 Excavations of a wheelhouse and other Iron Age structures at Sollas, North Uist by R.J.C. Atkinson in 1957. *Proceedings of the Society of Antiquaries of Scotland* 121, 117–73.

Campbell, E. 2002 The Western Isles pottery sequence. In B. Ballin Smith and I. Banks, 139–44.

Campbell, E. 2009 The raw, the cooked the burnt. *Archaeological Dialogues* 7, 184–98.

Canti, M.G. and Brochier, J.E. 2017 Plant ash. In C. Nicosia and G. Stoops *Archaeological Soil and Sediment Micromorphology,* 147–54. Oxford, John Wiley & Sons.

Cappers, R.T.J. and Bekker, R.M. 2013 *A Manual for the Identification of Plant Seeds and Fruits*. Groningen, Barkhuis and University of Groningen Library.

Cappers, R.T.J. and Neef, R. 2012 *Handbook of Plant Palaeoecology*. Groningen, Barkhuis and University of Groningen Library.

Cappers, R.T.J., Bekker, R.M. and Jans, J.E.A. 2006 *Digital Seed Atlas of the Netherlands*. Groningen, Barkhuis and Groningen University Library.

Carrott, J. and Kenward, H. 2001 Species associations among insect remains from urban archaeological deposits and their significance in reconstructing the past human environment, *Journal of Archaeological Science* 28, 887–905.

Carruthers, M. 2014 South Ronaldsay, The Cairns, Windwick Bay, excavation. *Discovery and Excavation in Scotland* New Ser 14, 142–3.

Carson, M. 1977 Iron Age finds from the Isle of Lewis. *Proceedings of the Society of Antiquaries of Scotland* 109, 370–5.

Carter, S. 1998 Red ash micromorphology. In N. Sharples (ed.), 29–31.

Cavers, G. 2006 Late Bronze and Iron Age lake settlement in Scotland and Ireland: the development of the 'crannog' in the north and west. *Oxford Journal of Archaeology* 25(4), 389–412.

Cavers, G. 2010 *Crannogs and Later Prehistoric Settlement in Western Scotland*. Oxford, Archaeopress. Available at: https://libcat.nms.ac.uk/uhtbin/cgisirsi.exe/?ps=luGqS27s25/NMS/X/9 [Accessed January 13, 2019].

Cavers, G. and Barber, J. 2018 *Dun Vulan, South Uist: Archaeological Excavation and Remedial Work, Data Structure Report*. Unpublished report for Historic Environment Scotland, AOC 23956-1.

Cavers, G. and Crone, A. 2017 *A Lake Dwelling in its Landscape: Iron Age Settlement at Cults Loch, Castle Kennedy, Dumfries and Galloway*. Oxford, Oxbow Books.

Cavers, G. and Hudson, G. 2010 *Assynt's Hidden Lives: An Archaeological Survey of the Parish*. Edinburgh. Available at: https://her.highland.gov.uk/Event/EHG3289.

Cavers, G. and Hudson, G. 2016 *Achlochan Coastal Heritage Project: Archaeological Survey*. Unpublished report for Coigach and Assynt Living Landscape Partnership.

Cavers, G. Barber, J. and Heald, A. 2015 *Clachtoll Broch: Conservation Strategy and Research Design*. Unpublished report for Coigach and Assynt Living Landscape Partnership, AOC 60073.

Cavers, G., Barber, J. and Johnstone, N. 2018 *Clachtoll Broch, Assynt: Conservation and Excavation: Data Structure Report*. Unpublished report, AOC 60094.

Cavers, G. Barber, J. and Ritchie, M. 2015 The survey and analysis of brochs. *Proceedings of the Society of Antiquaries of Scotland*, 153–76.

Cavers, G., Heald, A. and Barber, J. 2021 Monuments and memory in the Iron Age of Caithness. In S. Stoddart, E. Aines and C. Malone (eds.) *Gardening Time: monuments and Landscape from Sardinia, Scotland and Central Europe in the Very Long Iron Age*. Cambridge, Cambridge University Press.

Cavers, G., Hudson, G. and Barber, J. 2013 *Altbreck Broch, Dalchork: Archaeological Survey Report*. Unpublished report for Historic Environment Scotland, AOC 22483.

Cavers, M.G., Theodossopolos, T., Barber, J., Heald, A. and Martilla, J. 2009 *Clachtoll Broch, Assynt, Sutherland: Conservation Management Plan*, Unpublished Report for Historic Assynt, AOC 20867.

Ceron-Carrasco, R. 2006 The marine molluscs, with notes on the echinoidea remains and terrestrial snails. In I. Armit *Anatomy of an Iron Age Roundhouse The Cnip Wheelhouse Excavations, Lewis*, 180–2. Edinburgh, Society of Antiquaries of Scotland.

Chambers, F.M., Booth, R.K., De Vleeschouwer, F., Lamentowicz, M., Le Roux, G., Mauquoy, D., Nichols, J.E. and van Geel, B. 2012 Development and refinement of proxy-climate indicators from peats. *Quaternary International* 268, 21–33.

Charman, D.J. 2010 Centennial climate variability in the British Isles during the mid–late Holocene. *Quaternary Science Reviews* 29(13), 1539–1554.

Charman, D.J., Caseldine, C., Baker, A., Gearey, B., Hatton, J. and Proctor, C. 2001 Paleohydrological records from peat profiles and speleothems in Sutherland, Northwest Scotland. *Quaternary Research* 55(2), 223–34.

Charman, D.J., Barber, K.E., Blaauw, M., Langdon, P.G., Mauquoy, D., Daley, T.J., Hughes, P.D.M. and Karofeld, E. 2009 Climate drivers for peatland palaeoclimate records. *Quaternary Science Reviews* 28(19), 1811–19.

Charrié-Duhaut, A., Connan, J., Rouquette, N., Adam, P., Barbotin, C., de Rozières, M.F., Tchapla, A. and Albrecht, P. 2007 The canopic jars of Rameses II: real use revealed by molecular study of organic residues. *Journal of Archaeological Science* 34(6), 957–67

Charters, S., Evershed, R.P., Goad, L.J., Heron, C. and Blinkhorn, P. 1993 Identification of an adhesive used to repair a Roman jar. *Archaeometry* 35, 91–101.

Cheape, H. 1993 The 'straight spade' of the Highlands and Islands. in H. Cheape (ed.) *Tools and Traditions: studies in European ethnology presented to Alexander Fenton*, 76–84. Edinburgh, National Museums Scotland.

Childe, V.G. 1935 *The Prehistory of Scotland*. London, Keegan Paul.

Childe, V.G. 1936 Scottish tracked stones and their significance. *Proceedings of the Prehistoric Society* 2(2), 233–6.

Childe, V.G. 1946 *Scotland Before the Scots*. London, Methuen.

Chisholm, B.S., Nelson, D.E. and Schwarcz, H.P. 1982 Stable-carbon isotope ratios as a measure of marine versus terrestrial protein in ancient diets. *Science* 216, 1131–2.

Chittock, H. 2013 *A Useful Aesthetic: Re-examining the Aesthetic Effects of Weaving Combs from Glastonbury and Meare Lake Villages*. Unpublished MA thesis, University of Southampton.

Chittock, H. 2014 Arts and crafts in Iron Age Britain: reconsidering the aesthetic effects of weaving combs. *Oxford Journal of Archaeology* 33(3), 313–26.

Church, M. 2000 Carbonised plant macrofossils and charcoal. In D.W. Harding and T.N. Dixon, 120–30.

Church, M. and Cressey, M. 2006 Carbonized plant macrofossils and charcoal. In I. Armit (ed.), 182–94.

Church, M.J., Nesbitt, C. and Gilmour, S.M.D. 2013 A special place in the saltings? Survey and excavation of an Iron Age estuarine islet at An Dunan, Lewis, Western Isles. *Proceedings of the Society of Antiquaries of Scotland* 143, 157–226.

Clark, G. 1947 Whales as an economic factor in prehistoric Europe. *Antiquity* 82, 84–104.

Clarke, A. 1998 Stone. In L. Main, 377–89.

Clarke, A. 2006 *Stone Tools and the Prehistory of the Northern Isles*. Oxford, British Archaeological Reports British Series 406.

Clarke, A.D. 1960 Report on the animal remains. In A. Young and K.M. Richardson, Á Cheardach Mhor, Drimore, South Uist, *Proceedings of the Society of Antiquaries of Scotland* 93, 169–71.

Clarke, D.V. 1971 Small finds in the Atlantic Province: problems of approach. *Scottish Archaeological Forum* 3, 22–55.

Close-Brooks, J. 1972 Two steatite lamps. *Proceedings of the Society of Antiquareis of Scotland* 104, 295–7.

Close-Brooks, J. 1983 Dr Bersu's excavations at Traprain Law, 1947. In A. O'Connor and D.V. Clarke (eds.) *From the Stone Age to the 'Forty-Five*, 206–23. Edinburgh, John Donald.

Close-Brooks. J 1986 Excavations at Clatchard Craig, Fife. *Proceedings of the Society of Antiquaries of Scotland* 116, 117–84.

Close-Brooks, J. and Maxwell, S. 1974 The MacKenzie Collection. *Proceedings of the Society of Antiquaries of Scotland* 105, 287–93.

Cohen, A. and Serjeantson, D. 2015 *A Manual for the Identification of Bird Bone from Archaeological Sites*. London, Archetype (rev. edn).

Coles, J.M. 1987 *Meare Village East: The Excavations of A. Bulleid and H. St. George Gray 1932–1956, Somerset Levels Papers* 13. Exeter, Somerset Levels Project.

Conley, D.J. and Schelske, C.L. 2002 Biogenic Silica, in Smol, J.P., Birks, H.J.B. and Last, W.M. (eds.) *Tracking Environmental Change Using Lake Sediments. Developments in Paleoenvironmental Research. Volume 3: Terrestrial, Algal, and Siliceous Indicators*. Dordrecht, Springer, 281–293.

Copley, M.S., Hansel, F.A., Sadr, K. and Evershed, R.P. 2004 Organic residue evidence for the processing of marine animal products in pottery vessels from the pre-colonial archaeological site of Kasteelberg D east, South Africa, *South African Journal of Science* 100(5–6), 279–83.

Copley, M.S., Berstan, R., Dudd, S.N., Straker, V., Payne, S. and Evershed, R. 2005 Dairying in antiquity: evidence from absorbed lipid residues dating to the British Iron Age. *Journal of Archaeological Science* 32(4), 485–503.

Copley, M.S., Berstan, R., Dudd, S.N., Docherty, G., Mukherjee, A.J., Straker, V., Payne, S. and Evershed, R.P. 2003 Direct chemical evidence for widespread dairying in Prehistoric Britain. *Proceedings of the National Academy of Sciences of the United States of America* 100(4), 1524–9.

Correa-Ascencio, M. and Evershed, R.P. 2014 High throughput screening of organic residues in archaeological potsherds using direct acidified methanol extraction. *Analytical Methods* 6(5), 1330–40.

Coughtrey, M. 1872 Notes on materials found in a kitchen midden at Hillswick, Shetland, with special reference to long-handled combs. *Proceedings of the Society of Antiquaries of Scotland* 9, 118–51.

Courty, M.A, 1992 Soil micromorphology in archaeology. In M. Pollard (ed.), *New Developments in Archaeological Science*, 39–62. Oxford, Oxford University Press.

Courty, M., Goldberg, P. and Macphail, R. 1989 *Soils and Micromorphology in Archaeology*. Cambridge, Cambridge University Press.

Cowgill, J., de Neergaard, M. and Griffiths, N. 1987 *Medieval Finds from Excavations in London: 1. Knives and Scabbards*. London, H.M.S.O.

Cowley, D.C. 1999 Squaring the circle: domestic architecture in later prehistoric Sutherland and Caithness. In P. Frodsham, P. Topping and D.C. Cowley (eds.) *We Were Always Chasing Time: papers presented to Keith Blood, Northern Archaeology* (Special Edition) 17/18, 67–75.

Cowley, D. 2005. Architecture, landscape and the political geography of Iron Age Caithness and Sutherland. In V. Turner *et al.* (eds.), 180–9.

Cox, A. 2000 The artefacts. In D.R. Perry *Castle Park, Dunbar: Two Thousand Years on a Fortified Headland*, 113–78. Edinburgh, Society of Antiquaries of Scotland.

Cracknell, S. and Smith, B. 1983 Archaeological investigations at Mavis Grind, Shetland. *Glasgow Archaeological Journal* 10, 13–40.

Craig, O.E., Forster, M., Andersen, S.H., Koch, E., Crombe, P., Milner, N.J., Stern, B., Bailey, G.N. and Heron, C.P. 2007 Molecular and isotopic demonstration of the processing of aquatic products in northern European prehistoric pottery. *Archaeometry* 49, 135–52.

Cramp, L. and Evershed, R.P. 2013 Reconstructing aquatic resource exploitation in human prehistory using lipid biomarkers and stable isotopes. In T.E. Cerling (ed.) *Treatise on Geochemistry: archaeology and anthropology*, 319–9. Oxford: Elsevier

Cramp, L.J.E., Jones, J., Sheridan, A., Smyth, J., Whelton, H., Mulville, J., Sharples, N. and Evershed, R.P. 2014 Immediate replacement of fishing with dairying by the earliest farmers of the northeast Atlantic archipelagos. *Proceedings of the Royal Society B: Biological Sciences*, 281(1780), [20132372]. https://doi.org/10.1098/rspb.2013.2372

Crawford, I.A 1967 Whale bone artefacts and some recent finds in Berneray, Harris. *Scottish Studies* 11, 88–91.

Crawford R.A. 2018 *Into the Peatlands. A Journey through the Moorland Year*. Edinburgh, Birlinn.

Cressy, M. and Anderson, S. 2011 A later prehistoric settlement and metalworking site at Seafield West, near Inverness, Highland. *Scottish Archaeological Internet Reports* 47.

Crew, P. and Rehren, T. 2002 High temperature workshop residues from Tara: iron, bronze and glass. In H. Roche (ed.) *Excavations at Ráith na Ríg, Tara, Co. Meath, 1997*, 83–102. Discovery Programme Reports 6. Dublin, Royal Irish Academy.

Crone, B.A. 1993 A wooden bowl from Loch a' Ghlinne Bhig, Bracadale. *Proceedings of the Society of Antiquaries of Scotland* 123, 269–75.

Crone, A. 2000 *The History of a Scottish Lowland Crannog: Excavations at Buiston, Ayrshire 1989–90*. Scottish Trust for Archaeological Research Monograph 4. Loanhead, STAR.

Crone, A. 2008 The carbonised wood assemblage. In M. Cook and L. Dunbar *Rituals, Roundhouses and Romans; Excavations at Kintore 2000–2005. Vol. 1 Forest Rd*, 272–89. Scottish Trust for Archaeological Research Monograph 8. Loanhead, STAR.

Crone, A. 2012 Forging a chronological framework for Scottish crannogs: the dendrochronological evidence. In M. Midgeley and J. Sanders (eds.) *Lake Dwellings after Robert Munro*, 139–68. Leiden, Sidestone Press.

Crone, A. 2014 *Loch Paible, North Uist: The Waterlogged Wood Assemblage*. Unpublished report for SCAPE.

Crone, A., Cavers, G., Allison, E., Davies, K., Hamilton, D., Henderson, A., Mackay, H., McLaren, D., Robertson, J., Roy, L. and Whitehouse, N. 2018 Nasty, brutish and short? The life cycle of an Iron Age roundhouse at Black Loch of Myrton, SW Scotland. *Journal of Wetland Archaeology* 18(2), 138–62.

Cruickshanks, G.L. 2017 *Iron in Iron Age Scotland: A Long-Term Case Study of Production and Use c. 800 BC to AD 800*. Unpublished PhD thesis, University of Edinburgh.

Cruickshanks, G. and Hunter, F. 2020 Worked bone, antler, teeth and shell. In I. Armit and L. Büster *Darkness Visible. The Sculptor's Cave, Covesea, from the Bronze Age to the Picts*, 99–116. Edinburgh, Society of Antiquaries of Scotland.

Cunliffe, B. 1991 *Iron Age Communities in Britain*. London: Routledge

Cunliffe, B. 1984 *Danebury: An Iron Age Hillfort in Hampshire. Vol. 2, The Excavations: 1969–1978: The finds*. London, Council for British Archaeology Research Report 52.

Cunliffe, B. and Poole, C. 1991 *Danebury: An Iron Age Hillfort in Hampshire. Vol. 5, The Excavations: 1979–88: The finds*. London, Council for British Archaeology Research Report 73.

Curle, J. 1911 *A Roman Frontier Post and Its People: The Fort of Newstead in the Parish of Melrose*. Glasgow, Maclehose.

Curle, A.O. 1916 An account of the ruins of the broch of Dun Telve, near Glenelg, excavated by H.M. Office of Works in 1914. *Proceedings of the Society of Antiquaries of Scotland* 50, 241–54.

Curle, A.O. 1921. The Broch of Dun Troddan, Gleann Beag, Glenelg, Invernesshire. *Proceedings of the Society of Antiquaries of Scotland* 55, 83–94.

Curle, A.O. 1939 A Viking settlement at Freswick, Caithness. Report on the excavations carried out in 1937 and 1938. *Proceedings of the Society of Antiquaries of Scotland* 73, 71–110.

Curle, A.O. 1948 The 'Wag' of Forse, Caithness: excavations 1947–48. *Proceedings of the Society of Antiquaries of Scotland* 82 (1947–8), 275–86.

Curle, C. 1982 *Pictish and Norse Finds from the Brough of Birsay 1934–74*. Edinburgh, Society of Antiquaries of Scotland.

Curras, B.X. and Sastre, I. (eds.) 2020 *Alternative Iron Ages: Social Theory from Archaeological Analysis*. Abingdon, Routledge.

Cussans, J.E. 2010. Shellfish. In S.J. Dockrill, J.M. Bond, V.E. Turner, L.D. Brown, D. Bashford, J.E. Cussans and R.A. Nicholson *Excavations at Old Scatness, Shetland Vol. 1: The Pictish Village and Vicking Settlement*, 175–8. Lerwick, Shetland Heritage Publications.

Cussans, J.E. 2015. Shellfish. In S.J. Dockrill *et al.*, 249–50.

Cussans, J.E.M. and Bond, J.M. 2015. Mammal bone. In S.J. Dockrill *et al.*, 206–227.

Dalland, M. and MacSween, A. 1999 The coarse pottery. In O. Owen and C. Lowe (eds.), 178–200.

D'Anjou, R.M., Bradley, R.S., Balascio, N.L. and Finkelstein, D.B., 2012 Climate impacts on human settlement and agricultural activities in northern Norway revealed through sediment biogeochemistry. *Proceedings of the National Academy of Sciences* 109(50), 20332.

Davidson, P. 1998 Analysis of the deposits on sandstone mortars 302 & 473, in Main, L. Excavation of a timber round-house and broch at the Fairy Knowe, Bucklyvie, Stirlingshire, 1975-8, *Proc Soc Antiq Scot* 128, 293–417.

Davies, A.L. and Tipping, R. 2004 Sensing small-scale human activity in the palaeoecological record: fine spatial resolution pollen analyses from Glen Affric, northern Scotland. *The Holocene* 14(2), 233–45

Davies, S.J., Lamb, H.F. and Roberts, S.J. 2015 Micro–XRF core scanning in palaeolimnology: recent developments. In I.W. Croudace and R.G. Rothwell (eds.) *Micro-XRF Studies of Sediment Cores: Applications of a Non-Destructive Tool for the Environmental Sciences*, 189–226. London, Springer.

Dickson, C. 1994 Plant remains. In B. Ballin Smith (ed.), 125–39.

Dickson, C.A. and Dickson, J.H. 1984a The botany of the Crosskirk Broch Site In H. Fairhurst (ed.), 147–55.

Dickson, C. and Dickson, J. 2000. *Plants and People in Ancient Scotland*. Stroud, Tempus Publishing Ltd.

Dickson, J. 1992 North American driftwood, especially *Picea* (spruce) from archaeological sites in the Hebrides and Northern Isles of Scotland. *Review of Palaeobotany and Palynology* 73, 49–56.

Dixon, N. 2004 *The Crannogs of Scotland*. Stroud, Tempus.

Dixon, T.N. 1988 Eilean Domnhuill, Loch Olabhat: underwater excavations. *University of Edinburgh Department of Archaeology Annual Report* 35, 1988–9, 21–2

Djamali, M. and Cilleros, K. 2020 Statistically significant minimum pollen count in Quaternary pollen analysis; the case of pollen–rich lake sediments. *Review of Palaeobotany and Palynology* 275, 104156.

Dobney, K. and Ervynck, A. 2007 To fish or not to fish? Evidence for the possible avoidance of fish consumption during the Iron Age around the North Sea. In C. Haselgrove (ed.), *The Later Iron Age in Britain and Beyond*, 403–18. Oxford, Oxbow Books.

Dobney, K. and Rielly, K. 1988 A method for recording archaeological animal bones: the use of diagnostic zones. *Circaea* 5, 79–96.

Dockrill, S.J. 2007 *Investigations in Sanday, Orkney Vol 2: Tofts Ness, Sanday, An Island Landscape through 3000 Years of Prehistory*. Edinburgh.

Dockrill, S.J. and Bond, J.M. 2009. Sustainability and resilience in prehistoric North Atlantic Britain: the importance of a mixed paleoeconomic system. *Journal of the North Atlantic* 2, 33–50.

Dockrill, S., Outram, Z. and Batt, C. 2006. Time and place: a new chronology for the origin of the broch based on the scientific dating programme at the Old Scatness Broch, Shetland. *Proceedings of the Society of Antiquaries of Scotland* 136, 89–110.

Dockrill, S.J, Bond, J.M., Turner, V.E, Brown, L.D, Bashford, D.J, Cussans, J.E and Nicholson, R.A 2015 *Excavations at Old Scatness, Shetland Vol. 2: The Broch and Iron Age Village*. Lerwick, Shetland Heritage Publications.

Donnelly, E., Robertson, J. and Robinson, D. 2002 Potential and historical uses for bracken (*Pteridium aquilinum (L.) Kuhn*) in organic agriculture. In Powell, J (ed.) *UK Organic Research 2002: Proceedings of the COR Conference, 26–28th March 2002*, Aberystwyth; Aberdeen University Centre for Organic Agriculture 255–6; Available at https://orgprints.org/id/eprint/8312/1/Donnelly_Potential_historical_bracken.pdf

Downes, J. 2000 Site sequence and chronology. In J. Downes and R. Lamb, *Prehistoric Houses at Sumburgh in Shetland: Excavations at Sumburgh Airport 1967–74*, 35–76. Oxford, Oxbow Books.

Downes, J. and Ritchie, A. (eds.) 2003 *Sea Change: Orkney and Northern Europe in the Later Iron Age AD 300–800*. Balgavies, Pinkfoot Press.

Dryden, H. 1890 Notes of the brocks or "Pictish towers" of Mousa, Clickemin, Shetland, illustrative of part of the series of plans and sections deposited in the Library of the Society. *Archaeologica Scotica* 5, 199–212.

Dudd, S.N. and Evershed, R.P. 1998 Direct demonstration of milk as an element of archaeological economies. *Science* 282, 1478–81.

Duff, A. (ed.) 2018 *Checklist of Beetles of the British Isles*. Iver, Pemberley (3rd edition).

Dungworth D.B. 1995 *Iron Age and Roman Copper Alloys from Northern Britain*. Unpublished PhD thesis, University of Durham.

Dungworth, D.B. 1996 The production of copper alloys in Iron Age Britain. *Proceedings of the Prehistoric Society* 62, 399–421.

Dungworth, D.B. 1997 Iron Age and Roman copper alloys from northern Britain. *Internet Archaeology* 2. https://intarch.ac.uk/journal/issue2/dungworth_index.html. Accessed on 1/12/21.

Dungworth, D.B. 1999 The industrial waste. In M. Parker Pearson and N. Sharples, 230.

Dungworth, D.B. 2007 *Heckfield, Hampshire: An Examination of Middle Iron Age Smelting Slags*. Research Department Report 104/2007. London, English Heritage.

Dungworth, D. and McLaren, D. 2021 The manufacture of iron at Culduthel: ferrous metalworking debris and iron metallurgy. In C. Hatherley and R. Murray, *Culduthel: An Iron Age Craft Centre in North–East Scotland*, 142–67. Edinburgh, Society of Antiquaries of Scotland.

Dungworth, D.B. and Wilkes, R. 2009 Understanding hammerscale: the use of high–speed film and electron microscopy. *Historical Metallurgy* 43, 33–46.

Dunne, J., Evershed, R.P., Salque, M., Cramp, L., Bruni, S., Ryan, K., Biagetti, S. and di Lernia, S. 2012 First dairying in green Saharan Africa in the fifth millennium BC. *Nature* 486, 390–4.

Dunne, J., Gillard, T. and Evershed, R.P. 2019 *Organic Residue Analysis of East Barn Steatite Vessel for AOC Archaeology Group: Report*. Unpublished archive report produced by the Organic Geochemistry Unit, University of Bristol.

Dunning, G.C. 1934 The swan's neck and ring–headed pins of the Early Iron Age in Britain. *Archaeological Journal* 91, 269–95.

Dunwell, A. 1999 An Atlantic roundhouse at Durcha, Sutherland. *Proceedings of the Society of Antiquaries of Scotland* 129, 281–302.

Earwood, C. 1991 Two Early historic bog butter containers. *Proceedings of the Society of Antiquaries of Scotland* 121, 231–41.

Edwards, A.J.H. 1924 Report on the excavation of an earthhouse at Galson, Borve, Lewis. *Proceedings of the Society of Antiquaries of Scotland* 58, 185–203.

Edwards, K.J. and Whittington, G. 2001 Lake sediments, erosion and landscape change during the Holocene in Britain and Ireland. *Catena* 42(2–4), 143–73.

Edwards, K.J., Bennett, K.D. and Davies, A.L. 2019 Palaeoecological perspectives on Holocene environmental change in Scotland. *Earth and Environmental Science Transactions of the Royal Society of Edinburgh* 110(1–2), 199–217.

Edwards, K.J., Whittington, G., Robinson, M. and Richter, D. 2005 Palaeoenvironments, the archaeological record and cereal pollen detection at Clickimin, Shetland, Scotland. *Journal of Archaeological Science* 32(12), 1741–56.

Engl, R. and McLaren, D. 2016 The coarse stone. In M. Cook, Prehistoric settlement patterns in the north-east of Scotland: excavations at Grantown Road, Forres 2002–2013. *Scottish Archaeological Internet Reports* 61, 37–42. https://archaeologydataservice.ac.uk/archiveDS/archiveDownload?t=arch–310–1/dissemination/pdf/2056–742161_Grantown_Road.pdf. Accessed 12/11/2020.

Esper, J., Frank, D., Ulf, B., Anne, V., JГjrg, L. and Elena, X. 2007 Long–term drought severity variations in Morocco. *Geophysical Research Letters* 34(17), L17702–n/a.

Evans, C. 1989 Perishables and worldly goods: artefact decoration and classification in the light of wetlands research. *Oxford Journal of Archaeology* 8(2), 179–201.

Evans, P.A., Evans, I.M. and Rothero, G.P. 2002 *Flora of Assynt: flowering plants and ferns, Bryophytes*. Privately published, Evans & Evans.

Evershed, R.P. 1993 Biomolecular archaeology and lipids. *World Archaeology* 25(1), 74–93.

Evershed, R.P. 2008 Organic residue analysis in archaeology: the archaeological biomarker revolution *Archaeometry* 50(6), 895–924.

Evershed, R.P., Heron, C. and Goad, L.J. 1991 Epicuticular wax components preserved in potsherds as chemical indicators of leafy vegetables in ancient diets. *Antiquity* 65, 540–4.

Evershed, R.P., Copley, M.S., Dickson, L. and Hansel, F.A. 2008 Experimental evidence for the processing of marine animal products and other commodities containing polyunsaturated fatty acids in pottery vessels. *Archaeometry* 50(1), 101–13.

Evershed, R.P., Arnot, K.I., Collister, J., Eglinton, G. and Charters, S. 1994 Application of isotope ratio monitoring gas chromatography–mass spectrometry to the analysis of organic residues of archaeological origin. *The Analyst* 119, 909–14.

Evershed, R.P., Mottram, H.R., Dudd, S.N., Charters, S., Stott, A.W., Lawrence, G.J., Gibson, A.M., Conner, A., Blinkhorn, P.W. and Reeves, V. 1997a New criteria for the identification of animal fats preserved in archaeological pottery. *Naturwissenschaften* 84(9), 402–6.

Evershed, R.P., Vaughan, S.J., Dudd, S.N. and Soles, J.S. 1997b Fuel for thought? Beeswax in lamps and conical cups from late Minoan Crete. *Antiquity* 71, 979–85.

Fairhurst, H. 1971 The wheelhouse site Á Cheardach Bheag on Drimore machair, South Uist. *Glasgow Archaeological Journal* 2, 72–106.

Fairhurst, H. 1984. *Excavations at Crosskirk Broch, Caithness*. Edinburgh, Society of Antiquaries of Scotland, Monograph 3.

Farrell, M. 2015 Later prehistoric vegetation dynamics and Bronze Age agriculture at Hobbister, Orkney, Scotland. *Vegetation History and Archaeobotany* 24(4), 467–86.

Fenton, A. 1963 Early and traditional cultivating implements in Scotland. *Proceedings of the Society of Antiquaries of Scotland* 96, 264–317.

Fenton, A. 1968 Plough and spade in Dumfries and Galloway. *Transactions of the Dumfries and Galloway Natural History and Archaeology Society* 45, 147–83.

Fenton, A. 1973 Traditional elements in the diet of the Northern Isles of Scotland. *Ethnologische Nahrungsforschung Ethnological Food Research*, being *Kansatieteellinen Arkisto* 26, 2–16.

Fenton, A 1978 *The Northern Isles: Orkney and Shetland*. Edinburgh, John Donald Publishers Ltd.

Finlay, J.I. 1991 Animal bone. In E. Campbell, Excavation of a wheelhouse and other Iron Age structures at Sollas, North Uist. *Proceedings of the Society of Antiquaries of Scotland* 121, 147–8.

Fisher, R.A., Corbet, A.S. and Williams, C.B. 1943 The relation between the number of species and the number of individuals in a random sample of an animal population. *Journal of Animal Ecology* 12(1), 42–58.

Fojut, N. 2005a. Brochs and timber supply: a necessity born of invention. In V. Turner *et al*. (eds.), 190–201.

Fojut, N. 2005b. Towards a geography of Shetland brochs. In V. Turner *et al*. (eds.), 144–65.

Forster, A.K. 2009 Steatite use in the Middle and Later Iron Age: c. 500 BC to AD 800. In A.K. Forster and V.E. Turner (eds.) *Kleber: Shetland's Oldest Industry. Shetland Soapstone Since Prehistory*, 48–57. Lerwick, Shetland Amenity Trust.

Forster, A. and Jones R. 2017 From homeland to home. Using soapstone to map migration and settlement in the North Atlantic. In G. Hansen and P. Storemyr (eds.) *Soapstone in the North: quarries, products and people 7000 BC–AD 1700*, 225–48. Bergen, University of Bergen Archaeological Society.

Forster, A.K. and Turner, V.E. (ed.) 2009 *Kleber: Shetland's Oldest Industry. Shetland Soapstone Since Prehistory*. Lerwick: Shetland Amenity Trust.

Foster, S.M. 1990 Pins, combs and the chronology of later Atlantic Iron Age settlement. In I. Armit (ed.), 143–74.

Fowler, P.J. 1983 *The Farming of Prehistoric Britain*. Cambridge, Cambridge University Press.

Foxon, A. 1991 *Bone, Antler, Tooth and Horn Technology and Utilisation in Prehistoric Scotland*. Unpublished PhD thesis, University of Glasgow.

Freethy, R. 1987 *British Ferns*. Marlborough, The Crowood Press.

French, C 2003 *Geoarchaeology in Action. Studies in Soil Micromorphology and Landscape Evolution*. London, Routledge

Friesem, D.E., Tsartsidou, G., Karkanas, P. and Shahack-Gross, R. 2014 Where are the roofs? a geo-ethnoarchaeological study of mud structures and their collapse processes, focusing on the identification of roofs. *Archaeological and Anthropological Sciences* 6, 73–92.

Futty D.W. and Towers, W. 1982 *Northern Scotland Soil and Land Capability for Agriculture*. Handbooks of the Soil Survey of Scotland. Aberdeen, Macaulay Institute for Soil Research.

Froese, R. and Pauly, D. (eds.) 2019 *FishBase*. World Wide Web electronic publication. www.fishbase.org, Accessed 08/19.

Froyd, C.A. 2006 Holocene fire in the Scottish Highlands: evidence from macroscopic charcoal records. *Holocene (Sevenoaks)* 16(2), 235–49.

Gé, T., Courty, M.A., Matthews, W. and Wattez, J. 1993 Sedimentary formation processes of occupation surfaces. In P.Goldberg, D.T. Nash and M.D. Petraglia (eds.) *Formation Processes in Archaeological Contexts*, 49–163. Monographs in World Archaeology 17 Madison WI, Prehistory Press.

Geddes, G. 2006. Vernacular buildings of the Outer Hebrides 300 BC–AD 1930: temporal comparison using archaeological analysis. *Internet Archaeology* 19. Available at: https://doi.org/10.11141/ia.19.4. Accessed 1/12/21.

Giles, M. 2007 Making metal and forging relations: ironworking in the British Iron Age. *Oxford Journal of Archaeology* 26, 395–413.

Giles, M. 2008 Seeing red: the aesthetics of martial objects in the British and Irish Iron Age. In D. Garrow, C. Gosden and J.D. Hill (eds.) *Rethinking Celtic Art*, 59–77. Oxford, Oxbow Books.

Gilmour, S. 2005 Complex Atlantic roundhouses: chronology and complexity. In V. Turner *et al.* (eds.), 78–96.

Gilmour, S. and Cook, M. 1998 Excavations at Dun Vulan: a reinterpretation of the reappraised Iron Age. *Antiquity* 72, 327–37.

Glob, P.V. 1951 *Ard and Plough in Prehistoric Scandinavia*. Aarhus, Aarhus University Press.

Godwin, H. and Seward, A.C. 1940 Studies of the post-glacial history of British vegetation – III. Fenland pollen diagrams – IV. Post-glacial changes of relative land- and sea-level in the English Fenland. *Philosophical Transactions of the Royal Society of London B, Biological Sciences* 230(570), 239–303.

Goldberg, M. and Hunter, F. 2019 Objects made of iron and bone. In O. Lelong *Excavations at Milla Skerra, Sandwick, Unst: Rhythms of Life in Iron Age Shetland*, 107–11. Oxford, Oxbow Books.

Goodall, I.H. 2011 *Ironwork in Medieval Britain: An Archaeological Study*. London, Society for Medieval Archaeology Monograph 31.

Gourlay, R. 1996. *Sutherland: An Archaeological Guide*. Edinburgh.

Graeme, A.S. 1914 An account of the excavation of the broch of Ayre, St Mary's Holm, Orkney. *Proceedings of the Society of Antiquaries of Scotland* 49, 31–51.

Graham, A. 1949 Some observations on the brochs. *Proceedings of the Society of Antiquaries of Scotland* 81, 48–98.

Grant, A. 1982 The use of tooth wear as a guide to the age of domestic ungulates. In B. Wilson, C. Grigson and S. Payne (eds.) *Ageing and Sexing Animal Bones from Archaeological Sites*, 91–108. Oxford, British Archaeological Reports British Series 109.

Grant, I.F. 1961 *Highland Folk Ways*. London, Routledge.

Grant, W. 1842 United parishes of Cross and Burness. In Anon (ed.) *The Statistical Account of the Orkney Islands*, 85–113. Edinburgh, William Blackwood and Sons.

Grayson, D.K. 1984 *Quantitative Zooarchaeology*. New York, Academic Press.

Greenfield, H.J. 2006. Sexing fragmentary ungulate acetabulae. In D. Ruscillo (ed.) *Recent Advances in Aging and Sexing Animal Bones*, 68–86. Oxford, Oxbow Books.

Gregg, M.W., Banning, E.B., Gibbs, K. and Slater, G.F. 2009 Subsistence practices and pottery use in Neolithic Jordan: molecular and isotopic evidence. *Journal of Archaeological Science* 36(4), 937–46.

Gunstone, F. 2004 *The Chemistry of Oils and Fats: sources, composition, properties and uses*. Boca Raton FL, CRC Press.

Guttmann, E.B., Simpson, I.A., Nielsen, N. and Dockrill, S.J. 2008 Anthrosols in Iron Age Shetland: implications for arable and economic activity. *Geoarchaeology* 23(6), 799–823.

Hallén, Y. 1994 The use of bone and antler at Foshigarry and Bac Mhic Connain, two Iron Age sites on North Uist, Western Isles. *Proceedings of the Society of Antiquaries of Scotland* 124, 189–231.

Halmemies-Beauchet-Filleau, A., Vanhatalo, A., Toivonen, V., Heikkilä, T., Lee, M. and Shingfield, K. 2013 Effect of replacing grass silage with red clover silage on ruminal lipid metabolism in lactating cows fed diets containing a 60: 40 forage-to-concentrate ratio. *Journal of Dairy Science* 96(9), 5882–900.

Halmemies-Beauchet-Filleau, A., Vanhatalo, A., Toivonen, V., Heikkilä, T., Lee, M. and Shingfield, K. 2014 Effect of replacing grass silage with red clover silage on nutrient digestion, nitrogen metabolism, and milk fat composition in lactating cows fed diets containing a 60: 40 forage-to-concentrate ratio. *Journal of Dairy Science* 97(6), 3761–76.

Halstead, P. 2003 The animal bones from Baleshare and Hornish Point. In J. Barber, 142–8.

Hambleton, E. 1999 *Animal Husbandry Regimes in Iron Age Britain*. Oxford, Archaeopress.

Hamilton, C.A., Lloyd, J.M., Barlow, N.L.M., Innes, J.B., Flecker, R., Thomas, C.P., 2015. Late Glacial to Holocene relative sea-level change in Assynt, northwest Scotland, UK. *Quaternary Research* (United States) 84, 214–222.

Hamilton, J.R.C. 1956 *Excavations at Jarlshof, Shetland*. Edinburgh, HMSO.

Hamilton, J.R.C 1968 *Excavations at Clickhimin, Shetland*. Edinburgh, HMSO.

Hamilton-Dyer, S. 2006 Bird remains. In I. Armit, 172–3.

Hamlett, L.E. 2014 *Anthropic Sediments on the Scottish North Atlantic Seaboard: Nature, Versatility and Value of Midden*. Unpublished PhD thesis, University of Stirling.

Hansel, F.A. and Evershed, R.P. 2009 Formation of dihydroxy acids from Z-monounsaturated alkenoic acids and their use as biomarkers for the processing of marine commodities in archaeological pottery vessels. *Tetrahedron Letters* 50, 5562–4.

Hansel, F.A., Copley, M.S., Madureira, L.A.S. and Evershed, R.P. 2004 Thermally produced [omega]-(o-alkylphenyl) alkanoic acids provide evidence for the processing of marine products in archaeological pottery vessels. *Tetrahedron Letters* 45, 2999–3002.

Hanson, M.C. and Cain, C.R. 2007 Examining histology to identify burned bone. *Journal of Archaeological Science* 34, 1902–13.

Harding, D.W. 2000. *The Hebridean Iron Age: Twenty Years' Research.*, Edinburgh, University of Edinburgh, Dept of Archaeology Occasional Paper.

Harding, D.W. 2004 *The Iron Age in Northern Britain: Celts and Romans, Natives and Invaders*. London, Routledge.

Harding, D.W. 2005. The Atlantic Scottish Iron Age: external relations reviewed. In V. Turner *et al.* (eds.), 32–51.

Harding, D.W. 2009a Secondary occupation of Atlantic roundhouses: problems of identification and interpretation. In G. Cooney, K. Becker, J. Coles, M. Ryan and S. Sievers (eds.) *Relics of Old Decency: archaeological studies in later prehistory*, 471–84. Dublin, Wordwell.

Harding, D.W. 2009b *The Iron Age Roundhouse: Later Prehistoric Building in Britain and Beyond*. Oxford, Oxford University Press.

Harding, D.W. and Dixon, N. 2000 *Dun Bharabhat, Cnip. An Iron Age Settlement in West Lewis. Vol 1: The Structures and Material Culture*. Calanais Research Monograph 2. Edinburgh, University of Edinburgh.

Harding, D.W. and Gilmour, S. 2000. *The Iron Age Settlement at Beirgh, Riof, Isle of Lewis: Excavations 1985–1995. Vol. 1: The Structures and Stratigraphy*. Calanais Research Monograph. Edinburgh, University of Edinburgh.

Harkness, D.D. and Wilson, H.W. 1973 Scottish Universities Research and Reactor Centre Radiocarbon Measurements I. *Radiocarbon* 15(3), 554–65.

Harland, J.F. 2016 *Berst Ness Knowe of Skea: The Fish Remains*. Unpublished report for EASE Archaeology.

Harland, J.F. 2019 *Dunbeath Broch: The Fish Remains*. Unpublished report for AOC Archaeology, AOC 60097.

Harland, J.F. and Van Neer, W. 2018 Weird fish: defining a role for fish palaeopathology. In L. Bartosiewicz and E. Gal (eds.) *Care or Neglect? Evidence of Animal Disease in Archaeology*, 256–74. Oxford, Oxbow Books.

Harland, J.F., Barrett, J., Carrott, J., Dobney, K. and Jaques, J. 2003 The York System: an integrated zooarchaeological database for research and teaching. *Internet Archaeology*

13, https://intarch.ac.uk/journal/issue13/harland_index.html. Accessed 12/12/2021.

Hayward, P., Nelson-Smith, T. and Shields, C. 1996 *Seashore of Britain and Northern Europe*. New York, Harper Collins.

Heald, A. 2001 Knobbed spearbutts of the British and Irish Iron Age: new examples and new thoughts. *Antiquity* 75, 689–96.

Heald, A. and Barber, J. 2016 *Caithness Archaeology – Aspects of Prehistory*. Caithness, Whittles.

Heald, A. and Jackson A. 2001 Towards a new understanding of Iron Age Caithness. *Proceedings of the Society of Antiquaries of Scotland* 131, 129–47.

Heald, A. and Jackson, A. 2002 Caithness Archaeological Project: excavations at Everley broch, Freswick. *Antiquity* 76, 31–2.

Hedges, J.W. 1987 *Bu, Gurness and the Brochs of Orkney*. Oxford, British Archaeological Report 164.

Heiri, O., Lotter, A. and Lemcke, G. 2001 Loss on ignition as a method for estimating organic and carbonate content in sediments: reproducibility and comparability of results. *Journal of Paleolimnology* 25(1), 101–10.

Henderson, J.C. 2007 *The Atlantic Iron Age: Settlement and Identity in the First Millennium BC*. Oxford, Routledge.

Henshall, A.S. 1950 Textiles and weaving appliances in prehistoric Britain. *Proceedings of the Society of Antiquaries of Scotland* 16, 130–62.

Henshall, A.S. 1982 The finds. In D.B. Taylor, Excavation of a promontory fort, broch and souterrain at Hurly Hawkin, Angus. *Proceedings of the Society of Antiquaries of Scotland* 112, 225–44.

Heslop, D.H. 2008 *Patterns of Quern Production, Acquisition, and Deposition. A Corpus of Beehive Querns in Northern Yorkshire and Southern Durham*. Leeds, Yorkshire Archaeological Society Occasional Paper 6.

Hewer, H.R. 1974 *British Seals*. London, Collins.

Hillman, G. 1981. Reconstructing crop husbandry practices from charred remains of crops. In R. Mercer (ed.) *Farming Practice in British Prehistory*, 123–62. Edinburgh, Edinburgh University Press.

Hillson, S. 1986 *Teeth*. Cambridge, Cambridge University Press.

Hillson, S. 1992 *Mammal Bones and Teeth: An Introductory Guide to Methods of Identification*. London, University College London.

Hingley, R. 1992 Society in Scotland from 700 BC–AD 200. *Proceedings of the Society of Antiquaries of Scotland* 122, 7–53.

Hingley, R. 1997 Iron, ironworking and regeneration: a study of the symbolic meaning of metalworking in Iron Age Britain. In A. Gwilt and C. Haselgrove (eds.), *Reconstructing Iron Age Societies*, 9–18. Oxford, Oxbow Monographs 71.

Hingley, R. 2006 The deposition of iron objects in Britain during the later prehistoric and Roman periods: contextual analysis and the significance of iron. *Britannia* 37, 213–57.

Hodder, I. and Hedges, J.W. 1977 "Weaving combs": their typology and distribution with some introductory remarks on date and function. In J. Collis (ed.) *The Iron Age in Britain: A Review*, 17–28. Sheffield, Department of Prehistory and Archaeology, University of Sheffield.

Holden, T. 1998 Carbonised plant. In N. Sharples (ed.), 125–7.

Holden, T. and Boardman, S. 1998a Crops. In N. Sharples (ed.), 99–106

Holden, T. and Boardman, S. 1998b Carbonised plant. In N. Sharples (ed.), 125–7.

Howard, A.K. 1994. Marine molluscs. In B. Ballin Smith (ed.), 160–1.

Hubbard, C.E. 1984 *Grasses a Guide to Their Structure, Identification, Uses and Distribution in the British Isles*. London, Penguin Books (3rd edition).

Hubbard, R.N.L.B and al Azm, A. 1990. Quantifying preservation and distortion in carbonised seeds; and investigating the history of *friké* production. *Journal of Archaeological Science* 17, 103–6.

Hughes, P.D.M., Mauquoy, D., Barber, K.E. and Langdon, P.G. 2000 Mire-development pathways and palaeoclimatic records from a full Holocene peat archive at Walton Moss, Cumbria, England. *The Holocene* 10(4), 465–79.

Huntley, B., Daniell, J.R.G. and Allen, J.R.M. 1997 Scottish vegetation history: The Highlands. *Botanical Journal of Scotland* 49(2), 163–75.

Hunter, F. 1997 Iron Age hoarding in Scotland and northern England. In A. Gwilt and C. Haselgrove (eds.) *Reconstructing Iron Age Societies: New Approaches to the British Iron Age*, 108–33. Oxford, Oxbow Monographs 71.

Hunter, F. 1998 The iron In L. Main, 356–67.

Hunter, F. 2006a New light on Iron Age massive armlets. *Proceedings of the Society of Antiquaries of Scotland* 136, 135–160.

Hunter, F. 2006b The iron. In I. Armit, 154–5.

Hunter, F. 2007a Iron. In A. Dunwell (ed.) Cist Burials and an Iron Age Settlement and Dryburn Bridge, Innerwick, East Lothian. *Scottish Archaeological Internet Reports* 24, 79.

Hunter, F. 2007b Antler. In A. Dunwell, Cist burials and an Iron Age settlement at Dryburn Bridge, Innerwick, East Lothian. *Scottish Archaeological Internet Reports* 24, 79.

Hunter, F. 2007c Artefacts, regions and identity in the northern British Iron Age. In C. Haselgrove and T. Moore (eds.) *The Later Iron Age in Britain and Beyond*, 286–96. Oxford, Oxbow Books.

Hunter, F. 2015 Craft in context: artefact specialisation in later prehistoric Scotland. In F. Hunter and I. Ralston (eds.) *Scotland in Later Prehistoric Europe*, 225–46. Edinburgh, Society of Antiquaries of Scotland.

Hunter, F. and Carruthers, M. (eds.) 2012. *Iron Age Scotland: ScARF Panel Report*. Edinburgh, Society of Antiquaries of Scotland. Available at: https://scarf.scot/wp-content/uploads/sites/15/2015/12/ScARF%20Iron%20Age%20Sept%202012.pdf Iron Age Sept 2012.pdf, Accessed 1/12/21.

Hunter, F. and Heald, A. 2008 The metal finds. In M. Cook and L. Dunbar (eds.) *Rituals, Roundhouses and Romans: Excavations at Kintore, Aberdeenshire, 2000–2006*, 190–206. Scottish Trust for Archaeological Research. Edinburgh, STAR

Hunter, F., Gibson, A.M. and Gerken, J. 2013 The worked bone. In I. Armit and J. McKenzie *An Inherited Place. Broxmouth Hillfort and the South–East Scottish Iron Age*, 251–309. Edinburgh, Society of Antiquaries of Scotland.

Hunter, J. (ed.) 2007 *Investigations in Sanday, Orkney: Excavations at Pool, Sanday – A Multi–period Settlement from Neolithic to Late Norse Times, Vol. 1*. Kirkwall, Orcadian Association and Historic Scotland.

Hurrell, J.W. and Deser, C. 2009 North Atlantic climate variability: the role of the North Atlantic Oscillation. *Journal of Marine System*, 78(1), 28–41.

Hurrell, J., Kushnir, Y. and Ottersen, G. 2003 An overview of the North Atlantic Oscillation. In J.W. Hurrell, Kushnir, Y., Ottersen, G. and Visbeck, M. (eds) *The North Atlantic Oscillation: climatic significance and environmental impact*, 1–35. Washington DC. American Geophysical Union

Ilan, D. 2016 The ground stone components of drills in the ancient Near East: sockets, flywheels, cobble weights and drill bits. *Journal of Lithic Studies* 3, 261–77.

Jacomet, S. 2006. *Identification of Cereal Remains from Archaeological Sites*. Basel, Archaeobotany Lab IPAS, Basel University (2nd edition).

Jermy, C. and Tutin T.G. 1982 *Sedges of the British Isles*. London, Botanical Society of the British Isles Handbook 1.

Jessen, K. 1948 Studies in Late Quaternary deposits and flora-history of Ireland. *Proceedings of the Royal Irish Academy. Section B: Biological, Geological, and Chemical Science* 52, 85–290.

Joass, J.M. 1865. Two days' diggings in Sutherlandshire. *Proceedings of the Society of Antiquaries of Scotland* 5, 242–7.

Joass, J.M. and Aitken, T. 1890 The brochs or Pictish towers of Cinn–Trolla, Carnliath and Craig–Carril, in Sutherland, with notes on other northern brochs, with a report on the crania found in and about them. *Archaeologia Scotica* 5, 95–130.

Johnston, P. and Reilly, E. 2007 Plant and insect remains. In A. O'Sullivan, R. Sands and E.P. Kelly *Coolure Demesne Crannog, Lough Derravaragh: An Introduction to its Archaeology and Landscapes*, 55–62. Dublin, Wordwell.

Jones, G. 2003 The charred plant remains from Baleshare and Hornish Point. In J. Barber, 153–8.

Jones, R.E., Olive, V., Kilikoglou, V., Ellam, R., Bassiakos, Y., Bray, I. and Sanderson, D. 2007 A new protocol for the chemical characterisation of steatite: two case studies in Europe: the Shetland Isles and Crete. *Journal of Archaeological Science* 34, 626–41.

Karkanas P., Rigaud J-Ph., Simek J.F., Albert R.A., and Weiner S., 2002 Ash, bones and guano: a study of the minerals and phytoliths in the sediment of Grotte XVI, Dordogne, France. *Journal of Archaeological Science* 29, 721–32.

Kenward, H.K. 1975 The biological and archaeological implications of the beetle *Aglenus brunneus* (Gyllenhal) in ancient faunas. *Journal of Archaeological Science* 2, 63–9.

Kenward, H.K. 1997 Synanthropic decomposer insects and the size, remoteness and longevity of archaeological occupation sites: applying concepts from biogeography to past 'islands' of human occupation. In A.C. Ashworth, P.C. Buckland and J.T. Sadler (eds.) *Studies in Quaternary Entomology: an inordinate fondness for insects*, 135–52. *Quaternary Proceedings* 5.

Kenward, H.K. and Hall, A.R. 1995 *Biological Evidence from 16–22 Coppergate*. York, The Archaeology of York 14(7).

Kenward, H.K., Hall, A.R. and Jones, A.K.G. 1980 A tested set of techniques for the extraction of plant and animal macrofossils from waterlogged archaeological deposits. *Science and Archaeology* 22, 3–15.

Kenward, H.K., Hall, A.R. and Jones, A.K.G. 1986 *Environmental Evidence from a Roman Well and Anglian Pits in the Legionary Fortress*. London, Archaeology of York 14(5).

Kenward, H., Hall, A., Allison, E. and Carrott, J. 2011 Environment, activity and living conditions at Deer Park Farms: evidence from plant and invertebrate remains. In Lynn and McDowell 2011, 497–547.

Kilbride-Jones, H.E. 1980 *Celtic Craftsmanship in Bronze.* London, Taylor & Francis.

Kirk, W., Godwin, H. and Charlesworth, J.K. 1963 A Late-glacial Site at Loch Droma, Ross and Cromarty. *Transactions of the Royal Society of Edinburgh* 65(11), 225–49.

Kitchener, A.C. 1998 Extinctions, introductions and colonisations of Scottish mammals and birds since the last Ice Age. In R.A. Lambert (ed.) *Species History in Scotland*, 63–92. Edinburgh, Scottish Cultural Press.

Knowles, W.J. 1889 Tracked stones. *Journal Royal Historical and Archaeological Association of Ireland* 8:77, 497–502.

Kolattukudy, P.E. 1980 Biopolyester membranes of plants: cutin and suberin. *Science* 208, 990–1000.

Kolattukudy, P.E. 1981 Structure, biosynthesis, and biodegradation of cutin and suberin. *Annual Review of Plant Physiology and Plant Molecular Biology* 32, 539–67.

Kolattukudy, P.E., Croteau, R. and Buckner, J.S. 1976 Biochemistry of plant waxes. In P.E. Kolattukudy (ed.) *Chemistry and Biochemistry of Natural Waxes*, 289–347. Amsterdam: Elsevier

Kruuk, H. 2006 *Otters: Ecology, Behaviour and Conservation.* Oxford, Oxford University Press.

Kruuk, H., Carss, D.N., Conroy, J.W.H. and Gaywood, M.J. 1998. Habitat use and conservation of otters (*Lutra lutra*) in Britain: a review. In N. Dunstone and M.L. Gorman (eds.) *Behaviour and Ecology of Riparian Mammals*, 119–33. Cambridge, Cambridge University Press.

Kunst, L. and Samuels, A.L. 2003 Biosynthesis and secretion of plant cuticular wax. *Progress in Lipid Research* 42(1), 51–80.

Lamb, H.H. 1964 Trees and climatic history in Scotland. *Quarterly Journal of the Royal Meteorological Society* 90(386), 382–94.

Lambacher, N., Gerdau-Radonic, K., Bonthorne, E. and Valle de Tarazaga Montero, F.J. 2016 Evaluating three methods to estimate the number of individuals from a commingled context. *Journal of Archaeological Science Reports* 10, 674–83.

Lambrick, G. and Robinson, M. 1979 *Iron Age and Roman Riverside Settlements at Farmoor, Oxfordshire.* London, Oxford Archaeological Unit Report 2/Council for British Archaeology Research Report 32

Lane, A. 1987 English migrants in the Hebrides: 'Atlantic Second B' revisited. *Proceedings of the Society of Antiquaries of Scotland* 117, 47–66.

Lane, A. 1990 Hebridean pottery: problems of definition, chronology, presence and absence. In I. Armit (ed.), 108–30.

Lane, A. 2012 The Hebridean ceramic sequence. In N. Sharples (ed.), 20–21.

Lane, A. and Campbell, E. 2000 *Dunadd: An Early Dalriadic Capital.* Oxford, Oxbow Books.

Langdon, P.G. and Barber, K.E. 2005 The climate of Scotland over the last 5000 years inferred from multiproxy peatland records: inter-site correlations and regional variability. *Journal of Quaternary Science* 20(6), 549–66.

LaTrobe-Bateman, E. 1999 The pottery. In M. Parker Pearson and N. Sharples (eds.), 211–17.

LeQuesne, W.J. 1965 *Hemiptera Cicadomorpha (excluding Deltocephalinae and Typhlocybinae).* Handbooks for the Identification of British Insects 2(2a). London, Royal Entomological Society

Lethbridge, T.C. 1952 Excavations at Kilpheder, South Uist, and the problem of Brochs and Wheelhouses. *Proceedings of the Prehistoric Society* (NS) 18(2), 176–93.

Levi-Strauss, C. 1982 *The Way of the Masks.* Seattle WA, Washington Press.

Lindbo D.L., Stolt M.H. and Vepraskas M.J. 2010 Redoximorphic features. In Stoops *et al.* (eds.), 129–47.

Linford, J. 2009 *A Concise Guide to Trees.* Bicester, Baker and Taylor.

Ljungqvist, F.C. 2010 A new reconstruction of temperature variability in the extratropical northern hemisphere during the last two millennia. *Geografiska Annaler: Series A, Physical Geography* 92(3), 339–51.

Long, A. and Rippeteau, B. 1974 Testing contemporaneity and averaging radiocarbon dates. *American Antiquity* 39(2), 205–15. Available at: http://www.jstor.org/stable/279583

Lousley, J.E. and Kent D.H. 1981. *Docks and Knotweeds of the British Isles.* London, Botanical Society of the British Isles Handbook 3.

Low, G. 1813 *Fauna Orcadensis or The Natural History of the Quadrupeds, Birds, Reptiles, and Fishes of Orkney and Shetland.* Edinburgh, Archibald Constable and Company.

Lowther, P. 2000 Bone and antler artefacts. In C. Haselgrove and R. McCullagh (eds.) *An Iron Age Coastal Community in East Lothian: The excavation of Two Later Prehistoric Enclosure Complexes at Fishers Road, Port Seton, 1994–5*, 138–40. Edinburgh, STAR.

Lynn, C. J. 1988 Ulster's oldest wooden houses: Deer Park Farms, Co. Antrim. In A. Hamlin and C.J. Lynn (eds.) *Pieces of the Past: archaeological excavations by the Department of the Environment Northern Ireland.* Belfast, HMSO.

Lynn, C. J. and McDowell, J.A. 2011 *Deer Park Farms; The Excavation of a Raised Rath in the Glenarm Valley, Co. Antrim.* Northern Ireland Archaeological Monographs 9. Antrim, Stationery Office/Environmental Heritage Service.

MacGregor, A. 1974 The Broch of Burrian, North Ronaldsay, Orkney. *Proceedings of the Society of Antiquaries of Scotland* 105, 63–118.

MacGregor, A. 1985 *Bone, Antler, Ivory and Horn. The Technology of Skeletal Material since the Roman Period.* London, Croom Helm.

Mackay, J. 1892 Notice of the excavation of the Broch at Ousdale, Caithness. *Proceedings of the Society of Antiquaries of Scotland* 26, 351–7.

Mackay, H., Davies, K.L., Robertson, J., Roy, L., Bull, I.D., Whitehouse, N.J., Crone, A., Cavers, G., McCormick, F., Brown, A.G. and Henderson, A.C.G. 2020 Characterising life in settlements and structures: Incorporating faecal lipid biomarkers within a multiproxy case study of a wetland village. *J. Archaeol. Sci.* 121, 105202. https://doi.org/10.1016/j.jas.2020.105202

Mackenzie, W. 1795 Parish of Assint. In J. Sinclair (ed.) *The Statistical Account of Scotland*, 163–211. Edinburgh, William Creech.

MacKenzie, W.S and Adams A.E. 1994. *A Colour Atlas of Rocks and Minerals in Thin Section.* London, Manson.

MacKie E.W. 1963 A dwelling site of the earlier Iron Age at Balevullin, Tiree, excavated in 1912 by A. Henderson Bishop. *Proceedings of the Society of Antiquaries of Scotland* 96, 156–83.

MacKie, E.W. 1965a *Excavations on Two Galleried Duns on Skye in 1965: Interim Report.*

MacKie, E.W. 1965b The origin and development of the broch and wheelhouse building cultures of the Scottish Iron Age. *Proceedings of the Prehistoric Society* 31(7), 93–146.

MacKie, E.W. 1966 Iron Age pottery from the Gress Lodge Earth-house, Stornoway, Lewis. *Proceedings of the Society of Antiquaries of Scotland* 98, 199.

MacKie, E.W. 1969 Radiocarbon dates and the Scottish Iron Age. *Antiquity* 43, 15–26.

MacKie, E.W. 1971 English migrants and Scottish brochs. *Glasgow Archaeological Journal* 2, 39–71.

MacKie, E.W. 1972 Some new quernstones from brochs and duns. *Proceedings of the Society of Antiquaries of Scotland* 104, 137–46.

MacKie, E.W. 1974 *Dun Mor Vaul: An Iron Age Broch on Tiree.* Glasgow, University of Glasgow Press.

MacKie, E.W. 1980. Dun an Ruigh Ruaidh, Loch Broom, Ross & Cromarty Excavations in 1968 and 1978. *Glasgow Archaeological Journal* 7(1), 32–79.

MacKie, E.W. 1987 Impact on the Scottish Iron Age of the discoveries at Leckie Broch. *Glasgow Archaeological Journal* 14, 1–18.

MacKie, E.W. 1997 Dun Mor Vaul revisited: fact and theory in the reappraisal of the Scottish Atlantic Iron Age. In G. Ritchie (ed.) *The Archaeology of Argyll*, 141–80. Edinburgh, Edinburgh University Press.

MacKie, E.W. 2000a Excavations at Dun Ardtreck, Skye, in 1964 and 1965. *Proceedings of the Society of Antiquaries of Scotland* 130, 301–411.

MacKie, E.W. 2000b The Scottish Atlantic Iron Age: indigenous and isolated or part of a wider European world? In J. Henderson (ed.) *The Prehistory and Early History of Atlantic Europe*, 99–116. Oxford, British Archaeological Report S861.

MacKie, E.W. 2002 *The Roundhouses, Brochs and Wheelhouses of Atlantic Scotland c. 700BC–AD500: Architecture and Material Culture Part 1 – The Orkney and Shetland Isles.* Oxford, British Archaeological Report 342.

MacKie, E.W. 2005 Scottish brochs at the start of the new millennium. In V. Turner *et al.* (eds.), 11–31.

MacKie, E.W. 2007a Rotary quernstones. In W.S. Hanson, K. Speller, P. Yeoman and J. Terry (eds.) *Elginhaugh: A Flavian fort and its annexe*, 491–509. London, Society for the Promotion of Roman Studies Monograph 23.

MacKie, E.W. 2007b *The Roundhouses, Brochs and Wheelhouses of Atlantic Scotland c. 700 BC–AD 500: architecture and material culture, the northern and southern mainland and the Western Islands.* Oxford, British Archaeological Report 444.

MacKie, E.W. 2008 The broch cultures of Atlantic Scotland: origins, high noon and decline. Part 1: Early Iron Age beginnings *c.*700–200 BC. *Oxford Journal of Archaeology* 27(3), 261–79.

MacKie, E.W. 2010. The broch cultures of Atlantic Scotland. Part 2: The Middle Iron Age: high noon and decline *c.*200 BC–AD 550. *Oxford Journal of Archaeology* 29(1), 89–117.

MacKie, E.W. 2016 *Brochs and the Empire: The Impact of Rome on Iron Age Scotland as Seen in the Leckie Broch Excavations.* Oxford, Archaeopress.

MacLeod, F.T. 1915 Notes on Dun an Iardhard, a broch near Dunvegan excavated by Countess Vincent Baillet de Latour, Uiginish Lodge, Skye. *Proceedings of the Society of Antiquaries of Scotland* 49, 57–70.

MacPhail, R.I. and Goldberg, P. 2010 Archaeological materials. In Stoops *et al.* (eds.), 589–622.

Macphail, R.I., Cruise, G.M., Allen, M.J., Linderholm, J. and Reynolds, P. 2004 Archaeological soil and pollen analysis of experimental floor deposits; with special reference to Butser Ancient Farm, Hampshire, UK. *Journal of Archaeological Science* 31, 175–91.

MacSween, A. 1998a The coarse pottery. In C. Lowe (ed.) *Coastal Erosion and the Archaeological Assessment of an Eroding Shoreline at St Boniface Church, Papa Westray, Orkney*, 125–33. Stroud, Sutton.

MacSween, A. 1998b Ceramics. In N. Sharples, 132–6.

MacSween, A. 2002 Dun Beag and the role of pottery in interpretations of the Hebridean Iron Age. In B. Ballin Smith and I. Banks, 145–52.

MacSween, A. 2003 The coarse pottery from Balelone, Baleshare, Hornish Point, South Glendale and Newtonferry. In J. Barber (ed.), 126–33.

MacSween, A. 2006 Pottery. In I. Armit, 88–131.

MacSween, A. 2014 The pottery. In H. Moore and G. Wilson, 123–37.

MacSween, A. and Johnson, M. 2013 Pottery. In M.J. Church, C. Nesbitt and S.M.D. Gilmour, 177–83.

Main, L. 1998 Excavation of a timber round-house and broch at the Fairy Knowe, Buchlyvie, Stirlingshire, 1975–8. *Proceedings of the Society of Antiquaries of Scotland* 128, 293–419.

Malinsky-Buller, A., Hovers, E. and Marder, O. 2011 Making time: 'living floors', 'palimpsests' and site formation processes – a perspective from the open-air Lower Paleolithic site of Revadim Quarry, *Israel. Journal of Anthropological Archaeology* 30, 89–101.

Manning, W.H. 1981 Native and Roman metalwork in north Britain: a question of origins and influences. *Scottish Archaeological Forum* 11, 52–61.

Manning, W.H. 1985 *Catalogue of the Romano–British Iron Tools, Fittings and Weapons in the British Museum.* London, British Museum Press.

Manning, W.H. and Saunders, S. 1972 A Socketed Iron Axe from Maids Moreton, Buckinghamshire, with a Note on the Type, *Antiquaries Journal* 52(2), 276–92.

Martlew, R. 1985 The excavation of Dun Flodigarry, Staffin, Isle of Skye. *Glasgow Archaeological Journal* 12, 30–48.

Martynoga, F. 2012 *A Handbook of Scotland's Trees.* Glasgow, Saraband. (2nd edn.)

Mauquoy, D., Yeloff, D., Van Geel, B., Charman, D.J. and Blundell, A. 2008 Two decadally resolved records from north-west European peat bogs show rapid climate changes associated with solar variability during the mid–late Holocene. *Journal of Quaternary Science* 23(8), 745–63.

Mayyas, A.S., Khrisat, B.R., Hoffman, T. and El Khalili, M.M. 2017 Fuel for lamps: organic residues preserved in Iron Age lamps excavated at the site of Sahab in Jordon. *Archaeometry* 59(5), 934–48.

McCartney, E. 1984 Analysis of faunal remains. In H. Fairhurst, 133–47.

McCloy, J.S., Marcial, J., Clarke, J., Ahmadzadeh, M., Wolff, J., Vicenzi, E., Bollinger, D.L., Ogenhall, E., Englund, M., Pearce, C.I., Sjöblom, R. and Kruger, A.A. 2021 Reproduction of melting behavior for vitrified hillforts based on amphibolite, granite, and basalt lithologies. *Scientific Reports* 11(1), 1272. https://www.nature.com/articles/s41598–020–80485–w, Accessed 01/12/2021.

McCormick, F. 2006 Animal bone. In I. Armit, 161–73.

McCullagh, R.P.J. and Tipping, R. 1998 *The Lairg Project 1988–1996: The Evolution of an Archaeological Landscape in Northern Scotland.* Scottish Trust for Archaeological Research Monograph 3, Edinburgh, STAR.

McDonnell, J.G. 1994 Slag report. In B. Ballin Smith (ed.), 228–34.

McDonnell, J.G. 1998 Irons in the fire – evidence of ironworking on broch sites. In R.A. Nicholson and S.J. Dockrill (eds.), *Old Scatness Broch, Shetland: Retrospect and Prospect,* 150–62. Bradford, North Atlantic Biocultural Organisation Monograph 2/Bradford Archaeological Sciences Res 5.

McDonnell, J.G. 2000 Ironworking and other residues. In A. Lane and E. Campbell, 218–20.

McDonnell, J.G. and Dockrill, S.J. 2005 Cutting edge – the search for the Iron Age metals economy. In V. Turner *et al.* (eds.), 202–10.

McIlfatrick, O. 2013 *The Iron Age Pottery of Northern and Western Mainland Scotland and the Small Isles during the Long Iron Age: Typology and Aspects of Ceramic Social Narrative.* Unpublished PhD Thesis, University of Edinburgh.

McLaren, D. 2013 The rotary quern stones. In I. Armit and J. McKenzie, 309–30

McLaren, D. 2019 Ferrous metalworking: vitrified material. In D. Griffiths, J. Harrison and M. Athanson 2019 *Beside the Ocean: coastal Landscapes at the Bay of Skaill, Marwick, and Birsay Bay, Orkney: Archaeological Research 2003–18,* 215–24. Oxford, Oxbow Books.

McLaren, D. and Heald, A. 2006 The vitrified material. In I. Armit, 155–8.

McLaren, D. and Hunter, F. 2008 New aspects of rotary querns in Scotland. *Proceedings of the Society of Antiquaries of Scotland* 138, 105–28.

McLaren, D. and Hunter, F. 2014 The stone objects [Burland]. In Moore and Wilson, 284–305.

Meyers, P.A. and Teranes, J.L. 2001 Sediment organic matter. In W. Last and J. Smol (eds.) *Tracking Environmental Change Using Lake Sediments Volume 2: physical and geochemical methods,* 239–69. Dordrecht, Springer.

Miket, R. 2002 The souterrains of Skye. In B. Ballin Smith and I. Banks, 77–110.

Milek, K.B. 2012a Floor formation processes and the interpretation of site activity areas: an ethnoarchaeological study of turf buildings at Thverá, northeast Iceland. *Journal of Anthropology and Archaeology* 31, 119–37.

Milek K.B. 2012b Micromorphology. In N. Sharples (ed.), 54–61.

Miller, J. 2002 The Oakbank crannog: building a house of plants. In B. Ballin Smith and I. Banks, 35–43.

Mills, J.S. and White, R. 1977 Natural resins of art and archaeology: their sources, chemistry, and identification. *Studies in Conservation* 22(1), 12–31.

Moar, N.T. 1969 A Radiocarbon-dated pollen diagram from North-West Scotland. *New Phytologist* 68(1), 209–14.

Moore, H. and Wilson, G. 2014 *Ebbing Shores. Survey and Excavation of Coastal Archaeology in Shetland 1995–2008.* Edinburgh, Historic Scotland Archaeology Report 8.

Mortimer, C. 2000 Technological materials. In K. Branigan and P. Foster *From Barra to Berneray,* 270–1. Sheffield Environmental and Archaeological Research Campaign in the Hebrides 3. Sheffield, Sheffield University.

Mottram, H.R., Dudd, S.N., Lawrence, G.J., Stott, A.W. and Evershed, R.P. 1999 New chromatographic, mass spectrometric and stable isotope approaches to the classification of degraded animal fats preserved in archaeological pottery. Journal of Chromatography A 833(2), 209–21.

Mukherjee, A.J. 2004 The importance of pigs in the later British Neolithic: integrating stable isotope evidence from lipid residues in archaeological potsherds, animal bone, and modern animal tissues. Unpublished PhD thesis, University of Bristol

Mukherjee, A.J., Copley, M.S., Berstan, R., Clark, K.A. and Evershed, R.P. 2005 Interpretation of $\delta^{13}C$ values of fatty acids in relation to animal husbandry, food processing and consumption in prehistory. In J. Mulville and A. Outram (eds) *The Zooarchaeology of Milk and Fats,* 77–93. Oxford: Oxbow Books.

Mulville, J. 1999 The mammal bones. In M. Parker Pearson and N. Sharples, 210–11.

Mulville, J. 2002 The role of Cetacea in prehistoric and historic Atlantic Scotland. *International Journal of Osteoarchaeology* 12, 34–48.

Mulville, J., and Thoms, J. 2005 Animals and ambiguity in the Iron Age of the Western Isles. In V. Turner *et al.* (eds.), 235–44.

Munro, R. 1882 *Ancient Scottish Lake-dwellings or Crannogs: with a supplementary chapter on remains of lake dwellings in England.* Edinburgh.

Murphy, C.P. 1986 *Thin Section Preparation of Soils and Sediments.* Berkhamsted, AB Academic.

Murray, H. 1979 Documentary evidence for domestic buildings in Ireland *c.* 400–1200 in the light of archaeology. *Medieval Archaeology* 23, 81–97.

Naismith, R.S. 1962 A night at the Kuithes. *Scots Magazine,* 531–3.

Neighbour, T. 2000 Artificial platforms of possible Iron Age or Dark Age date on Dùn Mór, Dornie, Skye and Lochalsh. *Proceedings of the Society of Antiquaries of Scotland* 130, 283–300.

Nesbitt, C., Church, M.J. and Gilmour, S.M.D. 2011 Domestic, industrial, (en)closed? Survey and excavation of a Late Bronze Age/Early Iron Age promontory enclosure at Gob Eirer, Lewis, Western Isles. *Proceedings of the Society of Antiquaries of Scotland* 141, 31–74.

Newton, A.J. 2000 Two fragments of pumice. In E.W. MacKie 2000a, 405–6

Newton, A.J. and Dugmore, A.J. 2003 Analysis of the pumice from Baleshare. In J. Barber, 135–8.

Nicholson, R.A. 2000 Otter (*Lutra lutra* L.) spraint: an investigation into possible sources of small fish bones at coastal archaeological sites. In J.P. Huntley and S.M. Stallibrass (eds.) *Interpretation and Taphonomy in Environmental Archaeology*, 55–64. Oxford, Oxbow Books.

Nicholson, R.A. 2007 Marine molluscs In S.J. Dockrill, 227–8.

Nicholson, R.A. 2015a. Fish remains from Bronze Age and Iron Age deposits (Phases 2–6). In S.J. Dockrill *et al.*, 228–38.

Nicholson, R.A. 2015b. Bird bones from Bronze Age and Iron Age deposits In S.J. Dockrill *et al.* 239–45.

Nicholson, R.A and Davis, G. 2007 Mammal bones. In S.J. Dockrill, 169–95.

Noddle, B.A. 1980 Animal bones from Dun Cul Bhuirg. In J.N.G. Ritchie and A. Lane Dun Cul Bhuirg, Iona, Argyll. *Proceeding of the Society of Antiquaries of Scotland* 110, 209–29.

O'Brien, R. 2010 Spindle-whorls and hand-spinning in Ireland. In M. Stanley, E. Danaher and J. Eogan (eds.) *Creative Minds: Production, Manufacturing and Invention in Ancient Ireland*, 15–26. Dublin, National Roads Authority.

O'Connor, T. 2004. *The Archaeology of Animal Bones*. Stroud, Sutton.

O'Sullivan, T. 1988 Birds. In N. Sharples, 116–17.

O'Sullivan, T. 1998 Mammals. In N. Sharples, 127–30.

Olsen, J., Anderson, N.J. and Knudsen, M.F. 2012 Variability of the North Atlantic Oscillation over the past 5,200 years. *Nature Geoscience* 5(11), 808–12.

Ordnance Survey, *Name Book 1848–1878*. Object Name Books of the Ordnance Survey (6 inch and 1/2500 scale), Book 18, 102.

Ottoway, P. 1992 *Anglo-Scandinavian Ironwork from Coppergate*. Archaeology of York 17/6. York, Council for British Archaeology.

Outram, A.K., Stear, N.A., Bendrey, R., Olsen, S., Kasparov, A., Zaibert, V., Thorpe, N. and Evershed, R.P. 2009 The earliest horse harnessing and milking. *Science* 323, 1332–5.

Owen, O. and Lowe, C. 1999 *Kebister: the four-thousand-year-old story of one Shetland Township*. Edinburgh, Society of Antiquaries of Scotland Monograph 14.

Pálsson, H. and Edwards, P. 1978 *The Orkneyinga Saga: The History of the Earls of Orkney*. Harmondsworth, Penguin.

Parker Pearson, M. 1999 Summary of ceramic phases. In M. Parker Pearson and N. Sharples, 210–11.

Parker Pearson, M. 2014a The stone tools. In M. Parker Pearson and M. Zvelebil, 139–44.

Parker Pearson, M. 2014b Bone, ivory and antler tools and ornaments. In M. Parker Pearson and M. Zvelebil

Parker Pearson, M. and Sharples, N. 1999 *Between Land and Sea. Excavations at Dun Vulan, South Uist. Sheffield Environmental and Archaeological Research Campaign in the Hebrides*. Sheffield, Sheffield Academic Press.

Parker Pearson, M and Zvelebil, M. 2014 *Excavations at Cill Donnain: A Bronze Age settlement and Iron Age wheelhouse in South Uist*. Oxford, Oxbow Books.

Parker Pearson, M., Mulville, J., Smith, H. and Marshall, P. 2021 *Cladh Hallan: roundhouses and the dead in the Hebridean Bronze and Iron Ages, Part 1 – stratigraphy, spatial organisation and chronology*. Oxford, Oxbow Books.

Paterson, J.W. 1922 The Broch of Mousa: a survey by HM Office of Works. *Proceedings of the Society of Antiquaries of Scotland* 56, 172–83.

Patterson, R.T., Wright, C., Chang, A.S., Taylor, L.A., Lyons, P.D., Dallimore, A. and Kumar, A. 2002. British Columbia fish-scale atlas. *Palaeontologia Electronica* 4(1).

Payne, F.G. 1947 The plough in ancient Britain. *Archaeological Journal* 104, 82–111.

Payne, S. 1973 Kill–off patterns in sheep/goat and goats: the mandibles from Asvan Kale. *Anatolian Studies* 23, 281–303.

Payne, S. 1985. Morphological distinctions between the mandibular teeth of young sheep, Ovis, and goats, Capris. *Journal of Archaeological Science* 12, 139–47.

Payne, S. 1987 Reference codes for wear stages in the mandibular cheek teeth of sheep and goats. *Journal of Archaeological Science* 14, 609–14.

Peacock, D. 2013 *The Stone of Life. Querns, Mills and Flour Production in Europe up to c. AD 500*. Southampton, Highfield Press.

Pennington, W. 1995 Vegetation changes. In T.J. Lawson (ed.) *The Quaternary of Assynt and Coigach: Field Guide*, 104–31. Cambridge, Quaternary Research Association.

Pennington, W. and Bonny, A.P. 1970 Absolute pollen diagram from the British Late-Glacial. *Nature* 226, 871–3.

Pennington, W. and Godwin, H. 1947 Studies of the post-glacial history of British vegetation VII. Lake sediments: pollen diagrams from the bottom deposits of the north basin of Windermere. *Philosophical Transactions of the Royal Society of London B: Biological Sciences* 233, 137–75.

Pennington, W., Bonny, A.P., Lishman, J.P. and Haworth, E.Y. 1972 Lake sediments in northern Scotland, *Philosophical Transactions of the Royal Society B: Biological Sciences* 264, 191–294.

Peteranna, M. 2012 *Applecross Broch Community Archaeology Project 2006–2010*. Unpublished Data Structure Report Accessible on-line: https://her.highland.gov.uk/api/LibraryLinkWebServiceProxy/FetchResource/261558/full_261558.pdf, accessed 12/4/2022.

Photos–Jones, E. 2000 Metallurgical analysis of ferrous industrial waste and a shaft–hole axe from Dun Ardtreck. In E.W. MacKie, Excavations at Dun Ardreck, Skye, in 1964 and 1965. *Proceedings of the Society of Antiquaries of Scotland* 130, 399–405.

Piggott, C.M. 1953 Milton Loch crannog I: a native house of the 2nd century ad in Kirkcudbrightshire. *Proceedings of the Society of Antiquaries of Scotland* 87, 134–52.

Piggott, S. 1953 Three Metal–work Hoards of the Roman Period from Southern Scotland. *Proceedings of the Society of Antiquaries of Scotland* 87, 1–51.

Pollard, M., Beisson, F., Li, Y. and Ohlrogge, J.B. 2008 Building lipid barriers: biosynthesis of cutin and suberin. *Trends in Plant Science* 13(5), 236–46.

Pope, R. 2003 *Prehistoric Dwelling. Circular Structures in North and Central Britain c. 2500 BC–AD 500*. Unpublished PhD thesis, University of Durham.

Proctor, C., Baker, A. and Barnes, W. 2002 A three thousand year record of North Atlantic climate. *Climate Dynamics* 19(5), 449–54.

Proctor, C.J., Baker, A., Barnes, W.L. and Gilmour, M.A. 2000 A thousand year speleothem proxy record of North Atlantic climate from Scotland. *Climate Dynamics*, 16(10), 815–20.

PSAS 1960 Donations to and purchases for the museum. *Proceedings of the Society of Antiquaries of Scotland* 93, 252–62.

Raftery, B. 1996 *Trackway Excavation in the Mountdillon Bogs, Co. Longford, 1985–1991*. Irish Archaeological Wetland Unit Transactions 3. Dublin, University College Dublin.

Ralston, I. and Inglis, R. 1984 *Foul Hordes: The Picts in the north–east and their background*. Aberdeen, University of Aberdeen Anthropological Museum.

Ramat, A.G., Mauri, C. and Molinelli, P. 2013 *Synchrony and Diachrony: Introduction to a dynamic interface*. Philadelphia PA, John Benjamins North America.

Rasmussen, M.E. 2007 *Iron Age Houses in Flames*. Lejre, Lejre Historical-Archaeological Experimental Centre.

RCAHMS 1911 *The Royal Commission on the Ancient and Historical Monuments and Constructions of Scotland: Second report and inventory of monuments and constructions in the county of Sutherland*. Edinburgh, RCAHMS.

Rees, S.E. 1979 *Agricultural Implements in Prehistoric Britain*. Oxford, British Archaeological Report 69.

Reimer, P.J., Bard, E., Bayliss, A., Beck, J.W., Blackwell, P.G., Ramsey, C.B., Buck, C.E., Cheng, H., Edwards, R.L., Friedrich, M., Grootes, P.M., Guilderson, T.P., Haflidason, H., Hajdas, I., Hatté, C., Heaton, T.J., Hoffmann, D.L., Hogg, A.G., Hughen, K.A., Kaiser, K.F., Kromer, B., Manning, S.W., Niu, M., Reimer, R.W., Richards, D.A., Scott, E.M., Southon, J.R., Staff, R.A., Turney, C.S.M. and van der Plicht, J. 2013 IntCal13 and Marine13 radiocarbon age calibration curves 0–50,000 years cal BP. *Radiocarbon* 55(4), 1869–87.

Reimer, P.J. *et al.* 2020 The IntCal20 Northern Hemisphere Radiocarbon Age Calibration Curve (0-55 cal kBP). *Radiocarbon* 62(4): 725–757.

Renfrew, J. 1973 *Palaeoethnobotany: The Prehistoric Food Plants of the Near East and Europe*. London, Methuen.

Renfrew, J. 1993 Prehistoric Britain. In *A Taste Of History 10,000 Years Of Food In Britain*. London, British Museum Press, 11–49.

Reschreiter, H. and Kowarik, K. 2019 Bronze Age mining in Halstatt. A new picture of everyday life in the salt mines and beyond. *Archaeologia Austriaca* 103, 99–136.

Rhind, A.H. 1853 An account of an extensive collection of archaeological relics and osteological remains, from a "Pict's house" at Kettleburn, Caithness. *Proceedings of the Society of Antiquaries of Scotland* 1, 264–69.

Richardson, J.S. 1948 *The Broch of Gurness, Aikerness, Orkney*. Edinburgh, Ministry of Works.

Ritchie, A. 1972 Painted pebbles in early Scotland. *Proceedings of the Society of Antiquaries of Scotland* 104, 297–301.

Ritchie, J. 1941 A keg of 'bog-butter' from Skye and its contents. *Proceedings of the Society of Antiquaries of Scotland* 75, 5–22.

Ritchie, J.N.G. 1967 Keil Cave, Southend, Argyll: a late Iron Age cave occupation in Kintyre. *Proceedings of the Society of Antiquaries of Scotland 99*, 104–10

Ritchie, J.N.G. 1971 Iron Age finds from Dun an Fheurain, Gallanach, Argyll, *Proceedings of the Society of Antiquaries of Scotland* 103, 100–14.

Rivet, A.L.F. 1966. *The Iron Age in Northern Britain*. Edinburgh, Edinburgh University Press.

Rixson, D. 1989 Butchery evidence on animal bones. *Circaea* 6(1), 149–62.

Robertson, J. 2018. The macroplant assemblage. In G. Cavers and A. Crone, 82–7.

Robertson, J. and Roy, L. 2019 A Scottish Iron Age wetland village built from nature's bounty: understanding the formation of plant litter floors. *Environmental Archaeology: The Journal of Human Palaeoecology*, 1–16. https://doi.org/10.1080/14614103.2019.1618650.

Romankiewicz, T. 2009 Simple stones but complex constructions: Analysis of architectural developments in the Scottish Iron Age. *World Archaeology* 41(3), 379–95.

Romankiewicz, T. 2011 *The Complex Roundhouses Of The Scottish Iron Age*. Oxford, British Archaeological Report 550.

Ross, A. 1994 Pottery report. In B. Ballin Smith, 236–57.

Russ, H., Armit, I., McKenzie, J. and Jones, A.K.G. 2012. Deep–sea fishing in Iron Age Scotland? New evidence from Broxmouth hillfort, East Lothian. *Environmental Archaeology* 17(2), 177–84.

Rynne, E. 1983 Some early Iron Age sword-hilts from Ireland and Scotland. In A. O'Connor and D.V. Clarke (eds.) *From the Stone Age to the 'Forty-Five'*, 188–96. Edinburgh, John Donald.

Salque, M. 2012 *Regional and chronological trends in milk use in prehistoric Europe traced through molecular and stable isotope signatures of fatty acyl lipids preserved in pottery vessels*. Unpublished PhD Thesis, University of Bristol.

Schilder, J., van Hardenbroek, M., Bodelier, P., Kirilova, E.P., Leuenberger, M., Lotter, A.F. and Heiri, O. 2017 Trophic state changes can affect the importance of methane–derived carbon in aquatic food webs. *Proceedings of the Royal Society. B, Biological sciences* 284(1857), 20170278, https://doi.org/10.1098/rspb.2017.0278.

Schmid, E. 1972 *Atlas of Animal Bones*. London, Elsevier.

Schulz, B. 2018 *Identification of Trees and Shrubs in Winter Using Buds and Twigs*. London, Royal Botanic Gardens Kew.

Schweingruber, F. 1978 *Microscopic Wood Anatomy*. Birmensdorf, Swiss Federal Institute for Forest Research.

Scott, L. 1947 The problem of the brochs. *Proceedings of the Prehistoric Society* 13, 1–36.

Scott, L. 1948 Gallo-British colonies the aisled round-house culture in the North. *Proceedings of the Prehistoric Society* 14, 46–125.

Scott, W.L. 1935 The chambered cairn of Clettraval, North Uist. *Proceedings of the Society of Antiquaries of Scotland* 69, 480–536.

Sellwood, L. 1984 Objects of bone and antler. In B. Cunliffe, 371–95.

Serjeantson, D. 2007a Bird bones. In J. Hunter *et al.* (eds.), 279–85.

Serjeantson, D. 2007b Bird bones. In S.J. Dockrill *et al.* (eds.) 216–27.

Serjeantson, D. 2009 *Birds*. Cambridge, Cambridge University Press.

Sharman, P.M. 1998 Lamp. In N. Sharples, 149.

Sharples, N. 1991 Warfare in the Iron Age of Wessex. *Scottish Archaeological Review* 9, 79–89.

Sharples, N. 1998 *Scalloway. A Broch, Late Iron Age Settlement and Medieval Cemetery in Shetland.* Oxford, Oxbow Books.

Sharples, N. 2003 From monuments to artefacts: changing social relationships in the later Iron Age. In J. Downes and A. Ritchie (eds.), 151–65.

Sharples, N. 2012 *A Late Iron Age Farmstead in the Outer Hebrides. Excavations at Mound 1, Bornais, South Uist.* Oxford, Oxbow Books.

Sharples, N. 2020 Monumentalising the domestic: house societies in Atlantic Scotland. In B.X. Curras and I. Sastre (eds.) *Alternative Iron Ages: social theory from archaeological analysis,* 284–305. Abingdon, Routledge.

Shillito, L.M. and Matthews, W. 2013 Geoarchaeological Investigations of midden formation processes in the Early to Late ceramic Neolithic Levels at Çatalhöyük, Turkey ca. 8550–8370 cal BP. *Geoarchaeology* 28(1), 25–49.

Sills, J.D., Savage, D., Watson, J.V. and Windley, B.F. 1982 Layered ultramafic–gabbro bodies in the Lewisian of northwest Scotland: geochemistry and petrogenesis. *Earth and Planetary Science Letters* 58, 345–60.

Silver, I.A. 1969 The ageing of domestic animals. In D. Brothwell and G. Clark (eds.) *Science in Archaeology: a survey of progress and research,* 283–302. London, Thames & Hudson.

Smith, A.N. 1998 Miscellaneous bone tools. In N. Sharples, 152–9.

Smith, C. and Young, A. 1998 Animal bone. In L. Main, 316–20.

Smith, C.G.W., Hodgson, I., Armitage, P., Clutton-Brock, J., Dickson, C. and Holden, T. 1994. Animal bone report. In B. Ballin Smith (ed.), 139–52.

Smith, D.N., Osborne, P.J., and Barrett, J., 2000 Beetles as indicators of past environments and human activity at Goldcliff, in M Bell, A Caseldine and H Neumann, *Prehistoric intertidal archaeology in Welsh Severn Estuary,* Council for British Archaeology Research Report 120, York, 245–261.

Smith, D., Hill, G., Kenward, H. and Allison, E. 2020 Development of synanthropic beetle faunas over the last 9000 years in the British Isles. *Journal of Archaeological Science* 115. https://doi.org/10.1016/j.jas.2020.105075

Smith, H. 1999 The plant remains. In M. Parker Pearson and N. Sharples, 297–336.

Smith, R.A. 1905 The evolution of late–Keltic pins of the Hand type. *Proceedings of the Society of Antiquaries of London* (2nd ser.) 20, 344–54.

Smith, R.A. 1913 The evolution of the hand-pin in Great Britain and Ireland. *Opuscula Archaeologica Oscari Montelio Septuagenario Dicata,* 36–289. Stockholm, Häggström.

Smol, J.P. 2008 *Pollution of Lakes and Rivers: A Paleoenvironmental Perspective.* Malden, MA, Blackwell (2nd edition).

Spangenberg, J.E., Jacomet, S. and Schibler, J. 2006 Chemical analyses of organic residues in archaeological pottery from Arbon Bleiche 3, Switzerland – evidence for dairying in the late Neolithic. *Journal of Archaeological Science* 33(1), 1–13.

Stace, C. 2010 *New Flora of the British Isles.* Cambridge, Cambridge University Pres (3rd edition).

Starley, D. 2000 Metalworking debris. In K. Buxton and C. Howard–Davis (eds.) *Bremetenacum: Excavations at Roman Ribchester 1980, 1989–1990, 337–47.* Lancaster, Lancaster Imprints Series 9.

Steer, K.A. 1947 An iron implement and other relics from Falla Cairn, Roxburghshire. *Proceedings of the Society of Antiquaries of Scotland* 81, 183–5.

Steer, K.A. 1956 An Early Iron Age homestead at West Plean, Stirlingshire. *Proceedings of the Society of Antiquaries of Scotland* 89, 227–51.

Sterry, P. and Cleave A. 2012. *Collins Complete Guide to British Coastal Wildlife.* New York, Harper Collins.

Stevenson, R.B.K. 1955 Pins and the chronology of brochs. *Proceedings of the Prehistoric Soc* 21, 282–94.

Stevenson, R.B.K. 1963 Report on the objects of metal, stone and bone from Carlungie 1, in Wainwright 1963, 148–9.

Stevenson R.B.K. 1966 Metalwork and some other objects in Scotland and their cultural affinities. In A.L.F. Rivet (ed.) *The Iron Age in Northern Britain,* 17–45. Edinburgh, Edinburgh University Press.

Stewart, H., Bradwell, T., Bullard, J., Davies, S.J., Golledge, N. and McCulloch, R.D. 2017 8000 years of North Atlantic storminess reconstructed from a Scottish peat record: implications for Holocene atmospheric circulation patterns in Western Europe. *Journal of Quaternary Science* 32(8), 1075–84.

Stirling, L. and Milek, K. 2015 Woven cultures: new insights into Pictish and Viking culture contact using implements of textile production. *Medieval Archaeology* 59(1), 47–72

Stoops, G. 2003 *Guidelines for Analysis and Description of Soil and Regolith Thin Sections.* Madison WI, Soil Science Society of America.

Stoops, G., Marcelino, V. and Mees, F. (eds.) 2010 *Interpretation of Micromorphological Features of Soils and Regoliths.* Amsterdam and Oxford, Elsevier.

Stora, J. 2001 Skeletal development in the grey seal Halichoerus grypus, the ringed seal phoca hispida botnica, the harbour seal phoca vitulina, and the harp seal phoca groenlandica. Epiphseal fusion and life history. *Anthropozoologica* 11, 199–222.

Strachan, D. 2013 *Excavations at the Black Spout, Pitlochry.* Perth, Perth and Kinross Heritage Trust.

Strachan, R. 1999 Excavations at Albie Hill, Apple–garthtown, Annandale, Dumfries and Galloway. *Transactions of the Dumfriesshire and Galloway Natural History and Antiquarian Society* 73, 9–15.

Stuart, J. 1870 Report to the committee of the Society of Antiquaries of Scotland, appointed to arrange for the application of a fund left by the late Mr A Henry Rhind, for excavating early remains. *Proceedings of the Society of Antiquaries of Scotland* 7, 289–307.

Sugita, S. 1994 Pollen representation of vegetation in quaternary sediments: theory and method in patchy vegetation. *Journal of Ecology* 82(4), 881–97.

Summers, J. and Bond, J.M. 2015 The palaeobotanical remains. In S.J. Dockrill *et al.* (eds.), 250–88.

Swindles, G.T., Plunkett, G. and Roe, H.M. 2007a A delayed climatic response to solar forcing at 2800 cal. BP: multiproxy evidence from three Irish peatlands. *The Holocene,* 17(2), 177–82.

Swindles, G.T., Plunkett, G. and Roe, H.M. 2007b A multiproxy climate record from a raised bog in County Fermanagh, Northern Ireland: a critical examination of the link between bog surface wetness and solar variability. *Journal of Quaternary Science* 22(7), 667–79.

Swindles, G.T., Blundell, A., Roe, H.M. and Hall, V.A. 2010 A 4500–year proxy climate record from peatlands in the North of Ireland: the identification of widespread summer 'drought phases'? *Quaternary Science Reviews* 29(13), 1577–89.

Swindles, G.T., Lawson, I.T., Matthews, I.P., Blaauw, M., Daley, T.J., Charman, D.J., Roland, T.P., Plunkett, G., Schettler, G., Gearey, B.R., Turner, T.E., Rea, H.A., Roe, H.M., Amesbury, M.J., Chambers, F.M., Holmes, J., Mitchell, F.J.G., Blackford, J., Blundell, A., Branch, N., Holmes, J., Langdon, P., McCarroll, J., McDermott, F., Oksanen, P.O., Pritchard, O., Stastney, P., Stefanini, B., Young, D., Wheeler, J., Becker, K. and Armit, I. 2013 Centennial-scale climate change in Ireland during the Holocene. *Earth-Science Reviews* 126, 300–20.

Tabraham, C. 1977 Excavations at Dun Carloway broch, Isle of Lewis. *Proceedings of the Society of Antiquaries of Scotland* 108, 156–67.

Tams A. 2003 *Soil Micromorphology of Archaeological Deposits with Particular Reference to Floor Surfaces on Settlement Sites in the Western Isles, Scotland*. Unpublished PhD thesis, University of Edinburgh.

Taylor, D.B. 1982 Excavation of a promontory fort, broch and souterrain at Hurly Hawkin, Angus. *Proceedings of the Society of Antiquaries of Scotland* 112, 215–53.

Taylor, M. 1999 The wood. In M. Parker Pearson and N. Sharples, 188–92.

Theodossopoulos, D., Barber, J., Heald, A. and Cavers, G. 2012. The achievement of structural stability in the drystone Iron Age broch towers in North Scotland. In *Nuts and Bolts of Construction History: Culture, Technology and Society*, 1–11. Available at: http://www.editions–picard.com/product.php?id_product=38949, Accessed 1/12/21.

Tipper, J. 2012 *Experimental Archaeology and Fire: The investigation of a burnt reconstruction at West Stow Anglo-Saxon village, Bury Saint Edmunds*. Bury St Edmunds, Suffolk County Council Archaeological Services.

Tipping, R. 1994 The form and fate of Scotland's woodlands. *Proceedings of the Society of Antiquaries of Scotland* 124, 1–54.

Tipping, R. 2008 Blanket peat in the Scottish Highlands: timing, cause, spread and the myth of environmental determinism. *Biodiversity & Conservation* 17(9), 2097–13.

Tipping, R., Davies, A. and Tisdall, E. 2006 Long-term woodland dynamics in West Glen Affric, northern Scotland. *Forestry* 79(3), 351–9.

Tipping, R., Bradley, R., Sanders, J., McCulloch, R. and Wilson, R. 2012 Moments of crisis: climate change in Scottish prehistory. *Proceedings of the Society of Antiquaries of Scotland* 142, 9–25.

Tipping, R., Ashmore, P., Davies, A.L., Haggart, B.A., Moir, A., Newton, A., Sands, R., Skinner, T. and Tisdall, E. 2008 Prehistoric *Pinus* woodland dynamics in an upland landscape in northern Scotland: the roles of climate change and human impact. *Vegetation History and Archaeobotany* 17(3), 251–67.

Tite, M.S. 2008 Ceramic production, provenance and use – a review. *Archaeometry* 50(2), 216–31.

Topping, P. 1985a Later prehistoric pottery from Dun Cul Bhuirg, Iona, Argyll. *Proceedings of the Society of Antiquaries of Scotland* 115, 199–209.

Topping, P. 1985b *Later Prehistoric Pottery of the Western Isles*. Unpublished PhD thesis, University of Edinburgh.

Topping, P. 1987 Typology and chronology in the later prehistoric pottery assemblages of the Western Isles. *Proceedings of the Society of Antiquaries of Scotland* 117, 67–84.

Towsey, K. 2002 *Orkney and the Sea: An Oral History*. Kirkwall, Orkney Heritage Publication.

Traill, W. 1890 Results of the excavation at the broch of Burrian, North Ronaldsay, Orkney, during the summers of 1870 and 1871. *Archaeologia Scotia* 5, 341–64

Troalen, L. 2019. *SEM Investigation of Two Fragments from Clachtoll. Collections Sciences Section. Report no. AR 2019/03*. Unpublished archive report for AOC Archaeology, AOC 60094, Edinburgh.

Tulloch, A.P. 1976 Chemistry of waxes of higher plants. In P.E. Kolattukudy (ed.) *Chemistry and Biochemistry of natural waxes*, 289–347. New York: Elsevier.

Tuohy, T. 1995 Bone and antler working. In J. Coles and S. Minnitt (eds.) *Industrious and Fairly Civilised: The Glastonbury Lake Village*, 142–9. Taunton, Somerset Levels Project and Somerset County Council Museums Service.

Tuohy, T. 1999 *Prehistoric Combs of Antler and Bone*. Oxford, British Archaeological Report 285.

Tuohy, T. 2000 Long handled weaving combs: problems in determining the gender of tool-maker and tool-user. In M. Donald and L. Hurcombe (eds.) *Gender and Material Culture in Archaeological Perspective*, 137–52. Basingstoke, Palgrave Macmillan.

Urem-Kotsou, D., Stern, B., Heron, C. and Kotsakis, K. 2002 Birch-bark tar at Neolithic Makriyalos, Greece. *Antiquity* 76, 962–7.

Usep, A., Hashimoto, Y., Takahashi, H. and Hayasak, H. 2004. Combustion and thermal characteristics of peat fire in tropical peatland in Central Kalimantan, Indonesia. *Tropics* 14(1), 1–19.

Vander Voort, G.F. 1999 *Metallography, Principles and Practice*, New York: McGraw-Hill.

Von Den Driesch, A. 1976 *A Guide to the Measurement of Animal Bones from Archaeological Sites*. Cambridge MA, Peabody Museum of Archaeology and Ethnology, Harvard University.

Wainwright, F.T. 1963 *The Souterrains of Southern Pictland*. London, Routledge and Kegan Paul.

Walton, T.J. 1990 Waxes, cutin and suberin. In J.L. Harwood and J.R. Bowyer (eds.) *Methods in Plant Biochemistry* 4, 105–58. London: Academic Press.

Wang, T., Surge, D. and Mithen, S. 2012 Seasonal temperature variability of the Neoglacial (3300–2500BP) and Roman Warm Period (2500–1600BP) reconstructed from oxygen isotope ratios of limpet shells (*Patella vulgata*), Northwest Scotland. *Palaeogeography, Palaeoclimatology, Palaeoecology* 317–18, 104–13.

Wassenburg, J.A., Immenhauser, A., Richter, D.K., Niedermayr, A., Riechelmann, S., Fietzke, J., Scholz, D., Jochum, K.P.,

Fohlmeister, J., Schröder–Ritzrau, A., Sabaoui, A., Riechelmann, D.F.C., Schneider, L. and Esper, J. 2013 Moroccan speleothem and tree ring records suggest a variable positive state of the North Atlantic Oscillation during the Medieval Warm Period. *Earth and Planetary Science Letters* 375, 291–302.

Watson, H.C. 1986 *The Feeding Ecology of the European Otter (*Lutra lutra l*.) in a Marine Environment*. Unpublished MSc thesis, Durham University. Available from http://etheses.dur.ac.uk/6777/. Accessed 1/12/21.

Watt, J., Pierce, G.J. and Boyle, P.R. 1997 *A Guide to the Identification of North Sea Fish Using Premaxillae and Vertebrae*. Copenhagen, International Council for the Exploration of the Sea.

Wattez J. and Courty M.-A. 1987 Morphology of ash of some plant materials. In N. Fedoroff, L.–M. Bresson and M.-A. Courty (eds.) *Soil Micromorphology*, 677–83. Paris, Éditions de l'Association Française pour l'Etude des Sols.

Webley, L. 2007 Using and abandoning roundhouses: a reinterpretation of the evidence from late bronze age–early iron age southern England. *Oxford Journal of Archaeology* 26(2), 127–44.

West, B. 1990 A tale of two innominates. *Circaea* 6(2), 107–14.

Williams, M. 2003 Growing metaphors: the agricultural cycle as a metaphor in the later prehistoric period of Britain and North Western Europe. *Journal of Social Archaeology* 3(2), 223–55.

Young, A. 1953 An aisled farmhouse at the Allasdale, Isle of Barra. *Proceedings of the Society of Antiquaries of Scotland* 87, 80–105.

Young, A. 1956 Excavations at Dun Cuier, Isle of Barra, Outer Hebrides. *Proceedings of the Society of Antiquaries of Scotland* 89, 290–328.

Young, A. 1964 Brochs and duns. *Proceedings of the Society of Antiquaries of Scotland* 95, 171–98.

Young, A. 1966 The sequence of Hebridean pottery. In A.L.F. Rivet (ed.) *The Iron Age in Northern Britain*, 45–59. Edinburgh.

Young, A. and Richardson, K.M. 1960 Á Cheardach Mhor, Drimore, South Uist. *Proceedings of the Society of Antiquaries of Scotland* 93, 134–73.

Young, T. 2012 The slag. In N. Sharples, 289–95.

Zohary, D. and Hopf, M. 1993 *Domestication of Plants in the Old World*. Oxford, Oxford University Press (2nd edition).

Index

Numbers in *italic* denote pages with figures, those in **bold** denote pages with tables.